FROMMER'S

WHERE
TO STAY
USA

COUNCIL ON INTERNATIONAL
EDUCATIONAL EXCHANGE

Written by Marjorie A. Cohen

Edited by Margaret Sherman
and Janet Boltax

1982-1983 Edition

Published by the Council on International Educational Exchange
205 East 42nd Street
New York, NY 10017
and
Frommer/Pasmantier Publishers
A Simon & Schuster Division of
Gulf & Western Corporation
1230 Avenue of the Americas
New York, NY 10020

ISBN: 0-671-43402-0

Manufactured in the United States of America

Cover design by Steve Jenkins

*Although every effort was made to ensure the accuracy
of price information appearing in this book,
it should be kept in mind that prices
can and do fluctuate in the course of time.*

CONTENTS

About This Book

When we first sat down to write *Where to Stay USA* nine years ago, our purpose was simple enough: We wanted as many people as possible to enjoy an American experience, and we wanted them to be able to do it even on a limited budget. We've done what we set out to do, judging from the letters of praise and encouragement that we've received from readers. Many of these readers have sent us suggestions for additions, and we've followed up on all of them. You'll notice italicized quotes all the way through the book—these are from our readers.

To make this edition more useful, we've added Atlanta to our special sections on 15 of the most visited U.S. cities. We now cover New York, Washington, D.C., Denver, Houston, Phoenix, Los Angeles, San Francisco, San Diego, Chicago, Boston, St. Louis, Seattle, Miami, New Orleans, and Atlanta. In these sections we've tried to put enough information to give travelers a good start in a new, sometimes overwhelming city. We've included information on how to get around, where to stay, where to eat, what to see and do, and where to go for help and information. New in this edition are special discounts that some of the accommodation facilities are offering to ISIC holders and senior citizens. We have also indicated those places which provide access facilities for the handicapped. There is a key to these discounts and to access facilities on page 5.

The philosophy behind the book *Where to Stay* is uncomplicated—the book is primarily for use on the road, and it's meant to be carried with you. Although some of the introductory sections should be read before you begin your trip, the bulk of the book is meant to serve you as you travel. See page 20 for an explanation of how the listings are set up—and be sure to read Chapter 2 so that you know what to expect from some of the accommodation facilities.

We should probably explain how we at the Council on International Educational Exchange (CIEE) first came to write this book on low-cost travel in the U.S. CIEE was founded in 1947 as the Council on Student Travel (it became CIEE in 1967), and since then it has been actively involved in helping thousands of students plan their trips both abroad and in the U.S. It is a membership organization made up of nearly 200 colleges, universities, secondary schools, national organizations, and youth-serving agencies. Since its founding, CIEE has been arranging transportation and providing information and advisory services for both educational groups and individual students. Any U.S. student planning to travel abroad or in North America will want to get a free copy of CIEE's *Student Travel Catalog*, which describes the services offered by CIEE to both students and nonstudents. These services include the International Student Identity Card or ISIC (see page 3), charter flights to and within Europe, railpasses, insurance, car plans, and a variety of travel publications. Students from abroad should contact the local student travel organization for information on these services.

We couldn't do any of this without you. So if you have anything to tell us about low-cost travel in the U.S., we'd love to hear from you. Write to us at 205 East 42nd St., New York, NY 10017, and if we are able to use what you tell us in the next edition of *Where to Stay USA*, we'll send you a complimentary copy.

Acknowledgments

There are lots of people who need to be thanked for helping to put together this sixth edition of *Where to Stay USA*—some on CIEE's staff and some from other organizations, too.

We want to thank Mindy Feiger for her help and encouragement from the beginning to the end of the project, and special thanks, too, to the following people who helped us put the city sections together: Chris Arrott, Linda Meyer, Cindy Lake, Sabih Kent, José Millan, Robert Baudouin, Diane Capoverde, Ie Lin Leong, Jack O'Connell, Zelda Faigen, Ruth Purkaple, Pete Peterson, Debbie Shore, Richard Markow, and Aurora Aleu.

This is also the best place to thank the people who answered the letters and questionnaires that we sent all over the U.S. in order to collect firsthand information on each area. Some of the people to whom we wrote filled in the questionnaires and returned them, and we are grateful for that. But others who went even further and offered encouragement and additional information deserve our collective and special thanks.

Finally, to everyone who helped in the process of putting together *Where to Stay USA*, our thanks.

Marjorie A. Cohen
Margaret E. Sherman
Janet S. Boltax

Important Note: All information listed in this book, including prices, is subject to change. To the best of its ability, CIEE verified the accuracy of the information at the time *Where to Stay USA* went to press.

The International Student Identity Card

What Is the ISIC?

As soon as American students decide to make a trip abroad, they go out and buy an ISIC. For more than 12 years, American young people have been setting out on their travels with the ISIC tucked carefully into their wallets. Full-time high school and university students have found the ISIC to be their passport to low-cost travel—it is proof to anyone who needs to know, anywhere in the world, that the holder is a student and is eligible for special student privileges, discounts, and travel bargains. In more than 50 countries, ISIC holders can obtain lower air fares, tours and accommodations, and reduced or free admission to many museums, theaters, cultural and historic sites. With an ISIC, students are eligible, too, for discounts of up to 50% on a special network of student flights that crisscrosses Europe and connects Europe with several cities in Africa, Asia, and the Middle East.

The idea of the ISIC was initiated and is administered by the International Student Travel Conference (ISTC), a federation of national student travel bureaus representing more than 50 countries. The U.S. sponsor of the ISIC is the Council on International Educational Exchange (CIEE).

The ISIC in the U.S.

In mid-1980, with student discounts well established all over the world, CIEE began a campaign to develop a network of similar discounts in the United States for students who are holders of the International Student Identity Card. We've been quite successful and discounts have been obtained for accommodation facilities, car rentals, museums, etc. *ISIC discounts that had been arranged at the time we went to press with* Where to Stay USA *are noted and identified here by a* symbol: ➤. CIEE is continuing to negotiate new kinds of ISIC discounts in the United States, particularly those services that are of special interest to students who are traveling. Places that are currently offering ISIC discounts have been asked to display an ISIC window decal (see over), identifying them as ISIC-discounters.

No matter where you travel in the world, ISIC holders have gotten in the habit of always showing their ISIC before making any purchase and requesting an ISIC discount. If you are successful in obtaining a new ISIC discount, won't you let us know about it? Drop us a line telling us the name, address, and the type/size of the discount you were able to obtain. We'll contact the organization to see whether they want to be included in the growing U.S. discount network. And, for your effort, you'll receive a free copy of the next edition of *Where to Stay USA*.

Where to Get the ISIC

Full-time students may obtain their International Student Identity Card at one of more than 350 college campuses across the U.S. (check to see whether your campus issues the ISIC—try the international studies office, student travel office, or modern languages department, for examples). Or students may obtain the ISIC directly from CIEE. We've included a reply coupon for you below in case you would like to order the ISIC directly from CIEE.

Who Is Eligible

You are eligible to receive the ISIC if you are (1) at least 12 years of age or older; (2) a *full-time* high school / vocational school / college or university student; and (3) able to provide documentation as to your full-time student status.

Please send me an application for the International Student Identity Card.

Name _____

Address _____

_____

Return to: **CIEE - WTS**
205 East 42nd St.
New York, NY 10017

or

CIEE - WTS
312 Sutter St.
San Francisco, CA
94108

Your help in locating new ISIC discounts will be appreciated by all students who are traveling in the U.S. in the future, especially because the information you supply will help students to stretch their travel dollars. The kinds of new ISIC discounts you should look for are those made available by: hotels/motels and other accommodation facilities, restaurants, theaters, bookstores, record shops, clothing stores, museums, cinemas, etc. In short, any kind of product or service that students (U.S. as well as foreign) would be looking for as they travel through the United States. If you discover any new ISIC discounts, please complete the coupon below and return it to us. We will then contact your source and have it join the ISIC discount network. Don't forget to include your name and address so we can send you a free copy of the next edition (1984–85) of *Where to Stay*.

Here's my contribution to the ISIC discount network:

Name of organization granting discount _____
Name and title of contact _____
Address _____

Description of Discount _____

Your Name _____   Return to: **CIEE**
205 East 42nd St.
Address _____   **New York, NY 10017**

Explanation of Symbols

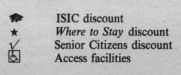

ISIC discount
Where to Stay discount
Senior Citizens discount
Access facilities

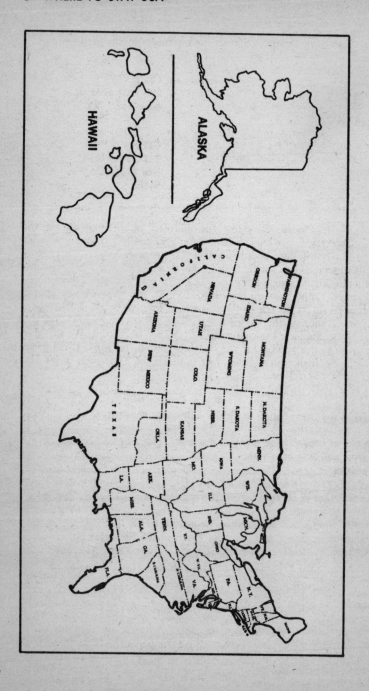

CHAPTER 1

Getting Around

How are you going to get from one place to another in this enormous and fascinating country? Will you fly? Drive? Hitchhike? What's best for you? What's economical? What kinds of "deals" are available?

In this first chapter we'll consider all of the possibilities, and then it's up to you. To make your decision you'll have to consider a number of variables. How much money you have to spend is important, of course, but so is understanding your own style. Some people wouldn't consider going any other way than hitchhiking; others would never be comfortable trying to thumb a ride from a stranger. A little old-fashioned know-thyself is what's called for first of all. Because so many of our readers are from abroad, it's important, too, to emphasize the enormous size of this country. The distance from New York to California is over 3000 miles or 5100 kilometers; from New York to Florida it's over 1000 miles or 1700 kilometers. Many people forget about the expanse that is the U.S. when they set out to plan their visit. They plan an unrealistic itinerary that has them covering too much, too quickly.

Going by Air

Except on very short trips, the quickest way to travel between two points in the U.S. is by air. There are ways of saving money on air fares, but the airlines are making it a bit difficult for us to tell you about them since they are constantly thinking up, instituting, and then canceling their own promotional fares. In addition, new airlines have recently appeared on the scene, causing even more rapid and dramatic change as established airlines alter their fares to compete. These new carriers generally offer low-cost service on short-haul routes. It's not realistic for us to say anything specific about prices since they are bound to change from the time we go to press to the time you read them. Air fares are going up and up because of the increase in fuel prices. So instead of giving prices we'll talk about percentages and leave you to find out the prices from the airlines or travel agents.

Unlimited Mileage: This fare was thought up by the people at Eastern Airlines. It allows 7 to 21 days of unlimited travel on their routes and costs $540 each for two traveling together or $640 if you're alone. For approximately $50 more you can also fly to Mexico and the Caribbean. The conditions: You must buy your ticket 14 days in advance and make at least two separate stopovers during the trip. You may not stop at the same city more than once during the trip, except when making an immediate connection to an onward destination. Reservations must be made for the entire itinerary at least 14 days in advance, but Eastern suggests that you don't wait that long if you want to be sure of your flights.

Super Saver: These fares are offered by most domestic airlines on routes connecting major U.S. cities. Discounts off normal coach fares range from 25% to 45%. Booking must be made 7 to 30 days in advance depending on the particular route involved. The departure and return dates must be fixed, but there is no cancellation penalty.

At press time, three noteworthy fares in effect were a one-way coach fare of $69 between cities of the Northeast and Florida, a round-trip Super Saver between New York and California for $390, and a one-way standby rate on the same route for $179. Be sure and ask whether these fares are still in effect.

New Airlines: Midway Airlines, one of the newer air carriers, will fly you between Chicago and New York for only $89, a savings of over 50% compared to normal coach fares. New York Air, People's Express, and Air Florida are other new carriers offering rates lower than those of the larger airlines. Besides all these "specials," there are still the standard discounts on night flights—up to 25% off on long-haul routes on flights that depart after 9 p.m.

"Night flights are cheap, it's true, but you arrive in a strange city at an ungodly hour in the morning."

Some well-traveled routes (e.g., New York-Boston, New York-Washington) have shuttle service—a no-frills arrangement where you just board, pay for your ticket on the plane, and get off without having any food or drinks. Shuttles generally run every hour during weekdays. Although shuttles offer the convenience of travel without reservations, they don't save you any money over the regular fares, except on weekends when there are special excursion fares available. The New York-Boston shuttle is $49, New York-Washington is $59, and the Saturday-Sunday round-trip excursion special is $58.

Foreign visitors are entitled to some special discounts on domestic air-fare arrangements. See Chapter 3 for details.

So you see, it's going to be a bit complicated sorting out the air-fare part of your trip, but the effort should result in a fairly substantial saving for you. For help, go to a CIEE office, travel agent, or to the airline itself. Ask lots of questions and don't settle for anything less than the best possible deal.

The Aviation Consumer Action Project puts out a pamphlet that's meant to inform air travelers of their rights, how to handle a complaint, how to learn about discount rates, etc. A free copy of *Facts and Advice for Airline Passengers* can be obtained by sending a 9″ stamped, self-addressed envelope to ACAP, P.O. Box 19029, Washington, DC 20036. Another booklet containing basic information especially for first-time travelers is *How to Fly*, published by the Air Transport Association of America. For a free copy, send a 9″ stamped, self-addressed envelope to Air Transport Association of America, Public Relations Dept., 1709 New York Ave. NW, Washington, DC 20006.

"Hitchhiking by small plane can be a quick, cheap way to get around the U.S. To do this, go to a small airport or the private hangar section of the larger airports. You may find a pilot who is willing to give you a lift in the direction you're going."

Going by Bus

"The bus is a terrific way to explore the U.S.A., especially for the first time. The bus goes everywhere and is on time. But you shouldn't spend too much time at the terminals, especially overnight. They're often not located in the best neighborhoods."

"Bus travel is usually a good thing but sometimes you miss the small cities, which is a real pity."

Bus travel has always been inexpensive so it's no wonder that the bus is such a popular way (especially with young people) to travel around the U.S. Buses are almost always air-conditioned in the summer, well heated in the winter. Service is efficient, connecting most cities and towns of the U.S. no matter how small, and if you break your trip into several short trips, you won't be too uncomfortable.

For years, the best bargains in bus travel have been the unlimited travel plans—Greyhound's Ameripass and Trailways' Eaglepass. This is how they work: As of press time, you pay $186.90 for 7 days, $240.30 for 15 days, and $347.10 for one month of practically unlimited travel in the continental U.S. and Canada. The Ameripass and Eaglepass are actually booklets of coupons which must be presented to an agent at each bus station. As long as the pass is valid you can use as many coupons as you need; i.e., you may cover as much territory as possible in the time allotted. The passes can be extended for a nominal daily charge, but the extensions must be made before the pass expires. There are some side trips, usually to specific attractions or national parks, which are not covered by the passes.

"One disadvantage of the pass is that it cannot be used in the national parks, although there are discounts on national park tours to pass holders."

We've talked to lots of people who have traveled with the Ameripass, and they're generally pretty enthusiastic about it. One friend from Minnesota told us:

"In two months I made four separate round trips lasting 9 to 12 days each. During that time I covered thousands of miles, 39 states, three Canadian provinces, and one Mexican city. In general, bus travel is best if you're not in a hurry and you've never been that route before. It's an excellent way to see the country and to meet people along the way. Most of the bus drivers are friendly and helpful."

"Bus trips are such an easy way to meet people—for me that advantage outweighs any of the discomforts I felt."

A little-publicized fare that nevertheless does exist is the "one-way anywhere fare." For $133.50, a passenger gets 15 days to reach wherever it is he or she is going. Stopovers are allowed just as long as they are on a direct route from the point of origin to the final destination.

Senior citizens are entitled to discounts on bus fares. Check with Greyhound and Trailways for details.

Don't overlook the fact that traveling by bus can also save you money on accommodations. If you travel at night, you can sleep on the bus and avoid paying for a place to stay. Ameripasses are available from CIEE; both Ameripasses and Eaglepasses may be purchased from travel agents or from the bus lines directly.

"For greater comfort on the bus, bring an AM-FM transistor radio (with earphones), a Thermos bottle, and a pillow and earplugs for sound sleep."

Besides the "establishment" bus companies, we have heard, off and on, about several alternative bus companies—private operators that drive minibuses between the East and West Coasts. We've heard varying reviews of these trips and suggest care in choosing this method of travel.

One of these alternative companies is the Grey Rabbit, which runs buses from coast to coast in three to four days. The fare from New York to California is $89. Stops are possible in between—the itinerary and route are left up to the driver and at times there are side trips to the Grand Canyon, Saratoga Hot Springs, etc. Buses are equipped with mattresses. For details, contact New York Ride Center, 159 West 33rd St., New York, NY 10001. Telephone: 212/279-3870, or in San Francisco, 415/524-5404.

Another similar operation is the Green Tortoise, which calls itself a camper bus-tour company. "We use sleep-aboard, fuel-efficient diesel coaches and have frequent stops for hot springs, swimming, hiking, rafting, and sailing. We do a lot of cooking out which helps to keep food costs low. . . ." The Green Tortoise connects San Francisco and Los Angeles, Boston and New York. It goes to New Orleans every year from San Francisco, Boston, and New York, and during Mardi Gras the buses remain in the French Quarter for two weeks in order to provide accommodation and sanitary facilities. The Green Tortoise also travels from the West Coast to Alaska, Baja California, and Mexico. At press time, a one-way, cross-country trip of seven to ten days was $199; the four-week Alaska trip was $499. For information, write to the Green Tortoise, P.O. Box 24459, San Francisco, CA 94124; or call: in Boston, 617/265-8533; in New York, 212/431-3348; and in San Francisco, 415/386-1798.

Going by Train

"If a person wants to have a relaxed—though long—trip and still see the country, he or she should take the train. I was on Amtrak from New York to New Mexico and from Kansas to Boston. I was able to do what I wanted to do. I saw the country without feeling cramped and met many people and I didn't have to pay for overnight accommodation since the coaches had comfortable seats. I found it more economical to bring fruits, biscuits, etc., on board rather than to have meals on the train."

Amtrak—the National Railroad Passenger Corporation, which has control of the nation's passenger railroads—is trying to entice people away from planes and buses and onto trains.

A spokesman for Amtrak's public relations department said: "We have made a special effort to attract young people back to the trains and have succeeded in many parts of the country. If you ride our *Montrealer*, for instance, between New York and Montréal, you will see many college students enjoying themselves hugely. Our *Coast Starlight,* which operates between Los Angeles and San Francisco and on to Seattle, is also heavily patronized by young people, who obviously are having a fine time. Our San Francisco *Zephyr* also attracts a lively crowd."

Unfortunately, Amtrak has stopped selling its unlimited-travel USA Rail Pass to Americans—it is available now only to foreign visitors. There are, however, some family plans available—the head of household pays full fare and the spouse and children ages 12 to 21 pay only half fare; children 2 to 11 pay one-quarter fare, and children under 2 travel free. To qualify for family fares, travel can begin any day of the week.

You can save money if you take advantage of round-trip excursion fares on certain routes between major cities, e.g., Boston-Washington, New York-Miami or New York-Orlando, Chicago-Denver, or Los Angeles-San Francisco. There are usually some restrictions on dates when the fares are valid and the return trip must be made within a certain period of time. For example, along the Northeast Corridor between Boston and Washington the round-trip excursion fares are good for travel anytime except between 11 a.m. and midnight on Friday and Sunday and some holiday dates. At press time, the excursion fare between New York and Washington was $48, the normal round-trip coach fare $64, and the round-trip Metroliner $74. Excursion travel must be completed within 30 days of the purchase of the ticket. Amtrak also offers a 25% discount on fares to people 65 and over and to those who are handicapped. (Amtrak recently renovated many of their passenger cars and stations to conform to the needs of the handicapped.)

"Traveling by train was an easy way to meet people and it was also comfortable. The only problem is that we were never on time."

Going by Car
Gasoline is expensive and all sorts of things can go wrong with a car en route. But if you want to be able to travel at your own pace and come and go as you please, travel by car is probably best for you. If you don't have your own car you can either rent one, buy a used one, or take advantage of the driveaway system, or find someone to ride with—all possibilities that are discussed below. (Special information for foreign visitors who intend to drive in the U.S. can be found in Chapter 3.)

If you're going to be driving in the U.S., you'll need a good map, which you can usually get at a gas station. The companies listed below will also send maps on request and will mark direct or scenic routes if you tell them where you want to go:

Exxon Touring Service, P.O. Box 10210, Houston, TX 77206.

ARCO Travel Service, P.O. Box 93, Versailles, KY 40383.

DRIVEAWAYS: There are several agencies throughout the U.S. that arrange the transport of cars from one part of the country to another. This provides an excellent opportunity for students over 21 years of age—or sometimes over 25—to go long distances at minimal cost. The car owner usually pays for the tolls and occasionally for the gas. A direct route must be followed, since the agencies usually contract to get the car to its destination by a certain time. The time allotted is reasonable, though; no one expects you to drive day and night. It's typical for a company to require that you cover about 400 miles per day.

Most large cities have driveaway companies, which are listed in the classified section of the telephone book—the Yellow Pages—usually under the heading "Automobile Transport and Driveaway Companies." Probably the most popular routes for driveaways are between New York, Philadelphia, or Boston and Florida or California. The classified sections of the daily newspapers are also a source of current driveaway possibilities.

The process of contracting with a driveaway company involves making a deposit of between $50 and $100 and being fingerprinted. If you get a choice of cars, take the smaller one so you can save on gasoline. Most cars are late model, privately owned, and are given to the driver with a full first tank of gas.

If you're a foreign student interested in a driveaway, your English must be fluent before most companies will let you have a car and you must have an International Driving Permit as well.

As with all things, before you sign on the dotted line for a driveaway you should be confident of the firm's reliability. One student who traveled across country via a driveaway said this: "*I strongly recommend checking into driveaway cars. My experience was with AAACON, a large agency with offices in over 80 cities. I walked in, filled out a detailed application, gave them four passport photos, my fingerprints, and a $50 deposit. I paid gas and oil and had my deposit refunded when I delivered the car. The advantages are many. It's cheap (the only cheaper way is hitchhiking); it's convenient—we were given six days to travel 2000 miles so we had time to sightsee along the way—and it's comfortable, especially compared to a bus. You may have difficulty getting a car to the exact city you're headed for. If so, get a car going to another city close by and hop a bus—you're still ahead moneywise. The cars are not always in tip-top shape, but the owner is responsible for any repair costs that are incurred.*"

Other companies with offices throughout the U.S. are Driveaway Service, Inc., Auto Driveaway Company, Dependable Car Service, Inc., and Nationwide Auto Transporters, Inc.

CAR RENTALS: In some cities of the U.S., car-rental companies require that you be 25 or over in order to rent one of their cars. Others will rent to anyone 21 or over. New York City is one place that requires you to be 25, but if a friend who is over 25 actually rents the car you may go along as a driver even if you are younger. Also, if you have a major credit card, companies will often adjust the minimum age requirement. Having a major credit card will make car rental easier—some companies won't rent to you without one, or if they do, they will charge an enormous deposit. (The situation for foreign visitors is a bit different. The minimum age is 18 as long as you have a valid International Driver's Permit and can show a return ticket and a passport.)

Most of you have heard of the major car-rental companies—National, Hertz, and Avis—but when you're thinking of renting a car, consider some of the smaller companies as well. Although the larger companies, with offices all over the world, offer such advantages as allowing you to pick up a car in one city and leave it in another, the smaller companies often charge less and may have more economy cars available than the larger ones.

Hertz will, however, give ISIC holders a 5% discount on daily rentals. You must have a special Hertz sticker affixed to your ISIC in order to get the discount, and the sticker is available at campus offices that issue the ISIC, or from CIEE.

The cost of car rental varies considerably from city to city. For instance, one week of unlimited mileage in Miami will cost you approximately $80, whereas a car rented for the same period in New York will cost approximately $180.

To give you a general idea of how much it will cost to rent a car, consider that most of the companies have special one-week rates that provide unlimited mileage for approximately $100. This rate does not include the cost of gasoline —and there's the rub, since gasoline prices have skyrocketed in the past few years. You can also get special weekday, weekend, and monthly rates that can make car rental an economical way to travel—especially if you have some friends along to share costs. Be sure to investigate all the possibilities.

"I don't know if two people can live cheaper than one but they sure can travel cheaper. Three is even better when you're splitting the gas, motel bills, and driving. We found a fellow traveler on our way home and the added savings and companionship were most welcome."

USED CARS: If you're the kind who enjoys taking chances, you can buy yourself a used car and hope for the best. An American car that is only a few years old may sell for half its original price; a car five to ten years old may sell for anywhere between $200 and $800 and can usually be resold at a small loss, as long as you can keep it in one piece. It's best to buy used cars through ads in the newspapers rather than from used car dealers. Here's one good suggestion we got from someone who has bought several used cars: check the tires, since their condition is a good measure of the care that the previous owner gave his car.

"We bought an old car in Boston to take cross-country to California. We paid $200 for it. On our way to see the Grand Canyon, a woman who wasn't paying attention to what she was doing ran into us. Not wanting to jeopardize her insurance renewal, she gave us $200 on the spot for repairs. When we got to California we sold the car for $200. Our trip was free!"

Once you've bought a car there are registration and insurance formalities that must be completed. Contact the nearest office of the American Automobile Association, the definitive source of information on anything auto related.

Going by Bicycle

A lot of people are deciding that two wheels are better than four. There's been an incredible boom in bicycling in recent years, and that's a good thing both for the people who are doing the bicycling and for the ones who aren't, since they're being spared the pollution of another car.

There are lots of bicycle clubs and organizations in the U.S. One of the best known organizations associated with bicycle travel is American Youth Hostels, Inc., which has been around since 1934. AYH was operating hostels throughout the U.S. and organizing bicycle tours for its members for years before the present bicycle boom began. Membership cards, available from AYH National Administrative Offices, 1332 I St. NW, Suite 800, Washington, DC 20005, or from any of AYH's 31 councils or 250 pass-selling agents, cost $7 for anyone under 18, $14 for anyone 18 to 59, and $7 for anyone over 60. See page 21 for more about AYH and its hostels.

Because of the recent bicycle boom, many communities are agitating for more bikeways. The word "bikeway" is a bit misleading—it is used to refer to a signposted route on streets and roads that are considered suitable for bicycling; it does not mean a roadway set aside only for bicyclists. According to the International Bicycle Touring Society (2115 Paseo Dorado, La Jolla, CA 92037), "Bikeways exist in hundreds of towns and cities, but they are of questionable value because they don't go anywhere." The average length of a bikeway in America is four miles. Only Wisconsin has a longer one. It stretches from Kenosha to La Crosse, a distance of 300 miles. For information and a copy of a new guide showing routes in 72 counties, write to Wisconsin Division of Tourism, P.O. Box 7606, Madison, WI 53707.

One of the newer groups of bicycle people is called Bikecentennial, an organization that celebrated America's birthday by inaugurating a 4500-mile Trans America Bicycle Trail. Besides running organized trips for bicyclists during the summer, Bikecentennial offers a routing service with 77 different routes. The two newest routes are a 370-mile extension to the Great Parks Route, which takes cyclists south from the Canadian Rockies and the parks of the western United States to Albuquerque, N.M., and the Central section of the Great River Bicycle Route, which runs from Davenport, Iowa, to Memphis, Tenn. All in all, Bikecentennial has 9000 miles of researched bicycle routes. The group's catalog, which includes its trips program, accessories, order forms for map routes, and books on cycling in the U.S. and abroad, costs $1 and is available from Bikecentennial, P.O. Box 8308, Missoula, MT 59807. Telephone: 406/721-1776.

The League of American Wheelmen (L.A.W.) is a membership organization that describes itself as being "of, by and for bicyclists in all 50 states as well as over 400 affiliated bicycle clubs." L.A.W., P.O. Box 988, Baltimore, MD 21203, actively works to protect the bicyclist's rights to the road; it provides accident and legal advice, bicycle safety information, and touring information. The *American Wheelman,* a monthly magazine, contains an extensive and timely listing of bicycle events in the U.S. Included in the group's yearly directory are a list of "Hospitality Homes," people willing to accommodate another cyclist for the night, and a list of Touring Information Directors, people willing to help you plan a bicycle trip through their state.

In general, bike books can be divided into two different categories: the ones that tell you how to buy, maintain, and repair your bike; and the ones that tell you where you can go with your bike. Three of the first type that are most often recommended are *The New Complete Book of Bicycling,* by Eugene A. Sloane, Simon and Schuster, 1980 ($19.95); *Anybody's Bike Book,* by Tom Cuthbertson, Ten Speed Press, Berkeley ($4.95); and *Two Wheel Travel: Bicycle Camping and Touring,* by Peter Tobey and others, Tobey Publishing Company ($4.95).

For information on bicycle routes, check *Northeast Bicycle Tours,* by Eric Tobey and Richard Wolkenberg, Tobey Publishing Company ($3.95)—130 tours in the New York and New England areas; *Bay Area Bikeways,* by Tom Standing, Ten Speed Press, Berkeley ($2.50); and *The American Bicycle Atlas,* by American Youth Hostels, Inc., E. P. Dutton ($6.25).

Going by Thumb
"Hitching is living by the seat of one's pants. It's surviving on guts and instinct. . . ."

This is a tricky subject. A lot of people are completely and absolutely turned off by the whole idea of hitchhiking. Many consider it too dangerous, too risky, to ever attempt. Others wouldn't think of traveling any other way. In an article in the *New York Times,* hitchhiking was called "an accepted mode of travel, well on its way to respectability." One French student who hitched from coast to coast told us: "Hitching was very easy. We never had to wait long in one place. We traveled 600 miles or more each day." We suspect that this had a lot to do with the fact that he is not American. Drivers respond more positively to hitchhikers from other countries.

"Foreigners may find it helpful to wave their national flag around when trying to thumb a ride. This I feel would apply especially to the British and was, in fact, recommended to me by an English chap who went from New York to Atlanta on one hop like this."

Since there is no cheaper way to travel, we discuss the subject of hitchhiking here. We sent a questionnaire to the state police of each of the 50 states; the responses, when helpful, are included in each state chapter. We've also included information on the attitude toward hitchhiking in each state—a more subjective view from readers and friends.

From what people told us, we sense a growing feeling of paranoia about hitchhiking-related crimes. Nowadays, it seems people are convinced that the potential for danger is greater for the hitchhiker than for the driver. In the past it was the driver who felt threatened.

For help in understanding the legal situation regarding hitchhiking in this country, we went to Tom Grimm, author of *Hitchhiker's Handbook* (published by New American Library, $2.95, now out of print but available by mail from New American Library, P.O. Box 120, Bergenfield, NJ 07621). Here's what we learned from him: Many people think that hitchhiking is illegal in the U.S., but this is not true. There are no nationwide laws regarding hitchhiking, and individual cities and states are able to make their own laws and regulations on the subject. And there's another wrinkle. Whether a law exists or not, the attitude of the police toward hitchhikers is something that can't be regulated and varies from area to area. Some police are cordial, even helpful, to hitchhikers, and others treat thumbers like escaped criminals. Perhaps the only way to know ahead of time what the prevailing attitudes are in any particular area is to ask someone who has hitched there. Law books can't tell you anything about attitudes, and we haven't room to tell you much in our state-by-state listings.

Most of the states prohibit hitchhiking on the "roadway," and usually "roadway" is defined as the traveled portion—the paved part—of the road. This means that soliciting a ride from the shoulder is permissible in most states. Since pedestrians are generally prohibited from walking on limited-access highways, like large Interstates, hitchhiking on these highways is, of course, prohibited too. However, it is still possible to thumb rides at the entrance roads to these highways.

If, after weighing the pros and cons, you decide to hitchhike, here's some general advice: If you are going to hitchhike, you will have to travel light. *"Travel light and smile."* It is best to carry your gear in a knapsack, since it leaves your hands free to hold a sign—clearly lettered—telling where you're headed. If you're in an area where people feel threatened by long hair, tuck your hair into a hat. Carry maps, clothing suited to the climate you're going to be traveling through, and a supply of water for hot, dusty, rideless days. How safe is hitchhiking? That depends on luck and your judgment. Follow your instincts —if you think for any reason that the ride you are being offered may lead to trouble, don't take it. Women should never hitch alone. A boy-girl combination is probably the most likely to get rides. Hitchhiking at night is not a good idea for anyone—drivers just can't see you. A sensible pamphlet on hitchhiking put out by the Travelers Aid Society of Detroit lists six suggestions for successful hitchhiking:

1. Be visible, wear bright clothing, and stand where you can be seen.
2. Carry as little as possible.
3. Choose morning and late afternoon for soliciting long rides—lunchtime is almost impossible.
4. Hitch on highways rather than expressways.
5. Try to find people who are already traveling—people at rest stops and gas stations. It's better for you to pick your driver than for your driver to pick you.
6. A little paranoia is fine.

One reader disagrees with this last one: *"No. No. No. Fear shows. An invitation to trouble. Paranoia is not fine. It is pointless, can keep one from enjoying the experience of a lifetime, and can be dangerously distracting. A little caution and common sense will do nicely."*

"Out of 29 different rides, all were good. Most people went out of their way to let us off at a convenient point. We were never stopped by officials. People who picked us up were usually wanting company, wanted to hear about our travels, and had a lot of interesting things to tell themselves."

"I usually tried to find a ride at a truck stop by asking the drivers at the entrance of a restaurant or coffeeshop. . . . Even though I was a little scared at the beginning, after listening to all the tales of mugging, I had a wonderful time talking with great Americans."

Going on Foot

If you like to walk with a group, you might want to find out about the many clubs throughout the U.S. that promote hiking and sponsor organized outdoor trips—generally in the parks and wilderness areas. Most of these organizations are regional or statewide.

A listing of more than 25 key hiking clubs along the East Coast can be obtained by writing to the Appalachian Trail Conference, P.O. Box 236, Harpers Ferry, WV 25425. This conference of trail clubs manages the 2000-mile Maine-to-Georgia Appalachian Trail, in conjunction with the National Park Service. For 50¢, they'll send you an information packet about the trail, membership, etc. Be sure to ask specifically for the list of clubs, or you can ask for the names of clubs in a particular area.

One of the hiking clubs on the East Coast is the Adirondack Mountain Club, 172 Ridge St., Glens Falls, NY 12801. The club publishes various trail guides and operates mountain lodges in the Adirondack High Peaks.

On the West Coast, there's the well-known Sierra Club, which has chapters in more than 40 states throughout the U.S. If you write to their headquarters at 530 Bush St., San Francisco, CA 94108, they can direct you to the nearest chapter. They can provide information about the Pacific Crest Trail, which stretches for 2400 miles along the Pacific Coast from Canada to Mexico.

A book especially for walkers is called *Walking: A Guide to Beautiful Walks and Trails in America,* by Jean Calder, published by William Morrow ($3.95). The book lists walks in every state and rates the walks from easy to hard.

Going by Boat

Had you thought of this one? It's a great way to do your part during the energy crisis. Paddlers can get all the information they need on canoes, kayaks, rafts, accessories, rentals, books, maps, and where to use them, from the Chicagoland Canoe Base, Inc., 4019 N. Narragansett Ave., Chicago, IL 60634. Send a stamped, self-addressed envelope for a copy of their book list.

The Appalachian Mountain Club publishes four books that would interest canoeists and kayakers: *AMC River Guide I: Maine* ($7.95); *AMC River Guide II: Central and Southern New England* ($9.95); *New England White Water River Guide,* 2nd edition, by Ray Gabler ($8.95); and *Whitewater Handbook,* 2nd edition, by John Urban and Walley Williams ($4.95). All are available by mail (add $1 shipping on orders for one book, 25¢ for each additional title) from AMC Books, 5 Joy St., Boston, MA 02108.

Some Books to Read

There are a few books that we can recommend to help you get some background on the places you are going to visit. To really get yourself in the mood for your trip you should read novels about the areas you're going to be visiting and see movies set in the places you'll eventually see. But for information on how to actually get around the various cities, where to eat cheaply and well, and for other practical advice, consult some of the following guidebooks:

The Moneywise Guide to North America. Written by Michael von Haag and Anna Crew. Published by Travelaid, this book was put together with the help of thousands of readers—mostly British and European—who have traveled in the U.S., Canada, and Mexico; they offer their candid comments on places to stay, to eat, and to see throughout North America. The 17th (1982) edition is available in the U.S. for $8.95 from Hippocrene Books, Inc., 171 Madison Ave., New York, NY 10016. Or you can order direct from the publisher, Travelaid, P.O. Box 28, Southwater Industrial Estate, Southwater, Sussex, England, enclosing the equivalent of £3.95 plus 55p postage anywhere in the world.

There are three series of guides, all published by Frommer/Pasmantier Publishers, that might interest you.

Books on Hawaii, New York, and Washington, D.C., started out as part of Frommer's well-known $5-a-Day series, but with things the way they are, they are now entitled *Hawaii on $25 a Day, New York on $25 a Day,* and *Washington, D.C. on $25 a Day.* The Hawaii book is $7.25; New York $5.95; and Washington $6.25.

Another Frommer production is the Frommer City Guide series, which includes guides to Washington, D.C., Boston, New York, New Orleans, Philadelphia/Atlantic City, Las Vegas, Los Angeles, San Francisco, and Honolulu. They cost $2.95 each.

And finally, Frommer has added four new guides to its Dollarwise series: *Florida, California and Las Vegas, New England,* and the *Southeast and New Orleans. California* is $5.95; *Florida* is $6.25; the others are $6.95.

A special guide called *How to Live in Florida on $10,000 a Year,* published by Frommer, costs $8.95. Frommer's brand-new *How to Beat the High Cost of Travel* tells how to save money on absolutely all travel items.

Frommer Guides are available at bookstores or from Frommer/Pasmantier Publishers, 1230 Avenue of the Americas, New York, NY 10020.

Another well-known series is the one by Fodor. The following regional titles are available in bookstores or from David McKay Co., 2 Park Ave., New York, NY 10016, all in paperback: *Fodor's Far West* ($8.95); *Colorado* ($6.95); *New England* ($7.95); *New York* ($7.95); *South* ($9.95); and *Southwest* ($7.95). *Fodor's USA,* which covers all 50 states, costs $10.95 in paperback and *Fodor's Budget Travel in America* costs $8.95.

The *Mobil Travel Guides,* published by Rand McNally, are also popular with travelers. There are six regional guides: *California and the West, Great Lakes Area, Middle Atlantic States, Northwest and Great Plains States, Southeastern States,* and *Northeastern States.* Each guide has about 300 pages and includes hotels, restaurants, and sightseeing information; the 1981 editions cost $6.95 each. Another Mobil guide is *The Mobil Travel Guide, Major Cities,* which concentrates on the 53 most-visited U.S. cities; the 1981 edition costs $6.95.

Farm, Ranch & Country Vacations, by Pat Dickerman, is a 240-page listing of ranches, farms, and lodges in the U.S. where city people can go to enjoy some country living. Some of these places are working farms, but don't be alarmed: "At a working farm or ranch guests don't do the work—they *watch* it—unless, of course, they have a special hankering for pitching hay or moving cattle." The 1981 edition costs $9.45 postpaid in the U.S. and $12 by check drawn on a U.S. bank for airmail delivery abroad; it is available from Farm and Ranch Vacations, 36 East 57th St., New York, NY 10022.

One of the newer entries in the field of travel books is *United States 1982,* a "Get 'em and Go Travel Guide" to the "finest in 40 cities," edited by Stephen Birnbaum, published by Houghton Mifflin ($9.95). It is revised and updated annually.

The long-awaited *Let's Go: USA,* one of the Harvard Student Agencies travel series, has appeared on the scene. It's published by E. P. Dutton and costs $5.95 in paperback.

And there are more:

A Literary Tour Guide to the United States: West and Midwest, by Rita Stein, William Morrow, 1979 ($5.95).

A Literary Tour Guide to the United States: Northeast, by Emilie C. Harting, William Morrow, 1978 ($4.95).

A Literary Tour Guide to the United States: South and Southwest, by Rita Stein, William Morrow, 1979 ($5.95).

Amazing America, by Jane and Michael Stern, Random House ($6.95). A guide to the more outlandish spots—the world's largest garbage dump, a museum of quackery, etc.

Adventure Travel, by Pat Dickerman, Adventure Guides, Inc., 1980 ($7.95). Who, what, where, when, and how much for outdoor vacations—

scaling rock, backpacking, and riding horseback into wilderness and more. Send $7.95 plus $1.50 postage and handling to Adventure Guides, Inc., 36 East 57th St., New York, NY 10022.

America's Wonderful Little Hotels and Inns, edited by Barbara Crossette, Congdon & Lattès, 1981 ($8.95). Three hundred places with a special charm in every state.

Guide to the Recommended Country Inns of New England, by Elizabeth Squier and Suzy Chapin, The Globe Pequot Press, 1980 ($6.95). A delightful book with the personal touch. Descriptions of menus at each inn will make your mouth water.

There's a series of guides describing inns in various parts of the country published by Burt Franklin and Co., Inc., 235 East 44th St., New York, NY 10017. The titles in the series are *Country New England Inns, Country Inns of the Mid Atlantic States, Country Inns of the Midwest/Rocky Mountains,* and *Country Inns of the West/Southwest.* The 1981–82 editions of these books cost $4.95 each and are available from the publisher.

Made in America: A Guide to Tours of Workshops, Farms, Mines and Industries, by Susan Farlow, Hastings House, 1979 ($7.95). Some American companies that invite you in to see how they work.

Walking Tours of America, Collier Books, 1979 ($7.95). The Kinney Shoe Corporation (get it?) together with a group of "tour experts" present 60 walks in major cities all over the U.S.

Walking Tours of New England, by Kenneth Winchester and David Dunbar, Doubleday, 1980 ($8.95). A footloose guide to mansions and museums, village ghosts and village greens, Yankee dreamers and doers.

New England Off the Beaten Path, by Corinne Madden Ross and Ralph Woodward, East Woods Press, 1981 ($4.95). By the same people who wrote *The New England Guest House Book,* mentioned in the next chapter. These are the places that the authors must have discovered while they researched guest houses.

Honky Tonkin', A Travel Guide to American Music, by Richard Wootton, Travelaid, 1980 ($6.95). It is distributed in the U.S. by East Woods Press, 820 East Blvd., Charlotte, NC 28203. You must send $1.30 for postage and handling. Where to go to hear what you like while you're on the road.

Roadnotes: A Student's Guide to North America's Adventures and Delights, by the editors of *America* magazine, Rand McNally ($6.95). Spring-break beaches, cheap ski resorts, white-water rivers, and uncrowded trails.

See Chapter 2 for additional books on accommodations in various parts of the U.S.

CHAPTER 2

Staying Awhile

When we first began searching out inexpensive places to stay in the U.S., we got mostly encouragement from the people we talked to. But one of our favorite responses was a letter that said: "You must be kidding or out of your minds. For that amount of money you can't even get accommodations in a tent—you are wasting your time."

We are delighted to say that the person who wrote that was completely and absolutely wrong. We have uncovered hundreds of places to stay that are under $25 per person per night. Some of the accommodations listed are spartan —room for a sleeping bag on a gymnasium floor for $3 a night—but we've also found luxurious rooms in a modern resort with just about every recreation facility imaginable for $20 a night. We've been able to list places suitable for people of all ages, although we do have some "students only" information. In general, we have listed any and every place we could find that offers a place to stay for under $25 for a single per night, our limit. (At times, in some of the larger cities, we've listed hotels where singles are more than $25 but doubles work out to $25 or less per person.) Needless to say, we haven't found everything that exists in this category. So if you come across a good place to stay that's under $25, let us know; we'll contact the people who run it and maybe list it in our next edition. Many of the additions to this year's listings have come via our readers and we're pleased about their willingness to help.

Accommodations are listed here by state and then by city. In order to make it easier for you to know where the cities listed are in relation to where you are, we have provided a map at the beginning of each state section and have put on that map the cities where we have listings. Fifteen of the largest U.S. cities have expanded sections incorporated into the state-by-state listings. These sections include information not only on accommodations but also on places to eat, things to do, how to get around, etc.

In each accommodation listing we have included the name of the facility, the address, the telephone number, and, when helpful, the name of the person to ask for when calling for information. Whenever a facility has agreed to offer a special discount rate to holders of the International Student Identity Card (ISIC), readers of *Where to Stay,* or senior citizens, or has access facilities for the disabled, we have indicated this with the following symbols:

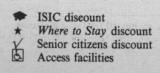

🎓 ISIC discount
★ *Where to Stay* discount
✓ Senior citizens discount
♿ Access facilities

We have listed the rates (per room unless otherwise indicated) and have noted whether accommodations are for men or women only and whether children can be accommodated. If the facility is open only at a certain time of the year, the dates are given, and if reservations are necessary this is also indicated. Any other information that we thought was either interesting or helpful or both, we put into the listings. To help you understand the types of accommodations in this book, we've described below the different kinds of places we have listed, what to expect from them, and, in some cases, what they expect from you.

"Where did I stay? In motels, campgrounds, youth hostels, with friends and relatives, in a barn, a school bus, on a picnic table, in a cave, and a university dorm."

American Youth Hostels

". . . Youth hostels were my salvation. Without fail, the houseparents were friendly and helpful, accommodation was good if sometimes basic, and prices were rock-bottom. I almost always found someone to travel with for a few days and saw none of the school parties and strictly enforced rules that so often mar English and European hostels. Altogether, a really good deal."

There are more than 250 youth hostels scattered through the U.S. that are operated by the American Youth Hostels, Inc., a member of the International Youth Hostel Federation. AYH hostels are often in private homes, and because they are meant for people who travel under their own steam—hikers, bicyclists, canoeists, skiers, or horseback riders—are often located in rural areas near parks, forests, or preserves. They are often in particularly beautiful settings, off the beaten path. There are now many AYH facilities in the larger cities as well—cities like Washington, D.C., Phoenix, Philadelphia, Seattle, San Francisco, Los Angeles, San Diego, Chicago, etc.

In order to use the hostel facilities of AYH, you must be a member of the organization. One year's membership costs $7 for anyone under 18 or over 59 years of age and $14 for anyone else. Membership passes are available from American Youth Hostels, 8th Floor, 1332 I St. NW, Washington, DC 20005, and from AYH councils and agencies in certain metropolitan areas. Check the telephone directory for listings or ask a travel agent. Visiting foreign students should have a membership card from their own national youth hostel association; in emergencies they may obtain an International Youth Hostel Pass from AYH National Headquarters (see above address).

"A youth hostel card, bought either in the U.S. or in a foreign visitor's home country, is strongly recommended. For example, in one place, if you don't have a card, the cost of an overnight will be $30; with the card it is $7.50."

Not all AYH facilities are the same; there are, in fact, three categories of hostels. By definition, a hostel is a low-cost, supervised, overnight accommodation for people traveling. It has maximum fees established by AYH, Inc., resident houseparents, separate dormitories and washing/toilet facilities, a kitchen, and a dining room and common room. A "home hostel" is someone's private residence and usually has all the basic elements of a hostel. The difference is size. A hostel usually has between 10 and 100 beds; a home hostel usually has only one to eight beds. Often the kitchen is the homeowner's private kitchen and, while meals may be provided, the hostelers cannot always expect to prepare their own meals. Overnight rates vary from hostel to hostel and sometimes change with the seasons. Rates are usually from $3 to $10 per night; exact rates that were in effect at press time are given in the individual listings.

And finally, there are supplemental accommodations (indicated in our book by "AYH-SA" in parentheses after the name), which provide most of the facilities of a regular hostel but are lacking one or more of the basic elements of a hostel—usually this is a kitchen or a houseparent, since the supplemental accommodations are often YMCAs, camps, etc. Rates at supplemental facilities are higher than standard hostel rates, and AYH membership is not usually required. Unless otherwise stated, the AYH-SA rates given in *Where to Stay*'s listings are for AYH members; nonmembers can expect a higher rate.

Reservations are generally recommended for overnight stays in hostels and should be made as far in advance as possible. To make a reservation, send the hostel a deposit equal to one night's accommodation. If reservations are absolutely required, the listings will indicate it.

A new International Advanced Booking Voucher scheme, whereby hostelers can make reservations at hostels all over the world before they set off on their trip, is now in operation. Write to the AYH National Headquarters for details.

All hostels share a common set of what *Hosteling USA* calls "customs": cooking, cleaning, and general hostel duties must be shared by hostelers; drinking, smoking, and illegal drugs are not allowed; check-out time is 9:30 a.m., and hostels are usually closed between 10 a.m. and 4 p.m.

For full information on AYH hostels in the U.S. and an extensive introduction to other hostel-related activities, including exact locations, facilities near each hostel, etc., you should have a copy of *Hosteling USA*. A somewhat less extensive manual called the *AYH Guide and Handbook* comes free with every AYH membership. Copies of *Hosteling USA* are available for $6.95 in bookstores or from AYH, Inc., at the above address. When ordering the book directly from AYH, add $1.30 for postage and handling.

Other Hostels

As you read through the accommodation listings in *Where to Stay USA*, you will find some facilities that call themselves hostels but are not affiliated with American Youth Hostels and do not have AYH written after their name. These are independent accommodation facilities set up by a variety of people and groups but all with one goal in common: to provide a cheap, relatively comfortable, and friendly place for people on the road to spend a night or two. Many of these hostels are in urban areas; often they have cooking facilities and sometimes even free kitchens. These independent hostels are operated by churches, community groups, and sometimes even by YMCAs.

Many of the hostels described above are open only a few hours a day for registration, since they are often short-staffed, so we suggest that you call ahead to find out the best time to arrive. All of these places are adamant about some basic rules which always include the prohibition of alcohol, drugs, or weapons on the premises. It is also common for the facilities to have a minimum age requirement. This is because in some states sheltering anyone under 18, or even 16, may be defined legally as "housing a runaway." If you are under 18 and traveling, it may be wise to carry a letter from your parents stating that they know you are traveling and that you have their permission to do so.

Most of these independent hostels also limit the length of your stay to two or three nights. They are, after all, for people passing through, and you must leave room for others who need what is usually rather limited space.

YMCAs and YWCAs

Young Men's Christian Associations (YMCAs) and Young Women's Christian Associations (YWCAs) are well known all over the world as organizations that will often provide inexpensive housing to transients. Ys are completely non-denominational in spite of their name and provide, besides accommodations, many recreational facilities such as swimming pools, gymnasiums, ball courts, and various programmed activities.

Not all Ys have accommodation facilities, but we contacted the ones that do and have listed the ones that responded. There are certain generalizations that we can make about staying in Y facilities. Usually rooms in Ys do not have private baths or showers, and you must share these facilities with others on your floor. Some YMCAs can accommodate both men and women, but most YWCAs can accommodate only women. This is indicated in the listings. Usually you may use the Y's recreational facilities at no extra cost when you spend the night there; sometimes if you are not a member of the YMCA or YWCA you will be required to pay a small membership fee along with the overnight rate. In well-traveled areas Ys are popular places to stay, so it is usually wise to call ahead to see if there is room for you. Some Ys require reservations; our listing will indicate if this is the case. It's possible to purchase prepaid vouchers for stays in 72 YMCA centers in 65 cities in the U.S. and Canada. The vouchers cost $11 single and $16 for twin rooms; a voucher guarantees a room in most of these Ys and reservations are recommended. Contact "The Y's Way to Visit the USA and Canada," YMCA, 356 West 34th St., New York, NY 10001. Telephone: 212/760-5856 or 760-5892.

Information on accommodations at the 124 YWCAs across the country can be obtained by writing to the National Board, YWCA, 600 Lexington Ave., New York, NY 10022. Telephone: 212/753-4700. Rates usually run from $10 to $15 per person per night. Advance reservations are usually recommended.

International Houses

Some large cities and university campuses have special residences where international students and American students live together, usually during the academic year. These International Houses are often filled to capacity, but sometimes they have room for transient students during the summer or school vacations. We list some of the International Houses that will rent space to travelers, but even if there is no room for you, the people at an International House can usually be counted on to help you get your bearings in their city, and you may even be able to participate in their programmed activities such as movies, dances, lectures, etc.

Dormitories and Residence Halls

There are many dormitories and residence halls at both large and small schools that are willing and able to put up traveling students in extra beds. We received a positive response from the housing offices of many U.S. colleges and universities and would certainly recommend that whenever you are in the neighborhood of a campus you check out its accommodation facilities. Even if a campus is not listed here, we would suggest your calling the housing office or asking at the student union about a place where you can spend the night. You will rarely be turned away.

Besides the dormitories and residence halls that are operated by colleges, there are residence halls that are operated privately to serve the local student population. Most of these residence halls are only a few years old and are quite luxurious. Usually they are divided into apartment-type areas with four single bedrooms, one kitchen, and one bathroom to each area. The buildings are often equipped with swimming pools, tennis courts, Ping-Pong tables, etc.

Although we don't have any to list, try sorority and fraternity houses too when you're on a campus. They may have room for you.

"I traveled with another guy for most of my trip. We found the easiest places to crash were fraternity houses. We stayed in them at Northwestern, Washington University (St. Louis, Mo.), and at the University of Utah in Salt Lake City. The best thing about frats is they usually have kitchens. Bring a sleeping bag to use on the floor."

Low-Cost Motel Chains

Something exciting has happened in the motel management field and that's the development of the low-cost motel chain. Based on the reasonable premise that travelers were getting tired of paying exorbitant prices for motel rooms, a few U.S. capitalists decided to build no-frills facilities that would not have to charge high rates to stay in business. This meant cutting out some of the extras such as restaurants on the property (they built their buildings across the street from the existing restaurants instead), wall-to-wall carpeting, etc. The first low-cost motel chain did so well that others have followed the lead, and now there are quite a few motels all over the U.S. where you can spend the night comfortably and cheaply. We've included the following low-cost motel chains in our listings:

Best Value Inns / Superior Motels, Budget Host Inns, California 6/ Western 6 Motels, Days Inns of America, E-Z 8 Motels, Econo-Travel Motor Hotel Corporation, Exel Inns, Friendship Inns, Imperial 400 Motor Inns, Motel 6, Red Roof Inns, Regal 8 Inns, Scottish Inns, Sixpence Inns, Susse Chalet Motor Lodges and Inns, and Thrifty Scot Motels.

The rates of the various low-cost motels vary from chain to chain, and sometimes even within the chain, but, in general, the more people you can fit into one room the more money you will save. It is always advisable to make reservations in advance at these motels, since they have become extremely popular with travelers.

"The budget motels are very heavily booked especially during the summer and the chance of getting a room after 2 p.m. is slim indeed."

For free directories of all the facilities in any of the low-cost chains, you can write to the following addresses. If a chain has a toll-free telephone reservation number it's included below:

Best Value Inns / Superior Motels
2602 Corporate Ave. East, Suite 125
Memphis, TN 38132
Toll-free reservations numbers:
Best Value: 800/238-2552
Superior: 800/238-2564
(In Tennessee, 800/582-2405)

Budget Host Inns
P.O. Box 10656
2601 Jacksboro Hwy., Suite 202
Fort Worth, TX 76114

California 6 / Western 6 Motels
Executive Offices
1156 South 7th Ave.
Hacienda Heights, CA 91745

Days Inns of America, Inc.
2751 Buford Hwy. NE
Atlanta, GA 30324
Toll-free reservations numbers for each state are given in free directory.
10% discount to those over 55 who join September Days Club. Write for
details.

E-Z 8 Motels
2484 Hotel Circle Pl.
San Diego, CA 92108

Econo-Travel Motor Hotel Corporation
20 Koger Executive Center
P.O. Box 12188
Norfolk, VA 23502
Toll-free reservations number: 800/446-6900
(In Virginia, 800/582-5882)
10% discount available to ages 55 and over.
Write for details.

Exel Inns of America, Inc.
4706 East Washington Ave.
Madison, WI 53704
Toll-free reservations number: 800/238-2552

Friendship Inns International
739 South 4th West
Salt Lake City, UT 84101
Toll-free reservations number: 800/453-4111

Imperial 400 National, Inc.
1830 North Nash St.
Arlington, VA 22209
Toll-free reservations number: 800/531-5300
(In Texas, 800/252-9649)

Motel 6
51 Hitchcock Way
Santa Barbara, CA 93105

Red Roof Inns
4355 Davidson Rd.
Amlin, OH 43002
Toll-free reservations number: 800/848-7878
(In Ohio, 800/282-7990)

Regal 8 Inns
P.O. Box 1268
Mt. Vernon, IL 62864

Scottish Inns, Inc.
Gate West, Suite 213
515 Two Mile Pkwy.
Goodlettsville, TN 37072
Toll-free reservations number: 800/251-1962
(In Tennessee, 800/342-1819)
10% discount available to those over 55 with Super Senior Saver 55 Club card.
Write for details.

Sixpence Inns of America, Inc.
1751 East Garry Ave.
Santa Ana, CA 92705

Susse Chalet Motor Lodges and Inns
Chalet Susse International, Inc.
2 Progress Ave.
Nashua, NH 03062
Toll-free reservations number: 800/258-1980
(In New Hampshire, 800/572-1880)

Thrifty Scot Motels, Inc.
1 Sunwood Dr.
P.O. Box 399
St. Cloud, MN 56302
Toll-free reservations number: 800/228-3222
(In Nebraska and Canada, call collect: 402/572-7722)

Pilot Books, 347 Fifth Ave., New York, NY 10016, publishes a *National Directory of Budget Motels.* The 1982 edition is available for $3.50 postpaid.

"Motels can be a great value. Particularly at touristy places out of season, it really pays to bargain. For example, when we were in Fort Lauderdale, Fla., the first two places told us it would be $26 for a double everywhere. Next door we got it down to $24 and next door to that, to $22. We checked next door to this last place and then returned to say the bloke next door was charging $18. We ended up with a magnificent room for $15."

Tourist Homes, Guest Houses, and Bed and Breakfast

For quite a while there were very few sources of information on tourist homes and guest houses, but happily we can now refer those in search of this kind of accommodation to two publications: *Guide to Guest Houses and Tourist Homes USA,* available from Tourist House Associates, Inc., RD 2, Box 355A, Greentown, PA 18426, for $5. The compiler of the directory, Betty Rundback, has listed 250 accommodations in 40 states and Nova Scotia. "These are all private residences where the owners rent their spare bedrooms to travelers and where you're made to feel more like a welcome guest than a paying customer." Rates are generally lower than motels and often include a continental breakfast. The guide also includes 13 bed-and-breakfast reservation services that give travelers entry to 1000 more homes.

Two other books on the subject are *The New England Guest House Book,* by Corinne Madden Ross, published by East Woods Press, 820 East Blvd., Charlotte, NC 28203 ($6.95), and *The Southern Guest House Book,* by the same author and publisher, and at the same price. Ms. Ross defines her subject matter as a place "that provides only lodging and is, on the average, smaller than an inn, with fewer rooms." Many of the places she lists are in popular resort areas where hotels and motels tend to be expensive and a guest house makes a terrific alternative.

It's probably due to the high cost of hotel and motel facilities, but whatever the reason, there seems to be quite a bit of interest lately in the idea of developing bed-and-breakfast facilities in the U.S. One organization that is involved in this movement is The International Spareroom, P.O. Box 518, Solana Beach, CA 92075. This organization keeps a list of people in many U.S. locations who have a room to rent in their homes for a minimum stay of three nights. Rates vary from home to home, and some provide access facilities. Write for details. If the idea of bed and breakfast in a private home is appealing to you and you're traveling in Washington, Oregon, Idaho, or California, contact Northwest Bed and Breakfast, 7707 Southwest Locust St., Tigard, OR 97227. The annual membership fee is $15 for one person, $20 for a family. Overnight rates vary from $14 to $22 for a single, $18 to $30 for a double, and $26 to $34 for a family. A descriptive listing of all homes in the Northwest network is available for $4; this amount will be credited to your membership fee.

Bed & Breakfast International, 151 Ardmore Rd., Kensington, CA 94707, is another organization that places people in private homes in the San Francisco Bay Area, the Napa Valley, Lake Tahoe, Carmel/Monterey, Los Angeles, San Diego, and other locations on the West Coast, as well as Hawaii, New York City, and Washington, D.C. A double, breakfast included, is $26 to $85 (students may request lower rates), and the minimum stay is three nights. For an application, write to the address above and enclose a stamped, self-addressed envelope. (Look for other bed-and-breakfast possibilities in the Colorado and California chapters.)

Camping

Camping in the U.S. can be a fabulous experience. The facilities are widespread and generally excellent, and it shouldn't be too difficult for you to avoid the trailer set and enjoy the great outdoors. Our favorites are the state and national parks, which are much more beautiful than most private campgrounds. Be warned, though, that state and national parks are extremely popular with campers, and it's possible that some will be filled to capacity when you decide to go.

In our state listings we have room to list only national parks, with a few exceptions. For complete information on state parks, just write or call the state tourist office listed for each state. Most publish lists and accompanying maps describing facilities and will send them to you—all free of charge, of course.

Anyone who intends to use the national park system extensively should purchase a *Golden Eagle Passport,* which is sold at all parks. The passport costs $10 and provides free entry to all areas of the national park system that charge entrance fees. The free entry applies to the permit holder and everyone accompanying him or her in a private, noncommercial vehicle; it is valid for the calendar year. Normally the entrance fees to the parks range from $1 to $3 per passenger vehicle.

The *Golden Age Passport* is issued free to any U.S. citizen age 62 or older upon presentation of proof of age at any park. It permits free admission to all areas of the national park system and a 50% discount on recreation fees. Applicants must apply in person.

Most campsites in the national park system are available on a first-come, first-served basis only. However, reservations can be obtained for campsites at Dinosaur National Monument, four campgrounds at Mount McKinley National Park (Alaska), and campgrounds at Acadia and Grand Canyon National Parks, Chickasaw National Recreation Area, and Cumberland Island and Point Reyes National Seashores. For reservations, write to the addresses given in the listings for these campgrounds, to the attention of the superintendent. Reservations may be made through Ticketron for Cape Hatteras National Seashore, Great Smoky Mountains National Park, Shenandoah National Park, Grand Canyon National Park, Rocky Mountain National Park, Sequoia-Kings Canyon National Park, and Yosemite National Park. Reservation forms are available at Ticketron outlets and the Ticketron Reservations Office, P.O. Box 2715, San Francisco, CA 94126.

Since campsites in the national parks are so much in demand, it has been necessary for the park service to limit the number of days a person may occupy a site at some of the parks during the peak season. This time limit, and all other information about the park, is available from the address listed in each state section. Remember that the address we list here for the park is not necessarily the location of the campground—it is a mailing address only. In some cases, campgrounds may be many, many miles from the town listed as the mailing address.

For a list of the 100 areas maintained by the National Park Service, and information on their facilities, send $2.25 to the Superintendent of Documents, U.S. Government Printing Office, Washington, DC 20402, and ask for *Camping in the National Parks.*

Three other useful publications available from the same source are *Lesser-Known Areas of the National Park System* ($3.50); *Visitor Accommodations, Facilities and Services* ($3.75), which lists overnight lodging accommodations and other facilities and services provided by concessioners in the National Park System; and *Back-Country Travel in the National Park System* ($1), which is geared toward the backpacker.

The Consumer Information Center, Pueblo, CO 81009, can send you *Camping in the National Parks*—188K ($2.25); as well as *Guide and Map to the National Parks*—190K ($2). Also available is a free brochure describing *Golden Eagle / Golden Age / Golden Access Passports*—595K.

Another book that has come to our attention is *Free Campgrounds, U.S.A.,* VanMeer Publications, Inc., 1982 ($8.95). It is a listing of over 6000 free campgrounds in the United States. To receive a copy, send $8.95 plus $1 for postage and handling to VanMeer Publications, Inc., P.O. Box 1289, Clearwater, FL 33517.

For a comprehensive listing of all campgrounds in the U.S., both public and private, we recommend the *Rand McNally Campground and Trailer Park Guide;* the 1981 edition costs $9.95 and is available in most bookstores. The Rand McNally guide is especially useful, since it contains maps of each state with every campground listed marked on them. This makes it easy to plan your travel route according to available campgrounds. Rand McNally also publishes its guide in regional editions; the 1981 edition of *The Western Campgrounds and Trailer Parks Guide* is $5.95, while the northeastern, southeastern, and midwestern editions are $4.95 each.

If the idea of camping on Indian lands interests you, write to the U.S. Department of the Interior, Bureau of Indian Affairs, Washington, DC 20242, and ask for its map of Indian Land Areas. On the back of the map are listed the addresses of area and agency offices of BIA where you can write for specific information on existing sites.

Crashing

There's not much one can say about this kind of accommodation. You find it where you can, and whether you do or not depends on your own resourcefulness. More and more areas of the country have gotten used to the idea of crashing, and if you carry a sleeping bag along you'll find crashing a lot easier. College towns are the most likely places to find crashing space; stop at some of the on-campus addresses given in the state listings to ask about the chances for crashing in the neighborhood. Or check out a local underground paper or a flourishing health food store—the people there will probably know where to send you. Many of the hotlines listed in *Where to Stay USA* will also be able to tell you whether there's any crashing space around.

Names of people who are willing to share their home with travelers who may someday make space for them can be found in the *Traveler's Directory.* The Directory is available only to people who are willing to be listed in it themselves. It is published by Tom Linn, 6224 Baynton St., Philadelphia, PA 19144. Telephone: 215/844-6111 (evenings). Write to ask for a questionnaire, and he'll send you what you need in order to be listed. Listings cost $15 each and the fee includes back issues of the Directory when available. Traveler's Directory members receive free copies of *The Vagabonds' Shoes,* the organization's quarterly newsletter, which includes travel features, transportation bargains, mutual-aid columns, and travel book reviews. Nonmembers may order a year's subscription for $7.

Last Resorts

Most communities have shelters for people who have absolutely no place else to turn. These are places run by organizations like the Salvation Army, which operates 200 centers for the homeless in the U.S. Most Salvation Army Centers serve transient men, but some have room for women. Leave places like the Salvation Army residences for the people who really need them.

"I met two guys who had had their packs ripped off in Colorado Springs and had nothing to their names. I went with them to the Salvation Army where they were able to get $4 worth of groceries and $6 worth of clothes—they also told them about churches, etc., that gave out free food. I'd advise anyone in trouble to check out a Salvation Army."

People Who Can Help

The idea of community switchboards, hotlines, free clinics, and help lines has caught on all over the country, and there isn't any place that you'll be where help is farther than a telephone call away. If you have a problem, need a place to stay or some medical care, or just want to hear a friendly voice, you can call the help lines listed in each state section.

In researching *Where to Stay USA,* we asked friends all over the country about the help lines and crisis centers that were located in their areas so that we could include them in our book. Hotlines seem to come and go with great rapidity; the telephone numbers that we have here were in service when we went to press and hopefully still are.

In the "Help" section of each state listing, besides the telephone numbers of hotlines and crisis centers you'll often find the addresses and telephone numbers of Travelers Aid offices. Travelers Aid (its full name is Travelers Aid Association of America) is a social work agency with branches in 25 airports, 31 bus stations, and 4 railroad stations that has been set up to assist people on the move by providing emergency assistance, protective care, and professional counseling service. Often you'll find Travelers Aid offices in bus, train, or air terminals. Feel free to call on them if you need help.

Two other organizations that should be mentioned here are CONTACT Teleministries and the National Runaway Switchboard. CONTACT is a network of crisis-intervention, information, and referral help lines. There are 100 centers in operation in 150 different calling areas. Thirty-two of these centers provide "Deaf CONTACT/TTY Services"—teletypewriter programs to serve the deaf. You can get a complete list of these services and their phone numbers by writing to CONTACT Teleministries USA, Inc., Room 125, 900 South Arlington Ave., Harrisburg, PA 17109, or by calling 717/652-3410.

The National Runaway Switchboard is operated by Metro-Help, Inc., in Chicago. It takes calls from around the country on a toll-free line. "Kids can call us from anywhere in the continental U.S. and get information on over 3000 runaway centers, central community switchboards, and counseling agencies around the country. In addition, we can also use a conferencing device on the phone to allow kids to talk directly with any of these agencies or their parents. If a runaway wants to let his or her parents know that he or she is all right, we'll also deliver the message. . . ." The toll-free number is 800/621-4000 and is available 24 hours a day. All services are confidential.

For the Handicapped

For much too long, handicapped travelers were ignored; there was very, very little information for them and facilities that could make their travel at the least possible, and at the most pleasurable, were minimal. That has changed and much has been done to develop facilities for these people and many new publications are available to them. Two of them that have come to our attention are *Air Travel for the Handicapped,* free from TWA offices, and the *Directory of Adventure Alternatives in Corrections, Mental Health, Special Education and*

Physical Rehabilitation, a list of 78 wilderness programs—with descriptions and populations they serve—photocopied from the *Journal of Experiential Education.* For a copy of the Directory, send $4 plus $1 postage and handling to the Journal of the Association for Experiential Education, P.O. Box 4625, Denver, CO 80204.

And finally, we refer you to a book called *Travel Ability: A Guide for Physically Disabled Travelers in the U.S.,* by Lois Reamy, published by Macmillan ($9.95). The intention of this book is to encourage the handicapped to travel—it provides answers to such questions as: How do you find a hotel with barrier-free rooms or a travel agent who specializes in booking for disabled clients? It's full, too, of personal experiences that make it all the more useful.

For Senior Citizens

The American Association of Retired Persons / National Retired Teachers Association (NRTA/AARP), with national headquarters at 1909 K St. NW, Washington, DC 20006, offers members a purchase privilege program which includes discounts on auto rentals with Hertz and Avis, on accommodations at Holiday Inns, Howard Johnson's Motor Lodges, Quality Inns, Ramada Inns, Rodeway Inns, Scottish Inns of America, Sheraton Hotels and Inns, Sonesta Hotels, and Treadway Inns. For information on this program and on membership in NRTA/AARP, write to the address above.

Another organization that serves senior citizens and has become extremely popular in the past few years is Elderhostel, a Boston-based group that sponsors study vacations on college campuses all over the U.S. Friends of ours who have participated in Elderhostel said that it was the best vacation they'd had in over 40 years of vacationing. For a catalog of Elderhostel programs, write to the organization at 100 Boylston St., Suite 200, Boston, MA 02116.

Also of interest to senior citizens is *The Discount Guide for Travelers Over 55,* by Caroline and Walter Weintz, E. P. Dutton ($5.75), and *Travel Tips for Senior Citizens,* a 21-page pamphlet which sells for $1 and is available from the Superintendent of Documents, U. S. Government Printing Office, Washington, DC 20402.

Many budget motel chains offer special discounts to senior citizens— check with the head offices of the individual chains (addresses on pages 24-26) for information.

Paying Your Way

As you travel, it may be possible to pick up odd jobs here and there to give you enough money to keep you going. This is probably going to be a difficult year for finding jobs, though, since unemployment is a serious problem in many areas.

State employment offices can usually offer good advice on the current work situation in any particular area—feel free to call on them for advice.

If you run out of money and need a job immediately in order to keep you going, you can try calling the help line numbers. Sometimes they can refer you to a temporary job that will give you enough money to move on.

There are some sweeping generalizations that can be made about job-finding in the U.S. One is, don't count on finding work in California, where too many others are job-seeking. If you're going across country and think you're going to need some more money to see you through, try Texas instead—the economy there is booming and jobs should not be too difficult to find. Big cities are good places to look for a job—especially in the service industries—as waiters, waitresses, sales help, etc.

Note: Foreign visitors with B (visitors) visas may not seek paid employment during their stay in the U.S. To work without the proper visa is illegal.

Volunteering

There's a lot to be done in the U.S. that must be done by volunteers. If you are interested in knowing what voluntary service opportunities exist in the U.S. for 1982, consult a copy of *Invest Yourself*, a catalog of service opportunities in the U.S. and abroad. *Invest Yourself* has been compiled by the Commission on Voluntary Service and Action, and is available by mail for $3 from *Invest Yourself*, c/o Susan Angus, P.O. Box 117, New York, NY 10009.

The National Park Service recruits volunteers for the national parks who are asked to perform a variety of tasks at the parks in the areas of interpretation (helping visitors understand the natural and human history of the area); arts and crafts; history, archeology, and natural science; environmental study; and resource management. You can get a brochure (*Volunteers in Parks*) and application from the National Park Service, U.S. Department of the Interior, Washington, DC 20240.

Eating

It's going to be tempting, as you travel, to do most of your eating at the fast-food chain restaurants that are springing up all over America. That's why we decided to list a few of our friends' favorite eating places in the state listings and have resisted mentioning any of the chains; we hope to prove that you can still find good, filling, low-cost meals without having to resort to the chains.

If you're trying to economize, why not forget eating in restaurants altogether, buy your food in supermarkets, and have yourself a picnic?

Many of the accommodations listed in *Where to Stay USA* have cooking facilities available; whenever this is true, be sure to take advantage of them. We have one friend who used to cook hamburgers in his hotel room on a travel iron that he carried around with him—there are all sorts of ways to save money if you put your mind to it.

If food is important and you want some help deciding where to eat wherever you are, you might be interested in the book called *Where to Eat in America*, edited by William Rice and Benton Wolf and published by Random House ($7.95). This book covers 50 cities and, according to the editors, is "intended for anyone away from home who is hungry or about to be hungry."

We can recommend one more book for those who care about what they eat. It is *Roadfood*, by Jane and Michael Stern, published by Random House ($7.95). According to the Sterns, "It is possible to escape homogenized cuisine that lines the highways and makes eating in Arizona indistinguishable from eating in Maine." They point the way, listing 400 of what they consider America's best regional restaurants within ten miles of a major highway.

CHAPTER 3

Especially for Foreign Visitors

The U.S., often judged so harshly by the natives, usually gets rave reviews from foreign visitors. If you're anything like the people from abroad who stopped by to see us after their trips around the U.S., you're going to have a wonderful time here. One of the reasons for this, and probably the most important, is that Americans really are a friendly bunch, especially the ones who live beyond the large cities and have more time for everything, including enjoying a visitor from another country. One young Frenchman put it neatly: "Everywhere we are welcome."

In this section we've organized a few things that you should know before you start out on your trip in the U.S. Some are related to special discounts available to you because you are an international visitor. (Remember that all special discounts are, unfortunately, subject to change or cancellation without warning.) Others are more practical, everyday bits of information designed to save you the common traumas of travel, e.g., your first phone call from a pay telephone or your first taxi ride.

Don't forget to read the introductory chapters too, since they contain information that everyone—American or foreign—needs when traveling in this country.

For those who plan to study in the U.S. for a few months or longer, we'd like to recommend a booklet compiled by the Institute of International Education, 809 United Nations Plaza, New York, NY 10017, titled *Practical Guide for Foreign Visitors* ($2.50). The 50-page publication describes higher education in the U.S., government regulations, arrival in the U.S., and the realities of the cost of living in the U.S., and it includes something about life in the U.S. When ordering by mail in the U.S., enclose 75¢ postage. The booklet is also available on some U.S. college campuses. To obtain the booklet abroad, go to the nearest U.S. International Communication Agency, located in the capital city of each country where there's a U.S. Embassy.

Hotline for Foreign Visitors

Besides all the switchboards and hotlines that are listed in each state section of this book, there's a special hotline for foreign visitors which is operated by TraveLodge and was set up with the help of the U.S. Travel Service. It's called the Travel Phone North American Desk, and although it's located way out in the middle of the country in Mission, Kan., the Travel Phone's hotline number is toll free—this means that you do not have to pay anything to call. The number is 800/255-3050. In Kansas it's 800/332-4350. There are people waiting at the number from 8 a.m. to 11 p.m., Monday to Friday, and from 11 a.m. to 7 p.m. on Saturday and Sunday (that's Central Standard Time) to answer your questions on sightseeing, accommodations, transportation, etc. The operators speak (besides English) German, Japanese, French, and Spanish, and if you speak a language other than these, they can still probably find someone to help you.

If you are in Canada and want information on travel in the U.S. before you get here, call toll free: 800/268-3330 from anywhere except British Columbia, where the number is 112-800/268-3330.

Transportation Discounts

BY AIR: Air travel is extremely popular in the U.S. There are planes flying in and out of 1000 different airports across the country, and with the help of air-taxi services it is possible to fly to many of the smaller cities and towns, too. For long-distance travel, it is often as inexpensive or even less expensive to go by air than by train for the same distances. And discounting airport delays and traffic jams getting to the airport, it's the fastest way to get from one place to another.

You will probably find that travel in the U.S. is less expensive mile for mile than it is at home, and if you take advantage of the following special discounts, you can travel by air and still keep to a modest budget:

● **Visit USA Fares:** This fare represents a 25% reduction of the regular one-way fare. You are eligible just as long as you are a resident of any country other than the U.S. and your travel begins and ends at least 100 miles beyond the borders of the U.S.

Tickets must be purchased either before arrival in the U.S. or within seven days after arrival—it all depends on the individual airline. The following airlines participate: Alaskan, American, Braniff, Delta, Eastern, National, Northwest, Pan Am, TWA, United, Western, and Hughes Airwest. (There are differences among the airlines, so be sure to check the details with any one you contact.)

● **Visit Florida Fares:** This is an unlimited-mileage deal offered by Air Florida primarily on routes within Florida. The fares are $99 for 14 days, $198 for 21 days, and $297 for 28 days.

● **Continental Airlines Excursion Fare:** Continental offers a special 30-day excursion fare of approximately $375 for travel in the continental U.S. Arrangements for this fare must be made before arrival in the U.S.

● **Eastern Airlines Unlimited Mileage Fare:** See Chapter 1, since this fare is available to foreign visitors and U.S. travelers as well.

BY BUS: Bus travel is inexpensive and a favorite with young people, both because of the cost and because you get to see a lot of the U.S. from a seat in a bus—everything that you'd miss if you went by plane. See page 9 for information on the Ameripass and Eaglepass and other bargains to which both foreign visitors and Americans are entitled.

BY TRAIN: An International U.S.A. Rail Pass is available to permanent residents of foreign countries. It must be purchased *before* your arrival in the U.S. The pass entitles the holder to unlimited coach travel for a choice of 7, 14, 21, or 30 days. The prices are as follows: 7 days, $220; 14 days, $330; 21

days, $440; 30 days, $550. Children between the ages of 2 and 12 pay one-half the above. (Residents of Canada and Mexico are not allowed to purchase the pass.) Passes are valid for 90 days from the date of purchase.

It will be necessary to present your pass at an Amtrak ticket office, where you will receive tickets for the particular trips you want to take.

The U.S.A. Rail Pass is good for travel on any part of the Amtrak system. According to the people in the public relations department of Amtrak, "a pass holder could simply ride a train to enjoy a reasonably priced meal on an Amtrak diner." Details and passes should be available in your country from most travel agents. Remember that on the more popular long-distance runs in the U.S. it is necessary to have reservations in advance of your train trip. U.S.A. Rail Pass holders should be sure to make reservations; there is no charge for them.

BY CAR: To drive in the U.S. all you'll need is a valid driver's license from your own country, as long as it is one of the 161 countries that have agreed to the Geneva Road Traffic Convention of 1949. (If you are not from one of these countries, you will have to obtain a U.S. driver's license at your point of entry into the U.S.) It is advisable to carry an International Driving Permit, which is printed in the official languages of the United Nations. It is especially helpful to local police speaking only English, and may be essential in case of an emergency.

Anyone from abroad who drives in the U.S. should have a copy of *U.S.A. Travel Information,* which is available free of charge from AAA's National Headquarters, 8111 Gatehouse Rd., Falls Church, VA 22042. This 69-page booklet contains all the information you need on traffic regulations, insurance requirements, highways, mileage, etc.; it also lists the 161 countries mentioned above.

If you plan to rent a car, you should investigate the special discount plans mentioned on page 12, which are available to anyone.

Most car-rental companies require that Americans be at least 21 years of age to rent a car (it's 25 in New York), but foreign visitors only have to be 18. When you rent a car, you'll have to make a fairly large deposit—the exact amount depends on the place where you pick up the car. Americans *must* pay the deposit with a credit card but foreign visitors may pay in cash.

Other Possibilities

Although there is no set nationwide policy, there are many hotels, motels, and tourist attractions that will give foreign visitors special rates. Always ask whether such a special rate exists—it never hurts to try.

Meeting Americans in Their Homes

Since there's no better way to get to understand the U.S. and Americans than to spend some time with them at home, you'll probably want to explore some of the following possibilities for arranging a visit to an American home. Chances are that if you do not prearrange such a visit through one of these organizations you will still get to meet Americans in their homes, since Americans are free with their invitations. When an American invites you to be his guest, don't feel he is just being polite—he wouldn't ask you to come if he didn't really want you to.

If you are interested in joining a summer or long-term program in the U.S. involving a family homestay, a partial listing of exchange programs is available on request from the Institute of International Education. Write for the *Family Homestay Information Sheet* to: Communications Division, IIE, 809 United Nations Plaza, New York, NY 10017.

SERVAS: One organization that sponsors a worldwide program of exchange hospitality for travelers in 80 countries including the U.S. is Servas. Its goal: to help build peace, goodwill, and understanding through home visits and other contact between people. Here's how Servas works: you apply and are interviewed; if accepted, you receive a personal briefing, written instructions, a list of Servas hosts in the area you are going to visit, and an introductory letter. You arrange your visits in advance by writing or calling the hosts. The usual stay with a Servas host is two nights. For information on Servas, contact the Servas office in your home country, or if you don't know where that is, write to the U.S. Servas Committee, Inc., 11 John St., Room 406, New York, NY 10038. Servas asks for a donation of $30 for its services.

BOY SCOUTS OF AMERICA: Any Boy Scout who has an International Letter of Introduction may stay at a camp run by the Boy Scouts of America during June, July, and August. During the rest of the year, the foreign scouts may stay in the homes of American scouts for a minimum of three nights. In both cases, prior arrangements must be made.

Community Organizations

There are also several community-based organizations around the country that have been set up specifically to cater to the needs of foreign visitors. These organizations are located all over the U.S., and most of them belong to a central organization, the National Council for International Visitors (NCIV), located in Washington, D.C.

Some of these organizations are equipped to place foreign students or visitors with families in their area for two- or three-day stays, although this is not necessarily their major function. These organizations should not be confused with accommodation bureaus: they are simply groups of people who wish to further international understanding and feel that one way to do this is to offer hospitality and program assistance to visitors from abroad. They are usually staffed by volunteers who give their time because they believe in what they are doing, and their help and hospitality should never be abused. Some community organizations can arrange home hospitality only for people who are visiting the U.S. as part of a prearranged program. Most of the ones we list below are willing to offer their sponsored services to unsponsored visitors. Understandably, all these organizations require advance notice of one week to one month to allow time to contact the host family and make arrangements.

In order to arrange a home visit with one of these groups, write to the address listed here giving basic information about yourself, your interests, and your background. Even if you are not planning a home visit, you can feel free to consult these organizations for general information on the area. Most are anxious to help you and many have 24-hour answering services so they can provide assistance in emergencies.

You may want to write to the NCIV and ask for a copy of its pamphlet *Where to Phone,* which provides a complete listing of the phone numbers of

NCIV members who are willing to assist international visitors, whether or not they are sent by a national programming agency. NCIV's address: Meridian House, 1630 Crescent Pl. NW, Washington, DC 20009.

ALABAMA: Birmingham Council for International Visitors, Suite 300, Commerce Center, Birmingham, AL 35203. Telephone 205/252-9825. Will provide homestay and home hospitality for sponsored visitors with ten-day advance notice. Open 8:30 a.m. to 5 p.m., Monday to Friday.

ARIZONA: World Affairs Council of Phoenix, Inc., 401 North 1st St., Ramada Inn Downtown, Room 233, Phoenix, AZ 85004. Telephone: 602/254-3345. Will provide homestays for sponsored foreign visitors and sightseeing advice and emergency help to others. Open 9:30 a.m. to 12:30 p.m. during the week.

CALIFORNIA: International Hospitality Center, 312 Sutter St., Room 402, San Francisco, CA 94108. Telephone: 405/986-1388. Open 9 a.m. to 5 p.m., Monday to Friday. Provides home hospitality in the form of dinner invitations, bus-sightseeing tours of the city for large groups; offers sightseeing information to walk-in and programmed visitors; arranges professional appointments; and provides hotel information.

COLORADO: International Hospitality Center of the Colorado Division, UNA, USA-UNESCO, 980 Grant St., Denver, CO 80203. Telephone: 303/832-4234. Open 10 a.m. to 4 p.m., Monday to Friday. Home hospitality is limited to sponsored visitors. Information and assistance available for drop-in visitors.

Institute of International Education, 700 Broadway, Suite 112, Denver, CO 80203. Telephone: 303/837-0788. Open 8:30 a.m. to 4:30 p.m., Monday to Friday. Brochures, maps, and general information about Denver for drop-ins. With one month's notice and an adequate description of the student, will arrange a two- or three-day homestay. Student must also give exact date and time of arrival and departure.

CONNECTICUT: World Affairs Center, Inc., 1380 Asylum Ave., Hartford, CT 06105. Telephone: 203/236-5277. Office open or answering service Monday to Friday, 9 a.m. to 4:30 p.m. Emergency phone: 203/633-2835. With adequate notice, home hospitality is available in addition to professional contacts and reservations for low-cost lodging.

DISTRICT OF COLUMBIA: Foreign Student Service Council, 1623 Belmont St. NW, Washington, DC 20009. Telephone: 202/232-4979. Open 9 a.m. to 5 p.m., Monday to Friday. Homestays of up to three nights may be arranged for international university students with host families or individuals in the area. At least two weeks' advance notice must be given. Send name, age, school, studies, nationality, date, time, and means of arrival in Washington, and address where you can be reached prior to your visit there. A $2-per-person registration fee, payable by check or money order, is required for this service. International Student Identity Cards are available, as well as advice on low-cost accommodations and sightseeing tours. Similar homestays can be arranged for national graduate students pursuing specific and advanced research. Three weeks' advance notice is necessary.

International Visitors Information Service, 1825 H St. NW, Washington, DC 20006. Telephone: 202/872-8747. Open 9 a.m. to 5 p.m., Monday to Friday. Provides tourist information, bilingual sightseeing (with 48 hours' notice), and language assistance when needed.

FLORIDA: Council for International Visitors of Greater Miami, Inc., 806 Olympia Building, 174 East Flagler St., Miami, FL 33131. Telephone: 305/379-4610 or 379-4615. Open Monday to Friday, 9 a.m. to 5 p.m. No homestays for unsponsored visitors, but "we never deny a welcome to foreign visitors. We welcome their inquiries, will assist by giving local orientation and in general make these students comfortable in our community."

INDIANA: Council for International Visitors, 8399 North Illinois St., Indianapolis, IN 46260. Telephone: 317/251-2414. If enough advance notice is given, a three-day homestay is possible. Overnight stays, sightseeing, and information would be more easily available. Some documentation would be required from the visitor.

MICHIGAN: International Visitors Council, 100 Renaissance Center, Suite 1405, Detroit, MI 48243. Telephone: 313/259-2680. Open 9 a.m. to 5 p.m. weekdays. Help with sightseeing information, maps, etc. No home hospitality for unsponsored visitors.

World Affairs Council of Western Michigan, Room 115, Federal Square Building, Grand Rapids, MI 49502. Telephone: 616/458-9535. Open Monday to Friday, 9 a.m. to 4 p.m. "Some of our members have expressed an interest in acting as host families for short-term visits by foreign guests. We could also arrange visits to local colleges and places of business."

NEBRASKA: Mayor's Committee for International Friendship, 4435 South 43, Lincoln, NB 68516. Telephone: 402/489-3339. "We can help visitors determine how best to spend their time in our city and area."

NEW MEXICO: Council on International Relations, 100 East San Francisco, P.O. Box 1223 (in La Fonda Inn), Sante Fe, NM 87501. Telephone: 505/982-4931. Open 9 a.m. to noon weekdays. Many members are willing to serve as host families for foreign travelers. "We ask for a donation of $9 per person per night, part of which goes to the host family, part to our office." Plenty of advance notice requested.

NEW YORK STATE: The International Center of Syracuse, 500 South Warren St., Hotel Syracuse, Syracuse, NY 13202. Telephone: 315/471-0252 or 471-1222. Open 9 a.m. to 5 p.m., Monday to Friday. They can no longer provide home visits but will gladly give information.

OHIO: International Visitors Center, 105 West 4th St., Room 1027, Cincinnati, OH 45202. Telephone: 513/241-7384. Open 9 a.m. to 3:15 p.m. weekdays. Although no home hospitality is available for unsponsored visitors, they'll help students with sightseeing information, maps, etc.

OREGON: World Affairs Council of Oregon, 1912 Southwest Sixth Ave., Room 252, Portland, OR 97201. "We can arrange schedules and itineraries and dinners in homes on occasion." Will recommend places to stay. Open 9 a.m. to 5 p.m. weekdays.

PENNSYLVANIA: Pittsburgh Council for International Visitors, 139 University Pl., 263 Mervis Hall, Pittsburgh, PA 15260. Telephone: 412/682-7929. Open 9 a.m. to 5 p.m., Monday to Friday. They are able to provide information about the city and make reservations for visiting foreign students.

Philadelphia Council for International Visitors, Civic Center Museum, 34th St. and Civic Center Blvd., Philadelphia, PA 19104. Telephone: 215/823-7261. Open weekdays from 9 a.m. to 5 p.m. Will provide sightseeing information and will arrange short-term overnight stays if applicant comes through International Student Service.

RHODE ISLAND: Newport Council for International Visitors, 40 Dearborn St., Newport, RI 02840. Telephone: 401/846-0222. Open Monday, Wednesday, and Friday, 9 a.m. to noon. "May be able to arrange home hospitality or hostel accommodations made available by Rhode Island educational institutions."

TENNESSEE: Office of International Student Affairs and International House at University of Tennessee, Knoxville, 1601 West Clinch Ave., Knoxville, TN 37916. Telephone: 615/974-4453 or 974-3177. Basic information and general assistance.

Tennessee Valley Authority, 400 Commerce Ave., EP B23 C-K, Knoxville, TN 37902. Telephone: 615/632-3974. Open 8 a.m. to 4:45 p.m. "General orientation to include visit to a project."

TEXAS: El Paso Council for International Visitors, 10 Civic Center, P.O. Box 9738, El Paso, TX 79987. Telephone: 915/544-7880, extension 32. "We have a volunteer on duty Monday to Friday from 9 a.m. to 4 p.m. to provide tourist information for foreign visitors, particularly students, and are also able to provide occasional home hospitality of varying types dependent on the amount of prior notification, i.e., after-dinner hospitality, supper, and sometimes an overnight stay" (at a cost of $6 per night for unsponsored visitors).

UTAH: International Visitors—Utah Council, Hotel Utah, P.O. Box 1020, Salt Lake City, UT 84111. Telephone: 801/532-4747. Open 8 a.m. to 4 p.m. Usually able to provide a meal in a member's home and someone to take a visitor sightseeing; always happy to provide information on the area and make suggestions about what to do and see.

Basic Survival Tips
This is the section that is meant to prepare you for some of the basic facts of life in the U.S.

THE TELEPHONE: Telephone numbers all over the U.S. have either seven digits or two letters and five digits (e.g., 661-0310 or MO 1-0310). All numbers also have area codes; for example, New York City's area code is 212. In addition, it recently became necessary to dial "1" before using any area code, so the above number would be 1-212/661-0310. The area code is used only when you are dialing from outside that particular area. The area code makes it possible to dial direct to any state by dialing 1, the three-digit area code, and the remaining seven digits. It eliminates the operator and makes the call cheaper.

If possible, make long distance calls within the continental U.S. when rates are lowered—check the front of the telephone directory for details.

You will find pay telephones in candy and drugstores, public buildings, and often in booths on the streets and at highway rest areas. The charge for a local call is 10¢ to 30¢ (It's 10¢ in Louisiana, 15¢ in Seattle, and 25¢ in the Dallas-Fort Worth airport). New pay telephones allow you to dial the local emergency number without putting in a dime. If you need assistance, you can dial the operator or "0" (zero, not the letter "oh") and when the operator answers you will get your money back. There are two types of telephone directories: the general directory or white pages, which lists alphabetically the telephone numbers and addresses for individuals and businesses, and the Yellow Pages, which classifies businesses alphabetically by type, listing together all bookstores, all cleaners, etc. In smaller cities or towns, the white and Yellow Pages will be combined into one book, with the Yellow Pages at the back.

TELEGRAMS: Telegrams are usually sent via Western Union, a privately owned company. The number of Western Union offices has diminished tremendously in the past few years. Telegrams are generally sent by telephone—check the telephone book under Western Union for the number to call. The price of a telegram depends on the number of words and where it is going. On telegrams sent overseas you are charged for the number of words in the address and for your signature, but not on telegrams sent within the U.S. A night letter, which is transmitted at night when the telegraph lines are less busy, is usually cheaper than a regular telegram; ask the Western Union operator for details.

You can also telegraph money to a stranded friend if necessary. Bring cash or a money order (they won't take checks), and for a fee—depending on where it is going—the money will be transferred to your needy friend.

MAIL: You can mail packages or letters at any of the post offices located throughout the cities and towns of the U.S., or, if you prefer, you can drop your stamped letters into a mailbox (they're located on many street corners and say "U.S. Mail" on them). Post offices are generally open from 8 a.m. to 5 p.m., Monday through Friday, and from 8 a.m. to noon on Saturday. Stamps may be purchased from a post office or a vending machine in stationery, drug, or variety stores. If possible, avoid using the machines since stamps cost more that way.

Aerograms are the cheapest and most efficient way to send letters abroad. You can buy them at any post office.

The following postage rates are now in effect:

U.S.A., Canada, Mexico

postcard (first class and airmail)	13¢
letter (first class and airmail)	20¢ per ounce

	Overseas
aerogram	30¢
airmail letter	35¢ per half ounce to Colombia, Venezuela, and the Caribbean area
	40¢ per half ounce to other areas
surface letter	23¢ for one ounce
airmail postcard	28¢
first-class surface postcard	19¢

When mailing a heavy letter or package, you must have it weighed at the post office. It's wise, too, to insure anything of value that you mail.

If you don't have a friend who can hold mail for you while you are traveling in the U.S., you can have mail addressed to you in care of General Delivery in any city of the U.S. The mail will be held at the main post office of that city for 30 days and will be returned to the sender if unclaimed by that time. To pick up mail sent to General Delivery, you will need to show official identification—your passport will do. Of if you'd like, you can have your friend write to you (as long as it's marked clearly) in care of CIEE Student Mail Service, New York Student Center, William Sloane House, 356 W. 34th St., New York, NY 10001.

MONEY AND BANKS: Ours is a decimal system based on the dollar, which contains 100 cents. There are six coins: a penny or 1¢, a nickel or 5¢, a dime or 10¢, a quarter or 25¢, a half dollar or 50¢, and a new dollar coin. As for paper money, the dollar bill is the most common denomination. There also are $2 bills (rare), and $5, $10, $20, $50, $100, $500, and higher bills.

You can check the exchange rate between your own currency and U.S. currency in any commercial U.S. bank or American Express office.

To protect yourself against loss or theft of money, you would be wise to buy travelers checks, which can be used just like cash. They usually cost one cent for every dollar's worth purchased.

Banks are usually open from 9 a.m. to 3 p.m., Monday through Friday. Some have evening hours on certain week nights, but these vary from bank to bank. Banks are always closed on the following national holidays, many of which fall on Monday as a result of legislation:

New Year's Day	January 1
Washington's Birthday	Monday closest to February 22
Memorial Day	Monday closest to May 30
Fourth of July	July 4 (How could it be any other date?)
Labor Day	First Monday in September
Columbus Day	Monday closest to October 12
Veteran's Day	Fourth Monday in October or November 11
Thanksgiving Day	Fourth Thursday in November
Christmas Day	December 25

TIPPING: You are generally expected to tip waiters and waitresses, taxi drivers, porters, hairdressers, and sometimes doormen. You do not have to tip the usher at the theater. Porters should get 25¢ per bag if they carry your bags to your room, waiters and waitresses 15% to 20% of the bill, and hairdressers approximately 20% of the bill.

A good way to save money is to avoid situations where you are expected to tip; carry your own bags, have a friend cut your hair, and eat in a self-service cafeteria.

DRINKING: In some states you must be 21 years old to be served in a bar or buy liquor from a liquor store; in others you may be 18 or 19. If you look as if you are under the drinking age, you should carry proof of your age if you intend to drink. There are all kinds of bars in the larger U.S. cities—bars for single people, bars for literary people, bars for gay people, bars for businessmen. Bars are good places to meet people, but puritan ethics die hard, and a girl alone just won't feel comfortable in many U.S. bars.

DRUGS: If you are going to get involved with the youth culture of the U.S. at all, you will probably come into contact with drugs. However, the whole drug thing is nowhere near as evident now as it was several years ago. At some point in your travels you may be offered marijuana or whatever happens to be in fashion and in supply at the time. In some places people will approach you right out in the street and you will be surprised at how open drug dealing seems to be. Remember that the possession of any narcotic—and marijuana is included—is against the law, and penalties can be severe. Besides the legal problems involved in narcotic usage, it is possible that drugs sold on the streets may be impure and may very well contain lethal ingredients.

MEDICAL ADVICE: Medical care in the U.S. is incredibly expensive. You must be aware of the fact that a visit to a doctor for a physical examination can cost $100 and that having a tooth extracted can cost as much. Hospitals charge as much as $300 per day per room—and that doesn't even include the doctor's fee, the high cost of medication, etc. *All this makes medical insurance a must.*

In case of emergency, you can get medical help, an ambulance, or the police by dialing "0" (zero) for Operator. In some communities there are free clinics that will attend to your needs as best they can, but they are usually limited by lack of funds and lack of staff so you can't count on them as a substitute for adequate insurance. To find out about free medical services, check the local underground papers or call the help lines listed in each state section.

CHAPTER 4

State by State

This chapter is divided alphabetically into states and further into cities within each state. Each state section begins with a map of the state, indicating the locations of cities listed in the section. It would be of no help to you to know that there is a place to spend the night somewhere if you have no idea how close or far away from that place you are. Each state section begins with some general, totally subjective commentary on the state, a list of some special events in the state that might be fun to see, a comment on the laws and attitudes about hitchhiking in the state, and the address of the state tourist office.

After the introductory material, the state is divided alphabetically into cities. We have further divided the city listings into the following subheadings: Tourist Information, Help, On Campus, Accommodations, and Camping. Not all cities have all subheadings; although we put in all the information we were able to uncover, for some cities we have lots to say and for others very little. For 15 of the major cities in the U.S. we have prepared special, more detailed sections. In general, the city listings will include: places to stay, places to eat, things to see and do, how to get around, where to shop, etc. For the other cities and towns listed, you will find some or all of the following information:

● **Tourist Information:** Indicates the address of the city tourist office; this is given only for large cities that can send you lots of glossy, slick brochures on their own territories. Use these information offices freely; beneath the public-relations exterior you'll usually find some helpful information and useful maps.

● **Help:** Here we list the telephone numbers of hotlines and crisis centers that can assist you in an emergency. Some are phone services; others are drop-in centers. Travelers Aid offices are also listed. See page 30 for a description of how they can help you.

● **On Campus:** This section tells you where to go on a particular campus to meet students, get information, find a good, cheap meal, or just enjoy yourself. We had the cooperation of a lot of people on a lot of campuses throughout the U.S. in getting information for the on-campus sections and are grateful for it all.

● **Accommodations:** These are the places to stay in each city or town. A variety of accommodation facilities are included, many of which offer various kinds of discounts and/or have access (for the handicapped) facilities. They are all described in Chapter 2.

● **Camping:** This heading is self-explanatory; it indicates the National Park Service campgrounds that are open to individual travelers.

Every once in a while you'll see a listing called "camping and accommodations"—this refers to campgrounds that have cabins to rent as well as tent space.

Now you are ready to use this book in the way it is meant to be used—to help you have fun, stay relatively comfortable, and get the most out of your travels in the U.S.

Alabama

Things are definitely looking up. In the first edition we complained that Alabama, with very few low-cost accommodations, made a discouraging beginning to a basically optimistic book. Since then, the Alabama listings have grown considerably. We're also delighted to pass on some good news about traveling in Alabama, and the South in general. "No more *Easy Rider* image, please," said a friend at the University of Alabama. "Things have changed a great deal since the early '60s, and although we are stereotyped as intolerant and conservative . . . people are very tolerant and congenial to outsiders, and especially those who come to our area to visit and learn more about us."

One of the cities that you will want to visit is Birmingham, with its mansions and landmarks reminiscent of the Old South including the Arlington Antebellum Home and Gardens. In Montgomery, the first capital of the Confederacy, you can visit the Capitol building and the W. A. Gayle Space Transit Planetarium. For space and rocket buffs, we recommend a visit to Huntsville, the home of the Alabama Space and Rocket Center, where you can take a simulated ride to the moon. South Alabama is the closest to the image of the Deep South as it's been portrayed in movies, books, and songs. Here the Spanish moss hangs heavy and the azaleas bloom. In Bayou LaBatre the city hall is a shrimp boat, Mobile has its own Mardi Gras, and near Mobile, in Theodore, is the quintessential reminder of the Deep South—Bellingrath Gardens and Home. A good introduction to Alabama is the booklet *Alabama the Beautiful,* available free from the Alabama Bureau of Publicity and Information (address below).

For those who enjoy bed-and-breakfast accommodations, the Tennessee Valley B&B of Alabama is the first to appear in the state. Members currently include 12 homes in five counties in the northeast section of Alabama, and the cost is $20 single, $25 double. Write to the Tennessee Valley B&B of Alabama, P.O. Box 1066, Scottsboro, AL 35768, for details, or call 205/259-1298.

Some Special Events: Jazz Festival in Mobile and Alabama Jubilee in Decatur (May); Chalaka Art Show in Sylacauga (June); Birmingham Area Callers Association Sing-Along in Fairfield and Alabama Mule Association Mule Show and Pull in Decatur (July); Arts Festival in Fayette (August); Coon Dog Cemetery Decoration and Barbecue in Cherokee (September); Bluegrass Contest in Huntsville (October); and W.C. Handy's Birthday Celebration in Florence (November).

Hitching: Officially, according to the Alabama Department of Public Safety, hitchhiking is permissible except on Interstate routes; "on other streets and highways people may not stand in the roadway for the purpose of soliciting a ride." "Roadway," in Alabama, means the paved portion of the highway. Our campus sources seem to agree that hitching "is acceptable, but not really recommended." A sergeant of the Highway Patrol says: "There are no good roads for hitchhiking. Don't hitchhike!"

Tourist Information: Alabama Bureau of Publicity and Information, 532 South Perry St., Montgomery, AL 36130. Telephone: toll free 800/633-5761 except from Alaska, Alabama, and Hawaii; 800/392-8096 in state; 832-5510 in Montgomery.

Birmingham

Tourist Information: Great Birmingham Convention and Visitors Bureau, Commerce Center, 2027 First Ave. North, 35203. Telephone: 205/252-9825.

Help: Travelers Aid, 3600 Eighth Ave. South, 35222. Telephone: 205/322-5426.

● Crisis Center, 205/323-7777.

Accommodations: YWCA, 🕊 ♿, 309 North 23rd St., 35203. Telephone: 205/251-1151. Women only. $8 per night transient. Weekly rates vary. Only 2½ blocks from bus station. Reservations recommended.

● Ranch House Motel, √ $2, 2127 Seventh Ave. South, 35233. Telephone: 205/322-0691. $18 for one; $20 for two in one bed; $24 for two in two beds.

● Days Inn, 1011 Ninth Ave. SW, Bessemer, 35020. Telephone: 205/424-9690. $20.88 to $23.88 for one; $24.88 to $27.88 for two.

● Days Inn, 5101 Airport Hwy., 35212. Telephone: 205/592-6110. $24.88 for one; $28.88 for two.

● Days Inn, ♿, 1813 Crestwood Blvd., 35210. 4½ miles from airport. Telephone: 205/956-3650. $21.88 to $23.88 for one; $24.88 to $26.88 for two.

● Econo-Travel Motor Hotel, 103 Greensprings Hwy., 35209. Near Sanford University and University of Alabama. Telephone: 205/942-1263. $19.95 for one; $25.95 for two in one bed; $27.95 for two in two beds—from April to October. Rates higher during other months.

● Econo Lodge, 2224 Fifth Ave. North, P.O. Box 10402, 35203. Telephone: 205/324-6688 or 324-3980. $23.95 for one; $27.95 for two in one bed; $31.95 for two in two beds.

Cullman

Accommodation: Days Inn, I-65 and U.S. 278, P.O. Box 693, 35055. Telephone: 205/739-3800. $20.88 to $21.88 for one; $24.88 to $25.88 for two.

Dothan

Accommodation: Days Inn, ⌖, 2841 Ross Clark Circle SW, P.O. Drawer 1890, 36301. Three miles from airport. Telephone: 205/793-2550. $21.88 to $22.88 for one; $25.88 to $26.88 for two.

Evergreen

Accommodation: Days Inn, ⌖, I-65 and Hwy. 83, P.O. Box 47, Bates Rd., 36401. Telephone: 205/578-4700. $18.88 for one; $22.88 for two.

Mobile

Tourist Information: Travel & Convention Department, Mobile Area Chamber of Commerce, 451 Government St., P.O. Box 2187, 36652. Telephone: 205/433-6951.

Help: Travelers Aid, Family Counseling Center, 6 South Florida St., 36606. Telephone: 205/471-3466.

● Helpline, 205/342-0711.

On Campus: Springhill College and the University of South Alabama are in Mobile. To find some of their students, try Solomons, Jag's, Thirstie's, or Mike's Public House.

Accommodations: YWCA, 1060 Government St., 36604. Telephone: 205/432-1848. One mile from bus station. Women only. $10 single; $8 per person double.

● Motel 6, I-10 and Alabama 163. To open in 1982. $12.95 for one; $16.95 for two; $19.95 for up to four.

● Econo Lodge, 1061 Government Blvd., 36604. Telephone: 205/438-4653. $23.75 for one; $25.75 for two in one bed; $30.75 for two in two beds.

● Days Inn, 3651 Government Blvd., 36609. Telephone: 205/666-7750. $22.88 for one; $27.88 for two.

Montgomery

Help: Travelers Aid, Family Guidance Center, 925 Forest Ave., 36106. Telephone: 205/265-0568 or 262-6669.

● Information and Referral, 205/279-7839.

Accommodations: Motel 6, 1051 Eastern Bypass, 36117. Telephone: 205/277-0600. See Mobile listing for rates.

● Scottish Inn, I-65 at Southern Blvd. Exit, U.S. 80 and U.S. 82, 36105. Telephone: 205/281-4250. $15 for one; $18 for two.

● Scottish Inn, U.S. 231 South, 36064. Telephone: 205/288-1501. $15 for one; $19 for two in one bed; $23 for two in two beds.

● Superior Doby's Hotel Court, 3453 Mobile Rd., 36108. Telephone: 205/288-8110. $17.50 to $21.50 for one; $20 to $24.50 for two in one bed; $24.50 to $28.50 for two in two beds.

● Days Inn, I-65 and 1150 West South Blvd., 36105. Telephone: 205/281-8000. $18.88 to $19.88 for one; $22.88 to $23.88 for two.

● Days Inn, Hope Hull Exit, I-65 and U.S. 31, Rte. 1, Box 152A, Hope Hull, 36043. Telephone: 205/281-7151. $20.88 for one; $24.88 for two.

Opelika

Accommodations: Days Inn, I-85 and U.S. 280, P.O. Box 2829, 36801. Telephone: 205/749-2002. $19.88 for one; $23.88 for two.
● Motel 6, 1015 Columbus Pkwy., 36801. Telephone: 205/749-0850. See Mobile listing for rates.

Oxford/Anniston

Accommodation: Days Inn, I-20 and Alabama 21, P.O. Drawer F, 36203. Telephone: 205/831-5463. $20.88 for one; $23.88 for two.

Phenix City

Accommodation: Econo-Travel Motor Hotel, 🔲, 1506 Phenix City Bypass, 36867. Telephone: 205/298-5255. $14.95 for one; $17.95 for two in one bed; $24.95 for two to four in two beds.

Scottsboro

Accommodation: Burton House, 112 College Ave., 35768. Telephone: 205/259-1298. $20 single; $25 double. Bed-and-breakfast in a 60-year-old home.

Selma

Accommodation: Days Inn, 2006 Highland Ave., 36701. Telephone: 205/875-9231. $20.88 for one; $24.88 for two.

Troy

Help: Help-a-Crisis, Emergency Telephone Counseling, c/o East Central Mental Health/Mental Retardation, Inc. Telephone: 205/566-3391.

Tuscaloosa (See University, below)

Help: University Switchboard, 205/566-3000.
Accommodation: Days Inn, 3600 McFarland Blvd., 35401. Telephone: 205/556-2010. $22.88 for one; $27.88 for two.

University

On Campus: According to a friend at the University of Alabama, which is (appropriately enough) in University (University is a zip code; the main campus is actually in Tuscaloosa), the school is "lovely and has a vibrant history." She told us that the Continuing Education Center on campus is open day and night and "offers housing for those on quasi-university business—that is, looking at the campus." If you're feeling lonely, go to the Side Track, Solomon's, or the Noose. Three good restaurants are Clancy McQ's, in downtown Tuscaloosa; the Landing, a steakhouse on McFarland Blvd.; or Storyville, right off campus. You'll easily find someone to talk to at any of these.

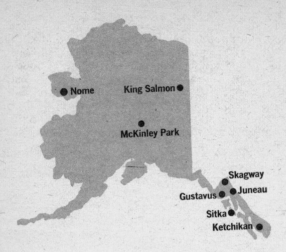

Alaska

Alaska is huge. Superimposed on a map of the U.S. it stretches from Seattle to Miami. And in all this space there are only 403,000 Alaskans.

Not many Americans get as far as Alaska, but one adventurous New York student told us about her two months in the town of Homer. "From Seattle I took a ferry that takes three days. I traveled fifth class and brought my own food. I got off at Haines, and hitchhiked to Homer on the Alaskan Highway. There are quite a few kids in Homer and if you settle down for more than a week you're no longer considered a stranger. Alaska is a rather expensive place—food especially."

The Alaska Division of Tourism gave us some good news and some bad news about low-cost accommodations in their state. The good news: The U.S. Forest Service rents 135 cabins in the Tongass National Forest for $5 a night. The bad news: Most of the cabins can be reached only after a plane ride in a single-engine De Havilland Beaver.

For all the tourist information you could want on Alaska, we recommend three publications:

One is *The Milepost,* published by the people who publish *Alaska Magazine,* Box 4EEE, Anchorage, AK 99509. The book is a mile-by-mile log of the northern highways, including the Alaska Highway, with maps and specifics for everyone from fishermen to rock hounds. Copies are $7.95 plus $1 postage and handling. Another is *Alaska Travel Guide,* published by Alaska Travel Guide, 241 West 1700 South, Salt Lake City, UT 84115. It costs $6.95 plus $1 postage and handling and contains information on hotels, motels, history, national parks, etc. It is released annually in March. The third recommended guide is

The Inside Passage Traveler, by Ellen Searby, Windham Bay Press, P.O. Box 1332, Juneau, AK 99802. It costs $5.50 plus $1.50 airmail postage. Written by a one-time member of a ferry crew, this book tells you how to make the most of the ferry system and how to find your way from the dock into town. It includes information on air, rail, and road connections, hotels, sights to see, etc.

Some Special Events: World championships including sled-dog races and snowmobile races (February); Fairbanks Winter Carnival (March); Break-Up Drama Festival in Dawson City, Yukon (May); Gold Rush Days in Valdez, an annual festival which celebrates the good old days of gold discovery in Alaska (August); and Alaska Festival of Music in Anchorage (September).

"Originally I was hitching from Houston to San Francisco to New York but then found a job with the U.S. Forest Service as a technician in Ketchikan and I'm still here."

Hitching: It's accepted but not generally recommended. To quote the law (from a large book of highway regulations), "a person may not stand on a roadway in a manner that will distract a driver's attention for the purpose of soliciting a ride, employment, or business from the occupant of a vehicle." Roadway is the main traveled portion of the highway. According to an Alaska state trooper, "a person may stand off the roadway and hitchhike as long as he or she doesn't interfere with the normal flow of traffic." Another piece of advice from the trooper: "Find out how far your ride is going so you are not let out in the middle of nowhere in a low-traffic area; in other words, try to get rides from town to town."

A German student who hitched in Alaska told us: "Hitchhiking in Alaska between Anchorage and Fairbanks is good. Hitchhiking into Alaska is a question of luck. On my way back by driver went straight from Delta Junction, Alaska, to Montana."

Tourist Information: Alaska Division of Tourism, Pouch E, Juneau, AK 99811. Ask for *The Worlds of Alaska and Canada's Yukon,* the official State of Alaska vacation booklet.

Anchorage

Help: Youth & Family Crisis Line, 907/279-0552.

Accommodation: Anchorage Youth Hostel (AYH), 32nd and Minnesota Blvd., 99509. Telephone: 907/276-3635. Two miles from bus station; three miles from train station; city bus stops right in front. Open year round. Reservations suggested. Recreation facilities nearby. $5 for AYH members (see page 21); $6 for nonmembers with purchase of $1 introductory AYH card.

On Campus: The bulletin board in the student center of Anchorage Community College is a good source of information on rides and accommodations. For an inexpensive meal, go to Lucy Cuddy Center at the college; for conversation, go to the Fly by Night Club.

Gustavus

Camping: Glacier Bay National Park, 99826. Wilderness camping from May to September. Access by aircraft or boat only.

Juneau

Accommodation: Juneau Youth Hostel, Inc. (AYH-SA), Northern Light United Church, 11th and B Sts., P.O. Box 1543, 99802. Telephone: 907/586-3131. Open June 1 to September 1. $2.

Camping: Glacier Bay National Park and Preserve, P.O. Box 1089, Gustavus, 99826. Wilderness camping; access by plane or boat only from Juneau. Open May to September.

Ketchikan

Accommodation: Ketchikan Youth Hostel (AYH-SA), United Methodist Church, Grant and Main Sts. Mailing address: P.O. Box 8515, 99901. Access to Ketchikan is by Alaska State Ferry or Alaska Airlines. Telephone: 907/225-2833. Open Memorial Day to Labor Day. Sleeping bags required. $2.

King Salmon

Camping: Katmai National Park and Preserve, P.O. Box 7, 99613. Brooks River camping area open June 1 to September 5.

McKinley Park

Camping: Denali National Park and Preserve, P.O. Box 9, 99755. Six campgrounds open June to September; Riley Creek open year round. Reservations accepted at the site adjacent to Teklanika River Campground; all others operated on a first-come, first-served basis. Some are free, others cost $4 per campsite per night.

Nome

Help: Crisis Line, 907/443-2255.

Accommodation: Community United Methodist Church (AYH), P.O. Box 907, corner of 2nd and C Sts., 99762. Telephone: 907/443-2865. Open year round. "Beautiful beaches for hiking and beachcombing, reindeer herds . . . and treeless tundra for hiking. . . ." $5 donation. The houseparents of this hostel recommend Milano's Pizza or the Polar Cub for "inexpensive" meals—in Nome, inexpensive means $4 for breakfast, $5 for lunch, and $6 to $11 for dinner!

Sitka

Accommodation: Sitka Youth Hostel (AYH-SA), Sitka United Presbyterian Church, 505 Sawmill Creek Rd., 99835. Telephone: 907/747-6332. Sitka can be reached by Alaska State Ferry or Alaska Airlines. Open June 1 to September 1. Sleeping bags required. $2 for AYH members (see page 21); $3 for nonmembers.

Skagway

Camping: Klondike Gold Rush National Historical Park, P.O. Box 617, 99840. Camping from May to September at primitive campsites.

Arizona

Lots of the people who come to Arizona are there to see the Grand Canyon, a multicolored fissure 217 miles long, 3 to 17 miles wide, about a mile deep, and very probably one of the most spectacular natural sights you will ever see. Since the largest crowds come during the summer, visit if you can in the spring or fall when you can enjoy the relative solitude.

The state's southern half—with its largest cities, Tucson and Phoenix—has the kind of warm, dry air that makes people feel good, so many come to the area's resorts to do just that. Arizona may well be one of the most beautiful of our states. Besides the Grand Canyon, the attractions of the state include Hoover Dam, Lake Mead, 15 national monuments, several Indian villages and reservations, the Painted Desert, and the Petrified Forest.

Some Special Events: Cinco de Mayo Celebrations in Prescott, Phoenix, Tucson, Scottsdale, Winslow, Willcox, and Mesa (May); Shakespeare Under the Stars in Tucson and Annual Old Timer's Picnic in Casa Grande (June); Navajo Pow Wow and Rodeo in Window Rock and Homemakers Ice Cream Social in Pine (July); Turkey Creek Rodeo in White River and Navajo County Fair in Holbrook (August); Annual Gold Camp Days in Oatman and Cochise County Fair in Douglas (September).

Hitching: The Arizona Department of Public Safety wrote to say that "Frankly, while it is not strictly illegal, we attempt to discourage hitchhiking on our highways. Also, while it is legal for the hitchhiker to solicit a ride if he is not standing on the roadway, a motorist who stops to pick up a hitchhiker is often in violation of the law, blocking traffic behind him." Pedestrians are not allowed on the Interstate highway system.

Tourist Information: Office of Tourism, 3507 North Central Ave., Phoenix, AZ 85004. Telephone: 602/255-3618.

Ajo

Camping: Organ Pipe Cactus National Monument, Rte. 1, P.O. Box 100, 85321. There's camping all year 1½ miles southwest of visitor center. $2.

Chinle

Camping: Canyon de Chelly National Monument, P.O. Box 588, 86503. Camping at Cottonwood, one mile south of entrance, year round.

Douglas

Accommodation: Motel 6, 111 16th St., 85607. Telephone: 602/364-5461. $12.95 for one; $16.95 for two; $19.95 for up to four.

Flagstaff

Help: Crisis Intervention, 519 North Leroux St. Telephone: 602/774-2727.

Accommodations: Weatherford Hotel (AYH-SA), 23 North Leroux St., 86001. Telephone: 602/774-2731. AYH members $6 to $8 (bring sleeping bags); regular hotel rooms $14 to $18 single, $16 to $20 double. Call and check on availability of rooms. Recommended by a reader who told us that "the Weatherford is named in Zane Grey's book *Call of the Canyon* and is very special."

● Pine Motor Hotel, 🛏 ★, 114 East Santa Fe, 86001. Telephone: 602/774-9969. $12 single; $10 per person in double-bedded room. These are special rates for ISIC-holders and *Where to Stay* readers. "Clean, economical and cozy."

● Motel 6, 2010 East Butler Ave., 86001. Telephone: 602/774-3533. See Douglas listing for rates.

● Friendship Inn-Carousel, 2918 East Santa Fe Ave., 86001. Telephone: 602/526-3595. $14 to $24 for one; $16 to $30 for two in one bed; $18 to $34 for two in two beds. Rates lower October to April.

● Friendship Ski Lift Lodge, Rte. 4, Box 957, 86001. Telephone: 602/774-0729. $16 to $22 for one or two in one bed; $16 to $30 for two in two beds.

● Friendship Inn-Autolodge, 1313 South Milton, 86001. Telephone: 602/774-6621. $24 for one; $24 to $26 for two in one bed; $28 to $30 for two in two beds.

● Regal 8 Inn, 2440 East Lucky Lane, 86001. Telephone: 602/774-8756. $15.88 to $19.88 for one; $18.88 to $22.88 for two in one bed; $21.88 to $25.88 for two to four in two beds.

Camping: Sunset Crater National Monument, Rte. 3, Box 149, 86001. Camping at Bonito Campground (opposite Visitor Center) April 1 to November 15. $3 per campsite per night.

Gila Bend

Accommodations: Friendship Inn–El Coronado Motel, 212 West Pima St., 85337. Telephone: 602/683-2281. $16 to $20 for one; $20 to $24 for two in one bed; $24 to $28 for two in two beds.

● Friendship–Sea Shell Inn, 515 Pima St. East. Telephone: 602/683-2294. $16 to $20 for one; $20 to $24 for two in one bed; $24 to $28 for two in two beds.

Globe

Accommodation: Friendship Ember, 1105 North Broad St., 85501. Telephone: 602/425-5736. $15 to $18 for one; $18 to $22 for two in one bed; $22 to $24 for two in two beds.

Grand Canyon

Camping: Grand Canyon National Park, P.O. Box 129, 86023. Four tenting campgrounds; two open year round, two open May to October. $2 to $3. Reservations for three hike-in campgrounds available at above address, c/o Superintendent.

Holbrook

Accommodations: Friendship Inn–Whiting Brothers Motor Hotel, 2402 East Navajo Blvd., 86025. Telephone: 602/524-6298. $16 to $20 for one; $18 to $22 for two in one bed; $22 to $26 for two in two beds.

● Motel 6, 2514 East Navajo Blvd., 86025. Telephone: 602/524-2666. See Douglas listing for rates.

Kingman

Accommodations: Motel 6, 3270 East Andy Devine Ave., 86401. Telephone: 602/757-4777. See Douglas listing for rates.

● Best Value Pony Soldier Motel, 2939 East Andy Devine Ave., 86401. Telephone: 602/753-5586. $16 to $18 for one; $20 to $23 for two in one bed; $22 to $25 for two in two beds.

● Imperial 400 Motor Inn, 1911 East Andy Devine Ave., 86401. Telephone: 602/753-2176. $16 to $18 for one or two in one bed; $20 to $22 for two in two beds.

● Friendship Space Age Motel, 1967 East Andy Devine Ave., 86401. Telephone: 602/753-5511. $15 to $20 for one; $15 to $21 for two in one bed; $18 to $23 for two in two beds.

Lake Havasu

Accommodation: E-Z 8 Motel, 105 Acoma, 96403. Telephone: 602/855-4023. $13.88 to $15.88 for one; $16.88 to $18.88 for two in one bed; $18.88 to $20.88 for two in two beds.

Mesa

Accommodation: Western 6 Motel, 630 West Main St., 85201. Telephone: 602/969-8111. $17.40 single; $24.90 double.

Nogales

Accommodation: Motel 6, 2210 Tucson Hwy., 85621. Telephone: 602/281-0703. See Douglas listing for rates.

Page

Camping: Glen Canyon National Recreation Area, P.O. Box 1507, 86040. Five campgrounds. All open year round. $2 entrance fee; $4.50 to $5 per campsite per night.

Phoenix

Wherever you go in Phoenix, you will be aware of the influence that Indian culture has had on its evolution.

The city that is now the capital of Arizona and began as a small settlement on the banks of the Salt River has become quite a popular tourist stop. One of the biggest attractions is the weather—one Phoenician promises "absolutely sunny skies 212 days of the year." The Phoenix and Valley of the Sun Convention and Visitors Bureau, 2701 East Camelback Rd., Suite 200H, Phoenix, AZ 85016, will be glad to send you information on their favorite city, including their *Valley of the Sun Visitors' Guide.* If you'd like more, you can get copies of the *Insiders' Guide,* by Boye de Mente (Phoenix Book Publishers, 6505 North 43rd Pl., Paradise Valley, AZ 85253; $3). Once you're in Phoenix, you'll want to check the *Phoenix Republic* and the *Gazette,* the local newspapers, and *New Times,* the "alternative" weekly publication.

Tempe, the location of Arizona State University, is not far from Phoenix and it has its own listing on page 61. There are some restaurants located in Tempe, though, that are listed here.

Getting There: From the airport, a taxi will cost between $4 and $6 to the downtown area. Airport limousine service costs $2.50 to downtown or $3 to Tempe, as long as there are other passengers; if not, it will cost $6. There's no airport bus service. The Continental Trailways terminal is at 433 East Washington (tel. 257-0257) and Greyhound's is nearby at 525 East Washington (tel. 248-4040). Amtrak is at 401 West Harrison (tel. 253-0121).

Getting Around: Once you're in the city, you can take a taxi for $1.65 for the first mile, 85¢ for each additional mile. Dial Yellow Cab Company (tel. 252-5071) and a taxi will come and get you. Since local bus service is very poor (no service after 7 p.m. or on Sunday), you may want to rent a car. To do this, check Budget Rent-a-Car, 219 South 24th St. To rent a Ford Escort or similar car costs $17.95 per day, with 100 miles included, 17¢ per mile after that, and $134 for the week with 1000 free miles. At Ajax Rental (tel. 244-9889), a Ford Escort costs $26.90 per day with unlimited mileage and $139 per week with 1050 free miles. If you insist on using the bus, you can get a printed schedule and route map from the Phoenix Transit Corporation's information booth, First St. and Adams.

Accommodations: YMCA, 🔲, 350 North First Ave., 85003. Telephone: 602/253-6181. Near the Civic Plaza. Men and women. This hotel is well kept and centrally located. Singles are $11 per night; $45 per week.

● Sand's Hotel, 3320 East Van Buren St., 85008. Telephone: 602/275-7848. For transportation from the bus station or airport, call for limousine service. This hotel-motel is near the Phoenix Zoo and a golf course and is not far from downtown. Rates in some of the budget rooms (in a separate building) are $20 single; $24 double.

● Motel 6, 2323 East Van Buren St., 85006. Telephone: 602/267-1397. See Douglas listing for rates.

● Motel 6, 5315 East Van Buren St., 85008. Telephone: 602/267-8553. See Douglas listing for rates.

● Motel 6, 2330 West Bell Rd., 85023. Telephone: 602/863-1666. See Douglas listing for rates.

● Friendship Inn 6, 201 North Seventh Ave., 85007. Telephone: 602/254-6521. $15 to $25 for one; $17 to $34 for two in one bed; $21 to $42 for two in two beds.

● Western 6 Motel, 214 South 24th St., 85034. Telephone: 602/244-1155. $17.40 single; $24.90 double.

● Western 6 Motel, 4130 North Black Canyon Hwy., 85017. Telephone: 602/277-5501. See above listing for rates.

● Del Ward's Romney Motor Hotel, 3037 East Van Buren St., 85008. Telephone: 602/273-1601. $16 to $18 for one; $18 to $23 for two in one bed; $20 to $24 for two in two beds.

● Days Inn, I-17 and 2735 West Sweetwater, 85029. Telephone: 602/993-7200. $19.88 to $24.88 for one; $22.88 to $27.88 for two.

● Days Inn, 8617 North Black Canyon Hwy., 85021. Telephone: 602/995-9500. $19.88 to $22.88 for one; $22.88 to $25.88 for two.

● Sixpence Inn, 1624 North Black Canyon Hwy., 85009. Telephone: 602/269-6281. $12.95 to $14.95 for one; $14.95 to $16.95 for two.

● Regal 8 Inn, 2548 West Indian School Rd., 85017. Telephone: 602/248-8881. $19.88 for one; $22.88 for two in one bed; $25.88 for two to four in two beds.

● International Hawaiian Inn, 1102 North Central, 85004. Telephone: 602/258-6341. $18 for one; $22 for two in one bed; $28.50 for two in two beds.

Where to Eat: Earthen Joy, 36 East 5th St., Tempe. Telephone: 602/968-4710. Open 11:30 a.m. to 10 p.m. From fresh carrot juice to delicious cheesecake, sandwiches on 14-grain bread, and salads. Every evening there's a special entree. The setting is informal and eating is done surrounded by bright colored pillows, an aquarium, and lots of plants.

● Monti's Casa Vieja, 3 West 1st St., Tempe. Telephone: 602/967-7594. Open 11:30 a.m. to midnight. "One of the best western steakhouses. The atmosphere is rustic; prices are reasonable."

● New Morning Café, 2911 North 16th St., northeast corner of 16th St. and Thomas. Telephone: 602/279-6322. Open 11 a.m. to 10 p.m. Centrally located and relaxed. The food is vegetarian and the specialties are frozen yogurt and honey ice cream for dessert.

● La Casita Café, 1021 South Central Ave. Telephone: 602/262-9322. Open from 11 a.m. daily except Tuesday. This Mexican café serves all the dishes you'd expect and has been a landmark for decades.

● Willy and Guillermo's, 1120 East Apache Blvd. (Tempe) and 5600 North Central Ave. Mexican food in a comfortable setting.

● Pinnacle Peak Patio, 10426 East Pinnacle Peak Rd., Scottsdale. This is about 12 miles north of Phoenix and is a popular tourist attraction. Steak and beans in a western atmosphere; entertainment includes a melodrama where it's perfectly acceptable—in fact encouraged—to hiss and boo the players.

What to See: Heard Museum of Anthropology and Primitive Art, 22 East Monte Vista Rd. Telephone: 602/252-8848. Open Monday to Saturday from 10 a.m. to 5 p.m.; Sunday from 1 to 5 p.m. One of the West's finest collections of Indian arts and crafts, prehistoric and modern, from all over the world. Every year, during the first week in March, the museum sponsors an Indian arts and crafts fair with dancing, food, and craft demonstrations. It's a very popular fair, indeed.

● Pueblo Grande Museum and Ruins, 4619 East Washington. Telephone: 602/275-3452. Open 9 a.m. to 5 p.m. weekdays, 1 to 5 p.m. Sunday; closed Saturday. Where the Hohokam Indians, the earliest inhabitants of Phoenix, lived. There's a museum with artifacts to visit, too.

● Japanese Flower Gardens. Along Baseline Rd. there's a two-mile stretch of flower farms. The peak of their beauty is from February to April. Citrus fruits and dates are sold at roadside stands along the way.

● South Mountain Park. The entrance to this municipal park is at the end of South Central Ave. Within the park's boundaries are petroglyphs, picnic areas, and superb views of the city.

● Desert Botanical Gardens, 5800 East Van Buren St. 3000 acres of Papago Park devoted to desert plants from all over the world.

● Taliesin West, East Shea Blvd. Telephone: 602/948-6670. Once the winter home and school of Frank Lloyd Wright, located in an area of virgin desert. Now open for visitors October to May, 10 a.m. to 4 p.m. daily; noon to 4 p.m. Sunday.

● Paola Soleri Cosanti Foundation, 6433 Doubletree Rd. Telephone: 602/948-6145. Workshop for innovative architectural designers where you can see models of future city projects.

● Gila River Indian Arts and Crafts Center. Approximately 20 miles southeast of Phoenix, just off the Phoenix–Tucson Freeway. Museum and a crafts shop that features pottery, baskets, and jewelry made by various Arizona tribes. Open 9 a.m. to 5:30 p.m.

At Night; Boojum Tree Restaurant, Second Ave. and Osborn. Telephone: 602/248-0222. Open until 1 a.m. A place to go to hear well-known jazz recording stars.

● El Bandido, 1617 East Thomas Rd. Open until 1 a.m. Good dancing and very good Mexican food.

● Chuey's, Mill Ave., Tempe. Near University St. and Mill Ave. Good jazz at this restaurant. No cover charge.

● Phoenix Little Theater, 25 East Coronado. Telephone: 602/254-2151. Curtain rises at 8:30 p.m. at this, the oldest continuously operated community theater in the U.S.

● Valley Art Theater, 509 Mill Ave., Tempe. If you're in the mood for a film, you'll find either a classic, a foreign film, an underground movie, or a current new feature at this theater near the university.

● Phoenix Symphony, Symphony Hall, 225 East Adams. Telephone: 602/264-4754. The season runs from October through May at Symphony Hall in the new Civic Plaza.

● Arizona Ballet Theater, Symphony Hall, or Scottsdale Center for the Arts. Telephone: 602/258-2354. This resident professional dance company performs classical and modern ballet, world premières, and classic revivals.

Shopping: Changing Hands, 9 East 5th St., Tempe. The emphasis here is on "humanistic self-growth books"—everything from solar energy to vegetarian cooking.

● Al's Family Bookstore, 1454 East Van Buren St. For a wide range of books, new and secondhand.

● Womansplace, 2401 North 32nd. A feminist bookstore.

● Lucky Toad's, 1024 South McClintock Dr., Tempe. Full line of records and tapes.

● Circles, 800 North Central Ave. An impressive variety of records.

● Odyssey Records and Tapes, 1127 East Camelback Rd. Jazz, rock, and classical music for sale.

● High Adventure Headquarters, 3925 East Indian School Rd. Books, topographical maps, dehydrated foods, etc.

● Yates, 3931 East Thomas Rd. Good outlet for discount-priced camping equipment.

● Morris Athletic Supply, 525 South Hayden, Tempe. Everything from handballs to skis.

Help: Valley of the Sun Convention Bureau, 602/957-0070.

● Doctor's Referral Service, 602/252-6094.

● Visitor Hot Line (what's happening in Phoenix), 602/956-6200.

Prescott

Accommodation: Motel 6, 1111 East Sheldon St., 86301. Telephone: 602/778-0200. See Douglas listing for rates.

Safford

Accommodation: Friendship Country Manor Motel, 420 East Hwy. 70, 85546. Telephone: 602/428-2451. $20 to $24 for one; $26 to $32 for two in one bed; $28 to $34 for two in two beds.

Scottsdale

Accommodation: Motel 6, 6848 East Camelback Rd., 85251. Telephone: 602/947-7321. See Douglas listing for rates.

Sierra Vista

Accommodation: Motel 6, 1551 East Fry Blvd., 85635. Telephone: 602/459-0666. See Douglas listing for rates.

Tempe

On Campus: Arizona State University is in Tempe and on the ASU campus is an auditorium designed by Frank Lloyd Wright; nearby is Wright's Taliesin West. To meet ASU students, go to Minderbinder's Restaurant, 715 South Hayden Rd., where you can get a huge hamburger "with fixings" for a moderate price. For inexpensive Mexican food try the Dash Inn, 731 East Apache, and for good food in a crowded atmosphere, Monti's La Casa Vieja, 3 West 1st St.

Note: See Phoenix listing for restaurants, etc., in Tempe, which is a suburb of that city.

Accommodations: Western 6 Motel, 513 West Broadway, 85282. Telephone: 602/967-8696. $17.40 single; $24.90 double.

● Western 6 Motel, 1612 North Scottsdale Rd., 85281. Telephone: 602/945-9506. $17.40 single; $24.90 double.

● Friendship Franciscan Inn Motel, 1005 East Apache, 85281. Telephone: 602/968-7871. $17 to $22 for one; $19 to $25 for two in one bed; $23 to $27 for two in two beds.

● Regal 8 Inn, 1720 South Priest Dr., 85281. Telephone: 602/968-4401. $16.88 to $18.88 for one; $19.88 to $21.88 for two in one bed; $22.88 to $24.88 for two to four in two beds.

Tonalea

Camping: Navajo National Monument, 86044. Open May 15 to October 31. Reservations must be made with the superintendent for trips to Keet Seel Ruin.

Tucson

Help: Tuscon Travelers Aid Society, 40 West Veterans Blvd., 85713. Telephone: 602/622-8900.

● Information and Referral, 602/881-1794.

● Free Clinic Switchboard, 602/622-8821.

On Campus: The Switchboard at the University of Arizona's Student Union (tel. 602/626-HELP) will help you find a place to crash and help you find your way around and deal with crises.

The Sixth Street Café, which we recommended in a previous edition, has changed hands, according to someone who stopped in Tucson for a while: "It's now a Greek restaurant called Marathon Gyros, still has great food and reasonable prices. I recommend their sandwiches, salads, and feta cheese pies. All the students working there will direct you to hangouts like the Stumble Inn, Green Dolphin, Night Train, Dooleys (at University and Euclid), and the Outlaw, the Wildcat House, and the Bum Stear (all on Stone Ave. south of Grant Rd.). Be sure and have your dancing shoes 'cause these bars really hop."

For food, try the Mosaic Café, 1065 Silverbell, for vegetarian fare; the Café Olé, 57 East Jackson, for sandwiches and salads; the New Life Health Center, 4841 East Speedway; the El Dorado, 1949 South Fourth Ave.; and the Blue Willow, 2616 North Campbell, and Cryin' Onion Café, 3936 East Ft. Lowell Rd., both known for good, home-style cooking and large portions.

Another friend, someone from New York who spent time in Tucson, passed on a few pieces of information about the city which he very obviously enjoyed: "Pick up copies of the University of Arizona's *Arizona Daily Wildcat.*" Food can be bought inexpensively at the Food Conspiracy, 412 North 4th, a nonprofit food co-op, and to get work to pay for the food, "you can get day-to-day employment from Casual Labor on 22nd St. and Ninth Ave., and weekend cash can be picked up selling flowers—check the newspapers for these ever-present ads."

Accommodations: YWCA, 738 North Fifth Ave., 85705. Telephone: 602/884-7810. Women only. $9. Dormitory accommodations for $6.50; $1 more for non-YWCA members.

● YMCA, 516 North Fifth Ave., 85705. Telephone: 602/624-7471. Men only. $10 per night plus $5 refundable key and towel deposit. Weekly rate: $59.50. $6 per night for six-bedded room. YMCA serves a noon meal for $1.50.

● Congress Hotel, 311 East Congress St., 85702. Telephone: 602/622-8848. One block from bus and train stations. $12 single; $15 double; $18 triple. *"Very clean and comfortable with a helpful manager . . . Really excellent."*

● Regal 8 Inn, 1222 South Freeway, 85713. Telephone: 602/624-2516. $15.88 to $18.88 for one; $18.88 to $21.88 for two in one bed; $21.88 to $24.88 for two to four in two beds.

● Budget Host–American Motel, 810 East Benson Hwy., 85713. Telephone: 602/884-5800. $19.95 for one; $22.95 for two; $25.95 for three. Rates slightly over our maximum January to May.

● Motel 6, 960 South Freeway, 85705. Telephone: 602/624-6345. See Douglas listing for rates.

● Motel 6, 1031 East Benson Hwy., 85715. Telephone: 602/884-8107. See Douglas listing for rates.

● Friendship Inn–Lamp Post Motel, 5451 East 30th St., 85711. Telephone: 602/790-6021. Rates start at $16 for one; $18 for two in one bed; $21 for two in two beds.

● E-Z 8 Motel, 720 West 29th St., 85713. Telephone: 602/624-8291. See Lake Havasu listing for rates.

● E-Z 8 Motel. 1007 South Freeway, 85705. Telephone: 602/624-9843. See Lake Havasu listing for rates.

● Western 6 Motel, 1388 West Grant Rd., 85705. Telephone: 602/622-4784. $17.40 single; $24.90 double.

● Western 6 Motel, 755 East Benson Hwy., 85713. Telephone: 602/622-4614. $17.40 single; $24.90 double.

Willcox

Accommodations: Motel 6, 331 North Haskell Ave., 85643. Telephone: 602/384-2256. See Douglas listing for rates.

● Imperial 400 Motor Inn, 340 South Haskell Ave., 85643. Telephone: 602/384-2237. $18 to $22 for one; $22 to $26 for two in one bed; $24 to $30 for two in two beds.

● Best Value Sands Motel, 400 South Haskell Dr., 85643. Telephone: 602/384-3501. $18 for one; $21 for two in one bed; $23 for two in two beds.

Williams

Accommodations: The Patio Motel, 🐟 ★, 128 East Bill Williams Ave., 86046. Telephone: 602/635-4791. $12 to $21 for one; $15 to $26 for two in one bed; $18 to $26 for two in two beds.
● Friendship Inn–Belaire, 620 West Bill Williams Ave. on Hwy. 66, 86046. Telephone: 602/635-4415. $18 to $22 for one; $22 to $26 for two in one bed; $26 to $30 for two in two beds.

Winslow

Accommodations: Imperial 400 Motor Inn, 1221 East 3rd St., 86047. Telephone: 602/289-4631. $16 to $18 for one; $18 to $20 for two in one bed; $22 to $24 for two in two beds.
● Motel 6, 725 West 3rd St., 86047. Telephone: 602/289-3903. See Douglas listing for rates.

Youngtown

Accommodation: Motel 6, 11133 Grand Ave., 85363. Telephone: 602/933-0541. See Douglas listing for rates.

Yuma

Accommodations: Motel 6, 2730 Fourth Ave., 85364. Telephone: 602/344-3550. See Douglas listing for rates.
● Motel 6, South Side of U.S. Hwy. 95 (16th St.), halfway between 4th Ave. and I-8. See Douglas listing for rates.

Arkansas

Here's one of the strangest stories ever told—how Arkansas got its name. It started with the name of a tribe called Quapaw which the Algonquins pronounced Oo-ka-na-sa. Marquette wrote it as Arkansoa, La Salle as Arkensa, De Tonti as Arkancas, and La Harpe as Arkansas. In 1881 the legislature had to appoint a committee to decide on the right pronunciation of the last syllable. May we suggest a similar committee, preferably of Algonquins, to decide how Quapaw could possibly have been pronounced Oo-ka-na-sa?

Probably the biggest tourist attraction in Arkansas is the world-famous Hot Springs National Park, with 47 thermal springs that are collected and distributed to bath houses throughout the park and the city of Hot Springs. Fifty-four miles from Hot Springs is Little Rock, the capital of Arkansas, where you can visit the Arkansas Art Center, Arkansas Territorial Restoration, and the first State Capitol. In Arkansas there are a number of state parks that offer housekeeping cottages for rent within the boundaries of each park. The overnight rental for two people is well within this book's budget and the settings are quite beautiful. For information, write to the Arkansas Department of Parks and Tourism at the address below.

A guide to the area that we can recommend is *The Greatest Ozarks Guidebook,* available from Greatest Graphics, Inc., P.O. Box 4467 G.S., Springfield, MO 65804 ($7.95 postpaid).

If you're going to spend any time at all in Arkansas, you'll want a set of the Arkansas Department of Parks and Tourism's Special Rate Coupons. They include reductions in the admission price to the Eureka Springs Passion Play and other tourist attractions and discounts at some hotels and restaurants throughout the state. Just write to the address below for your set.

Some Special Events: Rodeo of the Ozarks in Springdale and Miss Arkansas Pageant in Hot Springs (July); Alfred E. Brumley Annual Sun-down to Sun-up Gospel Sing in Springdale and White River Water Carnival in Batesville (August); Mid-America Banjo Rally in Eureka Springs and Arkansas Old-Time Fiddlers Association State Championship Competition in Mountain View (September).

Hitching: Hitching is prohibited on the roadways, and Arkansas law interprets roadway as including the shoulder, so if you hitch, stay off the road and the shoulder. A few words on the subject from friends in Arkansas: "Hitchhiking is difficult on the smaller, country roads" and "much depends on the prevailing mood of any police officer you may meet." The assistant commander of the Highway Patrol advised any hitchhiker to be sure to carry "adequate and proper identification."

Tourist Information: Arkansas Department of Parks and Tourism, One Capitol Mall, Little Rock, AR 72201. Telephone: toll free 800/643-8383 out of state; 800/482-8999 in state.

Bald Knob

Accommodation: Scottish Inn, Hwys. 64, 67, and 167, 72010. Telephone: 501/724-3204. $17.95 for one; $20.95 for two in one bed; $22.95 for two in two beds.

Benton

Accommodation: Superior Troutt Motel, I-30 West, 72015. Telephone: 501/778-3633. $16 to $19 for one; $19 to $21 for two in one bed; $22 to $24 for two in two beds.

Blytheville

Accommodation: Days Inn, I-55 and Arkansas 18, P.O. Box 1342, 72315. Telephone: 501/763-1241. $20.88 for one; $24.88 for two.

Brinkley

Accommodation: Friendship Inn Townhouse, on I-40 Exit 216; 1507 North Hwys. 17 and 39, 72021. Telephone: 501/734-2121. $21 to $22 for one; $26 to $27 for two in one bed; $29 to $30 for two in two beds.

Conway

Accommodations: Best Value Town House Motel, Hwy. 64-65B, 1200 Harkrider, 72032. Telephone: 501/329-3846. $16 to $18 for one; $18 to $20 for two in one bed; $22 to $24 for two in two beds.
 ● Motel 6, Hwy. 65B and I-40, 72032. Telephone: 501/327-6571. $12.95 for one; $16.95 for two; $19.95 for up to four.

Dardanelle

Accommodation and Camping: Mt. Nebo State Park, Rte. 2, P.O. Box 160 A, 72834. Telephone: 501/229-3655. Besides camping in the park ($4 to $6 per campsite), there are 13 natural stone cabins "with breathtaking views of the valley below," with all-electric kitchens, full baths, a bedroom, living room, and fireplace. Cabins rent for $25 to $29 per night, for two persons; $3 extra for each additional person up to six. You must be 21 or over to rent a cabin. Reservations are recommended two to three months in advance for cabins. Write to the Arkansas Department of Parks and Tourism, One Capitol Mall, Little Rock, AR 72201, for information on 11 other parks with similar facilities.

Eureka Springs

Tourist Information: Eureka Springs Chamber of Commerce, P.O. Box 551, 72632. Telephone: 501/253-8737.

Eureka Springs has been described as "the most unique and beautiful small town in the country and the center of an Ozark back-to-the-land movement." There are lots of young people passing through the Ozarks and many staying and homesteading. While you're in the area, "see the mountains, trees, lakes, rivers, Victorian architecture, and native crafts. Listen to the bluegrass, canoe, bicycle, or hike." Be sure to stop at Bon Appetit, 63 Spring St., in the New Orleans Hotel. The food is natural and reasonable.

Fayetteville

On Campus: We got lots of good information from the people who work on the school newspaper at the University of Arkansas. From what we can tell, if you're going to be in Arkansas at all you should be sure to get to Fayetteville. The counterculture seems to be alive and well there. There's a new Union building on Garland St. right in front of the library. In the Union you'll find the Student Programs Office and the Information Center—the two best sources of information on what's going on in the community. The Student Government Office has a small job list and an off-campus housing directory that they might let you share.

When you get hungry, go to the Restaurant on the Corner, 248 West Dickson; King Pizza, 203 West Dickson; Bogey's Restaurant, 9 South School; The Working Class Hero, 21 North Block; or Hugo's, 25½ North Block. Check the local newspaper, *The Grapevine,* for information on what's happening.

"The Ozark food co-op in the Green Warehouse on Watson and West Sts. has a Community Bulletin Board as well as a wide variety of patrons who would be good sources of information for folks traveling through."

Help: Information Desk, 402 Arkansas Union, University of Arkansas. Telephone: 501/575-2304.

Accommodation: Town House and Sands Motel, 215-229 North College (Hwys. 62 and 71), 72701. Telephone: 501/442-2313. Six blocks from University of Arkansas. Swimming pool. $14 to $15 single; $17 to $19 double, but that goes up for three big football weekends in the fall.

Fort Smith

Accommodations: Friendship Inn–Continental Motel, 1421 North 11th St., 72901. Telephone: 501/785-1471. $17.47 to $22.50 for one; $19.50 to $24.50 for two in one bed; $24.50 to $30.50 for two in two beds.

● Regal 8 Inn, 1021 Garrison Ave., 72901. Telephone: 501/785-2611. $17.88 for one; $20.88 for two in one bed; $23.88 for two to four in two beds.

● Motel 6, 6001 Rogers Ave., 72901. Telephone: 501/452-1924. See Conway listing for rates.

Harrison

Camping: Buffalo National River, P.O. Box 1173, 72601. Camping at Buffalo Point all year. Canoe rentals. $3 per campsite per night.

Hope

Accommodation: Friendship Inn–Dean's Motor Lodge, Hwy. 29 and I-30, P.O. Box 430, 71801. Telephone: 501/777-4665. $14 to $18 for one; $20 to $26 for two in one bed; $22 to $28 for two in two beds.

Hot Springs

Tourist Information: Hot Springs Chamber of Commerce, P.O. Box 1500, 71901. Telephone: toll free 800/643-1570 out of state; 800/272-2081 in state.

Camping: Hot Springs National Park, P.O. Box 1860, 71901. Campsites at Gulpha Gorge, two miles east of Hot Springs. Open year round. $3 per campsite per night.

Jonesboro

Accommodation: Motel 6, 2300 South Caraway Rd., 72401. Telephone: 501/972-6000. See Conway listing for rates.

Little Rock

Tourist Information: Little Rock Bureau for Conventions and Visitors, Markham and Broadway, 72201. Telephone: 501/376-4781.

Accommodations: YMCA, 6th and Broadway, 72201. Telephone: 501/372-5421. Men only. Weekly only, $35.

● Motel 6, 8401 New Benton Hwy., 72209. Telephone: 501/562-1914. See Conway listing for rates.

● Regal 8 Inn, 8421 New Benton Hwy., 72209. Telephone: 501/568-1200. See Fort Smith listing for rates.

● Best Value Acme Motel, 3301 West Roosevelt Rd., 72204. Telephone: 501/663-6361. $15 for one; $16 for two in one bed; $18 to $22 for two in two beds.

● Red Roof Inn, 🔾, I-30 at Scott Hamilton Dr. (Exit 134). Telephone: 501/562-2694. $19.95 for one; $22.95 for two in one bed; $24.95 to $26.95 for two to four in two beds.

Magnolia

Accommodation: Town House Motel, 301 East Main St., 71753. Telephone: 501/234-5286. $19 to $21 single; $22 to $25 double.

Marion

Accommodation: Scottish Inn, I-55, Exit 10, 72364. Telephone: 501/739-3186 or 732-1640. $18 for one; $24 for two in one bed; $28 for two in two beds.

Mountain Home

Accommodation: Best Value Town & Country Motel, 145 South Main St., 72653. Telephone: 501/425-3151. $16 to $18 for one; $18 to $20 for two in one bed; $20 to $22 for two in two beds.

North Little Rock

Accommodation: Days Inn, 2508 Jacksonville Hwy., 72117. Telephone: 501/945-4167. $23.88 for one; $27.88 for two. Rates slightly higher June to August.

Paragould

Accommodation: Sunset Motel, 1506 West Kingshighway, 72450. Telephone: 501/236-7631. $10.95 to $14 for one; $12.95 to $15 for two in one bed; $18 for two in two beds.

Russellville

Accommodations: Best Value Merrick Motel, Hwy. 64 East, 72801. Telephone: 501/968-6332. $12.95 to $14.95 for one; $15.95 to $17.95 for two in one bed; $17.95 to $19.95 for two in two beds.
● Motel 6, I-40 and County Rd., P.O. Box 242, 72801. Telephone: 501/968-3666. See Conway listing for rates.

Springdale

Accommodation: Scottish Inn, Hwy. 71 South, 72764. Telephone: 501/751-4874. $18 for one; $21 for two in one bed; $24 for two in two beds.

Los Angeles

California

Everyone wants to visit California. Ask any easterner, or anyone from abroad, and they'll all tell you their dreams about California. California is now as much myth as reality, but no one is making a mistake when they decide to go there. It's a complex, vibrant, and interesting piece of the U.S. and has a lot to offer any traveler. Because California is so beautifully situated between the Pacific Ocean and the mountains, visitors can sail, surf, swim, ski, or hike. Of course, there are Disneyland, Sea World, lots of zoos, and historical missions up and down the state, not to mention Hollywood and all that glamor capitol has to offer. California has television studios, some of the best shopping areas in the world, and a major university, the University of California, with nine campuses covering the entire state. California is the number one producer of agricultural products in the world and supplies most of the U.S. with its harvests. Of course, California is a leading wine-producing state, and some of the finest wines in the country—some might even say the world—come from the northern part of the state.

San Francisco is a jewel city, not to be missed. Los Angeles is another "must visit" place. The Huntington Library in San Marino, near Los Angeles, has a famous collection of paintings and illuminated manuscripts of great interest to anyone who's interested in art history.

Then there's the Getty Museum near Santa Monica and the Hearst Castle in San Simeon. The Carmel Valley, home of many fine artists and craftsmen, is a fascinating place to visit, and finally, Monterey, with its Cannery Row made famous by John Steinbeck, is a lovely city that should be on every visitor's itinerary.

While you're in California, stop at the offices of CIEE at 2511 Channing Way, Berkeley, CA 94704 (tel. 415/848-8604); 1093 Broxton Ave., Los Angeles, CA 90024 (tel. 213/208-3551); and 312 Sutter St., San Francisco, CA 94108 (tel. 415/421-3473). In addition to helping you find your way around California, they are a good source of information on low-cost travel, particularly to Asia and Australia.

"In California I slept under the stars lots of times, on beaches or in the woods. On the coast there are lots of state parks where you can stay for almost nothing."

Some Special Events: Tournament of Roses Parade and Football Game in Pasadena and Winter Carnival in South Lake Tahoe (January); Chinese New Year Celebration in San Francisco (February); Steinbeck Birthday Celebration in Salinas and San Luis Obispo Mardi Gras and Fiesta de la Golondrias (Return of the Swallows) in San Juan Capistrano (March); Renaissance Pleasure Faire in Agoura (April weekends); Dixieland Jazz Jubilee in Sacramento (May); Strawberry Festival in Los Gatos and San Francisco Birthday Celebration (June); World's Biggest Salmon Barbecue in Fort Bragg and County Fair in Sonoma (July); County Fairs in Stockton, Napa, Woodland, Ferndale, and San Jose (August); and Marin County (Blackpoint Forest) Renaissance Faire (weekends in August and September).

Hitching: Someone who returned from a trip across country had something to say about hitching in California, where it seems that hitching is a popular way to get around. He says that "hitching from San Francisco to Los Angeles can be done quickly if you use Interstate 5. Since there's nothing on the Interstate from Los Angeles to Oakland, you're pretty much assured of a ride all the way. But be prepared for a dull ride. If you aren't in a big hurry take U.S. 101, the coast road, instead. It may mean slow hitching, but it also means beautiful scenery and friendly rides. Going north from San Francisco you can choose Route 1, slow and beautiful; U.S. 101, which goes through wine and redwood country but is slow in summer because of all the other hitchhikers; or Interstate 5, for a fast ride north to Oregon or Washington."

A lieutenant of the California Highway Patrol, although anxious to point out the risks of hitching, did say that the best highways for hitching are Interstate 5 and U.S. 99 and 101 for north-south travel and Interstates 8, 10, 15, 40, and 80 for east-west routes. No hitchhiking is permitted on or along freeways.

Tourist Information: California Office of Visitor Services, P.O. Box 1499, Sacramento, CA 95805. Telephone: 916/322-1396. Offers an excellent visitor's map and other travel information.

N.B.: There's an interesting organization, Rent-A-Room International, located in Corona del Mar, which arranges bed and continental breakfast in private homes throughout southern California. The charge is $20 to $30 for two, and there's a minimum of three nights. Reservations must be made in advance. Information is available from Rent-A-Room International, 1032 Sea Lane, Corona del Mar, CA 92625. Telephone: 714/640-2330. If you write, enclose a stamped, self-addressed envelope.

A similar group that places people in private homes in the San Francisco Bay area, Lake Tahoe, Los Angeles, San Diego, Napa Valley, Carmel/Monterey, and other locations on the West Coast, is Bed and Breakfast International, 151 Ardmore Rd., Kensington, CA 94707 (Kensington borders Berkeley). The cost of a double, with breakfast included, is $26 to $85 (students may request lower rates); the minimum stay is three nights. To obtain an application, write to the address above and enclose a stamped, self-addressed envelope.

Anaheim

Accommodations: Motel 6, 921 South Beach Blvd., 92804. Telephone: 714/827-9450. $12.95 for one; $16.95 for two; $19.95 for up to four.
- Friendship Inn–Anaheim Motor Lodge, 1224 North Harbor Blvd., 92801. Telephone: 714/879-6440. $20 to $24 for one; $22 to $26 for two in one bed; $32 to $36 for two in two beds.
- Sixpence Inn, 2020 Via Burton, 92806. Telephone: 714/956-9690. $12.95 to $14.95 for one; $14.95 to $16.95 for two.

Arcadia

Accommodation: Motel 6, 225 Colorado Pl., 91006. Telephone: 213/445-2801. See Anaheim listing for rates.

Arcata

Help: Humboldt Open Door Clinic, 1000 H St., 95521. Telephone: 707/822-2957.
- Contact, 707/826-4400.
- Ride Line, 707/826-4444. Open from 9 a.m. to 10 p.m. Someone at the Humboldt Open Door Clinic told us that although hitchhiking is quite common, there are many rapes and robberies every year. She also mentioned that the Sprouted Seed is a good place for a meal. You can get hearty beans and cheese there for $1.60 or soup, fresh bread, and salad for $2.50.

Accommodations: Jolly Giant Conference Center, 🏠, Jolly Giant Commons, Humboldt State University, 95521. Telephone: 707/826-3451. "Must have a tie-in with HSU and be on educationally related business." Summer only. $10 single; $16 double. ISIC-holders who stay four to seven days pay $9 single, $12 double; those who stay 8 to 14 days pay $8.50 single, $11 double; and those who stay more than 15 days pay $6 single, $10 double.
- The Arcata Hostel, 1390 I St., P.O. Box 4958, 95521. Telephone: 707/822-9995 or 822-2876 from October to June. Open June 20 to September 19. $3.75 for AYH members; $5.75 for nonmembers. "The hostel is an old Victorian house with some excellent redwood burlwork. It is homey and quiet." Bring your own linen. Reservations suggested.
- Motel 6, 4755 Valley West Blvd., 95521. Telephone: 707/822-1745. See Anaheim listing for rates.

Atascadero

Accommodation: Motel 6, U.S. 101 and Santa Rosa Rd., 93422. See Anaheim listing for rates.

Baker

Accommodation: Friendship Inn–Royal Hawaiian Motel, 200 West Baker Blvd., 92309. Telephone: 714/733-4326. $12 to $20 for one; $14 to $22 for two in one bed; $16 to $26 for two in two beds.

Bakersfield

Accommodations: Motel 6, 350 Oak St., 93304. Telephone: 805/327-5913. See Anaheim listing for rates.
● Motel 6, 2727 White Lane, 93304. Telephone: 805/834-6411. See Anaheim listing for rates.
● Sixpence Inn, 8223 East Brundage Lane. Telephone: 805/366-7231. $12.95 to $14.95 for one; $14.95 to $16.95 for two.
● Imperial 400 Motor Inn, 906 Union Ave., 93307. Telephone: 805/327-7931. $17 to $19 for one; $19 to $23 for two in one bed; $22 to $26 for two in two beds.
● California 6 Motel, 1350 Easton Dr., 93309. Telephone: 805/327-1686. $14.40 single; $21.90 double.

Baldwin Park

Accommodation: Sixpence Inn, 14510 Garvey Ave., 91706. Telephone: 213/960-5011. See Anaheim listing for rates.

Barstow

Accommodations: Motel 6, 31951 East Main St., 92311. Telephone: 714/256-8778. See Anaheim listing for rates.
● Imperial 400 Motor Inn, 1281 Main St., 92311. Telephone: 714/256-6836. $18 to $24 for one; $23 to $28 for two in one bed; $25 to $30 for two in two beds.
● Friendship Desert Inn, 1100 East Main St., 92311. Telephone: 714/256-2146. $20 to $23 for one; $24 to $27 for two in one bed; $28 to $32 for two in two beds.

Beaumont

Accommodation: Golden West Motel, 625 East 5th St., 92223. Telephone: 714/845-2185. $17 to $22 for one; $19 to $24 for two in one bed; $22 to $27 for two in two beds.

Berkeley

Accommodations: International House, ♿, University of California, 94720. Telephone: 415/642-9470. To stay you "must have affiliation with the University of California as registered students, guests of residents, scholars visiting the campus, etc." Open to temporary visitors in summer only. One-week minimum stay. $161 single; $133 per person double. Includes 20 meals per week.
• YMCA, 2001 Allston Way, 94704. Telephone: 415/848-6800. Men only. $13.50 single; $24 double.

Bermuda Dunes

Accommodation: Motel 6, 78100 Varner Rd., Indio, 92201. Telephone: 714/345-2242. See Anaheim listing for rates.

Big Bear

Accommodation: Motel 6, 1200 Big Bear Blvd., P.O. Box M28-6, 92315. Telephone: 714/585-3996. See Anaheim listing for rates.

Bishop

Accommodation: Friendship Inn–Thunderbird, 190 West Pine St., 93514. Telephone: 714/873-4215. $24 for one; $26 for two in one bed; $28.50 for two in two beds.

Blythe

Accommodations: Motel 6, 500 West Donlon St., 92225. Telephone: 714/922-6661. See Anaheim listing for rates.
• E-Z 8 Motel, 900 West Rice St., 92225. Telephone: 714/922-9191. $13.88 to $15.88 for one; $16.88 to $18.88 for two in one bed; $18.88 to $20.88 for two in two beds.
• Friendship Desert Inn, 850 West Hobson Way, 92225. Telephone: 714/922-5145. $18 to $24 for one; $21 to $26 for two in one bed; $26 to $34 for two in two beds.

Bonita

Accommodation: Creepy Hollow Hostel (AYH), 3440 Valley Rd., 92002. Telephone: 714/475-1573. Ten miles from San Diego. $3. Reservations required. Map and hostel directions mailed with confirmed reservations. No smoking. If you are a folk music enthusiast, this is the place for you. AYH membership required (see page 21).

Buellton

Accommodation: Motel 6, 333 McMurray Rd., P.O. Box 1670, 93427. Telephone: 805/688-3293. See Anaheim listing for rates.

Burney

Accommodation: Best Value Charm Motel, 1803 Main, P.O. Box 57, 96013. Telephone: 916/335-2254. $18 to $24 for one; $19 to $26 for two in one bed; $21 to $28 for two in two beds.

Buttonwillow

Accommodation: Motel 6, 3810 Tracy Ave., 93206. Telephone: 805/764-5166. See Anaheim listing for rates.

Camarillo

Accommodation: Motel 6, 1641 East Daily Dr., 93010. Telephone: 805/482-5611. See Anaheim listing for rates.

Campbell

Accommodation: California 6 Motel, 1240 Camden Ave., 95008. Telephone: 408/371-8870. $14.40 single; $21.90 double.

Carpinteria

Accommodation: Motel 6, U.S. Hwy. 101 and Santa Monica Rd., 93013. Telephone: 805/684-4616. See Anaheim listing for rates.

Chico

Accommodation: Motel 6, 665 Manzanita Court, 95926. Telephone: 916/343-5806. See Anaheim listing for rates.

Chino

Accommodation: Sixpence Inn, 12266 Central Ave., 91710. Telephone: 714/591-3877. See Anaheim listing for rates.

Coalinga

Accommodation: Motel 6, 25278 West Dorris, 93210. Telephone: 209/935-2866. See Anaheim listing for rates.

Corning

Accommodation: Friendship Rancho Tehama Motel, 998 South Hwy. 99 West, 96021. Telephone: 916/824-5151. $14 to $16 for one; $17 to $19 for two in one bed; $20 to $22 for two in two beds.

Costa Mesa

Accommodation: California 6 Motel, 1441 Gisler Ave., 92626. Telephone: 714/957-3063. $14.40 single; $21.90 double.

Crescent City

Accommodation: Friendship Inn–Rustic Inn, 220 M St. (Hwy. 101 North), 95531. Telephone: 707/464-9553. $14 to $22 for one; $20 to $26 for two in one bed; $22 to $28 for two in two beds.

Davis

On Campus: There is a branch of the University of California in Davis, and you can get campus information by calling 916/752-2222. You will find a ride board in the undergraduate library, and housing possibilities in the Housing Office. There are two spots on campus where students tend to meet: the Coffee House, and the Pub. You can also find students off campus at Larry Blake's Restaurant in the evening.

Accommodation: Motel 6, 4835 Chiles Rd., 95616. Telephone: 916/756-6662. See Anaheim listing for rates.

Death Valley

Camping: Death Valley National Monument, Death Valley 92328. Nine campgrounds, five with sanitary stations. No entrance fee; $1 to $2 per campsite per night.

Delano

Accommodation: Friendship Inn–Stardust, 405 Cecil Ave. East on Hwy. 99, 93215. $18 to $22 for one; $28 to $30 for two in one bed; $30 to $32 for two in two beds.

Dunsmuir

Accommodations: Garden Motel, √, 4310 Dunsmuir Ave., 96025. Telephone: 916/235-4805. $21 to $26 for two in one bed; $22 to $27 for two in two beds.

● Friendship Cedar Lodge, 4201 Dunsmuir Ave., 96025. Telephone: 916/235-2836. $19 to $23 for one; $22 to $25 for two in one bed; $24 to $27 for two in two beds.

● Friendship El Rancho Motel, 400 Dunsmuir Ave., 96025. Telephone:

916/235-2884. $19 to $23 for one; $20 to $24 for two in one bed; $22 to $26 for two in two beds.

El Centro

Accommodations: Motel 6, 330 North Imperial Ave., 92243. Telephone: 714/352-8400. See Anaheim listing for rates.
● Motel 6, Smoketree Drive and I-86, 92243. See Anaheim listing for rates.
● E-Z 8 Motel, 455 Wake Ave., 92245. Telephone: 714/352-6620. See Blythe listing for rates.

El Monte

Accommodation: Motel 6, 3429 Peck Rd., 91731. Telephone: 213/442-7380. See Anaheim listing for rates.

Escondido

Accommodation: Motel 6, 509 West Washington Ave., 92025. Telephone: 714/743-1331. See Anaheim listing for rates.

Eureka

Accommodations: California 6 Motel, 1934 Broadway, 95501. Telephone: 707/445-9631. $14.40 single; $21.90 double.
● Best Value Safari Motel, 7th and Broadway, 95501. Telephone: 707/443-4891. $15 to $20 for one; $18 to $22 for two in one bed; $20 to $24 for two in two beds.
● Friendship Inn–Flamingo Motel, 4255 South Broadway. Telephone: 707/443-4556 or 4557. $14.50 to $18.50 for one; $17.50 to $22.50 for two in one bed; $20.50 to $25.50 for two in two beds.
● Friendship Inn–Town House Motel, corner of 4th and K Sts., 95501. Telephone: 707/443-4536. $16 to $22 for one; $20 to $25 for two in one bed; $24 to $28 for two in two beds. Rates slightly higher June to September.

Fairfield

Accommodation: Motel 6, 2353 Magellan Rd., P.O. Box U, 94533. Telephone: 707/422-4060. See Anaheim listing for rates.

Fontana

Accommodation: Motel 6, 10195 Sierra Ave., 92335. Telephone: 714/822-0541. See Anaheim listing for rates.

Fresno

Help: Job Hot Line, 209/435-1464.

Accommodations: YWCA, 1660 M St., 93721. Telephone: 209/237-4701. Women only. $10. Weekly rate: $25 to $40. Eight blocks from bus station.

● Motel 6, 949 North Parkway Dr. at Hwy. 99., 93728. Telephone: 209/268-1936. See Anaheim listing for rates.

● Motel 6, 4245 North Blackstone Ave., Hwy. 41 North, 93726. Telephone: 209/227-3523. See Anaheim listing for rates.

● Regal 8 Inn, 777 North Parkway Dr., 93728. Telephone: 209/237-2175. $15.88 for one; $18.88 for two in one bed; $21.88 for two to four in two beds.

● Friendship Inn–Vagabond Motor Hotel, 1807 Broadway. Telephone: 209/268-0916. $18 to $20 for one; $20 to $22 for two in one bed; $22 to $24 for two in two beds.

● California 6 Motel, 4080 North Blackstone Ave., 93726. Telephone: 209/222-2431. $14.40 single; $21.90 double.

Fullerton

Accommodation: California 6 Motel, 1415 South Euclid Ave., 92632. Telephone: 714/992-0660. $14.40 single; $21.90 double.

Gilroy

Accommodation: Motel 6, 6110 Monterey Hwy. (Hwy. 101), 95020. Telephone: 408/842-9306. See Anaheim listing for rates.

Glendale

Accommodation: Glendale YMCA, 140 North Louise St., 91206. Telephone: 213/240-4130. Ten blocks from bus station. Men only. $9.50 single. Weekly rate: $34 to $38.50.

Hacienda Heights

Accommodation: California 6 Motel, 1154 South Seventh Ave., 91745. Telephone: 213/968-9462. $14.40 single; $21.90 double.

Harbor City

Accommodation: Sixpence Inn, 820 West Sepulveda, 90710. Telephone: 213/549-9560. See Anaheim listing for rates.

Hayward

Accommodations: Friendship Inn–Mission Lodge, 24400 Mission Blvd., 94544. Telephone: 415/537-5404. $18 to $20 for one; $20 to $23 for two in one bed; $24 to $26 for two in two beds.

● California 6 Motel, 30155 Industrial Pkwy. SW, 94544. Telephone: 415/489-8333. $14.40 single; $21.90 double.

Indio

Accommodations: Friendship Inn–Indio Holiday Motel, 44-301 Sun Gold, 92201. Telephone: 714/347-6105. $16 to $20 for one; $18 to $25 for two in one bed; $21 to $35 for two in two beds.
● Motel 6, 82195 Indio Blvd., 92201. Telephone: 714/347-6582. See Anaheim listing for rates.

Julian

Accommodations: Camp Marston Hostel (AYH), Pine Hills Rd., 92036. Telephone: 714/765-0642. $3 summer; $3.50 winter. AYH membership required (see page 21).
● Camp Stevens Hostel (AYH), P.O. Box 367, 92036. Telephone: 714/765-0028. Open September 15 to May 15. Reservations required on weekends and always recommended. $3.50. AYH membership required (see page 21).

King City

Accommodations: Motel 6, 6 Broadway Circle, 93930. Telephone: 408/385-6666. See Anaheim listing for rates.
● Friendship Inn–Crown DD Lodge, 1130 Broadway, 93930. Telephone: 408/385-5921. $16 to $21 for one; $20 to $26 for two in one bed; $21 to $28 for two in two beds.

La Habra

Accommodation: California 6 Motel, 870 North Beach Blvd., 90631. Telephone: 213/694-2158. $14.40 single; $21.90 double.

La Mesa

Accommodation: California 6 Motel, 7621 Alvardo Rd., 92041. Telephone: 714/464-7151. $14.40 single; $21.90 double.

Lancaster

Accommodation: California 6 Motel, 43540 17th St. West, 93534. Telephone: 805/948-0435. $14.40 single; $21.90 double.

Lemon Grove

Accommodation: E-Z 8 Motel, 7458 Broadway. Telephone: 714/462-7022. $15.88 to $18.88 for one; $17.88 to $21.88 for two in one bed; $19.88 to $23.88 for two in two beds.

Lompoc

Accommodation: Motel 6, 1415 East Ocean Ave., 93436. Telephone: 805/736-4053. See Anaheim listing for rates.

Long Beach

Accommodation: California 6 Motel, 5665 East 7th St., 90804. Telephone: 213/597-1311. $14.40 single; $21.90 double.

Los Altos

Accommodation: Hidden Villa Hostel (AYH), 26870 Moody Rd., 94022. Telephone: 415/941-6407. Open September 1 to June 15. Located on 1800 acres of farm and ranch. $3 for AYH members; $5 for nonmembers.

Los Angeles

Los Angeles is a legend. Here's the movie kingdom, the home of the leisure suit, 20th-century America at its extreme. L.A. can be a confusing city for a visitor —its sprawl is mind-boggling, its freeways are restless, and its beaches are endless. In order to avoid culture shock when you arrive, consult Arthur Frommer's *Guide to Los Angeles* ($2.95) or *Around the Town with Ease,* by the Junior League of Los Angeles, Farmer's Market, 3rd and Fairfax Sts., Los Angeles, CA 90036 (free; enclose $1 to cover postage and handling). Three other books that might interest you are *Only in L.A.: A Guide to Exceptional Services,* by Roni Sue Malin and Judy Ruderman, Chronicle Books ($5.95); *L.A./Access,* by Richard Saul Wurman, an energy-conscious guide book ($8.95); and for fun, Los Angeles on $500 a Day, by Ferne Kadish and Kathleen Kirtland, Macmillan ($4.95).

Contact the Greater Los Angeles Visitors and Convention Bureau, 5051 South Flower St., 90071 (telephone 213/628-3101), for maps and information. And once you're there, check the *Los Angeles Times* entertainment section, *Los Angeles* magazine, *New West* magazine and *Reader,* a free weekly that comes out every Thursday.

Getting There: From the Airport: Los Angeles International Airport is 17 miles southwest of downtown L.A. The least expensive way to get from there to downtown is via Airport Bus Service (tel. 213/723-4636); the fare is $3.65. Bus service from the airport to Hollywood/Universal City costs $3.65; to West L.A. and the San Fernando Valley, $4.35; and to Beverly Hills and Century City, $3.65.

● From the Bus and Train Stations: The bus station is located at 208 East 6th St., and the train station, Union Station, is right off the Hollywood Freeway at 800 North Alameda. To call Continental Trailways, dial 742-1200; Greyhound, 620-1200; and Amtrak, 624-0171. RTD (Rapid Transit District) bus transportation is available from the bus and train stations to other parts of the city.

Getting Around: If you travel by taxi (Santa Monica Checker Cab can be summoned by dialing 394-1144), you'll pay $1.90 per mile; that is why we recommend taxis only for emergencies. L.A. Rapid Transit operates buses every 10 to 15 minutes that cost 65¢ locally and 5¢ for a transfer, but very few people depend on buses in L.A. Most people get around the city by car (or on skates). If you don't have a car but want to rent, some of the least expensive places to try are Rent a Convertible, 100 South La Brea (tel. 933-9508); Rent a Wreck (tel. 478-0676; $14.95 per day, first 75 miles free and 10¢ per mile after that); Budget Rent a Car (tel. 645-4500); and Bob Leach's Auto Rental, 4810 West Imperial Hwy., Inglewood (tel. 673-2727; $4 per day and 10¢ per mile for a subcompact car).

Keep in mind, when planning your trip to L.A., that the car is king there; if you do not have access to a car, stay near Westwood where the public transportation is better than in other parts of the city.

Accommodations: Westchester Family YMCA Youth Hostel (AYH-SA), 8015 South Sepulveda Blvd., 90045. Telephone: 213/776-0922. Two miles from Playa del Rey Beach, one mile north of L.A. International Airport, San Diego Freeway (405), and the Pacific Coast Hwy. (Rte. 1). $5 for AYH members; $6 for nonmembers. For men and women. Bring a bedroll or sleeping bag to put on the cots. You must be 18 or over to stay. Open June 1 to September 15. Breakfast and lunch available.

● Los Angeles International Hostel, 1502 Palos Verdes Dr. North, Harbor City, 90710. Telephone: 213/831-8109. Open year round. $4 for AYH members; $6 for nonmembers.

● YMCA, 1006 East 28th St., 90011. Telephone: 213/232-7193. About 20 minutes by local bus from central bus station. Men only. $10.64. "We are located in a black and Hispanic neighborhood and our building is old but being renovated."

● Mary Andrews Clark Home, YWCA, 306 Loma Dr., 90017. Telephone: 213/483-5780. Women only. $20 single, including two meals, for members; $21 for nonmembers. The building was built in 1912 and patterned after a French château.

● Hollywood YMCA and Youth Hostel (AYH-SA), 1553 North Hudson Ave., Hollywood, 90028. Telephone: 213/467-4161. Seven miles from the train station. From L.A. International Airport take RTD airport bus to the Hollywood Roosevelt Hotel. The Y is six blocks east on Hollywood Blvd., then one block south on Hudson. From the downtown bus station, take the RTD bus #91 on Hill St. to Hollywood and Wilcox, walk west one block to Hudson, then go one block south on Hudson. Men and women. Open year round as a youth hostel facility and an international center. $13.50 single; $18.75 double. For AYH members (18 and over), sleeping on cots with their own sleeping bags, $4.50 per night; $6.25 for others. There's a Garden Café, too. Ask for the Y's excellent *Guide to Restaurants in Hollywood* and the other useful tourist information they offer.

● American Student Hostel, 11024 Strathmore Dr., Westwood Village, 90024. Telephone: 213/208-9055. Take Bus 81 to Westwood Blvd. and Strathmore. Not far from UCLA and Westwood Village. $6.50 per night; bring a sleeping bag.

● Rainbow Hotel, 🛏 15%, ★, 536 South Hope St., 90071. Telephone: 213/627-9941. Airport bus service stop only one block west at Biltmore Hotel; from there go west one block on 6th St. to Hope and turn right. In the North Tower: single without bath $18; $22 twin. In the South Tower (for women and couples only): with bath, $23 single and $27 twin; without bath, $18 single and $22 twin.

● Seashore Motel, 2637 Main St., Santa Monica, 90405. Telephone: 213/392-2787. Six miles from airport and near Venice and Santa Monica beaches. $25 single; $31 double. Higher rates May to August.

● Royal Westwood Motel, 2352 Westwood Blvd., 90064. Telephone: 213/475-4551. Near UCLA, Westwood Village shops, Sunset Blvd., and Beverly Hills. About $36 for a double; single rates of $28 to $32 are a bit too high for our budget.

● Howard's Weekly Apartments, 1738 North Whitley, Hollywood, 90038 (tel. 213/406-6943); and 1225 North El Centro, Hollywood, 90038 (tel. 213/464-0948). Vacation apartments that rent by the week from $69.95 for one or $84.95 for two; kitchenettes available for $99.95 for two people. Reservations required.

Where to Eat: Farmer's Market, West 3rd St. at Fairfax. Telephone: 933-9211. This popular tourist attraction is an open market with souvenirs for sale, restaurants, fresh produce stands, bakeries, candy stands, etc. You can have a Chinese platter at one of the stands—a main dish, tea, and a cookie for under $4. If Chinese food doesn't interest you, you can choose from Mexican, Italian, and American. Hours: Monday to Saturday, 9 a.m. to 6:30 p.m.; Sunday, 10 a.m. to 5 p.m.

● Side Walk Café, 1401 Ocean Front Walk, Venice. Telephone: 399-5547. American food and innovative omelets and sandwiches. Early in the day, enjoy brunch while you watch the skaters, or later on admire the Pacific sunset as you sip a sangría. A meal will cost about $4 and someone may even pass by and offer you a role in *Rocky III*.

● Duke Tropicana Coffee Shop, 8585 Santa Monica Blvd. Telephone: 652-7949. A popular place with truck drivers, students, and artists in the heart of Hollywood's artist colony. There is a wait of at least a half hour on a Saturday.

● King's Head, 116 Santa Monica Blvd., Santa Monica. Telephone: 394-9458. Fresh fish and chips, good beers, and delectable desserts in a British pub atmosphere complete with darts. Half an order of fish and chips at $2.50 should fill you up.

● Atomic Café, 422 East 1st St. Telephone: 613-9233. In Little Tokyo near Chinatown. American and Japanese food; New Wave and Japanese music from 4 p.m. to 4 a.m. every day.

● Lares Mexican Café, 2909 Pico Blvd., Santa Monica. Telephone: 829-4559. Open 7:30 p.m. to 12:30 a.m. Mexican food for under $5. "The greatest margaritas and sunrises and a chance to practice your Spanish."

● Barney's Beanery, 8447 Santa Monica Blvd., Hollywood. Telephone: 656-0433. Open 10 a.m. to 2 a.m. every day. Sandwiches and a vast selection of imported beers. Good service, too.

What to See and Do: NBC Studios, 300 West Alameda, Burbank. Take a look at the inside of a television studio, controls, wardrobes, departments, and sound stages. Tours run from 9 a.m to 5 p.m. Monday through Sunday: $2.75 for adults; $2 for children 5 to 11; free for children under 5.

● Universal Studios, 3900 Lankershim Blvd. A two-hour guided tour aboard a tram winds through sound stages, the back lot, a star's dressing room. There are special effects demonstrations, animal shows, including *Jaws*. Tours are available daily 10 a.m. to 3:30 p.m. Call 985-8687, extension 271, for information.

● Disneyland, junction of Santa Ana Freeway and Harbor Blvd. in Anaheim, 27 miles from downtown Los Angeles. The world according to Disney—

a fantasyland of these parks, adventures, and rides. Call 533-4456 for hours and rates. "The happiest place on earth."

● Huntington Library, Art Gallery, and Botanical Gardens, 1151 Oxford Rd., San Marino. Telephone: 681-6601. The art gallery has 22 galleries of paintings, furniture, and tapestries; and the gardens cover over 200 acres. No admission fee; closed Monday.

● Chinatown and Little Tokyo are located in downtown L.A. and are worth a visit. There are shuttle buses that will take you from the heart of downtown to these two interesting areas.

● Farmer's Market. We mentioned it above under "Where to Eat," but it's a genuine tourist attraction too.

● J. P. Getty Museum, 17985 Pacific Coast Hwy., Malibu. You may enter only by car and must make parking reservations in advance by calling 454-6541. Called "Pompeii by the Pacific," it has a beautiful colonnaded garden with Greek and Roman sculpture to admire.

● Beverly Hills. If you're on foot, window shop from Wilshire and Rodeo Dr., going north on Rodeo. The prices are out of this world but window shopping is highly recommended.

At Night: In summer, there are concerts—classical, rock, and jazz—at the Hollywood Bowl, 2301 North Highland Ave., probably the world's most famous amphitheater. Admission varies with performance—from $1 to $15. Call 87-MUSIC for information.

● The Music Center for the Performing Arts, 1st St. and Grand Ave., telephone 626-7210, includes the Dorothy Chandler Pavilion, home of the Los Angeles Philharmonic Orchestra, the Ahmanson Theater, and the Mark Taper Forum. To find out what's on while you're in town, call.

● From June to September there are outdoor performances by big-name stars in the Greek Theater in a natural canyon in Griffith Park, 2700 North Vermont Ave. Call 660-8400 for up-to-the-minute information.

● If you like country and western music, go to the Palamino Club, 6907 Lankershim, North Hollywood. Telephone: 765-9256. "The best country and western music in L.A." Casual atmosphere, drinks, and dinner. Well-known stars like Linda Ronstadt appear ($2 to $10 admission) and on Thursday nights there's a talent showcase.

● To hear jazz, go to Come Back Inn, 1633 West Washington Blvd. in Venice. Telephone: 396-7255. A different group every night; Wednesday and Saturday are the liveliest. $1 donation for the band requested. The atmosphere is relaxed and the music is good.

● To disco, go to Odyssey I, 8471 Beverly Blvd., Hollywood. There's a $5 entrance charge and you can dance from 9 p.m. to 5 in the morning.

● For country and western music, try Banjo Café, 2906 Lincoln Blvd. Telephone: 392-5716. This bluegrass club in L.A. is open from 6 p.m. to midnight. The cover charge is $2.

● For a movie bargain, go to World Theater, 6025 Hollywood Blvd. Telephone: 469-5866. Three first-run movies cost only $2.25.

Shopping: B. Dalton Pickwick Books, 6743 Hollywood Blvd. Telephone: 469-8191. One of the largest bookstores in southern California.

● Westwood Book Store, 1021 Broxton Ave., Westwood Village. Telephone: 473-4923. Oriented toward students—"everything from student travel to a good novel."

● Papa Bach, 11317 Santa Monica Blvd. Telephone: 478-2374. If you can't find it at another bookstore, try this one—from L.A. underground magazines to how to cultivate your own garden.

● Tower Records, 8801 West Sunset Blvd. Telephone: 657-7300. Large selection, low prices.

● Warehouse Records, 1093 Broxton Ave., Westwood Village. Good sales. Right down the street from the Westwood Book Store.

● Pier One, 1087 Broxton Ave., Westwood. Handicrafts of wicker, glass, pottery. A good place to find a gift to take back home with you.

● Millers Outpost, Westwood Blvd. in Westwood. Good buys on the ever-popular jeans and shirts.

Help: KLOS Switchboard, 213/520-KLOS from L.A.; 213/981-KLOS from the San Fernando Valley; 714/534-KLOS from Orange County. (KLOS is a radio station—a good one to listen to for what's happening, where, etc.)

● Hollywood Life Line, 213/874-2951.

● Los Angeles Free Clinic, 213/660-2400.

● Travelers Aid, 646 South Los Angeles St., 90014. Telephone: 213/625-2501.

● Southern California Visitors Council, 213/628-3101.

Los Banos

Accommodation: Motel 6, 12733 South Hwy. 33, Gustine, 95322. Telephone: 209/826-6664. See Anaheim listing for rates.

Lost Hills

Accommodation: Motel 6, 14685 Warren St., 93249. Telephone: 805/797-2524. See Anaheim listing for rates.

Mammoth Lakes

Accommodation: Motel 6, 473372 Main St., P.O. Box 1260, 93546. Telephone: 714/934-4959. See Anaheim listing for rates.

Manteca

Accommodation: Friendship Travelers Inn, 1106 West Yosemite Ave., 95336. Telephone: 209/823-3141. $16 to $21 for one; $19 to $25 for two in one bed; $21 to $23 for two in two beds.

Marysville

Accommodations: Imperial 400 Motor Inn, 721 10th St., 95901. Telephone: 916/742-8586. $20 to $24 for one; $25 to $28 for two in one bed; $27 to $30 for two in two beds.

● Superior Holiday Lodge Motel, 530 10th St., 95901. Telephone: 916/742-7147. $17 for one; $21 for two in one bed; $24 for two in two beds.

● Friendship Inn–Capri Motel, 803 E St., Hwy. 70. Telephone: 916/743-5465. $13 to $21 for one; $17 to $25 for two in one bed; $21 to $29 for two in two beds.

Merced

Accommodations: California 6 Motel, 1215 R St., 95340. Telephone: 209/722-2737. $14.40 single; $21.90 double.
● Motel 6, 1983 East Childs Ave. and Hwy. 99 South, 95340. Telephone: 209/723-3271. See Anaheim listing for rates.
● Friendship Inn–Sierra Lodge, 951 Motel Dr., 95340. Telephone: 209/722-3926. $15 to $24 for one; $18 to $28 for two in one bed; $24 to $36 for two in two beds.

Midway

Accommodation: E-Z 8 Motel, 3325 Midway Dr., 92110. Telephone: 714/224-3166. See Lemon Grove listing for rates.

Mineral

Camping: Lassen Volcanic National Park, 96063. Eight campgrounds open May or June to September or October. Reservations needed. $1 to $2 per campsite per night.

Mission Valley

Accommodation: E-Z 8 Motel, 2484 Hotel Circle Pl., 92108. Telephone: 714/291-8252. See Lemon Grove listing for rates.

Modesto

Accommodations: California 6 Motel, 1920 West Orangeburg Ave., 95350. Telephone: 209/522-7271. $14.40 single; $21.90 double.
● Friendship Inn–Apex Motel, 2225 Yosemite Blvd., 95351. Telephone: 209/529-4750. $16 to $20 for one; $16 to $22 for two in one bed; $18 to $24 for two in two beds.
● Motel 6, 722 Kansas Ave., 95351. Telephone: 209/521-6130. See Anaheim listing for rates.

Mojave

Accommodations: Friendship Inn–Best Motel of Mojave, 15620 Sierra Hwy., 93501. Telephone: 805/824-4523. $16 to $20 for one; $21 to $23 for two in one bed; $22 to $30 for two in two beds.
● Motel 6, California 58 and 14, 93501. See Anaheim listing for rates.

Montara

Accommodation: Montara Lighthouse Hostel (AYH), Hwy. 1 and 16th St., 94037. Telephone: 415/728-7177. Hostel is on a cliff overlooking the Pacific. Men, women, and children. $3.50 for AYH members; $5.50 for nonmembers; one-half price for children. Reservations advised during summer.

Monterey

Help: Mental Health Crisis Team, Community Hospital, 408/624-5311, extension 1623.

Accommodations: Monterey Penninsula Youth Hostel (AYH), 🚶, 404 El Estero, 93940. Telephone: 408/373-4166. Open June 8 to August 21. $3.50. AYH membership required (see page 21).

● Motel 6, 2124 Fremont St. (Old Hwy. 1), 93940. Telephone: 408/373-3500. See Anaheim listing for rates.

Morro Bay

Accommodations: Best Value El Morro Lodge, 1206 Main St., 93442. Telephone: 805/772-2828. $20 to $22 for one or two in one bed; $28 to $32 for two in two beds.

● Best Value Leeward Motel, 3270 Main St., 93442. Telephone: 805/772-7135. $18 to $24 for one; $20 to $26 for two in one bed; $24 to $30 for two in two beds.

● Motel 6, 298 Atascadero Rd., 93442. Telephone: 805/772-8881. See Anaheim listing for rates.

Mount Shasta

Accommodations: Mount Shasta Youth Hostel (AYH), 200 Sheldon St., P.O. Box 801, 96067. Telephone: 916/926-4896. Less than a mile from bus station. However, if you have a lot to carry they might pick you up if you call. Men, women, and children. $4 summer; $5 winter. $2 more for nonmembers.

● Friendship Inn–Swiss Holiday Lodge, near junction of I-5 and California 89. Telephone: 916/926-4587. $20 for one; $23 for two in one bed; $25 for two in two beds.

Mountain View

Accommodation: E-Z 8 Motel, 1984 El Camino Real, 94040. Telephone: 415/967-6901. See Lemon Grove listing for rates.

Napa

Accommodation: Motel 6, 3380 Solano Ave., 94558. Telephone: 707/226-1811. See Anaheim listing for rates.

National City

Accommodations: E-Z 8 Motel, 1700 Plaza Blvd., 92050. Telephone: 714/474-6491. See Lemon Grove listing for rates.

● E-Z 8 Motel, 607 Roosevelt Ave., 92050. Telephone: 714/474-7502. See Lemon Grove listing for rates.

Needles

Accommodations: Motel 6, 1420 J St., 92363. Telephone: 714/326-4411. See Anaheim listing for rates.
● Imperial 400 Motor Inn, 644 Broadway, 92363. Telephone: 714/326-2145. $18 to $22 for one; $20 to $24 for two in one bed; $24 to $28 for two in two beds.
● Friendship Inn–River Valley Lodge, 1707 West Broadway, 92363. Telephone: 714/326-3839. $17 to $19 for one; $19 to $21 for two in one bed; $22 to $24 for two in two beds.

Newark

Accommodation: Motel 6, 5600 Cedar Court, 94560. Telephone: 415/791-1663. See Anaheim listing for rates.

Norden

Accommodation: Ski Inn Lodge (AYH-SA), P.O. Box 7, 95724. Open year round, by reservation only. Telephone: 916/426-3079. Ski lodge with ten rooms and two dorms. For AYH members, the rates are $14 per person double in summer; $16 per person double in winter; $3.50 during summer in the dormitory and $5.50 during winter.

Norwalk

Accommodation: California 6 Motel, 10646 East Rosecrans Ave., 90650. Telephone: 213/864-2567. $14.40 single; $21.90 double.

Oakland

Help: Travelers Aid, 1515 Webster St., 94612. Telephone: 415/444-6834.
Accommodations: YMCA, ☛, 2101 Telegraph Ave., 94612. Telephone: 415/451-8033. One block from bus station. Men and women. $10.20, including membership.
● Motel 6, 4919 Coliseum Way, 94601. Telephone: 415/534-8185. See Anaheim listing for rates.

Oceanside

Accommodation: Motel 6, 1403 Mission Ave., 92054. Telephone: 714/757-3492. See Anaheim listing for rates.

Ontario

Accommodations: Motel 6, 1515 North Mountain Ave., 91762. Telephone: 714/986-1915. See Anaheim listing for rates.
● Sixpence Inn, 1560 East 4th St., 91761. Telephone: 714/984-2424. See Anaheim listing for rates.

Orange

Accommodation: Sixpence Inn, 2920 West Chapman Ave., 92668. Telephone: 714/634-2441. See Anaheim listing for rates.

Oroville

Accommodation: Motel 6, 505 Montgomery St., 95965. Telephone: 916/534-9666. See Anaheim listing for rates.

Paicines

Camping: Pinnacles National Monument, 95043. Campgrounds at $2 per campsite.

Palm Springs

Accommodation: Motel 6, 595 East Palm Canyon Dr., 92262. Telephone: 714/327-2044. See Anaheim listing for rates.

Palmdale

Accommodation: Motel 6, 407 Palmdale Blvd., 93550. Telephone: 805/947-2866. See Anaheim listing for rates.

Palo Alto

Accommodation: Motel 6, 4301 El Camino Real, 94306. Telephone: 415/941-0220. See Anaheim listing for rates.

Pescadero

Accommodation: Pigeon Point Hostel (AYH), Pigeon Point Rd., 94060. Telephone: 415/879-0633. $3.50 for AYH members; $5.50 for nonmembers. Open year round. "Beautiful coastline view."

Petaluma

Accommodation: Motel 6, 5135 Old Redwood Hwy., 94952. Telephone: 707/795-8000. See Anaheim listing for rates.

Pismo Beach

Accommodation: Motel 6, U.S. 101 and 4th St. To open in 1982. See Anaheim listing for rates.

Pittsburg

Accommodation: Motel 6, 2101 Loveridge Rd., 94565. Telephone: 415/432-6699. See Anaheim listing for rates.

Pleasanton

Accommodation: California 6 Motel, 5102 Hopyard Rd., 94566. Telephone: 415/462-2626. $14.40 single; $21.90 double.

Point Reyes

Help: Mental Health Emergencies, 415/499-6666.
Accommodation: Point Reyes Hostel (AYH), √ half price, P.O. Box 247, 94956. Telephone: 415/669-9985 (after 4:30 p.m.). Open year round. $3.50 for AYH members; $5.50 for nonmembers. Beach two miles from hostel. One reader wrote that "the Point Reyes Hostel was definitely the Hilton of $3 accommodations—clean and comfortable and lots of good people. . . ." Closed 9:30 a.m. to 4:30 p.m. daily. Fully equipped kitchen. Children pay one-half price.
Camping: Point Reyes National Seashore, 94956. Four walk-in campgrounds open year round. Reservations required.

Pomona

Accommodation: Pomona Valley YMCA, 350 North Garey Ave., 91767. Two miles south of Interstate 10, San Bernardino Freeway. Telephone: 714/623-6433. Men only. $9 single. Weekly rate: $40.

Porterville

Accommodation: Motel 6, 935 West Morton Ave., 93257. Telephone: 209/781-6662. See Anaheim listing for rates.

Rancho Cordova

Accommodation: California 6 Motel, 10694 Olson Dr., 95670. Telephone: 916/635-8784. $14.40 single; $21.90 double.

Rancho Mirage

Accommodation: California 6 Motel, 69-570 Hwy. 111, 92270. Telephone: 714/324-8475. $17.40 single; $24.90 double.

Red Bluff

Accommodation: Motel 6, 20 Williams Ave., 96080. Telephone: 916/527-8107. See Anaheim listing for rates.

Redding

Accommodations: Budget Host–Shasta Lodge, 1245 Pine St., 96001. Telephone: 916/243-6133. $20 for one; $24 for two in one bed; $26 for two in two beds.

● Motel 6, 1640 Hilltop Dr., 96001. Telephone: 916/243-8700. See Anaheim listing for rates.

● Friendship Inn–Bel Air Motel, 540 North Market St., 96001. Telephone: 916/243-5291. $17 to $23 for one; $21 to $28 for two in one bed; $24 to $29 for two in two beds.

Redlands

Accommodations: Motel 6, 1160 Arizona St., 92373. Telephone: 714/793-3511. See Anaheim listing for rates.

● E-Z 8 Motel, 1235 West Colton Ave., 92373. Telephone: 714/793-6648. See Lemon Grove listing for rates.

Ridgecrest

Accommodation: Motel 6, 535 South China Lake Blvd., 93555. Telephone: 714/375-9666. See Anaheim listing for rates.

Riverside

"A desert community, well populated, one hour from L.A. with a campus of the University of California."

Help: Helpline, 714/686-HELP (24 hours).
Accommodations: Motel 6, 4045 University Ave., 92501. Telephone: 714/682-2250. See Anaheim listing for rates.

● Motel 6, 23581 Alessandro Blvd., 92508. Telephone: 714/653-2131. See Anaheim listing for rates.

● California 6 Motel, 1260 University Ave., 92507. Telephone: 714/784-2131. $14.40 single; $21.90 double.

Rohnert Park

"A basically rural area with rapidly growing suburban development and infant public transit."

Help: 707/544-HELP.
On Campus: One staff member of Sonoma State University told us that "both the campus facilities and those of the town have grown. We have ample off-campus housing facilitated by the best updated information source in the county, the Off-Campus Housing Board which lists shares to whole houses at Village 102. The dorms can hold up to 400 students, but come early."
Accommodations: Sonoma State University Inn, 1701 East Cotati Ave., 94928. Telephone: 707/664-2541. Open June 23 to August 15. $8 single; $5 per person double. The rooms are in town houses without kitchen facilities, but

there is the residence hall food service right nearby where you can get an all-you-can-eat breakfast, lunch, or dinner for $3.50, $4, and $4.50, respectively. Located about one hour's drive north of San Francisco.

● Regal 8 Inn, 6288 Redwood Dr., 94928. Telephone: 707/584-1005. $16.88 for one; $19.88 for two in one bed; $22.88 for two to four in two beds.

Rosemead

Accommodation: Motel 6, 1001 San Gabriel Blvd., 91770. Telephone: 213/288-5700. See Anaheim listing for rates.

Rubidoux

Accommodation: Motel 6, California 60 and Valley Rd. To open in 1982. See Anaheim listing for rates.

Sacramento

Help: Travelers Aid, 331 Jay St., Suite 160, 95814. Telephone: 916/443-1719.

On Campus: You will be able to find helpful information on the bulletin board at the Off-Campus Housing Office at this branch of California State University. A friend there recommends the Big Yellow House, which has "lots of good food," and the Coffee House on campus.

Accommodations: Motel 6, 1415 30th St., 95816. Telephone: 916/452-5581. See Anaheim listing for rates.

● Motel 6, 10271 Folsom Blvd., 95670. Telephone: 916/362-3262. See Anaheim listing for rates.

● California 6 Motel, 227 Jibboom St., 95814. Telephone: 916/441-0733. $14.40 single; $21.90 double.

● Sixpence Inn, 7850 College Town Dr., 95826. Telephone: 916/383-8110. See Anaheim listing for rates.

● Friendship Inn–Sands Motel, 2160 Auburn Blvd., 95821. Telephone: 916/925-8584. $19 to $22 for one; $24.50 to $26 for two in one bed; $29 to $32 for two in two beds.

● California 6 Motel, 5110 Interstate, 95842. Telephone: 916/331-8100. $14.40 single; $21.90 double.

● California 6 Motel, 1254 Halyard Dr., West Sacramento, 95691. See above listing for rates.

● Friendship Inn–Sky Ranch Motel, 1800 West Capitol Ave., 95691. Telephone: 916/371-8707. $16 to $18 for one; $20 to $22 for two in one bed; $24 to $28 for two in two beds.

● Friendship Inn–Arden Motel, 1700 Del Paso Blvd., 95815. Telephone: 916/925-3556. $20 to $22 for one; $22 to $24 for two in one bed; $26 to $28 for two in two beds.

Salinas

Accommodations: Friendship Inn–Sandstone, 214 John St., 93901. Telephone: 408/424-6468. $14 to $24 for one; $16 to $30 for two in one bed; $18 to $34 for two in two beds.

● Motel 6, 1010 Fairview Ave., 93901. Telephone: 408/758-2791. See Anaheim listing for rates.

San Bernardino

Accommodations: Motel 6, 111 Redlands Blvd., 92408. Telephone: 714/824-3535. See Anaheim listing for rates.
● Imperial 400 Motor Inn, 755 West 5th St., 92410. Telephone: 714/889-0401. $20 to $24 for one; $22 to $28 for two in one bed; $24 to $30 for two in two beds.

San Diego

"We have the finest year-round climate in the world, but if you miss shoveling snow you'll find some just one hour away."

San Diego is the first and oldest city in California. For a glimpse of its beginnings, you can visit Old Town, a park that recreates the setting of life in California during its Mexican and early American periods. Two buildings here that have been restored are the Casa de Estudillo and the Machado/Stewart Adobe. For a view of the more modern San Diego, you can take a cruise in San Diego Harbor and see the impressive skyline of the city, which has grown to be the second largest in the West. To read up on San Diego, we suggest the *Greater San Diego Metroguide,* San Diego Chamber of Commerce, 110 West C St., San Diego 92101 ($4.50). Designed for residents and prospective residents but includes tourist-type information as well. *The Student Survival Guide to San Diego,* by Barbara Peters and Phil Hopkins, Humbird Hopkins, Inc. ($2.50), includes all you'll need to know about the town from a student's point of view.

Getting There: From the Airport: The airport is only three miles northwest of the city. To get from there to downtown, you simply board a #2 bus—the fare is 60¢.
● From the Train and Bus Stations: The train station is at 1050 Kettner Blvd., the Greyhound bus station is at First Ave. and Broadway, and Trailways is at 310 West C St.

Getting Around: You can get a free copy of *Getting Around San Diego Without a Car* from CIEE's San Diego office, U.C. San Diego, Student Center, La Jolla, 92093. Telephone: 714/452-0630.
● City buses cost 60¢ and run every 15 to 20 minutes. A taxi will cost $1.80 for the first mile and 80¢ for every mile after that. Yellow Cab offers 24-hour service—call 714/234-6161.
● If you want to rent a car, consider AA, 5005 Voltaire (tel. 714/224-8235 or 224-8954; $8.95 per day plus 8¢ per mile); Safeway, 1320 Broadway (tel. 714/238-1305; $8 per day, 10¢ per mile); or Fairway Rent-A-Car, 2317 Pacific Hwy. (tel. 714/298-5555; $12.95 per day, with 150 free miles).

Accommodations: YMCA, 1115 Eighth Ave., 92101. Telephone: 714/232-7451. $9 to $10 single; $16 double (all prices include tax). Located in the heart of downtown; can be reached by bus #2, and the stop is at Eighth Ave. and Broadway. Men, women, and children can be accommodated and kitchen privileges are available.

● San Diego Armed Services YMCA (AYH-SA), ✦ ★, 500 West Broadway, 92101. Telephone: 714/232-1133. The Y has a section set aside as an American Youth Hostel with facilities for both men and women. AYH members may stay for $3.50 per night. The Y's usual accommodations are $9.50 to $11 single, $18.50 double, for men or women. Higher rates are for rooms with color television. Lunch counter, pool room, gym, library, and barbershop all in the building.

● Motel 6, 2424 Hotel Circle North, 92108. Telephone: 714/297-4871. See Anaheim listing for rates.

● Campus Hitching Post Motel, 6235 El Cajon Blvd., 92115. Telephone: 714/583-1456. Near the college districts. Convenient to public transportation. $22 single; $24 double.

● La Jolla Motel, ✦ ★, 4540 Mission Bay Dr., 92109. Telephone: 714/273-7515. Near beach and Sea World. $23 single; $30 double ($7 higher in summer).

● Point Loma Hostel (AYH), 3790 Udall St., 92107. Right off bus line #35. Near Mission Bay Park and Sea World. Telephone: 714/223-4778. A large, two-story stucco house with bunk beds and small rooms—room enough for 48 people. $4 for AYH members; $6 for nonmembers.

● Imperial Beach Hostel (AYH), 170 Palm Ave., 92032. Telephone: 714/423-8039. Five miles from the Mexican border and 20 miles south of downtown San Diego. $4 for AYH members; $6 for nonmembers. A converted fire station with bunk beds.

● Clarkslodge, 🛏, 1765 Union St., 92101. Telephone: 714/234-6787. Near downtown. $21.60 for one or two people; $27.50 for four people. Pool and color television.

● La Jolla Palms Motel, 6705 La Jolla Blvd., 92037. Telephone: 714/454-7101. One block from the beach. Room for one or two, $37; for two, $49; for three, $52. Lower rates October 1 to May 31.

● E-Z 8 Motel, 🛏, 2484 Hotel Circle Pl. North. Telephone: 714/291-8252. Mission Valley area. $21.88 single; $23 to $25 double.

● YWCA (AYH), 🛏, 1012 C St., 92101. Telephone: 714/239-0355. On bus lines #9 and #34. Women only. Community bathrooms and kitchen. For AYH members, $6 with linens, $4 without; others, $10 single, $15 double. Newly renovated. Indoor pool.

● Blue Bell Motel, 4444 Pacific Hwy. Ave., 92101. Telephone: 714/295-6444. $13 and up.

● Western Shores Motel, 4345 Mission Bay Dr., 92109. Telephone: 714/273-1121. $19 single; $24 double. Across the street from a public golf course.

Where to Eat: Alfonso's, 12151 Prospect, La Jolla. Telephone: 454-2232. Mexican food in an appropriate setting. Complete dinners from $4 to $6. Popular with UC San Diego students. Taco, burrito, rice, beans, and chips, $4.50.

● Boll Weevil (nine locations, check telephone directory). "Good prices, excellent food—$2.50 for a whole meal."

● Nordic Inn, 3577 Midway Dr. All-you-can-eat smörgåsbord for $4.75 at dinner time. Great if you're really hungry.

● Sir George's Smörgåsbord, 7840 Balboa Ave. Telephone: 277-0411.

Lunch, $3.95; dinner, $4.25. The choices are hot or cold—"good value for the price."

● Market Café, 650 Valley Ave., Solano Beach. Telephone: 755-5988. "Worth the 16-mile trip from downtown San Diego, this beach restaurant serves good, inexpensive meals in a relaxed atmosphere." The best margaritas in San Diego.

● Osaka's, 3645 University Ave. Telephone: 282-3688. Don't be discouraged by the outside; it's nice once you're inside. Japanese food.

● Souplantation, 6171 Mission Gorge Rd. Telephone: 280-7087. Soup, sandwiches, and all the salad you can eat in a mellow atmosphere.

● The Bratskellar, 1250 Prospect Lane. Telephone: 454-4244. In the heart of La Jolla. Fresh seafood and German specialties. Happy hour from 4 to 6 p.m. during the week.

● Julio's, 45th and University Ave. Telephone: 282-6837. Mexican food near San Diego State.

● V.G.'s, 106 Aberdene, Cardif-by-the Sea. Telephone: 753-2400. People come from miles around for their doughnuts.

● Aesop's Tables Greek Café, 5844 Montezuma Rd. Telephone: 287-3303. A gyros plate—meat, onions, cheese, tomatoes, and olives on pita bread—$3.99.

● Chinese Kitchen, 6160 University Ave. Telephone: 286-8778. A hole in the wall with good food.

● Soup Express, 737 Pearl St. Telephone: 454-3453. Downtown La Jolla. As much salad or soup as you want for $2.75.

● Casa de Pico, 2754 Calhoun Rd. Telephone: 296-3267. Traditional Mexican food with mariachi music every day from 1 p.m. on.

● Anthony's Fishette, 555 Harbor Lane, on the Embarcadero. Telephone: 232-2933. Other branches, too. "The best seafood in San Diego comes from Anthony's."

What to See and Do: Consult either the San Diego *Reader* or the San Diego *Union Tribune*'s entertainment section for a guide to what's going on.

● Balboa Park: 1400 acres of park with the famous San Diego Zoo and, from June to September, the city's Shakespeare Festival. The park's Aerospace Museum displays a replica of the *Spirit of St. Louis*. For information, call 236-5720.

● Old Town (see introduction).

● Harbor Excursion: You can choose from a one- or two-hour cruise that goes year round and daily from the foot of Broadway at Harbor Dr. Adults pay $4.90 for the two-hour cruise, $3.25 for the one-hour cruise. Call 234-4111.

● Sea World: Everything aquatic plus a dolphin quiz show. Leave a whole day for this one. $7.95 for adults, $4.95 for children 4 to 12 and senior citizens.

● Maritime Museum, 1306 North Harbor Dr. Telephone: 234-9153. Three restored ships to visit.

● Mission Bay: Sailing, swimming, Frisbee, jogging, picnicking, and lots of other things going on all the time.

● Beaches (as rated by a native): Black's Beach, for nude bathing; La Jolla Shores, "great"; Torry Pines, "fair, too much seaweed"; Mission Bay, "the best"; Ocean Beach, "good"; Imperial Beach, "great waves if it's not polluted."

At Night: Call 452-EDNA to find out what's going on on the campus of UC San Diego.

● Jazz: The Catamaran Hotel, 3999 Mission Blvd. Big-name performers appear weekly, and the admission is $4 on weeknights; $5 on weekends.

● Concerts: Often there are concerts in Balboa Park, or you can check with the University of California, San Diego (tel. 452-EDNA), which often presents a recital or concert.

● Dance: National dance companies perform year round at Mandeville Auditorium at the university. Tickets range from $3 to $5 for students, $5 to $7 for others. Call 452-3229 for details, Monday to Friday, 8:30 a.m. to 4:30 p.m.

● Rodeo, La Jolla Village Dr. Near UCSD. $2 cover charge. Top-name country and western bands. Other places to dance: Carlos and Charles in Pacific Beach or the Poseidon in Del Mar.

Shopping: Middle Earth Book Shop, 3731 Mission Blvd., Mission Beach. Science fiction, fantasy, general paperbacks, and books for the "inner self," e.g., on the occult, Zen, yoga, etc.

● Pacific Comics, 5011 Casa, Pacific Beach. 300,000 comics, rare and current.

● Bookstop III, 5065 El Cajon Blvd. Used books bought and sold.

● Groundwork Books, UCSD Student Center. Good prices.

● Map Centre, 2611 University Ave. Travel books of all kinds.

● Assorted Vinyl, UCSD, La Jolla. Co-op record store. New and used records at 30% to 50% off.

● Folk Arts, 3611 Adams. Complete selection of folk, blues, dixieland, bluegrass, and oldtime country records. Rare and out-of-print records available, too.

● Tower Records, 3601 Sports Arena Blvd. Super discount prices; open until midnight.

● The Mercado, 11844 Rancho Bernardo. Shops and boutiques with a variety of crafts and international merchandise; restaurants, too.

● Cal-Surplus, Clairmont Mesa. For backpacking equipment, tents, fishing gear, etc. Camping supplies available to rent.

Help: Help Center, 5059 College Ave. Telephone: 714/582-4357.

● Crisis Center/Hotline, 714/236-3339.

● Travelers Aid, 1122 Fourth Ave. Telephone: 714/232-7991. Has a travel board where drivers can find riders and vice versa.

● Free Clinic, 714/488-0644.

Tourist Information: San Diego Convention and Visitors Bureau, 1200 Third Ave., 92101. Telephone: 714/232-3101.

● Visitor's Information Center, 2688 East Mission Bay Dr. Telephone: 714/276-8200.

● CIEE Student Travel Center, UC San Diego Student Center, La Jolla. Telephone: 714/452-0630. Full service travel center.

San Francisco

A lovely city, San Francisco. The Convention and Visitors Bureau boasts that it has two big advantages over other cities—it's so very scenic and it's so compact. San Francisco is an easy place to be a visitor—it seems smaller than it is because the excellent public transportation makes it so easy to get around.

To read up on what Somerset Maugham called "the most civilized city in America," try:

The Native's Guidebook: San Francisco Free and Easy, edited by William Ristow. San Francisco: Bay Guardian Books, Downwind Publications ($5.95). The ultimate guide to the city's entertainment, restaurants, bars, and other interesting places.

The Dolphin Guide to San Francisco and the Bay Area, by Curt Gentry, Dolphin Books, Doubleday ($2.50). A good, basic guide to the Bay Area.

Arthur Frommer's Guide to San Francisco, Arthur Frommer Publications ($2.95).

San Francisco at Your Feet, by Margot Patterson Doss, Grove Press ($4.95). An excellent walking guide to the city.

The San Francisco Underground Gourmet, by R. B. Read, Simon & Schuster ($5.95). A helpful guide to ethnic restaurants in the Bay Area, but watch out, it was written a while ago and prices have skyrocketed since.

The weekly *Bay Guardian* lists coming events and the *City Arts Monthly,* available in cafés and restaurants around town, concentrates on art-related events. Or you can call Dial-An-Event, 415/391-2000, where there are information tapes in a number of foreign languages. At the San Francisco Visitors Information Center, Hallidie Plaza, Powell and Market Sts., a multilingual staff will answer questions and hand out all sorts of maps and brochures.

Getting There: From the Airport: The San Francisco Airport is 15 miles south of the city. You can go by Airporter bus from the airport to a downtown terminal for $3.25. These buses run every 10 to 15 minutes during the day, every half hour late at night. The bus station is at 50 7th St., and transportation from there is available by bus, cable car, city bus, and the subway, the relatively new Bay Area Rapid Transit (BART). The train station is at 1st and Mission Sts.

Getting Around: You have a choice of bus, taxi, subway, and cable car. Muni Metro opened in 1980 and it runs parallel to Market St., L Taravel goes to the zoo, North Judah to the Sunset, and the K to San Francisco State. The cost is 50¢ and transfers are available. BART is the extensive network of trains that will take you to the southern borders of the city and downtown. The cost will vary according to the distance you travel, from 50¢ to $2. Muni buses are ubiquitous. The cost is 50¢ and transfers are available. A monthly pass can be bought from outlets throughout the city—just ask at the MUNI Metro stations where you can buy the "Fast Pass." Taxis cost $1.20 for the first one-ninth mile and 20¢ for every one-sixth mile after that. There are taxi stands or you can call a taxi.

● To rent a car economically, try Bay Area Rent-A-Car, 111 Stevenson (across from the Sheraton). Telephone: 415/362-7564. The rate is $20 per day with no charge for mileage. They have special weekend rates—$40 for three days beginning at noon on Friday to noon on Monday.

Accommodations: YMCA Hotel, 351 Turk St., 94102. Telephone: 415/673-2312. Three blocks from Greyhound Station. Men, women, and children. $14 to $16.50 single; $20 double; $9 per person triple and quad. Reservations with deposit requested three to four weeks in advance at Christmas, Easter, and from June to September.

● Merced Hall, San Francisco State University, 802 Font Blvd., 94132. Off Interstate 280. Telephone: 415/469-1224. Students, faculty, and educationally related visitors only. $22 single, $11 per person double when available. Open

June 15 to August 15. Guest meals available in nearby University Dining Center.

• Hotel Regent, 562 Sutter St., 94102. One block from Union Square. Telephone: 415/421-5818. Rooms without bath are $24.50 single; $31.50 double; $33.50 triple. "A very nice, older hotel with friendly, helpful staff and clean, comfortable rooms."

• Ambassador Hotel, 55 Mason St., 94102. Telephone: 415/441-4188. Near bus station and air terminal. $12 single; $20.90 for a double with bath. Spartan, and in a neighborhood that's not the greatest for late-night walks.

• The University of California, Millberry Union Residence Hall, 🖔 (limited), 510 Parnassus Ave., 94143. Telephone: 415/666-2231. $24 single; $12 per person double. Open July 1 to September 15. Five minutes from Golden Gate Park and on main bus routes downtown. Swimming pool and cafeteria in building.

• YMCA, ➹ √ 10%, 166 The Embarcadero, 94105. Telephone: 415/392-2191. Men and women. $12 to $16 single; $18 to $29 twin. Discounts are for the period from November to May, and they also apply to AYH members. Inquire about *Discover San Francisco the Y's Way* packages, to which the discount also applies.

• Central YMCA, 220 Golden Gate Ave., 94102. Telephone: 415/885-0460. Men and women. $18 single; $25 double.

• Pension San Francisco, 1668 Market St., 94102. Telephone: 415/864-1271. $21 single; $26 to $28 double. No private baths. Hotel is convenient to BART, MUNI Metro, and several private bus lines. "Each room is individually designed by a designer who is one of the owners. Room themes focus on the American West, with photos, antiques, etc., that owners gathered while contemplating opening the hotel."

• Hotel Yerba Buena, ➹ ★ 20%, 🖔 55 5th St., 94103. Telephone: 415/543-3130. Toll-free telephone: 800/227-4673. Two blocks from the bus station. European rooms, with "detached bath," are $23 for a single; $31 for a double. "The building has been refurbished with new furniture, new plumbing, painting and carpeting. . . ."

• Continental Hotel, ➹ ★, 127 Ellis St., 94102. Telephone: 415/986-3772. Near downtown, Union Square. $30 single; $36 double. An older hotel that has been renovated and is well located.

• San Francisco International Hostel (AYH), 🖔 Bldg. 240, Fort Mason, 94123. Telephone: 415/771-7277. Two blocks inside Franklin and Bay Sts. Park entrance, behind park headquarters building. $5.50 for AYH members; $7.50 for others. "A spacious, historical Civil War building with an inspiring view of the bay."

• Golden Gate Hostel (AYH), Fort Barry, Marin Headland, Sausalito, 94965. Telephone: 415/331-2777. Located within the army facilities, so follow the signs from Van Ness Ave. On the bluffs overlooking the piers, the hostel was previously Officers' Headquarters and is listed in the National Register of Historic Places. $5.50 for AYH members; $7.50 for nonmembers. Sheets and sleeping sacks available. Residents must keep the hostel clean by doing five minutes of chores in the morning. All visitors must leave the hostel between 9 a.m. and 4 p.m. The accommodations here are simple but nice, and this is a perfect place to meet fellow travelers.

• Hotel El Dorado, 150 9th St., 94103. Telephone: 415/552-4660. Near the Civic Center, Symphony Hall, and the Museum of Modern Art. $23.50 single;

$27.50 double.

● Obrero Hotel, 1208 Stockton, 94133. Telephone: 415/986-9850. "Basque-type hotel with inexpensive dinners every night." $18 single; $23 double—includes a large breakfast.

● Ansonia Residence Club, 711 Post St., 94109. 2½ blocks from Union Square. Telephone: 415/673-2670. Men and women 18 to 35. Daily rate: $16 to $20. Weekly rate: $79 to $91, which includes breakfast and dinner six days a week. "Great place to meet students from abroad."

● Liberty Inn Hotel, 863 Bush St., 94108. Telephone: 415/928-6000. $20 to $36, depending on the room. An older hotel with clean rooms.

● Golden Gate Hotel, 775 Bush St., 94108. Telephone: 415/392-3702. Walking distance from bus and train; one-half block from cable car. Located very centrally. $17 to $26 single; $19 to $28 double. During off-season you pay for six days and get one free.

Where to Eat: Zim's. There are 12 throughout the city but the two most convenient are at the Holiday Inn at Sutter and Powell and at Powell and Geary. Open 24 hours with full-course meals ranging from $5.50 to $7.

● Salmagundi's, 442 Geary St. Telephone: 441-0894. Soup, salad, roll, and a drink are about $4. "Probably the best place in San Francisco for soup—homemade with several choices every day." Branches in other parts of town.

● Hong Kong Restaurant, 245 Church St., Castro area. Telephone: 621-3020. Chinese food that's good and very reasonable ($4 to $6 for a meal).

● Sam Who's, 813 Washington, North Beach. Telephone: 982-0596. More Chinese food. This one is known for its rude waiters and inexpensive food—"a real San Francisco experience."

● United States Restaurant, 431 Columbus in North Beach. Telephone: 362-6251. Full Italian dinners for $5 to $7 in what looks like a greasy spoon but isn't. "Old-fashioned Italian; soggy vegetables but excellent calamari."

● La Méditerranée, 2210 Fillmore. Telephone: 921-2956. Middle Eastern atmosphere. A dinner costs $5 to $7.

● Bangkok Café, 208 Clement. Telephone: 386-9669. Thai food in a small, friendly place. Lunch is $2.50, dinner about twice as much.

● Hamburger Mary's, 1582 Folsom. Telephone: 626-5767. All kinds of hamburgers. "An exotic clientele, often gay and usually friendly."

● Pasand Madras, 1857 Union St. Telephone: 522-4498. Southern Indian food like masala dosas, crêpes filled with vegetarian curry—about $8.50 for a full meal including an appetizer. (There's another Pasand in Berkeley on Shattuck.)

● Castro Gardens, 558 Castro. Telephone: 621-2566. Castro eggs with or without cheese, something like a soufflé, or a Denver omelet—$10 for two.

What to Do and See: Fisherman's Wharf. This is the home of the fishing fleet with seafood restaurants, shops, boat tours, and sailing ships. In October the fishing fleet is blessed and the Procession of Maria del Lume follows.

● Golden Gate Park. Museum, Hall of Flowers, Japanese Tea Garden, Botanical Gardens, an aquarium, and more in the world's largest artificial park.

● Chinatown. The largest and oldest Chinese colony outside of China. Grant Ave. is the heart of the area. Enjoy a dim sum lunch in a basement restaurant.

● The Cannery, Leavenworth and Beach Sts. Once a Del Monte fruit-packing plant, now restored with art galleries, restaurants, shops, etc.

● Ghirardelli Square, Northpoint and Larkin Sts. Once a chocolate and spice factory but now redone as a miscellany of shops, restaurants, and inviting plazas.

● North Beach. The city's Italian section which started out as the fishing center. Many artists live around Columbus Ave. Take a walk from Coit Tower. You'll get views of Alcatraz and find the quiet gardens of Telegraph Hill.

● Haight-Ashbury. Not what it was in the '60s but still worth a visit. Full of old Victorian homes that are being lovingly restored.

● Fort Mason Center, Laguna and Marina Blvd. Three old piers on the waterfront have been converted to a center for the arts, humanities, recreation, and ecology.

● Stern Grove Concert Series. Held every summer in the Julius Stern Park. Free. Call 558-3706 for information.

● Ferry Boat Ride. You can take a ferry from the San Francisco pier on the Embarcadero to Sausalito, across the bay in Marin County. Call 332-6600 for details.

● San Francisco Art Institute, 600 Chestnut St. Close to North Beach. Besides the art, the views from the cafeteria are remarkable.

At Night: To hear jazz, go to the Keystone Corner, 750 Vallejo St. Telephone: 781-0697. "One of the country's best jazz clubs." Cover charge is usually about $7. Call the KJAZ line (tel. 521-9336) for an update on concerts and jam sessions in the Bay Area.

● For disco dancing, try City, 936 Montgomery St. Telephone: 391-7920. $4 cover to use the large dance floor for disco dancing; a cabaret downstairs.

● More disco at Trocadero Transfer, 520 4th St. Telephone: 495-6620. $15 nonmember entrance fee. Gay and straight together, no alcoholic beverages, open all night.

● The Great American Music Hall, 859 O'Farrell. Telephone: 885-0750. Features all kinds of folk and country music. Call to see who's there when you're in town.

● Studio West, Vallejo at Front St. Telephone: 781-6357. The cover is $6. "A good crowd of both gays and straights."

● Magic Theater, ● $2, Fort Mason, Bay at Laguna. Telephone: 441-8822. Experimental theater in arts center that has been created by converting piers dating from World War I.

● One Act Theater Company, ●, 430 Mason St. Telephone: 421-6162. Near Union Square. Small theater where young and local playwrights get their chance to show what they can do. Tickets are $7.50 to $8.50.

● Castro Theater, 420 Castro. Telephone: 621-6120. They show old movies here for $3.50 and new ones for $4.50. Call for the schedule.

● York Theater, 24th St. at Portero Ave. Telephone: 282-0316. A neighborhood movie theater with a '30s decor. $1.50 for matinees; $2.50 at night.

● Ploughshares Coffeehouse, at Fort Mason. Telephone: 441-5705. About $3.50 cover. Good place for anyone serious about folk music.

● The Plough and the Star, 116 Clement St. Telephone: 751-1122. An authentic Irish pub with dancing and an open microphone.

● Davies Symphony Hall, Civic Center, McAllister St. Telephone: 431-5400. Where the San Francisco Symphony is located. Try to get to one of the morning open rehearsals—music, donuts, coffee, and time to talk to the musicians—all for $4.

● San Francisco Ballet. Civic Center, across from Davies Symphony Hall. Telephone: 431-1210. Some tickets for only $3.50 but expect a bird's-eye view.

There are many smaller dance companies in the Bay Area—check the pink section of the *Chronicle* on Sunday for when and where. Dance is an integral part of the cultural life of the San Francisco area.

Shopping: City Lights, 261 Columbus Ave. Lawrence Ferlinghetti's gift to San Francisco. One of the first paperback bookstores in the world and a literary meeting place.

● Green Apple Books, 506 Clement St. Friendly staff sells used books. You can browse for hours.

● Whole Earth Bookstore, Fort Mason Center, Bay at Laguna. Self-help books, nature books, something on just about every subject. Comfortable seating for browsers.

● Revolver Records, 520 Clement. Used records, all types of music.

● Discount Records, 656 Market St. The name says it all.

● Tower Records, Columbus and Bay Sts. Sells a large selection of records until midnight.

● Taylor and Ng, 2349 Market St. For gifts such as wooden goblets, ceramics, plants, jewelry, and glassware.

● Union St. all the way from Steiner to Gough St. has all types of stores—selling antiques, gifts, art, clothing, and flowers.

● California Surplus Sales, 1107 Mission St. For a large selection of camping equipment at reasonable prices.

● Cost Plus, 2552 Taylor St. at Fisherman's Wharf. A huge warehouse full of imports from all over the world. Two blocks of things to browse through.

● Clement St. Best part of town for bargain shopping. Many used clothing stores, factory outlets, small boutiques, coffeeshops, and cafés.

Help: Haight-Ashbury Switchboard, 415/621-6211. Stop in at their office at 1539 Haight St. and ask for a copy of the excellent, free *San Francisco Survival Manual.* Also pick up a copy of the one-page information sheet on *Job Resources in San Francisco.*

● Woman's Switchboard, 3543 18th St. Telephone: 415/431-1414.

● Travelers Aid, 38 Mason St., 94102. Telephone: 415/781-6738.

● Gay Switchboard and Counseling Service, 415/841-6224.

San Jose

Accommodations: Residence Halls, San Jose State University, ♿, 375 South 9th St., 95112. Telephone: 408/277-2114. Students, individuals, and groups affiliated with educational institutions only. June 1 to August 16. Single, $13 without linen; double, $9 per person without linen. You can get an all-you-can-eat meal at their Dining Commons.

● Motel 6, 2560 Fontaine Rd., 95121. Telephone: 408/274-2900. See Anaheim listing for rates.

● E-Z 8 Motel, 1550 North 1st St., 95112. Telephone: 408/292-1830. See Lemon Grove listing for rates.

● E-Z 8 Motel, 2050 North 1st St., 95131. Telephone: 408/295-4606. See Lemon Grove listing for rates.

● Sixpence Inn, 2081 North 1st St., 95131. Telephone: 408/288-5880. See Anaheim listing for rates.

● Friendship Inn–City Center Motel, 45 East Reed, 95112. Telephone: 408/998-5990. $22 for one; $25 for two in one bed; $28 for two in two beds.

San Luis Obispo

Accommodation: Motel 6, 1433 Calle Joaquin, 93401. Telephone: 805/544-8400. See Anaheim listing for rates.

San Pedro

Accommodation: Imperial 400 Motor Inn, 411 Pacific Ave., 90731. Telephone: 213/831-0195. $20 to $22 for one; $22 to $24 for two in one bed; $24 to $28 for two in two beds.

San Ysidro

Accommodation: Motel 6, 160 East Frontage Rd., 92073. Telephone: 714/428-4491. See Anaheim listing for rates.

Santa Ana

Accommodation: YMCA, 205 Civic Center Dr., 92701. Telephone: 714/542-3511. Men only. $12.50. Weekly rate: $45. Three blocks from bus, one-half mile from train.

Santa Barbara

Help: Helpline, 805/968-2556.
Accommodations: Motel 6, 443 Corona Del Mar, 93103. Telephone: 805/965-0300. See Anaheim listing for rates.
● Motel 6, 5897 Calle Real, Goleta, 93017. Telephone: 805/964-1812. See Anaheim listing for rates.
● Motel 6, 3505 State St., 93105. Telephone: 805/687-5400. See Anaheim listing for rates.

Santa Clara

Accommodations: Motel 6, 3208 El Camino Real, 95051. Telephone: 408/248-2479. See Anaheim listing for rates.
● E-Z 8 Motel, 3550 El Camino Real, 95051. Telephone: 408/246-3119. See Lemon Grove listing for rates.

Santa Fe Springs

Accommodation: California 6 Motel, 13412 Excelsior, 90670. Telephone: 213/921-0596. $14.40 single; $21.90 double.

Santa Maria

Accommodation: Motel 6, 839 East Main St., 93454. Telephone: 805/922-6461. See Anaheim listing for rates.

Santa Rosa

Help: Helpline, 707/544-HELP.
Accommodation: Motel 6, 2760 Cleveland Ave., 95401. Telephone: 707/546-9563. See Anaheim listing for rates.

Saratoga

Accommodation: Sanborn Park Hostel (AYH), ♿, 15808 Sanborn Rd., 95070. Telephone: 408/867-3993. $3 summer; $3.50 winter for AYH members ($1 extra for nonmembers). Not far from San Jose—about ten miles. Main hostel building is large redwood log building dating from 1908. AYH membership required (see page 21).

Sepulveda

Accommodations: California 6 Motel, 15711 Roscoe Blvd., 91343. Telephone: 213/894-9341. $14.40 single; $21.90 double.
● Friendship Inn–Tahiti, 9151 Sepulveda Blvd., 91343. Telephone: 213/894-4051. $18 to $20 for one; $20 to $22 for two in one bed; $22 to $24 for two in two beds.

Simi Valley

Accommodation: Motel 6, 2566 North Erringer Rd., 93065. Telephone: 805/526-3666. See Anaheim listing for rates.

Sonora

Accommodation: Motel 6, 21660 Parriots Ferry Rd., 95370. To open in 1982. See Anaheim listing for rates.

South Lake Tahoe

Accommodation: Motel 6, 2375 Lake Tahoe Blvd., P.O. Box 7756, 95731. Telephone: 916/541-6272. See Anaheim listing for rates.

Stanford

Help: The Bridge, 415/497-3392.
On Campus: A friend of ours at Stanford University told us that "Stanford University area residents stress lifestyle and are generally young, hip, artsy, but the campus atmosphere is not as intense as one might expect the 'Harvard of the West' to be." She suggested a few places where you can get a good meal inexpensively, and they are: Chungking Royale, 2209 El Camino, Palo Alto, where you can get a filling lunch for $2.95 and a gargantuan dinner for $3.95; La Fortuna, 3180 Middlefield Rd., Redwood City, which has good Mexican food; La Cumbre, Stanford Shopping Center, Palo Alto, which is known for its two-for-one drinks during the 5 to 6 p.m. happy hour on weekdays; Good Earth, 185 University Ave., Palo Alto, which has a health-food menu; New

Varsity, 456 University Ave., and Chez Justine at the Holiday Inn in Palo Alto, both known for their delicious brunches; and—for the big splurge—St. Michael's Alley, 800 Emerson, Palo Alto, has a moderately expensive but interesting menu. For just hanging out, you can meet students at the Stanford Coffeehouse, Tresidder Union Patio; Dutch Goose in Menlo Park; "Zot's" Alpine Beer Garden, Menlo Park; and Peet's Coffee, 899 Santa Cruz, Menlo Park.

Two good sources of travel information are in Tresidder Union; they are the Information Desk on the second floor, and the Sequoia Travel Service on the first floor.

Accommodation: Stanford University, Stern Hall Dormitory, Escondido Rd. off Campus Dr. Open June 21 to September 19. $14.25 single; $10.75 per person double. Prices are lower for a stay of more than four weeks. Send reservation requests, along with your reason for visiting Stanford, to: Stanford Conference Office, 123 Encina Commons, Stanford University, Stanford, CA 94305.

Stanton

Accommodation: Motel 6, 7450 Katella Ave., 90680. Telephone: 714/898-1179. See Anaheim listing for rates.

Stockton

Accommodations: Motel 6, 4100 Waterloo Rd., 95205. Telephone: 209/931-1710. See Anaheim listing for rates.
● California 6 Motel, 81817 Navy Dr., 95206. Telephone: 209/946-0923. $14.40 single; $21.90 double.
● California 6 Motel, 6717 Plymouth Rd., 95207. Telephone: 209/951-8120. $14.40 single; $21.90 double.
● Friendship Eden Park Inn, 1005 North El Dorado, 95202. Telephone: 209/466-2711. $21 to $23 for one; $25 to $27 for two in one bed; $26 to $29 for two in two beds.

Sunnyvale

Accommodation: Motel 6, 806 Ahwanee Ave., 94086. Telephone: 408/739-4450. See Anaheim listing for rates.

Sylmar

Accommodation: Motel 6, 12775 Encinitas Ave., 91342. See Anaheim listing for rates.

Thousand Oaks

"A beautiful new city midway between Santa Barbara and Los Angeles, 30 minutes from Malibu."

Accommodation: Motel 6, 2850 Camino Dos Rios, Newbury Park, 91320. Telephone: 805/498-1669. See Anaheim listing for rates.

Three Rivers

Camping: Kings Canyon National Park, 93271. Eight campgrounds at Azalea, Canyon View, Crystal Springs, Moraine, Sentinel, Sheep Creek, Sunset, and Swale. Azalea is open all year; the others are open from May or June to September or October. $2 per campsite per night.
● Sequoia National Park, 93271. Seven campgrounds at Atwell Mill, Buckeye Flat, Cold Springs, and Dorst, which are open during the summer season; and Lodgepole, Potwisha, and South Fork, which are open all year. $2 fee for some; others are free.
● Devils Postpile National Monument, c/o Sequoia and Kings Canyon National Parks, 93271. One campground open June 15 to October 1. $3 campsite fee.

Tracy

Accommodation: Motel 6, 3810 Tracy Blvd., 95376. Telephone: 209/835-8666. See Anaheim listing for rates.

Tulare

Accommodation: Motel 6, 1111 North Blackstone, 93274. Telephone: 209/688-8507. See Anaheim listing for rates.

Tulelake

Camping: Lava Beds National Monument, P.O. Box 867, 96134. Ten of the 40 campsites at Indian Well open all year; 30 campsites open May to September. $3 per campsite per night.

Turlock

Accommodations: Motel 6, 250 South Walnut Rd., 95380. Telephone: 209/632-6668. See Anaheim listing for rates.
● California 6 Motel, 185 North Tully Rd., 95380. Telephone: 209/634-2944. $14.40 single; $21.90 double.
● Accord Youth Hostel (AYH), 475 West Main, 95380. Telephone: 209/634-2691. AYH members preferred but students also accepted. Open year round. $3.50.

Tustin

Accommodation: Sixpence Inn, 1611 Laguna Rd., 92680. Telephone: 714/832-3220. See Anaheim listing for rates.

Twenty-Nine Palms

Camping: Joshua Tree National Monument, 74485 National Monument Dr., 92277. Eight campgrounds at Belle, Black Rock Canyon, Cottonwood Spring, Hidden Valley, Indian Cove, Jumbo Rocks, Ryan, and White Tank. Open all year. No entrance fee; $2 per campsite per night at Black Rock and Cottonwood Spring.

Ukiah

Accommodation: Motel 6, 1208 South State St., 95482. Telephone: 707/462-8763. See Anaheim listing for rates.

Vacaville

Accommodation: Motel 6, 107 Lawrence Dr., 95688. Telephone: 707/448-6663. See Anaheim listing for rates.

Vallejo

Accommodations: Motel 6, 101 Maritime Academy Dr., 94590. Telephone: 707/552-3666. See Anaheim listing for rates.
● California 6 Motel, 1455 Sears Point Rd., 94590. Telephone: 707/643-7611. $14.40 single; $21.90 double.
● Regal 8 Inn, 211 Lincoln Rd. West, 94590. Telephone: 707/552-6250. See Fresno listing for rates.

Ventura

Accommodation: Motel 6, 2145 East Harbor Blvd., 93003. Telephone: 805/648-3366. See Anaheim listing for rates.

Victorville

Accommodation: Motel 6, 16901 Stoddard Wells Rd., 92392. Telephone: 714/245-9548. See Anaheim listing for rates.

Walnut Creek

Accommodation: Motel 6, 2389 North Main St., 94596. Telephone: 415/939-8181. See Anaheim listing for rates.

Weed

Accommodation: Motel 6, 466 North Weed Blvd., 96094. See Anaheim listing for rates.

Westminster

Accommodation: Motel 6, 6266 Westminster Ave., 92683. Telephone: 714/894-9811. See Anaheim listing for rates.

Whiskeytown

Camping: Whiskeytown National Recreation Area, P.O. Box 188, 96095. Three campgrounds at Brandy Creek, Dry Creek, and Oak Bottom (walk-in only). Open all year. $3 per campsite per night at Oak Bottom.

Whittier

Accommodation: Motel 6, 8221 South Pioneer Blvd., 90606. Telephone: 213/695-0078. See Anaheim listing for rates.

Williams

Accommodation: Motel 6, 455 4th St., 95987. Telephone: 916/473-2995. See Anaheim listing for rates.

Woodland

Accommodation: Motel 6, 1564 East Main St., 95695. Telephone: 916/666-4611. See Anaheim listing for rates.

Yosemite

Accommodations: The Yosemite Park and Curry Company, Yosemite National Park, 95389, operates several accommodations within Yosemite National Park. Reservations are requested as far in advance as possible and may be made by phone. Call 209/373-4171. Some of these accommodations are out of the price range of this book, but the following aren't:

Yosemite: Lodge Cabins. Without bath or water. $17 for one or two people; $4 for each additional person. Use central bathhouse. Linen supplied.

Curry Village Tent Cabins. $12.50 for one or two people; $4 for each additional person. Use central bathhouse. Linen supplied.

Housekeeping Camp. Units for one to four persons. $14.50 per day. Summer only. You supply your own linens and use central bathhouse.

White Wolf Lodge tents. $16 for one or two people; $5 for each additional person. Use central bathhouse. Linen supplied.

In winter, check too about midweek ski packages. They're a good value.

Camping: Yosemite National Park, P.O. Box 577, Yosemite Village, 95389. Twenty-one campgrounds are available and most are open from May or June to September or October. Lower Pines in Yosemite Valley and Wawona are open year round. $1 to $6 per campsite per night.

Note: In summer, Yosemite Valley is jam-packed with people. Try other parts of the park if you want to see wildnerness.

Yreka

Accommodations: Thunderbird Lodge, 526 South Main St., 96097. Telephone: 916/842-4404. $17.50 to $20 for one; $20 to $24 for two in one bed; $22 to $25 for two in two beds.
- Motel 6, 1785 South Main St., 96097. Telephone: 916/842-1266. See Anaheim listing for rates.

Yuba City

Accommodation: Motel 6, 700 North Polara, 95991. Telephone: 916/673-1893. See Anaheim listing for rates.

Sterling
Dinosaur • Steamboat Springs • • Fort Collins
Craig • • • Greeley
Grand Lake • Estes Park • • Brush
Winter Park • Lafayette
Nederland • • Boulder
Georgetown • • Aurora
Glenwood Springs • Idaho Springs Denver • • Byers Burlington •
Palisade Breckenridge •
Fruita • • Aspen • • Fairplay
• Grand Junction
Manitou Springs • • Colorado Springs
• Gunnison
Salida • • Pueblo
Lamar •
• Silverton
Mosca • • Walsenburg
• Cortez • Pagosa Springs
Mesa Verde • • Durango • Trinidad

Colorado

Most of Colorado is located in the Rocky Mountains, and its natural beauty is extraordinary. Boulder is the student center of the state and Vail and Aspen are where everyone from the East Coast wants to go skiing.

The Colorado Office of Tourism promises 300 days of sunshine and crisp, clean air in what they call their 104,000-square-mile outdoor amphitheater. About one-third of Colorado is under government jurisdiction so it cannot be spoiled. There are 11 national forests, national parks, national monuments, national recreation areas, and national grasslands. Whatever your outdoor fun is, you can probably do it in Colorado. Before the snow falls, backpacking is a favorite Colorado activity and you can do it to your heart's content in the wilderness areas of Rocky Mountain National Park; south of Pikes Peak, near Colorado Springs; west of Denver in the Mount Evans area; in the San Juan mountain range in the southwest; north of Glenwood Springs, in the Flattops and Rabbit Ears Pass Area near Steamboat Springs; and in the Ten Mile Range south of Vail.

When winter comes, everyone in Colorado talks "ski." The Rocky Mountains have a powder snow that skiers dream about. For a guide to Colorado ski areas, write to Colorado Ski Country USA, Brownleigh Court, Suite A201, 1410 Grant St., Denver, CO 80203, or phone 303/837-0793.

Note: Colorado has an active and ever-growing number of youth hostels. At some you must be an AYH card holder; at others you may buy introductory passes. Call individual hostels to make sure.

Some Special Events: Mayfest Celebration in Estes Park (May); Rio Grande River Raft Races in Creede and University of Colorado Music Festival in Boulder (June); Cattlemen's Days Celebration in Gunnison and Buffalo Bill Days in Golden (July); Morgan County Fair in Brush, Hardrockers Holidays

Mining Celebration and Dance in Silverton, Rocky Mountain Watermedia Exhibit in Golden, and Old Settlers Picnic and Bar-B-Q in Springfield (all in August); Annual Harvest Festival in Windsor and Labor Day Festival in Fountain (September).

Hitching: A friend in Boulder says that people do hitchhike there, even though the police are against it. He recommends, however, that it be done with caution. Another, in Denver, says that hitching is accepted by most people and that if you stay on the curb while hitching and carry good identification with you, you shouldn't have difficulty with the police.

The Colorado State Police sent us a copy of the state law pertaining to hitchhiking, which states: "No person shall stand in a roadway for the purpose of soliciting a ride from the driver of any private vehicle." Added in 1975 was the sentence: "For the purposes of this subsection, 'roadway' means that portion of the road normally used by moving motor vehicle traffic."

Tourist Information: Office of Tourism, Colorado Division of Commerce and Development, 1313 Sherman, Room 500, Denver, CO 80203.

Aspen

Accommodation: Highlands Inn (AYH-SA), ☛ (same as AYH price), P.O. Box 4708, 1650 Maroon Creek Rd., 81611. Telephone: 303/925-5050. $7.50 summer, $10 winter for AYH members; for nonmembers, the rates for a double room are $40 to $60 during winter, $30 during summer, and $20 off season. The inn is open June through September and from Thanksgiving to early April. Free bus runs to Aspen every half hour. The inn is located at the base of Aspen Highlands ski area. "Here AYH'ers can enjoy all the facilities of a luxury hotel including pool, sauna, Jacuzzi, and free buses to town and to hiking areas—at what are probably the cheapest rates in all Aspen."

Aurora

Help: Comitis Crisis Center, 303/343-9890.
Accommodation: Riviera Motel, 9100 East Colfax, 80010. Six minutes from Denver airport. $21 to $25 for one; $24 to $29 for two in one bed; $26 to $32 for two in two beds.

Boulder

Help: Women's Line, 303/492-8910.
On Campus: A friend from the University of Colorado calls this "Mork and Mindy land, or East Coast/West Coast slick with a little hint of western laidback for flavor." He goes on to explain that a few years ago Boulder was summer headquarters for the street people and the locals didn't like it at all. Some of their feelings persist, but in general young travelers are welcome—"if you're reasonably clean, sober at noon and don't try to sleep in Central Park you won't be hassled."

When you're hungry in Boulder and want vegetarian food, try Hanna's New Age Foods (open at lunchtime only), located above the New Age Food Store at 10th and Pearl. For not-so-organic eating, try Don's Cheese and Sausage Mart, 28th and Baseline. Other possibilities: The Good Earth, at 18th and Pearl, for healthful food; Marie's on North Broadway, for reasonable prices and an occasional Czech specialty; and the New York Deli on the Pearl St. Mall. The best deal in town is probably the food service in the University Memorial Center on campus at either the Tabor Inn or the Alferd E. Packer Memorial Grill, named after the U.S.'s only convicted cannibal.

If you're in Boulder during the warm weather you'll surely walk along the Mall with a Häagen-Dazs ice cream cone and enjoy the jugglers, magicians, tightrope walkers, belly dancers, musicians, and all the other people. And if you're around in the beginning of April, you'll get to enjoy the annual campus Trivia Bowl.

To know what's going on, check the *Colorado Daily,* the campus paper, or the *Grapevine.* For disco, the place to be seen is Anthony's Gardens in the Harvest House Hotel, and if your desires run to an English/Irish pub-type place, try the James, just off the Mall. When it's time to leave Boulder, you can check the rider board next to the Packer Grill in the University Memorial Center—it's divided into geographical areas and gets lots of use.

"If you're clean, tan, and play Frisbee, there's a place for you."

Accommodation: Boulder International Youth Hostel (AYH-SA), 1107 12th St. (northwest corner of 12th and College Ave.), 80302. Telephone: 303/442-0522. $5.75 for AYH members in the dorm; $7.75 for introductory members. Family and private rooms are often available, too. Bring your own sleeping bag, sheet, sleeping sack, or linen, or rent linen for $2. The building is, according to the couple who run it, "relatively new, partially remodeled, roomy, spacious, and even plush." There's a kitchen, too, which can accommodate several cooks at once.

Breckenridge

Tourist Information: Breckenridge Resort Association, 303/453-2918.
Accommodation: Galbreath's Fireside Inn (AYH-SA), ☛ ★ ⓐ, P.O. Box 2252, 80424. Telephone: 303/453-6456. Open year round. Single: $18 summer, $29 winter; double: $26 summer, $29 winter; dorm: $10 summer, $15 winter. Breakfast included. "A cozy, friendly place in an interesting refurbished western mining town." Excellent summer and winter recreational facilities. Discount of 20% toward room and two meals per day; 10% discount toward room only.

Brush

Accommodation: Empire Motel, 1408 West Edison, 80723. Telephone: 303/842-2876. $19 for one; $22 to $23 for two in one bed; $28 for four in two beds.

Byers

Accommodation: Longhorn Motel, junction I-70 and Hwy. 36 at exit, P.O. Box 196, 80103. Telephone: 303/822-5205. $18 to $24 for one; $24 to $26 for two in one bed; $26 to $28 for two in two beds.

Burlington

Accommodation: Friendship Inn–Sloan's Motel, 1901 Rose Ave., 80807. Telephone: 303/346-5333. $20 for one; $24 to $26 for two in one bed; $26 to $30 for two in two beds.

Colorado Springs

Help: Terros, 303/471-4127. *"We would be sympathetic to and interested in helping any travelers who should contact us."* Terros can help you to find low-cost housing in this fast-growing town. They also mentioned that "the hitchhiker isn't really hassled but he isn't welcomed either."

Accommodations: Colorado Springs Hostel (AYH-SA), Farragut Hall, 17 North Farragut Ave., 80909. Telephone: 303/471-2938 or 634-9657. $4.25 summer and winter. Kitchens and laundry facilities.
● Motel 6, 3228 North Chestnut St., 80907. Telephone: 303/471-2340. $12.95 for one; $16.95 for two; $19.95 for up to four.
● Superior J's Motor Hotel, 820 North Nevada Ave., 80903. Telephone: 303/633-5513. $17 to $23 for one; $20 to $28 for two in one bed; $23 to $33 for two in two beds.
● Friendship Inn–Dale Downtown Motel, 620 West Colorado Ave., 80905. Telephone: 303/636-3721. $18 to $24 for one; $20 to $26 for two in one bed; $23 to $30 for two in two beds.

Cortez

Camping: Hovenweep National Monument, McElmo Route, 81321. Camping all year at Square Tower Ruin.

Craig

Accommodation: Friendship Inn–Alamo Motel, 205 East Victory Way, 81625. Telephone: 303/824-5592. $22 to $24 for one; $22 to $26 for two in one bed; $26 to $28 for two in two beds.

Denver

Denver is the mile-high capital of Colorado, exactly 5280 feet above sea level. One native says that anyone visiting the city should first "see Red Rocks Park—an incredibly beautiful natural amphitheater right outside Denver—and then move on to the mountains." Before heading for the mountains, though, there are some things that one should see in the city: Larimer Square, between 13th and 15th Sts., is a rebuilt section of downtown reminiscent of the 1890s that's fun to stroll through; the Denver Art Museum, adjacent to the City Center and housed in an ultramodern building, is worth a visit; and the Denver Museum of Natural History is well known for its collections, including dioramas of native birds and animals, meteorites, and Indian artifacts.

Getting There: Stapleton International Airport is four miles northeast of town and there's a #32 bus connecting the town with the airport that costs 50¢ from 6 to 8 a.m. and from 4 to 6 p.m.; 25¢ at other times. You can catch this bus on the lower level, between doors 1 and 5. A taxi ride on the same route would cost more than $5. The bus terminals are both located at 19th and Curtis; the train station is at 1735 19th St.

Getting Around: By Bus: The city buses run frequently, seven days a week from 5 a.m. until midnight. At rush hour, from 6 to 8 a.m. and from 4 to 6 p.m., the fare is 50¢; half that any other time. Call 778-6000 for information.

● By Taxi: Taxis charge $1.85 for the first mile, 80¢ each additional mile. Dial Zone Cab (tel. 861-2323), or Yellow Cab (tel. 892-1212). "Riding with Zone usually ends up costing less."

● By Car: To rent a car, try one of these: Budget Rent-a-Car, 1850 Broadway (tel. 861-4125; $25.95 per day with 150 free miles for an economy car); American International Rent-a-Car, 1919 Broadway (tel. 629-6153; $10.95 per day, 16¢ per mile for a Chevette); and Rent-a-Wreck (not a misprint!), 3737 Kalamath (tel. 477-1635; five- to ten-year-old cars rent for $9 per day, with the first 20 miles free and 9¢ per mile after that).

Accommodations: Denver Youth Hostel (AYH), 1452 Detroit, 80206. Telephone: 303/333-7672. 1½ miles east of the State Capitol and two blocks south of City Park. From the bus station, walk two blocks southwest to 17th St. and take bus #15 to Elizabeth St. stop. Then walk straight ahead two blocks to Detroit and turn right. From the airport, take a #65 bus to East Colfax, then transfer to a westbound A15 bus and get off at the Detroit St. stop. From the train station, get a #20 bus that goes to Fillmore. Then walk ahead one block to Detroit. Dormitory-style rooms, clean and friendly. Open year round. $3.75 summer; $4.25 winter. AYH membership required (see page 21). Three-night maximum stay.

● YMCA, 25 East 16th Ave., 80202. Telephone: 303/861-8300. Men and women. $10.25 single without bath; $14.90 single with bath; $17 to $19.50 double. Convenient to downtown. Small cafeteria.

● Ranch Manor Motor Inn, 1490 South Santa Fe, 80223. $15 for room with one bed; $20.50 for room with two beds. Unlimited number may use the same room. Two heated pools, air conditioning, and television.

● Coburn Hotel, 🐾, 980 Grant, 80203. Telephone: 303/837-0740. $25 single; $29 double, with ISIC.

● Regal 8 Inn, 12033 East 38th Ave. at Peoria St., 80239. Telephone: 303/371-0740. $17.88 for one; $20.88 for two in one bed; $23.88 for two to four in two beds.

● Regal 8 Inn, 3050 North 49th Ave. at Federal, 80221. Telephone: 303/455-8888. See above listing for rates.

● Friendship Inn–Red Coach Motor Inn, 9201 East Colfax Ave., Aurora, 80010. Telephone: 303/366-1586. $18 to $20 for one; $22 to $24 for two in one bed; $24 to $26 for two in two beds.

● Best Value Driftwood Motel, 1443 Oneida, 80220. Telephone: 303/388-4261. $20.50 to $25 for one; $22.50 to $26 for two in one bed; $24 to $28 for two in two beds.

● Motel 6, 12020 East 39th Ave., 80239. Telephone: 303/371-7410. See Colorado Springs listing for rates.

● Motel 6, 480 Wadsworth Blvd., 80226. Telephone: 303/238-6471. See Colorado Springs listing for rates.

Where to Eat: Beau Jo's, 2024 East Colfax. Telephone: 388-7600. Open 10 a.m. to midnight; until 2 a.m. on weekends. A pizza big enough for three costs $5.75.

- Red Moon Pizzeria, 329 East Colfax. Telephone: 861-9930. Open 11:30 a.m. to 9 p.m. during the week; Friday and Saturday 1 to 9 p.m.
- Zach's Ltd., 1480 Humboldt St. Telephone: 831-0870. Open 11 a.m. to 2 p.m., Monday through Saturday; 4 p.m. to midnight Sunday. Features natural foods.
- Chada Thai, 408 East 20th Ave. (downtown). Telephone: 861-7246. Authentic Thai food in a crowded spot; on weekends you'd better have reservations.
- Café Nepenthes, 1416 Market St. (downtown). Telephone: 534-5423. Vegetarian food in a coffeehouse atmosphere. Music from 9 p.m. to midnight every night.
- La Bola, 900 Jersey. Telephone: 333-3888. Mexican food dished out in generous portions. Busy neighborhood-type place. Margaritas are a specialty.
- Ohle's, 1520 East Colfax. Telephone: 832-5086. A German deli that shares space with a small food market. Open until 6 p.m.
- Rich's Café, 80 South Madison. Telephone: 399-4488. Popular watering hole for lunch and after work. Lots of young professional types.
- Le Central, 8th and Lincoln. Telephone: 863-3094. For French cuisine that's not too, too expensive.

What to See and Do: Larimer Square, between 13th and 15th Sts. on Larimer St. A recreation of the area as it appeared in the 1890s with antiques, restaurants, galleries, movies, etc. Often there are street fairs and other celebrations in the square.

- Denver Art Museum, in the Civic Center. Interesting collection in a controversial building designed by Gio Ponti. Admission is free. Closed Monday.
- U.S. Mint, Colfax Ave. and Cherokee St. Long lines wait for tours so get there early. "The tour is only 15 minutes long and all you see are coins being stamped."
- Denver Museum of Natural History, in City Park on Colorado Blvd. Everything you'd expect in a natural history museum, plus daily shows in the Gates Planetarium that are spectacular. "Definitely worth a visit." Admission is free to museum; planetarium $1.50 to $3.50.
- The Lift, 4501 East Virginia Ave. Telephone: 377-2701. Open 11:30 a.m. to 2 a.m. Monday through Friday; 5 p.m. to 2 a.m. Saturday; 6 p.m. to midnight Sunday. The cover charge is $2 on Saturday nights, and there's a one-drink minimum. This is the place to dance—it looks like a ski lodge and has a restaurant on the second floor.
- Swallow Hill Music Association presents programs of various types on Friday and Saturday evenings at the Monastery Restaurant, 1088 Delaware St. For information, call 778-8711.
- Café Promenade, 1430 Larimer St. Telephone: 893-2692. Open 9 a.m. to midnight; closed Sunday. An elegant place, serving homemade breads and pastries accompanied by live chamber music performances by moonlighting members of the Denver Symphony Orchestra.

Shopping: Together Books, 200 East 13th Ave. (13th and Sherman). Telephone: 832-5171. Books on philosophy, survival, women, yoga, the occult, etc.

- Budget Tapes and Records, 2701 East Third Ave. Telephone: 333-2088.

The Capitol Hill branch of this chain that has lots of other stores in the city.

● Denver Folklore Center, 440 South Broadway. Telephone: 778-8711. For pop, folk, and specialty records.

● Eastern Mountain Sports, 1428 East 15th St. Telephone: 571-1160. Backpacking, camping, climbing, ski touring supplies, and jogging gear.

● Gart Brothers, 1000 Broadway. Telephone: 861-1122. A large retail store specializing in sports and photographic equipment. (By now you've caught on to the fact that Denverites are very outdoorsy types.)

● Cherry Creek Shopping Center. This is a large complex in the middle of a residential area bounded by University Ave., Third Ave., Steele St., and North Cherry Creek Dr. It includes a wide variety of stores, large and small— from Sears to exclusive specialty shops, restaurants, and cinemas. Some shops in the center are open on Sunday.

Help: Denver Convention and Visitors Bureau, 225 West Colfax Ave., 80202 (one block west of Civil Center Park). Telephone: 303/892-1112. (Information booth at airport.)

● Travelers Aid, 504 East 14th Ave., 80204. Telephone: 303/832-8194.

● COMITIS, 9840 East 17th Ave., Aurora. Telephone: 303/343-9890. 24-hour switchboard for information, referrals, and help.

Dinosaur

Camping: Dinosaur National Monument, P.O. Box 210, 81610. Backcountry river sites; many accessible by boat only. Some open all year, some just summer and fall. $2 fee for Rainbow Park and Split Mountain.

Durango

Accommodation: Durango Hostel (AYH), ★, 543 East Second Ave., 81301. Telephone: 303/247-5477 or 247-9905. $6 to $8 summer; $7 to $9 winter. Late-night arrivals can call for a ride; train is one-half block away, bus is eight blocks. In a Victorian lodging house originally meant to house railroaders and miners. AYH membership required (see page 21). A temporary pass is available for nonmembers. If you have a copy of *Where to Stay* with you and pay in advance, you can have your third night free. The hostel has discount rental cars available. Reservations should be made well in advance during summer and holiday seasons.

Estes Park

Accommodation: H-Bar-G Ranch Hostel (AYH-SA), P.O. Box 1260, 3500 H-G Rd., 80517. Six miles northeast of Estes Park, near Rocky Mountain National Park. Telephone: 303/586-3688. Open May 25 to September 10. $4.25 for AYH members; membership available at hostel. Reservations requested. Six miles from bus station. Hostel owner will pick you up at the Chamber of Commerce Tourist Information Center at 5 p.m. Bring food to cook because the nearest grocery store is six miles away. "Superbly situated with views of Rocky Mountain Park."

Camping: Rocky Mountain National Park, 80517. Six campgrounds at Aspenglen, Glacier Basin, Longs Peak, Moraine Park, Timber Creek, and Trail Camps (accessible by trail only). $4 per campsite per night.

"For family-style cooking, go to Coulters Waffle Shop, Estes County Kitchen, the Mountaineer, or Heidis."

Fairplay

Accommodation: Fairplay Hotel, 500 Main St., 80440. Telephone: 303/ 836-2565. $14 to $20 single; $15 to $21 double. A resort hotel in the Rocky Mountains with a restaurant and bar.

Fort Collins

Help: Community Crisis Center, 303/493-3888.

On Campus: Fort Collins is the home of Colorado State University, and the town has a good attitude toward young people. A student there told us that hitchhiking is common but that it is sometimes difficult to catch rides.

The United Campus Ministry at 629 South Howes might be able to help you find an inexpensive or free place to stay. You can call them at 303/482-8487.

There are inexpensive movies at the Student Center throughout the weekends and a number of concerts and theater performances on and off campus throughout the year.

The Collegian, Triangle Review, and *The Paper,* all student newspapers, can provide you with all kinds of useful information on entertainment, rides, accommodations, and the like.

CSU students tend to congregate at the Ramskeller in the Student Center; Chesterfield, Bottomley and Potts, 1415 West Elizabeth; and Washington's Bar and Grill, 132 West Laporte.

Accommodation: Motel 6, 3900 East Mulberry, 80521. Telephone: 303/ 484-6662. See Colorado Springs listing for rates.

Fruita

Camping: Colorado National Monument, 81521. Camping at Saddle Horn, four miles south of the West Entrance. Open all year. $2 per campsite per night.

Glenwood Springs

Accommodation: Pinon Pines Apartments, 🔲 3210 County Rd. 114, 81601. Telephone: 303/945-8102. Ten miles from train station; three miles from bus station. $29 for room with twin beds; $39 for room with four beds. Reservations required. Kitchen available. Not far from Aspen.

Grand Junction

Accommodation: Motel 6, 776 Horizon Dr., 81501. Telephone: 303/245-6668. See Colorado Springs listing for rates.

Grand Lake

Accommodations: Shadowcliff Lodge (AYH), P.O. Box 658, 80447. Telephone: 303/627-9966. Upon entering Grand Lake Village, take Tunnel Rd. for three-quarters of a mile. Sign on left, just before bridge. Open June 1 to October 1. $4 for AYH members in dormitory; $5 to $10 for private room for nonmembers. 16 miles from bus and train station in Granby. You can hitch a ride to Grand Lake with local residents. Reservations preferred.
• Dougal's Mountain Inn (AYH), P.O. Box 1, 612 Grand Ave., 80442. Telephone: 303/627-3385. Open November 15 to April 15. $4 to $5. One mile from Rocky Mountain National Park. Hostel is constructed entirely from logs.

Greeley

On Campus: For general information about this college town, home of the University of Northern Colorado, stop at the Office of International Education, Carter Hall, Room 209. The University Center is the central spot on the UNC campus; it's there that you'll find a bulletin board with rides and a cafeteria that's a popular meeting place on campus. During the summer, contact the director of housing at the university—there may be a place for you to stay on campus. For collectors of curious facts: Greeley is the home of the number one cattle feed manufacturer in the world—Monfort of Colorado. You can visit one of their feed lots if you'd like.
Accomodations: Motel 6, U.S. Hwys. 85 and 34, Evans, 80620. Telephone: 303/353-6665. See Colorado Springs listing for rates.
• Friendship Inn–Greeley Lamplighter Motel, 2905 Eighth Ave., Evans, 80620. Telephone: 303/352-7070. $22 to $25 for one; $25 to $30 for two in one bed; $27 to $35 for two in two beds.

Gunnison

Camping: Curecanti National Recreation Area, P.O. Box 1040, 81230. Camping at Elk Creek, Lake Fork, Old Stevens Creek, and Cimarron, all on Blue Mesa Lake. $2 per campsite per night. Open May to October.

Idaho Springs

Accommodation: Best Value Six & Forty Motel, 2920 Colorado Blvd., 80215. Telephone: 303/567-2691. $13 to $15 for one or two in one bed; $18 to $25 for two in two beds.

Lafayette

Accommodation: Lafayette Hostel (AYH-SA), 409 East Oak St., 80026. Telephone: 303/665-5997. Leave message on tape recorder. $3.75 for AYH members in bunk rooms. Nonmembers: $7 per person double; $5 per person triple; $3 per person quad. Nonmembers must also pay a $1 introductory membership fee.

Lamar

Accommodations: Friendship Plaza Motel, 905 East Olive, 81052. Telephone: 303/336-7701. $18 to $22 for one; $21 to $26 for two in one bed; $24 to $30 for two in two beds.

● Motor Way Motel, √, 500 East Olive, 81052. Telephone: 303/336-2201. $15 for one; $18 for two in one bed; $20 for two in two beds.

Manitou Springs

Accommodation: Walks Superior Motel, 45 Manitou Ave., 80829. Telephone: 303/685-9982. $20 to $25 for one; $20 to $28 for two in one bed; $25 to $30 for two in two beds.

Mesa Verde

Camping: Mesa Verde National Park, 81330. Campground at Morefield Canyon. Open May 1 to October 31. $2 per campsite per night.

Mosca

Camping: Great Sand Dunes National Monument, 81146. Campgrounds at Dunes open October to April; Pinyon Flats open April to October. $3 per campsite per night during summer season.

Nederland

Accommodation: Nederland Youth Hostel (AYH), 1005 Jackson, P.O. Box 391, 80466. Telephone: 303/258-9925. Leave message on tape recorder. $3.50. Open year round. In the heart of mining country.

Pagosa Springs

Accommodation: Best Value San Juan Motel, Rte. 160, P.O. Box 729, 81147. Telephone: 303/264-2262. $19 to $21 for one; $22 to $24 for two in one bed; $25 to $27 for two in two beds.

Palisade

Accommodation: Superior Mesa View Motel, Hwys. 6 and 24, 81526. Telephone: 303/464-5618 or 464-5619. $16.50 to $18.50 for one; $20.50 to $24.50 for two in one bed; $22.50 to $28.50 for two in two beds.

Pueblo

Accommodations: Pueblo YWCA (AYH), 801 North Santa Fe Ave., 81003. Telephone: 303/542-6904. $3.75 for AYH members.

● Regal 8 Inn, 960 U.S. 50 West, 81008. Telephone: 303/543-8900. See Denver listing for rates.

● Motel 6, I-25 and U.S. 50, 81008. See Colorado Springs listing for rates.

● Friendship Claymar Inn, 115 East 8th St., 81103. Telephone: 303/542-1061. $13 to $18 for one; $18 to $22 for two in one bed; $20 to $24 for two in two beds.

● Friendship Inn–Rambler Motel, 4400 North Elizabeth St., 81008. Telephone: 303/543-4173. $20 to $22 for one; $22 to $24 for two in one bed; $26 to $28 for two in two beds.

Salida

Accommodation: Superior Shawano Motel, 525 Rainbow Blvd., 81201. Telephone: 303/539-6689. $18 to $23 for one; $21 to $25 for two in one bed; $23 to $29 for two in two beds.

Silverton

Accommodation: French Bakery Restaurant and Teller House Pension (AYH-SA), 🍴 ★ 5%, 1250 Greene St., P.O. Box 457, 81433. Telephone: 303/387-5423. Two blocks from bus station; two blocks from narrow-gauge train from Silverton to Durango (June to October). European-style hotel with breakfast included in price of room. In a small gold mining town (population 800) in the San Juan Mountains. $16 single; $24 double. Rates for AYH members and ISIC-holders in the dormitory are $8 per person.

Steamboat Springs

Accommodation: Haystack Lodge Youth Hostel (AYH-SA), 🍴, 2030 Walton Creek Rd., P.O. Box 1356, 80499. Telephone: 303/879-0587. Reservations required. $5 summer, $12 winter for AYH members; others must pay more at this ski lodge. Skiing only three blocks away. Discount applies to ski rentals too. Discount does not apply to period between December 20 and January 1.

Sterling

Accommodation: Friendship Inn–El Patio Motel, 100 Logan St., 80751. Telephone: 303/522-5353. $21 to $24 for one; $26 for two in one bed; $29 for two in two beds.

Trinidad

Accommodations: Friendship Inn-Derrick Motel, RR #1, Box 427B, 81082. Telephone: 303/846-3307. $15.95 to $17.95 for one; $17.95 to $20.95 for two in one bed; $19.95 to $22.95 for two in two beds.

● Best Value Derrick Motel, Rte. 1, Box 427B, 81082. Telephone: 303/846-3307. $11.95 to $15.95 for one; $13.95 to $18.95 for two in one bed; $15.95 to $20.95 for two in two beds.

Walsenburg

Accommodations: Friendship Inn–Country Host, P.O. Box 190, 81089. Telephone: 303/738-3800. $24 for one; $26 for two in one bed; $30 for two in two beds.

● Crescent Motel, 802 Walsen Ave., 81089. Telephone: 303/738-2435. $19 for one or two in one bed; $23 for two in two beds.

Wheat Ridge

Accommodation: Sixpence Inn, 9920 West 49th Ave., 80033. Telephone: 303/424-0658. $12.95 to $14.95 for one; $14.95 to $16.95 for two.

Winter Park

Accommodation: Winter Park Hostel (AYH), Vasquez Rd., P.O. Box 3323, 80482. Telephone: 303/726-5356. Open year round. $4 summer, $7 winter for AYH members; nonmembers must pay higher rate. Equipped kitchen. Continental Trailways stops 50 yards from hostel door.

Connecticut

Connecticut can be quite a lovely place to be. The southwestern part of the state has some of New York's bedroom communities, but the rest has its very own identity and is often very interesting. No point in the state is more than two hours from any other, so even if your time is limited, you can see quite a bit of Connecticut.

The capital city, Hartford, was enjoying a renaissance of its downtown area when the roof on its civic center caved in. The newly rebuilt Civic Center attests to the city's determination to revive its downtown. Hartford is as proud of its past as it is of its present and within the city are several interesting historic sites to visit: the Mark Twain House and, right next to it, the Harriet Beecher Stowe House are faithfully restored reminders of a gracious, literary 19th century; the Old State House on Main St., the oldest in the nation, has just recently become a tourist attraction with its restored Senate and House chambers; and the Wadsworth Atheneum, Hartford's art museum, has an appealing collection of paintings, sculpture, silver, textiles, etc.

New Haven is another Connecticut town that's worth a visit. The home of Yale University, it has two museums worth a stop—the Yale Center for British Art and the Yale University Art Gallery—and all of the cultural events you'd expect from a university town. The Long Wharf Theater, also in New Haven, in a former food terminal warehouse, can usually be counted on for top-rate performances of new and revived plays.

In summer, the place to go is the Connecticut shore—to Westbrook, Saybrook, Lyme, and to Mystic with its Seaport, which is the state's number one tourist attraction, a living museum that re-creates a 19th-century maritime village with ships, shops, homes, and the last of the wooden whalers, the *Charles W. Morgan*. Throughout the state there are wooded hillsides, lakes, streams, colonial villages, and historic homes.

For general information on Connecticut and its attractions, send for *Connecticut Vacation Guide* from the address given under tourist information below. For more specific books on Connecticut, consider the following:

Coastal Connecticut, Eastern Region, by Barry and Susan Hildebrandt, and *Coastal Connecticut, Western Region,* by Marcy Beaubelle, Peregrine Press, Old Saybrook, CT 06475 ($4.95). Covers the Connecticut shore from Guilford to Stonington giving historical sketches, things to do, and restaurant recommendations.

Fifty Hikes in Connecticut, by Gerry and Sue Hardy, New Hampshire Publishing Co., P.O. Box 70, Somersworth, NH 03878 ($6.95; add $1.50 postage and handling).

Connecticut Outdoors, by Paul Cohen, Charles & Co., Inc., P.O. Box 606, Southport, CT 06490 ($3.95). Places to fish, rent boats, hunt, eat, and stay.

Connecticut Walk Book, Connecticut Forest and Park Association, Inc., P.O. Box 389, East Hartford, CT 06108 ($8.25 by mail). Detailed description of trails with maps.

Globe Pequot Press, Old Chester Road, Box O, Chester, CT 06412, publishes a variety of books on Connecticut including a *Guide to Hartford, Short Bicycle Rides, The Fine Restaurants of Connecticut,* etc. Write to them for a list.

Some Special Events: Shad Festival in Windsor and Dogwood Festival in Fairfield (May); Rose and Arts Festival in Norwich and Barnum Festival (P. T. Barnum, founder of the Greatest Show on Earth was also the mayor of Bridgeport for a while) in Bridgeport (late June to early July); Audubon Festival in Sharon (late July); the Oyster Festival in Milford and Outdoor Arts Festival in Mystic (August); Chrysanthemum Festival in Bristol (late September to early October); and the Apple Harvest Festival in Southington (early October).

Hitching: In 1975, Public Act 75220 permitting hitchhiking in Connecticut came into effect. It states that soliciting a ride is permissible from the shoulder except on limited-access highways. A friend from the University of Hartford recommends hitching; a state trooper does not. "Hitchhiking is a practice which is not condoned by the Connecticut State Police Department."

Tourist Information: Connecticut Department of Economic Development, Vacation-Travel Promotion, 210 Washington St., Hartford, CT 06106. Telephone: toll free 800/842-7492 in Connecticut, and 800/243-1645 in Maine through Virginia.

Bolton

Accommodation: Bolton Home Hostel (AYH), 42 Clark Rd., 06040. Telephone: 203/649-3905. Open May 1 to mid-October. Reservation necessary. Must arrive on foot or by bicycle; no cars allowed. $4.50. AYH membership required (see page 21).

Bridgeport

Help: Infoline, 203/333-7555.

Accommodation: YMCA, 🡒 ★, 651 State St. at Park Ave., 06604. Five blocks from I-95. Telephone: 203/334-5551. Men only. $10, plus $5 key deposit. Weekly rate: $45 to $53. All buses stop at the Y; the train station is on the same street, five blocks away.

East Hartford

Accommodation: Imperial 400 Motor Inn, 927 Main St., 06108. Telephone: 203/289-7781. $22 to $24 for one; $24 to $26 for two in one bed; $26 to $28 for two in two beds.

Hartford

Help: University of Hartford General Info, 203/243-4204.
● Info Line, 999 Asylum Ave., 06105. Telephone: 203/521-7150. "Information, referral, advocacy."
● Travelers Aid, 30 High St., Suite 4, 06103. Telephone: 203/522-2247.
● Art Line, 203/247-4433. For what's happening art-wise.
On Campus: Trinity College is in Hartford. You can go to the movies at the Cine Studio there for $1.50 with a student ID card. Check the bulletin board at the Mather Campus Center for listings of apartments, rides, etc. To meet students go to Trinity's Cave in Mather Center, Trinity's Pub in the same place, and the Corner Tap Bar.
On the campus of the University of Hartford you can go to the Gengras Student Union to meet people—the campus is at 200 Bloomfield Ave. Or when you're hungry for a delicious, low-priced vegetarian meal, follow the advice of U of H students and head for Cheese and Stuff at 137 Sisson Ave. If you crave a hearty Italian meal, Pippie's at 682 Wethersfield Ave. is the place. Our U of H contact seems to think Hartford is "getting better and is becoming more than just a stopover between New York and Boston." You'll meet others who probably think the same thing at Mad Murphy's, 22 Union Pl., an excellent place to sit, talk, drink, and listen to good music. There's an upstairs and a downstairs—look at both and decide which best suits your mood. A newer spot in Hartford is the Congress Street Café at 7-9 Congress St. "Happy hour here could be rated as the best in the city!" Walk through the newly reborn downtown area around the Civic Center, and while you're there, stop for a drink at the lovely bar/restaurant called the Russian Lady.
Accommodations: YMCA, 160 Jewell St., 06103. Telephone: 203/522-4183. Men and women. $16 to $20. "One of the newest YMCAs in America. All rooms are carpeted and air-conditioned." Weekly rate: $87 to $105.
● YWCA, 135 Broad St., 06105. Telephone: 203/525-1163. Women only. $13 to $19 single; $8 per person quad. This is a new building with a kitchen and a laundry on each of the seven floors. Reservations necessary one or two weeks in advance. Two blocks from bus and train stations.
● Susse Chalet Inn, I-91 (Exit 27) on Brainard Rd., 06114. Telephone: 203/525-9306. $24.70 for one; $28.70 for two; $34.70 for four.

Lakeside

Accommodation: Bantam Lake Youth Hostel (AYH), East Shore Rd., 06758. Telephone: 203/567-9258. Open year round. $3.50 summer; $5 winter. Groups must make advance reservations. AYH membership required and may be purchased at hostel (see page 21). Five miles from bus stop, but if you call, someone might be available to pick you up. "Historic area of great natural beauty offering a variety of outdoor activities in all seasons."

Meriden

Help: Info Line, 203/235-7974.

Accommodations: YMCA, 110 West Main St., 06450. Telephone: 203/235-6386. Men and women. $10 single. Weekly rate: $28.50 to $30.50. Near bus and train.

● Best Value Home & Travel Motor Hotel, 1102 East Main St., 06450. Telephone: 203/634-4700. $20.50 for one; $23.75 for two in one bed; $28 for two in two beds.

Milford

Accommodation: Best Value Mayflower Motel, 219 Woodmount Rd., 06460. Telephone: 203/878-6854. $22 to $25 for one; $28 for two in one bed; $30 to $35 for two in two beds.

New Britain

Accommodation: YMCA, 50 High St., 06050. Two miles from Exit 35 off Hwy. 84, via Rte. 72 to Columbus Avenue exit. Telephone: 203/229-3787. Men only. $12 plus membership. Weekly rate: $35 plus membership. Two blocks from bus station.

New Haven

Help: Travelers Aid, 1 State St., 06511. Telephone: 203/787-3959.
● Info-Line, 203/624-4143.

Accommodations: Hotel Duncan, 🐟 ★, 1151 Chapel St., 06511. Telephone: 203/787-1273. Walking distance from bus and train. $16 to $23 single; $24 to $32 double; $50 to $75 weekly rate. Some rooms have hotplates.

● International Center Residence Halls, 406 Prospect St. 06511. Telephone: 203/787-3531 or 562-8896. Men and women. Summer only. Closed last two weeks in August. $7. (There may be room for one person to stay for a night or two during the academic year—call ahead to check.) "This was once a private home and is situated in an attractive residential area."

● YMCA, 🐟 ★ 20%, 52 Howe St., 06511. Telephone: 203/865-3161. Men and women. $20 single. Weekly rate: $41 to $46. Restaurant in building.

New London

Accommodation: Susse Chalet Motor Lodge, I-95 (Exit 74), 06357. Telephone: 203/739-6991. $19.70 for one; $23.70 for two; $29.70 for four.

Norwich

Accommodation: YMCA, 337 Main St., 06360. Telephone: 203/889-7349. Men only. $9 first night. Weekly rate: $39.

Southington

Accommodations: Sixpence Inn, 625 Queen St., 06489. Telephone: 203/621-7351. $13.95 to $15.95 for one; $15.95 to $17.95 for two.
● Susse Chalet Motor Lodge, I-84 (Exit 32). Telephone: 203/621-0181. See New London listing for rates.

Stamford

Help: Info-Line, 203/324-1010.
Accommodations: YMCA, 909 Washington Blvd., 06901. Telephone: 203/357-7000. Men and women 18 and over. Although the single rate is $22 in this high-rise facility with private baths, color TV, phones, and maid service, a double is $29.70, and the weekly rate is within our budget at $93.50. Reservations are necessary.

"Forget any story you may have heard before about other Ys—some facilities are suffering 'old age' symptoms but not here."

● YWCA, 422 Summer St., 06902. Telephone: 203/348-7727. One mile from bus and train. Women only, on a permanent basis; must be working or going to school in area. $26 to $36 per week.

Waterbury

Help: Source, 203/574-2944.
● Info-Line, 203/753-0171.
Accommodation: YMCA, 🐟 ★ 10%, 136 West Main St., 06702. Telephone: 203/754-2181. Men only. $10.50 to $12. Weekly rates: $38 to $47. One block from bus station, one-half mile from train.

Newark ● ● Wilmington
● New Castle

Delaware

It's a mini-state, and most of it either belongs or belonged to the Du Ponts, one of the world's richest families. In 1802, Eleuthere Du Pont built a powder mill on Brandywine Creek, and in the 150 years since, Delaware has, with the help of the Du Ponts, become the chemical capital of the world. Other corporations have been lured by the state's attractive incorporation and tax laws.

One of the nicest things the Du Ponts did for Delaware was to give it the Henry Francis Du Pont 100-room pied-à-terre in Winterthur. Now the Winterthur Museum contains a collection of American decorative arts from the 17th through the 19th centuries and is definitely worth seeing. Day-long tours are available by reservation only. Another tourist attraction in Delaware is also Du Pont-related. It's the Hagley Museum, an 185-acre complex where visitors are told the story of American industry from the Du Pont point of view. Admission is free and a jitney takes visitors from one exhibit to another.

Some Special Events: Spring Festival in Wilmington and Old Dover Days in Dover (May); Crafts Fair at Delaware Arts Museum in Wilmington (June); An Old Fashioned Fourth with fireworks on the boardwalk in Rehoboth (July); Arts Festival in Bethany (August); and Nanticoke Tribe Pow Wow, six miles east of Millsboro (September).

Hitching: Illegal on highways, and in Delaware "highway" means the road, the shoulders, and even beyond the shoulders. A friend from the University of Delaware says that people caught hitchhiking are generally fined from $10 to $100. This advice comes from a captain in the Delaware State Police: "If someone must travel through Delaware on foot, I would suggest that they solicit rides on private property such as restaurant parking lots, service stations, etc. This should be done only with the approval of the proprietor."

Tourist Information: Delaware State Travel Service, Division of Economic Development, Department of Community Affairs and Economic Development, 630 State College Rd., Dover, DE 19901.

New Castle

Accommodation: Superior Tremont Motel, 196 North DuPont Hwy., 19720. Telephone: 302/328-6211. $18 for one; $20 for two in one bed; $22 for two in two beds.

Newark

On Campus: This is where you'll find the University of Delaware. To meet the students, go to the Student Center Scrounge or to the international center at 52 West Delaware Ave. To get something inexpensive to eat, someone at the university suggests Jimmy's Diner or the Post House Restaurant, both on East Main St. A popular Sunday brunch spot is Klondike Kate's, also on East Main St. To meet students, try the Deer Park, the Stone Balloon, or the Glass Mug—all on (you guessed it) Main St. The Glass Mug also has nightly all-you-can-eat specials. According to someone on the staff at the U of D, the school is "a commuter institution, and consequently loses most of its students over the weekends when they go home."

Wilmington

Help: Travelers Aid, 809 Washington St., 19801. Telephone: 302/658-9885.

Accommodations: YWCA, 908 King St., 19801. Telephone: 302/658-7161. Women only. $8 or $9 single; $7 per person in a semiprivate room; $6 per person in a dorm with four beds. Reservations preferred one week in advance. Nine blocks from bus and train stations.

● YMCA, West 11th and Washington Sts., 19801. Telephone: 302/571-6900. Men only. $12.50 single. Weekly rate: $45. Reservations preferred.

● YMCA, 10th and Walnut Sts., 19801. Telephone: 302/571-6935. Men only. $6 single. Weekly rate: $25. Room for nine transients; reservations requested. Within walking distance of train and bus stations.

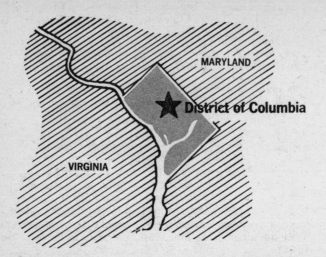

District of Columbia (Washington, D.C.)

Washington, D.C., is ready if you are. When you get there you'll want to stop by one of the information centers that are available to assist visitors to the capital district. They include the International Visitor Information Service, with offices at Dulles Airport and at 1825 H Street NW (tel. 872-8747), which provides 24-hour language assistance in over 50 languages; the Public Citizens Information Center, founded by Ralph Nader's Center for the Study of Responsive Law, at 215 Pennsylvania Ave. SE; Washington Area Convention and Visitors Bureau, 1575 I St. NW (tel. 789-7000); and the information Center for Handicapped Individuals, 120 C St. NW (tel. 347-4986).

Three guidebooks that you can buy in just about any bookstore are *Washington: The Official Bicentennial Guidebook,* edited by Nancy Love, Washingtonian Books ($3), which, although a bit dated by its title, is still useful as a general guide to things to do and see; *Washington, D.C., on $25 a Day,* by Beth Bryant, Frommer/Pasmantier Publishers ($6.25), a guide that you can depend on; and *The Walker Washington Guide,* by John and Katherine Walker, Guide Press ($4.95), a guide that includes maps and details on what to do and how to do it.

Getting There: Washington's National Airport is about five miles south of town. The best way to get from there to downtown is to take the Metro, an elevated train. The average fare is 60¢ during nonrush hours and 85¢ during rush hours (Metro fare is calculated according to distance). Taxi fare from the airport is about $4.50. The Greyhound Station is at 1110 New York Ave. (tel.

565-2662), and Trailways is across the street at 12th St. and New York Ave. NW (tel. 737-5800). The train station, Union Station, is at 50 Massachusetts Ave. NE (tel. 484-7540).

Getting Around: The best way to get from place to place is the new, quiet, and fast subway system or Metro. There's a hitch, though: Metro runs only from 6 a.m. to midnight on weekdays, 8 a.m. to midnight on Saturday, and 10 a.m. to 6 p.m. on Sunday. Trains run every five minutes during rush hours (6 to 9:30 a.m. and 3 to 6:30 p.m.); every ten minutes during nonrush hours. Fare is 60¢ during nonrush hours; during rush hours the fare depends on distance traveled. Many of the buses connect with the Metro—the fare on the bus is 60¢. You can call 637-2437 for bus and Metro information.

● Taxis charge by the zone for out-of-town service they charge $1.60 for the first mile and 90¢ for each additional mile. One Washingtonian advises: "When taking a cab, always establish the fare before you get in—otherwise it may double or triple by the time you get to where you're going—especially at night."

● If you're going to tour within the city, avoid using a car. If you do bring your car, you'll just end up buying it back from the parking lot at the end of the day. The most popular sites are close together and the subway, bus, and tourmobiles are inexpensive and uncomplicated. The tourmobiles stop at 17 sites, and tourists are able to get on and off wherever they want, as often as they want. Fares are $5 for adults and $3 for children for a full-day ticket, 9:30 a.m. to 4:30 p.m. For touring outside the center city area, you might consider renting a car from Hertz (tel. toll free 800/654-3131), Budget Rent-A-Car (tel. 628-2750), or Avis (tel. toll free 800/331-1212).

Accommodations: Since so many people visit Washington and need a place to stay, there's an organization that specializes in helping them do just that: it is Women's Information Center, 3918 W St. NW, 20007. Telephone: 202/333-9696. The staff there finds housing especially for women and foreign visitors. "We have information on both short- and long-term housing—bed and breakfast, houses, rooms, apartments, etc. We also have information on jobs, rides, and local organizations."

● Washington International Hostel, 1332 I St. NW, 20005. Telephone: 202/347-3125. One block west of bus stations. On Metro rail line from train station and airport, hostel is one-half block east of 14th St. exit of the McPherson Square Station. Within walking distance of the White House, shopping and theater districts, and the Smithsonian Institution. Dormitory rooms have from four to eight beds per room (some bunk beds). The overnight rate is $6.70 per night for AYH members; $10.05 plus $1 introductory fee for nonmembers. There's a dining room and cooking facilities, too. *"One of the best hostels I've seen in the whole U.S.A."*

● Franklin Park Hotel, 1332 I St. NW, 20005. Telephone: 202/347-3125. This is the same hotel that houses the Washington International Hostel above. Single rooms are $29.40; doubles $40.40; and triples $53.60. All rooms are comfortable and air-conditioned.

● International Student House, 1825 R St. NW, 20009. Telephone: 202/232-4007. Students only. Very few vacancies, but worth a try. $335 to $440 single per month; $325 to $370 double per month. All rates include breakfast and dinner. Reservations requested. This is a grand mansion built in 1912 with a dormitory wing built in 1969. It is primarily for long-term graduate students, but transients planning to stay at least a week are welcome if there's room. Weekly rates are $115 to $130 per week single; $105 to $125 per week double.

● YWCA, 901 Rhode Island Ave. NW, 20001. Telephone: 202/667-9100. Women only. $20 single. Reservations are advisable.

● Catholic University Dormitory. Contact: Director of Housing. Telephone: 202/269-6740. Students and faculty only. Open mid-May to August. Men and women. $20 single; $16 per person double. Air-conditioned, dining room on-campus.

● Presidential Hotel, 900 19th St. NW, 20006. Telephone: 202/331-9020. Three blocks from the White House. $25 single; $32 double.

● Bed & Breakfast Ltd. of Washington D.C., 1307 Rhode Island Ave. NW, 20005. Telephone 202/232-9150. Thirteen historic homes provide bed and breakfast. Prices range from $15 to $35 for a single; $25 to $60 for a double.

● Connecticut-Woodley Tourist Home, 2647 Woodley Rd. NW, 20008. Telephone: 202/667-0218. Two miles from bus; three miles from train. $14 to $25 single; $18.50 to $29 twin. "Large old house converted into a tourist home."

● Howard Johnson Hotel at Washington National Airport, 2650 Jefferson Davis Hwy., Arlington, VA 22202. Telephone: 703/684-7200. The regular rates are too high for us ($58 single) but there's a special weekend rate (Friday to Sunday) of $32 for a room for one to four people. If you're traveling with three other friends, this would mean only $8 per person.

● The "2005" Guest House, 🐟 ★ 10%, 2005 Columbia Rd. NW, 20009. Telephone: 202/265-4006. $12 to $17 single; $18 to $30 double. AYH members pay $6.75 for dorm-style accommodations. One-half block from Hilton, "a large patrician mansion."

● Hawthorne Hotel, 🐟 ★ 20%, 2134 G St. NW, 20037. Telephone: 202/338-7810. Foggy Bottom stop on Metro is three blocks from hotel. $20 single; $29.50 double. Near George Washington University and six blocks from the White House.

● 1440 Hotel, 🐟 ★ 20%, 1440 Rhode Island Ave. NW, 20005. Telephone: 202/232-7800. Farragut Metro Station is three blocks from hotel. $20 single; $29.50 double.

● Columbia House, 🐟 ★ 20%, 800 E St. NE, 20002. Telephone: 202/543-8800. Within walking distance of the congressional offices, monuments, and galleries. $20 single; $29.50 double. Rooms are without private bath.

● International Guest House, 1441 Kennedy St. NW, 20011. Telephone: 202/726-5808. Steps away from the bus station. $11 per person. Internationals are preferred, but anyone including children can be accommodated. "A home away from home for traveling internationals."

Where to Eat: Scholl's Cafeteria, 1990 K St. NW, or 1433 K St. NW. These cafeterias are open every day of the week and offer a wide variety of food, large portions, and moderate prices.

● Golden Eagle Restaurant, 1411 I St. NW. You can have dinner here for under $5. Open for breakfast, lunch, and dinner, Wednesday to Sunday only.

● Holloway House Cafeteria, 14th St. and New York Ave. NW. The service is fast and pleasant and the food is inexpensive.

● Patent Pending, in courtyard between National Collection of Fine Arts (8th and G Sts. NW) and the National Portrait Gallery (7th and F Sts. NW). Perfectly located if you're sightseeing around the Mall. This cafeteria offers an interesting menu including courtyard salad, nitrite-free hot dogs made interesting, and big bowls of soup. You can eat outdoors or in. Open every day for lunch.

- Kramerbooks and Afterwards, 1517 Connecticut Ave. NW. Telephone: 387-1400. Just north of Dupont Circle. Popular indoor/outdoor café with an adjoining bookstore. Croissants for breakfast, quiches and salads for dinner.
- Tucson Cantina, 2605 Connecticut Ave. NW. Telephone: 462-6410. Near the National Zoo. The food is Mexican via the Southwest—tacos, burritos, enchiladas. Service is fast and entrees are $3.50 or under.
- The Dubliner, 4 F St. NW, directly across from Union Station. Telephone: 737-3773. Irish-American food; conveniently located near Capitol Hill, Irish traditional music live every night with no cover charged.
- Steak and Eggs Kitchen, 4700 Wisconsin Ave. NW. About two miles from Georgetown. A small diner open 24 hours and busiest between 2 and 5 a.m. A mammoth breakfast of three eggs, bacon, toast, hash browns, juice, and coffee is only $3.19.
- The Booeymonger, 5250 Wisconsin Ave. NW. Telephone: 686-5805. Indoor and outdoor seating attracts a young crowd who like the salads and sandwiches like "The Exorcist," roast beef "possessed" by bleu cheese with sprouts on french bread, $3.25. Open 24 hours.
- The Tune Inn, 331½ Pennsylvania Ave. SE. Telephone: 543-2725. On a popular strip; filled with people who work on Capitol Hill. Burgers and fries. A pitcher of beer is $3.25.
- The Omega, 1856–58 Columbia Rd. NW. Telephone: 462-1732. Spanish food very close to Dupont Circle. "Lots of food for your money."
- Universal Cafeteria, 1834 Connecticut Ave. NW. Telephone: 234-2502. A large cafeteria right in the Dupont Circle area with complete meals for about $5.
- Columbia Station, 1836 Columbia Rd. NW. Telephone: 667-2900. Bar/restaurant with outdoor seating, too. Food (hamburger with fries, $3.25; pita stuffed with lamb and chutney, $3.45) and music every night.

What to See: For an up-to-the-minute guide to what's going on, check the Amusement Section of the *Sunday Washington Post*, the monthly *Washingtonian* magazine, and radio station Q 107 FM.

- The Mall and its Museums: From the Capitol to the Washington Monument lies the National Mall, laid out in 1791. All along the Mall are buildings that you'll want to visit. Seven of these are Smithsonian Institution Museums, including the Freer Gallery of Art, Arts and Industries Building, the Hirshhorn Museum and Sculpture Garden (20th-century art indoors and sculpture outdoors), the National Museum of History and Technology, the National Museum of Natural History, the Smithsonian Institution Building (where the Visitors Information Center is located), the National Gallery of Art, and the new, extraordinarily popular National Air and Space Museum. At the National Air and Space Museum you can trace the history of flight as you look at the Wright Flyer, Lindbergh's *Spirit of St. Louis*, John Glenn's Mercury Capsule, Gemini 4, the Apollo 11 command module *Columbia*, and finally, a moonrock. The Albert Einstein Spacearium on the second floor presents sky and space spectaculars. For information on the Smithsonian Institution buildings, hours, exhibits, etc., call 381-6270.
- National Portrait Gallery (7th and F Sts. NW). Life portraits of "men and women who have made significant contributions to the history, development, and culture of the people in the United States." Is yours there? This is a Smithsonian Institution, and although it's not in the Mall, it's not far away at all.

● National Collection of Fine Arts (8th and G Sts. NW). Another Smith-sonian Institution, right across from the Portrait Gallery, which contains a panorama of American painting, graphic art, and sculpture from the 18th century to now.

● The U.S. Capitol, Capitol Hill. Of all the buildings in Washington, this most symbolizes the federal government. You can visit the House and Senate galleries with passes that can be obtained from your representative or senator. There are tours every day starting from the Rotunda from 9 a.m. to 3:45 p.m. Call 224-3121 for information.

● U.S. Supreme Court, 1st St. and Maryland Ave. NE. Tours of the highest court in the land are conducted from 9:30 a.m. to 4 p.m. Call 252-3211.

● Washington Monument, Constitution Ave. at 15th St. NW. You can take an elevator up (10¢ if you're over 16) and enjoy the view from 9 a.m. to 5 p.m. every day. Call 426-6841.

● The White House, 1600 Pennsylvania Ave. NW. Nancy and Ron would like you to come and see their home. Tours are conducted from 10 a.m. to noon, Tuesday to Saturday. If there's an official function on the day you want to go and you haven't received a personal invitation, you won't be able to take the tour.

● Lincoln Memorial, foot of 23rd St. NW. A very moving tribute to Lincoln and worth a quiet visit.

● Federal Buildings: Just about every government agency offers a tour of its premises. Some possibilities are: Bureau of Engraving and Printing (tel. 566-2000), Federal Bureau of Investigation (tel. 324-3447), Department of State (tel. 632-3241).

● Dumbarton Oaks and Gardens, 1703 32nd St. NW. Telephone: 342-3200. The house is headquarters for the Colonial Dames of America. Adjacent to it you can enjoy 16 acres of beautiful gardens with terraces and reflecting pools.

● Washington National Zoo, 3000 Connecticut Ave. Telephone: 381-7300. Easily reached by buses L-2, L-4, and L-6. The stars of the zoo are the two giant pandas. The zoo is divided into six trails that are well marked and easy to follow.

● Beyond Washington: Two recommended day trips are to Annapolis (40 minutes away), a charming small town that's the home of the U.S. Naval Academy, and to Harpers Ferry in West Virginia (about 1½ hours away), a national historic park with a visitors' center that explains the history of the community and John Brown's raid and capture here in 1859. Visitors can explore the park grounds and even do a bit of mountain climbing.

At Night: Kennedy Center, New Hampshire Ave. at F St. NW. This is where you can see a play, enjoy a concert, listen to opera, see a dance perfor-mance, or watch a film. For information on what is going on at the Eisenhower Theater, the Opera House, the Concert Hall, the American Film Institute, or the Terrace Theater, call 202/872-0466. Student discounts are available at times.

● Blues Alley, 1073 Wisconsin Ave. NW. Telephone: 337-4141. This restau-rant/nightclub presents big-name and local jazz performers and serves New Orleans—style food.

● Pier 9, 1824 Half St. SW. Telephone: 488-1205. There's room for 700 people to dance to a disco beat. Minimum every night; closed Monday.

● Déjà Vu, 2119 M St. NW. No cover or minimum. Enormous stained-glass windows, palm trees, and working fireplaces set the scene of this very colorful dance hall/bar that's always busy. Every night there's bopping (remember that?) to the tunes of the '50s and '60s. You can let loose on the dance floor or go to one of the quieter adjoining rooms. No food is served and the drinks are reasonable.

● Biograph Theater, 2819 M St. NW. $3 will buy you a double feature of either a golden oldie or a more recent classic; film festivals, celebrity actors, directors, countries, etc. are featured periodically.

● One Step Down, 2517 Pennsylvania Ave. NW. Telephone: 331-8863. Big-name jazz bands in a small, smoky, and crowded atmosphere. Cover charge on weekends can go as high as $6; during the week it may be only $1.50 on some nights.

● Pier Street Annex, 1210 19th St. NW. Telephone: 466-4040. Enormous dance hall with disco and rock. Drinks served outdoors. "Attracts all kinds."

● Gallagher's Pub, 3319 Connecticut Ave. NW. Telephone: 686-9189. A large pub that serves great hamburgers and often features folk and country music.

Shopping: National Book Store, Union Station, 50 Massachusetts Ave. NE. A store devoted to books that cover the various aspects of American life—history books, guidebooks, etc.

● Discount Records and Books, 1340 Connecticut Ave. NW. A popular place—the name tells you why.

● Crown Books, 1710 G St. NW, and 2020 K St. NW. General selection of books at a hefty discount.

● International Learning Center, 1715 Connecticut Ave. NW. The stock includes international cookbooks, travel guides to the U.S., and dictionaries in 100 languages.

● Record and Tape Limited, 19th and L Sts. NW, or 1239 Wisconsin Ave. NW. Everything at a discount.

● Serenade Record Shop, 1710 Pennsylvania Ave. NW, and 1800 M St. NW. Jazz, popular, classical, rock, and soul at a discount.

● Gary's Discount Records, 1445 K St. NW. All kinds of records and tapes discounted.

● Garfinckels, 1401 F St. NW. Washington's best known department store —with a nice selection of gifts if you don't have to worry too much about prices.

● Mandy TH, 1118 19th St. NW. Women's clothes at a discount.

● Hudson Bay Outfitters, 4437 Wisconsin Ave. NW. Sleeping bags, clothing, and other outdoor gear.

● Georgetown. The whole area—an eight-square-block area with hub at Wisconsin Ave. and M St. NW—teems with galleries, specialty shops, boutiques, and eateries.

Help: Travelers Aid, 1015 12th St. NW, 20005. Telephone: 202/347-0101; and Washington National Airport, 202/684-3472.

● International Visitors Information Service, 1825 H St. NW. Telephone: 202/872-8747. Language assistance in over 50 languages is available 24 hours a day.

Florida

Florida means vacation for most people. When the winter winds blow up north, down they all come. The biggest tourist attraction in all of Florida is Disney World, about 20 miles south of Orlando. Everyone seems to agree that the place is a lot of fun. One friend's favorite Florida sight is the Stephen Foster Memorial on the Suwannee River (near White Springs), which is a sight in itself with its oak-lined banks and Spanish moss.

There are lots of sea attractions in Florida, like Sea World in central Florida, Marineland in St. Augustine, and the Seaquarium in Miami. A real must-see, if you can stand the traffic, is Miami Beach with its famous hotel row where each hotel vies with the next for splendor.

The farthest point south in the U.S. is Key West, with the Atlantic on one side and the Gulf of Mexico on the other. Here you can still see men practicing the old art of shelling conch.

If you're attracted by state capitals, then you'll want to visit Tallahassee. But one city that you really should try to include in your plans is St. Augustine, just 50 miles south of the Georgia-Florida line. This was the first place in the U.S. settled by the Spaniards in the 1500s and its original fort still stands. Tampa still has an Hispanic flavor.

The southern portion of Florida, from the Keys to the Broward County area, has become home for many who have left Castro's Cuba. Many sections of Miami are called Little Cuba, 20 years after the first exodus. Southern Florida is still home to many natives, but in the last 30 years many northerners have relocated to take advantage of the climate. Central and northern Florida are still mostly "home-grown" people, but they too are being "colonized" by people who can't stand the northern winters.

Some Special Events: Orange Bowl in Miami (January, on New Year's night); Seafood Festival in Grant (February); Old Island Days in Key West (February to March); Frontier Days in Orange City and Ponce de Leon Festival in Port Charlotte (March); Rodeo in Palatka and Catfish Festival in Crescent City (April); Billy Bowlegs Festival (Billy Bowlegs was a pirate) in Fort Walton Beach (May); Sea Turtle Watch in Jensen Beach (June); Everglades Outdoor Music Festival (the annual festival of the Miccosukee Tribe) in Miami (July); Fun Day and Possum Festival in Wausau (August); International Worm Fiddling Contest (who can create the best vibration on a wooden stake to bring up the most worms) in Caryville and Seafood Festival in Pensacola (September); and Hispanic Heritage Week in Dade County (October).

Hitching: According to the Florida Highway Patrol, hitchhiking is legal in Florida, except on Interstates or turnpikes or when a specific prohibition is posted. In practice, it seems, from the reactions we got from people at several of the colleges in Florida, that the attitude toward hitchhiking in the state is conservative and that Floridians are hesitant to pick up hitchhikers. When we asked about the general attitude toward young people "on the road" in the Miami area, we got two opposite views. One person said it was good: "Miami is heavily populated with tourists so young people visiting Miami or surrounding areas are not considered unusual." The other person said the attitude was discouraging: "This is a tourist-industry economy and flocks of students are considered disruptive." It must be all in the way you look at it.

Tourist Information: Division of Tourism, Florida Department of Commerce, 107 West Gaines St., Suite 410-D, Tallahassee, FL 32301. Telephone: 904/488-8230.

Boca Raton

Help: Crisis Line, 305/272-1121.

Accommodation: College of Boca Raton, Military Trail, 33431. Three miles from beach. Telephone: 305/994-0770. For groups of ten or more. December 15 to January 30 and May 15 to August 30. $18.50 single, with three meals included.

Bradenton

Accommodation: Superior Plaza Motel, 4410 14th St. West (U.S. 41), 33507. Telephone: 813/755-9032. $18 to $25 for one or two in one bed; $22 to $35 for two in two beds.

Brooksville

Accommodation: Days Inn, I-75 and Fla. 50, Rte. 3, P.O. Box 430, 35512. Telephone: 904/796-9486. $17.88 to $22.88 for one; $21.88 to $26.88 for two.

Chattahoochee

Accommodation: Superior Morgan Motel, U.S. 90 East, 32324. Telephone: 904/663-4336. $15 to $18 for one; $18 to $20 for two in one bed; $19 to $22 for two in two beds.

Cocoa Beach

Accommodations: Motel 6, 3701 North Atlantic Ave., 32931. Telephone: 305/783-0890. $12.95 for one; $16.95 for two; $19.95 for up to four. Fifteen minutes from Kennedy Space Center.

● Econo-Travel Motor Hotel, ♿, 5500 North Atlantic Ave., 32931. Telephone: 305/784-2550. $16 to $18 for one; $20 to $22 for two in one bed; $23 to $25 for two to four in two beds.

● Days Inn, I-95 and Fla. 524, P.O. Box 1418, 32922. Telephone: 305/636-2580. $22.88 to $25.88 for one; $26.88 to $29.88 for two.

Crestview

Accommodation: Scottish Inn, 564 U.S. 90 West, 32536. Telephone: 904/682-3832. $18 for one; $22 for two in one bed; $24 for two in two beds.

Dania

Accommodation: Motel 6, north side of Dania Beach Blvd; 200 feet east of Gulfstream Rd. (Northeast Seventh Ave.), 33004. See Cocoa Beach listing for rates.

Davenport

Accommodation: Susse Chalet Motor Lodge, I-4 and U.S. 27, 33837. Telephone: 813/424-2521. $19.70 for one; $25.70 for two to four.

Daytona

Accommodation: Friendship Inn–Granada Royale, I-95 and U.S. 1, 32074. Telephone: 904/672-7341. $19 for one; $24 for two. Rates higher March to May.

Daytona Beach

Help: Travelers Aid of Daytona Beach (Volusia County), 1050 North Beach St., 32017. Telephone: 904/252-4752.

Tourist Information: Convention and Tourism Department, Daytona Beach Area Chamber of Commerce, City Island, 32015. Telephone: 904/255-0981.

Accommodations: Days Inn, I-95 and U.S. 92, 32015. Telephone: 904/255-0541. $21.88 to $23.88 for one; $25.88 to $27.88 for two.

● Econo-Travel Motor Hotel, 2250 Volusia Ave., 32014. Telephone: 904/255-3661. $16 for one; $19 for two in one bed; $22 for two in two beds.

● Econo Lodge, 1220 North Atlantic Ave., 32018. Telephone: 904/252-3681. $9.95 to $19.95 for one; $11.95 to $23.95 for two in one bed; $17.95 to $27.95 for two in two beds.

● Best Value Rip Van Winkle Motel, 1025 North Atlantic Ave., 32018. Telephone: 904/252-6213. $10 to $18 for one; $12 to $20 for two in one bed; $14 to $22 for two in two beds.

Deerfield Beach

Accommodation: Days Inn, 1250 West Hillsboro Blvd., 33441. Telephone: 305/427-2200. $22 to $24 for one; $26 to $28 for two. Rates higher December 15 to April 30.

DeLand

On Campus: At Stetson University, your first stop, if you want help finding your way around, is the Carlton Union. Stetson students should be easy to meet at the Commons.

Englewood

Accommodation: Days Inn, 🔥, 2540 South McCall Rd., 33533. Telephone: 813/474-5544. $21.88 for one; $24.88 for two. Rates higher December to April.

Fort Lauderdale

Accommodation: Motel 6, 1801 State Rd. 84, 33315. Telephone: 305/525-1363. See Cocoa Beach listing for rates.

Fort Myers

Accommodations: Days Inn, 🔥, 1099 U.S. 41 North, Cleveland Ave., 33903. Telephone: 813/995-0535. $23.88 for one; $27.88 for two. Rates higher December 16 to April 30.
● Days Inn, 🔥, 5499 Cleveland Ave., 33907. Telephone: 813/936-1311. $21.88 for one; $25.88 for two. Rates higher December 15 to April 26.
● Sea Chest Motel, 2571 1st St. (Rte. 80), 33901. Telephone: 813/332-1545. $20 for two in one bed; $25 for two in two beds. Rates higher December 15 to April 15.
● Superior Le Mar Motel, 3511 Cleveland Ave. (U.S. 41), 33901. Telephone: 813/936-1959. $14 to $23 for one; $16 to $25 for two in one bed; $18 to $45 for two in two beds.
● Econo-Travel Motor Hotel, 1089 U.S. 41, 33903. Telephone: 813/995-0571. $17.95 to $24.95 for one; $19.95 to $28.95 for two in one bed; $22.95 to $31.95 for two in two beds.

Fort Walton Beach

Accommodations: Econo-Travel Motor Hotel, 100 Miracle Strip Pkwy. SW, 32548. Telephone: 904/244-0121. $17.95 to $24.95 for one; $19.95 to $26.95 for two in one bed; $22.95 to $29.95 for two to four in two beds.
● Days Inn, U.S. 98 West, 135 Miracle Strip Pkwy., 32548. Telephone: 904/244-6184. $21.88 to $23.88 for one; $25.88 to $27.88 for two. Rates higher May 22 to September 7.

136 WHERE TO STAY USA

Gainesville

On Campus: The University of Florida is in Gainesville, and according to one student, "there are so many students in Gainesville that strangers will blend right in." For food, go to the Copper Monkey, the Olde College Inn, Orient Express, or Knife and Fork. At night, try Richenbacher's for jazz, XTC for rock n' roll at the Great Southern Music Hall, and Spectrum Disco for dancing. The J. Wayne Reitz Union on the U. of Florida campus has a ride board on the ground floor and cheap movies are shown on the second floor. Buses in town are a bargain at 25¢. The student newspaper *Independent Florida Alligator* is distributed all over town free, and the Corner Drug Store has leads on places to stay.

Accommodations: Econo-Travel Motor Hotel, 2649 SW 13th St., 32608. Telephone: 904/373-7816. $19.95 for one; $21.95 for two in one bed; $23.95 for two in two beds.

● Econo-Travel Motor Hotel, 700 NW 75th St., 32601. Telephone: 904/378-2346. $19.95 for one; $23.95 for two in one bed; $27.95 for two in two beds.

Gulf Breeze

Camping: Gulf Islands National Seashore, Fort Pickens Area, P.O. Box 100, 32561. Campground with 165 sites open all year. $4 per campsite per night.

Homestead

Camping: Everglades National Park, P.O. Box 279, 33030. There are 29 backcountry campgrounds and two regular campgrounds (Long Pine Key and Flamingo) with a total of over 300 sites. Backcountry campgrounds are accessible by boat only, and a permit is required for their use. $2 to $3 per campsite per night.

● Biscayne National Monument, P.O. Box 1369, 33030. Camping all year at Elliott Key. Access by boat only.

Jacksonville

Tourist Information: Convention and Visitors Bureau of Jacksonville and Jacksonville Beaches, 206 Hogan St., 32202. Telephone: 904/353-9736.

Help: Travelers Aid, 217 West Church St., 32202. Telephone: 904/356-0249.

● Central Crisis Center, 904/384-2234.

Accommodations: YWCA, 325 East Duval St., 32202. Telephone: 904/354-6681. Women and up to two children (boys up to age 8). $9.50 to $11.50 single; $7.50 per person double. 50¢ per night extra for nonmembers.

● Econo Lodge, 5018 University Blvd. West, 32216. Telephone: 904/731-0800. $19 for one; $21 for two in one bed; $24 for two in two beds.

● Econo-Travel Motor Hotel, 6560 Ramona Blvd., 32205. Telephone: 904/786-2794. $17.95 for one; $21.95 for two in one bed; $25.95 for two in two beds.

● Days Inn, 1153 Airport Rd., 32229. Telephone: 904/757-5000. $20.88 to $22.88 for one; $24.88 to $26.88 for two.

- Days Inn, 🔲, 5929 Ramona Blvd., 32205. Telephone: 904/786-6600. $23.88 for one; $28.88 for two. Ask about special rates some weeks.
- Days Inn, 5649 Cagle Rd., 32216. Telephone: 904/733-3890. $20.88 to $22.88 for one; $24.88 to $26.88 for two.
- Superior Stevens Motel, Rte. 1, Box 714, Yulee, 32097. Telephone: 904/225-5166 or 225-5538. $15 for one; $18 for two in one bed; $20 for two in two beds.
- Scottish Inn, Arlington Rd. and U.S. Alt. 90, 32211. Telephone: 904/725-9600. $19 for one; $22 for two.
- Scottish Inn, I-10 at Lane Ave. Exit, 460 South Lane Ave., 32205. Telephone: 904/786-7550. $19 for one; $21 for two.

Kissimmee

Accommodation: Days Inn, 2095 East Spacecoast Pkwy., 32741. Telephone: 305/846-7136. $20.88 for one, September 8 to December 15; $23.88 for one, January 4 to May 31. Rates higher at other times.

Lake City

Accommodations: Days Inn, I-75 and U.S. 90, P.O. Box 1300, 32055. Telephone: 904/752-9350. $17.88 to $19.88 for one; $21.88 to $23.88 for two.
- Scottish Inn, I-75 and Fla. 47, 32055. Telephone: 904/752-6450. $15.88 for one; $18.88 for two.
- Econo Lodge, U.S. 90 West at I-75 Interchange, P.O. Box 1238, 32055. Telephone: 904/752-7550. $14.95 for one; $16.95 for two in one bed; $19.95 for two in two beds.

Lake Wales

Accommodations: Econo-Travel Motor Hotel, Hwy. 27 and Rte. 60, P.O. Box 1637, 33853. Telephone: 813/676-7963. $16.50 for one; $19.50 for two in one bed; $22.50 for two to four in two beds.
- Superior Emerald Motel, 530 South Scenic Hwy., 33853. Telephone: 813/676-3310. $15 to $22.50 for one; $18 to $24 for two.

Lake Worth

Help: Crisis Line Information and Referral Service, 305/588-1121.

"Population comprised mostly of elderly people."

Lakeland

Accommodation: Days Inn, I-4 and U.S. 98, 3223 U.S. 98, 33805. Telephone: 813/688-6031. $23 to $25 for one; $27 to $29 for two. Rates higher December 15 to April 30.

Marianna

Accommodation: Best Value Motel Sandusky, U.S. 90 West, 32446. Telephone: 904/482-4973. $16 for one; $18 for two in one bed; $20 for two in two beds.

Melbourne

Accommodations: Days Inn, 🔾, I-95 and U.S. 192, 10909 New Haven Ave., 32901. Telephone: 305/724-5840. $22.88 for one; $26.88 for two. Rates slightly higher January 15 to April 26.
● Econo-Travel Motor Hotel, 4505 West New Haven Ave., 32901. Telephone: 305/724-5450. $21.50 to $24.50 for one; $24.50 to $27.50 for two in one bed; $25.50 to $30.50 for two in two beds.

Miami/Miami Beach

Sixty years ago this was swampland but now it's high-rise hotel land. People flock to Miami every winter for the sun and the ocean and many have decided to stay, so the Miami area is full of transplants from other, more northerly spots. Because Miami is such a popular resort area, prices can be high. If you want to keep your expenses down, keep in mind this advice from the Miami Beach Visitor and Convention Authority: "Hotels and restaurants in the southern end of Miami Beach are the least expensive—that is, from Lincoln Road south." When to visit? One friend writes: "In September the hotels are empty and the rates are still low; later on it's too crowded and earlier it's too hot." To know what's going on in Miami, check with *Miami Magazine* or contact the Miami Beach Visitor and Convention Authority, 555 17th St., 33139. Telephone: 305/673-7080.

Getting There: Miami International Airport is five miles northwest of the city. A taxi ride from the airport will cost about $9, but you can take a bus—the #20 Miami or #3 East—and it will cost only 75¢. The bus station is at 300 NW 32nd Ave. in Miami (tel. 638-6700).

Getting Around: Taxi fares start at $1, and 50¢ is added for every half mile. The bus fare is 75¢, with a discount for senior citizens between 9 a.m. and 4 p.m. and after 6 p.m. Bus information is available by calling 638-6700. To rent a car, you might try Alamo Rent-A-Car, 1490 Northwest Lejeune Rd. (tel. 526-6510 or 871-3710). An air-conditioned Chevy Scooter will cost $69 per week or $276 per month—with unlimited mileage as long as you stay in Florida.

Accommodations: Haddon Hall Hotel, ★ (AYH-SA), 1500 Collins Ave., 33139. In Miami's art deco area, one block from Greyhound station. Telephone: 305/531-1251. Men, women, and children. From May 1 to July 1 and from September 1 to November 15: $15 to $20 single or double; from July 1 to September 1: $15 to $18 single; $18 to $25 double. Higher rates in winter. Rooms have refrigerators, sinks, and cooking facilities. "We have our own Olympic-size pool and are a block from the ocean. We're in the heart of Miami Beach." Air-conditioned and free parking. The above rates are special for *Where to Stay* readers. Ask about AYH rates.
● Alamo Hotel Apartments, 4121 Indian Creek Dr., Miami Beach, 33140.

"One block from the Fontainebleau." Telephone: 305/531-8462. $18 single; $26 double. Rates higher in winter. Ocean bathing one block away. A small, family-oriented type of place.

● Best Value Clevelander Hotel, 1020 Ocean Dr., Miami Beach, 33139. Telephone: 305/531-3485. $13 to $24 for one; $15 to $26 for two in one bed; $15 to $26 for two in two beds.

● Hotel Netherland, 1330 Ocean Dr., Miami Beach, 33139. Telephone: 305/534-4791. Summer: $12 to $18 single; $13 to $20 double. In winter the rates are $15 to $39 single; $17 to $39 double.

"A very friendly and helpful staff. I traveled in America for five months and the Netherland may be the best value in the whole country!"

● Miramar Hotel and Apartments, 1744 North Bayshore Dr., 33132. Telephone: 305/379-1865. Seven blocks from bus, ten miles from train station. $16 single; $20 double; $24 triple. Higher in winter.

● Winterhaven Hotel, 1400 Ocean Dr., 33139. Telephone: 305/531-5571. $15 to $25 single. Rooms face the ocean and have kitchenettes. Recommended by a reader who said the management was "very friendly."

● Willard Garden Hotel, 124 NE 14th St., 33132. Telephone: 305/394-9112 or 374-5115. $15.50 to $22.50 single; $18.50 to $33.50 double. Weekly rates are lower. "We deliver comfortable, hospital-clean bed and bath facilities. Quiet and uniquely secure lodging." A photo ID is required at the door.

Where to Eat: Bananas, 3500 Main Hwy., Coconut Grove (near the playhouse). Telephone: 446-4652. Twenty kinds of hamburgers, with a happy hour on Friday from 3 p.m. on. Lots of students.

● Steak and Burger, 1150 South Dixie Hwy., Coral Gables. Telephone: 446-9461. Small café that's so relaxed they won't mind if you go in your shorts and bare feet.

● D'Pizza of U.M., 1118 South Dixie Hwy., Coral Gables, near University of Miami. Telephone: 666-5841. What you'd expect—pizza, lasagne, pasta, plus a popular Italian fish soup.

● Bagel Emporium, 1238 South Dixie Hwy., Coral Gables, across from University of Miami. Telephone: 666-9516. Nine varieties of the popular little roll with the hole in the middle.

● Canton of Westchester, 2501 SW 87th Ave., near Dadeland Shopping Center. Telephone: 552-5292. Lunch from $2 to $2.80; full dinner from $3.75 to $5.35.

● Uncle Tom's Cabin Barbecue, SW 8th St. and 40th Ave. Telephone: 446-9528. Relaxing, old-style western setting. $3.75 to $5.25 for a meal consisting of barbecued chicken, ribs, or pork with cole slaw and bread.

What to See: You'll probably want to stay horizontal on the sand for most of your stay, but if the weather is bad or you get tired of sun and sand, there are lots of tourist attractions in the area. These include the Miami Seaquarium, a 60-acre aquatic park on Rickenbacker Causeway in Biscayne Bay with performing whales. Call 361-5703 for information.

● Monkey Jungle, 14805 SW 216th St. Telephone: 235-1611. Gorillas, orangutans, and chimpanzees doing what they do in the open while the visitors watch from enclosed walkways. Performing chimps, besides.

● Villa Vizcaya, 3251 South Miami Ave. Telephone: 579-2708. This 70-room Italian-style extravaganza was once the home of industrialist James

Deering and is now the property of the Dade County Art Museum. Inside the villa you'll see rugs, tapestries, and sculpture, and outside you can walk through formal gardens.

At Night: The big hotels have shows at night—big-name stars and some not-so-big-name stars. Check *Miami Magazine* to see who's where while you're in town. Some other possibilities:

● Bananas, 3500 Main Hwy. Telephone: 446-4652. Live jazz in a dark, relaxed bar-restaurant combination.

● Flamenco, 991 NE 79th St. Telephone: 751-8631. Two shows every night and dancing. A $3 minimum.

● Dade County Auditorium, 2901 West Flagler St. Telephone: 547-5414. This is the heart of Miami's cultural life—call to see whether there's a concert, a play, or a dance company booked into this popular theater and whether there are any tickets left.

Shopping: The Grove Book Worm, 3025 Fuller St. Telephone: 443-6411. All hard- and softcover books.

● Star Ship Enterprises, 1788 NE 163rd St., North Miami Beach. Telephone: 940-9539. Everything for the sci-fi nut—books, magazines, and posters.

● Spec's Music Shop, Dadeland Mall, 7535 North Kendall Dr. Telephone: 666-5941. Records galore.

Help: Travelers Aid, United Family and Children Services, 2190 NW 7th St., 33125. Telephone: 305/643-5700. Or West Dade office, 9370 Sunset Dr., 33173 (tel. 305/279-3322), or South Dade office, 18861 South Dixie Hwy., 33157 (tel. 305/232-1610). "We offer casework services to people who have been in Dade County less than six weeks."

Someone at Travelers Aid mentioned that the area around the bus terminals is hazardous, although the neighborhood improves rapidly within a few blocks.

Micanopy

Accommodation: Days Inn, I-75 and Fla. 329, Rte. 2, Box 804, 32667. Telephone: 904/466-3152. $17.88 to $18.88 for one; $21.88 to $22.88 for two.

Naples

Accommodation: Days Inn, 🔄, U.S. 41 and Fla. 84, Alligator Alley, 1925 Davis Blvd., 33942. Telephone: 813/774-3117. $19.99 for one; $23.99 for two. Rates higher December 15 to May 31.

North Palm Beach

Accommodation: Econo-Travel Motor Hotel, 757 U.S. 1, 33408. Telephone: 305/848-1424. $19.95 to $24.95 for one; $21.95 to $31.95 for two in one bed; $23.95 to $34.95 for two to four in two beds.

North Port

Accommodation: North Port Motor Inn, 200 Bolander Terrace, 33596. Telephone: 813/426-2606. $16 to $25 for one; $19 to $28 for two in one bed; $19 to $31 for two in two beds.

North St. Petersburg

Accommodation: Days Inn, U.S. 19 and Mainland Blvd., 9359 U.S. 19 North, Pinellas Park, 33565. Telephone: 813/577-3838. $20.88 for one; $24.88 for two. Rates higher December 16 to May 31.

Ocala

Accommodations: Days Inn, I-75 and Fla. 40, 4040 SW Broadway, 32671. Telephone: 904/629-8850. $17.88 to $21.88 for one; $21.88 to $25.88 for two.
● Western Motel, 4013 NW Blitchton Rd., 32670. Telephone: 904/732-6940. $15 for one; $18 for two.
● Scottish Inn, I-75 and Fla. 40, 32671..Telephone: 904/629-6902. $14 for one; $16 for two.
● Econo Lodge, 3951 NW Blitchton Rd., 32670. Telephone: 904/629-7021. $16.95 for one; $19.95 for two in one bed; $20.95 for two in two beds.

Orlando

All of the budget motels in the Orlando area are here to accommodate all the people who come to Disney World and Sea World.
Help: Information and Referral, 305/841-8911.
● We Care, Inc., 112 Pasadena Park, 32803. Telephone: 305/628-1227. Someone from We Care, Inc., told us that if you are really in a bind, a place called Daily Bread will serve you a free meal at noon and very cheap breakfasts and dinners. But for the most part, "people who are stranded find little help."
Accommodations: Young Women's Community Club (AYH-SA), 107 East Hillcrest St., 32801. Telephone: 305/425-2502. Women 16 to 37 only. $5 in dorm-style room. No advance reservations accepted. Breakfast and dinner served on the premises.
● Superior Motel South, 1820 North Mills Ave., 32803. Telephone: 305/896-3611. $18 for one or two in one bed; $22 to $24 for two in two beds.
● Days Inn, I-4 and Fla. 436, 450 North Douglas Rd., 32701. Telephone: 305/862-7111. $23.88 for one; $27.88 for two. Rates slightly higher December 15 to May 31.
● Days Inn, U.S. 27 and Fla. 19, Sunshine State Pkwy. Exit 85, P.O. Box 105K, Rte. 2, 32711. Telephone: 904/429-2151. $16.88 to $23.88 for one; $20.88 to $27.88 for two. Rates slightly higher from December 18 to January 3.
● Days Inn, I-4 and Fla. 436, 235 South Wymore Rd., 32701. Telephone: 305/862-2800. $23.88 for one, $27.88 for two. Rates slightly higher December 15 to May 31.
● Days Inn, U.S. 441 and East-West Expressway, 720 South Orange Blossom Trail, 32805. Telephone: 305/843-3410. See above for rates.
● Days Inn, I-4 and 33rd St., 2500 West 33rd St., 32805. Telephone: 305/841-3731. See above for rates.

- Days Inn, McCoy Rd. and Fla. 528 (Beeline Expressway), 2323 McCoy Rd., 32809. Telephone: 305/859-6100. See above for rates.
- Days Inn, I-4 and Fla. 528A, 7200 Sandlake Rd., 32811. Telephone: 305/351-1900. See above for rates.
- Days Inn, ♿, I-4 and International Dr., 7200 International Dr., 32809. Telephone: 305/351-1200. See above for rates.
- Days Inn, U.S. 441 and Sunshine State Pkwy., Exit 70, 1221 West Land Street Rd., 32809. Telephone: 305/859-7700. See above for rates.
- Days Inn, I-4 and U.S. 192 West, 7980 Spacecoast Pkwy., 32741. Telephone: 305/846-1000. See above for rates.
- Days Inn, I-4 and U.S. 192 East, 5840 Spacecoast Pkwy., 32741. Telephone: 305/846-7969. See above for rates.
- Econo-Travel Motor Hotel, 5870 Orange Blossom Trail South, 32809. Telephone: 305/859-5410. $18.50 for one; $20.50 for two in one bed; $23.50 for two in two beds.
- Econo-Travel Motor Hotel, 9401 Orange Blossom Trail South, 32809. Telephone: 305/851-1051. See above listing for rates.
- Friendship Inn—Orlando Motor Lodge, 1825 North Mills Ave., 32803. Telephone: 305/896-4111. $17 to $20 for two in one bed; $24 to $27 for two in two beds.

"Malcolm's Hungry Bear has an unlimited buffet. It is quite near Greyhound, opposite Holiday Inn; ask anyone where it is. All you can eat for $4 includes soup, fish, chicken, roast beef, turkey, eight desserts, and a loaf of bread—if you're hungry there is nowhere else."

Ormond Beach

Accommodation: Econo-Travel Motor Hotel, U.S. 1 and I-95, 32074. Telephone: 904/672-6222. $14 for one; $17 for two in one bed; $20 for two in two beds.

Panama City

Accommodations: Sangraal By-the-Sea #2 Myrtlewood Lodge (AYH-SA), 226 College Ave., 32401. Telephone: 904/785-6226. Reservations necessary. $4.50. Inexpensive meals provided.
- Days Inn, U.S. 231 to U.S. 98, 4810 West U.S. 98, 32401. Telephone: 904/769-4831. $21.88 to $23.88 for one; $25.88 to $27.88 for two. Rates higher May 22 to September 7.

Pensacola

Help: Help Line, 904/438-1617.
- Information & Referral, 904/436-9777.

"Tokyo Chaya, 53 East Chase St., serves excellent Japanese food at a reasonable price."

Accommodations: Motel 6, 5829 Pensacola Blvd., 32505. Telephone: 904/477-2152. See Cocoa Beach listing for rates.

● Scottish Inn, one-half mile south of I-10 on Hwy. 29, 32505. Telephone: 904/477-3100. $22 for one; $30 for two.

● If you are really in a bind, you might be able to stay at the Waterfront Mission for a night or two.

Plant City

Accommodation: Days Inn, ♿, I-4 and Fla. 39, 301 South Frontage Rd., 33566. Telephone: 813/754-3531. $22.98 for one; $26.88 for two. Rates higher during February and March.

Pompano Beach

Accommodations: Days Inn, 1411 West Atlantic Blvd., Exit 24 off Sunshine Pkwy., 33060. Telephone: 305/972-3700. $23.88 for one; $27.88 for two. Rates higher December 15 to April 30.

● Motel 6, southeast quadrant of the intersection of Florida Turnpike with Hammondville Rd. (Pompano Beach Interchange #24), 33060. To open in 1982. See Cocoa Beach listing for rates.

Ridge Manor

Accommodation: Ridge Manor Motel, 7555 Hwy. 301 North, 33525. Telephone: 904/583-2109. $18 to $20 for one; $20 to $22 for two in one bed; $22 to $24 for two in two beds.

St. Augustine

Accommodations: Econo Lodge, 3101 Ponce de Leon Blvd., ♿, 32084. Telephone: 904/829-3461. $16.50 to $19.50 for one or two in one bed; $19.50 to $22.50 for two in two beds.

● Econo-Travel Motor Hotel, Rte. 2, Box 278, 32084. Telephone: 904/824-4436. $12.50 to $16.50 for one; $14.50 to $19.50 for two in one bed; $16.50 to $22.50 for two in two beds.

● Scottish Inn, 110 San Marco, 32084. Telephone: 904/824-2871. $17 for one; $20 for two in one bed; $22 for two in two beds.

● Scottish Inn, I-95 and Fla. 16, 32084. Telephone: 904/829-5643. $14 to $17 for one; $16 to $19 for two in one bed; $19 to $22 for two in two beds.

● Days Inn, I-95 and Fla. 16, Rte. 2, Box 227Y, 32084. Telephone: 904/824-4341. $17.88 to $19.88 for one; $21.88 to $23.88 for two.

● Days Inn, ♿, U.S. 1 and Fla. 16, 2800 Ponce de Leon Blvd., 32084. Telephone: 904/829-6581. $18.88 to $22.88 for one; $22.88 to $26.88 for two.

St. Cloud

Accommodation: Friendship Polynesian Inn, 2900 13th St., 32769. Telephone: 305/892-5131. $19 to $30 double.

St. Petersburg

Tourist Information: Convention and Tourist Division, St. Petersburg Convention Bureau, St. Petersburg Area Chamber of Commerce, P.O. Box 1371, 33731. Telephone: 813/821-4069.

Accommodations: YMCA, 116 5th St. South, 33701. Telephone: 813/822-3911. Men only. $12.

● Friendship Inn–Tops Motel, 7141 4th St. North, 33702. Telephone: 813/526-9071. $18 to $25 for one; $18 to $28 for two in one bed; $20 to $35 for two in two beds.

Sanford

Accommodation: Days Inn, I-4 and Fla. 46, 32771. Telephone: 305/323-6500. $19.88 to $21.88 for one; $23.88 to $25.88 for two.

Sarasota

Accommodations: Friendship Inn–Imperial Motel, 4807 North Tamiami Trail, 33580. Telephone: 813/355-5247. $14 to $24 for one; $16 to $30 for two in one bed; $18 to $32 for two in two beds.

● Days Inn, 🔣, U.S. 41 (between Mecca Dr. and 47th St.), 4900 North Tamiami Trail, 33580. Telephone: 813/355-9721. $21.88 for one; $25.88 for two. Rates higher December 15 to April 26.

● Econo Lodge, 5340 North Tamiami Trail, 33580. Telephone: 813/355-8867. $19.95 for one; $21.95 for two in one bed; $23.95 for two in two beds. Rates higher December 15 to April 30.

● Superior Cadillac Motel, 4021 North Tamiami Trail, 33580. Telephone: 813/355-7108. $15 to $24 for one or two in one bed; $18 to $26 for two in two beds.

Starke

Accommodation: Superior Dixie Motel, 744 North Temple Ave., 32091. Telephone: 904/964-5590. $10 to $12 for one; $12 to $14 for two in one bed; $14 to $18 for two in two beds.

Tallahassee

On Campus: If you're in Tallahassee and want to meet some of Florida State University's students, stop at Poor Paul's Poorhouse, the Alley, or Bullwinkle's, all friendly local pubs with music.

For rides, odd jobs, accommodation information, and the like, stop at the Campus Consumer Affairs office or check ride and job boards.

A great lunch buffet of Thai food can be found at the Bhan Thai restaurant.

Accommodations: Days Inn, U.S. 27 and U.S. 319, 3100 Apalachee Pkwy., 32301. Telephone: 904/877-6121. $23.88 for one; $27.88 for two. Rates slightly higher December 15 to May 31.

● Scottish Inn, 1402 West Tennessee St., 32304. Telephone: 904/224-4174.

$15 to $18 for one; $17 to $20 for two in one bed; $19 to $22 for two in two beds.
- Econo-Travel Motor Hotel, ♿, 2681 North Monroe St., 32303. Telephone: 904/385-6155. $21.95 for one; $23.95 for two in one bed; $25.95 for two to four in two beds.

Tampa

On Campus: You can contact the Overseas Information Center, SOC 107–Room 301, at the University of South Florida (tel. 813/974-2249), for help in finding temporary accommodations "with someone from the university community." You might also find apartment listings in the *Oracle,* the University of South Florida's newspaper.

A good place to meet people is the Empty Keg, the student bar at the University Center. There are also several pubs along Fletcher Ave. where students burn the midnight oil.

For good pizza, ask directions to the popular C.D.B. Pizza, and Duff's Smörgåsbord will fill you up at 3825 South Dale Mabry Hwy. and 8805 North Florida Ave.

"One can reach Tampa by car, bus, train, boat or plane. Tampa International Airport has been rated the finest airport in the world. It should be seen!"

Tourist Information: Convention and Visitors Bureau, Greater Tampa Chamber of Commerce, P.O. Box 420, 33601. Telephone: 813/228-7777.

Help: Travelers Aid, 301 North Ashley Dr., 33602. Telephone: 813/229-1703.
- University Center Desk, 813/974-2635.

Accommodations: Econo-Travel Motor Hotel, 11414 Central Ave., 33612. Telephone: 813/933-7831. $19.95 for one; $24.95 for two in one bed; $29.95 for two in two beds.
- Regal 8 Inn, 4011 East Columbus, 33605. Telephone: 813/621-7836. $17.88 for one; $20.88 for two in one bed; $23.88 for two to four in two beds.
- Days Inn, I-75 and Fla. 54 West, Zephyrhills, 33599. Telephone: 813/973-0155. $24.88 for one; $28.88 for two. Rates slightly higher December 15 to May 31.
- Days Inn, I-75 and East Fletcher Ave., 701 East Fletcher Ave., 33612. Telephone: 813/977-1550. See above for rates.
- Days Inn, I-4 and Fla. 579N, 6010 Fla. 579N, Seffner, 33584. $24.88 for one; $29.88 for two. Rates slightly higher December 16 to May 31.

Tarpon Springs

Accommodation: Days Inn, ♿, U.S. 19 at Lake Tarpon, 816 U.S. 19 South, P.O. Box 786, 33589. Telephone: 813/934-0859. $21.88 for one; $25.88 for two. Rates higher December 15 to April 26.

Titusville

Accommodations: Econo Lodge, 3655 Chaney Hwy., 32780. Telephone: 305/269-7110. $19.95 for one; $23 for two.
● Superior Three Oaks Motel, 707 South Hopkins Ave., 32780. Telephone: 305/267-6272. $18 to $20 for one; $20 to $22 for two in one bed; $22 to $24 for two in two beds.
● Days Inn, ♿, I-95 and Fla. 406, 3480 Garden St., 32780. Telephone: 305/269-9310. $24.88 for one; $28.88 for two. Rates higher December 15 to May 31.

Venice

Accommodations: Motel 6, 281 Venice Bypass, 33565. Telephone: 813/488-7395. See Cocoa Beach listing for rates.
● Kent Motel, 625 South Tamiami Trail, 33595. Telephone: 813/484-2684. $16 to $25 for one or two in one bed; $18 to $31 for two in two beds.

West Palm Beach

Help: Travelers Aid, 208 Clematis St., Suite 403, 33401. Telephone: 305/655-4483.
● Crisis Line, 305/588-1121.
Accommodation: YWCA, 901 South Olive Ave., 33401. Telephone: 305/833-2439. Women only. $15 single; $20 double. Ten blocks from ocean. Only three rooms for transients, so reservations are recommended.

Wildwood

Accommodations: Days Inn, U.S. 301 and Sunshine Pkwy. (Exit 90), 32785. Telephone: 904/748-3197. $15.88 to $19.88 for one; $19.88 to $23.88 for two.
● Cindy's Budget Motel, I-75 and Fla. 44, 32785. Telephone: 904/748-3121. $14.50 for one; $16.50 for two in one bed; $17.50 for two in two beds.

Georgia

Georgia is a bit confusing. Its image as part of the Deep South just doesn't jibe with what goes on in its most popular city, Atlanta.

The Tourist Office people have recently mounted a campaign to entice visitors their way and they've divided Georgia into seven travel regions: Pioneer Territory, in the northwest, which includes Chickamauga Battlefield, scene of one of the Civil War's bloodiest battles; the Northeast Georgia Mountains, where the attractions are out-of-doors; the Classic South, with hundreds of antebellum mansions, the Cotton Exchange Building and the Old Slave Market Column in Augusta, and the preserved home of Alexander H. Stephens, vice-president of the Confederacy, in Crawfordsville; the Colonial Coast, where you'll find the lovely city of Savannah and the vast and intriguing Okefenokee Swamp; the "Heart of Georgia," center of the state which includes the city of Macon with its restored Grand Opera House and 24-room Renaissance Hay House and Ocmulgee National Monument, the largest archeological restoration of ancient Indian civilization in the East; Plains Country, with Jimmy Carter's hometown (remember him?) and the national headquarters of the American Camellia Society; and finally, what the tourist people call the Big "A," with Atlanta at its hub.

For full descriptions of each area, write to the Georgia Department of Industry and Trade (address below) and ask for the 76-page *Georgia: This Way to Fun.*

Some Special Events: Pecan Festival in Albany (September); Crowe Springs Craftsmen's Fair and Sorghum Festival in Blairsville (October); Marigold Festival in Winterville and Spring Lake Bluegrass Festival (June); Blessing of the Fleet in Thunderbolt (July); Georgia Mountain Fair in Hiawassee and

Old Time Fiddlin' Convention in Dalton (August); and Georgia Week in Savannah (February).

Hitching: Georgia law states: "No person shall stand in a roadway for the purpose of soliciting a ride."

Tourist Information: Tourist Division, Georgia Department of Industry and Trade, P.O. Box 1776, Atlanta, GA 30301. Telephone: 404/656-3590.

Albany

Accommodation: Motel 6, 301 South Thornton Dr., 31705. Telephone: 912/439-8028. $12.95 for one; $16.95 for two; $19.95 for up to four.

Ashburn

Accommodation: Ashburn Motor Inn, I-75 at Exit 28, 31714. Telephone: 912/567-3346. $19.88 single or double.

Athens

On Campus: A friend at the University of Georgia describes Athens as "a serene and ruggedly beautiful southern town with very hospitable people." Athens and the surrounding areas are rich in Civil War history, particularly Madison, "the town Sherman would not burn," and the many pre-Civil War plantations that still stand.

The university students can most often be found at O'Malley's, the Madhatter, Smokes, and the Speakeasy. You can find them eating at El Dorado Natural Foods, 199 West Washington (quiche and salad for $2), or at Hunan, where you can get a complete lunch for $2.25.

Look into the welcome center in the middle of Athens for information about the area, and get a copy of the *Red & Black* student newspaper for information on student events, rides, etc. If you happen to be in Athens during the first weekend in May, you won't want to miss the annual downtown bedrace.

Accommodation: Days Inn, U.S. 78 West, 2741 Atlanta Hwy., 30606. Telephone: 404/546-9750. $17.88 for one; $22.88 for two.

Atlanta

Atlanta started out as a railroad worker's camp right near today's Omni International Complex. The camp was called "The Terminus," and one civil engineer at the time noted that the place had little future. Atlanta is now home to 1.8 million people, a veritable boom town American style. The phoenix is the symbol of Atlanta, commemorating its amazing resurrection after General Sherman put the town to torch. That was in 1864, when eight out of every nine homes were burned. Who can ever forget the scene of a burning Atlanta in Margaret Mitchell's *Gone With the Wind*?

In the '80s Atlanta is thriving. The city celebrates itself several times a year: at the Piedmont Park Art Festival in early May, where hundreds of artisans display their works in the city's largest park; the Dogwood Festival, a nine-day celebration at the peak of dogwood season including parades, music, dance, and drama productions scheduled throughout the city; the July 4th Peachtree Parade and Peachtree Road Race; and the annual Atlanta Independent Film and Video Festival, the first week in April.

To find out what's happening and when, check the "Weekend" supplement to the Saturday *Atlanta Constitution and Journal; Creative Loafing,* an alternative newspaper; and the monthly *Atlanta Magazine.*

To get a panoramic look at Atlanta, consider the tours that Metro Atlanta Rapid Transit Authority (MARTA) operates. They leave from the International Blvd. side of the bus station, across from a small park. There are two tours to choose from. Tour 1 includes Central City Park, Martin Luther King Jr. Memorial, the State Capitol, Atlanta/Fulton County Stadium, and Stone Mountain Park, 16 miles from Atlanta. On the way back to the city you'll see Emory University, Lenox Square, Phipps Plaza, the Governor's Mansion, and the Atlanta Historical Society's Swan House, once the home of an Atlanta real estate and railroad magnate. Tour 2 is exactly the same except that it substitutes a visit to the High Museum of Art for the trip out to Stone Mountain. Tour 1 costs $10 for adults, $5 for children; Tour 2 costs $7 for adults, $3.50 for children. Information is available by calling 524-7176. Reservations are required.

Getting There: From the Airport: The Atlanta airport, with the largest passenger terminal complex in the world, is about eight miles from the city. You can get from the airport to town on MARTA bus #72 for 50¢. A taxi from the airport will cost about $10. The Atlanta Airport Shuttle has regular service to the downtown and metropolitan area from 5:30 a.m. to 2:00 a.m.; the ride costs $4.50.

● From the Bus Stations: The Greyhound Terminal is at 81 International Blvd., right behind the Peachtree Center area (522-6300); Trailways is at 200 Spring St. (524-2441).

Getting Around: Atlanta streets follow old rail rights-of-way and cow paths; no symmetrical grid-like pattern here. The city is divided into quadrants, which come together at the junction of Peachtree St., Edgewood Ave., and Marietta-Decatur Sts.

● MARTA is constructing a rapid rail system (see those "MARTA at work" signs). MARTA bus fares are 50¢ with no extra charge for a transfer. Loop buses circle the downtown area and run from 8 a.m. to 6 p.m. Call 522-4711 for MARTA information. Taxis cost $1 for the first one-fifth mile and 10¢ for each additional one-fifth mile, with 25¢ extra for each additional passenger.

Accommodations: Alamo Plaza Motel, 2370 Stewart Ave. SW, 30315. Telephone: 404/767-1521. On MARTA routes 19 and 41. $12.50 single; $22 double. An older building.

● Atlanta Downtown Motel, 330 West Peachtree St., 30308. Telephone: 404/525-2771. Just north of Peachtree Center Complex. Regular rates are too high for us ($35 single; $40 double), but international visitors can stay for $27 single, $36 double; and students, for rooms not yet redecorated, pay $20 for one or two.

● Atlantan Hotel, √10%, 111 Luckie St. NW, 30303. Downtown. Telephone: 404/524-6461. $25 single; $29 double.

● Georgian Motel, ⚑ √$1, 4300 Buford Hwy., 30329. Telephone: 404/636-4344. Accessible from downtown on MARTA bus #44, #65, or #130. $17 single; $19 double.

● Georgian Terrace Hotel (AYH-SA), ⚑ ★ 10%, 659 Peachtree St., 30308.

Telephone: 404/872-6671. At the north end of downtown area. $24 single; $30 double; $36 triple; $42 quad. AYH rates are $16 single; $9.50 each for a double; $8 each for triple; and $7.50 each for a quad. There's a multilingual staff.

● Rodeway Inn Downtown, √10% (AARP members), ⌂, 144 14th St. NW, 30318. Telephone: 404/873-4171. Six blocks from Georgia Tech to the southwest and Piedmont Park to the east. Take MARTA bus #23 from downtown. $26 single; $34 double.

● Sky Host Inn, √10%, 1360 Virginia Ave., 30344. Telephone: 404/761-5201. Take MARTA bus #72 from downtown. One mile from airport; free-shuttle available. $25 single; $32 double.

● Bed and Breakfast Atlanta, 1221 Fairview Rd. NE, 30306. Telephone: 404/378-6026. "Each host home has been visited and selected to provide a comfortable, convenient and more personal alternative to commercial lodging." $20 to $28 single; $24 to $32 double; price includes a continental breakfast. There is a slightly higher charge for one-night stays.

● YMCA, 22 Butler St. NE, 30303. Telephone: 404/659-8085. Men only. $6.42 single without bath. Weekly rate: $35.60.

● Friendship Inn–Dogwood Motel, 5140 Buford Hwy., Doraville, 30340. Telephone: 404/457-7246. $22 to $24 for one; $23 to $25 for two in one bed; $24 to $26 for two in two beds.

● Motel 6, 4427 Commerce Dr., 30344. Telephone: 404/762-1606. See Albany listing for rates.

● Motel 6, 4100 Wendell Dr. SW, 30336. Telephone: 404/696-4084. See Albany listing for rates.

● Days Inn, Exit 33 to Buford Hwy. and 2461 Old Stone Mountain Rd., Chamblee, 30341. Telephone: 404/458-9323. $20.88 for one; $24.88 for two.

● Days Inn, I-85 and Chamblee Tucker Rd., Exit 34, 2768 Chamblee Tucker Rd., 30341. Telephone: 404/458-8711. $20.88 to $22.88 for one; $24.88 to $26.88 for two.

● Days Inn, I-85 and Shallowford Rd., Exit 33, 4815 Buford Hwy., Chamblee, 30341. Telephone: 404/458-8011. $20.88 for one; $24.88 for two.

● Days Inn, I-85 and Clairmont Rd., Exit 32, 2910 Clairmont Rd., 30329. Telephone: 404/633-8411, $20.88 to $22.88 for one; $24.88 to $26.88 for two.

● Days Inn, I-20 and Fulton Industrial Blvd. (Exit 14), 4120 Fulton Industrial Blvd., 30336. Telephone: 404/696-4690. $21.88 to $23.88 for one; $25.88 to $27.88 for two.

● Days Inn, I-20 East and Wesley Chapel Rd., 4200 Wesley Club Dr., Decatur, 30034. Telephone: 404/288-7110. $22.88 to $23.88 for one; $26.88 to $27.88 for two.

● Days Inn, I-75 and Cleveland Ave., 2788 Forest Hills Dr., 30315. Telephone: 404/768-7750. $21.88 to $23.88 for one; $25.88 to $27.88 for two.

● Days Inn, I-75 Frontage Rd. and Farmer's Market, Forest Park, 30050. Telephone: 404/363-0800. $20.88 to $22.88 for one; $24.88 to $26.88 for two.

Where to Eat: Café de la Paix, Atlanta Hilton Hotel, 255 Courtland and Harris Sts. Telephone: 659-2000. Eat as much as you'd like; choose from eight entrees, three vegetables, fruit, fresh baked breads, and desserts. $5.95 Monday to Saturday; $9.50 Sunday brunch.

● Snack Shack, 37 Pryor St. SW. Telephone: 523-5054. About two blocks from Central City Park in downtown. "Sandwiches are huge and excellent."

• Ivy Street Library and Pub, 22 Ivy St. Telephone: 521-2584. Downtown, one block from Central City Park. Soups, chili, quiche, and burgers. "Great place for a literary lunch or after-work libation."

• Mary Mac's, 224 Ponce de Leon Ave. NE. Telephone: 876-6604. About ten minutes by car from Peachtree Plaza. Family-style down-home cooking in just the right atmosphere. Soup, country fried steak, two vegetables, and dessert costs $4.75 at dinnertime.

• Eat Your Vegetables Café, 438 Moreland Ave. Telephone: 523-2671. Healthy food like a mushroom melt, hummus sandwich, soyburger, salads, a fruit plate, tempura, etc. A friendly and comfortable place where a full lunch costs under $4.

• The Mansion, 179 Ponce de Leon Ave. NE. Telephone: 876-0727. An unusual and charming restaurant in an old Victorian house surrounded by trees. Lunch is about $5; dinner from $10 to $15.

• Grandma's Biscuits, 54 Broad St. NW. Telephone: 523-3168. Simple southern cooking. Meat, two vegetables, and biscuit or cornbread is only $3.05.

• Thelma's Kitchen, 223 Marietta St. No telephone. Southern cooking in a corner restaurant frequented by lots of regulars. Thelma would like to talk to you; tell her how you find her place. Fried chicken, okra, and sweet potatoes is $2.90.

• Capo's Café, 992 Virginia Ave. NE. Telephone: 876-5655. Lovely menu includes chicken salad nora (chunks of chicken, apples, walnuts, and raisins with a curry cream dressing), $3.75; a seafood casserole Parisienne (scallops, shrimp, and mushrooms in a sauce and topped with puff pastry), $6.95; and fettucine Alfredo, $3.95. "One of the least expensive good restaurants around."

What to See and Do: Stone Mountain Park. About 16 miles east of Atlanta. A 3200-acre park complete with museums, skylift, riverboat, scenic railroad, campground, and more. MARTA bus marked "20 Stone Mountain" will get you there.

• Six Flags Atlanta. 15 minutes from downtown Atlanta. Telephone: 948-9290. A family entertainment park with 100 rides, shows, and attractions. Open weekends during the fall and spring, daily from May 20 to September 1. Accessible from downtown by MARTA rail and bus: take rail line to Hightower Station and from there take bus marked "201 Six Flags." The trip costs $1.50 each way; a one-price ticket to Six Flags costs $9.95 and entitles you to all rides and shows.

• Toy Museum of Atlanta, 2800 Peachtree St. Telephone: 266-8697. Antique toys and dolls dating from the 1850s. $2 adults; $1.50 children 6 to 12.

• Martin Luther King Historic District. This two-block area includes King's birthplace, the Ebenezer Baptist Church where he preached, and Dr. King's gravesite. Information center for the area is on the site.

• Grant Park and Atlanta Zoo, Georgia and Cherokee Aves. SE. Telephone: 622-4839. The largest reptile collection in the country, and an ape who likes to watch soap operas. $1.50 admission.

• Fernbank Science Center, 156 Heaton Park Dr., Decatur. Telephone: 378-4311. Science exhibits, botanical gardens, 65-acre forest with two miles of walking trails, and the third-largest planetarium in the U.S.

• Gone With the Wind Museum, 152 Nassau St. NE. Telephone: 522-1526. Rhett's top hat, the original movie script, and Margaret Mitchell's china. $2 adults; $1 children 12 to 17.

• Wren's Nest, 1050 Gordon St. Once the home of Joel Chandler Harris, creator of the Uncle Remus stories, with some of the original furniture on display. $12 adults; $1 teens; 50¢ children.

● Omni International, Marietta St. at International Blvd. A commercial and recreation center with a hotel, skating rink, restaurants, six movie theaters (only $1 admission), and lots of shops.

● Peachtree Center, bounded by Baker, Ellis, Williams, and Courtland Sts. A commercial and entertainment center, including the world's tallest hotel, the Peachtree Plaza.

● Atlanta Memorial Arts Center, 1280 Peachtree St. NE. Home of the High Museum of Art, the Atlanta Symphony Orchestra, and the Alliance Theater.

● Underground Atlanta, 84 Pryor St. SW. Entrance at Central Ave. and Martin Luther King Dr. In the 1960s this part of Atlanta, which had been lively in the 1890s, was restored and several blocks were turned into shops and restaurants meant to be reminiscent of the gaslight era. The area isn't as interesting now as it was in the '70s.

At Night: For jazz: Carlos McGee's, 3035 Peachtree St. NE; Harvestmoon Saloon, 2423 Piedmont; E.J.'s, 128 East Andrews Dr.; Clarence Foster's, 1915 Peachtree Rd.

● To dance: Limelight, 3330 Peachtree Rd. An entertainment complex which includes disco, a screening room, and room to eat.

● For dinner or drinks and a film: Buckhead Cinema 'n' Drafthouse, 3110 Roswell Rd. NE.

● For inexpensive films: Six theaters at Omni International, $1 at all times; or Toco Hills, 298 North Druid Hills Rd., 99¢ at all times.

● To hear country music: Scooter's Neon Cowboy, 6521 Roswell Rd.; The Blue Eagle, 280 Hildebrand in the Balconies; Mama's Country Showcase, 3952 Covington Hwy., Decatur.

Shopping: Atlantans love shopping centers and there are three enormous ones in town—Lenox Square at 3393 Peachtree Rd. NE, Peachtree Center Shopping Gallery at 225 Peachtree St., and Omni International at Marietta St. and International Blvd.

● Rizzoli International Book Store, Omni International. Art, foreign language, and general fiction and nonfiction.

● Brentano's, Peachtree Center and Lenox Square Shopping Center. All kinds of books.

● Peaches Records and Tapes, 2282 Peachtree St. All kinds of records and tapes at a discount.

● Turtle's Records and Tapes, 3337 Buford Hwy. NE and ten other locations. More records and tapes at discount.

● Blue Ridge Mountain Sports, Ltd., Lenox Square Shopping Center. Sells all kinds of outdoor equipment and rents backpacking and canoeing equipment.

● Old Sarge Army-Navy Surplus Store, 5316 Buford Hwy., Doraville. All kinds of surplus outdoor gear.

● Marshall's, in the mall at Buford Hwy. and Clairmont Rd. Name-brand clothing at substantial discounts.

Tourist Information: Atlanta Convention and Visitors Bureau, 233 Peachtree St. NW, Suite 200, 30303. Telephone: 404/659-4270.

Help: Travelers Aid, 110 Spring St. NW, 30303. Telephone: 404/523-0585.

● Contact, 404/261-3644. 24-hour telephone counseling service.

Augusta

Accommodations: YMCA, 945 Broad St., 30902. Telephone: 404/722-4801. Men only. $10.49 single, first night; $6.24 on succeeding nights. $32.33 first week; $28.33 succeeding weeks.
- Days Inn, I-20 and 3026 Washington Rd., 30907. Telephone: 404/738-0131. $21.88 for one; $24.88 for two.
- Econo-Travel Motor Hotel, 906 Molly Pond Rd., 30901. Telephone: 404/722-6841. $17 for one; $22 for two in one bed; $25 for two in two beds.
- Best Value Uptowner Inn, 801 Reynolds St., 30903. Telephone: 404/722-5361. $18 to $20 for one; $24 to $26 for two in one bed; $26 to $28 for two in two beds.

Bainbridge

Accommodation: Glen Oaks Motel and Campground, Hwy. 27 South, 31717. Telephone: 912/246-4343. $18.85 for one; $19.85 for two in one bed; $21.85 for two in two beds.

Brunswick

Help: Crisis Line, 912/264-7307.
Accommodations: Hostel in the Forest (AYH-SA), P.O. Box 1496, 31522. Telephone: 912/264-9676, 265-0220, or 638-2623. Open year round. $4 plus $1 for linens. Call hostel for transportation from bus station. "A geodesic dome with private rooms and a bunk room."
- Days Inn, I-95 and U.S. 341, Exit 7, 409 New Jessup Hwy., 31522. Telephone: 912/264-4330. $24.88 for one; $26.88 for two. Rates slightly higher December 15 to May 31.

Byron

Accommodation: Byron Inn, √10%, I-75 and Ga. 49, 31008. Telephone: 912/956-5100. $17.88 for one; $21.88 for two.

Calhoun

Accommodations: Days Inn, I-75 and Ga. 53, Exit 129, P.O. Box 392, 30701. $16.88 to $18.88 for one; $20.88 to $22.88 for two.
- Shepherd Motel, junction of I-75 and Ga. 53, 30701. Telephone: 404/629-8644 or toll free 800/238-2552. $14.88 for one; $17.88 for two in one bed; $19.88 for two in two beds.
- Best Value Shepherd Motel, on Ga. 53, junction I-75, 30701. Telephone: 404/629-8644. $14.88 to $15.88 for one; $16.88 to $17.88 for two in one bed; $18.88 to $19.88 for two in two beds.

Cartersville

Accommodations: Best Value Pioneer Motel, P.O. Box 746, 30120. Telephone: 404/386-0700. $16.88 for one; $20.88 for two.

● Days Inn, I-75 and Cassville-White Rd., Exit 127, P.O. Box 1088, 30120. Telephone: 404/386-0350. See Calhoun listing for rates.

Claxton

Accommodation: Superior Resthaven Motel, P.O. Box 874, U.S. 301 North, 30417. Telephone: 912/739-2214. $15 for one; $17 for two in one bed; $19 for two in two beds.

Columbus

Accommodations: YMCA, 118 East 11th St., 31902. Telephone: 404/322-8269. Men only. $8 single. Weekly rate: $30.
● Days Inn, I-185 and Macon Rd. Exit, 3452 Macon Rd., 31907. Telephone: 404/561-4400. $24.88 for one; $28.88 for two.
● Motel 6, 3050 Victory Dr., 31903. Telephone: 404/689-0020. See Albany listing for rates.

Cordele

Accommodation: Days Inn, I-75 and Tremont Rd., P.O. Box 736, 31015. Telephone: 912/273-6161. $16.88 to $18.88 for one; $20.88 to $22.88 for two.

Dalton

Accommodation: Best Value San Quinton Motel, 1407 Chattanooga Rd., 30720. Telephone: 404/278-3693. $16.64 for one; $20.80 for two in one bed; $22.88 for two in two beds.

Eulonia/Townsend/North Brunswick

Accommodation: Days Inn, ♿, I-95 and Ga. 99, Exit 11, Townsend, 31331. Telephone: 912/832-4411. $20.88 to $21.88 for one; $24.88 to $25.88 for two.

Forsyth

Accommodation: Days Inn, I-75 and Ga. 42, Exit 63, Rte. 2, Box 273, 31029. Telephone: 912/994-5168. $16.88 to $18.88 for one; $20.88 to $22.88 for two.

Gainesville

Accommodation: Days Inn, ♿, U.S. 129 and Ga. 365, P.O. Drawer CC, 30503. Telephone: 404/532-7531. $20.88 for one; $24.88 for two.

Hahira/North Valdosta

Accommodation: Days Inn, I-75 and Ga. 122, Hahira-Barney Exit, Rte. 2, Box 3, 31632. Telephone: 912/794-3000. $16.88 for one; $20.88 for two.

LaGrange/Callaway Gardens

Accommodation: Days Inn, I-85 and Ga. 219, Exit 2, 30240. Telephone: 404/882-8881. $19.88 to $21.88 for one; $23.88 to $25.88 for two.

Lake Park

Accommodation: Days Inn, I-75 and Exit 1, 31636. Telephone: 912/559-7902. $16.88 to $18.88 for one; $20.88 to $22.88 for two.

Locust Grove

Accommodation: Friendship Inn–Russell's Travel Inn, Hampton Rd. and I-75, Exit 68, 30248. Telephone: 404/957-2671. $16.88 for one; $17.88 for two in one bed; $19.88 for two in two beds.

Macon

Accommodations: Days Inn, I-75 and Pio Nono, Exit 49, 4295 Pio Nono Ave., 31206. Telephone: 912/788-8910. See Lake Park listing for rates.
 • Motel 6, 4991 Harrison Rd., 31206. Telephone: 912/474-9212. See Albany listing for rates.

Marietta

Accommodation: Scottish Inn, 2390 Delk Rd., 30062. Telephone: 404/952-3365. $21 for one; $25 for two.

McDonough

Accommodation: Days Inn, I-75 and Ga. 20 (Exit 70), P.O. Box 681, 30253. Telephone: 404/957-5818. See Lake Park listing for rates.

Milledgeville

Accommodation: Days Inn, 🦽, U.S. 441N, 30034. Telephone: 912/453-3551. $17.88 to $18.88 for one; $21.88 to $22.88 for two.

Perry

Accommodation: Best Value Georgian Inn Motel, P.O. Box 539, 31069. Telephone: 912/987-2200. $13.88 for one; $15.88 for two in one bed; $17.88 for two in two beds.

Richmond Hill

Accommodation: Days Inn, I-95 and U.S. 17, Exit 14, P.O. Box 519, 31324. Telephone: 912/756-3371. $20.88 to $22.88 for one; $24.88 to $26.88 for two.

Savannah

Help: Family Counseling Center of Savannah, Inc. (Travelers Aid), 428 Bull St., 31401. Telephone: 912/233-5729.
● Helpline, 912/232-3383.
Tourist Information: Savannah Visitors Center, 301 West Broad St., 31499. Telephone: 912/233-6651. Free 12-minute slide show, literature, and tour information to give you an idea of what to see. Open every day except Christmas.
Accommodations: Bed and Breakfast Inn, c/o Robert McAlister, 117 Gordon St. West at Chatham Square, 31402. Telephone: 912/233-9481. Accommodation and continental breakfast in a private home. Rates begin at $20 single; $24 double.
● Budget Inn, 3702 Ogeechee Rd. (Hwy. 17 South at Loop 26), 31405. Telephone: 912/233-3633. $18.50 single; $23.50 double. The Cherokee Restaurant is right next door.
● Days Inn, I-95 and I-16 to Loop 26 South to Abercorn St. (Ga. 204 South) to Mall Blvd., 114 Mall Blvd, 31406. Telephone: 912/352-4455. $21.88 to $23.88 for one; $25.88 to $27.88 for two.
● Econo-Travel Motor Hotel, 🔳, I-95 and U.S. 17, Richmond Hill, 31324. Telephone: 912/756-3312. $17.95 for one; $21.95 for two in one bed; $23.95 for two in two beds. Rates higher January 1 to February 14.

Savannah Beach

Accommodation: Days Inn, Rte. 80 East, P.O. Box. 696, 31328. Telephone: 912/786-4576. $18.88 for one; $22.88 for two. Rates higher June 1 to September 7.

Suwanee

Accommodation: Days Inn, 🔳, I-85 and Ga. 317, 3103 Hwy. 317, 30174. Telephone: 404/945-8372. $20.88 for one; $24.88 for two.

Thomasville

Accommodation: Days Inn, U.S. 19 Bypass and U.S. 319, P.O. Box 796, 31792. Telephone: 912/226-6025. $17.88 to $19.88 for one; $21.88 to $23.88 for two.

Tifton

Accommodations: Days Inn, I-75 and U.S. 82, Exit 18, P.O. Box 1310, 31794. Telephone: 912/382-8100. See North Tifton listing for rates.

● Days Inn, I-75 at Chula-Brookfield Exit 23, P.O. Drawer 40, Chula, 31733. Telephone: 912/382-2686. $16.88 to $18.88 for one; $20.88 to $22.88 for two.

Unadilla

Accommodation: Days Inn, I-75 and U.S. 41, Exit 39, P.O. Box 405, 31091. Telephone: 912/627-3211. See North Tifton listing for rates.

Valdosta

Accommodations: Azalea City Motel, √10%, 2015 West Hill Ave., 31601. Telephone: 912/244-4350, 244-4351, or 244-4647. $13 to $16 for one; $17 to $25 for two.
● Econo Lodge, intersection of I-75 and Hwy. 84, P.O. Box 911, 31601. Telephone: 912/247-2440. $15 for one; $18 for two in one bed; $21 for two in two beds.

Warner Robins

Accommodation: Days Inn, I-75 Exit 45, Rte. 3, Byron, 31008. Telephone: 912/956-5300. See Lake Park listing for rates.

Waycross

Accommodation: Days Inn, U.S. 1 South at 2016 Memorial Dr., 31501. Telephone: 912/285-4700. $17.88 to $20.88 for one; $21.88 to $24.88 for two.

Woodbine

Accommodation: Stardust Lodge, I-95, Exit 4 to U.S. 17, Bedell Ave. (P.O. Box 537), 31569. Telephone: 912/576-5345. $17 single; $19 double. "Home-like atmosphere."

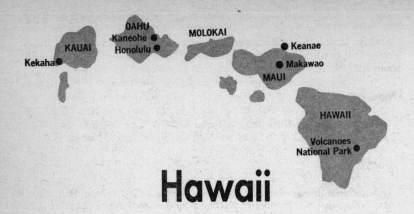

Hawaii

James Michener calls the islands of Hawaii "unbelievably beautiful. They rise from the sea like a strand of pearls, each one with its own peculiar beauty, yet all suffused with the same grace and charm." Mark Twain called them "the loveliest fleet of islands that lies anchored in any sea." The state of Hawaii, 2000 miles west of California, is actually a cluster of islands and Hawaii is only one of these islands. The other largest ones are Kauai, Oahu (where Honolulu is), Molokai, Lanai, and Maui. Downtown Honolulu is a busy city with typical urban problems, but beyond it the islands are not heavily populated and are characterized by mountains, volcanoes, tropical foliage, sandy beaches, and rocky coast.

Because Hawaii is so far away from the mainland, air fares to and from it are high.

One friend suggests that you do what she did for six months: "Get a camping permit at Oahu's Department of Parks and Recreation, 650 South King St., rent camping equipment if you don't have your own (the Visitors Bureau will supply names and addresses), and camp around the island. The weather is always good, between 69 and 90 degrees . . . and as long as you renew your permit every two weeks you can go on like this forever."

"Hawaii's a great place, but don't be fooled into expecting a paradise or utopia."

A good guide to the islands is *Hawaii on $25 a Day,* by Faye Hammel and Sylvan Levey, Frommer/Pasmantier Publishers ($7.25).

Some Special Events: Orchid Society Flower Show in Hilo and Fiesta Filipina in Honolulu (July); Queen Kaahumanu Festival in Hana Bay and Hula Festival in Waikiki (August); and Aloha Week Festivals on all islands (September and October).

Hitching: Hitchhiking is accepted and is fairly common on most of the islands. One friend from Hawaii says that hitchhiking is best on Kauai ("the police told us to") and okay on Hawaii. Since it costs 50¢ to get anywhere on the island of Oahu by bus, with unlimited transfers allowed, it seems unnecessary, doesn't it? The Visitors Bureau wants to go on record as saying that hitchhiking "is never recommended."

Tourist Information: Hawaii Visitors Bureau, Waikiki Business Plaza, 2270 Kalakaua Ave., Honolulu, HI 96815. Telephone: 808/923-1811. (On the mainland, there are branch offices in Chicago, Los Angeles, New York, and San Francisco.) The Visitors Bureau has a free hotel list with rates, which includes some inexpensive accommodations as well as the more luxurious.

Note: Since accommodations are generally so expensive in Hawaii you might find Bed & Breakfast International, an organization that places people in private homes, an appealing alternative to standard accommodations. A double, breakfast included, is $26 to $85 (students may request lower rates); the minimum stay is three nights. For an application, write to the organization at 151 Ardmore Rd., Kensington, CA 94707, and enclose a stamped, self-addressed envelope.

Hawaii Volcanoes National Park, Hawaii

Camping and Accommodation: Hawaii Volcanoes National Park, 96718. Besides three campgrounds that are open year round, the park has camper cabins available. The Namakani Paio Cabins are unfurnished except for mattresses. You can rent linen, pillows, blankets, and towels, but must bring your own cooking utensils, wood, etc. The cabins are $12 for up to four people, with a $5 key deposit. Reservations recommended as far in advance as possible. Write or call for reservations to: Kilauea Volcano House, Hawaii, HI 96718. Telephone: 808/967-7318.

Honolulu, Oahu

Help: Information and Referral, 808/521-4566.
● Suicide and Crisis Center, 808/521-4555.
● Institute for Human Services, 127 North Beretania St. Telephone: 808/538-7684. Provides meals and someone to talk to.
Tourist Information: Hawaii Visitors Bureau, 808/923-1811.

"Try to get out of the city and into the rural areas—great scenery!"

Accommodations: YWCA, 1566 Wilder Ave., 96822. Telephone: 808/941-2231. Women only. $15 for a room shared with one other person and bath shared with three others (dorm style). Rate includes breakfast and dinner. Bus service to the beach and the U. of Hawaii. Lower weekly and monthly rates available.
● Armed Services YMCA, 250 South Hotel St., 96813. Telephone: 808/524-5600. Men, women, and children. $16 single; $20 double. Reservations suggested three to four weeks in advance for all except single men. Please write to The Y's Way, 356 West 34th St., New York, NY 10001, for reservations. The YMCA is located in downtown Honolulu and can be reached from the airport by city bus.
● YMCA, 401 Atkinson Dr., 96814. Telephone: 808/941-3344. Men only. $11 single without bath; $13 with bath. $9.50 to $11.50 per person double. Call from airport to see if there is a room. Coffeeshop in building; restaurants in Ala Moana Shopping Center across the street.
● YMCA, 1441 Pali Hwy., 96813. Telephone: 808/536-3556. Men 18 and older. $11 single with community showers; $13 single with private bath. Cafeteria in building. There is a bus stop right in front.

• Honolulu International Youth Hostel (AYH), 2323 Seaview Ave., 96822. Telephone: 808/946-0591. Open year round. $4. AYH membership required (see page 21). Enclose stamped return envelope when making reservations. A 2½-mile walk to Ala Moana Beach and one-mile walk to Waikiki Beach.

"Don't expect to live on the beach or in any free housing. Jobs are difficult to find. Living expenses are very high. Don't carry expensive jewelry or large amounts of cash."

Keanae, Maui

Help: Kohua Service–Cameron Center, 808/244-7405.

Accommodation: Maui YMCA Camp Keanae, S.R. Box 60, Wailuku, Maui, 96708. Telephone: 808/248-8355. Open year round. $4 for AYH members; $4.50 for nonmembers. Bring your own food—there's a big kitchen. "Cabins with bunk beds, toilets, cots in gym room, tenting sites."

Kekaha, Kauai

Accommodation: Kokee Lodge, P.O. Box 518, Kekaha, Kauai, 96752. Telephone: 808/335-6061. Cabins that sleep six and come equipped with linens and kitchen supplies, hot showers, and fireplaces. $6 to $10 per person per night. Breakfast and lunch available in restaurant on premises.

Makawao, Maui

Camping: Haleakala National Park, P.O. Box 537, 96768. Four campgrounds open year round. No charge. Three cabins equipped with most essentials available in crater; $3 per person per night. Accessible by horseback or on foot only. $2 per person per night. Reservations required 60 days in advance.

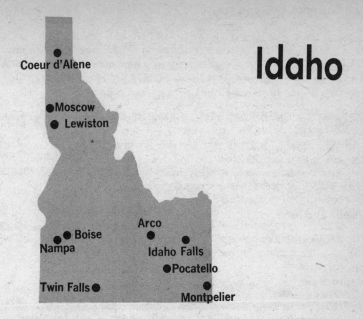

Idaho

We're convinced, having read through so many tourist office brochures, that there's one public relations man or woman who puts out the materials for all 50 states and just changes the name of the state to suit the latest client. All the brochures say that *blah* has it all, *blah* has something for everyone, *blah* is a year-round playground, and Lewis and Clark passed through *blah*. But in the case of Idaho it's all really true. There may not be many people in Idaho, but there certainly is a variety of landscape. The brochures don't fib. In central Idaho there's the Primitive Area where there are no roads, the Salmon River, and the Craters of the Moon National Monument. (This is a weird and wild landscape where the astronauts trained for their moon walk.) Northern Idaho has beautiful rivers, lakes, and mountains. In southeastern Idaho there are more mountains and rivers, plus an incredible combination of dry desert plains and rich farmland. Try to forgive Idaho's obsession with potatoes (Spud Cellar Lounge, the potato-processing capital of the world, Ski the Big Potato) and enjoy some of its extraordinary variety.

Some Special Events: Salmon River Rodeo in Riggins (May); picnic in Craigmont featuring a noon buffalo barbecue (last Saturday in June); Old Timer's Celebration in Harrison, featuring a theater revue, dance, and parade, and Idaho State Square and Round Dance Festival (July); a Roundup in Lewiston, including a cowboy breakfast and a rodeo, and Labor Day Festival in Bellevue, which includes a parade, a shootout, oldtime fiddlers, and a barbecue (September).

Hitching: It should be okay to hitchhike in Idaho—just be sure to stay on the shoulder. In some of the less populated areas you may have to wait a while for a ride to come along. One Idaho resident told us that hitchhikers he picks up while traveling around the state say that rides come quite easily there.

Tourist Information: Division of Economic and Community Affairs, State Capitol Building, Boise, ID 83720.

Arco

Camping: Craters of the Moon National Monument, P.O. Box 29, 83213. At Lava Flow Campground you can camp from April 15 to October 15. (Bring a foam pad—the stone is hard.) $2 per campsite per night.

Boise

Help: Hotline, 208/345-7888 (evening hours only).
● Information and Referral, 208/378-0111 (during business hours).
Accommodation: Motel 6, 2323 Airport Way, 83705. Telephone: 208/342-7733. $12.95 for one; $16.95 for two; $19.95 for up to four.

Coeur D'Alene

Accommodation: Motel 6, 416 Appleway, 83814. Telephone: 208/664-6660. See Boise listing for rates.

Idaho Falls

Help: Information Referral Agency, 208/524-2433.
Accommodations: Motel 6, 1448 West Broadway, 83401. Telephone: 208/523-9265. See Boise listing for rates.
● Best Value Bonneville Motel, 2000 South Yellowstone Hwy., 83401. Telephone: 208/522-7847. $17 to $18 for one; $19 to $20 for two in one bed; $22 for two in two beds.

Lewiston

Help: Crisis Center, 204 Main, 208/743-1521.

"It is very difficult here for travelers. Police will stop and question and possibly search young people who look too grubby."

Accommodation: Motel 6, U.S. 95 and U.S. 12, 83501. To open in 1982. See Boise listing for rates.

Montpelier

Accommodations: Best Value Park Motel, 745 Washington, 83254. Telephone: 208/847-1911. $22 to $23 for one; $25 to $26 for two in one bed; $27 to $29 for two in two beds.
● Friendship Inn–Sunset, 453 South 4th, 83254. Telephone: 208/847-1551. $12 to $14 for one; $14 to $16 for two in one bed; $18 to $22 for two in two beds.

Moscow

Accommodation: Motel 6, 101 Baker St., 83843. Telephone: 208/882-6639. See Boise listing for rates.

Nampa

Accommodation: Nampa Chief Motel, √10%, 908 3rd St. South, 83651. Telephone: 208/466-3594. $20 for one; $23 for two in one bed; $26 for two in two beds; $11 per person for dormitory.

Pocatello

Accommodations: Motel 6, 291 West Burnside Ave., 83201. Telephone: 208/237-6667. See Boise listing for rates.
● Imperial 400 Motor Inn, 1055 South Fifth Ave., 83201. Telephone: 208/233-5120. $18 to $22 for one; $22 to $26 for two in one bed; $24 to $30 for two in two beds.

Twin Falls

Accommodation: Motel 6, 1472 Blue Lakes Blvd. North, 83301. Telephone: 208/733-6663. See Boise listing for rates.

Rockford●
Morton Grove Elgin
●Libertyville
●Evanston
●La Grange
DeKalb●
●Chicago
Aurora
Moline
●
Lombard
Naperville
●Joliet
●Galesburg
●Kankakee
Peoria ●
●Pontiac
Bloomington●
●Normal
Macomb Lincoln●
●Urbana
●
Springfield● Decatur
●Champaign
Jacksonville

●Effingham
● Pocahontas
Belleville ●
Mount Vernon ●
Campbell Hill●
● Marion

Illinois

Chicago is the pulse of Illinois, and, in many ways, of the Midwest. It's where many of the young people from midwestern states head when they leave school and it's most definitely worth a visit. See the special section on Chicago to help plan your days there.

If you have more time to explore the state, go beyond Chicago to the area around Springfield where Abraham Lincoln spent many years of his life. Lincoln's New Salem State Park is a restoration of the town where Lincoln lived from 1831 to 1837. This is where he studied law, and this is where Ann Rutledge, his first love, was buried, according to legend (but not, as we've been told, according to fact; she's buried *near* here). Lincoln memorabilia are exhibited in a museum in this park and tourists can visit 26 buildings that are meant to conjure up Lincoln's past.

Although it is the state of Utah that is most often thought of when Brigham Young is mentioned, it was in Illinois, on the banks of the Mississippi, where Joseph Smith founded the headquarters of the Church of Latter-Day Saints. The group was persecuted there and, after Smith was murdered, Brigham Young led the exodus to Utah. Left behind in the town of Nauvoo are Smith's first log homestead, the restored Joseph Smith Mansion House, and the Brigham Young Home.

Anyone planning to visit Illinois should send for a free copy of *The Weekend Book—A Guide to Small Adventures in Illinois,* which includes information on festivals, camping, hiking, biking, skiing, etc. Copies are available from the Illinois Travel Information Center, 208 North Michigan Ave., Chicago. IL 60601.

Some Special Events: Old Settler Days in Sumner (fourth weekend in April); Dogwood Festival in Quincy and Des Plaines River Canoe Marathon in Libertyville (May); Olde English Fair at Jubilee College State Park in Brimfield (June); Ravinia Festival in Highland Park, summer home of Chicago

Symphony (all summer long); ChicagoFest, and Illinois State Fair in Springfield (August); and Abe Lincoln Railsplitting Contest in Lincoln (September).

Hitching: The attitude toward hitching in Illinois seems lukewarm. It is legal except on limited-access highways, tollways, and in a roadway. No one we talked to refused to recommend it, but no one seemed very enthusiastic about the possibilities. The official word from the Illinois State Police is that hitchhiking is "not recommended," and "fraught with danger."

Tourist Information: Office of Tourism, Illinois Department of Commerce and Community Affairs, 222 South College St., Springfield, IL 62706; or Illinois Travel Information Center, 208 North Michigan Ave., Chicago, IL 60601. Telephone: 302/793-2094.

Aurora

Accommodation: Regal 8 Inn, 2380 North Farnsworth Ave. and East West Tollway #5, 60507. Telephone: 312/851-3600. $18.88 for one; $21.88 for two in one bed; $24.88 for two to four in two beds.

Belleville

Accommodation: Imperial 400 Motor Inn, 600 East Main St., 62220. Telephone: 618/234-9670. $20 to $24 for one; $24 to $28 for two in one bed; $26 to $30 for two in two beds.

Bloomington

Accommodations: Friendship Inn–Coachman Motel, 408 East Washington St., 61701. Telephone: 309/827-6186. $16.50 to $18.50 for one; $19.50 to $21.50 for two in one bed; $20.50 to $22.50 for two in two beds.

● Regal 8 Inn, 2304 Washington, 61701. Telephone: 309/662-4381. $17.88 for one; $20.88 for two in one bed; $23.88 for two to four in two beds.

● Best Inns of America, I-74, I-75, and Market St., 61701. Telephone: 309/827-5333. $18.88 to $22.38 for one; $24.38 to $27.88 for two.

Campbell Hill

Accommodation: Ruebke Youth Hostel (AYH-SA), Hwy. 4 at Taggart, 62916. Telephone: 618/426-3136. $4.50. On the Trans America Bicycle Trail. Call five hours in advance if you want dinner.

Champaign-Urbana

On Campus: The University of Illinois is in this fair-size town on the Illinois prairie. You may be able to stay at the Student Union for $23.10 per night—contact the Illini Union Travel Center, 131 Illini Union (tel. 217/333-7360). For a true "taste" of Champaign-Urbana, you have to visit Murphy's Pub for a steak sandwich or the Deluxe Lunch for a fish sandwich on Friday or Saturday. To meet students, you can also go to Cochrane's, Round Robin, or Garcia's Pizza. The Deluxe Lunch & Billiards, Inc. has a delicious fish sandwich and is open Friday and Saturday.

The *Daili Illini* newspaper can help you find out about rides and accommodations.

"Champaign-Urbana is an oasis of culture, fun, and entertainment on an otherwise barren prairie. It's a good stopover for anyone going cross country since it's at the intersection of Interstates 74 and 57."

Accommodations: Best Inns of America, 914 West Bloomington Rd., 61820. Telephone: 217/356-6000. $17.88 to $21.38 for one; $23.38 to $26.88 for two.
● Regal 8 Inn, 1701 Neil St., 61820. Telephone: 217/359-8888. See Bloomington listing for rates.

Chicago

Chicago's most striking feature is its lakefront. Because of Lake Michigan, Chicago has beaches, parks, and marinas that give lots of pleasure to Chicagoans and visitors as well. While you're in Chicago, be sure to walk, bicycle, or jog along the lakefront, admiring the skyline on one side and the lake on the other. For anyone with an interest in architecture, Chicago is a dream—you'll find the works of Louis Sullivan, Frank Lloyd Wright, and Mies van der Rohe, and two outstanding examples of the architecture of the '70s—the Sears Tower and the John Hancock Building.

Chicago starts to celebrate every year as soon as the weather gets nice. From June to August, there are concerts by the Chicago Symphony Orchestra at the Ravinia Festival in Highland Park (can be reached by special train during concert season). During the summer there are also free concerts in Grant Park. Just bring a picnic supper along and make yourself comfortable on the lawn. At midsummer there's Chicagofest, a ten-day festival of music and food at the Navy Pier. Chicagofest is linked with the Lakefront Festival, which features air and water shows.

The "Loop" is the commercial heart of Chicago—it is a five- by seven-block area west of Michigan Ave. Michigan Ave. itself is a busy and elegant shopping street.

The Lincoln Park area is bounded by North Ave. on the south, Diversey on the north, and the lake on the east; its western border is rather fuzzy. This area includes high-rise buildings on the lake and rehabilitated low-rise and restored homes in the interior.

Lakeview may be thought of as Chicago in microcosm. It begins at Diversey on the south, goes to Irving Park on the north, the lake on the east, and Ashland on the west. Within its boundaries are the rich and the poor and ethnic communities where Spanish, German, Korean, Filipino, and Japanese are heard more often than English. In this area, too, are some of the old, established shopping areas and the part of Chicago, dubbed "New Town," where new singles bars, discos, boutiques, and records stores open every day.

The triangle between North Clark Street and West North and Ogden Aves. is called "Old Town." It is the part of the city where you'll find the lovely old Victorian homes built after the fire of 1871. Hyde Park, the area that borders the lakefront from 51st to 59th Sts. and goes west to Washington Park, is dominated by the presence of the University of Chicago.

Two recommended guides to the city are *Chicago on Foot: Walking Tours of Chicago's Architecture,* by Ira J. Bach, Rand McNally ($7.95), and *The Chicago Gourmet,* by Sue Kupcinet and Connie Fish, Simon and Schuster ($3.95).

Another book for people exploring the city is *Norman Mark's Chicago: Walking, Bicycling and Driving Tours of the City,* Chicago Review Press ($6.95). To know what's going on in Chicago while you're visiting, check the *Sun Times,* the *Tribune,* or the alternative paper called *The Reader,* which can be picked up free in just about any store, especially on the North Side. *Chicago Magazine* is another good source of information—it comes out monthly and includes articles, restaurant listings, etc.

Getting There: From the Airport: O'Hare is about 17 miles from the city and Midway is about 10 miles away. Continental Air Transport services both airports and the fare is $5.45 from O'Hare and $4.20 from Midway to the Loop.

Or you can go by public transport from O'Hare to the Loop. Take the #40 express bus at the lower level east to Jefferson Park Rapid Transit, then transfer to the el going south to the Loop—it will cost 90¢.

● From the Train and Bus Stations: The Greyhound station is at Clark and Randolph and the Trailways station is at Randolph and State, in the heart of downtown. From these terminals you can catch a bus, an el, or a subway. Union Station, the train terminal, is located at Canal and Adams. There are four city bus routes that go to and from the train station.

Getting Around: Taxis are expensive: it will cost you 75¢ to get in, then 80¢ per mile, plus 10¢ for every three-quarters of a minute of waiting time and 50¢ for each additional passenger between the ages of 12 and 65.

● There's a subway and an elevated system that goes north, south, and west of the city and "loops" the central business and shopping district—hence the name "Loop." The fare is 80¢ plus 10¢ for a transfer.

● The bus fare is the same and buses run every 5 to 15 minutes, usually. Look for rectangular signs that say CTA, with the number and route of the bus, at each bus stop. Exact change is required.

● The Chicago Transit Authority (CTA) distributes a Downtown Transit Map, which explains its routes in both English and Spanish. Their travel information number is 836-7000.

Accommodations: For a brochure describing *Chicago Holidays* (two-in-a-room weekend specials), write to the Chicago Convention and Tourism Bureau, McCormick Place and the Lake, 60616.

"Some of the most elegant Chicago hotels offer special weekend rates that are not very widely publicized. A few phone calls might get you an elegant double for about $30 per person for two nights."

● International House at the University of Chicago (AYH-SA), 1414 East 59th St., 60637. Telephone: 312/753-2270. Men and women connected with a university. More room in summer. $12 and up per night. Bring your own soap. Reservations required three to seven days in advance.

● YMCA, 501 North Central Ave., 60644. Telephone: 312/287-9120. Men only. $18 single. Bus stops at the door.

● YMCA, 1621 West Division St. One-half block from train and bus. Telephone: 312/278-4380. Men only. $12 single first night; $7 per night after that. Weekly rate: $49 first week; $35.50 second week. No advance reservations.

● YMCA, 3333 North Marshfield Ave., 60657. Telephone: 312/248-3333. Men over 18 only. $6.50 plus $1 key deposit per night in private room with shared bathroom. Weekly rate: $30 to $35. No telephone reservations; personal interview required.

● Lawson YMCA, 30 West Chicago Ave., 60610. Telephone: 312/944-6211. Men and women. $13.70 to $21.20 single; $13.10 to $14.30 per person double.

● The Blackstone Hotel, 636 South Michigan Ave. at Balbo, 60605. Telephone: 312/427-4300. This is a small, intimate hotel furnished in French Renaissance style. It is generally expensive, but they do have a special summer promotion at $29 for a single and $32 for a double.

● Friendship Inn–Edgebrook Motor Hotel, 6401 West Touhy Ave., 60648. Telephone: 312/774-4200. $20 to $22 for one; $23 to $25 for two in one bed; $25 to $27 for two in two beds.

● Regal 8 Inn, 2448 North Mannheim, Franklin Park, 60131. Telephone: 312/455-6500. See Bloomington listing for rates.

● Days Inn, ♿, I-65 and U.S. 30, 8290 Louisiana St., Merrillville, IN 46410. Telephone: 219/738-2701. $22.88 for one; $27.88 for two.

● Best Value Admiral Oasis Motel, 9353 Waukegan Rd., Morton Grove, 60053. Telephone: 312/965-4000. $17.71 for one; $19.71 for two.

● Red Roof Inn, I-80/294 at Halsted Rd., South Holland. To open in 1982. $19.95 for one; $22.95 for two in one bed; $24.95 to $26.95 for two to four in two beds.

Where to Eat: There are two chains that can be recommended because of both the quality of their food and their low prices. These are the Steak and Eggers, open seven days a week and 24 hours a day (check the Yellow Pages of the phone book for locations), and the Original Pancake House (at 2020 North Lincoln Park West and 30 other Chicago locations). At the Steak and Egger, you can get hamburgers, steak and eggs, etc. The Original Pancake House serves an apple pancake that's more like a soufflé with apple slices and a cinnamon glaze on top. There's usually a long wait on weekends and the Pancake House is a popular restaurant for people with children.

● Manny's, 1141 South Jefferson. Telephone: 939-2855. Open Monday to Saturday from 5 a.m. to 5:30 p.m. This is a huge cafeteria with lots of choices. The food is delicatessen—"from knishes to brisket."

● Family House, 2421 West Lawrence. Telephone: 334-0552. Open 11:30 a.m. to 2 a.m. daily. The food is Greek and fresh fish is flown in three times a week. The lamb dishes are excellent and the salads are fresh in this restaurant in a Greek neighborhood.

● The Berghoff, 17 West Adams. Telephone: 427-3170. Open Monday to Saturday, 11 a.m. to 9:30 p.m. In this German restaurant right in the heart of the Loop, you'll find one of the best food bargains in the city. Portions are generous and the price is reasonable. The restaurant is huge, one of the oldest in the city, and extremely busy at lunchtime.

● La Paella, 2920 North Clark. Telephone: 528-0757. Not an inexpensive restaurant, but it's worth a bit of a splurge to have their paella at $10.95. There's a wonderful flan for dessert, too.

"To try stuffed pizza, which is a layered deep-dish pie, go to one of the branches of Giordano's (North Rush St., Lincoln Ave., among others), which Chicago Magazine *voted the best in the city."*

What to See: Art Institute of Chicago, Michigan Ave. at Adams. Telephone: 443-3500. The well-known institute houses one of the best collections of French impressionist paintings in the world. Admission is $3 for adults, $1.50 for students, children, and senior citizens; and Thursday it's free for all.

● Field Museum of Natural History. Telephone: 922-9410. In Grant Park, Roosevelt Rd. at Lake Shore Dr., this museum features animal dioramas, Indian art and archeology collections, and exhibits tracing the history of man. On Friday admission is free; otherwise it's $2 for adults, $1 for students with an ID. Right near the Field Museum are the Adler Planetarium (tel. 322-0300) and the John G. Shedd Aquarium (tel. 939-2426). Both are worth a side trip.

● Sears Tower. You'll find this 110-story building at the intersection of Wacker Dr. and Adams. For $1.50 you can enjoy a view from the top, seeing not only Chicago but also the suburbs, and parts of Indiana, Michigan, and Wisconsin, too.

● Museum of Science and Industry, East 57th St. and South Shore Dr. Telephone: MU4-1414. The admission is free and the exhibits include an enormous model of the human heart and the Apollo 8 lunar module. Fun for anyone who likes to know how things work.

● Boat ride. There are two sightseeing companies that operate boat trips from the Michigan Ave. docks, down the Chicago River to the Merchandise Mart and back through the locks and up along Lake Michigan's shoreline. Both begin their season in the spring and rates are not available at press time. Call either Wendella Sightseeing, 400 North Michigan (tel. 377-1446), or Mercury Sightseeing, Wacker Dr. and Michigan Ave. (tel. 332-1353), for details.

At Night: Rick's Café American, in the Holiday Inn, 644 North Lake Shore Dr. Telephone: 943-9200. In this re creation of Rick's from the film *Casablanca,* the jazz is good, whether there are big names featured or local talent.

● Wise Fools Pub, 2270 North Lincoln. Telephone: 929-1510. This is the place to hear the best that local jazz and blues performers have to offer. On weekends there's a $2 admission charge and a two-drink minimum.

● Holsteins, 2464 North Lincoln Ave. Telephone: 327-3331. Cover charge is $2 to $5. For the best in national and international folk stars. Good, inexpensive hamburgers; fish and chips, too.

● B.L.U.E.S., 2519 North Halsted St. Telephone: 327-3331. It's near to Lincoln Park's nightlife area and features blues seven nights a week.

● The League of Chicago offers half-price tickets for over 40 Chicago theaters on the day of the performance. Go to the Hot Tix booth in Daley Center Plaza near the corner of Clark and Washington. Open Tuesday to Friday, 11 a.m. to 5:15 p.m.; Saturday, 10 a.m. to 5 p.m. Call 977-1755 for information.

● Victory Gardens Theater, ●➤$2, 3730 North Clark St. This is a professional theater that usually mounts new productions. Programs include experimental studio productions and free readings of original scripts every other Saturday night at 11 p.m. Tickets for the main stage productions are $6 to $11, with $2 discount for ISIC-holders. Next door to the theater is an interesting experimental theater called the Remains Theater.

● Orchestra Hall, 220 South Michigan. Telephone: 435-8111. This is the home of the Chicago Symphony Orchestra, whose principal conductor is Georg Solti. Guest artists perform during the symphony's season which runs from fall through spring.

● Civic Opera House, 20 North Wacker. Telephone: 346-0270. The Lyric

Opera, a first-rate company, attracts top operatic talent during its fall season. Chicago is also visited each year by many famous dance companies, e.g., the Joffrey, Alvin Ailey, American Ballet Theater, etc.

● Parkway Theater, 2736 North Clark. Telephone: 929-9555. Film revivals. Before 5 p.m. on weekdays, $3.

● Second City, 1616 North Wells St. Telephone: 337-3992. This improvisational comedy theater was the starting place for most of "Saturday Night Live"'s original cast as well as Alan Alda. There are shows every night at 9 p.m., Sunday to Thursday, and at 8:30 and 11 p.m. Friday and Saturday night. Sunday to Thursday at 11 p.m. and Saturday at 1 p.m. there are free improvisation sessions.

● Tut's, 959 North Belmont. Telephone: 447-3365. This New Wave club has the best of both local and national bands.

Shopping: Barbara's Book Store, 1434 North Wells, 2907 North Broadway, and 121 North Marion, Oak Park. A fine selection of paperbacks, especially "counterculture." Good photography, theater, poetry, and fiction sections.

● Joseph O'Gara, 1311 East 57th St. For used paperbacks and hardcovers.

● Rizzoli's, Water Tower Place, 835 North Michigan Ave. Books, records, foreign and domestic newspapers and magazines.

● Rose Records, 214 South Wabash and 165 West Madison. Huge selection of records and tapes, especially well stocked in the classics, opera, and jazz departments. The second floor of the Wabash store has budget and out-of-print records.

● Sounds Good, 3155 North Broadway and 3259 North Ashland. For rock, jazz, blues, folk, and disco records at low prices. The Ashland store has Chicago's best selection of old 45-rpm records.

● Marshall Field, 111 North State. One reader insists that all visitors take a look at this, the city's most famous department store.

● Handmoor, 200 West Adams. Clothes for women at 20% below the suggested retail price.

● Traveler's Abbey, 2934 North Broadway. Camping and hiking equipment; clothes, too.

● Eddie Bauer, Inc., 123 North Wabash Ave., across from Marshall Field. Specializes in backpacking, skiing, and down gear of high quality.

● Crate and Barrel, 1510 North Wells and 850 North Michigan Ave. Here you'll find anything and everything you'd need to equip a kitchen—glassware, dishes, good gift possibilities. Most things are reasonably priced. The Michigan Ave. store has a room for "seconds" which is always worth a look.

Tourist Information: Chicago Convention and Tourism Bureau's Water Tower Information Center, Michigan and Chicago Aves. Telephone: 312/225-5000, extension 276. All you need to know in this new center for tourists. Open seven days a week.

Help: Travelers Aid, 327 South LaSalle. Telephone: 312/435-4500. Offices at Greyhound Station, Union Station, and O'Hare Airport.

● Jazz Hotline, 312/666-1881.

Decatur

Accommodation: Regal 8 Inn, 16 South Country Club Rd., 62521. Telephone: 217/428-4677. See Bloomington listing for rates.

De Kalb

Help: Crisis Line, 815/758-6655.

On Campus: Northern Illinois University is in De Kalb, and if you don't mind spending $21 for a single or $24.15 for a double, you can stay in one of the hotel-like rooms in the University Student Center there. Also in the Holmes Student Center is the Pow Wow Room where a full meal—meat, potatoes, vegetables, roll, and beverage—will be inexpensive. There are three other restaurants in the Student Center to choose from.

Accommodation: Motel 6, 1116 West Lincoln Hwy., 60115. Telephone: 815/756-6605. $12.95 for one; $16.95 for two; $19.95 for up to four.

Effingham

Accommodations: Days Inn, West Fayette Rd. and I-57 and 70, Exit 159, Box 1168, 62401. Telephone: 217/342-9271. $19.88 to $21.88 for one; $24.88 to $26.88 for two.

● Friendship Inn–Lincoln Lodge, Rte. 45 North, P.O. Box 634, 62401. Telephone: 217/342-4133. $15.95 to $19.95 for one; $19.95 to $23.95 for two in one bed; $21.95 to $25.95 for two in two beds.

Elgin

Accommodation: Friendship Inn–Colonial Lodge, 788 Villa St., 60120. Telephone: 312/742-2790. $18.50 to $20.50 for one; $19.50 to $21 for two in one bed; $21 to $26 for two in two beds.

Evanston

Help: Crisis Intervention Referral Services, 312/492-6500.

On Campus: In Evanston, the suburban area adjacent to Chicago, you'll find the campus of Northwestern University. Northwestern students gather at The Spot, Fritz's, Jay's, Yesterday's, and The Main. There's a bulletin board you might want to check at Norris Center; pick up a copy of the *Daily Northwestern* to see what's going on when you arrive.

Accommodations: YMCA, 1000 Grove, 60201. Telephone: 312/475-7400. In downtown Evanston, one block south of Davis Street El Station. Men only. Must be 18 or over. $14 single plus $3 key deposit. Reservations usually required. There's a cafeteria in the building. "Spartan."

● Margarita Inn, 🔄, 1566 Oak Ave., 60201. Telephone: 312/869-2273. Men and women. $22 single; $28 double. Weekly rates: $80 to $90 single; $110 double. "The inn is European-style . . . there are very few rooms with private bath but there are ample facilities on each floor."

Galesburg

Accommodation: Regal 8 Inn, 1487 North Henderson, 61401. Telephone: 309/344-2401. See Bloomington listing for rates.

Jacksonville

Accommodation: Motel 6, 1716 West Morton Dr., 62650. Telephone: 217/243-5322. See De Kalb listing for rates.

Joliet

Accommodations: Regal 8 Inn, 2219½ West Jefferson, 60435. Telephone: 815/744-1220. See Bloomington listing for rates.
● Red Roof Inn, I-80 at Larkin Ave. To open in 1982. $19.95 for one; $22.95 for two in one bed; $24.95 to $26.95 for two to four in two beds.

Kankakee

Accommodations: Regal 8 Inn, Ill. 50 and Armour Rd., Bourbonnais, 60914. Telephone: 815/933-2300. See Bloomington listing for rates.
● Imperial 400 Motor Inn, 1225 East Court St., 60901. Telephone: 815/933-1681. $17 to $21 for one; $19 to $23 for two in one bed; $21 to $25 for two in two beds.

La Grange

Accommodation: West Suburban YMCA, 31 East Ogden Ave., 60525. Telephone: 312/352-7600. Men and women. $14 single; $16 double. Cafeteria on the premises.

LaSalle

Accommodation: Motel 6, 1900 May St., Peru, 61354. Telephone: 815/224-2734. See De Kalb listing for rates.

Libertyville

Accommodation: Best Value Doe's Motel, Rtes. 45 and 137, 60048. Telephone: 312/362-0800. $21 to $22 for one; $22 to $23 for two in one bed; $25 to $26 for two in two beds.

Lincoln

Accommodation: Regal 8 Inn, U.S. 66, 62656. Telephone: 217/732-9641. See Bloomington listing for rates.

Lombard

Accommodation: Friendship Inn–Highland Manor, 19 West 545 Roosevelt Rd., 60148. Telephone: 312/627-5700. $19 to $23 for one; $21 to $26 for two in one bed; $24 to $29.50 for two in two beds.

Macomb

Accommodation: Tanner Conference Center, Western Illinois University, University Dr., 61455. Telephone: 309/298-2461. $7.88 to $14.70 single. Rooms have two single beds, which are used as couches during the day. Each floor of the guest area has a lounge and a community bathroom. Meals in adjacent building. On Western Illinois University campus, one-half mile from bus and train stations.

Marion

Accommodation: Regal 8 Inn, I-57 and Rte. 13, 62959. Telephone: 618/993-2631. See Bloomington listing for rates.

Moline

Accommodations: Regal 8 Inn, Quad City Airport Rd. (Ill. 92), 61265. Telephone: 309/764-8711. See Bloomington listing for rates.
● Exel Inn of Moline, 🛆, 2501 52nd Ave., 61265. Telephone: 309/797-5580. $17.95 for one; $22.95 for two in one bed; $24.95 for two in two beds.

Mount Vernon

Accommodations: Regal 8 Inn, I-57 and U.S. 460, 62864. Telephone: 618/244-2383. See Bloomington listing for rates.
● Best Inns of America, Rte. 15 and I-57, 62864. Telephone: 618/244-4343. $18.88 for one; $22.38 for two in one bed; $24.38 for two in two beds.

Morton Grove

Accommodation: Best Value Admiral Oasis Motel, 9353 Waukegan Rd., 60053. Telephone: 302/965-4000. $17.71 for one; $19.71 for two.

Naperville

Accommodation: YMCA, 34 South Washington, 60540. Telephone: 312/420-6270. Men only. $11. Weekly rate: $35. Reservations required.

Normal

Accommodation: Motel 6, 1600 North Main St., 61761. Telephone: 309/452-9481. See De Kalb listing for rates.

Peoria

Accommodations: YWCA, 301 NE Jefferson St., 61602. Telephone: 309/674-1167. Women only. $13 single. Weekly rate of $50 includes linens. Centrally located. "1928 building with front parlors, tearoom, swimming pool, and a sauna."

● Motel 6, 104 West Camp St., 61611. Telephone: 309/694-3294. See De Kalb listing for rates.

● Imperial 400 Motor Inn, 202 NE Washington, 61602. Telephone: 309/676-8961. $20 to $24 for one; $24 to $29 for two in one bed; $26 to $30 for two in two beds.

● Red Roof Inn, I-74 at War Memorial Dr., U.S. 150 (Exit 89), 61614. Telephone: 309/685-3911. See Joliet listing for rates.

● Days Inn, ⓑ, Exit 89 off I-74, 2726 West Lake Ave., 61614. Telephone: 309/688-7000. $20.88 to $21.88 for one; $24.88 to $25.88 for two.

● Best Value Townehouse Motel, 1519 North Knoxville Ave., 61603. Telephone: 309/688-8646. $20.25 for one; $23.50 for two in one bed; $25.50 for two in two beds.

● Best Value Townehouse Motel, 705 Hamilton Blvd., 61603. Telephone: 309/674-6135. See above listing for rates.

Pocahontas

Accommodation: Best Value Wikiup Motel, Inc., Box 156, Johnson and Plant St., 62275. Telephone: 618/669-2293. $16 to $22 for one; $18 to $22 for two in one bed; $20 to $25 for two in two beds.

Pontiac

Accommodation: Best Value Fiesta Motel, Rtes. 66 and 116, 61764. Telephone: 815/844-7103. $16.80 for one; $21 for two in one bed; $23.10 for two in two beds.

Rockford

Help: Contact Rockford, 815/964-4044.

Accommodations: YWCA, 220 South Madison St., 61101. Women only. YWCA membership required for stay of more than one week. $15. Weekly rate: $20 to $25. Reservations requested. Snackbar in the building.

● Motel 6, 4205 11th St., 61109. Telephone: 815/399-6266. See De Kalb listing for rates.

● Regal 8 Inn, U.S. 20 and 51, 61109. Telephone: 815/398-6080. See Bloomington listing for rates.

● Exel Inn, ⓑ, 220 South Lyford Rd., 61108. Telephone: 815/332-4915. $17.50 for one; $22.50 for two in one bed; $24.50 for two in two beds.

● Imperial 400 Motor Inn, 733 East State St., 61104. Telephone: 815/964-3361. $18 to $24 for one; $22 to $28 for two in one bed; $24 to $30 for two in two beds.

● Red Roof Inn, ⓑ, I-90 at East State St. (Business Rte. 20). Telephone: 815/398-9750. $17.95 for one; $20.95 for two in one bed; $22.95 to $24.95 for two to four in two beds.

Springfield

"An historical, amusing, clean, and educational town."

On Campus: Sangamon State University is here. For accommodations in the university area, stop at the Office of the Dean of Students on Sheppard Rd.; telephone: 217/786-6581.

Accommodations: Best Value Capitol City Motel, 1620 North 9th St., 62702. Telephone: 217/528-0462. $13 to $18 for one; $14 to $20 for two in one bed; $16 to $22 for two in two beds.

● Red Roof Inn, 🛆, I-55 at South Grand Ave. (Exit 96B). Telephone: 217/753-4302. See Rockford listing for rates.

● Regal 8 Inn, I-55 and Toronto Rd., 62707. Telephone: 217/529-1633. See Bloomington listing for rates.

● Motel 6, 3125 Wide Track Dr., 62703. Telephone: 217/789-0520. See De Kalb listing for rates.

Urbana (see also Champaign-Urbana)

Accommodation: Motel 6, 1906 North Cunningham Ave., 61801. Telephone: 217/344-8660. See De Kalb listing for rates.

Indiana

Most people think of the Indianapolis 500 when they think of Indiana; the race is probably Indiana's biggest claim to fame. It's held on Memorial Day and has attracted huge crowds since 1911 (with time off for the two World Wars). Other things to see in Indiana are Indiana Dunes National Lakeshore; Wayandotte Cave, a five-level cavern; the Indianapolis Motor Speedway, once a test ground for vehicle performance and now the scene of the 500 and a museum of the racing art; Lincoln Boyhood National Memorial, the cabin and the grave of Lincoln's mother with a visitor center that features a film on the family's four years in Indiana; and New Harmony, the remains of what was once a utopian village.

Some Special Events: Parke County Maple Fair in Rockville (February); Dogwood Festival in Orleans, Indianapolis 500 Festival, and Civil War Weekend in Fort Wayne (all in May); Victorian Lockerbie Square Summer A'Fair in Indianapolis and Rose Festival in Richmond (June); Circus City Festival in Peru (once winter headquarters for many great circuses) and Three Rivers Festival in Fort Wayne (July); War of 1812 Weekend in Fort Wayne and State Fair in Indianapolis (August); James Whitcomb Riley Festival (a three-day celebration in honor or the Hoosier poet) in Greenfield, Village Tour of Homes in Zionville, and the Parke County Covered Bridge Festival in Rockville (all in October).

Hitching: According to the State Police, you may not stand on the traveled part of the road to solicit a ride. Otherwise, it's okay except, of course, on Interstates. The best routes for hitching are U.S. 40, 41, 31, and 30. We got one typical reaction to our question about hitchhiking in Indiana: "Parents don't like it, but the kids do it anyway." According to another friend who took no risks with his answer to our question about the attitude to people on the road, "the attitude varies from extreme rejection to total acceptance."

Tourist Information: Tourism Development Division, Department of Commerce, 440 North Meridian St., Indianapolis, IN 46204. Telephone: 317/232-8860. Ask for their *SceniCircle Drives* booklet, which lists the state's major historical, recreational, and scenic attractions organized in a series of 17 mini-tours.

Anderson

Accommodation: Motel 6, 5810 Scatterfield Rd., 46013. Telephone: 317/642-3333. $12.95 for one; $16.95 for two; $19.95 for up to four.

Bedford

Accommodation: Best Value Rosemount Motel, 1923 M St., 47421. Telephone: 812/275-5953. $16 for one; $19 for two.

Bloomington

On Campus: Have you seen the film *Breaking Away*? That's Bloomington, scene of the Little 500 bicycle race and home of the University of Indiana, one of the "Big Ten."

Two places on campus where you may be able to spend a night are the Indiana Memorial Union and the Poplar's Research and Conference Center. If you're hungry, try Nero's Olde World Chili Parlor on Walnut, and the Tao, a vegetarian restaurant on 10th St. Or for food and drink, student favorites are Nick's English Hut and Kilroy's on Kirkwood, and Bear's Place on 3rd St. The Indiana Memorial Union is the largest in the U.S.—it has restaurants, bowling alleys, and nightspots.

If a problem comes up while you're on campus, dial 332-0211.

Accommodation: Motel 6, 126 South Franklin Rd., 47401. Telephone: 812/336-0689. See Anderson listing for rates.

Clarks Hill

Accommodation: Best Value Lincoln Lodge, RR #1, on U.S. 52 and Ind. 28, 47930. Telephone: 317/523-2111. $18 for one; $22 for two in one bed; $26 for two in two beds.

Elkhart

Help: Switchboard Concern, 219/293-8671.

Accommodations: Red Roof Inn, I-80/90 at Ind. 19 (Exit 92). Telephone: 219/262-3691. $17.95 for one; $20.95 for two in one bed; $22.95 to $24.95 for two to four in two beds.

● Days Inn, I-80/90 and Ind. 19 (Exit 92), 2820 Cassopolis St., 46514. Telephone: 219/262-3541. $17.88 to $19.88 for one; $21.88 to $23.88 for two.

Evansville

Accommodations: YWCA, 118 Vine St., 47708. Telephone: 812/422-1191. Women only. $5.25 single or double; $7.50 triple. Short walk from bus station.
● Regal 8 Inn, 4201 Hwy. 41 North and Yokel Rd., 47711. Telephone: 812/424-6431. $18.88 for one; $21.88 for two in one bed; $24.88 for two to four in two beds.

Fort Wayne

Tourist Information: Fort Wayne Convention and Visitors Bureau, 826 Ewing, 46802. Telephone: 219/424-1435.
Help: Switchboard, Inc., 316 West Creighton Ave. Telephone: 219/456-4561. 24-hour crisis and information line.
Accommodations: YMCA, 226 East Washington Blvd., 46802. One-quarter of a mile from bus station; one-half mile from the train station. Telephone: 219/422-6486. Men and limited facilities for women. $10 plus membership fee. Weekly rate: $36.
● Susse Chalet Motor Lodge, U.S. 24 and City Rte. 30 at junction with U.S. 30, 46803. Telephone: 219/424-1980. $19.70 for one; $23.70 for two; $29.70 for four.
● Motel 6, 1020 U.S. 30 Bypass North, 46802. Telephone: 219/422-3840. See Anderson listing for rates.
● Motel 6, 3003 Coliseum Blvd. West, 46808. Telephone: 219/483-9225. See Anderson listing for rates.
● Econo-Travel Motor Hotel, 1401 West Washington Center Rd., 46825. Telephone: 219/489-3588. $19.95 for one or two in one bed; $21.95 for two in two beds.
● Red Roof Inn, I-69 at U.S. 30 and 33 (Exit 109A), 46808. Telephone: 219/484-8641. See Elkhart listing for rates.
● Days Inn, I-69 and U.S. 30 and 33, P.O. Box 8035, 3527 Coliseum Blvd., 46808. Telephone: 219/482-4511. $18.88 to $19.88 for one; $22.88 to $23.88 for two.

Goshen

On Campus: If you find yourself in need of conversation, the Oasis, a popular watering hole, is the place to go in Goshen. The Student Union of Goshen College has a bulletin board which might provide helpful information about rides, accommodations, and so forth. Goshen has been described by a friend at the college as "the town that voted for George Wallace when he ran in the presidential primary—need I say more?"
Accommodation: Goshen Motor Inn, 🐟★, 65522 U.S. 33 East, 46526. Telephone: 219/642-4388. $16.50 for one; $23.50 for two.

Howe

Accommodation: Best Value Bailey Motel, RR #2, on Hwy. 9 off Exit 11, 46746. Telephone: 219/562-3481. $18.72 for one; $20.80 for two in one bed; $22.88 for two in two beds.

Indianapolis

Tourist Information: Indianapolis Convention and Visitors Bureau, Inc., 100 South Capital Ave., 46225. Telephone: 317/635-9567.

Accommodations: YMCA, 860 West 10th St., 46202. Telephone: 317/634-2478. Men and women. $16.06 single. Weekly rate: $37.88 or $41.15. "The people there were very friendly. Don't walk from the bus station—you have to go through a pretty raunchy neighborhood." Higher rates during race week.

● Superior Clover–West, 9745 West Washington St., 46231. Telephone: 317/839-2324. $14 for one; $16 to $18 for two in one bed; $18 to $22 for two in two beds.

● Motel 6, 2851 Shadeland, 46219. Telephone: 317/546-1501. See Anderson listing for rates.

● Budget Motor Inn, √, 5855 East Washington, 46219. Telephone: 317/357-8323, or toll free 800/648-4920. $17.95 for one; $19.95 for two in one bed; $23.95 for two in two beds.

● Susse Chalet Motor Lodge, I-465, Exit 42, then west one mile, 46226. Telephone: 317/546-4971. See Fort Wayne listing for rates.

● Friendship Inn–Catalina Motel, 8010 West Washington St., 46231. Telephone: 317/244-9558. $16 to $19 for one; $19 to $22 for two in one bed; $22 to $26 for two in two beds.

● Regal 8 Inn, 5241 West Bradbury at Lynhurst, 46241. Telephone: 317/248-1231. $17.88 for one; $20.88 for two in one bed; $23.88 for two to four in two beds.

● Regal 8 Inn, 3731 Shadeland, 46262. Telephone: 317/545-6051. See above listing for rates.

● Red Roof Inn, ♿, I-465 at U.S. 421 North (Exit 27), 46268. Telephone: 317-872-3030. See Elkhart listing for rates.

● Red Roof Inn, I-465 at South Emerson Ave. (Exit 52), 46203. Telephone: 317/788-9551. See Elkhart listing for rates.

● Days Inn, ♿, I-70 and Shadeland Exit, 7314 East 21st St., 46219. Telephone: 317/359-5500. $20.88 for one; $25.88 for two.

● Days Inn, I-465 and Emerson Rd., 5151 Elmwood Dr., 46107. Telephone: 317/783-5471. $20.88 to $22.88 for one; $24.88 to $26.88 for two.

● Days Inn, ♿, I-465 at U.S. 31 South, Exit 2B, 450 Bixler Rd., 46227. Telephone: 317/788-0811. $19.88 for one; $23.88 for two.

Kokomo

Accommodations: Days Inn, South Edge, on U.S. 31 Bypass South, 46901. Telephone: 317/453-7100. $17.88 to $19.88 for one; $21.88 to $23.88 for two.

● Susse Chalet Motor Lodge, U.S. 31 Bypass and East Blvd., 46901. Telephone: 317/457-7561. See Fort Wayne listing for rates.

Lafayette

Accommodations: Red Roof Inn, I-65 at Ind. 26, 47905. Telephone: 317/448-4671. $19.95 for one; $22.95 for two in one bed; $24.95 to $26.95 for two to four in two beds.
● Regal 8 Inn, 1217 Sagamore Pkwy., 47906. Telephone: 317/463-1531. See Indianapolis listing for rates.

Merrillville

Accommodation: Red Roof Inn, I-65 at U.S. 30 West. Telephone: 219/738-2430. See Elkhart listing for rates.

Michigan City

Accommodations: Red Roof Inn, I-94 at U.S. 421 North (Exit 34B), 46360. Telephone: 219/874-5251. See Elkhart listing for rates.
● Superior ABC Motel, 3948 Franklin St., 46360. Telephone: 219/879-0335. $16 to $22 for one; $18 to $22 for two in one bed; $20 to $26 for two in two beds.

Miller

Accommodation: Susse Chalet Motor Lodge, I-65, Indiana Toll Rd. (Exit 3 or 17), 46402. Telephone: 219/938-6065. See Fort Wayne listing for rates.

Muncie

Accommodations: YWCA, 310 East Charles St., 47305. Telephone: 317/284-3345. Women only. $7.50 nonmembers; $5.50 members.
● Best Value Roberts Downtown Inn, 420 South High St. at Howard, 47305. Telephone: 317/286-0900. $14 for one; $25 for two in one bed; $32 for two in two beds.

New Albany

On Campus: Indiana University Southeast is located in New Albany. According to one friend there, the place to eat is Lancaster's, one-half mile from campus on Grant Line Rd. Also recommended is the Cellar at 13th and Floodwall.

New Castle

Accommodation: YMCA, 1201 Church St. 47362. Telephone: 317/529-3804. Men only. $11 single. Weekly rate: $32. No one can be checked in on Sunday or after 1 p.m. on Saturday.

Plymouth

Accommodation: Motel 6, 2535 North Michigan, 46563. Telephone: 219/936-3106. See Anderson listing for rates.

Portage

Accommodation: Motel 6, 6101 Melton Rd., Rte. 20, 46368. Telephone: 219/762-3129. See Anderson listing for rates.

Remington

Accommodation: Days Inn, ♿, I-65 and U.S. 24, Rte. 2, Box 240B, 47977. Telephone: 219/261-2178. $20.88 for one; $24.88 for two.

Richmond

Accommodation: Susse Chalet Inn, I-70 at junction U.S. 40, 47374. Telephone: 317/966-7511. $22.70 for one; $26.70 for two; $32.70 for four.

San Pierre

Accommodation: River Bend Campground (AYH-SA), RR1, P.O. Box 128, 46374. Telephone: 219/896-3339. Open May 1 to October 1. $2.

"This is a private campground with dorm. It is family run and on some weekends we have hog roasts and corn roasts. I have two families in the area I have promised to call in case anyone comes by from either Switzerland or Norway."

Schererville

Accommodation: Superior Underwood Motel, 110 South Lincoln Hwy., Rte. 30, 46375. Telephone: 219/865-2451. $17.50 to $21 for one; $21 to $25 for two in one bed; $27 to $30 for two in two beds.

Seymour

Accommodation: Days Inn, I-65 and U.S. 50 East, 302 Frontage Rd., 47274. Telephone: 812/522-3678. $19.88 to $20.88 for one; $23.88 to $24.88 for two.

South Bend

"We have beautiful parks, two Frank Lloyd Wright houses, the Notre Dame and Indiana State University campuses, and an auto museum."

Help: Hotline-Crisis Intervention, 219/232-3344.
- Information and Referral, 219/232-2522.

On Campus: Indiana University and Notre Dame are here, and you can meet some of their students at the bars along Eddy St., south of the Notre Dame campus, or at the Huddle, right on campus.

In addition to eating at the school cafeterias, you can find an excellent Chinese lunch at China Garden, 910 East Ireland Rd. for $2.95, or a Hungarian dinner at the Budapest Night for $4 to $6.

Indiana University has a good film series which costs $1.25 per film; a similar series exists at Notre Dame.

Accommodations: YWCA, ♿, 802 North Lafayette Blvd., 46601. Telephone: 219/233-9491. Women only. $10.50 single. Weekly rate: $22 to $31. Reservations preferred. Cooking facilities available.

● Motel 6, 52624 U.S. Hwy. 31 North, 46637. Telephone: 219/277-1661. See Anderson listing for rates.

Spencer

Accommodation: McCormick's Creek State Park, ♿, RR1, P.O. Box 71, 47460. Telephone: 812/829-4881. Two miles from Bloomington. Accommodations at the Canyon Inn, and at cabins in the park; cabins available for a full week only, April to October. These cabins accommodate six people and have two sleeping rooms, a kitchen, a lavatory, and showers. They rent for $73 per week. At Canyon Inn, the rates are $26 to $30 for a double room. The inn has access facilities.

Terre Haute

Accommodations: Friendship Inn of Terre Haute, 4800 Dixie Bee Rd., 47802. Telephone: 812/299-1181. $19 to $21 for one; $23 to $25 for two in one bed; $26 to $30 for two in two beds.

● Regal 8 Inn, I-70 and U.S. 41, 47802. Telephone: 812/238-1586. See Evansville listing for rates.

Warsaw

Accommodation: Regal 8 Inn, U.S. 30 East, 46580. Telephone: 219/269-2601. See Indianapolis listing for rates.

Iowa

You probably never thought about it before, but wherever you are in the U.S. you're no more than 2½ driving days away from Iowa. Lots of people pass through Iowa on their way across country on Interstate 80 and some, who like farmland and open spaces, decide to stay.

It was, in fact, Iowa's rich prairie soil that attracted people from all over Europe from the mid-1800s on. The farmer is king in Iowa—the state is patterned with farms that grow corn and soybeans and raise hogs and cattle. The major attractions in Iowa are the Amana Colonies, not far from Cedar Rapids, which represent an experiment in communal utopianism; the Herbert Hoover National Historic Site in West Branch, which includes the two-room cottage where the one-time president was born, a replica of his father's blacksmith shop, the Quaker meeting house where the family worshipped, and the Hoover Presidential Library Museum; Fort Dodge Historical Museum, Fort, and Stockade, reproduction of a fort where pioneers withstood hostile Indians; and Vesterheim in Decorah, a folk museum honoring the Norwegian pioneers of the area.

The Iowa Development Commission has seven information centers located on Interstate highways throughout the state which are open from mid-May to mid-September; check with them for maps and travel advice.

Some Special Events: Tulip Time in Pella (May); International Folk Festival in Bettendorf and Steamboat Days in Burlington (June); All Iowa Fair in Cedar Rapids, Riverboat Days in Clinton, and Bix Beiderbecke Memorial Jazz Festival in Davenport (July); National Hobo Convention in Britt and Iowa State Fair in Des Moines (August); Tri-State Rodeo in Fort Madison (September); and Covered Bridge Festival in Winterset (October).

Hitching: Hitching is legal as long as you stay off the traveled portion of the road. Local cities and towns can prohibit hitchhiking within city limits. In Des Moines, for instance, hitching is illegal on I-235 within Des Moines and

West Des Moines. Hitchhiking seems to be accepted in Iowa, and the attitude toward people on the road is good, more so in the larger cities than in the smaller towns. A friend from Iowa City writes that hitching, especially in the Iowa City area, is good: "Most people are willing to pick you up—everyone from farmers to truckers—if you look clean and you smile. . . . the highway patrol may stop but usually just to talk with you and give you some good tips."

Tourist Information: Iowa Development Commission, Tourism and Travel Division, 250 Jewett Building, Des Moines, IA 50309. Telephone: 515/281-3100.

Albia

Accommodation: Friendship Inn–Holiday Motel, one mile south on U.S. 34, one block east of junction Iowa 5, RFD #1, 52531. Telephone: 515/932-7181. $18 for one; $20 for two in one bed; $22 for two in two beds.

Ames

Help: Open Line, 515/292-7000. "We are a free, confidential listing and info-referral service."
● University Switchboard, 515/294-4357.
● Fish and Loaves Center for Peace and Justice, 2631 Knapp Ave. (near campus). "Provides housing, food for transients and others in need."

On Campus: The campus of Iowa State University is in Ames. A place for the night on campus may be found at the Memorial Union ($22 for a single, $30 for a double); or by contacting the Office of International Educational Services, whose personnel will assist you in finding accommodations (tel. 515/294-1120). For rides, etc., check the bulletin board in the Memorial Union; to meet students, go to the Library, 204 Welch Ave.; Baxter's, 2418 Lincoln; That Place, 205 Main St.; Grand Daddy's, 202 Market; or the Memorial Union's Commons. For good food, all in the university area and all in a $2 to $5 price range, try Grubstake Barbecue, 2512 Lincoln Way (ribs, sandwiches, beer); Thumbs Up, 113 Welch Ave. (pizza, salad bar, beer); Dugan's Deli, 2900 West St. (deli sandwiches and salads); or Quarterstove Café, in the basement of Alumni Hall on ISU campus, open at lunchtime (you can get a huge vegetarian meal here for $1.75 or even work for your meal).

Cedar Falls

Accommodation: Motel 6, 4117 University Ave., 50613. Telephone: 319/277-6900. $12.95 for one; $16.95 for two; $19.95 for up to four.

Cedar Rapids

Accommodations: Red Roof Inn, ⓖ, I-380 at 33rd Ave. SW, 52404. Telephone: 319/366-7523. $17.95 for one; $20.95 for two in one bed; $22.95 to $24.95 for two to four in two beds.
● Exel Inn, ⓖ, 616 33rd Ave. SW, 52404. Telephone: 319/366-2475. $17.95 for one; $22.95 for two in one bed; $24.95 for two in two beds.

Clear Lake

Accommodations: Days Inn, ⬛, I-35 and Hwy. 18, 1306 North 25th St., 50428. Telephone: 515/357-7181. $18.88 for one; $22.88 for two.

● Motel 6, I-35 and Iowa 18, 50428. To open in 1982. See Cedar Falls listing for rates.

Clinton

Accommodation: Imperial 400 Motor Inn, 1111 Camanche Ave., 52732. Telephone: 319/243-4621. $20 to $24 for one; $24 to $28 for two in one bed; $26 to $30 for two in two beds.

Council Bluffs

Accommodation: Motel 6, 1846 North 16th St., 51501. Telephone: 712/328-3851. See Cedar Falls listing for rates.

Davenport

Help: Information, Referral, and Assistance Service of Rock Island, Illinois and Scott County, 315 Ripley Kahl Building, 52801. Telephone: 319/324-0625.

Accommodations: Friendship Inn–Bronze Lantern Motel, 1661 West Kimberly, 52806. Telephone: 319/391-5570. $16 to $17 for one; $20 to $22 for two in one bed; $22 to $24 for two in two beds.

● Motel 6, 6111 North Brady St., 52806. Telephone: 319/391-1300. See Cedar Falls listing for rates.

● Exel Inn, ⬛, 6310 North Brady St., 52804. Telephone: 319/386-6350. See Cedar Rapids listing for rates.

● Town House Budget Host, ➤ ★ ⬛, 7222 Northwest Blvd., 52806. Telephone: 319/391-8222. $21 to $24 for one; $23 to $26 for two in one bed; $25 to $29 for two in two beds.

Des Moines

Tourist Information: Des Moines Convention and Visitors Bureau, 800 High St., 50307. Telephone: 515/286-4971.

Help: Travelers Aid, 1321 Walnut, Suite 200, 50309. Telephone: 515/288-9020.

● Information Referral Center, 515/244-8646.

Accommodations: YMCA, 101 Locust, 50309. Telephone: 515/288-0131. Men only. $12.10 single; $34.95 per week (available after a three-day stay at the regular rate).

● YWCA Residence, 717 Grand Ave., 50309. Telephone: 515/244-8961. Eight blocks from bus station. $17.97 single; $52.30 per week in shared room. Eight-year-old building with pool and gym. Women only.

● Motel 6, 4817 Fleur Dr., 50321. Telephone: 515/285-4720. See Cedar Falls listing for rates.

● Friendship Inn–Beacon, 4144 Hubbell Ave., 50317. Telephone: 515/266-

1166. $16 to $18 for one; $18 to $20 for two in one bed; $20 to $22 for two in two beds.
● Friendship Inn–Plaza Motel, 5626 Douglas, 50310. Telephone: 515/278-1601. $20.50 for one; $24.50 for two in one bed; $27.50 for two in two beds.

Dubuque

Accommodation: Regal 8 Inn, 2670 Dodge St., 52001. Telephone: 319/556-0880. $17.88 for one; $20.88 for two in one bed; $23.88 for two to four in two beds.

Fort Dodge

Accommodation: Best Value Towers Motor Inn, West on Hwy. 20, 50501. Telephone: 515/955-8575. $16 to $20 for one; $18 to $22 for two in one bed; $22 to $30 for two in two beds.

Iowa City

Help: Crisis Center, 112½ East Washington. Telephone: 319/351-0140.
On Campus: The University of Iowa has a ride board in the Wheel Room of the Iowa Memorial Union. For help with U.S. travel information, stop at the Office of Overseas Study and Travel, 200 Jefferson Building, and ask for a copy of the *People's Yellow Pages* for Iowa City. Three eating places recommended by an Iowa City native are the Best Steak House, 1 South Dubuque St.; Bushnell's Turtle, on the Mall on East College ("for large subs, homemade soup, and hot apple cider"); and Taco Grande, 331 East Market (for a good bargain in fast food). The Bijou, the movie theater at the Iowa Memorial Union, shows old and new films for only $1.50.
Accommodations: Wesley House Youth Hostel (AYH), 120 North Dubuque, 52240. Two miles south of I-80. Telephone: 319/338-1179. Open year round. Men, women, and children. $3. Gas stove and oven available. Beds enough for 20 and rollaway cots for 20 or more. AYH membership (see page 21) or current student registration required. First floor of an old house adjacent to Campus Ministry Building.
● Friendship Inn–MarKee, P.O. Box 5426, 707 First Ave., 52241. Telephone: 319/351-6131. $16.50 to $20.50 for one; $20.50 to $24.50 for two in one bed; $24.50 to $30.50 for two in two beds.
● Friendship Inn–Alamo, Exit 242, I-80, west on U.S. 6 and 218 in Coralville, 52241. Telephone: 319/354-4000. $19.85 to $24.85 for one; $22.85 to $27.85 for two in one bed; $24.85 to $29.85 for two in two beds.
● Motel 6, 810 First Ave., Coralville, 52241. Telephone: 319/351-0586. See Cedar Falls listing for rates.

Keokuk

Accommodation: Best Value Globe Motel, Main St. Rd. on Hwy. 218 North, 52632. Telephone: 319/524-4312. $13.75 to $17.75 for one; $19.75 to $24.25 for two in one bed; $28.75 for two in two beds.

Lamoni

On Campus: According to a friend from Graceland College, area people are generally friendly toward strangers. When it's time to eat, all of the restaurants are "good and inexpensive compared with big-city prices." If you're in Lamoni on a Thursday night, go over to the cattle auction held at the Sale Barn. The café attached to the barn serves "a very country, very wholesome, filling meal for $3.50." To meet students, stop in at Bob's Place, K Bar C, the Wagon Wheel, the Pizza Shack, the Out Post, or the Snack Cafeteria at Graceland.

Le Mars

On Campus: Westmar College is here and you can spend a night or two at the College Residence Hall—contact the dean of students for information. "We're just corn fields—Sioux City is 25 miles south." Three good eating spots are the Pantry Café, Central Ave. and 1st St. NE; the Club Café, 20 Plymouth St. SW; or Munro's, south on Hwy. 75. For a bit of culture in Westmar, ask someone about the "excellent collection of exotic musical instruments in the south edge of town."

Mason City

Accommodations: Thrifty Scot Motel, 2301 4th St. SW, 50401. Telephone: 515/424-0210. $16.90 to $21.90 for one; $20.90 to $22.90 for two in one bed; $25.90 to $27.90 for two in two beds.
● YMCA, 15 North Pennsylvania Ave., 50401. Telephone: 515/423-5526. Men only. $9.50.

Mount Vernon

On Campus: Cornell College (the oldest coed college west of the Mississippi) is in this town, which is, according to one student, "friendly, small, picturesque, safe, and typical of Middle America. We welcome travelers into our homes as well as into the community." The college has guest rooms for under $25 per night and, if they're full, there are rooming houses nearby. Free tours of the campus and some of its more than 30 buildings are available for those with a historic bent.

Muscatine

Accommodation: YMCA, 312 Iowa Ave., 52761. Telephone: 319/263-4813. Men only. Singles are $11.75. Weekly rate: $39. Meals available in several places within a six-block radius; the Mississippi River is close by.

Newton

Accommodation: Thrifty Scot Motel, 1605 West 19th St. South, P.O. Box 1031, 50208. Telephone: 515/792-2330. $19.90 to $21.90 for one; $23.90 to $25.90 for two in one bed; $28.90 to $32.90 for two in two beds.

Oskaloosa

Accommodation: Friendship Inn–Mahaska Motel, 1321 A Ave. East, 52577. Telephone: 515/673-8351. $19 to $22 for one; $21 to $25 for two in one bed; $22 to $29 for two in two beds.

Sioux City

Help: AID Center, YMCA Building, 722 Nebraska St., 51101. Telephone: 712/252-1861.

Accommodations: Sioux City YMCA (AYH-SA), 722 Nebraska St., 51101. Telephone: 712/252-3276. Men only. $10 single; less for AYH members. Weekly rate: $35. Within walking distance from bus station.

● Motel 6, 6166 Harbor Dr., c/o General Delivery, Sergeant Bluff, 51054. Telephone: 712/277-2620. See Cedar Falls listing for rates.

Spirit Lake

Accommodation: Friendship Inn–Motel Shamrock, Hwys. 9 and 71 West, 51360. Telephone: 712/336-2668. $16 to $25 for one; $20 to $28 for two in one bed; $24 to $30 for two in two beds.

Villisca

Help: Villisca Emergency, 712/826-2222.

Accommodation: Camp Aldersgate, ♿, Rte. 1, 50864. Telephone: 712/826-6647 or 826-6643. Men, women, and children. $5 first night; $4 each succeeding night for multibedded rooms in a lodge or lodge annex. Bring a sleeping bag. Cooking facilities available. There's a state lake across the road.

Walnut

Accommodation: Friendship Colonial Motor Inn, P.O. Box 408, 51577 (Exit 46, south of I-80). Telephone: 712/784-2233. $16 to $20 for one; $17 to $24 for two in one bed; $20 to $26 for two in two beds.

Waterloo

Accommodations: YWCA, 425 Lafayette, 50703. Telephone: 319/234-7589. Women only. $5. Weekly rate: $20. Reservations requested two weeks in advance. One block from bus station.

● Exel Inn, ♿, 3350 University Ave., 50701. Telephone: 319/235-2165. $18.50 for one; $23.50 for two in one bed; $25.50 for two in two beds.

Williams

Accommodation: Best Value, Boondocks USA Motel, I-35 and U.S. 20, 50271. Telephone: 515/854-2201. $16 for one; $19 for two in one bed; $22 for two in two beds.

Kansas

Capitalizing on the ever-popular movie *Wizard of Oz,* in which the heroine, Dorothy, comes from Kansas, Kansas calls itself the "Land of Ah's."

Kansas is the geographic center of the U.S. and the breadbasket of the world. When Dwight Eisenhower told a European audience "I come from the heart of America," he was referring to Abilene, Kansas, the town where he grew up. The Eisenhower family home is preserved and the Eisenhower library and museum were opened in 1962.

Many historic trails crossed through early Kansas—you can almost hear the wagonmaster's cry of "Wagons Ho!" in parts of the Chisholm Trail, along which Indian trader Jesse Chisholm drove his cattle on the way from Texas to Abilene; Lewis and Clark's route, which follows the Missouri River along the northeastern boundary of the state; the Oregon Trail, which was so heavily traveled in the years after 1848 by people heading for California gold; the Santa Fe Trail, which was used as a trade route with Mexico; and the Smoky Hill Trail, which was the quickest way to the Denver goldfields discovered in 1859. There's an organization that operates one-day covered-wagon trips following the Flint Hill Trail. Write to Flint Hills Overland Wagon Train Trips, P.O. Box 1076, El Dorado, KS 67042. For those who prefer their adventures on water, the Kansas Canoe Association (P.O. Box 2885, Wichita, KS 67201) puts out brochures describing three different canoe trails—from 14 to 59 miles long. Included are points of interest along the trail, water conditions, and access information.

Some Special Events: Messiah Festival in Lindberg (during Easter Week); After Harvest Czech Festival in Wilson and Mexican Fiesta in Topeka (July); Walnut Valley Bluegrass Festival and Flat-Picking Championship Contest in Winfield and Mexican Fiesta in Garden City (September); Arkansas City's Arkalah Festival, Neewollah Celebration in Independence, Wichita's Harvest Home Festival, and Maple Leaf Festival in Baldwin City (all in October). Write to the Department of Economic Development for a *Calendar of Events.*

Hitching: The State Police say that it is legal to hitchhike on any road in Kansas except the Interstate system and the Kansas Turnpike. They advise that you "carry plenty of identification and enough money to sustain yourself." It seems to be an accepted means of transportation, for students especially. Someone from Kansas State University says to go ahead and hitchhike but "be wary of police and weird people." Sound enough advice.

Tourist Information: Travel and Tourism Division, Kansas Department of Economic Development, 503 Kansas, 6th Floor, Topeka, KS 66603. Telephone: 913/296-3487.

Dodge City

Accommodation: Thunderbird Motel, 2300 West Wyatt Earp Blvd., 67801. Telephone: 316/225-4143. $20 for one; $22 for two in one bed; $26 for two in two beds.

Goodland

Accommodation: Motel 6, I-70 and Hwy. 27, Rte. 1, Box 96E, 67735. Telephone: 913/899-6466. $12.95 for one; $16.95 for two; $19.95 for up to four.

Greensburg

Accommodation: Friendship Inn–Kansan Inn, 800 East Kansas Ave., 67054. Telephone: 316/723-2141. $13 to $15 for one; $15.50 to $20.50 for two in one bed; $17.50 to $22.50 for two in two beds.

Hays

Accommodations: Friendship Inn–Fort Hays, 527 East 8th St., 67601. Telephone: 913/625-2581. $12 to $16 for one; $14 to $20 for two in one bed; $16 to $24 for two in two beds.
- Motel 6, 3404 Vine St., 67601. Telephone: 913/628-1037. See Goodland listing for rates.
- Villa Inn, 810 East 8th St. at Vine, 67601. Telephone: 913/625-2563. $12 to $13 for one; $16 to $23 for two in one bed; $22 to $25 for two in two beds.
- Frontier City Best Value Inn, I-70 and U.S. 183 Alt., 67601. Telephone: 913/628-1076. $9.75 for one; $12.75 for two in one bed; $22.50 for two in two beds.

Hill City

Accommodation: Western Hills Motel, 800 West Hwy. 24 (Box 389), 67642. Telephone: 913/674-2141. $19 to $21 for one; $22 to $26 for two in one bed; $26 to $30 for two in two beds.

Hutchinson

Accommodations: Sunset Motel, √10%, 2605 East 4th St., 67501. Telephone: 316/662-4429. $19 for one; $23 for two in one bed; $26 for two in two beds.

● Imperial 400 Motor Inn, 114 West 4th St., 67501. $20 to $24 for one; $24 to $28 for two in one bed; $26 to $30 for two in two beds.

Kansas City

Accommodations: YMCA, 900 North 8th St., 66101. Telephone: 913/371-4400. Men only. $5 single. Usually 99% full, so call ahead.

● Best Value Mission Inn Motel, 7508 West 63rd, Mission, 66202. Telephone: 913/262-9600. $22 for one; $25 for two in one bed; $27 for two in two beds.

● Days Inn, &, I-35 South and 95th St., 9630 Rosehill Rd., Lenexa, 66215. Telephone: 913/492-7200. $23.88 for one; $26.88 to $27.88 for two.

Lawrence

On Campus: The University of Kansas is in Lawrence and the Union is a good place to meet U of K students. At night the scene switches to the mini-bars and restaurants on Massachusetts, the town's main street. You'll find Bogarts, the Crossing, Hawk and Wheel, among others. However, Kansas is "a dry state except for 3.2 beer. The real bars have to be private clubs." When hunger strikes, there's the Cashbah Deli, where you can get sandwiches and salads for $2, or La Tropicana, serving Mexican food for $3 to $4. There is also an American Indian Junior College in Lawrence—Haskell.

Help: KU Information Center, 105 Strong, 66044. Telephone: 913/864-3506. Open 24 hours. "We'll help with questions about directions, where to eat, what to do, etc."

"The country around Lawrence is beautiful with a number of small and large lakes for swimming and fishing. The Information Center is here to tell you what is happening."

Help and Emergency Accommodation: Headquarters, Inc., 1602 Massachusetts, 66044. Telephone: 913/841-2345. Headquarters is a crisis intervention center with a bedroom that accommodates five people per night. There is a one-night limit and one hour's worth of housework is required as payment.

Lenexa

Accommodation: Motel 6, southeast quadrant of I-35 and 95th St., 66015. See Goodland listing for rates.

Liberal

Accommodations: Spur Motel, 101 East Pancake, 67901. Telephone: 316/624-6231. $13 to $15 for one; $16 to $18 for two in one bed; $17 to $21 for two in two beds.

● Friendship Inn–Western-Ho Motel, U.S. 54 East, P.O. Box W, 67901.

Telephone: 316/624-1921. $13.50 to $15.50 for one; $17 to $19 for two in one bed; $19 to $21 for two in two beds.

● Friendship Ranch Motel, 304 U.S. 54 East, 67901. Telephone: 316/624-3897. $14 for one; $16 to $16.50 for two in one bed; $18 for two in two beds.

Lindsborg

Accommodation: Viking Motel, 446 Harrison, 67456. Telephone: 913/227-3336. $16.48 for one; $18.54 for two. "Lindsborg is better known as 'Little Sweden.' "

Manhattan

Tourist Information: Chamber of Commerce, 505 Poyntz, 66502. Telephone: 913/776-8829.

Help: Fone-Crisis Center, 1221 Thurston, 66502. Telephone: 913/532-6565.

On Campus: A friend at Kansas State University says that Manhattan has a lot to offer for being "stuck out in the middle of Kansas." Since it's the home of the Kansas State University Wildcats, the students have one of the biggest and best student unions around, the K-State Union. KSU also has an International Student Center to accommodate foreign visitors. The off-campus hang-out is Aggieville, a section right off campus. It's been said that if you put a roof over Aggieville, you'd have the biggest bar in the country. Since Kansas State is a state institution there are restrictions on alcoholic beverages allowed on campus, so you'll find the action either in Aggieville or at Tuttle Creek Reservoir when the weather's nice (there's camping there, too). The University Master Calendar, located in the Reservations Office, second floor of the K-State Union, is the place to find out what's going on—call 532-6591.

Manhattan has all the typical hamburger, taco, and fried-chicken places you'd expect, but for good down-home cooking try the Chef at 111 South 4th or Reynard's at 622 Tuttle Creek Blvd. (across the street from Motel 6).

For rides out of town, there's a ride board on the second-floor concourse in the K-State Union that really works.

Accommodation: Motel 6, 510 Tuttle Creek Blvd., 66502. Telephone: 913/776-4033. See Goodland listing for rates.

Mankato

Accommodation: Dreamliner Motel, √, Rte. 1, Box 95, 66956. Telephone: 913/378-3107. $16 to $20 for one; $19 to $22 for two in one bed; $21 to $25 for two in two beds.

Marion

Accommodation: Stone Prairie Life Center (AHY-SA), ✎, RR1, 66861. Telephone: 316/382-2057. Open May to November. $4.50 for AYH members. (For AYH membership details, see page 21). $6.50 single; $11 double for nonmembers. "Stone Prairie is a large stone building surrounded by wheat fields and covered by an immense sky. It is a peaceful, quiet, and unusual place." Meals are served, and chores are required. No smoking. "You can find an excellent buffet at the Owl Car Café in town."

Marysville

Accommodation: Friendship Inn–Thunderbird Motel, U.S. 36 West, 66508. $15.75 to $19.75 for one; $19.75 to $23.75 for two in one bed; $21.75 to $26.75 for two in two beds.

McPherson

Accommodation: Wheat State Motel, ➤ ★ √ 10%, West Hwys. 56 and 153 (Box 374), 67460. Telephone: 316/241-4230. $15 to $16 for one; $18 to $19 for two in one bed; $22 to $23 for two in two beds.

Newton

Accommodation: Best Value Newtonian Motor Lodge, 105 Manchester, 67114. Telephone: 316/283-6500. $18 to $22 for one; $21 to $28 for two in one bed; $23 to $28 for two in two beds.

Ottawa

Accommodation: Friendship Inn–Royal Manor, 1641 South Main St., 66067. Telephone: 913/242-4842. $17 to $21 for one; $20 to $23 for two in one bed; $22 to $26 for two in two beds.

Phillipsburg

Accommodation: Friendship Inn–Silver Saddle, P.O. Box 322, East Phillipsburg, 67661. Telephone: 913/543-2125. $13 to $14 for one; $16 to $17 for two in one bed; $18 to $19 for two in two beds.

Pittsburg

Help: Help Now, Inc., 316/232-1000.

On Campus: To get your bearings and a friendly word, contact the Student Union Program Office of Pittsburg State University at 1701 South Broadway. Telephone: 316/231-7000, extension 276. A student there says that the acceptance of hitchhiking in Pittsburg is "better than most" and the attitude toward young travelers is "pretty good."

Pratt

Accommodation: Friendship Inn–Catalina Motel, 1401 East 1st St., 67124. Telephone: 316/672-5588. $18 to $20 for one; $20 to $24 for two in one bed; $24 to $28 for two in two beds.

Quinter

Accommodation: Q Motel, I-70 and Hwy. 212, 67752. Telephone: 913/754-3337. $17 to $19 for one; $20 to $22 for two in one bed; $22 to $24 for two in two beds.

Sabetha

Accommodation: Koch Motel, U.S. 75 (Box 235), 66534. Telephone: 913/284-2145. $14.50 to $20.50 for one; $17 to $24 for two in one bed; $22 to $28 for two in two beds.

Salina

Accommodations: Vagabond II Inn, 🐟 ★ (during off-season), 🖢, 217 South Broadway, 67401. Telephone: 913/825-7265. $16 to $18 for one; $18 to $22 for two in one bed; $26 to $30 for two in two beds.
● Friendship Inn–Tradewinds Motel, 1700 North 9th St., 67401. Telephone: 913/827-0371. $18 to $22 for one; $22 to $27 for two in one bed; $26 to $30 for two in two beds.

Seneca

Accommodation: Friendship Inn–Starlite Motel, U.S. 36 at 4th St., 66538. Telephone: 913/336-2191. $16 to $17.50 for one or two in one bed; $22 to $28 for two in two beds.

Sharon Springs

Accommodation: Friendship Traveler Motel, intersection of U.S. 40 and Kans. 27, 67758. Telephone: 913/852-4293. $14 for one; $16 for two in one bed; $18 for two in two beds.

Smith Center

Accommodation: Friendship Inn–U.S. Center Motel, 116 East Hwy. 36, 66967. Telephone: 913/282-6611. $13 to $18 for one; $17 to $22 for two in one bed; $19 to $22 for two in two beds.

Topeka

Accommodations: Motel 6, 3846 South Topeka Ave., 66609. Telephone: 913/267-3800. See Goodland listing for rates.
● Motel 6, 709 Fairlawn Rd., 66605. Telephone: 913/273-6582. See Goodland listing for rates.

WaKeeney

Accommodation: Friendship Inn–Sundowner Lodge, I-70 and U.S. 283 West Exit, 67672. Telephone: 913/743-2129. $13 to $16 for one; $15 to $22 for two in one bed; $17 to $23 for two in two beds.

Wichita

Tourist Information: Wichita Convention and Visitors Bureau, 111 West Douglas, Suite 804, 67202. Telephone: toll free 800/835-2027 from out of state; 800/362-1194 from in state. Locally, dial 265-2800.

Accommodations: Best Value Western Trails Lodge, 4701 West Kellogg, 67209. Telephone: 316/943-4231. $15 for one; $17 for two in one bed; $20 for two in two beds.

● Friendship Inn–Western Trails Lodge, 4701 West Kellogg, 67209. Telephone: 316/943-4231. $15 to $17 for one; $20 to $24 for two in one bed; $20 to $24 for two in two beds.

● Motel 6, 5736 West Kellogg, 67209. Telephone: 316/945-9452. See Goodland listing for rates.

Kentucky

The theme is horses. They take them very seriously in Kentucky from the breeding to the racing. If you're planning to go to the Kentucky Derby in May this year, be sure to check to see if there's room at the Derby Hostel at the University of Louisville.

Some of the major attractions in Kentucky are: in the north-central part of the state, the Abraham Lincoln Birthplace, Stephen Foster's "Old Kentucky Home" in Bardstown, Churchill Downs, and several famous horse farms; in eastern Kentucky, Cumberland Gap, Daniel Boone National Forest, and Black Mountain; in western Kentucky, Kentucky Lake, Lake Barkley, and 170,000-acre Land Between the Lakes; and in the south-central part of the state, Mammoth Cave National Park and Lake Cumberland—which lead the list of things to see.

Kentucky's State Park system includes 15 resort parks with both lodge and camping facilities. Some also have cottages and houseboat rentals. Information on the parks and their facilities is available in a brochure, distributed by *Travel,* Frankfort, KY 40601. Rate information is available by calling toll free 800/372-2961 from Kentucky or 800/626-8000 from much of the eastern U.S.; or by writing to the Kentucky Department of Parks, Capital Plaza Tower, Frankfort, KY 40601.

For more about the state and its outdoors, consider the following publications:

A Guide to Kentucky Outdoors, by Arthur B. Lander, Jr., Thomas Press, 2030 Ferndon Rd., Ann Arbor, MI 48104 ($9.95).

A Guide to Backpacking and Day-Hiking Trails of Kentucky, by Arthur B. Lander, Jr., Thomas Press ($9.95).

A Canoeing and Kayaking Guide to the Streams of Kentucky, by Bob Sehlinger, Thomas Press ($12.95).

A free booklet, *The Kentucky Travel Guide,* is available from the Department of Tourism (address below), and the *Guide to Trails and Natural Areas,* which lists trails and areas for backpacking, day hiking, bikeways, equestrian trails, and canoe routes, is available for not more than $5 (it wasn't out when we went to press so the price is uncertain) from the State Naturalist, Kentucky Department of Parks (address above).

According to the Kentucky Department of Public Information, "Natural Bridge State Resort Park and the Red River Gorge are a fantastic draw among young people. They flock there for beauty and solitude, camping and canoeing."

Some Special Events: Kentucky Derby Festival in Louisville (end of April and beginning of May); Capital Expo in Frankfort and Heritage Weekend in Louisville (June); Shaker Festival in South Union (July); Farm Festival Days in Frenchburg and International Banana Festival (featuring a one-ton banana pudding) in Fulton (August); and Our Appalachia Day in Pippa Passes (September).

Hitching: Officially, no one may hitchhike from the roadway. The attitude seems to be mixed—leaning toward indifference.

Tourist Information: Department of Tourism, Capital Plaza Tower, Frankfort, KY 40601.

Bardstown

Accommodation: Scottish Inn, U.S. 31 East and 150 North, 40004. Telephone: 502/348-3073. $22 for two in one bed; $26 for two in two beds.

Benton

Accommodation: Friendship Inn–Shamrock, 806 Main St., 42025. Telephone: 502/527-1341. $14 to $16 for one; $16 to $18 for two in one bed; $20 to $22 for two in two beds.

Berea

Accommodation: Econo-Travel Motor Hotel, I-75 and Ky. 21, P.O. Box 183, 40403. Telephone: 606/986-9323. $16 for one; $18 for two in one bed; $22 for two in two beds.

Bowling Green

On Campus: A friend at Western Kentucky University told us that his campus is not really used to transients, but that if you want to help them get more used to them you should probably head for the Downing Center on campus. He says there are good camping areas—it costs only $5 to get a campsite at Beech Bend Park. For good eating he recommends a popular truck stop on the Bypass called Mary's Restaurant.

Accommodations: Motel 6, 3139 Scottsville Rd., 42101. Telephone: 502/781-6010. $12.95 for one; $16.95 for two; $19.95 for up to four.

● Days Inn, I-65 and U.S. 231, 1110 Cumberland Trail, 42101. Telephone: 502/781-6330. $22.88 to $24.88 for one; $26.88 to $28.88 for two.

● Scottish Inn, I-65 and U.S. 231, 42101. Telephone: 502/781-6550. $19 for one; $21 for two in one bed; $23 for two in two beds.

● Econo-Travel Motor Hotel, I-65 and U.S. 31 West, Rte. 14, Box 61, 42101. Telephone: 502/781-6181. $17.95 for one; $23 for two in one bed; $25 for two in two beds.

Central City

Accommodation: Best Value Rambler Rose Motel, Hwys. 62 and 431 and West Kentucky Pkwy., 42330. Telephone: 502/754-2441. $14.95 for one; $16.95 for two in one bed; $18.95 for two in two beds.

Corbin

Accommodation: Days Inn, I-75 and U.S. 25 West, Rte. 6, Box 10, Cumberland Falls Rd., 40701. Telephone: 606/528-8150. $19.88 to $20.88 for one; $23.88 to $24.88 for two.

Elizabethtown

Accommodations: Days Inn, 🛆, I-65 and U.S. 62, P.O. Box 903, 42701. Telephone: 502/769-5522. $18.88 to $20.88 for one; $22.88 to $24.88 for two.
  ● Friendship Inn–Clover Leaf, 711 East Dixie Ave., 42701. Telephone: 502/765-2194. $12 to $16 for one; $16 to $22 for two in one bed; $18 to $28 for two in two beds.
  ● Motel 6, U.S. 62 and I-65, 42701. Telephone: 502/769-3376. See Bowling Green listing for rates.

Frankfort

Accommodation: Days Inn, I-64 and U.S. 127 South, 40601. Telephone: 502/875-2200. $23.88 for one; $27.88 for two.

Georgetown

Accommodations: Scottish Inn, I-75 and U.S. 460, 40324. Telephone: 502/863-0713. $18.50 for one; $21.50 for two in one bed; $24.50 for two in two beds.
  ● Days Inn, I-75 and Delaplain Rd. (Exit 129), 40324. Telephone: 502/863-5000. $17.88 to $18.88 for one; $21.88 to $22.88 for two.

Jackson

Accommodation: Best Value Paul's Motel, 1186 Main St., 41339. Telephone: 606/666-2471. $19 for one; $23 for two in one bed; $24 to $26 for two in two beds.

Lexington

"The place to visit if you are interested in horses or bluegrass."

Help: Crisis Intervention, 606/254-3844.
On Campus: "Visiting students can call Student Housing (tel. 257-3721) to rent a room for $10 a night. Favorite eating places near campus are High on Rose, a crowded bar with beer and Mexican food; Alfalfa, a mostly vegetarian restaurant; and Joe Bologna, for pizza and Italian food."

Accommodations: YMCA, 239 East High St., 40507. Telephone: 606/255-5651. Men only. $12.30. Weekly rate: $52.50.

● YMCA, 535 West 2nd St., 40508. Telephone: 606/252-7543. Men and women. Walking distance from bus station. $10 for a single plus $2 key deposit. $30 per week. "Very desirable accommodations for the average person looking for economic facilities."

● Red Roof Inn, 🚻, I-75/64 at U.S. 27/68 (Exit 113). Telephone: 606/293-2626. $19.95 for one; $22.95 for two in one bed; $24.95 to $26.95 for two to four in two beds.

Louisville

Help: Family and Children's Agency, Travelers Aid Service, P.O. Box 3775, 40201. Telephone: 502/584-8186.

● Louisville also has a service called "We Speak Your Language." The phone number is 502/589-4450 for French, Spanish, German, and Vietnamese speakers.

● Crisis and Information Center, 502/589-4313.

Tourist Information: Louisville Visitors Bureau, Founders Square, 40202. Telephone: 502/582-3732. The people at the Visitors Bureau sent us two interesting pieces of information. First, the excellent Actors Theater of Louisville offers student rush tickets 15 minutes before a production for $4. And second, bus fares in Louisville go up from 35¢ to 60¢ during rush hours, so plan accordingly.

On Campus: The University of Louisville's International Center can help foreign visitors find their way around. Telephone 502/588-6602 to find out how to get to the center. To meet students, stop at the Butchertown Pub, 1335 Story Ave.; Bristol Bar and Grill, 1321 Bardstown Rd.; City Lights, 117 West Main; or the Sub and Cardinal's Nest, restaurants in the student center. The people at the university's Union for Student Activity run a hostel during Derby weekend. At other times call the housing office at 502/588-6636 for possible on-campus accommodations. We have one more good tip—Alpha Cinemas provides discount tickets for students.

A visiting group of students in 1980 agreed that: "We were as touched by your hospitality as by the beauty of your horses."

Accommodations: Kentucky Derby Student Hostel, 🎓★, 2011 South Brook St., 40292. Telephone: 502/588-6691. "A tent city located in a secure area of campus offering indoor showers, continental breakfasts, and parking areas." Open Thursday through Sunday afternoon of Derby weekend. Advance reservations necessary. $5 per night.

● Days Inn, I-65 and North Hamburg Exit, P.O. Box 7618, Sellersburg, IN 47172. Telephone: 812/246-4451. $18.88 for one; $22.88 for two.

● Days Inn, I-65 and Eastern Blvd., 350 Eastern Blvd., Jeffersonville, 47130. Telephone: 502/583-3421. $20.88 for one; $25.88 for two.

● Days Inn, I-71 and Ky. 53, LaGrange, 40031. Telephone: 502/222-7192. $20.88 for one; $24.88 for two.

● Days Inn, 🚻, I-65 and Ky. 44, 40165. Telephone: 502/543-3011. $19.88 for one; $23.88 for two.

● Motel 6, 3304 Bardstown Rd., 40218. Telephone: 502/458-3201. See Bowling Green listing for rates.

● Red Roof Inn, 🚻, I-64 at Hurstbourne Lane North (Exit 15). Telephone:

502/426-7621. $17.95 for one; $20.95 for two in one bed; $22.95 to $24.95 for two to four in two beds.
● Continental Inns of America, 🔀, 1620 Arthur St., 40217. Telephone: 502/636-3781. $18.95 for one; $22 for two in one bed; $28 for two in two beds.

Madisonville

Accommodation: Econo-Travel Motor Hotel, U.S. 41 and U.S. 70, P.O. Box 187, 42431. Telephone: 502/821-0364. $19.95 for one; $22.95 for two in one bed; $25.95 for two in two beds.

Mammoth Cave

Camping: Mammoth Cave National Park, 42259. There's camping at headquarters and at Houchin's Ferry all year.

Middlesboro

Camping: Cumberland Gap National Historical Park, P.O. Box 840, 40965. There's walk-in camping at four sites all year. Cabins are available at Martin's Fork.

Mount Sterling

Accommodations: Days Inn, 🔀, I-64 and U.S. 460, Ragland Ave., 40353. Telephone: 606/498-4680. $17.88 to $19.88 for one; $21.88 to $23.88 for two.
● Brier Hill Motel, √, 443 Maysville Rd., 40353. Telephone: 606/498-3424. $15.50 for one; $18.60 for two in one bed; $20 for two in two beds.

Owensboro

Accommodations: Motel 6, 4585 Frederica St., 42301. Telephone: 502/684-9636. See Bowling Green listing for rates.
● Days Inn, 🔀, U.S. 231 and 60 Bypass, P.O. Box 1707, 42301. Telephone: 502/684-9621. $18.88 for one; $22.88 for two.

Paducah

Accommodations: Regal 8 Inn, 2150 South Beltline, 42001. Telephone: 502/442-6171. $17.88 for one; $20.88 for two in one bed; $23.88 for two to four in two beds.
● Days Inn, 🔀, I-24 and U.S. 60 West, 42001. Telephone: 502/442-7501. $21.88 to $22.88 for one; $25.88 to $26.88 for two.

Pippa Passes

Accommodation: Old Knott County High School (AYH-SA), P.O. Box 15, 41844. Telephone: 606/368-2753. Open all year. $2.50.

Richmond

Accommodation: Days Inn, I-75 and U.S. 421, Exit South 90-A, North 90, 40475. Telephone: 606/623-0880. $17.88 to $19.88 for one; $21.88 to $23.88 for two.

Russell

Accommodation: YMCA, P.O. Box A.C., 41169. Telephone: 606/836-6884. Men only. $8.

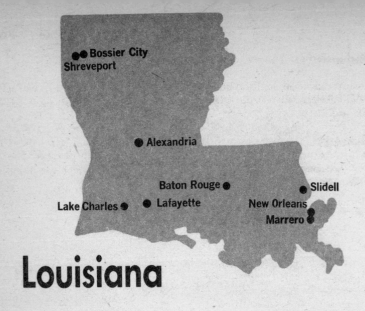

Louisiana

The big attraction is New Orleans with its Vieux Carré, Preservation Hall Jazz, and two weeks of Mardi Gras celebration that fall 47 days before Easter. It's a shame that most travelers making the typical cross-country trips never make it as far south as Louisiana—a detour might be worth considering.

Although New Orleans is probably the reason you'll be coming to Louisiana, there is more to see if you have the time. (See the New Orleans section, page 204.) To get a feeling for the state's past there are two historic sites, each about three hours from New Orleans, that deserve a visit. The first, the Acadian House Museum in St. Martinville, in the very heart of Cajun country, displays artifacts of the early French period of the area. Some say that this home may have once belonged to Louis Arcenaux, the model for Longfellow's Gabriel in his poem "Evangeline." The Acadians, or Cajuns, still keep their distinct subculture alive and well in the 20th century. The second is the Rosedown Plantation and Gardens, a restoration of an 1835 mansion that is lavishly furnished and surrounded by fabulous formal gardens designed in the 17th-century French manner; a tour of the house is available.

On the River Roads, on both sides of the Mississippi River between New Orleans and Rosedown, are several other plantations that also capture the flavor of Louisiana's past. They are San Francisco, Destrehan, and Houmas House on the east bank, and Oak Alley and Nottoway on the west. All are open to the public for a fee of from $3 to $4 and some have restaurant facilities.

Two books recommended by the Office of Tourism for those interested in Louisiana are *Louisiana,* by Joe Gray Taylor, W. W. Norton ($8.95), for a history of the state, and *The Pelican Guide to Plantation Homes of Louisiana,* by Nancy Harris Calhoun and James Calhoun, Pelican ($3.95). The Louisiana Office of Tourism (address below) offers a guidebook and highway map free of charge to travelers.

Some Special Events: Louisiana Pine Tree Festival in Walker (April); New Orleans Jazz and Heritage Festival and Bluegrass Festival in Natchitoches (May); Louisiana Peach Festival in Ruston (June); New Orleans Food

Festival and Cajun Festival in Montegut (July); Seafood Festival in Lafitte (August); and the North Louisiana Cotton Festival and Fair in Bastrop (September).

Hitching: Officially, as in most states, Louisiana law prohibits standing on the "roadway" for the purpose of soliciting. The attitude toward hitching is improving, according to one friend, and students traveling near a campus are the most likely to get rides. It may mean a long wait in some areas, though. The Department of Public Safety adds that if you do hitchhike you should carry proper identification, but it warns of the dangers of hitching.

Tourist Information: Louisiana Office of Tourism, P.O. Box 44291, Baton Rouge, LA 70804. Telephone: 504/925-3860.

Alexandria

Tourist Information: Alexandria–Pineville Tourist Center, 214 Jackson St., 71301. Telephone: 318/442-6671.

Accommodations: Friendship Alexandria Inn, 1212 MacArthur Dr., 71301. Telephone: 318/443-1826. $16 to $18 for one; $19 to $21 for two in one bed; $22 to $24 for two in two beds.

● Imperial 400 Motor Inn, 601 3rd St., 71301. Telephone: 318/443-0484. $22 to $24 for one; $24 to $28 for two in one bed; $28 to $30 for two in two beds.

Baton Rouge

Tourist Information: Baton Rouge Area Convention and Visitors Bureau, Old State Capitol, 70801. Telephone: 504/383-1825.

On Campus: You may be able to spend a night or two on campus in Pleasant Hall, but first you must obtain special permission from the International Student Office at Louisiana State University.

If you go to Murphy's or the Bengal you'll be able to meet LSU students. They suggest Dragon Hall Cafeteria, 161 West State St., for inexpensive Chinese food, and Round-the-Corner, 3347 Highland.

There is a bulletin board located in the Union near "Tiger Lair" cafeteria, and you might be able to find helpful information in the Student Government Office, 327 Union.

Accommodations: Friendship Inn–Shades Motel, 8282 Airline Hwy. on U.S. 61 and 190 Bypass, 70815. Telephone: 504/925-2401. $15.12 to $16.20 for one; $16.20 to $17.28 for two in one bed; $18.36 to $19.44 for two in two beds.

● Motel 6, I-10 and La. 415, 70767. To open in 1982. See Shreveport listing for rates.

Bossier City

Accommodation: Days Inn, I-20 East at Old Minden Rd. (Exit 21), 200 John Wesley Blvd., 71112. Telephone: 318/742-9200. $23 for one; $29 for two. Rates higher May 7 to October 4.

Lafayette

Tourist Information: Lafayette Parish Convention and Visitors Commission, P.O. Box 52066, 70505. Telephone: 318/232-3737.

On Campus: The University of Southwestern Louisiana is in Lafayette. A friend from there told us that the local folklore of Acadiana is worth investigating—if you speak French you'll especially enjoy the back country of Acadiana. "We also have a Mardi Gras, like New Orleans, but ours is more like it started out to be—simple but fun." You may be able to stay at the Conference Center on campus for about $16 per night. Call to check (tel. 318/233-9350).

Lake Charles

Accommodation: Friendship Inn–Lakeview, 1000 North Shore Pkwy., 70601. Telephone: 318/436-3336. $18 to $19 for one; $21 to $23 for two in one bed; $23 to $25 for two in two beds.

Marrero

Accommodation: Scottish Inn, 6613 Westbank Expressway, 70072. Telephone: 504/347-1502. $20 for one or two in one bed; $24 for two in two beds.

New Orleans

Two hundred fifty years of French, Spanish, Italian, West Indian, and finally American influence have made New Orleans the appealing place it is today, probably the most European city in all of North America. Narrow streets, antebellum mansions, oldtime jazz, Créole culture, and the busy Mississippi are all reminiscent of another time, one recalled so well in the books of Mark Twain, William Faulkner, and Tennessee Williams. In spite of the ultracontemporary hotels and the space-age Superdome, much of New Orleans is not new at all. Many old ways are alive and well in this city. Mardi Gras is, of course, New Orleans's big, big event. It always falls on the Tuesday 47 days before Easter. New Orleans's Carnival Parades begin many days before the actual Mardi Gras, on Fat Tuesday.

"During Mardi Gras, the French Quarter is just one long party."

Getting There: New Orleans (Moisant) International Airport is 12 miles west of the central business district and the French Quarter. Cab fares vary: the fare for one person to downtown is about $14; for three or more it's $5 each. Cheaper still is the Orleans Transportation Service's limousine service between the airport and the downtown hotels which costs $5 per person. Call 722-3158 for reservations. And least expensive of all is the Louisiana Transit Company's express bus service, which will get you from the airport to a terminal on Tulane Ave. (near the Civic Center, downtown) for only 65¢. Call 737-9611 for information. Trailways' bus terminal is at 1314 Tulane Ave. (tel. 525-4201, near downtown), and Greyhound's terminal is at 1001 Loyola Ave. (tel. 525-9371, downtown).

Getting Around: If you need a map of the city, get a free one at the Tourist Commission, 334 rue Royal, in the French Quarter. The city bus system (NOPSI) also has an information desk in the French Quarter, at 317 Baronne (tel. 529-4545), where you can pick up a map of bus routes. Bus service is inexpensive (40¢ for regular service) and generally efficient. The trolley line that links the French Quarter with the uptown district of the city is more than just a relic—it's a popular source of public transportation, day and night; at 40¢ there is no better self-guided tour of the city. Several bus companies provide transportation to the outlying parishes. St. Bernard Bus Lines, Inc. (tel. 279-5556) goes to Arabi, Chalmette, and places nearby. Gretna, Harvey, and various suburbs across the river are served by Westside Transit Lines, Inc. (tel. 366-3258). The airport and the surrounding East Jefferson Parish are served by the Louisiana Transit Company (tel. 737-9611). Algiers and communities on the West Bank are connected by a free ferry which leaves from the Canal and Jackson St. docks; the trip takes ten minutes.

Accommodations in the French Quarter: A Créole House, 1013 St. Ann St., 70116. Telephone: 504/524-8076; toll free 800/535-7785. $29 single; $40 double. No two rooms are the same. There's a courtyard, and complimentary continental breakfast.

● L'Auberge Hostel, 717 Barracks St., 70116. Telephone: 504/523-1130. Seven-person maximum. Minimum stay of two nights; three nights during July and August. $17.50 per person. Highly recommended by many of our readers. Bright and spotless, with kitchen privileges too. "Homey atmosphere." The only hostel in New Orleans and at a good location. (The rate doubles for Mardi Gras.)

● St. Peter Guest House, 1005 St. Peter, 70116. Telephone: 504/524-9232. Rates begin at $28. Balcony and courtyard rooms.

Accommodations near the French Quarter within easy access via trolley: Columns Hotel, 3811 St. Charles, 70115. Telephone: 504/899-9308. Rates begin at $20. Rooms with balconies in a nice neighborhood.

● Hedgewood Guest House, 2427 St. Charles, 70130. Telephone: 504/895-1894. $30 to $40 for singles and doubles.

● YMCA, ●10%, ★🛏, 936 St. Charles, 70130. Telephone: 504/568-9622. Men, women, and children. $16 single; $24 double. "More than a room, with safety, comfort, convenience, cleanliness."

● India Hotel, 1328 Prytania St., 70130. Telephone: 504/568-1724. $15 to $25 single; $9 for dormitory room. Special discount rates for foreign visitors. Complimentary breakfast. Clean but spartan accommodations in a marginal neighborhood.

● La Salle Hotel, ●10%, 1113 Canal St., 70112. Telephone: 504/523-5831. $28 single; $33 double. *"I stayed at the La Salle and liked it; they gave me a discount for being an Ameripass holder."* Discount does not apply from February 20 to 24 or December 28 to January 1.

● Lafayette Hotel, ● ★ 10%, 628 St. Charles, 70130. Telephone: 504/525-3372. $17.95 and up single; $24.95 double.

● Hummingbird Hotel, 804 St. Charles, 70130. Telephone: 504/561-9229 or 523-9165. $8 single; $16 double. *"Convenient location, but in a rundown neighborhood."* Breakfast, lunch, and dinner served in the grill, which is open 24 hours every day of the year.

● Parkview Guest House, 7004 St. Charles, 70118. Telephone: 504/866-

5580. Next to Audubon Park and across from Tulane University. $23 to $35 per room.

Accommodation near the Airport: Days Inn, 1300 Veterans Blvd., Kenner, 70062. Telephone: 504/469-2531. $25 single; $30 double.

Where to Eat: New Orleans is known for its food and its restaurants. Here's a list of some of the more popular, but not too expensive, restaurants. Keep in mind the fact that many of the city's restaurants are closed on Mondays. For more on eating in New Orleans, see a copy of *The New Orleans Restaurant Guide,* by Richard and Rima Collin, Strether and Swann Publishers ($3.95).

In the French Quarter and Downtown: Buster Holmes, 721 Burgundy St. Telephone: 561-9375. Average meal $1.50 to $4.

● Café du Monde Coffee Stand, in the French Market, by the river. Try the beignets.

● Central Grocery, 923 Decatur St. Telephone: 523-1620. Sandwiches are $2; try the muffulettas.

● Chez Helene, 1540 North Robertson St. Telephone: 947-9155. A good soul-food restaurant where a meal costs anywhere from $8 to $14.

● Felix, 739 Iberville St. Telephone: 522-4440. Have oysters on the half shell, at the bar.

● Gumbo Shop, 630 St. Peter St. Telephone: 525-1486. The gumbo is among the best in town; a meal costs from $5 to $9.

● Mother's, 401 Poydras St. Telephone: 523-9656. Taste the roast beef poor boy, dressed. $2.75 to $3.50. *"Probably the most famous and best poor boys in town."*

● The Coffee Pot, 714 St. Peter. Telephone: 523-8215. For a breakfast served in a courtyard. "The food is delicious."

● Café Maspero's, 601 Decatur. Telephone: 523-8414. Nice setting with lots of dark varnished wood. A small menu but huge sandwiches that are excellent.

● Houlihan's, 315 Bourbon. Telephone: 523-7412. A Créole bistro featuring French onion soup, spinach salad, and quiche Lorraine.

Uptown: Camellia Grill, 626 South Carrollton Ave. Telephone: 861-9311. Located on the trolley line. The cheeseburger is always a winner, but if you're feeling more adventurous try a "Cannibal Special." The freezes and the pecan pie are excellent.

● Casamento's, 4330 Magazine St. Telephone: 895-9761. Many people think that their oyster loaf is the best in town. Closed in summer.

● Tyler's Beer Garden, 5234 Magazine. Telephone: 891-4989. Oysters on the half shell at $2 per dozen are one of the best bargains in town. The atmosphere at Tyler's is relaxed and there's live music every night.

● Bud's, 3137 Calhoun and Claiborne Sts. Telephone: 866-9294. A typical New Orleans–style seafood restaurant with tile floors and Formica tables. Meals are about $7. Near Tulane University.

What to Do: "The best things to do in New Orleans are walk and eat and drink. Other activities include antique shopping on Magazine St. and plantation tours outside the city."

● In the French Quarter, begin by walking; stroll around Jackson Square, see the Cabildo and the Presbytère. Ride the New Orleans Steamboats for a fascinating journey on the Mississippi or into bayou country. Boats dock at Toulouse St. and Canal St. wharves. Phone the tourist office for information (tel. 568-5661). Be sure, too, to walk along the Moonwalk in the evening. It's along the river, just opposite Jackson Square. Some places that we recommend visiting are:

● New Orleans Museum of Art, 🐟, Lelong Ave., City Park, 70179. Telephone: 488-2631. Open Tuesday through Sunday from 10 a.m. to 5 p.m. Free admission to ISIC-holders.

● Casa Hove, 723 Toulouse St., one of the oldest buildings in the Mississippi Valley, furnished in period pieces and open Monday to Saturday, 10 a.m. to 4:30 p.m. A tour costs $1.50.

● Gallier House, 1118-1132 Royal St. To tour this fine example of 19th-century architecture and furnishings costs $2.50. The house is open Monday to Saturday, 10 a.m. to 4:30 p.m.; Sunday, 1 to 4:30 p.m.

● Musée Conti Wax Museum, 917 Conti St. Telephone: 525-2605. Here you'll see the history of New Orleans from 1682 to the 20th century unfold. Open Monday to Friday, 9:30 a.m. to 5:30 p.m.; Saturday and Sunday, 10 a.m. to 9 p.m. Admission is $3.

● Voodoo Museum, 739 Bourbon St. Telephone: 523-2906. Exactly what its name says it is.

● At the corner of Canal and Carondelet Sts. you can step onto the St. Charles streetcar for a journey along broad St. Charles Ave. into uptown New Orleans and its magnificent Garden District. Between 1st and 7th Sts., from St. Charles to Magazine, the area has some of the finest antebellum architecture in the South. See the Old Cemetery in the Garden District, bounded by 6th, Coliseum, Prytania, and Washington Sts.; Audubon Park and Zoo, farther uptown than the Garden District, near the trolley line; and Audubon Pl., across from the park, a palm-tree-lined boulevard which is literally out of another century.

At Night: As with our restaurant suggestions, the following listing is only meant as an appetizer. After all, jazz was born in New Orleans and it can be heard all over the French Quarter. Some favorites: Preservation Hall, 726 St. Peter, the classic place to hear oldtime jazz; Al Hirt's, 501 Bourbon St.; Pete Fountain's Place, Hilton Hotel, Poydras St. and the river; or Crazy Shirley's, 640 Bourbon St.

● You'll find jazz outside the Quarter too, as well as blues, rock, Cajun, reggae, and just about any other type of music you can name. Pick up a copy of *Figaro,* the weekly entertainment and newspaper, for listings of who's playing where and when. Some popular music spots beyond the Quarter are Tipitina's, 501 Napoleon Ave. ("Very 'laid back' with some of the best live progressive jazz and blues"); Jed's, 8301 Oak, for country music and sometimes punk rock; the Dream Palace, 534 Frenchmen, a popular nightclub near the French Quarter; the Maple Leaf Bar, 8316 Oak, featuring a relaxed atmosphere and music anywhere from ragtime to blues; and Jimmy's, around the corner from Jed's at 8200 Willon, where you'll hear mostly rock, country, and New Wave.

Shopping: Maple Street Bookshop, 7529 Maple. All kinds of books.

● Leisure Landing Records, 5500 Magazine. Best in the city for whatever kind of music you like.

● Canoe and Trail Shop, 624 Moss. For all types of camping equipment.

● Uptown Square Shopping Center, 200 Broadway. Lots of boutiques with tempting things inside.

Tourist Information: Greater New Orleans Tourist and Convention Commission, Inc., 334 Royal St., 70130. Telephone: 504/566-5011. Maps, hotel information, and a calender of events are all here and are free.

● Volunteer and Information Agency, 504/524-HELP. "During Mardi Gras, a Mardi Gras coalition is formed to help visitors."

● Travelers Aid, 211 Camp St., Suite 400, 70130. Telephone: 504/525-7131. A United Way agency that can help travelers with almost any kind of problem.

Shreveport

Tourist Information: Shreveport-Bossier Convention and Tourist Bureau, P.O. Box 1761, 629 Spring St., 71166. Telephone: 318/222-9391.

Accommodation: Motel 6, 4915 Monkhouse Dr., 71109. Telephone: 318/636-6452. $12.95 for one; $16.95 for two; $19.95 for up to four.

Slidell

Accommodations: Scottish Inn, I-10 at U.S. 190 (Gause Rd.), P.O. Box 9, 70458. Telephone: 504/641-0576. $19.95 for one; $23.95 for two.

● Econo-Travel Motor Lodge, P.O. Box 1358, 70459. Telephone: 504/641-2153. $21 for one; $24 for two in one bed; $27 for two to four in two beds.

Maine

Maine is a beautiful state—its coastline attracts lots of visitors in the summer months, and Acadia National Park on Mount Desert Island is a mecca for campers, hikers, fishermen, and nature lovers. In this park you'll find mountains, lakes, seashore, and more than 75 carriage trails that are a hiker's dream. If you can get to Acadia in the spring or early fall you'll be able to appreciate it all the more. If the summer crowds get to you, head north of Bar Harbor to the miles of unspoiled wilderness and wooded areas that stretch to the Canadian border.

Many tourists favor the southern coast of Maine from York to Bath, which includes Ogunquit, home of a well-known summer playhouse. And those who have even the mildest interest in camping and things out-of-doors really should treat themselves to a visit to the headquarters of L. L. Bean, a store that campers and sportsmen dream about. Located in Freeport, L. L. Bean is open every single day of the year, 24 hours a day.

"We stopped at L. L. Bean at midnight on a summer Tuesday night and you might have thought, by the size of the crowd, that it was the day before Christmas!"

More attractions in Maine are Mt. Katahdin, the state's highest peak and the beginning of the Appalachian Trail, and Lily Bay State Park on Moosehead Lake, the largest natural lake within one state in the U.S.

When you get hungry in Maine, take advantage of the bean suppers, barbecues, and seafood festivals that are held in small towns all over the state, especially during the summer. The food is inexpensive, plentiful, and, best of all, homemade with love. Check for posters outside supermarkets and along the road.

The Appalachian Mountain Club publishes two very good outdoor guides to Maine, both of which are available from AMC, 5 Joy St., Boston, MA 02108.

They are *AMC Maine Mountain Guide* ($6.95) and *AMC Trail Guide to Mount Desert and Acadia National Park* ($2.50).

Some Special Events: Annual Chicken Barbecue and Fiddlers Contest in Bowdoinham, Clam Festival in Yarmouth, and Seacoast Festival in Kennebunkport (July); Blueberry Festival in Union and Downeast Jazz Festival in Camden (August); and Fair in Fryeburg (September).

Hitching: The law states: "It shall be unlawful for any person to hitchhike on the traveled portion of any public highway, including but not limited to the Maine Turnpike or any portion of any public highway during the nighttime. . . ." The act goes on to say that it is still possible for municipalities to post signs prohibiting hitching in their own areas.

Tourist Information: Maine Publicity Bureau, 97 Winthrop St., Hallowell, ME 04347. Telephone: 207/289-2423.

Auburn

Accommodation: YMCA, 62 Turner St., 04210. Telephone: 207/784-7222. One-half mile from bus station. Men only. $9.40. Call ahead—there's more room in summer than in winter.

Augusta

Help: Project Open Line, 207/623-4511.
Accommodation: Susse Chalet Motor Lodge, Maine Turnpike I-95, Exit 30, on Whitten Rd., 04330. Telephone: 207/622-3776. $19.70 for one; $23.70 for two.

Bangor

Accommodation: Susse Chalet Motor Lodge, I-95, Rte. 2 (Hermon Exit) on Hammond St., 04401. Telephone: 207/947-6921. $19.70 for one; $23.70 for two; $29.70 for four.

Bar Harbor

Help: Dial Help, toll free 800/432-7810.
Accommodation: YWCA, 36 Mount Desert St., 04609. Bus stops one block away. Telephone: 207/288-5008. Women only. $9 single; $8 per person double. A bed in the Solarium, a dorm which is open from June to September, costs $7. Reservations essential from June to Labor Day.
Camping: Acadia National Park, Rte. 1, P.O. Box 1, 04609. Blackwoods and Seawall are the two campgrounds with over 500 sites altogether. Blackwoods, five miles south of Bar Harbor, is open April to November. Seawall is open May 15 to October 4. $4 per campsite per night.

Blanchard Corner

Accommodation: Crossroads Inn (AYH), Rte. 1, Box 54, Abbott Village, 04406. Telephone: 207/848-3781 or 997/3920. Call the inn and someone will pick you up at a charge of 10¢ per mile (20 miles from bus station). Open May

15 to October 15, and possibly during February for skiing. $2 per person; discount possible for small groups or families. Sleeping bags required. Meals served on premises. Reservations strongly advised. AYH members receive preference.

"Appalachian Trail passes the door; canoeing the Piscataquis River even closer."

Brewer

Accommodation: Best Value Twin City Motel, 453 Wilson St., 04412. Telephone: 207/989-5450. $20 to $24 for one; $22 to $30 for two in one bed; $24 to $34 for two in two beds.

Caribou

Accommodation: Best Value Red Brick Motel, RFD 3, Presque Isle Rd., 04736. $16 for one; $20 for two in one bed; $22 for two in two beds.

Jonesboro

Accommodation: Superior Blueberry Patch Motel, RFD, on U.S. 1, 04648. Telephone: 207/434-5411. $14.90 for one; $19.80 for two in one bed; $23.90 for two in two beds.

Lincoln

Accommodation: Big Lake Hostel (AYH), Stanhope Mill Rd., 04457. Telephone: 207/794-8200. Open May 15 to October 15. $3.50. AYH membership required (see page 21). Call the hostel and someone will pick you up at the bus station (five miles) for a small fee.

Ogunquit

Accommodation: Admiral's Loft Guest House, 97 Main St., 03907. Telephone: 207/646-5496. A three-story Victorian sea captain's home that's over 150 years old. Fifteen minutes from a three-mile-long sandy beach. Open May 1 to October 12. $26 to $30 for a double with shared bath; $35 for a double with a private bath. "Newly done and very clean."

Orono

Help: Off-Campus Board, 207/581-2664.
On Campus: The University of Maine is in Orono and the Memorial Union Building is the hub of life there. For good Mexican food, go to Barstans on Mill St.; to meet students, just stop at the Bear's Den in the Union. You might be able to pay a reasonable price for a dorm room in summer—just check with the Student Affairs Office on the Main Floor of Memorial Union.

"I'm from Tennessee and I think this place is great—the people are friendly and there's lots and lots of snow for winter fun."

Portland

Help: Hotline, 207/773-5516.

Accommodations: YWCA, 87 Spring St., 04101. Telephone: 207/772-1906. Women only, at least 18 years of age. $15 single; $11 per person double. $2.50-per-day charge for linen. Inquire about a possible weekly discount for readers of *Where to Stay*. Minimum stay is one week, unless arrangements are made with residence director.

● YMCA, 70 Forest Ave., 04101. Telephone: 207/773-1736. Two blocks from bus station. Men only. $13.55 single. Weekly rates: $38.65.

● Susse Chalet Motor Lodge, Maine Turnpike I-95, Exit 8, on Brighton Ave. Telephone: 207/774-6101. See Bangor listing for rates.

Rumford

Accommodation: Friendship Inn–Linnell, U.S. 2 West and Prospect Ave., 04276. Telephone: 207/364-4511. $20 to $24 for one; $24 to $28 for two in one bed; $28 to $32 for two in two beds.

Southwest Harbor

Accommodation: Harbor Light Tourist Home, Main St., 04679. Telephone: 207/244-3835. A large, old Victorian home with a very thoughtful family in charge. $20 to $25 per room in high season (July 1 to Labor Day); $12 to $15 at other times. An excellent place to stay if you plan to explore the fabulous Acadia National Park. Call the owners about the possibility of arranging transportation (Harbor Light is 20 miles from the bus).

Maryland

Although many people limit their travel in Maryland to the suburban belt around Washington, D.C., there's lots of breathtaking farmland beyond. One of the most interesting features about Maryland is the Eastern Shore, named after the three states of Delaware, Maryland, and Virginia—the Delmarva Peninsula. On "The Shore" is a mixture of farmland, fishing villages, colonial towns, large estates, and a seaside resort. To set the mood for a visit, read James Michener's *Chesapeake.*

Annapolis, Maryland's historic capital, was the country's first peacetime capital and since 1845 it has been the home of the U.S. Naval Academy. The U.S. Department of the Interior has designated one square mile of downtown Annapolis as a historic district—and many landmarks still stand. A walking tour of Annapolis should include a look at the City Dock area with its restored City Market, shops, and seafood restaurants.

Baltimore is a city with a maritime atmosphere and a reputation for excellent seafood. Also well known for its association with the national anthem (Francis Scott Key wrote "The Star-Spangled Banner" there), it has many landmarks worth visiting: Fort McHenry, U.S.S. *Constellation,* B & O Railroad Museum, Harborplace, and the brand-new National Aquarium.

For help in finding your way around Maryland, write to the Office of Tourist Development (address below) and ask for *Maryland Guidebook.*

Some Special Events: NASA Goddard Flight Center Model Rocket Launching, in Greenbelt (the first and third Sunday of every month); Winterfest in McHenry and Maryland Day Celebration in St. Mary's City (March); Sugarloaf's Spring Arts and Crafts Festival in Gaithersburg (April); Revolutionary War Days in Marbury and Montpelier Spring Festival in Laurel (May); Craft Fair in Frederick and Chicken Festival in Princess Anne (June); and Barbara Fritchie Motorcycle Race in Frederick (July).

Hitching: A person may hitchhike, but not on major highways that have controlled-access ramps or on controlled-access roads leading to the highways.

Hitchhiking is permitted on a shoulder or curb, but never on a roadway. It is prohibited in Ocean City.

Tourist Information: Office of Tourist Development, 1748 Forest Dr., Annapolis, MD 21401. Telephone: 301/269-3517.

Baltimore

Help: Travelers Aid, 601 North Howard St., 21201. On mezzanine of Greyhound Terminal. Telephone: 301/685-5874.

Tourist Information: Baltimore Office of Promotion and Tourism, 110 West Baltimore St., 21201. Telephone: 301/752-8632.

Accommodations: Abbey Hotel, 723 St. Paul St., corner of Madison St., 21202. Telephone: 301/332-0405. $23.75 single; $31.75 double. "European-style" hotel. Free continental breakfast served.

● You might be able to find lodging in a dorm room at the Peabody Conservatory on 606 St. Paul Street. Ask at the housing office.

"Make sure you stop at the Lexington Market on Lexington and Eutaw Sts., for the freshest seafood around. Another place I really enjoyed was the Peabody Book Store on Charles St. It was an old, comfortable, dusty bar which looks like a library and has a wonderful fireplace."

Berlin

Camping: Assateague Island National Seashore, Rte. 2, P.O. Box 294, 21811. Campground on the island about ten miles south of Ocean City. Open April to October. $3 per site. Reservations required.

Cambridge

Accommodation: Cambridge Maryland Home Hostel (AYH), 1311 Race St., 21613. Telephone: 301/228-7455. One mile from bus station. $10 single; $16 double. AYH membership required (see page 21). Reservations necessary.

Cumberland

Accommodation: YMCA, 205 Baltimore Ave., 21502. Telephone: 301/724-5445. One block from bus station; two blocks from train station. Men only. $9.95. Weekly rate: $27.75. Meals available across the street at Lynn's Restaurant.

Easton

Accommodation: Econo-Travel Motor Lodge, U.S. 50 Intown, 21601. Telephone: 301/822-6330. $21.95 for one; $25.95 for two in one bed; $29.95 for two in two beds.

Elkridge

Accommodation: Econo-Travel Motor Lodge, 5895 Bonnie View Lane, 21227. Telephone: 301/796-1020. $22.95 for one; $26.95 for two in one bed; $29.95 for two in two beds.

Greenbelt

Camping: Greenbelt Park, 6501 Greenbelt Rd., 20770. Twelve miles from Washington, D.C. 174 sites open all year. $2 per campsite per night.

Hagerstown

Accommodations: YMCA, 149 North Potomac St., 21740. Telephone: 301/739-3990. Four blocks from the bus station. Men only. $9 single. Weekly rate: $23. Reduction for Y members.
● Friendship Inn–Mid-Town Motel, 16 North Prospect St., 21740. Telephone: 301/790-0800. $20 to $24 for one; $24 to $28 for two in one bed; $28 to $34 for two in two beds.

Havre-de-Grace

Accommodation: Best Value Midtown Motel, 912 Pulasky Hwy. (U.S. 40), 21078. Telephone: 301/939-4567. $16 to $18 for one; $18 to $20 for two in one bed; $21 to $24 for two in two beds.

Jessup

Accommodation: Econo Lodge, Rte. 175 and Baltimore–Washington Pkwy., Box 367, 20794. Telephone: 301/799-0300 or 776-5510. $20.95 for one; $23.95 for two in one bed; $25.95 for two in two beds.

Joppa

Accommodation: Friendship Inn–Lakeside Motel, 1015 Pulaski Hwy., 21085. Telephone: 301/676-2700. $18 to $21 for one; $21 to $24 for two.

Knoxville

Accommodation: Kiwanis Youth Hostel (AYH), Rte. 2, P.O. Box 304, Sandy Hook Rd., 21758. Telephone: 301/834-7652. Open April 1 to November 1. Appalachian Trail passes by hostel. $3. AYH membership required (see page 21), or introductory three-day pass available at hostel for $1. Shuttle service available twice daily for $1.50 from train station. Call in advance. Camping on hostel grounds available for $1.50 per person. Campers may use hostel facilities (kitchen and bathroom).

Laurel

Accommodation: Valencia Motel, on U.S. 1 via Laurel exit from I-95 or Baltimore and 10131 Washington Blvd., 20810. Telephone: 301/725-4200. $22 for one or two in one bed; $27 for two in two beds.

Oakland

Accommodation: Camp Minnetoska Youth Hostel (AYH), P.O. Box 26, 21550. Telephone: 301/334-8292. $1.50. AYH membership required (see page 21). Open November 1 to April 1 for winter camping in cabins without insulation (must be cold!).

Salisbury

Accommodations: Friendship Inn–Temple Hill Motel, 2½ miles off Rte. 50 to South Salisbury Blvd. on Hwy. 13, 21801. Telephone: 301/742-3284. $19 to $22 for one; $20 to $24 for two in one bed; $22 to $26 for two in two beds.
● Superior Lord Salisbury Motel, P.O. Box 1696, U.S. 13 North, 21801. Telephone: 301/742-3251. $18 to $22 for one; $22 to $24 for two in one bed; $24 to $26 for two in two beds.
● Days Inn, ⌖, Rte. 13 North, P.O. Box 3, 21801. Telephone: 301/749-6200. $19.88 to $23.88 for one; $23.88 to $27.88 for two.

Sharpsburg

Camping: Chesapeake and Ohio Canal National Historical Park, P.O. Box 158, 21782. Camping along the mileposts. Open all year. Also hiker-biker units, accessible by trail, boat, bike, and horseback, are located at intervals between Seneca and Cumberland.

Thurmont

Camping: Catoctin Mountain Park, 21788. Owens Creek campground open from mid-April to October 31. $2 per campsite per night.

Waldorf

Accommodation: Best Value Waldorf Motel, Rte. 301, 20601. Telephone: 301/645-5555. $20 to $22 for one; $22 to $24 for two in one bed; $24 to $26 for two in two beds.

Westminster

Accommodation: Elderdice Hall, Western Maryland College, 21157. Telephone: 301/848-7000, extension 241. Students only. "Students from other colleges must submit a statement of good citizenship." June 1 to August 20; very limited space at other times. $8 first night; $4 each additional night.

Williamsport

Accommodations: Falling Waters Youth Hostel (AYH), RR1, Box 238-B, 21795. Telephone: 301/223-9208. Five miles outside Williamsport, 300 yards east of the C & O Canal at Falling Water. $3. Cooking faciliites and showers available. Open year round. AHY membership required (see page 21).

● Days Inn, 🛇, I-81 and U.S. 11, 310 East Potomac, 21795. Telephone: 301/582-3500. $20.88 for one; $23.88 for two.

Massachusetts

At first look, the Commonwealth of Massachusetts seems typically New England, but it has lots about it that's unique. Massachusetts's beauty, although somewhat showy in the fall, is more hidden and unexpected in the other seasons. Winter is a difficult time to travel in this state since the weather, at best, is unpredictable. Summer and fall, although unbearably hot or disappointingly short, are the most sensible times to travel and sightsee.

If you travel through Massachusetts, try to include the Berkshires and the musical events at Tanglewood, the Amherst region with its rich cultural life that is rooted in the area's many colleges and universities, lovely but sometimes overcrowded Cape Cod, and of course the cities of Boston and Cambridge. Massachusetts can show you rocky shores, sandy beaches, salt marshes, cranberry bogs, gentle hills, valleys, woods, meadows, and fields. Nearly every town has a river, a lake, or a pond to be proud of.

Because so much of the important early history of the U.S. took place in Massachusetts, there are many historic sights to visit—Lexington and Concord, Boston Harbor, Salem. But there's more than the reminders of the past to see. There are lots of offbeat, less well-known sights that will amuse: a medieval castle in Gloucester, a church built like an upturned ship in Hingham, the "Littlest House," also in Hingham, and on and on. According to one native, every town has its oddity—just ask.

You'll have no trouble at all gathering information about Massachusetts. Not only is there information from a vast number of public sources, but most of the people you'll meet will be happy to pass information on, to tell the legends and scandals of their town, and of course, to throw in a few complaints about their government.

Two books about Massachusetts that are recommended for the city-weary are the *AMC Massachusetts and Rhode Island Trail Guide* ($9.95) and the *AMC Guide to Country Walks Near Boston,* by Alan Fisher ($6.95). Both books are available from the Appalachian Mountain Club, 5 Joy St., Boston, MA 02108.

Some Special Events: The 26-Mile Patriot's Day Marathon Race in Boston (April); Ethnic Heritage Festival in Fall River and Ten-Day Lowell Festival in Lowell (May); Hilltown Banjo Convention in Cummington (June);

Heritage Days in Scituate and Summer Music Festival in Great Barrington (July); Homecoming Week in Beverly, Native American Festival in Lowell, and Harbor Festival in Hull (all in August); Labor Day Weekend Clambake in West Stockbridge and Barrington Fair in Great Barrington (September).

Hitching: The Massachusetts State Police told us that it is legal to hitchhike but not on the Mass. Turnpike where it is an arrestable offense. The State Police made it clear, though, that they don't endorse hitchhiking. One friend said that most people have mixed feelings about hitching in Massachusetts—"students hitch and parents are concerned."

Tourist Information: Division of Tourism, Massachusetts Department of Commerce and Development, 100 Cambridge St., Boston, MA 02202.

Amesbury

Accommodation: Susse Chalet Motor Lodge, I-95 at Rte. 110, 01913. Telephone: 617/388-3400. $19.70 for one; $23.70 for two; $29.70 for four.

Amherst

Help: Direct Information Service, Jones Library (University of Massachusetts). Telephone: 413/256-0121.

On Campus: This is a lovely New England college town—just what you'd expect—with Amherst College, the University of Massachusetts, and Hampshire College. There's a free bus that connects these schools and two others nearby—Smith in Northampton and Mount Holyoke in South Hadley. The place to meet students is the Blue Wall in the University of Massachusetts Campus Center or the Pub on East Pleasant St. For what's going on in town, check the Five College Calendar at the Campus Center's Information Desk. If you're looking for an inexpensive place to stay and have a car, consider the Motel 6 in South Deerfield—it's not far from Amherst. During the summer, check with Summer Conference Housing at UMass for possibilities.

Accommodation: Hampshire College, ★50¢, Office of Summer Programs (AYH), 01002. Telephone: 413/549-4600, extension 524. Open June 7 to August 22. $4.75. AYH membership required (see page 21). You can get an inexpensive, all-you-can-eat meal at the campus dining commons.

Beverly

Help: Project Rap, 617/922-0000.

Accommodation: YMCA, 245 Cabot St., 01915. Telephone: 617/922-0990. Men only. $12. Weekly rate: $25 for members only.

Boston/Cambridge

The Boston/Cambridge area is an absolute haven for students. Harvard, Radcliffe, MIT, Boston University, Northeastern, and Boston College are the largest schools in town and there are lots of smaller ones. You'll see students everywhere, but probably nowhere in greater concentration than in Harvard Square in Cambridge. Boston is a well-loved city that's easy to walk around and easy to get to know in a fairly short time. A city of neighborhoods, Boston has Beacon Hill; Back Bay, with the Boston Common and the Public Gardens; and the North and South Ends. Adjacent to the North End are Haymarket Square, the Faneuil Hall Marketplace, which attracts tourists by the droves, Waterfront Park, and Boston's historic wharves. Boston's Chinatown is the third largest in the U.S. and a nice place for wandering.

To know what's going on in the area while you're there, check the section of the *Boston Globe* that comes out on Thursday and is called *Calendar*. *Boston Magazine* is a weekly guide to what's happening, and an alternative paper, *The Phoenix*, can be counted on to provide a good rundown on what to do, what movies and plays are around, etc.

Most bookstores have a good selection of books on the city. Two that are worth looking at are:

Car-Free in Boston: A User Guide to Public Transportation in Greater Boston and New England (Association for Public Transportation, Inc., $2.50.) Explains how to use the transit system with routes and schedules.

Arthur Frommer's Guide to Boston, by Faye Hammel (Frommer/Pasmantier, $2.95). The familiar guidebook to points of interest, hotels, shopping, and nightlife.

Getting There: From the Airport: Logan Airport is only about two miles from the city. To get to town from Logan, simply take the shuttle bus that stops at each major airline terminal and takes passengers to the Airport station on the Blue Line of the MBTA (subway). Take the Blue Line to Government Center (the fourth stop), change to the Green Line, and go one stop to the Park St. station, the heart of the city, or ask for directions on getting where you want to go. The fare is 75¢ (25¢ on the shuttle and 50¢ on the MBTA).

● From the Bus Station: The Greyhound station is at 10 St. James Ave. near the Arlington St. subway station. The Trailways station is at 555 Atlantic Ave., across from South Station. Both are close to the center of town.

● From the Train Stations: Trains may stop at North Station or South Station. Both North and South Stations are stops on the subway system.

Getting Around: Taxi: There are taxi stands at major intersections. You can either hail a cab or call one. The fare is $1 plus 20¢ for each one-sixth of a mile.

● Subway: The fare is 50¢ for rides underground; 20¢ or more if you go above ground. All MBTA stations are color coded according to line (orange, red, blue, and green) and are marked with a large "T."

● Bus: The bus fare is 25¢.

● Car Rentals: Just check the Yellow Pages for the rates. Expect to be quoted about $40 per day for a compact car.

Accommodations: (See also listings for Charlestown, Newton, and Medford, which are nearby suburbs and convenient to the city.)

● Berkeley Residence Club, 40 Berkeley St., 02116. Between Copley Square and Arlington St. MBTA stations. Telephone: 617/482-8850. Women only. $17 single; $16.50 per person double. Reservations required two to three days in advance. There's a cafeteria in the building, "a lovely walled garden," and a swimming pool.

● International Fellowship House, 386 Marlborough St., 02115. Telephone: 617/247-7248, and ask for manager. June 1 to August 15 for transients. Male foreign students only. "The International Fellowship House is sponsored by several Christian businessmen who desire to provide a family-like atmosphere for international students far from their own homes." $8 per person double or triple. Breakfast and dinner available.

● Boston YMCA, 316 Huntington Ave., 02115. Telephone: 617/536-7800. Men and women. Near Northeastern University and the Museum of Fine Arts. On MBTA's Arborway/Huntington Ave. line. Students: $13 single; $18.50 double.

● Garden Halls Dormitories, 164 Marlborough St., 02116. Telephone: 617/267-0079 or 266-5232. Men, women, and children. June 20 to August 20. $8 ($24 minimum charge). Weekly rate: $50. Meals can be arranged. Reservations and advance payment required. Bring a sleeping bag—there's no linen.

● Kirkland Inn, 67 Kirkland St., Cambridge, 02138. Telephone: 617/547-4600. Singles start at $20 and doubles at $35. Located close to Harvard Square, the center of Cambridge.

● Strathmore House (AYH-SA), 45 Strathmore Rd., Brookline, 02146. Four miles from Boston, near public transportation. Telephone: 617/566-8936. Open year round. This is a rooming house with hostel facilities, including cooking privileges. $5 for AYH members; $7 for nonmembers.

● YMCA, 820 Massachusetts Ave., Cambridge, 02139. Telephone: 617/876-3860. Men only. $18 single. Restaurant in building. Near Harvard and MIT.

● YWCA, 7 Temple St., Cambridge, 02139. Telephone: 617/491-6050. Near Central Square. Women only. $22 single. Inexpensive restaurants nearby; swimming pool.

● Armed Services YMCA (AYH-SA), ✒, 32 City Square, 02129. Telephone: 617/242-2660. $6 for AYH members; $11 single, $13 double, for nonmembers. "YMCA front desk is open and available 24 hours and 365 days of the year—will refer and offer help."

● Susse Chalet Motor Lodge, 800 Morrissey Blvd., 02122. Telephone: 617/287-9100. Off the Southeast Expressway. $21.70 for one; $25.70 for two.

● Susse Chalet Inn, Rte. 2, Cambridge, 02140. Telephone: 617/661-7800. $21.88 for one; $24 to $26.11 for two.

● The Longwood Avenue Guest House, 83 Longwood Ave., Brookline, 02146. Telephone: 617/277-1620. Only 1½ blocks from MTA at Beacon St., which will transport you to the Boston area in 5 to 12 minutes. $15 single; $25 double. "An old Victorian home converted to a ten-room guest house."

Where to Eat: Note—we've included both Cambridge and Boston possibilities here.

● Blue Parrot, 123 Mt. Auburn St., Cambridge. Telephone: 491-1551. Open 11:30 a.m. to midnight; until 1 a.m. weekends. This is a coffeehouse with an easy-going atmosphere. If you're not hungry for a quiche, salad, or a light casserole, you can have just a glass of wine, coffee, or tea.

● Legal Seafoods, in the Park Plaza Hotel, Arlington St. and Columbus Ave. Telephone: 426-4444. Fish is featured, but the meat and chicken are just as good. This is a very popular place so expect up to an hour's wait at dinnertime.

● Jacob Wirth, 33–37 Stuart St. Telephone: 338-8586. Open Monday through Saturday. The food is German and American and you can choose from a generous-size sandwich to a full dinner. This is an old, popular eating place with a saloon atmosphere that's best known for its specially brewed dark beer.

● One Potato Two Potato, 1274 Massachusetts Ave., Cambridge. Telephone: 492-7682. Good, sensible food in an informal atmosphere.

● Wursthaus, 4 Boylston St., Cambridge. Telephone: 491-7110. Another

German/American place with good hot pastrami, a wide choice of beers, and a friendly Bavarian atmosphere.

● Joe Tecce's Restaurant, 55 North Washington St. Telephone: 742-6210. In the Italian North End, off Haymarket Square and right by Government Center. A meal of pasta, meat, and vegetables can cost $10, and according to one fan, "is worth every penny."

● Rubin's Kosher Deli, 404a Harvard St., Brookline. Telephone: 566-8761. A short MBTA ride out of the city but worth it when you crave real kosher deli. A full meal will cost almost $6, but a good and filling sandwich is under $3.

● Back Yard, inside the Garage Mall at 36 Boylston St., Cambridge. Telephone: 661-8979. Deep-dish pizza is the house specialty. Soup, sandwiches, omelets, and crêpes are available, too.

● No-Name Restaurant, 15½ Fish Pier (just past Anthony's Pier Four on the Wharf). Telephone: 338-7539. Fresh seafood at reasonable prices; well known for the chowder. Bring your own wine and expect a waiting line.

● Durgin Park, Faneuil Hall Marketplace, North Market Building. Telephone: 227-2038. "Established before you were born." In the same spot since the late 1800s, this place is a very definite part of the Boston tradition and a favorite with tourists.

What to See and Do: Boston Common and Public Garden: The Common is the oldest park in the U.S. and provides a nice piece of green in the heart of downtown. The Public Garden, right across Charles St. from the Common, is where you'll find the swan boats in summer.

● Freedom Trail: There are two trails and you can walk along either or both. One is the Freedom Trail–Downtown, which includes the sites connected with the Revolution—Faneuil Hall, Old South Meeting House, Boston Tea Party Ship and Museum, and the Granary Burying Ground. The other is the Freedom Trail—North End, which includes the Old North Church, Paul Revere's House, and Copp's Hill Burying Ground.

● Hancock Tower Observatory: Go the top of this Copley Square building for a view of the city.

● Prudential Center: For a different view of the city, go up to the Skywalk on the 50th floor of the "Pru."

● Museum of Fine Arts, 465 Huntington Ave. Telephone: 267-9377. Egyptian, Classical, and Asiatic art; impressionist painting; and early American furniture. The Huntington Ave. streetcar stops right in front of the museum and there's a restaurant inside and a place for you to eat if you bring your own lunch.

● Museum of Science, Science Park. Telephone: 723-2500. Take the Green Line from Park St. to Science Park station. Exhibits about man's natural world and the things he has invented. Wonderful for all ages. Open every day.

● Isabella Stewart Gardner Museum, 280 The Fenway. Telephone: 734-1359. Isabella Gardner was a fascinating, eccentric Bostonian whose fabulous art collection is housed in this reconstruction of a Florentine palace. Included is a Titian, some Vermeers, and paintings by Botticelli, Corot, etc.—all arranged by Mrs. Gardner with the stipulation that they must never be moved. There are free chamber music concerts at the museum; call for the schedule, which varies with the season.

● Faneuil Hall Marketplace: One of the major tourist attractions in the country, Faneuil Hall/Quincy Market is a conglomeration of small shops and restaurants. Be prepared to elbow through crowds wherever you go, but do go.

● Beacon Hill: Originally, the hill was twice as high and it had a beacon on top of it so that sailors could find the city. The New Statehouse (the old one stands on Washington St.) was designed by Charles Bulfinch and built in 1797, and is the prototype for many other capitols including the one in Washington. Louisburg Square with its lovely town houses and Charles St. are the epitome of Boston charm.

● Haymarket: In the North End near Faneuil Hall, this open-air market attracts crowds, especially on Friday and Saturday.

● For a free walking tour of the Harvard campus, go to the Admissions Office in Byerly Hall, 8 Garden St., Cambridge. Telephone: 495-5000. Tours on weekdays and Saturday. For a look at MIT's campus, go to the school's information office inside the main entrance at 77 Massachusetts Ave.

● All in the Harvard area of Cambridge are the Fogg Art Museum, 32 Quincy St., with medieval, Oriental, and impressionistic works; the Busch-Reisinger Museum, a collection of the art of central and northern Europe; and the Peabody Museum, 11 Divinity Ave., a collection of archeological, botanical, and geological exhibits and home of the famous glass models of nearly every flower on earth.

At Night: Jack's, 952 Massachusetts Ave., Cambridge. The cover here is $1 to $3 and the style is casual. The music is blues, southern rock, rock and roll, and New Wave. There's a small dance floor.

● Oxford Ale House, 36 Church St., Harvard Square, Cambridge. Open daily until 3 a.m. A casual place where young people like to dance. Night cover charge.

● Symphony Hall, 251 Huntington Ave. Telephone: 266-1492. The home of the Boston Symphony. Call for performance schedule and prices—the season runs from September through April. "One of the most acoustically perfect concert halls in the world."

● Boston Ballet Company, the Metropolitan, 553 Tremont St. The season runs from November to March. Call 542-3945 for information.

● Resident theater groups like Boston Shakespeare, the Lyric Stage, the Next Move Theater, and the American Rep offer good theater at prices that are reasonable.

Shopping: Barnes and Noble, with several branches in the city, has popular books at discount prices.

● Brentano's, 91 D Plaza, Prudential Center. Just about everything you might want to read.

● Reading International, corner of Brattle and Church Sts., Cambridge (Harvard Square). Mostly paperbacks; large selection of periodicals and some foreign language magazines, journals, and papers.

● Wordsworth, 30 Brattle St., Cambridge. Good selection, all books discounted—10% for paperbacks and 15% on hardcovers.

● Harvard Coop, 1400 Massachusetts Ave., Cambridge. Books, records, clothing, and just about everything else.

● Strawberries, 709 Boylston St., Boston, and 30 Boylston St. in Harvard Square, Cambridge. Contemporary records and tapes.

● Filene's, 426 Washington St. A specialty store with a well-known bargain basement that's the oldest in the U.S. All the merchandise is dated and every 15 days the price drops 30%.

Tourist Information: There are information booths on Tremont St. next to the Park St. subway station or in the National Park Building at 15 State St. next to the Old State House.

● Greater Boston Convention and Tourist Bureau, Prudential Tower, P.O. Box 490, 02199. Telephone: 617/536-4100. Call 338-1976 for events of the day.

● MBTA Information: 617/722-5657 or 722-5700.

● Bostix, in Quincy Hall Marketplace. For information and tickets to concerts, plays, and other special events. Some tickets are discounted.

Help: Travelers Aid, 312 Stuart St. Telephone: 617/542-7286 or 542-7296.

● Project Place, 32 Rutland Pl. Telephone: 617/267-9150. Drop in or call 24 hours a day, seven days a week. "From stubbed toes to suicide calls."

● Bridge Over Troubled Waters, Inc., 23 Beacon St. Telephone: 617/227-7114. Counseling and free medical service.

● For information about Cambridge and just about anywhere else you're going, contact Harvard Student Agencies, 4 Holyoke St., Cambridge, 02139. Telephone: 617/864-0380.

Braintree

Accommodation: Susse Chalet Motor Lodge, Rte. 3 at Union St., 02184. Telephone: 617/848-7890. $21.70 for one; $25.70 for two; $31.70 for four.

Brockton

Accommodation: Old Colony YMCA, 320 Main St., 02401. Telephone: 617/583-2155. Men only. $15. Weekly rate: $50. Cafeteria in the building.

Cambridge

(See Boston/Cambridge listing.)

Cedarville

Accommodation: Camp Massasoit (AYH-SA), Sandy Pond Rd., RFD 5, P.O. Box 636, Plymouth, 02360. Telephone: 617/888-2624. Open June 15 to Labor Day. $3.50.

Danvers

Accommodation: Motel 6, 110 Newbury St., 01923. $12.95 for one; $16.95 for two; $19.95 for up to four.

Dudley

Accommodation: Dudley Home Hostel (AYH). Telephone: 617/943-6520. $5. AYH members given preference. Reservations necessary.

East Bridgewater

Accommodation: Train Hostel (AYH), ✦11%, ♿, 234 Central St., 02333. Telephone: 617/378-4046. Open year round. $5.75 winter; $4.50 summer. AYH membership required (see page 21). Call hostel and someone will pick you up at the bus station.

Eastham

Accommodation: Starfish Youth Hostel (AYH), RR1, Box 138, 02642. Telephone: 617/255-1441. Bus will stop in front of hostel at your request. $4.50 for AYH members; $6 for nonmembers. Will accept men, women, and children.

Falmouth

Accommodation: Schofield's Guest House, ★, 335 Grand Ave., Falmouth Heights, 02540. Telephone: 617/548-4648. $18 to $20 per person. On the ocean. Discount to *Where to Stay* readers if you stay for a fair amount of time. Reservations necessary.

Framingham

Accommodation: Red Roof Inn, Mass. 30 at I-90, 01701. To open in 1982. $19.95 for one; $22.95 for two in one bed; $24.95 to $26.95 for two to four in two beds.

Haverhill

Accommodation: YMCA, 81 Winter St., 01830. Telephone: 617/374-0506. Men over 18 only. $7.50 per night; $35 per week.

Holyoke

Accommodation: Susse Chalet Inn, Rte. 5, I-91 (Exit 17, 17A), 01040. Telephone: 413/536-1980. $22.70 for one; $26.70 for two; $32.70 for four.

Hyannis

Accommodations: Hy-land Youth Hostel (AYH), 465 Falmouth Rd., 02601. Telephone: 617/775-2970. Reservations required. $4.50. Space is limited in winter. AYH membership required (see page 21).

● Yellow Door Guest House, 6 Main St., 02601. Telephone: 617/775-0321. Ten-minute walk from bus station. $16 during high season; $5 to $8 off-season. Rates per person, double occupancy. Reservations recommended.

Lawrence

Accommodation: YMCA, ★ 10%, 40 Lawrence St., 01840. Telephone: 617/686-6191. Men over 18 only. $12. Weekly rate: $35.

Lenox

Accommodation: Susse Chalet Motor Lodge, 428 Lenox-Pittsfield Rd., Rtes. 7 and 20, 01240. Telephone: 413/637-3560. No singles. $23.70 to $29.70 for a double room. Near Tanglewood and ski areas. Cable color TV, pool, and coffeeshop.

Leominster

Accommodations: Susse Chalet Motor Lodge, Rte. 2 at Rte. 13 Exit near Searstown, 01453. Telephone: 617/537-8161. See Amesbury listing for rates.
● Best Value Leominster Motor Inn, 665 Central St., 01453. Telephone: 617/537-1741. $17.50 for one; $19.50 for two in one bed; $21.50 for two in two beds.

Littleton

Accommodation: Friendly Crossways Youth Hostel (AYH), two miles from Littleton Depot on Whitcomb, 01460. Telephone: 617/456-3649. Open year round. $5 summer, $7.50 winter for AYH members; $12.50 for nonmembers. A privately owned country conference center that prides itself on being homey.

Lunenburg

Accommodation: Superior Coach House Inn, junction of Rtes. 2A and 13, 01642. Telephone: 617/582-9921. $20 to $21.50 for one; $23 to $25 for two.

Martha's Vineyard

Help: Project Hotline, 617/693-1199.
Accommodations: Titticut Follies Guest House, 43 Narragansett Ave., Oak Bluffs, 02557. Telephone: 617/693-4986. Two blocks from bus station. Open May 15 to September. $32 for a double. Reservations recommended. "An old house restored to its original gingerbread style in the tradition of the Victorian seaside resort."
● Manter Memorial Youth Hostel (AYH), Edgartown Rd., West Tisbury, 02575. Telephone: 617/693-2665. Open April 1 to November 30. Send stamped, self-addressed envelope for reservations form and information sheet. "Bikers and hikers only; no hitchhikers or motorists." $4.75. AYH membership required (see page 21).

Nantucket

Accommodation: Star of the Sea Youth Hostel (AYH), ♿, Surfside, 02554. Three miles from Nantucket town on south side of the island. Telephone: 617/228-0433. Open April to October. $4.50. The hostel, built in 1873, is an old Coast Guard Station. Reservations are necessary. AYH membership required (see page 21).

Newburyport

Help: Turning Point, 5 Middle St. Telephone: 617/465-8800 or 462-8251.
Accommodation: Civic Center YMCA (AYH-SA), 🐟★, 96 State St., 01950. Telephone: 617/462-6711. Open June 15 to Labor Day. $3.50 for AYH members.

Newton

Accommodations: YMCA, 276 Church St., 02158. Telephone: 617/244-6050. Men only. $32 to $47 per week. Minimum stay is two weeks.

Northampton

On Campus: Not far from Amherst is Northampton, home of Smith College. One of the most popular spots in town is the Iron Horse Coffeehouse on Center St., where a light meal costs under $2.50 and there's live folk or jazz music every night. Another good place to eat is the Soup Kitchen, on Main St. Not far from Northampton, on Main St. in Florence, is the Miss Florence Diner, which the *New York Times* rated as one of the ten best diners in New England.

Northfield

Accommodation: Monroe Smith Memorial, Daly House (AYH), Highland and Pine Sts., 01360. Telephone: 413/498-5311, extension 502. Open June 21 to August 22. $4.50. AYH membership required (see page 21).

Orleans

Accommodation: Mid-Cape Youth Hostel (AYH), 140-H Bridge Rd., 02642. One-quarter mile from junction of Rtes. 6 and 28. Telephone: 617/255-2785. Open May 26 to Labor Day. $4.50. Reservations absolutely required. AYH membership required (see page 21).

Quincy

Accommodation: YMCA, 79 Coddington St., 02169. Telephone: 617/479-8500. Men only, 18 years and over. $12 single. Weekly rate: $47.50.

Sheffield

Accommodation: Mount Everett Youth Hostel (AYH), Rte. 1, P.O. Box 161, 01257. Appalachian Trail is 1½ miles away. Telephone: 413/229-2043. Open May 15 to September 5. $3. You can set up camp there for $2.75. In the Berkshires. AYH membership required (see page 21).

South Deerfield

Accommodation: Motel 6, Rte. 5-10, 01373. Telephone: 413/665-2681. See Danvers listing for rates. Restaurant on premises.

Springfield

Help: Hotline, 413/739-7339. Open Thursday to Sunday, 7 to 11 p.m.

Accommodations: YMCA, 275 Chestnut St., 01104. Telephone: 413/739-6951. Men and women. Single $17 per night for the first week. Weekly rate is $58.50 thereafter. "New building with plenty of free parking."

● Susse Chalet Motor Lodge, Mass. Turnpike (Exit 6), 01020. Telephone: 413/592-5141. See Amesbury listing for rates.

● Springfield College Camp Youth Hostel (AYH-SA), 🐟★, 701 Wilbraham Rd. (Box 592, Springfield College, 01109). Telephone: 413/782-0461. Three miles from the center of town. Open July 1 to August 31. $1.50. "Camp facilities with log cabins containing bunk cots—81 acres on lake."

Truro

Accommodation: Little America Youth Hostel (AYH), P.O. Box 402, 02666. Telephone: 617/349-3889. Open June 15 to September 7. Advance reservations required. During closed period, contact AYH National Office, 1332 I St. NW, Washington, DC 20005. $4.50. An old Coast Guard Station converted to dorm-like accommodations. AYH membership required (see page 21).

Washington

Accommodation: Bucksteep Manor, Camp Karu/Bucksteep (AYH-SA), Washington Mountain Rd., 01223. Ten miles east of Pittsfield. Telephone: 413/623-5535. In the Berkshires. "We are a place of quiet majesty; a place of refuge and sanctuary. We offer you a mellow blend of the rural life, mixed as you like it with sports, entertainment and cultural attractions." Cabins, $6; lodge, $15; AYH members, $3.50. They also have rooms in the Manor Inn which cost $22.50 single and $25 double.

West Boylston

Accommodation: Best Value West Boylston Motel, 90 Sterling St., Rte. 12, 01583. Telephone: 617/835-6247. $19 for one; $26 for two in one bed; $28 for two in two beds.

Worcester

Help: Crisis Center, 617/791-6562.

Accommodations: YWCA, 2 Washington St., 01604. Telephone: 617/791-3181. Women only. $12.50 single; $9.50 per person double. Weekly rate: $30 to $35. Self-service cafeteria in the building.

● YMCA, 766 Main St., 01608. Telephone: 617/755-6101. Men only. $14 single. Weekly rate: $56 for the first four weeks; $34 thereafter.

Wrentham

Accommodation: Superior Stardust Motor Inn, Rte. 1 at I-495, 02093. Telephone: 617/384-3176. $23 for one; $25 for two in one bed; $28 for two in two beds.

Michigan

Your first thoughts when you hear "Michigan" are probably Detroit and cars. Michigan is, after all, America's leading producer of automobiles and the headquarters of the United Auto Workers, the second-largest union in the country.

But there's much of Michigan beyond Detroit—much that's beautiful, rustic, and serene. The state motto, "If You Seek a Pleasant Peninsula, Look Around You," can quite accurately describe the Upper Peninsula of Michigan, where there are streams to fish, forests to camp and hike, mines to explore, and where in winter there's skiing, snowmobiling, tobogganing, and skating. You'll enjoy taking a ferry from Mackinaw City to Mackinac Island during the summer; there are no cars on the island, but hundreds of bicycles are available to rent for exploring this popular summer resort.

The Henry Ford Museum and Greenfield Village, not far from Detroit in Dearborn, is a popular tourist attraction where Americana is king: Ford had famous homes, laboratories, stores, and other buildings gathered from all over the U.S. and deposited in his park.

Ann Arbor, the home of the University of Michigan, is a lively town, certainly worth a visit, especially if you're a student.

Some Special Events: Blossomtime Festival in Benton Harbor (April); Tulip Festival in Holland (May); Rose Festival in Jackson and Seaway Festival in Muskegon (June); National Cherry Festival in Traverse City and Bass Festival in Crystal Falls (July); Country Festival in Canton and Indian Pow Wow in Cross Village (August); Peach Festival in Romeo and Riverfest in Lansing (September).

Hitching: The issue of hitchhiking in Michigan is a controversial one. Some of our friends said that it is accepted among the students, but they recommend caution for both the driver and the hitchhiker. Others wrote to us that they would definitely not recommend hitchiking, warning that the crime rate in the Detroit area is particularly high. Officially, hitching is legal except on limited-access highways. Some cities may prohibit hitchhiking within their corporate limits, but the cities that do this vary from year to year.

Tourist Information: Travel Bureau, Michigan Department of Commerce, P.O. Box 30226, Lansing, MI 48909.

Ann Arbor

"A unique blend of cosmopolitan opportunities and small-town charm."

Help: Ann Arbor Conference and Visitor Hotline, 313/995-7281.
● Washtenaw Crisis Center, 313/996-4747 or 994-1616.
On Campus: The University of Michigan is in Ann Arbor, and according to one Ann Arborite "the university is the whole town." A good source of help there, especially for foreign visitors, is the University of Michigan International Center, 603 East Madison St., 48109. Telephone: 313/764-9310.

Be forewarned: Finding low-cost accommodations in Ann Arbor is difficult, according to one person who's tried it and another who lives there, and on football weekends it's next to impossible. It may be possible for students to stay at the residence halls of the University of Michigan during the summer—call the International Center for information.

For an inexpensive Mexican meal, try the Central Café, 332 South Main St. or the Pan Tree on Liberty St. between 5th and Division. There you will find homemade soups, salads, omelets, etc.

Accommodations: Allen's Tourist Home, ➡10%, ♿, 1126 East Ann, 48104. Telephone: 313/662-2763. One-half mile from train station; three-quarters of a mile from bus. $12 single; $13 twin; $14 triple. Baths in the hall, communal kitchen. Next to University of Michigan campus.
● Ann Arbor YMCA, ♿, 350 South Fifth Ave., 48104. Telephone: 313/663-0536. Men and women. Near bus and train station. $15. Weekly rate: $56.
● Red Roof Inn, ♿, U.S. 23 at Plymouth Rd. Telephone: 313/996-5800. $19.95 for one; $22.95 for two in one bed; $24.95 to $26.95 for two to four in two beds.

Battle Creek

Accommodations: Best Value Michigan Motel, 20475 Michigan 66 North, 49017. Telephone: 616/963-1565. $18 to $20 for one; $22 for two in one bed; $26 for two in two beds.
● Regal 8 Inn, 4775 Beckley Rd. (Capital Ave. at I-94), 49017. Telephone: 616/979-1141. $18.88 for one; $21.88 for two in one bed; $24.88 for two to four in two beds.

Bay City

Accommodations: YMCA, 111 North Madison, 48706. Telephone: 517/895-8596. Men only. $12 plus $3 key deposit. Weekly rate: $36. Within walking distance from bus station.
● Friendship Inn–Bertrands, 910 South Euclid, 48706. Telephone: 517/684-4100. $17 to $19 for one; $20 to $22 for two in one bed; $22 to $24 for two in two beds.

● Empire House Motel, √10%, 1305 Washington, 48706. Telephone: 517/894-2711. $19 to $21 for one; $22 to $24 for two in one bed; $26 to $28 for two in two beds.

● Imperial 400 Motor Inn, 50 6th St., 48706. Telephone: 517/892-4554. $20 to $22 for one; $22 to $24 for two in one bed; $28 to $30 for two in two beds.

Benton Harbor

Accommodation: Red Roof Inn, 🛇, I-94 at Pipestone Road (Exit 29), 49022. Telephone: 616/927-2484. $17.95 for one; $20.95 for two in one bed; $22.95 to $24.95 for two to four in two beds.

Bessemer

Accommodation: Bessemer-Indianhead Youth Hostel (AYH), 1110 East Iron St., 49911. Two miles south of Bessemer. Telephone: 906/667-0915 or 663-4465. Open December to March for skiing (four mountains to choose from). For groups only in summer. $18.65 with breakfast and dinner. AYH membership required (see page 21).

Brevport

Accommodation: Best Value Gustafson's Resort, U.S. 2, 49760. Telephone: 906/292-5541. $14 to $16 for one; $16 to $18 for two in one bed; $20 to $22 for two in two beds.

Center Line

Accommodation: Home Hostel (AYH), 8585 Harding Ave., 48015. Telephone: 313/756-2676. $4. AYH membership required (see page 21). Ten miles from Detroit. Three blocks from bus station. A unique home filled with odds and ends from all over the world and assorted pets. *"We spent a wonderful time with Gloria and Harold, the houseparents."*

Charlevoix

Accommodation: Home Hostel (AYH), 541 North Mercer, 49720. Telephone: 616/547-2937. $2 with your own sleeping bag. Small fee for linen and kitchen privileges.

Cheboygan

Accommodation: Cheboygan Motor Lodge, 1355 Mackinaw Ave., 49721. Telephone: 616/627-3129. $23 for two in one bed; $26 for two in two beds.

Coloma

Accommodation: Camp Warren (AYH), 2456 Maple Ave., 49038. Telephone: 616/849-1433. $3 summer; $4 winter. Camping, too. AYH membership required (see page 21). Bring linen or sleeping bag.

Delton

Accommodation: Circle Pines Center (AYH), 8650 Mullen Rd., 49046. Telephone: 616/623-5555. $8 adults; $4 children (age 0 to 2 free). Rooms sleep four to six. Twenty-five miles from bus or train station. Chores required. Kitchen available for $1 per day or you can eat meals served there at a reasonable price. Bring your own linen. "We are an educational cooperative established in 1938. We own 284 acres of woods and meadows, with one-third mile of lakefront with a sandy beach. There are 40 buildings: a lodge, a farmhouse, and many cabins."

Detroit

Help: Travelers Aid, 1509 Broadway, 48226. Telephone: 313/962-6740.
• Travelers Aid, 130 East Congress (Greyhound Bus Station), 48226. Telephone: 313/961-1532. There is also a branch at Metropolitan Airport.
• Hotline, 313/298-6262. What's happening in Detroit.
Tourist Information: Detroit Visitor Information Center, 2 East Jefferson, 48226. Telephone: 313/963-0879.

"Detroiters do not wear mechanics' coveralls to the symphony!"

Except possibly when it plays under the stars at Meadowbrook at Oakland University on summer nights (call 377-2100 for information). Also look into the free jazz and blues concerts sponsored by the Jefferson-Chalmen Citizens' District Council in summer (call 822-0006). Check with the housing office of Oakland University in suburban Rochester, or the University of Detroit—they might have a room available for a night or two.
Accommodations: YMCA (AYH-SA), 2020 Witherell, 48226. Telephone: 313/962-6126. Men and women. Open year round. Reservations recommended. $2.25 for AYH members; $12.48 for nonmembers.
• YWCA (AYH-SA), 🔊, 2230 Witherell, 48201. Telephone: 313/961-9220. Women only. Open all year. $15.25 single. AYH members: $5.20.
• YMCA, 1601 Clark Ave., 48209. Telephone: 313/554-2136. Men only. $10 per night plus $6 key deposit.
• Manning Hall, Mercy College, 8200 West Outer Dr., 48219. Telephone: 313/592-6170. Ask for Director of Housing. Men, women, and children. May to August. Reservations requested one month in advance.
• Red Roof Inn, 🔊, I-275/I-696 at Grand River, Farmington Hills, 48018. Telephone: 313/478-8640. See Ann Arbor listing for rates.
• Red Roof Inn, I-275 at Ann Arbor Rd., Plymouth, 48170. Telephone: 313/459-3300. See Ann Arbor listing for rates.
• Red Roof Inn, I-94 at Little Mack Rd., Roseville, 48066. Telephone: 313/296-0310. See Ann Arbor listing for rates.
• Red Roof Inn, 🔊, I-75 at Rochester Rd., Troy, 48084. Telephone: 313/689-4391. See Ann Arbor listing for rates.

East Lansing

Help: Listening Ear, 547½ East Grand River Ave., 48823. Telephone: 517/337-1717. Phone or drop in, seven days a week.

On Campus: Michigan State University is here, and, according to a member of the Union Activities Board, the attitude toward people on the road in the area is "liberal because of the college atmosphere." Nearly all of the local meeting places are just across the street from campus on Grand River Ave. When hunger strikes, you can find an inexpensive meal at Beggar's Banquet, 218 Abbott; Al Azteco, 203 M.A.C.; or Olga's Kitchen, 131 East Grand River.

Accommodation: Michigan State University Student Housing Corporation (AYH-SA), ♿, 311 B Student Services Building, 48824. Telephone: 517/355-8313. Men, women, and children may stay at any of the student cooperative houses in the campus area. Beds are more likely to be available during the summer but there's always floor space. $4 for adults, $2 for children. "Call first and we'll give you directions on how to reach whichever co-op has room for that night." Meals are available for $2 per day. Bring your own linen.

Flint

Tourist Information: Flint Area Convention and Tourist Council, North Bank Center, Suite 101A, 400 North Saginaw St., 48502. Telephone: 303/232-8900 or toll free within Michigan 800/482-0989.

Help: Voluntary Action Center, 202 East Boulevard Dr., 48503. Telephone: 313/767-0500. For information and referral.

Accommodations: YWCA, 310 East 3rd St., 48502. Women only. Telephone: 313/238-7621. $10.40 for members; $10.65 for nonmembers. Reservations required at least three days in advance.

● Mott Lake Hostel (AYH), 🏕 ★ (discount on equipment rentals), G-6511 North Genesee Rd., 48506. Telephone: 313/736-5760. Bring a sleeping bag or your own linens. Their backyard is a 4000-acre park that includes a 600-acre lake. $3.50 for those under 18; $4 for others. Anyone who reserves with full payment at least one day ahead receives $1 discount per night. Bike, canoe, and sled rentals available. Kitchen facilities provided; bring your own food. AYH membership required (see page 21).

● Red Roof Inn, I-75 at Miller Rd., 48507. Telephone: 313/733-1660. See Ann Arbor listing for rates.

Frankfort

Camping: Sleeping Bear Dunes National Lakeshore, 400 Main St., 49635. Camping all year at D. H. Day and Platte River for $2 per campsite per night, and at South Manitou Island (you must take a boat to the island and get a permit from the island office).

Gaylord

Accommodation: Royal Crest Motel, six blocks south of Mich. 32 on Old U.S. 27. Telephone: 517/732-6451. $18 for one; $22 for two in one bed; $25 for two in two beds.

Grand Marais

Accommodation: Welker's Lodge, end of Mich. 77 on Lake Superior Coast Guard Point, Canal St. (Box 277), 49839. Telephone: 906/494-2361 or 494-2562. $19 to $20 for one; $21 to $22 for two in one bed; $24 to $25 for two in two beds.

Grand Rapids

Help: Community Crisis Intervention Center, 616/774-3535. Open 24 hours.

Accommodations: YMCA, 33 Library NE, 49503. Telephone: 616/458-1141. Men only. $9 (for Y members there's a discount). Weekly rate: $40. Reservations required at least two days in advance.

● Home Hostel (AYH), c/o Charles French, 1117 Paradise Lake SE, 49506. Telephone: 616/676-9247. Open all year. AYH membership required (see page 21).

● Red Roof Inn, I-96 at 28th St. (Exit 43A). Telephone: 616/942-0800. See Ann Arbor listing for rates.

● Best Value Beltline Motel, 171 28th St. SE, 49508. Telephone: 616/241-0151. $20 for one; $22 for two in one bed; $25 for two in two beds.

● Exel Inn, 🔟, 4855 28th St. SE, 49508. Telephone: 616/957-3000. $18.50 for one; $23.50 for two in one bed; $25.50 for two in two beds.

● Motel 6, 3524 28th St. SE, 49508. Telephone: 616/949-8112. $12.95 for one; $16.95 for two; $19.95 for up to four.

Hart

Accommodation: Hart Home Hostel (AYH), 19 Courtland. Telephone: 616/873-4565. $4.50. Bicyclists only—no cars.

Holland

Help: Crisis Intervention, 616/396-4357.

Accommodations: Home Hostel (AYH). Telephone: 616/392-1311. $2.50. AYH membership required (see page 21). Inexpensive meals served by houseparent.

● Wooden Shoe Motel, √, U.S. 31 Bypass and 16th St., 49423. Telephone: 616/392-8521. $20 to $25 for one; $26 to $34 for two in one bed; $30 to $38 for two in two beds.

● Days Inn, 🔟, U.S. 31 Holland Bypass and 32nd St., 49423. Telephone: 616/392-7001. $24.88 for one; $28.88 for two. Rates higher May to September.

Houghton

Camping: Isle Royale National Park, 87 North Ripley St., 49931. Thirty-one campgrounds, some accessible only by trail, some only by boat. Open May to October. The park is a large island on Lake Superior and some distance from Houghton. There is a ferry service from Houghton to Isle Royale.

Houghton Lake

Accommodation: Best Value Sands Resort Motel, 9192 Old U.S. 27, 48629. Telephone: 517/422-5295. $18 to $22 for one; $20 to $24 for two.

Inkster

Accommodation: Friendship Inn–Dearborn Motel, U.S. 12, 25925 Michigan Ave., 48141. Telephone: 313/565-7200. $22 to $24 for one; $24 to $26 for two in one bed; $28 to $32 for two in two beds.

Iron Mountain

Accommodation: Best Value Cooney's Mountaineer Motel, Rtes. 2 and 141, 49801. Telephone: 906/774-2918. $14 to $20 for one; $22 to $25 for two in one bed; $25 to $30 for two in two beds.

Iron River

Accommodation: Best Value Iron Inn, 202 West Adams, 49935. Telephone: 906/265-5111. $17 to $21 for one; $21 to $26 for two in one bed; $23 to $29 for two in two beds.

Kalamazoo

Help: Helpline, 616/381-4357.
- Lodging Assistance Hotline, 616/385-8199.

On Campus: Kalamazoo College and Western Michigan University are in Kalamazoo. A friend of ours who is a student there describes his town as having a "strong academic and cultural flavor" and a friendly attitude toward young people on the road. Gaspare's and Knollwood Tavern are popular student spots, and you can find a low-priced meal in the college dining rooms.

Accommodations: Red Roof Inn, I-94 at Sprinkle Rd. (Exit 80), 49001. Telephone: 616/382-6350. See Benton Harbor listing for rates.
- Red Roof Inn, ⬢, U.S. 131 at Stadium Dr. (Exit 36B), 49009. Telephone: 616/375-7400. See Benton Harbor listing for rates.

Lakeview

Accommodation: Home Hostel (AYH), 10350 Orchard Lane, 48850. Telephone: 517/352-6351. AYH membership required (see page 21).

Lansing

Help: Emotional Crisis, 517/372-8460.
Accommodations: YMCA, 301 West Lenawee, 48914. Telephone: 517/489-6501. Men only. $9.26 plus $3 key deposit. Three blocks from bus station.

- Red Roof Inn, ♿, I-496 at Jolly Rd., 48910. Telephone: 517/332-2575. See Benton Harbor listing for rates.
- Red Roof Inn, ♿, I-96 at West Saginaw Hwy. (Exit 93B), 48917. Telephone: 517/321-7246. See Benton Harbor listing for rates.
- Motel 6, 112 East Main St., 48933. Telephone: 517/372-2666. See Grand Rapids listing for rates.
- Regal 8 Inn, 6501 South Cedar St., 48910. Telephone: 517/393-2030. $17.88 for one; $20.88 for two in one bed; $23.88 for two to four in two beds.

Marquette

Accommodation: Friendship Inn–Birchmont Motel, 2090 South U.S. 41, 49855. Telephone: 906/226-9275. $16 to $24 for one; $20 to $26 for two in one bed; $24 to $32 for two in two beds.

Midland

Accommodation: Northwood Institute, NADA Center, ★, 3225 Cook Rd., 48640. Telephone: 517/835-7755. Ask for Kathy Clouse. Open year round. $18 single; $24 double. College cafeteria available to guests.

Milford

Accommodations: Foote Youth Hostel (AYH), ♿, Kevin and Linda Lundquist, houseparents, 1845 Dawson Rd., 48042. Telephone: 313/684-9775. Open April 1 to November 1. Reservations required. $2.50 for students under 18; $3 for adults. $1 for camping. AYH membership required (see page 21). Good recreational facilities nearby.
- Heavner Home Hostel and Ski Center (AYH), 2775 Garden Rd., 48042. Telephone: 313/685-2379. $3. Canoe rentals, cross-country skiing, bicycling, horseback riding, hiking, and skating nearby. Bring your own linens. "Cozy tri-level home in the country." AYH membership required (see page 21).

Munising

Camping: Pictured Rocks National Lakeshore, 49862. Campgrounds at Little Beaver Lake, 12-Mile Beach, and Hurricane River. Open May to November. No fee.

Muskegon

Accommodation: Days Inn, ♿, Business I-96 and U.S. 31 and Hoyt St., 150 Seaway Dr., 49444. Telephone: 616/739-9429. $19.88 to $23.88 for one; $24.88 to $28.88 for two. Rates higher from May 9 to 15.

Newberry

Accommodation: The New Falls Hotel, 301 Newberry Ave., 49868. Telephone: 906/293-5111. $17 to $21 for one; $22 to $27 for two in one bed; $24 to $30 for two in two beds.

Petoskey

Accommodation: Friendship Inn–Golf View Motel, 1011 U.S. 31 North, 49770. Telephone: 616/347-8281. $18 to $22 for one; $22 to $25 for two in one bed; $25 to $34 for two in two beds.

Reading

Accommodation: Kimball YMCA Center (AYH), Long Lake Rd., 49274. Telephone: 517/283-2427. Open September 1 to May 31; some arrangements may be possible during summer. Advance booking necessary. $3.50 summer; $4.50 winter. AYH membership required (see page 21).

Saginaw

Accommodations: University Center, Saginaw Valley (AYH), ⬜, Department of Residence Halls, Saginaw Valley State College, 2250 Pierce Rd., 48710. Telephone: 517/790-4255. Open May to August. $4. AYH membership required (see page 21). Reservations necessary at least one day in advance.
● Red Roof Inn, I-75 at Holland Ave. West., 48601. Telephone: 517/754-8414. See Benton Harbor listing for rates.

Sault Ste. Marie

Accommodation: Lake Superior State College (AYH-SA), 1000 College Dr., 49783. Telephone: 906/632-6841, extension 411. Open June 15 to August 15. $4.85. Advance reservations preferred.

Sturgis

Accommodation: Friendship Green Briar Inn, P.O. Box 12, 49091. Telephone: 616/651-2361. $21 for one; $25 for two in one bed; $27 for two in two beds.

Traverse City

Accommodations: Days Inn, ⬜, U.C. 31 North and 8th St. at City Limits, 420 Munson Ave., 49684. Telephone: 616/941-0208. $17.88 to $24.88 for one; $21.88 to $34.88 for two. Rates higher July 1 to September 6.
● Friendship Colonial Inn, 460 Munson Ave., 49684. Telephone: 616/947-5436. $20 to $24 for one; $30 to $34 for two in one bed; $34 to $42 for two in two beds.

Three Rivers

Accommodation: Redwood Motel, 59389 U.S. 131, 49093. Telephone: 618/278-1945. $22 for one; $26 for two in one bed; $29 to $31 for two in two beds. Lower rates off-season.

Twin Lake

Accommodation: Home Hostel (AYH), c/o M. Payne, 3175 1st St., 49457. Telephone: 616/828-6675. Open all year. AYH membership required (see page 21). Canoeing on the lake in summer; cross-country skiing in winter. Bring your own linen. Reservations required. No fee.

Walker

Accommodation: Motel 6, 777 Three Mile Rd., 49504. Telephone: 616/784-1616. See Grand Rapids listing for rates.

White Pigeon

Accommodation: Home Hostel (AYH), c/o E. Hostetter, U.S. 12, 49099. Telephone: 616/483-7236. Open all year. $2. AYH membership required (see page 21).

"White Pigeon is a very small, rural, and traditional town. U.S. 12, which passes through it, is the old route (once an Indian trail) between Chicago and Detroit."

Williamston

Accommodation: Home Hostel (AYH), Ed and Lynnae Ruttledge, house-parents, 115 East Riverside, 48895. Telephone: 517/655-2830. Open all year. Reservations necessary. AYH membership required (see page 21).

Ypsilanti

On Campus: If you're at Eastern Michigan University, call the Office of International Studies (tel. 313/487-2424) for information on possible accommodations at the Hoyt Conference Center.

Minnesota

Roseau ● International Falls ● Grand Marais ● Bemidji ● Hibbing ● Moorhead ● Cloquet ● Duluth ● Brainerd ● Barnum ● Alexandria ● Sauk Centre ● Collegeville ● Cambridge ● St. Cloud ● Minneapolis ● Roseville ● Hamel ● St. Paul ● Burnsville ● Northfield ● Owatonna ● Wabasha ● Mankato ● Rochester ● St. Charles ● Winona ● Worthington ● Fairmont ● Albert Lea

Summer activities in Minnesota revolve mainly around the water, since it is so accessible in all areas but the far west. The Boundary Waters Canoe Area is one of the best canoeing and wilderness camping areas in the country. In the winter many hardy Minnesotans even go camping with their snowshoes and cross-country skis. There is more camping, fishing, and boating available up near the northern border of the state in International Falls at Voyageurs National Park. French-Canadian voyagers transported their furs through this forested lake country in the 1700s and 1800s—hence the name.

Fishing, waterskiing, and swimming are also very popular and can be done easily in or near the Twin Cities—the metropolitan area of Minneapolis/St. Paul has over 100 lakes within its limits.

One of the most beautiful canoe trips in the country is down the St. Croix River, which divides Minnesota and Wisconsin. It is possible to rent canoes at several points along the river and to canoe for from four hours to several days, camping along the shores as you go. At the end you can leave your canoe and get transportation back at a moderate price.

Another interesting camping area is Rainy Lake, at the Canada-Minnesota border. A number of islands in the lake have tidy campsites on them, owned and kept in shape for the general public by an area lumber company. The lake is rock bottomed, very deep, and has many underwater rock mountains. The cold water is excellent for fishing, scuba diving, and snorkeling.

For those who like the bigger cities, Minnesota's twin cities of Minneapolis and St. Paul have lots to offer. Cultural activities include the nationally renowned Guthrie Theater, Minneapolis Children's Theater, St. Paul Chamber Orchestra concerts, the Science Museum of St. Paul and its Omnitheater, and the Minneapolis Museum of Art. The University of Minnesota has a number of concert, ballet, and opera series throughout the year. Minnesota Orchestra concerts, held year round, are exceptional and shouldn't be missed on any trip to the area.

In Minnesota, the Scandinavian and German influence is quite noticeable. Other groups exist, but not in any great numbers, comparatively. In fact, it's been said that there are as many Lutheran churches in Minnesota as there are lakes.

Some Special Events: Smelt Fry in Garrison (April); Festival of Nations in St. Paul, and Syttende Mai Fest in Spring Grove featuring Norwegian food, crafts, and dances (May); Good Times Days in Boyd, Noble County Dairy Days in Ellsworth, Swedish Festival in Cambridge, and International Polka Festival and Tug of War in Pine City (all in June); Whiz Bang Days in Robbinsdale, Lake of the Woods County Fair in Baudette, Lumberjack Days in Cloquet, and Song of Hiawatha Pageant in Pipestone (all in July); Strawhat and Sunbonnet Days in Verndale, Victorian Crafts Festival in St. Paul, and Sweet Corn Festival in Ortonville (August); Cherry Area Fair and Rodeo in Iron and Lac Qui Parle County Fair in Madison (September).

Hitching: A friend says that hitchhiking across the state is fair to good but that "highway patrolmen on Interstate 94 may escort a hitchhiker to an entrance ramp." Forget hitching in winter, though—it's miserable in the cold. Officially, no one may solicit a ride from the roadways and pedestrians are prohibited on controlled-access highways.

Tourist Information: Tourism Information Center, 480 Cedar St., St. Paul, MN 55101. Telephone: 612/296-5029. Minnesota residents outside the Twin Cities area can call toll free 800/652-9747; from other parts of the U.S. call 800/328-1461. The center is open Monday through Friday from 8 a.m. to 4:30 p.m.

Albert Lea

Accommodation: Friendship Country Side Inn, 2102 East Main St., 56007. Telephone: 507/373-2446. $17 to $20 for one; $20 to $23 for two in one bed; $25 to $28 for two in two beds.

Alexandria

Accommodation: Thrifty Scot Motel, 4810 Hwy. 29 South, 56308. Telephone: 612/762-1171. $20.90 to $22.90 for one; $24.90 to $26.90 for two in one bed; $27.90 to $29.90 for two in two beds.

Barnum

Accommodation: YWCA Camp Wanakiwin (AYH-SA), c/o 202 West 2nd St., Duluth, 55802. Telephone: 218/722-7425 or 389-6981. Open September to May. Three weeks' advance registration necessary. AYH membership required for individuals (see page 21).

Bemidji

Accommodations: Best Value Paul Bunyan Motel, 915 Midway Dr., 56601. Telephone: 218/751-1314. $14 to $24 for one; $20 to $35 for two.

● Thrifty Scot Motel, Hwy. 2 West, P.O. Box 39, 56601. Telephone: 218/751-0390. $18.90 to $23.90 for one; $22.90 to $24.90 for two in one bed; $27.90 for two in two beds.

Brainerd

Accommodation: Thrifty Scot Motel, P.O. Box 364, Hwys. 210 and 371, 56401. Telephone: 218/829-0391. $19.90 to $22.90 for one; $23.90 to $24.90 for two in one bed; $26.90 to $28.90 for two in two beds.

Burnsville

Accommodation: Red Roof Inn, I-35 at Burnsville Pkwy., 55337. To open in 1982. $19.95 for one; $22.95 for two in one bed; $24.95 to $26.95 for two to four in two beds.

Cambridge

Accommodation: Friendship Inn–Imperial Lodge, Hwy. 65 North, 55008. Telephone: 612/689-2200. $17.50 to $22.50 for one; $20.50 to $26.50 for two in one bed; $26.50 to $28.50 for two in two beds.

Collegeville

Accommodation: St. John's University Summer Programs, 56321. Telephone: 612/363-3487. Greyhound bus stops on campus. Open June 1 to August 15. $11.50 single ($8.50 if you bring your own sleeping bag or linen). Reservations requested. Tennis courts, indoor pool, lake swimming, and boating nearby. "We are a Benedictine monastic community also—respect our quiet."

Cloquet

Accommodation: Best Value Driftwood Motel, 1413 Hwy. 33 South, 55720. Telephone: 218/879-4638. $17 for one; $21 for two in one bed; $23 for two in two beds.

Duluth

Help: Information and Referral, 218/727-8538.
Accommodations: College of St. Scholastica, 🔲, Kenwood Ave., 55811. Ask for Director of Residential Life. Telephone: 218/723-6483. Men, women, and children. $10 single; $15 double. Weekly rate available. Reservations requested 24 hours in advance. Open June 13 to September 1.
● YWCA (AYH-SA), 202 West 2nd St., 55802. Telephone: 218/722-7425. Women only in residence, $10.60 per night. Men and women in AYH facility, $3.50 per night.
● Best Value Interstate Budget Motel, I-35 and 27th Ave. West, 55806.

Telephone: 218/723-1123. $14.99 to $19.99 for one; $17.99 to $23.99 for two in one bed; $19.99 to $26.99 for two in two beds.
 ● Thrifty Scot Motel, 909 Cottonwood Ave., 55801. Telephone: 218/727-3110. $18.90 to $23.90 for one; $25.90 to $30.90 for two in one bed; $27.90 to $32.90 for two in two beds.

Fairmont

Accommodation: Best Value Lakeside Inn, 101 Albion Ave., 56031. Telephone: 507/238-4406. $13 to $15 for one; $18 to $20 for two.

Grand Marais

Accommodations: Seagull Canoe Trips/Hostel (AYH-SA), P.O. Box 119-H, 55604. Telephone: 218/388-2271. Open May 15 to September 15. $3. Note: The mailing address is Grand Marais; the actual hostel is 55 miles away, adjacent to Seagull Resort. For canoeists. "Rustic old cabins with no plumbing or electricity."
 ● Friendship Inn–Lamplighter, southwest on U.S. 61, P.O. Box 667, 55604. Telephone: 218/387-2633. $16 to $18 for one; $18 to $22 for two in one bed; $20 to $26 for two in two beds.

Hamel

Accommodation: Pinewood Youth Hostel (AYH), 4535 Willow Dr., 55340. Telephone: 612/478-6930. Open June 1 to Labor Day. $2.50. Reservations required one week in advance. AYH membership required (see page 21).

Hibbing

Accommodation: Thrifty Scot Motel, P.O. Box 662, 55746. Telephone: 218/263-8306. $18.90 to $23.90 for one; $25.90 to $30.90 for two in one bed; $27.90 to $32.90 for two in two beds.

International Falls

Accommodation: Thrifty Scot Motel, P.O. Box 182, Hwy. 53, 56679. Telephone: 218/283-9441. $19.90 to $22.90 for one; $23.90 to $25.90 for two in one bed; $26.90 to $28.90 for two in two beds.
 Camping: Voyageurs National Park, 56649. Campgrounds accessible only by boat. Open all year.

Mankato

Help: Blue Earth Co. Information and Referral Service, 507/625-3031, extension 239.
 Accommodation: McElroy Center, Mankato State University, Ellis Ave., 56001. Telephone: 507/389-1011. 1½ miles from bus station. Open June 6 to August 12. $8 single; $7 per person double. You can get a good meal at the Centennial Student Union one-half block away.

Minneapolis

Note: See St. Paul, too, since Minneapolis and St. Paul are "twin cities" divided only by the Mississippi River.

Help: First Call For Help (Travelers Aid), 404 South 8th St., 55404. Telephone: 612/340-7431.

● Contact-Twin Cities, 612/341-2896.

● Information Referral, 300 South 6th St. Telephone: 612/348-8125. Open Monday to Friday, 8 a.m. to 4:30 p.m. Phones open 24 hours.

Tourist Information: Minneapolis Convention and Tourism Commission, 15 South 5th St., 55402. Telephone: 612/348-4330.

On Campus: The University of Minnesota is, according to one student there, lucky enough to be in the middle of a "liberal and progressive city." On campus you can always call on the Assistance Center (tel. 373-1234) for help. A good place to go on campus for travel information (primarily international travel) is the International Study and Travel Center, 40 Coffman Memorial Union. To meet students right in the Coffman Union stop at the Whole Coffeehouse, or go into Dinkytown, the area adjacent to the campus, and check into the Artist's Quarter, Sergeant Preston's, or Bullwinkle's. For an inexpensive, filling meal in the university area try the Tokyo Café, Sammy D's, or Valley Pizza, all in Dinkytown. Also recommended is the New Riverside Café, corner of Riverside and Cedar Aves., for natural foods. If you like theater, you owe it to yourself to see a performance at the Guthrie Theater, 725 Vineland Pl., the home of one of the U.S.'s best repertory companies. Students are entitled to reduced rates on tickets available 30 minutes before curtain.

Accommodations: YMCA, 30 South 9th St., 55402. Telephone: 612/332-2431. Men and women. $12.25 and up per night; $51 and up per week.

● Best Value Cross Keys Motel, 5812 Lyndale Ave. South, 55419. Telephone: 612/861-6006. $20 for one; $22 for two in one bed; $26 for two in two beds.

● Snelling Motor Inn, 5346 Minnehaha Ave. South, 55417. Telephone: 612/721-4841. $18 to $22 for one; $22 to $26 for two in one bed; $24 to $28 for two in two beds.

● Exel Inn, 🏛, 2701 East 78th St., Bloomington, 55420. Telephone: 612/854-7200. $24.95 for one; $29.95 for two in one bed; $31.95 for two in two beds.

Moorhead

On Campus: Moorhead State University is in this town. For information while you're there, call Campus Information (tel. 218/236-2011), or the Exchange in the Comstock Union (tel. 218/236-2261). At night, try Mick's Office, the Trader, or Trapper to meet people.

Nimrod

Accommodation: Crow Wing Trails Youth Hostel (AYH), 56478. Telephone: 218/472-3250. Open June 10 to September 15. $2. AYH membership required (see page 21).

Northfield

On Campus: St. Olaf College is here in Northfield, the town that is famed for "its defeat of Jesse James." A student there describes it as "a typical small midwestern town with a college emphasis."

For a full meal at lunchtime for $1.50, the Cage on the St. Olaf campus is the place to go. You can meet St. Olaf students at Rueb-n-Stein in Northfield, and the A & M Bar in Dundas, a small community three miles away.

Owatonna

Accommodation: Thrifty Scot Motel, P.O. Box 655, I-35 and Hwy. 14, 55060. Telephone: 507/451-0380. $16.90 to $21.90 for one; $20.90 to $22.90 for two in one bed; $25.90 to $27.90 for two in two beds.

Rochester

Accommodations: Best Value Colony Inn Motel, Hwy. 52 and 2nd St. SW, 55901. Telephone: 507/282-2733. $17.20 for one; $20.09 for two in one bed; $22.90 for two in two beds.

● Friendship Center Towne Travel Inn, 116 SW 5th St., 55901. Telephone: 507/289-1628. $21 to $23 for one; $23 to $26 for two.

● Motel 6, 2107 West Frontage Rd., 55901. Telephone: 507/282-8947. $12.95 for one; $16.95 for two; $19.95 for up to four.

Roseau

Accommodation: Guest House Motor Inn, 216 North Main Ave., 56751. Telephone: 218/463-2542. $12 to $22 for one; $16 to $26 for two.

Roseville

Accommodation: Northwestern College, ♿ (partial), 3003 North Snelling Ave., 55113. Telephone: 612/636-4840, extension 217. $16 to $18 single; $26 to $28 double. If you stay longer than one night the rates become lower. "Spectacular—new—similar to a fine hotel room."

Sauk Centre

Accommodation: Palmer House Hotel and Restaurant, 500 Sinclair Lewis Ave., 56378. Telephone: 612/352-3431. $10 to $15 single; $15 to $22 double. A restored 1901 hotel which is the model for Sinclair Lewis's "Minniemashie House" in his novel *Main Street.* There's a restaurant on the premises which will prepare on occasion a nine-course gourmet meal at a very reasonable price.

St. Charles

Accommodation: Friendship Inn–White Valley Motel, Rte. 3, Box 1, 55972. Telephone: 507/932-3142. $14.75 to $15.75 for one; $17 to $19 for two in one bed; $21 to $22 for two in two beds.

St. Cloud

On Campus: A student at St. Cloud State University says the people there are "friendly and interested in conversing and finding things that they have in common." You can meet this talkative group at the Pub Bar or the Press Bar downtown.

Accommodations: Thrifty Scot Motel, 130 14th Ave. NE, 56301. Telephone: 612/253-6320. $20.90 to $22.90 for one; $24.90 to $26.90 for two in one bed; $27.90 for two in two beds.

● Thrifty Scot Motel, 40 South 10th Ave., Waite Park, 56387. $18.90 to $23.90 for one; $22.90 to $24.90 for two in one bed; $27.90 for two in two beds.

St. Paul

Help: Family Service of St. Paul (Travelers Aid), 333 Sibley, Suite 500, 55101. Telephone: 612/222-0311.

Tourist Information: St. Paul Convention, Exhibition, and Tourism Commission Landmark Center, B Level, 55102. Telephone: 612/297-9303.

On Campus: The people at Hamline University in St. Paul recommended the food at Al's Breakfast at 413 14th Ave. SE in Minneapolis. Al obviously thinks that breakfast is not only the most important meal of the day, but also the only meal of the day, since his restaurant is open only for breakfast. Not far from the St. Paul campus of the University of Minnesota you'll find the Muffuletta, 2260 Como Ave., a friendly neighborhood restaurant. For a good meal in St. Paul, you can go to the Caravan Serai, an Afghani restaurant, at 2046 Pinehurst Ave., where dinner will cost approximately $8 to $12.

Students at the St. Paul campus of the University of Minnesota congregate at the student center, Valli Pizza, and Sammy D's. They also recommended contacting the Hennepin City and Ramsey City Historical Societies for information on the wonderful architecture in St. Paul, which includes art deco and late Victorian. The Ramsey number is 222-0701; Hennepin's is 870-1329.

Accommodation: Red Roof Inn, I-494 at Valley Creek Rd. (Woodbury), 55125. Telephone: 612/738-7160, $19.95 for one; $22.95 for two in one bed; $24.95 to $26.95 for two to four in two beds.

Wabasha

Accommodation: The Anderson House Youth Hostel (AYH), 333 Main St., 55981. Telephone: 612/565-4525 or 4524. This hostel is located in the oldest registered hotel in Minnesota. Open year round. $5. AYH membership required (see page 21).

Winona

Help: Winona Volunteer Services, 507/452-5591.

Accommodations: Prentiss-Lucas Dormitory, ⌂, Winona State University, 265 West King St., 55987. Telephone: 507/457-2179. Seven blocks from bus; five blocks from train. $10 per person per night for a single; $7 per person double. Open June 1 to August 23. *"It is kept sparkling clean, and very, very quiet. I was treated like a member of the family."*

● Best Value Sterling Motel, Junction 14-61 and Gilmore Ave., 55987. Telephone: 507/454-1120. $11 to $15.50 for one; $14 to $20 for two in one bed; $22 to $26 for two in two beds.

● Thrifty Scot Motel, 420 Cottonwood Dr., 55987. Telephone: 507/454-6930. $16.90 to $21.90 for one; $20.90 to $22.90 for two in one bed; $25.90 to $27.90 for two in two beds.

Worthington

Accommodation: Best Value Oxford Motel, Inc., 1801 Oxford St., 56187. Telephone: 507/376-6126. $14 for one; $15 to $16 for two in one bed; $18 and up for two in two beds.

Mississippi

Mississippi has made rich contributions to the literature of the U.S. with such native authors as William Faulkner, Eudora Welty, and Richard Wright. Rural and quite poor by national standards, Mississippi has much beauty to be seen, especially in some of its state parks. For a free guide to these parks, write to Department of Natural Resources, Bureau of Recreation and Parks, P.O. Box 10600, Jackson, MS 39207.

Must-see sights in Mississippi would have to include the Natchez antebellum homes, the largest and—some say—most beautiful collection of preserved homes from the era before the Civil War. Cotton was king in Natchez, a Mississippi River port, and wealth was everywhere in the beginning of the 1800s. Natchez Trace Parkway is administered by the National Park Service, and on the portion between Tupelo and Natchez, drivers can stop at well-marked sites of historic or natural interest. Probably the most unsettling sight near the parkway is the view of the ruins of Windsor—40 columns are all that's left of a once-fabulous mansion.

And for those who are interested in the history of the Civil War, there's a national military park at Vicksburg, site of the 47-day Union siege after which the field was surrendered to General Grant. At the Visitors' Center, the story of the battle is told through film and a variety of exhibits.

Some Special Events: Governor's Fishing Rodeo in Hollandale and Mississippi Chicken Cooking Contest in Jackson (May); Bluegrass Festival in Houston and Barter Day Festival in Morton (June); Lake Festival in Grenada and Seafood Festival in Pass Christian (July); Folk Art Festival in Batesville and Tippah County Fair in Ripley (August); Prairie Arts Festival in West Point (September); and Gumbo Festival of the Universe in White Cypress (October).

Hitching: Although hitchhiking is not illegal in Mississippi as long as it's not done from the roadway, we've been told that the attitude toward young people on the road is generally unfriendly and suspicious. If you want to hitchhike, concentrate your efforts on Interstates 55, 59, 10, and 20.

Tourist Information: Division of Tourism, Mississippi Department of Economic Development, Box 849, Room 1301, Walter Sillers Building, Jackson, MS 39205. Telephone: 601/354-6715.

Dennis

Camping and Accommodation: Tishomingo State Park, Rte. 1, P.O. Box 310, 38838. Telephone: 601/438-6914. Family cabins equipped for light housekeeping. $20 for a one-bedroom cabin; $22 for a two-bedroom cabin which sleeps up to six. Reservations needed. 13 miles of nature trails, canoeing, and lodge built by CCC.

Durant

Camping and Accommodation: Holmes County State Park, Rte. 1, P.O. Box 153, 39063. Telephone: 601/653-3351. Rustic cabins in great condition and modern duplex cabins for $24 to $32 per night. Room for three to six in cabins. Cabins are very well equipped. Reservations recommended.

Grenada

Accommodation: Days Inn, I-55 and Miss. 8, Exit 54, Rte. 3, Box 300, 38901. Telephone: 601/226-6222. $18.88 for one; $22.88 for two.

Hattiesburg

Camping and Accommodations: Paul B. Johnson State Park, 39401. Telephone: 601/582-7721. Besides camping at $4 to $7 per campsite, there are cabins that hold up to six people and rent for $30 to $33 per night. Bed linens and cooking utensils are furnished and some cabins have a fireplace.

Accommodations: Days Inn, ⬧, I-59 and U.S. 49, 39401. Telephone: 601/268-2251. $22 to $23 for one; $26 to $27 for two.

● Motel 6, 3109 Hwy. 49 North, 39401. Telephone: 601/544-5016. $12.95 for one; $16.95 for two; $19.95 for up to four.

Holly Springs

Accommodation and Camping: Wall Doxey State Park, ⬧, Rte. 5, 38635. Telephone: 601/252-4231. Vacation cabins with kitchens. $24 to $32 per night per cabin. "A family-oriented park."

Iuka

Accommodation and Camping: J. P. Coleman State Park, Rte. 5, 38852. Telephone: 601/423-6515. Vacation cabins with bedroom, bath, kitchen, and some with living rooms. $28 to $34 per night per cabin.

Jackson

Accommodations: Motel 6, 970 I-20 West, North Frontage Rd., 39202. Telephone: 601/948-3692. See Hattiesburg listing for rates.
● Days Inn, &, I-55 and 616 Briarwood Dr., P.O. Box 12864, 39211. Telephone: 601/957-1741. $22.88 to $23.88 for one; $26.88 to $27.88 for two.
● Days Inn, &, Jackson I-20, U.S. 49 and U.S. 80 East, P.O. Box 6034, 39208. Telephone: 601/939-8200. $21.88 to $22.88 for one; $25.88 to $26.88 for two.
● Days Inn, &, I-55 South and Savanna St. (Exit 26), 3880 I-55 South, 39212. Telephone: 601/373-3320. $19.88 for one; $23.88 for two.

McComb

Accommodation: Percy Quin State Park, &, Rte. 3, 39648. Telephone: 601/684-3931. Men and women over 21. Besides rustic camping there are cabins furnished with linens and a kitchen. $29 to $39 per night. Some of the cabins can hold up to 12 people. Reservations necessary well in advance for cabins. Camping area is first come, first served.

Meridian

Accommodation: Days Inn, I-20 DeKalb Exit and I-59, 1521 Tom Bailey Dr. (U.S. 80 East), 39301. Telephone: 601/483-3812. $23.88 for one; $27.88 for two. Rates slightly higher December 15 to May 31.

Morton

Camping and Accommodation: Roosevelt State Park, &, Star Route, 39117. Telephone: 601/732-6316. One-bedroom cabin with two double beds, $24 to $32 per night; two-bedroom cabin with four double beds, $32 per night; three-bedroom cabin with six double beds, $36 per night. Three-night minimum in summer; two nights at other times. Reservations recommended.

Natchez

Accommodations: Days Inn, &, 109 U.S. 61 South, 39120. Telephone: 601/445-8291. $20.88 to $21.88 for one; $24.88 to $25.88 for two. Rates higher from October 9 to 25 and from March 6 to April 4.
● Scottish Inn, 40 Sargent Prentiss Dr., 39120. Telephone: 601/442-9141. $16 for one; $20 for two in one bed; $22 for two in two beds.

Oakland

Accommodation and Camping: George Payne Cossar State Park, Rte. 1, 38948. Telephone: 601/623-7356. Eight cabins with central air conditioning and heat, kitchens, screened porch, and fireplace—"very modern." $33.60 per night per cabin.

Ocean Springs

Camping: Gulf Islands National Seashore, Davis Bayou, 4000 Hanley Rd., 39564. In both Florida and Mississippi. The Davis Bayou campground has 51 sites and is open year round. $3 per campsite per night.

Oxford

Help: Rapline, 601/232-5900. Student organized. "An ear to listen or a source of help."

On Campus: According to a friend at the University of Mississippi's Student Travel Information Service (tel. 232-7106), you can go to the Grill at the Student Union and find someone there who will be glad to help you find a place to stay. According to this same friend, the people at the university are very helpful and friendly. Foreign student visitors who need help may call the foreign student advisor's office (tel. 232-7315).

Since the legal age for beer drinking was lowered to 18 a few years ago, several bars have sprung up in Oxford. One friend's favorites are the Gin, in an old cotton gin, because it's "cheap, informal and has good sandwiches and loud music," and the Warehouse, "because it has a lovely patio and a nice atmosphere, especially when the weather's nice."

To find a ride to wherever you're going, check the Ole Miss Union Ride Board.

Oxford was the home of William Faulkner and one Oxfordian wants you to be sure to visit the Faulkner home there. At the end of July there's a week-long Faulkner festival in the town which attracts writers from all over the world.

Accommodation: Ole Miss Motel, 1517 East University Ave., 38655. Telephone: 601/234-2424. About four blocks from the campus of U Miss. Single with black-and-white television, $15; single with color television, $17; double, $20 and up.

Sardis

Camping and Accommodations: John Kyle State Park, Rte. 1, P.O. Box 115, 38666. Telephone: 601/487-1345. Cabins that rent for $24 to $28 per night. Reservations should be made at least two months in advance for summer. Three-night minimum May 1 to Sept. 15; two-night minimum at other times.

• Best Value Gulf Trail Motor Lodge, I-55 at Miss. 315, 38666. $17 to $20 for one; $23 to $32 for two in one bed.

Tupelo

Camping: Natchez Trace Parkway, RR 1, NT-143, 38801. Campgrounds at Jeff Busby, Meriwether Lewis, and Rocky Springs open all year.

Camping and Accommodation: Tombigbee State Park, Rte. 2, P.O. Box 336E, 38801. Telephone: 601/842-7669. There are cabins large enough for four that rent for $21 per night.

Vicksburg

Accommodation: Scottish Inn, 3955 Hwy. 80 East, 39180. Telephone: 601/638-5511. $20 for one; $23 for two in one bed; $24 for two in two beds.

Missouri

Missouri is partly southern and partly western in philosophy and has produced such diverse personalities as Jesse James, Mark Twain, T. S. Eliot, and Harry S Truman.

The northwestern part of the state is called the Pony Express Region, since it was from St. Joseph, in 1860, that the first Pony Express rider galloped on his way. Camping, picnicking, and water sports abound—and some people like to take a look at the home where the outlaw Jesse James was shot and killed. In the Mark Twain Region in the northeast, the town of Hannibal has preserved the author's boyhood home and has a Twain museum and the restored Becky Thatcher home.

In the center of the state, the huge Lake of the Ozarks attracts water lovers. And then there are the cities—Kansas City and St. Louis. Going south, the Ozark Playground Region has two of the area's best known attractions: Silver Dollar City, a re-created 1870s town and entertainment park, and the outdoor pageant at Shepherd of the Hills Farm, which depicts the story of Ozarks frontier life.

Some Special Events: Women's Jazz Festival in Kansas City (March); Dogwood Festival in Camdenton (April); Valley of Flowers Festival in Florissant and Family Bluegrass Music Weekend in Hermitage's Pomme de Terre State Park (May); International Festival in St. Louis and Hillbilly Days in Bennett Spring State Park, Lebanon (June); National Tom Sawyer Fence Painting Contest in Hannibal (July 4); Bootheel Rodeo in Sikeston (August); Cotton Carnival in Sikeston (September); and Crafts Festival in Arrow Rock (October).

Hitching: Missouri is one of the states mentioned in the introduction that does not have laws against hitching—except on Interstates. The State Highway Patrol put it this way: "Hitchhiking is legal in Missouri with no statutory limitations." However, some municipalities have local ordinances which prohibit hitchhiking within their city limits. The people of Missouri are used to seeing hitchhikers in the St. Louis, Columbia, and Kansas City areas on their way across country.

Tourist Information: Missouri Division of Tourism, P.O. Box 1055, Jefferson City, MO 65102. Telephone: 314/751-4133.

Blue Springs

Accommodation: Motel 6, 901 West Jefferson St., 64015. $12.95 for one; $16.95 for two, $19.95 for up to four.

Cape Girardeau

Accommodation: Friendship Inn–Sands Motel, I-55 Business Loop, 63701. Telephone: 314/334-2828. $19 to $21 for one; $21 to $23 for two in one bed; $25 to $28 for two in two beds.

Cassville

Accommodation: Holiday Motel, 85 South Main St., 65625. Telephone: 417/847-3163. $13 for one; $16 for two in one bed; $18 for two in two beds.

Columbia

Help: Everyday People, 209 Price Ave., 65201. Telephone: 314/443-0424. (They're under accommodations too.)

Accommodations: Everyday People, 🛏, 209 Price Ave., 65201. Telephone: 314/443-0424. Overnight accommodation is free in the house that Everyday People own. There are a few beds but mostly cushions; a sleeping bag would be a good idea since there's no linen. Everyday People recommends Ernies, 100 SE Walnut, as a good place to get a meal.

● Motel 6, 1718 North Providence Rd., 65201. Telephone: 314/442-3155. See Blue Springs listing for rates.

● Regal 8 Inn, 1800 I-70 Dr. SW, 65201. Telephone: 314/445-8433. $17.88 for one; $20.88 for two in one bed; $23.88 for two to four in two beds.

Fremont

Accommodation: Ozark Wilderness Hostel (AYH), P.O. Box 278, 63941. Telephone: 314/251-3549. Open April to December. AYH membership required (see page 21). Near the Ozark National Scenic Riverway. Swimming, canoeing, hiking, and biking trails.

Harrisonville

Accommodations: Cortez Motel, √ $1, 1302 North Commercial (Box 58), 64701. Telephone: 816/884-3208. $19 for one; $26 for two in one bed; $28 for two in two beds.

● Friendship Inn–Caravan Motel, P.O. Box 483, 64701. Telephone: 816/884-4100. $20 for one; $22 for two in one bed; $24 to $26 for two in two beds.

Jefferson City

Accommodation: Regal 8 Inn, 808 Stadium Dr., 65101. Telephone: 314/634-2848. See Columbia listing for rates.

Kansas City

Help: Services to Mobile Persons, 1111 Holmes, 64106. Telephone: 816/221-1559.

Tourist Information: Convention and Visitors Bureau of Greater Kansas City, Visitor Information Office, City Center Square, 1100 Main, Suite 2550, 64105. Telephone: 816/221-5242. Visitor Information phone: 816/474-9600.

On Campus: Once you're in Kansas City, stop by the University Center Building at 5100 Rockhill Rd. on the University of Missouri campus. The center can give you information on upcoming lectures, concerts, films, off-campus housing, and tuition-free classes through Kansas City's free university.

Accommodations: YMCA, 404 East 10th St., 64106. Telephone: 816/842-8920. Men over 18 only. $10 to $11 single. Two blocks from bus station. You can get an inexpensive meal at Tom's Café, 410 East 10th.

● The Martinique (AYH-SA), 3014–16 Harrison St., 64109. Telephone: 816/561-2044. $5. Families accepted.

● Red Roof Inn, 🛦, I-435 at Mo. 210 (Exit 210B), 64161. Telephone: 816/452-8585. $17.95 for one; $20.95 for two in one bed; $22.95 to $24.95 for two to four in two beds.

● Red Roof Inn, I-70 at Noland Rd., Independence, 64055. Telephone: 816/373-2800. $19.95 for one; $22.95 for two in one bed; $24.95 to $26.95 for two to four in two beds.

● Red Roof Inn, I-435 at Metcalf Rd. (Mo. 169), Overland Park. To open in 1982. $19.95 for one; $22.95 for two in one bed; $24.95 to $26.95 for two to four in two beds.

● Best Value Green Crest Motel, 15014 East Hwy. 40, 64136. Telephone: 816/373-7500. $14 to $20 for one; $16 to $22 for two in one bed; $18 to $26 for two in two beds.

Lebanon

Accommodation: Friendship Inn–Holiday Motel, City Rte. 66 East, 65536. Telephone: 417/532-7176. $12 to $15 for one; $15 to $17 for two in one bed; $16 to $22 for two in two beds.

Mexico

Accommodation: Air Park Motel, Hwy. 54 East, 65265. Telephone: 314/581-2795. $20 for one; $23 for two in one bed; $27 for two in two beds.

Mount Vernon

Accommodation: Ranch Motel, ⚿ (limited), junction I-44 and Hwy. 39, RR 1, Box 6B, 65712. Telephone: 417/466-2125. $16 to $18 for one; $24 for two in two beds.

Rolla

Accommodations: Best Value Rustic Motel, Hwy. 63 South, 65401. Telephone: 314/364-6943. $10 to $14 for one; $12 to $18 for two in one bed; $15 to $19 for two in two beds.

● Superior Town House Motel, 1207 Kings Hwy., 65401. Telephone: 314/341-3700. $14.95 to $16.95 for one; $17.95 to $19.95 for two in one bed; $20.95 to $22.95 for two in two beds.

● Interstate Motel, 1631 Martin Spring Dr., 65401. Telephone: 314/341-2158. $12 to $16 for one or two in one bed; $16 to $20 for two in two beds.

St. Charles

Accommodation: Monarch Motel, 3717 I-70, 63301. Telephone: 314/724-3717. $19 to $20 for one or two in one bed; $24 to $25 for two to four in two beds.

St. Louis

Lewis and Clark launched their two-year expedition from St. Louis, at the confluence of the Mississippi and Missouri Rivers. The Gateway Arch is the symbol of modern St. Louis, but not far from it are reminders of St. Louis's past: the Old Courthouse and the Basilica of St. Louis King of France, the oldest cathedral west of the Mississippi River. Not far, too, is Laclede's Landing, the last remaining historic area of the city's waterfront where buildings dating from 1830 have been restored and converted into restaurants, shops, and offices. A long time ago, in 1904, St. Louis hosted a World's Fair in 1400-acre Forest Park, which has since become a well-loved tourist attraction with its Zoo, Planetarium, Municipal Opera, Art Museum, and Historical Society.

Good sources of information on what's happening in St. Louis are *St. Louis Magazine* and the *St. Louis Magazine's Annual Guide* ($2.95), radio station KSHE-AM, or Fun Phone (tel. 421-2100). You'll also want to have a copy of the Convention and Visitors Bureau's *St. Louis Visitor's Guide.* It's free.

Getting There: The airport is about ten miles from town and a limousine connection costs $5.50 one way. The limousine will also take you to St. Louis and Washington Universities. A taxi costs about $15. The Greyhound Terminal is at 801 North Broadway; Trailways is just a few steps away at no. 706. The train station is at 550 South 16th St. Transportation from both stations is available by bus or taxi.

Getting Around: The bus fare is 50¢; 60¢ if you want a transfer. Bus stop signs are posted on lampposts, at just about every corner. Taxis can be flagged or called ahead. They charge 75¢ to 85¢ a mile.

Accommodations: Washington University Guest Housing, 6515 Wydown Blvd., P.O. Box 1075, 63105. Telephone: 314/889-5073. Ask for Tootie Williams, conference director. Men, women, and children (but no cribs available). Open June 1 to August 15. $13 single; $11 per person double. Meals available on campus. Airport limousine will take you there. *"Very good air-conditioned rooms, more than clean."*

• YWCA, 2709 Locust Blvd., 63103. Telephone: 314/533-9400. Women only, 18 and over. $8 single; $7 per person double. $1 off rates for AYH members.

• Huckleberry Finn Youth Hostel (AYH), 1904–1906 South 12th St., 63104. Telephone: 314/241-0076. Reservations required April to September. $4.

• The Tripper (AYH), Portage, De Sioux, 63373. Telephone: 314/725-1616 (day) or 872-7570 (night). Open during summer only. The hostel is a houseboat for river trips. Write or call for itinerary packages. During closed period, write to 172 Forest Brook Lane, St. Louis, MO 63141. $55 for a two-day trip; $75 for a three-day trip.

• Ivy Motel, 10143 Old Olive St., 63141. Telephone: 314/993-9785. A small hotel. $16 single; $22 double. Cribs available.

• Westward Motel, 🐾, 1580 South Kirkwood Rd., 63127. Telephone: 314/822-7171. $25 single; $27 double; $29 twin. Reservations necessary during summer.

• St. Louis University, Graduate Dormitory, Lewis Memorial, 3701 Lindell, 63108. Telephone: 314/658-3060. Lindell bus west stops in front. Near downtown. Men, women, and children. $12 single; $18 double. Reservations necessary 24 hours in advance; they must be made during regular office hours or by letter.

• Regal 8 Inn, 3655 Pennridge, Bridgeton, 63044. Telephone: 314/291-6100. See Columbia listing for rates.

• Motel 6, 4576 Woodson Rd. (at airport), 63134. Telephone: 314/427-6100. See Blue Springs listing for rates.

• Red Roof Inn, 🛏, I-270 at St. Charles Rock Rd., Bridgeton. Telephone: 314/291-3350. $19.95 for one; $22.95 for two in one bed; $24.95 to $26.95 for two to four in two beds.

• Red Roof Inn, I-270 at Graham Rd., Florissant, 63044. Telephone: 314/831-7900. See above listing for rates.

Where to Eat: Busch Center Cafeteria, 20 North Grand Blvd. Telephone: 658-2822. On St. Louis University campus, near downtown and Forest Park. Cafeteria style with lots of students.

• Caleco's, 3818 Laclede. Telephone: 534-7878. Italian-American food near St. Louis University and downtown.

• Spaghetti Factory, Laclede's Landing, 727 North 1st St. Telephone: 621-0276. A spaghetti dinner here will cost about $4.50.

• Majestic, Euclid and Laclede. Telephone: 361-2011. Casual, home-type atmosphere; dinners from $3. Open seven days a week, 6 a.m. to 10 p.m. Bar is open until 1:30 a.m.

• Rigazzi's, 4945 Dagget, on "The Hill," the city's Italian district on the south side. Telephone: 772-4900. A pleasant place where dinner averages $7.95. Closed Sunday.

• Lettuce Leaf, 107 North 6th St. Telephone: 241-7773. A busy, pleasant place to have a salad.

● Fourth and Pine, 401 Pine. Telephone: 241-2184. Downtown spot with piano player at lunch and a band in the evening. The food is good, the atmosphere cozy.

● Stegton, Hwy. 70 West and 5th St. Telephone: 946-6860. Buffet-style food overlooking the Missouri River.

What to See and Do: Gateway Arch, 111 North 4th St. Telephone: 425-4465. Designed by Eero Saarinen, the 630-foot arch is the nation's tallest memorial. Each leg of the arch has a passenger train to carry visitors to the top for a 30-mile-wide view. The ride costs $1 for adults, 50¢ for children.

● Museum of Westward Expansion, in the underground area beneath the arch, which tells the story of the pioneers and the people who made St. Louis.

● Grant's Farm, 10501 Gravois. Telephone: 843-1700. Land once farmed by Ulysses S. Grant. A train without tracks takes you through a game preserve.

● Jewel Box, Forest Park. Telephone: 535-4111. A floral conservatory that's open all year.

● Six Flags Over Mid-America, in Eureka. A big theme park with rides, games, shops, etc. Admission for the day, $10.99.

● St. Louis Art Museum, Forest Park. Telephone: 721-0067. Over 70 galleries displaying representative pieces of art of the last 3000 years. Free admission. Tours on Wednesday, Friday, Saturday, and Sunday.

● Municipal Opera, in Forest Park. Telephone: 361-1900. World's largest outdoor summer musical theater—seats 12,000. In summer, features a ten-week repertory of light operas, musicals, and dance performances.

● Huck Finn, Samuel Clemens and Tom Sawyer Riverboat, foot of Washington Ave. Telephone: 621-4040. Cruises from Memorial Day to Labor Day. $4. Dinner-dance cruises are $17.50 and include dinner and cocktails.

● Soulard Market, 7th and Lafayette. An interesting public market in South St. Louis.

● Laclede's Landing. Near the Gateway Arch and Mississippi River. Neighborhood of stores, bars, and restaurants—the "original" St. Louis. Park at the riverfront, go to the Arch, and walk around. In the evening, enjoy jazz at the Lt. Robert E. Lee Riverboat.

At Night: For jazz: La Casa, 309 North Jefferson. Telephone 534-5929.

● To dance: Mali Kai–Henry VIII, 4960 North Lindbergh (near airport). Telephone: 731-3040. Three dance floors, quite elegant, with a $2 cover charge on weekends.

● For folk/country music: Bogart's on the Landing, 809 North 2nd St. Three bars and a live band.

● During the summer, Washington University has outdoor concerts beginning May 22. Call 534-1700. Student rates are available for tickets—$2 to $2.50.

● Call Arts Line (tel. 531-1111) for a list of current cultural events.

Shopping: Waldenbooks, 251 Chesterfield Mall and several other locations. All kinds of books.

● Streetside, 6314 Delmar. Jazz, disco, and soul.

● Peaches Records and Tapes, 9995 West Florissant and two other locations. All kinds of records.

Tourist Information: Convention and Visitors Bureau of Greater St. Louis, 1300 Convention Plaza, 63102. Telephone: 314/421-1023.

Help: Mullanphy Travelers Aid, Greyhound Bus Station, 809 North Broadway, 63102. Telephone: 314/241-5820.
● St. Louis Help Line, 314/725-3022.

Salem

Accommodation: Montauk State Park, ⬗, Rte. 5, RFD Box 278, 65560. Telephone: 314/548-2434. Accommodations include a modern motel with a restaurant, 14 housekeeping cabins, and 10 individual nonhousekeeping cabins. Facilities are open March 1 to November 1 and cost from $21 to $39. Specialties of the area are trout fishing and floating on Current River.

Sikeston

Accommodation: Econo-Travel Motor Hotel, I-55 and Hwy. 62, P.O. Box 701, 63801. Telephone: 314/471-7400. $19 for one; $23 for two in one bed; $25 for two in two beds. Rates higher November to March.

Springfield

Help: CODAC/Hot Line, 417/864-4100 or 865-2616.
Accommodations: Regal 8 Inn, 3114 North Kentwood, 65803. Telephone: 417/833-0880. See Columbia listing for rates.
● Motel 6, 2455 North Glenstone Ave., 65803. Telephone: 417/865-1151. See Blue Springs listing for rates.

Stockton

Accommodation: Lake Stockton Motel, √, 506 East Hwy. 32 (Box 310), 65785. Telephone: 417/276-5151. $13.75 for one; $16.75 for two in one bed; $18.75 for two in two beds.

Van Buren

Camping: Ozark National Scenic Riverway, P.O. Box 490, 63965. Eleven campgrounds open year round. Canoe rentals available at three of them. $3 per campsite per night.
Accommodation: Smalley's Motel, √ $1, Hwy. 60, Box 358, 63965. Telephone: 314/323-4263 or 323-4264. $18 for one; $23 for two in one bed; $25 for two in two beds.

Waynesville

Accommodation: Friendship Inn–Deville Motor Inn, P.O. Box A, Business Rte. I-44 East, 65583. Telephone: 314/336-3113. $14 to $16 for one; $16.50 to $18 for two in one bed; $18 to $22 for two in two beds.

Wentzville

Accommodation: Interstate Budget Motel, I-70 at Hwy. 61, 63385. Telephone: 314/327-5212. $19 to $20 for one or two in one bed; $24 to $25 for two to four in two beds.

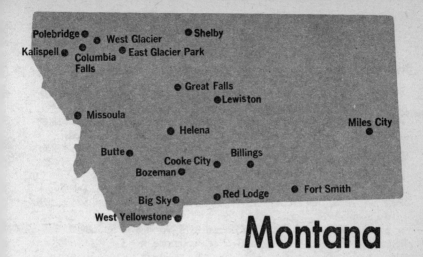

Polebridge●
Kalispell●   ●West Glacier   ●Shelby
Columbia   ●East Glacier Park
Falls
    ●Great Falls
     ●Lewiston
●Missoula
    ●Helena   Miles City●
Butte●   Billings●
Cooke City●
Bozeman●
Big Sky●   ●Red Lodge   ●Fort Smith
West Yellowstone●

Montana

Montana, especially the western part with its mountains and mountain valleys, is camping, hiking, and horseback-riding country. The scenery is spectacular and there's enough space for everyone. Montana is home to seven North American Indian tribes. If you visit any of the reservations you'll discover some very small museums, filled with samples of some absolutely exquisite Indian crafts. Approach the reservations, the museums, and the people with respect and love—two things they've been denied for too long. (Three of the entrances to Yellowstone National Park are in Montana, but since most of the park is in Wyoming, see the section on that state for the Yellowstone listing.)

Some Special Events: Community College Rodeo in Miles City (April); Memorial Day Powwow in Lame Deer (May); Centennial Celebration in Glendive (July); Dawson County Fair and Rodeo in Glendive, Eastern Montana Fair in Miles City, Northern Cheyenne Labor Day Rodeo in Busby, and White River Cheyenne Powwow in Busby (all in September).

Hitching: The law states that no one "shall stand in a roadway for the purpose of soliciting a ride." When we asked the State Police whether they had any special advice for hitchhikers in Montana, they answered: "Don't thumb from the traveled portion of any roadway. Stay in the southern and western part of the state."

A friend in Great Falls advises hitchhikers to stay away from that city and use a more southerly route through Montana—people just aren't interested in helping hitchhikers in that area of the state.

Tourist Information: Travel Promotion Bureau, Montana Department of Commerce, Helena, MT 59620.

Big Sky

Accommodation: Big Sky Telemark Inn, ●, P.O. Box 808, 59716. Telephone: 406/995-4269. Men, women, and children. $20 single; $26 double; $30 triple; $34 quad. 10% discount for AYH members. This is a new resort with tennis, golf, horseback riding, skiing, fishing, and just about everything else you can think of.

Billings

Accommodations: Motel 6, 5400 Midland Rd., RR 1, 59102. Telephone: 406/248-7759. $12.95 for one; $16.95 for two; $19.95 for up to four.

• Regal 8 Inn, I-90 and Midland, 59102. Telephone: 406/248-7551. $18.88 for one; $21.88 for two in one bed; $24.88 for two to four in two beds.

• Superior Kings Rest Motel, 1206 East Main St., 59101. Telephone: 406/252-8451. $22 to $24 for one; $24 to $26 for two in one bed; $26 to $28 for two in two beds.

• Best Value Lewis & Clark Inn, 1709 First Ave. North, 59101. Telephone: 406/252-4691. $18 to $20 for one; $22 to $24 for two in one bed; $24 to $26 for two in two beds.

• Friendship Inn–Westward Ho Lodge, 1315 North 27th St., 59101. Telephone: 406/245-4128. $22 for one; $26 for two in one bed; $28 for two in two beds.

Bozeman

Accommodations: Friendship Inn–Rainbow, 510 North Seventh Ave., 59701. Telephone: 406/587-4201. $12 to $22 for one; $14 to $24 for two in one bed; $16 to $26 for two in two beds.

• Imperial 400 Motor Inn; 122 West Main St., 59715. Telephone: 406/587-4481. $18 to $22 for one; $20 to $24 for two in one bed; $22 to $26 for two in two beds.

• Motel 6, junction of I-90 and U.S. 10, 59715. See Billings listing for rates.

• Thrifty Scot Motel, 1321 North Seventh Ave., 59715. Telephone: 406/587-5251. $17.90 to $22.90 for one; $21.90 to $23.90 for two in one bed; $26.90 to $30.90 for two in two beds.

Butte

Accommodation: Motel 6, 3645 Harrison Ave., 59701. To open in 1982. See Billings listing for rates.

Columbia Falls

Accommodation: Best Value Mountain Shadows Motel, Box 0, junction U.S. 2 and Mont. 40, 59912. Telephone: 406/892-4333. $15 for one; $18 for two in one bed; $22 for two in two beds.

Cooke City

Accommodation: Friendship Inn–Mus-Rest Motel, west on Hwy. 212, P.O. Box 1056, 59020. Telephone: 406/838-2272. $16 to $18 for one; $20 to $22 for two in one bed; $22 to $24 for two in two beds.

East Glacier Park

Accommodation: Bear Creek Ranch, Hwy. 2, P.O. Box 151, 59434. Telephone: area code 406, Bear Creek #1 (ask to be connected with operators in Shelby to reach Bear Creek #1). The Bear Creek Ranch provides space for AYH members as well as private lodge rooms and cabins for nonmembers. $4 per night for AYH members; $27 per day for nonmembers (including three meals in lodge rooms).

Fort Smith

Camping: Bighorn Canyon National Recreation Area, P.O. Box 458, 59035. Camping May 1 to November 1 at Black Canyon Boat Camp (access by boat only) and all year at Horseshoe Bend, Barry's Landing, and Black Canyon Boat Camp (access by boat only). $2 per campsite per night at Horseshoe Bend.

Great Falls

Help: Crisis Center, 406/453-6511.

Accommodations: YWCA, 220 2nd St. North, 59401. Telephone: 406/452-1315. Women only. $4. Weekly rate: $20. Community kitchen. Six blocks from bus station.

● Best Value Wright Nite Wagon Wheel Motel, 2620 Tenth Ave. South, 59405. Telephone: 406/761-1300. $19.50 to $22.50 for one; $22.50 to $24.50 for two in one bed; $24.50 to $28.50 for two in two beds.

● Imperial 400 Motor Inn, 601 Second Ave. North, 59401. Telephone: 406/452-9581. $21 to $24 for one; $23 to $27 for two in one bed; $29 to $35 for two in two beds.

Helena

Accommodation: Motel 6, 800 North Oregon, 59601. Telephone: 406/442-1311. See Billings listing for rates.

Kalispell

Accommodations: Rocky Mountain Hostel (AYH), 845 First Ave. East, 59901. Telephone: 406/257-2937. A large old house with a friendly, relaxed atmosphere. Open June 1 to September 25. $3 for AYH members. Bring your own sleeping bag. Good recreational facilities nearby.

● Motel 6, 1540 Hwy. 93 South, 59901. Telephone: 406/755-6669. See Billings listing for rates.

Lewiston

Accommodation: Best Value B & B Motel, 520 East Main St., 59457. Telephone: 406/538-5496. $22 for one; $26 for two in one bed; $29 for two in two beds.

Miles City

Accommodation: Motel 6, 1314 South Haynes Ave., 59301. Telephone: 406/232-6662. See Billings listing for rates.

Missoula

Help: Crisis Center, 406/543-8277.

Accommodations: University of Montana Residence Halls, c/o Room 101 Turner Hall, 59812. Telephone: 406/243-2611 or 243-5324. Ask for Ron Brunell. For men and women who are affiliated with the university in some capacity, e.g., visiting faculty, students, those attending workshops on campus, prospective students, etc. Open June 15 to August 14. $6.50 single; $5.50 per person double (rates subject to change).

● The Birchwood Youth Hostel (AYH-SA), 600 South Orange St., 59801. Telephone: 406/728-9799. Open April to September; open October to March by reservation only. $3.75 to $5. Priority given to members of AYH/IYHF, bicycle tourists, backpackers, and foreign visitors; others welcome as space permits. Reservations recommended. Fully equipped kitchen.

Polebridge

Accommodation: North Fork Hostel (AYH), ✿ ★ 20%, end of Beaver Dr., 59928 (mailing address: P.O. Box 1, 59928). No phone at hostel. Telephone: area code 406, Polebridge #2 for information. Open year round. Large rustic log cabin adjacent to Glacier National Park. No electricity. $4 for AYH members; $5 for others. Shower and complete kitchen. Bring sleeping bag.

Red Lodge

Accommodation: Best Value Valli Hi Motor Lodge, 320 South Broadway, P.O. Box 849, 59068. Telephone: 406/446-1414. $18 to $22 for one; $20 to $22 for two in one bed; $22 to $24 for two in two beds.

Shelby

Accommodation: Best Value O'Haire Manor Motel, 204 2nd St. South, 59474. Telephone: 406/434-5555. $20 for one; $24 to $26 for two in one bed; $28 to $30 for two in two beds.

West Glacier

Camping: Glacier National Park, 59936. Sixteen campgrounds open June to September (except for Apgar, which is open May to October). Horseback riding at three: Sprague Creek, Many Glacier, and Apgar. $2 to $3 per campsite per night.

West Yellowstone

Help: Social Services Center, 236 Yellowstone Ave. Telephone: 406/646-7311.

Accommodations: Alpine Motel, ✒ ★, 120 Madison, 59758. Telephone: 406/646-7544. Across from bus station. Open May 1 to October 15. $13 to $16 for one or two in one bed; $18 to $20 for two to four in two beds. Recommended by a reader from West Germany.

● Best Value City Center Motel, Box 211, 214 Madison, 59758. Telephone: 406/646-7337. $20 for one; $22 for two in one bed; $24 for two in two beds.

● Best Value Traveler Lodge, 225 Yellowstone Ave., Box 384, 59715. Telephone: 406/646-7773. $20 to $24 for one; $20 to $26 for two in one bed; $24 to $30 for two in two beds.

Nebraska

Not surprisingly, the people at the Division of Travel and Tourism in Nebraska want you to save time for what they call "the Good Life of Nebraska." Nebraska's "good life" is available both indoors and out. Canoeists should write for *Canoeing Nebraska* and bikers should ask for *Backpacking: Trails to Nebraska's Great Outdoors,* both available free from the address below.

For those who prefer museums, Nebraska has three that may interest you: the Joslyn Art Museum in Omaha, which has a well-received collection of art from ancient to modern times and a group of paintings and artifacts from the Maximilian expedition to the upper Missouri in the mid-1800s; the Museum of the Fur Trade, near Chadron, which tells the story of that lively enterprise from the point of view of the traders, trappers, and Indians; and the University of Nebraska State Museum in Lincoln, a museum of natural history which features, among other things, "Ceres the Transparent Woman."

Since the sport of rodeo began in Nebraska in 1882, it would seem appropriate to attend at least one while you're in that state. North Platte, Burwell, and Omaha host three of the biggest rodeos.

Some Special Events: Western Federation Square Dance Festival in North Platte (April); Good Old Days Jubilee in Crete (May); Buffalo Bill Rodeo in North Platte (June); Republican River Canoe Race in Franklin (July); Frontier County Fair in Stockville, and lots of other fairs throughout the state (August).

Hitching: A friend at Nebraska Free University in Lincoln says that hitching in Lincoln is acceptable, but in Omaha it's more difficult. He suggests sticking to main roads and standing on the curb. "If you're planning to go into Colorado from Nebraska, make sure you can get a ride through to your destination because Colorado police are tough on hitchhikers." Officially, hitchhiking is legal in Nebraska on all roads except the Interstate system.

Tourist Information: Division of Travel and Tourism, Nebraska Department of Economic Development, P.O. Box 94666, 301 Centennial Mall South, Lincoln, NB 68509. Telephone: 402/471-3111.

Auburn

Accommodation: Friendship Inn–Palmer House, U.S. 73 and 75 South, 68305. Telephone: 402/274-3193. $17.75 to $22.75 for one; $19.75 to $24.75 for two in one bed; $22.75 to $27.75 for two in two beds.

Beatrice

Accommodation: Friendship Holiday Villa Motel and Cafe, 1720 North 6th, 68310. Telephone: 402/223-4036. $16 to $21 for one; $20 to $24 for two in one bed; $24 to $27 for two in two beds.

Chadron

Accommodations: Friendship Inn–Grand Motel, West Hwy. 20 (two blocks east of 385 Junction), 69337. Telephone: 308/432-5595. $18 to $24 for one; $20 to $24 for two in one bed; $24 to $28 for two in two beds.
● Best Value Westerner Motel, 300 Oak, P.O. 1205, 69337. Telephone: 308/432-5577. $18 for one; $22 for two in one bed; $24 for two in two beds.

Columbus

Accommodations: Best Value Country Club Inn, junction U.S. 30 and 81, P.O. 482, 68601. $18 for one; $20 for two in one bed; $22 for two in two beds.
● Friendship Inn–Gembol's, 3218 8th, 68601. Telephone: 402/564-2729. $14 to $20 for one; $18 to $24 for two in one bed; $20 to $28 for two in two beds.

Geneva

Accommodation: Friendship Inn–Goldenrod Motel, 328 South 13th, 68361. Telephone: 402/759-3176. $13.50 to $16.50 for one; $18.50 to $22.50 for two in one bed; $20.50 to $24.50 for two in two beds.

Grand Island

Tourist Information: Chamber of Commerce, P.O. Box 1486, 68802.
Accommodation: Friendship Inn–Lazy V Motel, 2703 East Hwy. 30. Telephone: 308/384-0700. $10 to $11 for one; $14 to $16 for two in one bed; $16 to $18 for two in two beds.

"I-80 Holiday Inn has an excellent buffet. Around $4 at noon and $5 at night. All you can eat!"

Holdrege

Accommodation: Friendship Inn–Plains Motel, six blocks west of junction U.S. 183 and 6-34. Telephone: 308/995-8646. $16 to $22 for one; $20 to $24 for two in one bed; $24 to $32 for two in two beds.

Kearney

Accommodations: Friendship Inn Western, 824 East 25th St., 68847. Telephone: 308/234-2408. $16 to $20 for one; $20 to $24 for two in one bed; $22 to $28 for two in two beds.
● Motel 6, 515 Second Ave. East, 68847. To open in 1982. $12.95 for one; $16.95 for two; $19.95 for up to four.

Kimball

Accommodation: Friendship Inn–Motel Kimball, east on Hwy. 30, 69145. Telephone: 308/235-4606. $14 to $19 for one; $16 to $22 for two in one bed; $22 to $25 for two in two beds.

Lexington

Accommodations: Friendship Inn–Toddle Inn, South Hwy. 283, 68850. Telephone: 308/324-5595. $20 for one; $24 for two in one bed; $26 to $30 for two in two beds.
● Best Value L-R Ranch Motel, East Hwy. 30, 68850. Telephone: 308/324-4621. $14 to $16 for one; $18 to $20 for two in one bed; $20 to $22 for two in two beds.
● Hollingsworth Motel, East Hwy. 30, 68850. Telephone: 308/324-2388. $16.50 to $18.50 for one; $19.50 to $22.50 for two. Rates lower in winter.

Lincoln

Help: Personal Crisis Line, 402/475-5171.
On Campus: There are three universities in Lincoln. The University of Nebraska is the largest—25,000 students. There are also Nebraska Wesleyan University and Union College. For travel information and advice on accommodations, stop at the Overseas Opportunities Center, Suite 345 in the Nebraska Union, and for counterculture-type information go to Dirt Cheap, 217 North 11th St.

The people from the University of Nebraska were anxious to recommend places to eat in the city-center area, where the food is good, and inexpensive, too. Here's their list: Greenwich Café, 1917 O St., great fish and chips; Duffy's Bar, 1412 O St., a college tradition, with beef stew for 90¢; Kuhl's, 1038 O St., home-cooked chicken dinners for $1.95; Taco Hut, 249 North 11th, the best Mexican food in eastern Nebraska; and for late-night eaters there's R. J. Willy's, open at night only and best known for its cinnamon rolls and breakfasts.

"Football Saturdays are a great time for strangers to see what football mania can do to a town."

Accommodations: YMCA, 139 North 11th St., 68508. Telephone: 402/475-9622. Men, women and children. $16.50 single with bath, $10 without bath. Weekly rate: $35 to $49. The YMCA is approximately one block from the bus stations. If you choose a room without bath, you should know that the only shower facilities are the gym showers, opening and closing when the gym does.

● Wesley House Youth Hostel (AYH), 640 North 16th, 68508. On U. of Nebraska Campus. Telephone: 402/476-0355. Open year round. $2. Groups only. AYH membership required (see page 21).

● Days Inn, I-80 and Cornhusker Hwy., 2400 NW 12th St., 68521. Telephone: 402/474-1311. $22.88 for one; $26.88 for two.

● Thrifty Scot Motel, 2920 NW 12th St., 68521. Telephone: 402/475-3616. $19.90 to $21.90 for one; $23.90 to $25.90 for two in one bed; $28.90 to $32.90 for two in two beds.

● Motel 6, 3001 NW 12th St., 68521. Telephone: 402/475-9502. See Kearney listing for rates.

"In Lincoln we ate at the most fantastic Chinese restaurant, Peking Garden, 6811 O St. It had great gourmet Mandarin food and was truly cheap for a huge meal."

North Platte

Accommodations: Friendship Inn–Rambler, 1420 West Hwy. 30, 69101. Telephone: 308/532-9290. $14 to $19 for one; $18 to $24 for two in one bed; $20 to $26 for two in two beds.

● Friendship Inn–Stanford Lodge, 1400 East Hwy. 30, 69101. Telephone: 308/532-9380. $15 to $20 for one; $19 to $24 for two in one bed; $22 to $26 for two in two beds.

● Motel 6, 1520 South Jeffers St., 69101. Telephone: 308/534-3510. See Kearney listing for rates.

Ogallala

Accommodations: Friendship Inn–Western Paradise, 221 East 1st, 69153. Telephone: 308/284-3684. $15.50 to $20.50 for one; $18.50 to $22.50 for two in one bed; $22 to $26 for two in two beds.

● Lakeway Lodge Motel, √, 918 North Spruce, 69153. Telephone: 308/284-4004. $16 to $19 for one; $19 to $21 for two in one bed; $21 to $25 for two in two beds.

Omaha

Help: Personal Crisis Service, 4102 Woolworth. Telephone: 402/444-7442 or 444-7443. They recommend Together, Inc., an organization that helps stranded travelers, should you find yourself in that position.

Tourist Information: Omaha Convention and Visitors Bureau, Suite 1200 —Civic Center, 1819 Farnam St., 68183. Telephone: 402/444-4660.

On Campus: The University of Nebraska has a campus in Omaha that goes from 60th to 66th Sts. When you get hungry, try the Bohemian Café, 1406 South 13th St. (Czech food and atmosphere—the duck is good); Joe Tess's Fish Place, 5460 South 24th St., for delicious fish sandwiches and dinners at good prices; and Chicago, 3259 Farnham (two blocks from Dodge St.), for great hamburgers and reasonable prices. One more place recently recommended to us is Caviglia's at 7th and Pierce, where for $5 to $6 you can get a steak, salad, soup, potato, spaghetti, fried ravioli, pizza bread . . . and drink.

Although the drinking age is 19 in Omaha, it's 18 nearby in Council Bluffs, Iowa. Howard Street Tavern, a bar in the Old Market area of Omaha, at 1112 Howard, is a popular place with young people. In fact, on weekends the entire Old Market area (where the once-upon-a-time market space has been rejuvenated) is a good place to meet people. There are a number of restaurants in the area.

A friend from Omaha wrote to say that "besides claiming the world's largest stock yard, Omaha is Gerald Ford's birthplace."

Accommodations: YMCA, 430 South 20th, 68102. Telephone: 402/341-1600. Men and women. $14.75 single, one night; $11.75 each night thereafter. $3 refundable key deposit.

"The Omaha/Council Bluffs Downtown YMCA is interested in welcoming all international travelers. Tours of the city as well as the rural area near Omaha are available at the front desk."

● Imperial 400 Motor Inn, 2211 Douglas St., 68102. Telephone: 402/345-9565. $20 to $22 for one; $24 to $26 for two in one bed; $26 to $28 for two in two beds.
● Friendship Ben Franklin Motel, I-80 and Hwy. 50, Exit 440, 68046. Telephone: 402/895-2200. $18.95 to $21.95 for one; $23.95 to $25.95 for two in one bed; $25.95 to $28.95 for two in two beds.
● Best Value Ben Franklin Motel, I-80 and Hwy. 50, 68138. Telephone: 402/895-2200. $18.95 to $20.95 for one; $23.95 to $24.95 for two in one bed; $25.95 to $26.95 for two in two beds.
● Motel 6, 10708 M St., 68127. Telephone: 402/331-2331. See Kearney listing for rates.

Scottsbluff

Accommodation: Friendship Inn–Sands Motel, 814 West 27th St., 69361. Telephone: 308/632-6191. $16 for one; $20 for two in one bed; $22 for two in two beds.

Seward

Accommodation: Concordia College, 800 North Columbia Ave., 68434. Telephone: 402/643-3651, extension 410. Men, women, and children. Open all year, but space is limited while school is in session. $5 per person; $3 if you have sleeping bag. Reservations necessary.

Sidney

Accommodation: Friendship Inn-El Palomino, 2220 Illinois St., 69162. Telephone: 308/254-5566. $17 to $22.50 for one; $19 to $28 for two.

South Sioux City

Accommodation: Friendship Inn–Park Plaza, 1201 First Ave., 68776. Telephone: 402/494-2021. $18 to $24 for one; $24 to $28 for two in one bed; $26 to $30 for two in two beds.

Valentine

Accommodation: Friendship Inn–Raine Motel, west on U.S. 20, 69201. Telephone: 402/376-2030. $16 to $20 for one; $20 to $24 for two in one bed; $24 to $28 for two in two beds.

York

Accommodation: Best Value Y Motel, North Hwy. 81, Rte. 1, P.O. Box 192, 68467. $14 to $15 for one; $17 to $18 for two in one bed; $19 to $20 for two in two beds.

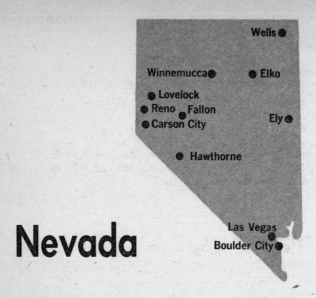

Nevada

Nevada has more neon lights than people, and Las Vegas wins the plastic city award hands down.

In case you hadn't heard, gambling is legal in Nevada, and practically all of the population depends on the industry for its livelihood. One good thing about Las Vegas and Reno: any poor traveler over 21 years old can get a good, cheap meal in the casinos and hotels. The idea behind the "bargain" is that once you're there you'll gamble, so if you just eat and run you can save quite a bit.

"You hit the secret of Vegas on the nose—if you stay away from gambling, you can really get off cheap. Pick up some of the tourist newspapers in every hotel lobby. They feature free coupons for nickels to play the slots and free meals at some casinos and other give-aways like a three-minute phone call to anywhere in the U.S."

Try desert camping in Nevada; the stars are fantastic, the air is cold and clean, and the sand makes a good mattress.

Some Special Events: Winter Carnival in South Lake Tahoe (January); All-Breed Bull Sale in Fallon (February): Fireman's Ball in Gardnerville (March); World Series Poker in Las Vegas—where else? (April); Mexican Fiesta in Moapa Valley (May); Carson Valley Days in Gardnerville and Rodeo in Reno (June); National Basque Festival in Elko (July); Arts Alliance Festival in Carson City (August); Camel Races and 100-Mile Horse Endurance Ride in Virginia City (September).

Hitching: It is illegal to hitchhike in most places in Nevada, although a friend there told us that police surveillance is not very tight, and that the general attitude toward hitchhikers is "mostly indifferent." The trooper we contacted had this to say: "There is a large amount of desert area. Great distances between towns. Lots of rattlesnakes."

Tourist Information: Tourism Division, Department of Economic Development, Carson City, NV 89710.

Boulder City

Camping: Lake Mead National Recreational Area, 601 Nevada Hwy., 89005. Ten campgrounds open all year. Be prepared to share most of the campgrounds with trailers. $2 per campsite per night.

Carson City

Accommodations: Friendship Inn–Desert Hills Motel, 1010 South Carson St., 89701. Telephone: 702/882-1932. $18 to $24 for one; $24 to $30 for two in one bed; $26 to $32 for two in two beds.
● Motel 6, 2749 South Carson St., 89701. Telephone: 702/883-1150. $12.95 for one; $16.95 for two; $19.95 for up to four.

Elko

Accommodation: Motel 6, north side U.S. 40, east end of Elko, 89801. To open in 1982. See Carson City listing for rates.

Ely

Accommodation: Motel 6, 7th and Ave. O, 89301. Telephone: 702/289-3566. See Carson City listing for rates.

Fallon

Accommodation: Friendship Inn–Ranch Motel, South Taylor St. on U.S. 95, 89406. Telephone: 702/423-2277. $18 to $20 for one; $20 to $22 for two in one bed; $22 to $24 for two in two beds.

Hawthorne

Accommodation: Friendship Inn–Holiday Lodge, 5th and J Sts., Hwy. 95, 89415. Telephone: 702/945-3316. $14 to $16 for one; $18 to $20 for two in one bed; $20 to $24 for two in two beds.

Las Vegas

"Eating out in Las Vegas is cheaper than cooking at home. Most of the casinos have smörgåsbords with all of the extras for less than you can buy groceries ($1.79 for a typical lunch, $2.49 for dinner). Every casino has what are called 'fun books,' and if you utilize them you can have a lot of fun for very little money. I have a free pancake, egg, and coffee breakfast every morning, and where it's not free, breakfast can be found in many hotels for 99¢. As a rule, prices are cheaper downtown than in the luxurious Strip hotels. If you are a gambler, you'll find the odds more in your favor downtown."

Tourist Information: Las Vegas Convention and Visitors Authority, Las Vegas Convention Center, P.O. Box 14006, 89114. Telephone: 702/733-2323.

Accommodations: Motel 6, 195 East Tropicana Blvd., 89109. Telephone: 702/736-4904. See Carson City listing for rates.

● Western 6 Motel, 4125 Boulder Hwy., 89121. Telephone: 702/457-8051. $16.40 single; $23.90 double.

● Western 6 Motel, 5085 South Industrial Rd., 89118. Telephone: 702/739-6747. $16.40 single; $23.90 double.

● E-Z 8 Motel, 5201 South Industrial Rd., 89118. Telephone: 702/739-9513. $15.88 to $18.88 for one; $17.88 to $21.88 for two in one bed; $19.88 to $23.88 for two in two beds.

Lovelock

Accommodation: Friendship Inn–LaFon's Motel, 515 Cornell Ave., 89419. Telephone: 702/273-2973. $19 to $23 for one; $20 to $26 for two in one bed; $26 to $30 for two in two beds.

Reno

Help: Crisis Call Center, 702/323-6111 or toll free 800/992-5757. For 24-hour telephone crisis counseling, information and referral.

On Campus: A friend at the University of Nevada wants you to know that "although Reno is basically known for its gambling aura, you shouldn't forget that it's an all-around tourist area with summer sports, winter skiing, hiking, etc."

One friend wrote to tell us about her stay in Reno. She described the Reno campus as "the most beautiful in the country and the center of all of the cultural life of Reno."

Accommodations: Senator Hotel, ☞ ★, 136 West 2nd St., 89501. Telephone: 702/322-2125. Older hotel that's centrally located. $14 to $16 single; $16 to $20 double.

● Motel 6, 1901 South Virginia, 89502. Telephone: 702/825-8401. See Carson City listing for rates.

● Motel 6, 866 North Wells, 89512. Telephone: 702/786-0180. See Carson City listing for rates.

● Motel 6, 1400 Stardust St., 89503. Telephone: 702/747-2676. See Carson City listing for rates.

● Western 6 Motel, 666 North Wells Rd., 89502. Telephone: 702/329-3681. $16.40 single; $23.90 double.

● Friendship Inn–Blue Fountain Motel, 1590 B St., 89431. Sparks area. Telephone: 702/359-0359. $18 to $22 for one; $22 to $28 for two in one bed; $27 to $36 for two in two beds.

Wells

Accommodations: Friendship Inn–Griff's Wagon Wheel, 316 6th St., 89835. Telephone: 702/752-3331. $14 for one; $18 for two in one bed; $22 for two in two beds.

● Motel 6, I-80/U.S. 40 and U.S. 93, 89835. Telephone: 702/752-3696. See Carson City listing for rates.

Winnemucca

Accommodation: Motel 6, 1600 Winnemucca Blvd., 89445. Telephone: 702/623-5775. See Carson City listing for rates.

Randolph ● ● Gorham
● Twin Mountain
● Franconia

North Haverhill ●

Lyme ●
● Waterville Valley

Grantham ●

● Durham
Keene ● ● Manchester
Peterborough ● ● Nashua

New Hampshire

New Hampshire is one place to go when you've had enough of cities. Its mountains, lakes, and wilderness are delicious to anyone who has been cramped up for any time and needs some space to move around in. Since New Hampshire has the highest mountains in the Northeast, the state is especially popular with people who like mountain hiking and skiing. The Appalachian Mountain Club, 5 Joy St., Boston, MA 02108, has published the *AMC White Mountain Guide,* which is recommended for anyone who'd like to try some hiking or climbing (509 pages, with maps; $9.95, or $10.95 postpaid).

Some Special Events: Spring Fair in Hampton and National Historic Preservation Week in Concord (May); Old Timers Fair in Hanover (June); Merchants Street Fair in Keene (July); Old Time Farm Day in Milton and Blue Grass Festival in West Ossipee (August); Fireman's Parade and Muster in Keene (October).

Hitching: As of 1974, hitchhiking became lawful in New Hampshire—as long as the hitchhiker stays off the paved portion of the road. The Department of Safety says that it is "opposed to hitchhiking per se; however, in as much as the legislature saw fit to make it permissible, we will adhere to the spirit of the law." A representative of the State Police advised hitchhikers to "Be alert and wear clothing that can be easily seen by motorists."

Tourist Information: New Hampshire Vacations, P.O. Box 856, Concord, NH 03301.

Alton

Accommodation: Green Tops Youth Hostel (AYH), R.D. 1, from Rte. 28, Robert's Cove Rd., 03809. 400 yards from Lake Winnipesaukee. Telephone: 603/569-9878. Open May 30 to September 7. $5 for AYH members; $1 more plus credentials for nonmembers. Waterskiing, sailing, lake swimming, "with an island yet!"

Belmont

Accommodation: Lakes Region Youth Hostel (AYH), Rte. 106, P.O. Box 342, 03220. Telephone: 603/524-2880. 2½ miles from Laconia. Open June 30 to August 15. $4.75. Advance reservations necessary at other times.

Durham

Accommodation: University of New Hampshire, Randall Hostel (AYH-SA), c/o Residence Office, 03824. Telephone: 603/862-2120. Men, women, and children 6 years and over. Open June 7 to August 13. $10 single; $8 per person double. $3 for AYH members. Reservations advisable one week in advance.

Franconia

Accommodation: Pinestead Farm Lodge, Easton Rd., Rte. 116, 03580. Telephone: 603/823-8121. $15 for first night; $9 for second night. Built in 1852 and situated on almost 200 acres of a working farm. Call the owners from the bus station (four miles) and they'll pick you up.

Gorham

Accommodation: Appalachian Mountain Club, Pinkham Notch Camp, 03581. Telephone: 603/466-2727. Men, women, and children. $16 to $18 for one adult including one meal, $8 to $9 for children; $21.50 including two meals, $10.75 for children (at least one meal must be purchased). $3 discount for AMC members. "Relatively modern, rustic lodge with small bunk rooms with two, three, or four beds per room."

Grantham

Accommodation: Gray Ledges Youth Hostel (AYH-SA), 03755. Telephone: 603/863-1002. Open year round. $5.

Keene

Accommodation: Doyle House (AYH-SA), Keene State College, 03431. Telephone: 603/352-1909, extension 230. Open June 24 to August 14. $4. AYH membership required (see page 21).

Lyme

Accommodation: Loch Lyme Lodge and Cottages, Rte. 10, 03768. Telephone: 603/795-2141. Cabins open from late May to September; the main lodge, a farmhouse built in 1784, is open all year. Reservations strongly advised for cabins. $11 to $17 for one; lower rates for children. In the winter this includes breakfast. Various meal plans are available during the summer (the menu looks wonderful!). All types of summer and winter recreational facilities are available, from swimming to skiing to ice fishing.

Manchester

Accommodation: YMCA, 30 Mechanic St., 03101. Telephone: 603/623-3558. Two blocks from bus station. Men only. $7. Weekly rate: $30. Reservations requested.

Nashua

Accommodations: Best Value Hannah Dustin Motel, 172 D.W. Hwy. South, 03060. Telephone: 603/888-2315. $21 to $22 for one or two in one bed; $23 to $25 for two in two beds.
● Susse Chalet Motor Lodge, Everett Turnpike, Rte. 3, Exits 5 West (North), 5 East (South), 03062. Telephone: 613/889-4151. $19.70 for one; $23.70 for two; $29.70 for four.

North Haverhill

Accommodation: The Lime Kilns Youth Hostel (AYH), 🗪 ★ 🔲, Lime Kiln Rd., 03774. Telephone: 603/989-5656. Open Memorial Day to Columbus Day. Swimming at hostel. $3. Check first with hostel if arriving by car. Housekeeping units available for non-AYH members at $5.50 for one and $4.50 per person for two or more. Campsites available as well. If you take the bus to Wells River, Vt., they will pick you up.

Peterborough

Accommodation: Sharon Studio Barn Hostel (AYH), 🗪 ★, c/o Shapley, Box 310, RFD 2, Sharon, 03458. Telephone: 603/924-6928. Open May through October. New England barn set in the woods. Many recreational and cultural facilities in the area as well as meditation workshops. $12 per night; $70 per week ($7 for AYH members). Meals served at hostel through prior arrangement. Discounts indicated above are for extended stays.

Randolph

Accommodation: Bowman Base Camp (AYH), U.S. 2, 03570. Telephone: 603/466-9487. Open June 1 to September 15. Reservations preferred. $5.50.

Twin Mountain

Accommodation: Ammonoosuc Campground Hostel (AYH), 🗪, P.O. Box 178, 03595. Telephone: 603/846-5527. Open year round, but at least four hostelers needed to open in winter. $4.50 summer; $5.50 winter. Rates $7 to $7.50 for nonmembers. Ideal for hikers, cyclists, downhill skiers, and cross-country skiers. Complete kitchen.

Waterville Valley

Accommodation: Waterville Valley Bunkhouse (AYH-SA), 03233. Telephone: 602/236-8326. Open Thanksgiving to April 30; May 29 to October 16 with advance reservation. $6 per night in low season (before December 17 and after March); $7 in high season; $9 on holidays.

On the map: Layton, Paterson, Parsippany, Passaic, Montclair, Orange, Hoboken, Jersey City, Newark, Union, Somerville, Elizabeth, Bayonne, Linden, Plainfield, Westfield, New Brunswick, Princeton, Maple Shade, Mount Holly, Mount Laurel, Ocean City

New Jersey

New Jersey is a much maligned member of the Middle Atlantic States. It's true that the northeastern part of New Jersey represents the worst of what can happen when industrialization hits an area. But trust us: the state really does deserve to be called the Garden State. Once you're off the New Jersey Turnpike, you'll enter a New Jersey that's unknown to most of the rest of the country.

The New Jersey coast—Cape May, Long Beach Island, and Barnegat Light—is an area of exceptional beauty. The further south you go, the more beautiful it seems to become. Its 127 miles of wide beaches are quiet on the mild days of fall and spring and busy with vacationers in summer.

On the western border of New Jersey is the Delaware River and in the far northwest, along the river, there are rolling hills, streams, and ponds. The Appalachian Trail passes through the area at the Delaware Water Gap, which has been made a national recreation area. Along this part of the river there are a number of places to rent canoes. If you do so, you'll experience rapids and calm stretches, passing high banks, cliffs, and rolling fields.

The Pine Barrens, in southeastern New Jersey, are more than 100 miles of scraggly pine and cedar trees that live in a series of swamps and on the banks of freshwater streams. This region is ideal for spring and fall camping and canoeing. The Bass River State Forest in New Gretna is the center of activity for the area.

New Jersey boasts more than 800 lakes and ponds, more than 100 rivers and creeks, more than 1400 miles of freshly stocked trout streams, 40 state parks, and 11 state forests.

There's no lack of historic sites to visit in New Jersey. Over 100 Revolutionary War battles were fought on New Jersey soil, including the important Battle of Trenton. Some of the names from New Jersey's proud past are Von Steuben, Livingston and Molly Pitcher, Edison, Whitman, and Wilson. For those who want to visit New Jersey's history preserved, we recommend the New Jersey Division of Travel and Tourism's booklet *Your 1980s Vacation*

Guide. Other recommended reading for the history-minded is *Tours of Historic New Jersey,* by Adeline Pepper, Rutgers Press ($7.50).

Some Special Events: New Jersey Folk Festival at Rutgers University in New Brunswick (April); Spring Festival of the Arts in Atlantic City (May); Italian, Ukrainian, Polish, and Irish Heritage Festivals at Garden State Arts Center in Holmdel (June); Cape May County 4-H Fair in Cape May (July); and the New Jersey State Fair in Trenton (September).

Hitching: New Jersey is one of those states that uses "highway" in its law (see page 15). When we asked local people about hitching, we got generally negative responses. Students hitching around the area of their schools usually manage to get rides.

Tourist Information: Division of Travel and Tourism, CN 384, Trenton, NJ 08625.

Bayonne

Accommodations: YMCA, 259 Ave. E, 07002. Telephone: 201/339-2330. Men only. $9.50. Weekly rate: $34.50.

● YWCA, 44 West 32nd St., 07002. Telephone: 201/339-7676. Women only. $10. Possible emergency shelter for any woman and her children in need. Very little room available for transients.

Elizabeth

Help: Elizabeth General Hospital Free Clinic, 201/289-8600.

Accommodation: YMCA, 135 Madison Ave., 07201. Telephone: 201/355-9622. Men over 18 only. $12 to $13 per night; $42 to $46 weekly. $15 refundable key and towel deposit.

Hoboken

Accommodation: YMCA, 1301 Washington St., 07030. Telephone: 201/963-4100. Men only. $10. Weekly rate: $34 to $39.

Jersey City

Help: CONTACT Hudson County, 201/831-1870 (covers Bayonne, Jersey City, North Bergen, Weehawken, Guttenberg, West New York, and Union City).

Accommodation: YMCA, 654 Bergen Ave., 07304. Telephone: 201/434-3211. Men and women. $12. Weekly rate: $55 first week; $39.50 second week. Reservations necessary. Twenty minutes from New York City.

Layton

Accommodation: Old Mine Road Youth Hostel (AYH), two miles north of Dingman's Ferry Bridge on Sussex County Rte. 521, P.O. Box 172, 07851. Telephone: 201/948-6750. Open year round. $3.50. In the Delaware Water Gap National Recreation Area. River swimming one-quarter mile away. AYH membership required (see page 21).

Linden

Accommodation: Friendship Inn–Benedict, 401 West Edgar Rd, 07036. Telephone: 201/862-7700. $20 to $24 for one; $22 to $26 for two in one bed; $26 to $30 for two in two beds.

Maple Shade

Accommodation: Superior Track and Turf Motel, Rte. 73, 08052. Telephone: 609/235-6500. $20 to $23 for one or two in one bed; $23 to $26 for two in two beds.

Montclair

Help: Help Line, 201/744-1954.
Accommodation: YMCA, 25 Park St., 07042. The bus from New York City stops at Y. Telephone: 201/744-3400. Men only. $11. Weekly rate: $37.

Mount Holly

Accommodation: Friendship Inn–Mount Holly Concord Motor, Rte. 38, 08060. Telephone: 609/267-7900. $19 for one; $21 for two in one bed; $25 for two in two beds.

Mount Laurel

Accommodation: Red Roof Inn, N.J. 73 between I-295 and New Jersey Turnpike, 08054. To open in 1982. See Parsippany listing for rates.

Newark

Help: North Jersey Community Union, 201/642-0280.
Accommodation: YMCA, 🛏 ♿, 600 Broad St., 07102. Telephone: 201/624-8900. Men and women. $14 per night; $43 per week.

New Brunswick

Accommodation: YMCA, 9 Livingston Ave., 08901. Telephone: 201/545-1900. Men only. $9 Weekly rate: $40. Reservations necessary.

Ocean City

Accommodation: Sassafras Lodge Hostel (AYH-SA), 1145 Central Ave., 08226. Telephone: 609/399-4555. Advance booking required. $4.50 summer; $5 winter; $3.50 spring or fall. Closed on Saturday from Memorial Day through Labor Day, including Memorial Day and Labor Day weekends.

Orange

Accommodation: YMCA, 125 Main St., 07050. Telephone: 201/673-5100. Men only. $10 single. Weekly rate: $39 and up.

Parsippany

Accommodation: Red Roof Inn, I-80 at N.J. 46, 07054. To open in 1982. $19.95 for one; $22.95 for two in one bed; $24.95 for two to four in two beds.

Passaic

Accommodation: YWCA, 114 Prospect St., 07055. Telephone: 201/779-1770. Women only. $10 single. Weekly rate: $35 to $45. Reservations requested two weeks in advance.

Paterson

Accommodation: YMCA, 128 Ward St., 07505. Telephone: 201/684-2320. Men and women. Single: $12 plus $3 key deposit. Weekly rate: $36 to $55.

Plainfield

Accommodation: YMCA, 518 Watchung Ave., 07060. Telephone: 201/756-6060. Men only. $10 single; $12 double. $10 key deposit required. Transient rooms are scarce.

Princeton

Help: Hotline, 201/924-1144.

On Campus: The well-known Princeton University is here as well as the Institute for Advanced Studies. It's a good place to see "well preserved, lived-in American architecture of the 18th and 19th centuries." While you're there you can visit the university's excellent art museum or take the "Orange Key" tour of the campus.

A popular student hangout which also happens to have very good, inexpensive meals is the Annex, 128½ Nassau St. For Greek food and pizza, try the Athenian, 25 Witherspoon St.

Somerville

Accommodation: Best Value Arch Motel, 1034 Rte. 22 East, 08876. Telephone: 201/722-3555. $21 for two in one bed; $24 for two in two beds.

Stone Harbor

Accommodation: Fairview Guest House, 8700 Pennsylvania Ave., 08247. Telephone: 609/368-9872 or 368-2065 in season, 609/468-5397 off-season. $18 to $30 double in season; $13 to $21 double off-season.

Trenton

Accommodation: YMCA, ✏, 2 South Clinton Ave., 08609. Telephone: 609/392-5168. Men only. $14.50.

Union

Help: Kean College of New Jersey Communication-Help Center Hot Line, Morris Ave., 07083. Telephone: 201/289-2101, 527-2360, or 527-2330. "If you're down about anything, drop by or call."

Westfield

Accommodation: YMCA, 138 Ferris Pl., 07090. Telephone: 201/233-2700. Men only. $15 single. Weekly rate: $35. You can eat not too far away at Town Lunch on East Broad St.

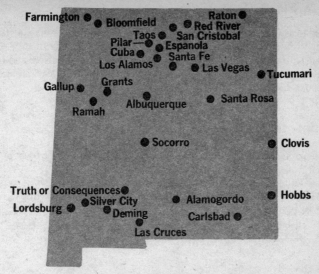

New Mexico

Certain states attract dreamers and New Mexico is one. In the late '60s and early '70s, young Americans considered New Mexico as their Utopia. Communes formed, young people arrived, and all seemed well. By now lots of those communes have dissolved and the people have moved on. But the reality of New Mexico is almost as beautiful as their dream, so do try to spend some time there.

What shall you see while you're there? Carlsbad Caverns National Park, with more than 50 caves; White Sands National Monument (where the first atomic bomb was detonated in 1945); Taos Pueblo, 2½ miles north of Taos, where you can wander and watch some of the 1400 Indians who make their home in this terraced pueblo. New Mexico is a state to explore and a state where there is much to be learned about the Spanish and Indian cultures of the American Southwest. For some background information on New Mexico's Indian population, ask the Tourism and Travel Division (address below) for a copy of their booklet *Indians of New Mexico*.

Some Special Events: Arts and Crafts Fair in Gallup (March); Four Corners Hot Air Balloon Rally in Farmington Lake (May); Old Town Fiesta in Albuquerque (June); Indian Pueblo Arts and Crafts Fair in Albuquerque, and Fiesta de Taos (July); Indian Market in Santa Fe and Inter Tribal Indian Ceremonial in Gallup (August); State Fair in Albuquerque (September); High Altitude Glider and Soaring Festival in Eagle Nest (November).

Hitching: Hitchhiking is not legal on any Interstate highway in New Mexico. Otherwise, hitchhiking is officially legal from the road shoulder, but may be prohibited in some municipalities. The State Police advise: carry photo identification if possible and, if you're under 18, be able to provide a phone contact to verify that you are allowed to be on your own. The State Police stand prepared to assist any traveler in any way possible during his or her stay in New Mexico. Visitors are always welcome in the "Land of Enchantment!"

Tourist Information: New Mexico Travel Division, Commerce and Industry Department, Bataan Memorial Building, Santa Fe, NM 87503. Telephone: toll free 800/545-2040.

Alamogordo

Accommodations: Motel 6, 251 Panorama Blvd., 88310. To open in 1982. $12.95 for one; $16.95 for two; $19.95 for up to four.

● Best Value Alamo Inn, 1400 North White Sands Blvd., 88370. Telephone: 505/437-1000. $14 to $18 for one; $16 to $20 for two in one bed; $18 to $20 for two in two beds.

● Friendship Satellite Inn, White Sands Blvd. at 23rd St., 88310. Telephone: 505/437-8454. $21 to $24 for two in one bed; $24 to $26 for two in two beds.

Albuquerque

Help: AGORA, UNM Student Crisis Center, 505/277-3013. "Stop and talk or ask us about what to see and do."

Tourist Information: Albuquerque Convention and Visitors Bureau, P.O. Box 26866, 87125. Telephone: 505/243-3696.

Accommodations: Canterbury Youth Hostel (AYH-SA), 1906 Central Ave. SE, 87106. Open all year. $4 summer. AYH membership required (see page 21). Reservations required during summer.

● Days Inn, I-40 and Central Ave. NE (Exit 167), 13031 Central Ave. NE, 87123. Telephone: 505/292-3490. $19.88 for one; $25.88 for two.

● Friendship Inn–Crossroads, 1001 Central Ave. NE, 87106. Telephone: 505/242-2757. $16 to $20 for one; $18 to $22 for two in one bed; $20 to $24 for two in two beds.

● Friendship Inn–Tropicana·Lodge, 8814 Central Ave., SE, 87112. Telephone: 505/299-7696. $12 to $13 for one; $14 to $15 for two in one bed; $15 to $16 for two in two beds.

● Western 6 Motel, 3400 Prospect Ave. NE, 87107. Telephone: 505/883-8813. $15.40 single; $22.90 double.

● Motel 6, 13141 Central Ave. NE, 87123. Telephone: 505/296-4891. See Alamogordo listing for rates.

● Motel 6, 1701 University Blvd. NE, 87102. Telephone: 505/843-6100. See Alamogordo listing for rates.

● Regal 8 Inn, 5701 Iliff, NW at Coors, 87105. Telephone: 505/831-8888. $17.88 for one; $20.88 for two in one bed; $23.88 for two to four in two beds.

Bloomfield

Camping: Chaco Canyon National Monument, Star Rte. 4, P.O. Box 6500, 87431. Campground with 35 sites at Gallo Wash, one mile east of Visitor Center. Open year round.

Carlsbad

Camping: Guadalupe Mountains National Park, c/o Carlsbad Caverns National Park, 3225 National Parks Hwy., 88220. Campgrounds at Pine Springs Canyon with ten tent sites. Open year round.

Accommodations: Best Value Stagecoach Inn, 1819 South Canal, 88220. Telephone: 505/887-1148. $16 to $18 for one; $18 to $24 for two in one bed; $22 to $26 for two in two beds.

● Motel 6, 3824 National Parks Hwy., 88220. Telephone: 505/885-8807. See Alamogordo listing for rates.

Clovis

Accommodations: Motel 6, 2620 Mabry Dr., 88101. Telephone: 505/762-3186. See Alamogordo listing for rates.

● Best Value Sands Motel, P.O. Box 1777, 1400 Mabry Dr., 88101. Telephone: 505/763-3439. $16 to $24 for one; $18 to $26 for two.

Cuba

Accommodation: Circle "A" Ranch (AYH), 🐟 ★, P.O. Box 382, 87013. Telephone: 505/289-3350. Open full time June through September; weekends only during other months. $8 single; $7 double; $5 quad for AYH members, $1 more for nonmembers. Rates slightly higher in winter. Houseparents will pick you up at the bus station (six miles) morning and evening. "Extremely beautiful, peaceful, and friendly."

Deming

Accommodation: Motel 6, Country Club Rd., P.O. Box 970, 88030. Telephone: 505/546-9663. See Alamogordo listing for rates.

● Plainsman Motel, 🐟 ★ $1, 1309 West Pine St., 88030. Telephone: 505/546-2787. $12.95 single; $17.95 double.

Espanola

Accommodation: Friendship Inn–Western Holiday Motel, one mile south on U.S. 64/68/285, Rte. 1, Box 249, 87532. Telephone: 505/753-2491. $20 to $22 for one; $24 to $28 for two in one bed; $28 to $34 for two in two beds.

Farmington

Accommodations: Regal 8 Inn, 510 Scott Ave., 87401. Telephone: 505/327-0242. See Albuquerque listing for rates.

● Motel 6, 1600 Bloomfield Hwy., 87401. Telephone: 505/327-7600. See Alamogordo listing for rates.

Gallup

Accommodations: Motel 6, 3306 West Hwy. 66, Star Rte. 2, Box 18. Telephone: 505/722-4084. See Alamogordo listing for rates.
● Best Value El Rancho Hotel and Motel, 1000 East Hwy. 66, 87301. Telephone: 505/863-4411. $12 to $18 for one; $14 to $20 for two in one bed; $16 to $22 for two in two beds.
● Friendship Inn–Road Runner, 3012 East Hwy. 66, 87301. Telephone: 505/863-3804. $19 to $22 for one; $23 to $26 for two in one bed; $27 to $29 for two in two beds.

Grants

Accommodations: Friendship Inn–Grants Motel, 1009 East Santa Fe Ave., 87020. Telephone: 505/287-4477. $19 to $23 for one; $21 to $25 for two in one bed; $24 to $28 for two in two beds.
● Motel 6, East Santa Fe Ave. (I-40 Interchange), P.O. Box 1478, 87020. Telephone: 505/287-7566. See Alamogordo listing for rates.

Hobbs

Accommodations: Best Value Lamplighter Motel, 110 East Marland, 88240. Telephone: 505/397-2406. $16 for one; $19 for two in one bed; $22 for two in two beds.
● Motel 6, 509 North Marland Blvd., 88240. Telephone: 505/397-2879. See Alamogordo listing for rates.

Las Cruces

Accommodations: Motel 6, 235 La Posada Lane, 88001. Telephone: 505/526-3276. See Alamogordo listing for rates.
● Friendship Inn Town House, 2205 West Picacho, Hwy. 70, 88001. Telephone: 505/524-7733. $12.50 to $14.50 for one; $14.50 to $16 for two in one bed; $17 to $22 for two in two beds.

Las Vegas

Accommodation: Friendship Inn–Palomino Motel, 1330 Grand Ave., 87701. Telephone: 505/425-7524. $13 to $15 for one; $15 to $17 for two in one bed; $17 to $19 for two in two beds.

Lordsburg

Accommodation: Friendship Inn–Sea Shell Motel, 816 East Railroad, 88045. Telephone: 505/542-3567. $11 to $13 for one; $13 to $15 for two in one bed; $16 to $18 for two in two beds.

Los Alamos

Camping: Bandelier National Monument, 87544. Campground at Juniper (one-tenth mile inside entrance). Open March 15 to November 1. $3 per campsite per night.

Pilar

Accommodation: The Plum Tree, ♠ 10%, Old Taos Hwy., 87571. Telephone: 505/758-4696. $16 single; $22 double. The Plum Tree is also a restaurant which has a delicious, reasonably priced, creative menu. Discount applies to rooms and meals.

Ramah

Camping: El Morro National Monument, 87321. Campground one-half mile from headquarters with nine free sites. Open all year.

Raton

Accommodations: Best Value Melody Lane Motel, Restaurant and Lounge, 136 Canyon Dr., 87740. Telephone: 505/445-3655. $16 to $22 for one; $22 to $30 for two in one bed; $22 to $34 for two in two beds.
● Friendship Inn–Capri Motel, 304 Canyon Dr., 87740. Telephone: 505/445-3641. $16 to $20 for one; $20 to $26 for two in one bed; $26 to $32 for two in two beds.
● Friendship Village Inn Motel, 1207 South 2nd St., 87740. $22 to $25 for one; $25 to $28 for two in one bed; $28 to $32 for two in two beds.
● Motel 6, 1600 Cedar St., 87740. Telephone: 505/445-9666. See Alamogordo listing for rates.

Red River

Accommodation: Best Value Golden Eagle Lodge, P.O. Box 866, East Main St., 87558. Telephone: 505/754-2227. $18 to $22 for one; $22 to $28 for two.

San Cristobal

Accommodation: San Cristobal Trading Post, P.O. Box 106, 87564. Telephone: 505/776-8454. Four log cabins adjacent to country store. Fully equipped with kitchens, bath, etc. $17 for two per night; rates slightly higher in winter. Fifteen miles north of Taos off Hwy. 3.

Santa Fe

"The very old Indian and Spanish heritage and culture of the majority of people here is almost sacred."

Help: Crisis Intervention Center, 505/982-2771.

Accommodations: Private homes of members of Council on International Relations, P.O. Box 1223, 100 East San Francisco St. (La Fonda Hotel, Suite #3, Mezzanine), 87501. Telephone: 505/982-4931 (mornings only). Foreign visitors only. Donation of $9 per night requested for a stay of no more than three to four days, breakfast included. Reservations preferred. Office hours: 9 a.m. to noon, September 10 to June 30 (closed weekends and holidays); from July 1 to September 9, office is also open 2 to 5 p.m. weekdays and 9 a.m. to noon on Saturday.

"The Council is really fantastic. The members are very friendly and helpful."

● Motel 6, 3007 Cerrillos Rd., 87501. Telephone: 505/471-2442. See Alamogordo listing for rates.

"It is always worth checking at both the College of Santa Fe and St. John's College for dormitory space."

"The Palace on San Francisco Street (on Burro Allen Plaza) is great for all-night jazz. Another good bar with live entertainment is the Ore House on the plaza, which is the center of things. Two cheap, full-course New Mexican-type restaurants (about $4 for a main course, including sopaipillas) are Josie's and Molly's Kitchen, both near the center of town."

Santa Rosa

Accommodations: Motel 6, 3400 Will Rogers Dr., 88435. Telephone: 505/472-3266. See Alamogordo listing for rates.
● Friendship Inn–Tower Motel, Business I-40, U.S. 54-66 and 84, 88435. Telephone: 505/472-3463. $16 to $18 for two in one bed; $18 to $20 for two in two beds.
● Friendship Inn–Will Rogers Motel, 924 Will Rogers Dr., 88435. Telephone: 505/472-3481. $12 to $16 for one; $14 to $24 for two.
● Best Value Western Motel, 860 Will Rogers Dr., 88435. Telephone: 505/472-3466. $16 to $18 for one; $18 to $20 for two in one bed; $20 to $22 for two in two beds.

Silver City

Camping: Gila Cliff Dwellings National Monument, Route 11, Box 100, 88061. Camping all year at Lower Scorpion and Upper Scorpion, both one-half mile from the visitor center.

Socorro

Accommodation: Motel 6, U.S. 85 approximately one-half mile west of I-25, 87801. To open in 1982. See Alamogordo listing for rates.

Taos

Accommodations: The Abominable Snowmansion (AYH-SA), 🎓 ★, P.O. Box 3271, Arroyo Seco, 87571. Telephone: 505/776-8298. Closed Easter to May 31 and October 1 to Thanksgiving. $6 summer, $8 winter, for AYH members; $12 bed and breakfast for nonmembers. Slightly higher during ski season. Reservations suggested during ski season. Meals available at hostel.
● Silvertree Lodge of Taos, √, P.O. Box 1528, 87571. Telephone: 505/758-3071. Although a single on weekends is above our maximum at $26, the rate for a single from Sunday to Thursday is $18 (except holidays). The lodge has a river running just behind it, a swimming pool, and cable color TV.

Truth or Consequences

Accommodation: Friendship Inn–Ace Lodge, 1014 Date St., 87901. Telephone: 505/894-2151. $14 to $16 for one; $16 to $18 for two in one bed; $18 to $20 for two in two beds.

Tucumcari

Accommodations: Motel 6, 2900 East Tucumcari Blvd., 88401. Telephone: 505/461-4316. See Alamogordo listing for rates.
● Palomino Motel, 🦅, 1215 East Tucumcari Blvd., 88401. Telephone: 505/461-3622. Standard motel. $16 for one.

Massena ● ● Hogansburg
● Malone ● Plattsburgh
Canton ●
● ─ Paul Smiths
Star Lake ● ● Lake Placid
Watertown ● Old Forge ● ● Blue Mountain Lake
Lacona ● ● Newcomb
Oswego ● ● Warrensburg
Clyde ● ● Lake George
Niagara
Falls ● Syracuse ● Owasco ● Utica
Rochester ● Auburn ● Canajoharie Little Falls ● Gloversville
Buffalo ● ● Amsterdam
Skaneateles Sharon Springs ● ● Schenectady
Springville ● Geneseo ● Dresden Willet Gilbertsville ● Troy
Ithaca ● ● Oneonta ● Albany
Dundee ● Marathon ● ● New Baltimore
Alfred ● Vestal ● Oliveria ● Big Indian
Jamestown ● Elmira ● ● Woodstock ● Kingston
Binghamton ● Staatsburg

● White Plains
Yonkers ●
New York City ● ● Patchogue

New York

What can you say about New York that hasn't already been said? Like California, New York is a place that people want to see. But most people think of New York as New York City. It's especially hard for New York City residents to remember that all those other people in the state are New Yorkers, too. If you visit New York, don't leave without immersing yourself in New York City for at least a few days, but leave yourself enough time to see some of the beautiful rural areas of the state too.

With a little exploring, you'll find that much of New York State is rural with miles of farmland, small towns, and abundant wildlife. Outdoor recreational opportunities are endless. The southwestern part of the state offers beautiful countryside, especially during early to mid-October, unbounded recreation in the Finger Lakes region, and some very special tourist possibilities like Watkins Glen for racing, Corning Glass Works and Museum, and the many wineries that dot the area from Watkins Glen to Hammondsport. For hikers or campers, what could be more inviting than the Adirondacks or the Catskills? Anyone with a car should try to do some exploring, too, along the Hudson where there are so many restored homes, museums, and pretty little towns just a few hours' ride from the New York City area.

And without going too far from the city, you can also enjoy some lovely hikes and walks—just consult the *New York Walk Book,* Doubleday ($7.95).

Some Special Events: Peach Blossom Square Dance Festival in Canajoharie and Civil War Encampment in Youngstown (May); Art Show and Tuna Tournament in Bay Shore, St. Lawrence County Dairy Princess Parade and Festival in Canton, and Northeast Craft Fair in Rhinebeck (June); Old Catskill Days in Catskill, Newport Jazz Festival in Saratoga, and Bluegrass Festival in Upper Jay (July); Shaker Museum Festival in Old Chatham and Annual Summer Bazaar and Crafts Fair in Sackets Harbor (August); Chowder Society Celebration in Old Bethpage and New York State Fiddler's Contest in Osceola

(September); Fall Festival in Lake Luzerne and Harvest and Arts Festival Salute to the Farmers of America in Elmira (October).

Hitching: To quote the New York State Police: "Soliciting a ride is prohibited at the entrances and exits and any space within the limits of a State Expressway or Interstate Route Highway." On all other state highways, outside of cities and villages, "no person shall stand in a roadway for the purpose of soliciting a ride." The term "roadway" is defined as the improved or paved portion of the highway. "Therefore, hitching is permitted if the person is standing on the shoulder of the highway. Each town, village and city has the authority to enact laws regarding hitchhiking. . . ."

Most of the people we talked to from upstate (northern New York) consider hitchhiking common and acceptable, except on the New York State Thruway. Although they recognize that it's a common means of travel, they hesitate to recommend it because of "occasional tragedies." A golden rule for hitchhiking out of New York City (and any major city, for that matter) is to get out of the city limits first. Hitching within New York City is virtually impossible, and, frankly, you'd have to be a little crazy to even consider it.

Tourist Information: Bureau of State Information, New York State Department of Commerce, 99 Washington Ave., Albany, NY 12245. Telephone: 518/474-4116.

Albany

Help: The Albany area is serviced by Capital District Travelers Aid Society, 142 State St., 12207. Telephone: 518/463-2124.

Tourist Information: Albany County Convention and Visitors Bureau, 90 State St., Suite 200, 12207. Telephone: 518/434-1217.

Accommodations: Albany International Center, Wellington Hotel, ⬧, 136 State St., 12207. Telephone: 518/436-9741. Men, women, and children. International students given preference. Open year round. $16 to $21 single; $22 to $30 double. Reservations are preferred at Wellington Hotel (tel. 518/434-4141). Someone at the hotel recommended Ribbon Grass on Central Ave. as a good health-food restaurant.

● YMCA, 274 Washington Ave., 12203. Telephone: 518/449-7196. Men only. $12.50 single without bath; $15 with bath. Weekly rate: $30 to $45. $5 key deposit necessary.

Alfred

On Campus: If you find yourself in Alfred and want to meet some of the State University students, stop by Alex's College Spot or Gentleman Jim's in the evening. You might also find them eating at the Collegiate, where sandwiches cost only $1. You can find rides listed on the bulletin board in the Campus Center; they are also listed on radio station WALF. Apartments are listed in the Office of Student Living.

Amsterdam

Accommodation: Best Value Windsor Motel, Rte. 30, 12010. Telephone: 518/843-0243. $20 for one or two in one bed; $22 for two in two beds.

Auburn

Accommodations: Superior Sleepy Hollow Motel, RD 4, Box 380, 13021. Telephone: 315/253-3281. $21 for one; $24 to $26 for two in one bed; $28 to $32 for two in two beds.

● Auburn YMCA-WEIU (AYH-SA), 27–29 William St., 13021. Telephone: 315/253-5304. Reservations preferred. $4.

Big Indian

Accommodation: Cold Spring Lodge, 🪶 ★ 5%, 🔲, Oliverea Rd., 12410. Telephone: 914/254-5711. Modern efficiency cabins with fireplaces which accommodate up to eight people. $55 per cabin per night or $17 per person. Firewood supplied. They also have boarding-house-style rooms for $18 single and $12 per person double. "We own 40 acres of land situated in a beautiful valley in the Catskill Mountains."

Binghamton

Help: Off Campus College, 607/798-2767. During business hours only.
● High Hopes, 607/798-HELP or 798-DRUG.
Accommodation: YWCA, Hawley and Exchange Sts., 13901. Telephone: 607/772-0340. Women only. No transients; must plan to stay three months or longer.
On Campus: A friend of ours at the State University of New York at Binghamton says that the fall there is spectacular, the winter is cold and overcast, and the summer is bright, warm, and laid back. She also told us about the Johnson City Coffeehouse, where you can meet students, play Dungeons & Dragons, listen to music, play chess, or see films. When you're hungry, go to Whole in the Wall, 43 South Washington St., where you'll find foods such as fish tempura, whole-wheat pizza, and felafel; or El Cholo Café, 119 Harry L Dr., Johnson City, for large portions of Mex-Tex food.

During the summer, and possibly at other times during the year, you can stay in a dorm room for $5 per night plus $1 for linen. You must make advance reservations through Residential Life Office (tel. 607/798-2321), located in the basement of O'Connor Hall. The YMCA at 61 Susquehanna St. and the YWCA at the corner of Hawley and Exchange Sts. usually have a few transient rooms available for emergency shelter, but please use these only when you really need them.

Blue Mountain Lake

Accommodation: The Steamboat Landing (AYH-SA), 12812. Telephone: 518/352-7323. Open June 1 to October 1. $4 to $5. You must provide your own linen. Bus stops there only on weekends from July to Labor Day. Otherwise you must take the bus to Warrensburg and hitchhike. The hostel is in a summer resort hotel on the lake. There is no cooking allowed on premises but there are restaurants within walking distance.

Buffalo

Help: Travelers Aid, 656 Ellicott Square Bldg., 14203. Telephone: 716/854-8661. Open 24 hours per day.

On Campus: There are five colleges and universities in Buffalo—the State University of New York at Buffalo, Buffalo State College, Daemen College, Canisius College, and D'Youville College. All of them will have a great deal of helpful information on their bulletin boards. Many students congregate on the Elmwood Strip, where you'll find Cole's, Mr. Goodbar, Bullfeathers, Pano's, Upstairs Downstairs, Casey's, and Graffiti's. For a good meal in a warm, comfortable atmosphere, try Sign of the Steer on Main St. near the SUNY Buffalo campus. They have burgers, Mexican food, fried potato skins, and fantastic drinks. If you can make it to Fort Erie, Canada, which is ten minutes from Buffalo, go to George's Good Food Restaurant for an inexpensive Chinese meal. It's a real establishment.

Accommodations: YWCA (AYH-SA), 245 North St., 14201. Telephone: 716/884-4761. Women only; mothers can bring young children age 6 and under. $8.50 single; $11.50 double. Reservations requested with advance deposit of $2. Cafeteria in the building. AYH members, $3.25 without linen.

● Best Value Fountain Court Motor Inn, 9560 Main St., Clarence, 14031. Telephone: 716/759-6835. $20 to $22 for one; $22 to $24 for two in one bed; $24 to $26 for two in two beds.

● Best Value Modern Aire Motel, 1346 Sheridan Dr., Kenmore, 14217. Telephone: 716/876-4489. $16 to $23 for one; $20 to $26 for two in one bed; $22 to $28 for two in two beds.

● Red Roof Inn, ♿, I-90 at Camp Rd. (Exit 57), Hamburg, 14075. Telephone: 716/648-7222. $17.95 for one; $20.95 for two in one bed; $22.95 to $24.95 for two to four in two beds.

Canajoharie

Accommodation: Best Value Mohawk Motor Lodge, P.O. Box 130, Hwy. 5, 13428. Telephone: 518/673-3233. $18 to $20 for one; $22 to $24 for two in one bed; $23 to $26 for two in two beds.

Canton

On Campus: Half of Canton's population consists of students. If you need more convincing that Canton is a real college town, a friend there wrote us when asked where students tend to congregate, that "most any bar (and there are plenty) or local restaurant would suffice." There are four colleges in the area, two in Canton (Canton ATC and St. Lawrence University) and two more in Potsdam, which is ten miles away.

Clyde

Accommodation: Honey Farm Home Hostel (AYH), RD 1, Kelsey Rd. East, 14433. Telephone: 315/923-7102. $2.50. Reservations necessary by telephone. Natural foods are sold at hostel and there is Russian stove or wood stove cooking only. You can go horseback riding at the hostel, which is a farmhouse undergoing renovations.

Dresden

Accommodation: Camp Whitman (AYH), RD 1, Penn Yan, 14527. Telephone: 315/536-8391. Open April 1 to October 31. Reservations required April, May, September, and October. $3. "Over 100 acres of woods, ravines, meadows and trails."

Dundee

Accommodation: The Household Center Youth Hostel (AYH), 🎓 25%, Old Bath Rd., RD 1, 14837. Telephone: 607/292-3842. Open May 1 to November 1. $4. AYH membership required (see page 21). Early reservations are a must—this is primarily a conference center.

Elmira

Help: Info-Line, 607/737-2077.
Accommodation: YMCA, 201 East Church St., 14902. Across from bus station. Telephone: 607/734-1609. Men only. Minimum of two weeks. The rate is $60 for two weeks plus $5 key deposit.

Geneseo

On Campus: Information on accommodations in the campus area is available at the school's Travel Center, located in the College Union, Room 326; telephone: 716/245-5864 or 245-5851.

For inexpensive meals in the area, the student staff of the Travel Center recommend the Normal Café, located on Main St., open 24 hours Friday and Saturday; Jack Carr's Restaurant, which is also open 24 hours; and Fat Augie's, Pontillo's Italian Restaurant, and Shakti Foods, all on Main St. On campus, it's the College Union Snackbar. For good, inexpensive food and drink, try the Yard of Ale, just a few miles northwest of the village on Rte. 63 in Piffard. On Conesus Lake, it's the Tee and Gee, the Cottonwood Inn, and the Loganberry Barn.

For drinks and new friends, it's the Idle Hour on Center St., with "happy hours" daily. Gentleman Jim's (GJ's) on School St. near campus offers specials most weeknights and live rock and blues music every weekend. The In Between (in between GJ's and the Vital Spot), offers specials on weeknights, and one more spot to try is Uncle Waldo's, on Main Street.

Gilbertsville

Accommodation: The Major's Inn (AYH-SA), P.O. Box 136, 13776. Telephone: 607/783-2412. Open May 15 to October 1. Reservations preferred. $2.50. "Somewhat primitive but interesting." AYH membership required (see page 21).

Gloversville

Accommodation: YMCA, 19 East Fulton St., 12078. Telephone: 518/725-0627 or 725-0628. Men only. $6. Weekly rate: $22.

Hogansburg

Accommodation: Lost Dauphin's Cottage (AYH), P.O. Box 366, 13655. Telephone: 518/358-2829. Open all year. $3.50 summer; $4.50 winter. AYH membership required (see page 21). "Hostel is historic architectural A-frame house, lived in by son of France's Louis XVI and Marie Antoinette."

Ithaca

On Campus: There are thousands of students in Ithaca—at Cornell or Ithaca College—and either campus will welcome you. To find out what's happening on the two campuses, pick up copies of the *Ithaca Journal,* the *Cornell Daily Sun,* the *Grapevine,* or the *Ithaca New Times.* For a bulletin board with rides and apartments listed, go to Willard Straight Hall at Cornell and to the third floor of the Student Union building at Ithaca.

Our friend at Ithaca College tells us that "the city is on a lake, and during the warm months, there are boating trips and sailing facilities. There's also a wide selection of summer stock theaters in the area. . . ."

Accommodation: International Living Center, North Campus 8, Cornell University, 14853. Telephone: 607/256-5299. Men and women (children with difficulty). Accommodation only for those with official business at Cornell. Preference is given to foreign students. June 1 to August 16. $5.50 single; $4 per person double. $1 charge for linen, which can be waived if you bring a sleeping bag. Reservations recommended. Cooking facilities available.

Jack's Reef

Accommodation: Whitmore Home Hostel (AYH), 7213 Kingdom Rd., Memphis, 13112. Telephone: 315/689-9064. Reservations necessary. Located on a working farm.

Jamestown

Accommodation: YMCA (AYH-SA), 101 East 4th St., 14701. Telephone: 716/664-2802. Men only, 18 or over. $3 for AYH members (must bring own bedding); $11 for nonmembers. No registration Sunday.

Kingston

Accommodations: YMCA, 507 Broadway, 12401. Telephone: 914/338-3810. Men only. $13. Weekly rate: $30.
● Hidden Valley Lake Youth Hostel (AYH), 🔄, CPO Box 190, 12401. Telephone: 914/338-4616. Reservations preferred. Open all year. Men, women, and children. $5.75 winter; $4.50 summer. Bring sleeping bag. "Beautiful, serene, clean."

● Best Value Roma Inn, Rte. 28, 12401. Telephone: 914/331-1919. $23 for one; $28 for two in one bed; $32 for two in two beds.

Lacona

Accommodation: Smart House Nature Center (AYH), 🎓 ★ (AYH rates), Smartville Rd., Box 199, 13083. Telephone: 315/387-5521. Open all year. Reservations preferred. $5 summer; $6.75 winter. Approximately $2 higher for nonmembers. Accommodations available for families. "More snow than anywhere else in the East."

Lake George

Accommodation: Lake George Youth Hostel (AYH), 🦽 (partial), Upper Bay Rd., P.O. Box 176, 12845. Telephone: 518/793-1627 (July 1 to August 31) or 518/668-2634 (May 1 to June 30). Open June 15 to August 31. $4. Reservations necessary in June; helpful at other times. AYH membership required (see page 21).

Lake Placid

Accommodation: Lake Placid Youth Hostel (AYH-SA), 54 Main St., 12946. Telephone: 518/523-2008. $5. Advance booking required.

Little Falls

Accommodations: YMCA, 15 Jackson St., 13365. Take Herkimer exit off New York State Thruway. Ten miles from Adirondack Mountains. Telephone: 315/823-1740. Men only. $8. Weekly rate: $23.
● Holy Family Renewal Center (AYH-SA), 639 East John St., 13365. Telephone: 315/823-1548. Open all year. Reservations suggested. $5. AYH membership required (see page 21).

Malone

Accommodation: Home Hostel, 65 Park St., 12953. Telephone: 518/483-7334. Reservations necessary. $3. AYH membership required (see page 21).

Marathon

Accommodation: Best Value Three Bear Inn and Motel, 3 Broome St., 13803. Telephone: 607/849-3258. $18 for one; $21 for two in one bed; $24 for two in two beds.

Massena

Accommodation: Burke's Superior Motel, RD 1, Rte. 37, 13662. Telephone: 315/764-0246. $20 for one; $26 for two in one bed; $28 for two in two beds.

New Baltimore

Accommodation: New Baltimore Home Hostel (AYH), P.O. Box 205, River Rd., 12124. Telephone: 518/756-9097. One-half mile from bus station. Open year round. Will not accept people traveling by car. One night stay only. $3. Reservations necessary one week in advance. AYH membership required (see page 21).

New York City

"I agree with Comden and Green, 'a wonderful town.'"

It doesn't matter how you get to New York just as long as you make sure to get there. New York is an incredible city. There's no place quite like it anywhere and everyone should see it for themselves at least once. Most people aren't satisfied with just one visit—they keep coming back again and again. Since New York is so big and so fast-paced, you can use a little help getting used to this small and crowded island. Here are some books that will help:

Arthur Frommer's Guide to New York, by Faye Hammel, Frommer/Pasmantier Publishers ($2.95). A good, general guide to what there is to see and do.

New York on $25 a Day, by Joan Hamburg and Norma Ketay. Frommer/Pasmantier ($5.95). Another Frommer guide, this with emphasis on the bargain spots.

Michelin Guide to New York City, Michelin ($7.95). (Available in bookstores or from CIEE.) Covers all the points of interest in a thoroughly researched and fascinating way.

I Love New York Guide, by Marilyn J. Appleberg, Collier Macmillan ($3.95). Dedicated to helping you find it in New York—whatever "it" may be. This is a good pocket guide to everything and everywhere in New York.

The City Observed: A Guide to Architecture, by Paul Goldberger, Vintage Press ($7.95). A thorough and thoughtful guide to our buildings.

Nooks and Crannies: An Unusual Walking Tour Guide to New York City, by David Yeadon. The Scribner Library ($8.95). If you have time for more than the usual tourist attractions, this book will introduce you to some of the lesser known pleasures of the city.

Also, to know what's going on when you're in town, refer to the *Soho Weekly News,* the *Village Voice, New York* magazine, the *New Yorker,* or the *New York Times* (especially the Sunday *Arts and Leisure* section and the Friday *Weekend* section).

"This is a city that's culturally diverse, intellectually alive and vigorous."

A first stop in New York, especially for student visitors, should be CIEE's New York Student Center, which offers up-to-the-minute information on what's happening in the city, as well as organized walking tours and discount tickets for a variety of activities in town. The Student Center also offers a Travel Service which provides help in planning travel throughout the United States and the world. What's more, the Student Center is an ideal place to stay (see listing on page 301), as well as a great spot to meet other travelers. The Student

Center is located in the William Sloane House, 356 West 34th St., New York, NY 10001 (tel. 212/695-0291).

Getting There: From the Airports: You'll land in the borough of Queens at either JFK or LaGuardia, or in New York's somewhat less glamorous neighbor, New Jersey, at Newark Airport. Banish thoughts of a taxi—the fare is $20 or more from JFK. Fortunately, there are several alternatives. In 1978, a new subway route called the JFK Express was inaugurated with much hoopla and attendant publicity. The "Express," which is really a combination bus and train ride, takes about one hour and costs $5. From JFK, the bus takes passengers to the Howard Beach-JFK Airport station where they board the train for stops at Jay St. in Brooklyn, and seven stops in Manhattan: Broadway-Nassau, Chambers Street (World Trade Center), West 4th St. (Washington Square), 34th St. (Sixth Ave.), 42nd St. (Fifth Ave.), 47th-50th Sts. (Rockefeller Center), and 57th St. (Sixth Ave.).

A somewhat slower but less expensive ($1.20) bus/train combination has been around a lot longer than the JFK Express: From JFK take a Q10 bus to the Union Turnpike-Kew Gardens station or the Lefferts Blvd.-Liberty Ave. station of the IND subway. From the first station you can take an E or F train; from the second, board an A train right into the heart of Manhattan.

From LaGuardia, take the Q33 bus to 74th St./Broadway in Jackson Heights and then switch to the #7 train which goes to 42nd St. If you have lots of luggage or are a bit unwilling to spend your first hour in New York on the subway, take a Carey Bus from either airport to the East Side Airlines Terminal at 38th St. and First Ave. From JFK the ride costs $5; from La Guardia it's $3.50. There's a free shuttle van between the World Trade Center and the Terminal, too, which leaves from the World Trade Center every hour on the hour between 11 a.m. and 5 p.m., Monday to Friday.

A bus will also take you from Newark Airport to the Port Authority Bus Terminal on the West Side of Manhattan at Eighth Ave. and 40th St. The 30-minute trip costs $2.25.

● By Train: If you come by train, you'll arrive at either Grand Central Station on the East Side at 42nd St. and Vanderbilt Ave. or at Pennsylvania Station at 32nd St. and Seventh Ave. Both stations have information booths where you can find out how to get where you're going by public transportation. There are subway stations in both terminals and bus stops right outside.

● By Bus: Anyone coming by bus will arrive at the Port Authority Bus Terminal, 40th St. and Eighth Ave. There's a subway station entrance in the terminal and buses outside.

Getting Around: The best way to get around Manhattan is on foot. Just remember that most streets and avenues are laid out on a grid, that streets are numbered consecutively north of 4th St., and that the avenues (with some exceptions) are numbered from the East to the West Side. Fifth Avenue divides East and West; uptown is north of where you are, downtown is south, and crosstown is east or west toward either river. The New York Convention and Visitors Bureau has a free map, but it's not very detailed, so we recommend either buying the paperback *New York in Flash Maps,* by Toy Lasker, which costs $2.50, or a Hagstrom map.

Note: Bus, subway, and taxi fares will probably be higher than the rates listed below by the time you read this. However, we have no way of knowing, at press time, how much higher they'll be.

● By Bus: For visitors who don't want to walk, the bus is best. Buses go up and down the avenues and across the major streets, and they run frequently and all day and all night. The bus fare is 75¢ (exact change or a subway token), and free transfers are available on some routes. There are two Culture Bus Loops, too, that connect some of the major cultural attractions of Manhattan and Brooklyn on weekends. The fare on both is $2.50 in coins. Call 330-1234 for bus information.

● Subway: Since 1904, New Yorkers have been riding on and complaining about the subway. It's noisy, it's dirty, and it's graffiti-scarred—but it's fast and costs only 75¢ to go anywhere on the system. You need to buy a token before you can enter the platform. Token booths are supposed to have a supply of subway maps.

● Taxis: You'll be able to tell whether or not a taxi's free by the light on top—if it's lit up, it's vacant. A taxi ride costs $1 for the first one-seventh mile and 10¢ for each additional one-ninth mile. At night and on weekends you must pay a 50¢ surcharge. The minimum tip is 25¢ or 20% of the fare, whichever is greater. Try to avoid taking a taxi because they're expensive and slow—especially when you're making a crosstown trip. Most taxis are yellow—these are the ones licensed by the City of New York. Taxis by any other color are called gypsy cabs and their drivers boast: "We're not yellow—we'll go anywhere."

Accommodations: New York now has its own bed-and-breakfast service. It's called Urban Ventures and it's run by Mary McAulay and Frances Dworan. "We inspect every room, we list and interview every host." Here's one sample listing: "A twin-bedded room on East 80th St. and York Ave. in the home of a vivacious teacher. $32 for one; $38 for two. The bus to Bloomingdale's stops right in front of the door." Prices range from about $22 to $40 for a single; $30 to $45 for a double. For details, write to: Urban Ventures, 322 Central Park West, New York, NY 10025. Telephone: 212/MO2-1234.

● The Chelsea Hotel, ★, 222 West 23rd St., 10111. Telephone: 212/243-3700. The Chelsea has been and is an artistic and creative haven for many of New York's and the world's most famous characters, including Thomas Wolfe, Arthur Miller, Jane Fonda, Dylan Thomas, and Lenny Bruce. From $25 for a single room with semiprivate bath; $45 for a double room. Reservations are necessary. *Where to Stay* readers will receive a 15% discount if they stay one week.

● New York Student Center, 🐾, William Sloane House, 356 West 34th St., 10001. Telephone: 212/695-0291. Six blocks from Port Authority; two blocks from Penn Station. Huge 1485-room facility. Rates: $17 single with ISIC, $19 without; $11 per person for a twin-bedded room with ISIC, $13 without. Rates are for rooms without baths, although a few rooms with bath are available at a higher price. Long-term rates and meal plans are also available for resident students. Cafeteria, lounges, reading rooms, game room, television room, gymnasium, and laundry. CIEE and YMCA cooperate in offering the services at the Student Center, and CIEE staffs a Student Travel office at Sloane House which arranges low-cost transportation and tours and helps students to plan their travels in the U.S. and abroad. The Hospitality Center offers information on activities in New York, including walking tours and discount tickets to plays and other events. The Student Center is also a good meeting place, especially in summer. Other pluses are the ride and message boards at the center.

● Prince George Hotel (AYH-SA), 14 East 28th St., 10016. Telephone: 212/685-9207. $13 to $26 summer; $11 to $24 winter.

- International House, ♿ (limited), 500 Riverside Dr., 10027. Telephone: 212/678-5036. Men and women. During academic year for full-time graduate students, visiting scholars or researchers, with a few guest suites available. During summer vacation anyone associated with higher education, research, traineeships, or nonprofit international work can be accommodated. Weekly rate: $75. Guest suite rate: $25 to $40 per day; $150 to $240 per week. All rates include a food plan which entitles guests to reduced rates in the dining room.

- John Jay Student Hostel, c/o 125 Livingston Hall, Columbia University, 10027. Street address is 515–519 West 114th St., 10027. Telephone: 212/280-2775 or 280-2776. You must be a student with ID. Open late May to mid-August. $7 single ($6 for Columbia students); $13 double ($11 for Columbia students). If you pay for two weeks or more in advance, there's a 10% discount. There is a mandatory weekly linen charge of $2.75.

- McBurney YMCA, 215 West 23rd St., 10011. Telephone: 212/741-9226. Men only. $17 single.

- International Student Center, 38 West 88th St., 10024. Telephone: 212/787-7706. Open year round. $6. Foreign students only.

- FIT Residence Hall, ♿, 230 West 27th St., 10001. Telephone: 212/255-0018. Men and women. Open June 14 to July 31. $10 for a double; no singles available. Communal bathroom. Reservations necessary one week in advance.

- West Side YMCA, 5 West 63rd St., 10023. Telephone: 212/787-4400. Male and female students. $18 to $23 single, plus a few doubles at $23. Reservations preferred three weeks in advance with $18 deposit. Cafeteria in the building.

- Vanderbilt YMCA, 224 East 47th St., 10017. Telephone: 212/755-2410. Men and women. $16 single; $22 double. Excellent cafeteria.

- YMCA, 99 Meserole Ave., Greenpoint, Brooklyn, 11222. Telephone: 212/389-3700. Men only. $11.50. One block from Nassau Ave. subway stop. Newly renovated. One-half hour by subway from midtown Manhattan.

- YWCA, 30 Third Ave., 🍴, Brooklyn, 11217. Telephone: 212/875-1190. Women only. $15.50 single. Weekly rate: $50. Reservations required at least two weeks in advance. Twenty minutes from Times Square by subway. 10% discount toward a week's stay, 15% discount for one night.

- YMCA, 138-46 Northern Blvd., Flushing, Queens, 11354. Telephone: 212/961-6880. Men only. $17.25 single. Weekly rate: $46 to $51.

- Parkside Evangeline Residence, 18 Gramercy Park South, 10003. Telephone: 212/677-6200. Women only. "This is a business women's residence for permanent residency for 300 women, serving predominantly young business women." The weekly rate of $75.70 includes breakfast and dinner. Reservations and an interview are required.

- Vacation Accommodation Centers, 🍴 ★ 15%, c/o Travel Inn, 42nd St. and 11th Ave. Telephone: 212/582-9760. This is a new facility especially for students or AYH members. The single rate is above our maximum, but if you are traveling alone and don't mind sharing a room, they'll match you up with one or more single travelers. The rates are $28 to $32 for a single, $35 to $40 for a double, and $15 to $18 per person for a triple or quad. The inn has a pool and sauna. You must present your student ID, AYH membership card, or a copy of *Where to Stay*. They also offer a 20% discount to ISIC-holders on the purchase of their Vacation Card, which applies to discount accommodations in other parts of the country. Ask them for details.

Where to Eat: There are two kinds of eating to be done in New York. First is the grab-it-while-you-can-get-it type and second are the more peaceful, more leisurely meals that are best when shared with someone else. For the first kind you can depend on some of the chains like Chock Full O' Nuts, Blimpies, Zum Zum, Nathan's Famous, or Amy's. You'll never be far from one of these wherever you are in the city.

For the second type of eating, here are some possibilities. We've chosen these because we feel that they offer, above all, good value. (Remember that to save money it's always best to have your big restaurant meal at lunchtime since the prices on the dinner menu are much higher.) For more suggestions look through a copy of *The New York Underground Gourmet,* by M. Glaser and J. Snyder, Fireside ($3.95). Don't let the title fool you, though—it's a 1977 edition and some of the restaurants listed may have disappeared by now.

If you're interested in saving money at dinnertime, why not take advantage of the "happy hour" that many midtown restaurants observe. Usually the happy hour lasts from 5 to 7 p.m., and during these two hours it's possible to have a drink and all the hors d'oeuvres you can eat for the cost of the drink alone. Some places serve quite substantial hors doeuvres—like fried chicken, pepper steak, meatballs, etc. Some places you might consider are the Old Stand, 893 Third Ave.; Molly Mog's, 65 East 55th St.; Tandoor, 40 East 49th St.; the Cowboy, 60 East 49th St.; and Pronto, 30 East 60th St. and 801 Second Ave.

● The Front Porch, 253 West 11th St. (in the West Village), 2272 Broadway at 82nd St. (Upper West Side), and 119 East 18th St. (Gramercy Park). The specialty here is thick soups that are accompanied by homemade breads, sandwiches, and rich desserts.

● Pink Tea Cup, 310 Bleeker St. (between Grove and Barrow Sts). A soul-food luncheonette with a reputation for tasty meals. Their pecan pancakes are known far and wide.

● Chumley's, 86 Bedford St. (the West Village). The quintessential Village bar and restaurant that was once a speakeasy. Hearty food, surprisingly low prices, and plenty of beer.

● Spring Street Natural Restaurant and Bar, 149 Spring St. (in Soho). The food is good—soups, vegetable tempura, etc.—and the staff, at least when we've been there, is anxious to please.

● Spring Street Restaurant, 401 West Broadway (in Soho). One of the first restaurant/bars in Soho and still one of the most popular. The management doesn't mind if you sit and talk a while over your drink or your meal.

● Leshko's, 111 Ave. A (near 7th St.). An order of meat-filled pirogi (a pocket of dough with meat inside) is filling and inexpensive. Other Polish and Ukrainian specialties, too.

● Odessa Restaurant, 117 Ave. A (at East 7th St.). Foods of the Ukraine that are reasonably priced and served by amiable waitresses. We recommend the potato pirogies, fried and served with sour cream, the stuffed cabbage, or lamb stew. The check shouldn't go over $5 for a filling meal.

● Mitali, 334 East 6th St. (between 1st and 2nd Aves.). An Indian restaurant on a block that's filled with Indian restaurants. Entrees are $3 to $4. Bring your own wine.

● Puglia's, 189 Hester St. (Little Italy). Lots of Italian food in a joyous atmosphere—everyone sings and seems to have a great time while eating.

● King Crab, 871 Eighth Ave. (at 52nd St.). A good seafood meal here is inexpensive and the restaurant is well located, not far from the theater area.

● Nom Wah Tea Parlor, 113 Doyers St. Featured in this Chinatown restaurant is the dim sum lunch consisting of an assortment of dumpling-like creations that are stuffed with pork, seafood, bean curd, and vegetables.

● Hee Seung Fung Restaurant and Teahouse, 46 Bowery. Another very popular Chinatown restaurant. At lunchtime waiters carry around trays of dim sum specialties and you pick what looks good. At the end of the meal you pay according to the number of empty plates left on your table.

● Hunan Garden, 1 Mott St. A popular Chinatown restaurant with enclosed sidewalk café. Varied menu with Hunan specialties—hot and spicy dishes printed in red on the menu.

● Hwa Yuan Szechuan Inn, 40 East Broadway. Another Chinatown favorite (there's nearly always a waiting line in the evening). Superb Szechuan cuisine.

● Luna's, 112 Mulberry St. In the very heart of Little Italy, Luna's serves southern Italian-style food. Usually crowded, always noisy, and lots of fun.

● Akasaka, 715 Second Ave. The sushi, the tempura, and all else is delicious. The restaurant is Japanese; the owners are from Japan via France.

● Manganaro's Hero-Boy Restaurant, 492 Ninth Ave. In the middle of the Italian market section; serves all kinds of hero sandwiches.

● Molfeta's, 307 West 47th St. Greek food that's good and reasonably priced. Only steps from most of the Broadway theaters.

● Symposium, 544 West 113th St. (near Columbia University). Friendly, popular Greek restaurant with a pleasant summertime garden.

● Sou-En, 2444 Broadway (Upper West Side). In case you thought that macrobiotic food was just good for you, Sou-En will show you that it can be delicious too.

● Z, 117 East 15th St. (near Irving Place), is a nice place for a not-too-expensive Greek meal. Try the avgolemono soup, the poikilia (a mixed Greek antipasto), and the lamb dishes. "A dinner for three of us including poikilia, the main course, wine, and coffee cost about $28 with tax and tip included." That's a bargain for New York City.

● Second Avenue Deli, 156 Second Ave. at 10th St. Everything you've always wanted from a kosher deli—pastrami, borscht, chicken soup—and reasonably priced too, when compared with similar establishments.

● West End Café, Broadway between 113th and 114th Sts. (near Columbia). You can eat here—omelets, sandwiches, etc.—but it's the music that we recommend. Starting at 8:30 every night, in a side room that's all dark and smoky, you can hear terrific swing jazz played by the people who worked with Ellington and others as famous.

● Delphi Restaurant, 109 West Broadway, corner of Reade St. (a short walk from the World Trade Center). More Greek food in a pleasant atmosphere. *"Everything I tasted was so good and I was amazed at the low prices."*

● Rathbones, 1702 Second Ave. (at 88th St.). Full meals cost from $3.95 to $6.95. Relaxed, comfortable setting but can be noisy at times. The bar is buzzing at night.

● Jackson Hole, 232 East 64th St. Other locations too, but this is the best. "Great burgers with exotic toppings and low prices. Very trendy and always, always crowded. Expect to wait."

● And then there's Brooklyn. A short subway ride from Manhattan (the #2 or #3 train to Court Street or the #4 or #5 train to Borough Hall) are the glories of Atlantic Ave. and its Middle Eastern restaurants. Two we can recommend are the New Near East, on Court St. just off Atlantic Ave. (not to be confused with the Near East across the street), and the Tripoli, on Atlantic Ave. at Clinton St. After you've eaten at these or any other Atlantic Ave. spot, walk over to the Brooklyn Heights Promenade for a beautiful view of the Lower Manhattan skyline.

What to See and Do: Free in the Parks: The New York Philharmonic, the Metropolitan Opera, and the Shakespeare Festival Company all perform in the parks of New York every summer for free. Take a picnic along and enjoy some of the world's most creative people in a superb setting. Call 472-1003 for a recorded message about what's going on in the parks.

"I'd encourage visitors to check the papers for any street fairs that might be on during their stay; they strike me as New York at its very best."

● Museums: There are 75 museums in New York, each with something special to offer. With a limited time to spend in the city you will probably want to choose from some of the better known: the American Museum of Natural History, 79th St. and Central Park West; the Metropolitan Museum of Art, Fifth Ave. between 80th and 84th Sts.; the Museum of Modern Art, 11 West 53rd St.; the Guggenheim Museum, Fifth Ave. at 89th St.; the Cooper-Hewitt Museum (the Smithsonian Institution's National Museum of Design) at 2 East 91st St.; and the Frick Collection, 1 East 70th St.

To find out what exhibits are where, the hours of the museums, and admission policies (most have fees), check a copy of *New York* magazine, *The New Yorker,* or the free calendar of events distributed by the New York Convention and Visitors Bureau.

● One museum with a difference is the South Street Seaport Museum, along the East River in Lower Manhattan. "This is not a building or a ship; it is what remains of New York's great 19th-century port." The Seaport is a group of historic properties, restored or to be restored, to the area's 19th-century glory.

● The Museum of Holography, ★ 50%, 11 Mercer St., near Canal, features a form of 3-D photography which involves the use of lasers. This is the place for a unique, interesting, "wave of the future" experience in Soho. Open noon to 6 p.m., Wednesday to Sunday.

● The United Nations. Hour-long tours of the U.N. are available every 15 minutes from 9 a.m. to 4:45 p.m., Monday to Friday. Tickets are $1.50 for students, $2.50 for others. Free tickets to open sessions of the General Assembly are also available on a first-come, first-served basis; they are distributed at the information booth at the 45th St. entrance. Call 754-7713 for information.

● The Buildings: For a view from the top that you won't forget, go to the 107th floor of the World Trade Center on the Lower West Side. It costs $2.50 for adults ($1.25 for children) to go to the observation deck and from there you can go to an open walkway on the roof. The Empire State Building, 34th St. and Fifth Ave., has another view of Manhattan to offer from its 102nd floor. Cost: $2.50 for adults; $1.35 for children under 12. To combine a beautiful view of New York on one side and New Jersey on the other with a drink, go to the Top of the Park Restaurant, 60th St. and Broadway (no sneakers, please).

● Staten Island Ferry. For 25¢ round trip you can take this poor man's cruise across New York harbor. You'll pass the Statue of Liberty en route but if you want to actually visit the statue, walk around her, and climb into her crown, you can reach her by boat from South Ferry. The round trip costs $1.50

for adults (50¢ for children) and includes admission to the American Museum of Immigration in the statue's base.

● Circle Line. One of the nicest ways to see the island of Manhattan is from a boat which cruises around all of it in three hours. The boat ride is a good way to begin a trip to New York, helping you to orient yourself to what's where on the island. The ride costs $3.75 for children under 12, $7.50 for adults, and it begins at Pier 83 on the Hudson River at the foot of 43rd St.

● Tour of Harlem. Since most visitors are curious about Harlem, a black-operated tour company called Penny Sightseeing has a tour of the area on Monday, Thursday, and Saturday. Call 247-2860.

● Neighborhoods. A walk in and around the neighborhoods of New York is the most fun of all. You can choose from the Financial District, Chinatown, Little Italy, the Lower East Side, Soho, Greenwich Village, the Garment Center, Midtown, the Upper East Side, and the Upper West Side. Leave yourself lots of time to stroll, go in and out of shops, and explore any place that attracts you.

● Theater. See at least one play while you're in New York. For up-to-the-minute listings of what is playing either on Broadway, off-Broadway, or off-off-Broadway, check the *New York Times* (the Sunday *Arts and Leisure* section especially) or *New York* magazine. Take advantage, too, of the bargains offered at the TKTS booths at 47th St. and Broadway in Duffy Square and at 100 William St. in Lower Manhattan. At 3 p.m. on the day of the performance, leftover tickets go on sale for half their original price at the 47th St. booth; the William St. booth opens at 11:30 a.m. The line can be long and you may not get your first choice, but after all, a bargain is a bargain.

● Lincoln Center. Whether it's dance, opera, symphony, or theater that interests you, you'll find some or all of them going on at once in the Lincoln Center complex. The Metropolitan Opera, Avery Fisher Hall, the New York State Theater, the Vivian Beaumont Theater, Alice Tully Hall are all at Lincoln Center. At times, student rush tickets are available to performances in the Lincoln Center halls—call the individual box offices for details.

● Film. If you want to see a commercial release, it's easy enough to find out what's playing where in the listings in the daily newspapers. But for those who are attracted to the lesser known films—films by "undiscovered" directors, independent films, or early or overlooked films by known directors—there are several possibilities. The Museum of Modern Art, the Whitney Museum, and the Little Theater in Joseph Papp's Public Theater are the most obvious; a bit less well-known are Film Forum, 15 Vandam St.; Millennium, 66 East 4th St.; and Collective for Living Cinema, 52 White St.

Shopping: Does anyone pay full price for anything in New York? We sometimes wonder. For people who are here to shop, there's a new guide book that's an absolute must—*The Shopper's Guide to New York,* by Marjorie A. Cohen, published by Two Zee's ($6.95) and distributed by Dutton. The book, written especially for visitors to New York, takes you in and out of almost 300 stores and uncovers fabulous merchandise and some bargains that will amaze you. Arranged by neighborhood, the book makes it easy to find what you want at the price you wanted to pay.

Some specific suggestions for the shoppers among us:

● Barnes and Noble Sale Annex, two main locations, at 600 Fifth Ave., and at 17th St. and Fifth Ave., and branches all over town. A bookstore offering such good reductions on all bestsellers and others that it's worth a trip from wherever you are.

● The Complete Traveller, 199 Madison Ave. (at 35th St.). Telephone: 679-4339. The only bookstore in New York City that specializes in travel. Books, guides, and maps—old and new. Has a large section on New York City.

● For real bookstore aficionados, there's a 75-page book called *The Bookstore Book: A Guide to Manhattan Booksellers*, which doesn't overlook a single one. It's written by Robert Egan, is published by Avon, and costs $5.95.

● Sam Goody's, Third Ave. and 43rd St.; 235 West 49th St.; and 1290 Ave. of the Americas. Check Goody's ads in the Sunday *New York Times* for special bargains on all kinds of records and tapes.

● The Record Hunter, 507 Fifth Ave. One reader insists it's "better than Sam Goody's."

● Disco-Mat, branches all over Manhattan. Cheap, cheap records and tapes.

● Bloomingdale's, 59th St. and Lexington Ave. Even *Time* magazine was inspired to superlatives by this extraordinary department store. Stop at Fiorucci's, up the block at 125 East 59th—it's a "must-see" store for the '80s.

● Hudsons, Third Ave. and 13th St. For camping equipment, jeans, outdoor clothing, etc., head downtown to one of New York's best loved stores.

● The Pottery Barn, 24th St. and Tenth Ave. There are other branches of this chain in other parts of the city but this is the biggest. It's filled with cooking accessories, ceramic ware, and gift-type things to bring home with you.

● United Nations Gift Shop, at the United Nations, 46th St. and First Ave. Usually forgotten by New Yorkers, this is an excellent place to buy gifts for everyone. Merchandise is selected from all over the world and whoever does the choosing has excellent taste.

● The Lower East Side. What bargains you'll find, along Orchard St. especially—stylish clothing for men, women, and children. Durable underwear, pretty lingerie, fashionable shoes—all at least 20% below "uptown" prices. Remember that most of the stores here are closed Saturday but open on Sunday.

Help: Travelers Aid Society of New York, 204 East 39th St., 10016. Telephone: 212/679-0200.

Tourist Information: New York Convention and Visitors Bureau, 2 Columbus Circle, 10019. Telephone: 212/397-8222. Everything here is free—from maps to calendars of events to tickets for television shows.

● Jazz-Line. Dial 421-3592 to find out what's going on jazz-wise.

● New York Magazine Information Service. Call 880-0755 to find out what tickets are still available on the day you call. They can also provide hotel and restaurant information. Hours: noon to 6 p.m.

Newcomb

Accommodation: The House of Grace (AYH), P.O. Box 234, 12852. Open June through October. $3. Must bring own linen. Near beaches and hiking trails. AYH membership required (see page 21).

Niagara Falls

Help: Travelers Aid, Family and Children's Service of Niagara Falls, Inc., 826 Chilton Ave.,14301. Telephone: 716/285-6984.

Accommodations: YMCA, 1317 Portage Rd., 14301. Telephone: 716/285-8491. Men only in single and double rooms, which are $10. Women and children (men too) with sleeping bags can be accommodated for $3. By the time this book is in print, the YMCA might have access facilities.

● Superior Henwood's Motel, 9401 Pine Ave., 14304. Telephone: 716/297-2660. $10 to $24 for one; $20 to $30 for two in one bed; $22 to $32 for two in two beds.

Old Forge

Accommodation: Brooker Family Lodge (AYH), ☞ ★ ($1), Rte. 28, 13420. Telephone: 315/369-6072. Open year round. $6. AYH membership preferred. Closed during Easter. Three weeks' advance reservations necessary during winter. To quote the owners, this is the "best AYH facility in New York State." Tell us if you find out.

Oliverea

Accommodation: Mountain Gate Lodge, 12462. Telephone: 914/254-4770. An alpine lodge run by the Appalachian Mountain Club. Offers a shuttle service to and from the bus stop, which is four miles away. Open year round. 15 minutes from ski area. $13.50 per person per night. You are required to take either breakfast or dinner there. Advance reservations necessary.

Oneonta

Help: Project, 85 Chestnut St. Telephone: 607/432-2111.

On Campus: A branch of the State University of New York is here, and a student mentioned that Market St. has several bars where students meet. Perkins Pancake and Steak House on Rte. 7, East End, is a good place to get a reasonable meal.

You'll find the most informative bulletin boards in the basement of Schumacher Hall and in the Administration Building across from the Housing Office.

Oswego

On Campus: The State University of New York has another branch here. The Hewitt Union is the center of on-campus student activity at SUNY Oswego; off-campus, people tend to congregate at Broadwell's on Rte. 104 West and Nunzy's off Lake Shore Rd. West.

Owasco

Accommodation: Camp Y-Owasco (AYH-SA), P.O. Box 341, Sam Adam Lane, Auburn, 13021. Telephone: 315/784-5451. Open May 1 to October 1. Reservations necessary May 1 to May 15 and September 1 to October 1. $2.

Patchogue

Camping: Fire Island National Seashore, 120 Laurel St., 11772. Watch Hill, a campground in East Davis Park, is open all year. Campsites are available by reservation only and are accessible by private boat or ferry only.

Paul Smith's

Accommodation: Rotary Youth Hostel (AYH), 50%, Keese Mill Schoolhouse, 12970. $3.50 May to September; $4.50 October to April. AYH membership required (see page 21).

Plattsburgh

Accommodations: Mountain Air Residence (AYH-SA), 63 Broad St., 12901. Telephone: 518/561-1620. Open May 24 to August 31. $5.
● Econo Lodge, 610 Upper Cornelia St., 12901. Telephone: 518/561-1500. $17.95 to $22.95 for one; $20.95 to $26.95 for two in one bed; $25.95 to $31.95 for two to four in two beds.

Rochester

Help: Life Line—Got A Problem, 716/473-6550.
Tourist Information: Rochester/Monroe County Convention and Visitors Bureau, Inc., 120 Main St. East, 14604. Telephone: 716/546-3070.
On Campus: A friend at the University of Rochester suggests that for U.S. travel information you check the International Student Office, Psychology Building, Room 217. For help in finding accommodations, contact University Apartments, 70 Goler House, 14620. Bulletin boards listing apartments, rides, etc., are in Wilson Commons on the university's River Campus. Wilson Commons also has a snackbar where you can get a cheap meal—hamburgers, hot dogs, sandwiches, hot dishes. A Chinese restaurant that everyone's raving about is the Shanghai Restaurant, 2920 West Henrietta Rd., and you can get an interesting assortment of foods at Fridays, 125 White Spruce Blvd., or the Red Creek Inn, 300 Jefferson Rd.
Accommodations: YMCA, 10%, ★, 100 Gibbs St., 14605. Telephone: 716/325-2880. Men only. $14. Weekly rate: $44. Within walking distance from bus and train stations.
● Best Value Trail Break Motor Inn, 7340 Pittsford–Palmyra Rd., 14450. Telephone: 716/223-1710. $18 to $20 for one; $20 to $22 for two in one bed; $24 to $26 for two in two beds.
● Red Roof Inn, I-90 at N.Y. 15 (Exit 46), Henrietta. Telephone: 716/359-1100. $19.95 for one; $22.95 for two in one bed; $24.95 to $26.95 for two to four in two beds.

Schenectady

Help: INFOLINE of Schenectady, 518/374-2244.

Accommodations: YMCA, 13 State St., 12305. Telephone: 518/374-9136. Men only. $10.50 to $11.50 single (includes membership). Reservations requested.

● YWCA, 44 Washington Ave., 12305. Telephone: 518/374-3394. One block from bus station. Women only. $12 single for members; $15 for nonmembers.

Sharon Springs

Accommodation: Sharon Springs International Hostel (AYH), 181 Union St., 13459. Telephone: 518/284-2460, 284-2836, or 284-2367. Open July and August; open the rest of year by prearrangement only. $5. AYH membership required (see page 21).

Skaneateles

Accommodation: Bel-Aire Motel, 797 West Genesee, 13152. Telephone: 315/685-6720. $15 for one; $16 to $18 for two in one bed; $17 to $19 for two in two beds. Lower rates October to May.

Springville

Accommodation: Home Hostel, 16 Woodward Ave., 14141. Telephone: 716/592-3864. Open May 1 to November 1. Reservations preferred. $4.50. "One-hundred-years-plus old building, beautiful architecture, artistic plaster work."

Staatsburg

Accommodation: Hi Vu Youth Hostel (AYH-SA), 🔲, 12580. Telephone: 914/338-4616. Open May 1 to October 1. $5. Bring your own linen.

Star Lake

Accommodation: Star Lake Campus (AYH-SA), 🔲, 13690. Telephone: 315/268-4980 or 848-2480. Open year round. By reservation only. $5 for AYH members; $6 for nonmembers.

Syracuse

Tourist Information: Syracuse Convention and Visitors Bureau, 1500 One Mony Plaza, 13202. Telephone: 315/422-1343.

Help: Contact, 315/474-7011.

On Campus: Some suggestions for anyone who gets hungry around the campus of Syracuse University: try Jaberwocky in the basement of Kimmel Hall on campus at Comstock and Waverly Ave. for good, cheap vegetarian and meat dishes; Dreck Sub Shop on Marshall St. for submarine sandwiches; Caroma's on Lodi St. for Italian food; Danzer's on Park St. for "dynamite corned beef and roast beef sandwiches"; and King David's on Marshall St. for Middle Eastern cuisine. The bulletin boards listing rides, apartments, etc., can be found in the basement of the Library, in H. B. Crouse Hall, and in the basement of the Hall of Languages and Hendrick's Chapel. For film buffs, inexpensive films are shown at the H. B. Crouse Building on campus; most are open to the public.

Accommodations: Downing International Hostel (AYH), 459 Westcott St., 13210. Telephone: 315/472-5788. Open year round. $5 to $5.50. AYH membership required (see page 21).

● YMCA (AYH-SA), 340 Montgomery St., 13202. Telephone: 315/474-6851. Men only. $12. $6 for AYH members.

● Syracuse University Internationational Living Center, 401 Euclid Ave., 13210. Telephone: 315/423-8418. Summer only. $8 per night. Weekly rate: $35.

Troy

Accommodation: YWCA, ⌂, 21 1st St., 12180. Telephone: 518/274-7100. Women only. $12 to $15. Reservations preferred.

Utica

Help: Travelers Aid, Family Services of Greater Utica, Inc., 239 Genesee St., Suite 500, 13501. Telephone: 315/735-2236.

● Crisis Intervention, 315/736-0883.

Accommodation: Mohawk Valley Community College, 1101 Sherman Dr., 13501. Telephone: 315/797-9530, extension 394. Ask for Office of the Director of Student Life. Men, women, and children. June 1 to August 15. $6 per night plus linen (you can bring your own).

Vestal

Accommodation: Home Hostel (AYH), RD 2, P.O. Box 257, Noyes Rd., 13850. Telephone: 607/748-3529 or 729-1981. $2.50. Must be traveling by bicycle or on foot. AYH membership required (see page 21). Bring your own linen.

Warrensburg

Accommodation: The Glen House (AYH-SA), The Glen, Rte. 28, 12885. Telephone: 518/494-3250 or 623-9951. Open year round. $4. If you call ahead, they will pick you up at certain times during the weekend. Reservations advised. You must be an AYH member, student, or alumni of SUNY at Albany.

Watertown

Accommodation: Best Value New Parrot Motel, Washington St., 13601. Telephone: 315/788-5080. $16 to $20 for one; $24 to $28 for two in one bed; $26 to $34 for two in two beds.

White Plains

Accommodations: YWCA, 69 North Broadway, 10603. Telephone: 914/428-1130. Women over 18 only. $15.25 single. Cots available for $4 per night. Only one room is available for transients, so reservations are strongly recommended.

● YMCA, 250 Mamaroneck Ave., 10605. Telephone: 914/949-8030. Men only. Daily rates start at $15 or $20 per room. Half the rooms have air conditioning, private bath, and television. There's a new diner one-half block away with reasonable prices.

Willet

Accommodation: Home Hostel, Willet Produce Farm, Mooney Hill Rd., 13863. Telephone: 607/863-4435. Several miles from bus and train stations, so if you want to get there you can do one of several things, to quote the host: "thumb a ride, walk, use your imagination, rent a bike, look distressed, dress like a woman. . . . call, someone from the farm may be likely going to town to do errands and might arrange to pick you up." You must pay $5 or lend a hand. Bring sleeping bag. Reservations preferred.

Woodstock

Help: Family of Woodstock, 16 Rock City Rd., 12498. Telephone: 914/338-2370 or 679-2485. "Family provides 24-hour, seven-day-a-week crisis intervention and referral services for Ulster County. We operate a free employment service—most of the jobs are local, part-time, or temporary." They can also provide emergency housing for a work exchange, but there's a three-night limit. According to the people at Family, "Woodstock is real crowded in summer, always hard to find work and housing in, and rents are high, salaries low." Once you're in Woodstock it won't take long for you to find your way to Joshua's for Middle Eastern food and Misty's Behind the Guild for a good lunch that will cost no more than $3. Three Penny has weekly poetry readings and is a good place to meet people.

Yonkers

Accommodation: YWCA, 87 South Broadway, 10701. Telephone: 914/963-0640. Women only. $15. Reservations are accepted in advance; registration from 9 a.m. to 5 p.m.

North Carolina

North Carolina shares the Blue Ridge Parkway with Virginia and the Great Smoky Mountains National Park with Tennessee. Both are spectacular to see. For those who like the seashore best, North Carolina has some of that too: the well-known Outer Banks project a jagged coastline where currents can sometimes be treacherous, marine life is prolific, and there are some of the loveliest beaches on the entire Atlantic Coast. In this same area you'll find Kitty Hawk, the stretch of land where the Wright Brothers made their flying tests in 1903. Campers love North Carolina and hikers can enjoy any or all of the 68 miles of the Appalachian Trail that run through the state.

The cities of North Carolina include Asheville in the mountainous west, where you can tour the Vanderbilts' Biltmore House and Gardens; Winston-Salem, "cigaretteville," a combination of the Moravian-founded town of Salem and the contemporary industrial town of Winston; Raleigh, the state capital; Chapel Hill, the home of the University of North Carolina (Thomas Wolfe's alma mater), the Ashland Memorial Art Center, the Coker Arboretum, and the Morehead Planetarium; and Durham, the home of Duke University and the place where the tobacco industry got started.

Some Special Events: Fiddler's Convention in Denver and Folk Music and Dance Festival in Louisburg (March); Shad Festival in Grifton and Azalea Festival in Wilmington (April); Strawberry Festival in Chadbourn and Potato Festival in Bayboro, which includes a male beauty pageant (May); Bluegrass and Old Time Fiddlers Convention in Mount Airy and National Hollerin' Contest in Spivey's Corner (June); Lumber River Raft and Canoe Regatta in Wagram (July); Festival of Outer Banks Folk Music at Cape Lookout National Seashore and the Strange Seafood Exhibition (tasting marinated octopus, fried squid, and charcoaled shark) in Beaufort (August); Rowan County Fair in Salisbury and Masters of Hang Gliding Championship in Linville (September).

Hitching: Hitchhiking is legal, except on the Interstate system, as long as you stay off the main traveled portion of the road. The Highway Patrol doesn't recommend it but most friends at North Carolina colleges seem to think that hitching in the area of the school is okay; with all the student traffic, the wait for a ride shouldn't be too long.

Tourist Information: North Carolina Travel and Tourism, Department of Commerce, 430 North Salisbury St., Raleigh, NC 27611. Telephone: 919/733-4171.

Asheboro

Accommodation: Econo-Travel Motor Hotel, N.C. 220 Bypass and U.S. 64 on Albemarle Rd., 27203. Telephone: 919/625-1880. $17.95 for one; $21.95 for two in one bed; $25.95 for two in two beds.

Asheville

Accommodations: Econo-Travel Motor Hotel, 190 Tunnel Rd., 28805. Telephone: 704/254-9521. $17.95 to $21.95 for one; $19.95 to $26.95 for two in one bed; $21.95 to $29.95 for two to four in two beds.
● Econo Lodge, Exit 55, off I-40, P.O. Box 9676, 28815. Telephone: 704/298-5519. $20.95 to $22.95 for one; $23.95 to $26.95 for two in one bed; $26.95 to $29.95 for two in two beds.
● Days Inn, I-40 and 70 East (Exit 55), 28815. Telephone: 704/298-5140. $19.88 to $22.88 for one; $23.88 to $26.88 for two.
● Days Inn, 🖫, I-40 at Candler and East Canton Exit 37, Rte. 5, P.O. Box 95, 28715. Telephone: 704/667-9321. $24.88 for one; $28.88 for two. Rates slightly higher June to October.
● Days Inn, 🖫, I-26 and Airport Rd., Rte. 2, Box 273A, Fletcher, 28732. Telephone: 704/684-2281. See above listing for rates.
● Four Seasons Motor Inn, 820 Merrimon Ave., 28804. Telephone: 704/254-5324. $17 to $23 for one or two in one bed; $21 to $26 for two in two beds.
Camping: Blue Ridge Parkway, 700 Northwestern Bank Bldg., 28801. Nine campgrounds, five in North Carolina and four in Virginia. Four open year round, weather permitting. $3 per campsite per night.

Beaufort

Camping: Cape Lookout National Seashore, P.O. Box 690, 28516. Primitive camping all year. Access by boat only.

Benson

Accommodation: Days Inn, I-95 and N.C. 50 (Exit 79), 27504. Telephone: 919/894-2031. $17.88 to $19.88 for one; $21.88 to $23.88 for two.

Blowing Rock

Accommodation: Blowing Rock Assembly Grounds (AYH), 🐟 ★ 10%, 🖫, P.O. Box 974, 28605. Telephone: 704/295-7813. Open all year. $4 summer, $6 winter for AYH members; $8 for nonmembers. A mountaintop retreat furnished with paneling and carpets.

Bryson City

Accommodation: Nantahala Outdoor Center (AYH-SA), 🛏 (for hostel beds), ♿, Star Rte., Box 68, 28713. Telephone: 704/488-2175. Open year round. $3 for AYH members. A hostel and a motel. Double-bedded rooms in the motel are $19. Located 13 miles southwest of Bryson City on U.S. 19, where the Appalachian Trail crosses the Nantahala River in Wesser. The bus will stop at the center (west of Bryson City) if you request. No linen available in hostel rooms. Reservations advisable during summer. Nantahala is largely a white-water and outdoor recreation and instruction center.

Chapel Hill

"Chapel Hill has had a reputation for being progressive, diverse, and activist since the '60s. It's a great town. I grew up here, left for college, and chose to move back. Please come!"

Help: Access Inc., Switchboard, 919/929-7177.

On Campus: Some 23,000 students inhabit Chapel Hill, many of them studying at the University of North Carolina. One of them recommends that you check with the Department of University Housing, Carr Building, UNC Campus 103A, about possible dorm space for a night or two. You might check the bulletin board or information desk in Frank Porter Graham Union for details on special events, rides, etc., or the *Village Advocate,* campus newspaper. Students meet at Harrisons, 149½ East Franklin St., and He's Not Here, 112½ West Franklin. You can find an inexpensive home-style meal at the Porthole on Old Fraternity Row, or Dip's Country Kitchen, 405 West Rosemary.

Accommodation: Tar Heel Motel, 15-501 Bypass (Eastgate Shopping Center), 27514. Telephone: 919/929-3090. Near the University. $15.60 for one; $18.20 for two.

Charlotte

Help: Traveler's Aid, 301 South Brevard, Room 217, 28202. Telephone: 704/334-7288.

Accommodations: YWCA, 3420 Park Rd., 28209. Telephone: 704/525-5770. Women over 17 only. $14 with private bath; $12.50 without. Cafeteria open Monday to Friday; on weekends you can eat at a nearby shopping center.

• YMCA, 400 East Morehead St., 28202. Telephone: 704/333-7771. Men only. $9 single. Weekly rate: $65 first week, $32 second week.

• Motel 6, 512 Clanton Rd., 28210. Telephone: 704/527-0230. $12.95 for one; $16.95 for two; $19.95 for three.

• Motel 6, 3433 Mulberry Church Rd., 28208. Telephone: 704/394-0189. See above listing for rates.

• Days Inn, ♿, I-85 and N.C. 27, 4419 Tuckaseegee Rd., Tuckaseegee, 28208. Telephone: 704/394-5181. $24.88 for one; $29.88 for two.

• Days Inn, ♿, I-85 and Sugar Creek Rd., 1408 Sugar Creek Rd., Sugar

Creek, 28213. Telephone: 704/597-8110. See above listing for rates.

● Econo Lodge, 2222 East Independence Blvd., 28205. Telephone: 704/372-6250. $20.95 for one; $24.95 for two in one bed; $27.95 for two in two beds.

● Econo Lodge, I-85 and Sugar Creek Rd., P.O. Box 26623, Sugar Creek, 28213. Telephone: 704/597-0470. $21.95 for one; $25.95 for two in one bed; $29.95 for two in two beds.

Concord

Accommodation: Days Inn, ⬛, I-85 and N.C. 73, P.O. Box 3322, 28025. Telephone: 704/786-9121. $20.88 for one; $25.88 for two.

Durham

Help: Hassle House Crisis Line, 1022 Urban Ave., 27701. Telephone: 919/688-4353.

Accommodations: Duke University International House, 🐟 ★ (summer only), 2022 Campus Dr., 27706. Telephone: 919/684-3585. Foreign students only in winter, with a two-night limit. $7 single; $10 double. If space permits, American students accepted in summer. Reservations eight to ten days in advance.

● Days Inn, I-85 and Redwood Rd., 27704. Telephone: 919/688-4338. $18.88 to $19.88 for one; $22.88 to $23.88 for two.

● Econo-Travel Motor Hotel, 2337 Guess Rd., 27705. Telephone: 919/286-7746. $18.95 for one; $22.95 for two in one bed; $24.95 for two in two beds.

● Motel 6, 2101 Holloway St., 27701. Telephone: 919/682-8043. See Charlotte listing for rates.

Fayetteville

Accommodations: Days Inn, I-95 and U.S. 13 (Exit 58), Rte. 1, Box 216BB, 28395. Telephone: 919/323-1255. $19.88 to $21.88 for one; $23.88 to $25.88 for two.

● Motel 6, 525 South Eastern Blvd., 28301. Telephone: 919/323-1957. See Charlotte listing for rates.

Gastonia

Accommodation: Days Inn, ⬛, I-85 and Edgewood Rd., P.O. Box 338, Bessemer City, 28016. Telephone: 704/867-0231. $20.88 for one; $25.88 for two.

Goldsboro

Accommodations: Days Inn, ⬛, U.S. 70 Bypass and 2000 Wayne Memorial Dr., 27530. Telephone: 919/734-9471. $18.88 for one; $22.88 for two.

● Motel 6, 701 U.S. 70 Bypass East, 27530. Telephone: 919/736-7140. See Charlotte listing for rates.

● Econo-Travel Motor Hotel, 704 U.S. 70 Bypass East, 27530. Telephone:

919/736-4510. $14.95 for one; $16.95 for two in one bed; $18.95 for two in two beds.

Greensboro

Help: Family Service of Greater Greensboro, Inc. (Travelers Aid), 1301 North Elm St., 27401. Telephone: 919/373-1341.

Accommodations: Econo Lodge, 512 Farragut St., 27406. $15.95 to $17.95 for one; $17.95 to $20.95 for two in one bed; $19.95 to $23.95 for two in two beds.

● Motel 6, 831 Greenhaven Dr., 27406. Telephone: 919/294-1305. See Charlotte listing for rates.

● Days Inn, 🛇, I-40 West on Hwy. 68, North Airport Exit, Rte. 9, Box 319, 27409. Telephone: 919/668-0476. $19.88 to $21.88 for one; $24.88 to $26.88 for two.

Greenville

Accommodation: Econo-Travel Motor Hotel, 810 Memorial Dr., 27834. Telephone: 919/752-0214. $17.95 for one; $21.95 for two in one bed; $23.95 for two in two beds.

Henderson

Accommodation: Days Inn, I-85 and Ruin Creek Rd., P.O. Box 808, 27536. Telephone: 919/492-4041. $18.88 to $19.88 for one; $22.88 to $23.88 for two.

Hendersonville

Accommodation: Briarwood Motel, 1510 Greenville Hwy., 28739. Telephone: 704/692-8284. $17 to $20 for one double bed; $20 to $26 for two double beds.

High Point

Accommodation: Motel 6, 200 Ardale Dr., 27260. Telephone: 919/886-5041. See Charlotte listing for rates.

Jefferson

Accommodation: Mount Jefferson Motel, √ 10%, 216 South Main St., 28640. Telephone: 919/246-4386. $20 for one; $24 for two in one bed; $25 for two in two beds. Winter rates lower.

Kinston

Accommodation: Econo-Travel Motor Hotel, 212 East Newbern Rd.,

28501. Telephone: 919/523-8146. $16.95 for one; $19.95 for two in one bed; $22.95 for two in two beds.

Lexington

Accommodation: Best Value Royal 8 Motel, 402 National Blvd., 27292. Telephone: 704/246-5111. $17 to $20 for one; $20 to $30 for two in one bed; $30 to $40 for two in two beds.

Lumberton

Accommodations: Days Inn, I-95 and N.C. 211 Exit, P.O. Box 937, 28358. Telephone: 919/738-6401. $19.88 to $20.88 for one; $23.88 to $24.88 for two.
 ● Motel 6, 2365 I-95 Service Rd., Rte. 3, 28358. Telephone: 919/738-8930. See Charlotte listing for rates.
 ● Susse Chalet Motor Lodge, I-95 (Exit 14) at junction of U.S. 74, 28358. Telephone: 919/738-1444. $19.70 for one; $23.70 for two; $29.70 for four.
 ● Scottish Inn, I-95 and Hwy. 211, Exit 211, 28358. Telephone: 919/738-7121. $14 for one; $17 for two in one bed; $22 for two in two beds.

Maggie Valley

Accommodation: Scottish Inn, Hwys. 276 and 19, 28751. Telephone: 704/926-1251. $24 for one or two.

Manteo–Cape Hatteras

Camping: Cape Hatteras National Seashore, P.O. Box 675, 27954. Five campgrounds at Cape Point, Frisco, Ocracoke, Oregon Inlet, and Salvo. $4 per campsite per night.

Monroe

Accommodation: Friendship Inn–Hilltop Motel, junction of Hwy. 74 and U.S. 601, 28110. Telephone: 704/289-1581. $17.25 to $25 for one; $21 to $25 for two in one bed; $24 to $28 for two in two beds.

Morganton

Accommodation: Days Inn, I-40 and Hwy. 18 South, 28655. Telephone: 704/433-0011. $22.88 for one; $26.88 for two.

New Bern

Accommodation: Friendship Inn–Curtis Motel, north of New Bern, 28560. Telephone: 919/638-3011. $14 to $16 for one; $18 to $22 for two in one bed; $20 to $24 for two in two beds.

Raleigh

Help: Family Services of Wake County, 3803 Computer Dr., Suite 101, 27609. Telephone: 919/781-9317.

Accommodations: YMCA, 1601 Hillsborough St., 27605. Telephone: 919/832-6601. Men only. $8.50 with shared bath; $10.50 with private bath.

● YMCA, 600 South Bloodworth St., 27611. Telephone: 919/833-1256. Men only. $5 single.

● Econo-Travel Motor Hotel, 5110 Hollyridge Dr., 27612. Telephone: 919/782-3201. $20 for one; $23 for two in one bed; $26 for two in two beds.

Roanoke Rapids

Accommodation: Econo-Travel Motor Hotel, 1615 Roanoke Rapids Rd., Weldon, 27890. Telephone: 919/536-2131. $17.95 for one; $20.95 for two in one bed; $22.95 for two in two beds.

Rocky Mount

Accommodations: YWCA, 215 Lexington St., 27801. Telephone: 919/442-0186. Women only. Ten-year-old, three-story building is usually filled with permanent residents, but call and see if there's room. $2.60 per night.

● Days Inn, I-95 and N.C. 48, Goldrock Exit 145, Rte. 1, Box 155, Battleboro, 27809. Telephone: 919/446-0621. $19.88 to $20.88 for one; $23.88 to $24.88 for two.

● Econo-Travel Motor Hotel, Rte. 1, Box 161-B, Battleboro, 27809. Telephone: 919/446-2411. $16.95 for one; $19.95 for two in one bed; $22.95 for two in two beds.

● Imperial 400 Motor Inn, Rte. 1, Box 162A, 27809. Telephone: 919/977-3505. $16 to $24 for one; $20 to $28 for two in one bed; $24 to $32 for two in two beds.

Rowland

Accommodation: Days Inn, ♿, I-95 and U.S. 301, at South of the Border, P.O. Box 147, 28383. Telephone: 919/422-3366. $16.88 to $19.88 for one; $20.88 to $23.88 for two.

Salisbury

Accommodations: Days Inn, ♿, I-85 and Klumac Rd., 28144. Telephone: 704/636-8910. $20.88 for one; $25 for two.

● Econo Lodge, 1011 East Innes St., 28144. Telephone: 704/633-8850. $18.95 for one; $22.95 for two in one bed; $25.95 for two to four in two beds.

Sanford

Accommodation: Econo Lodge, 404 Carthage St., 27330. Telephone: 919/775-2328. $18.95 for one; $22.95 for two in one bed; $25.95 for two in two beds.

Selma

   Accommodations: Econo-Travel Motor Hotel, P.O. Box 786, 27576. Telephone: 919/965-5756. $13.95 for one; $16.95 for two in one bed; $19.95 for two in two beds.
   ● Days Inn, I-95 and U.S. 70A (Exit 97), Rte. 3, Box 22, 27576. Telephone: 919/965-3762. $18.88 for one; $22.88 for two. Rates higher December 15 to May 31.

Southern Pines

   Accommodation: Superior Charlton Motel, U.S. 1, 28387. Telephone: 919/692-2232. $22 for one; $24 for two in one bed; $28 for two in two beds.

Statesville

   Accommodations: Scottish Inn, I-40 Exit at Hwy. 21, 28677. Telephone: 704/872-9891. $18 for one; $22 for two in one bed; $24 for two in two beds.
   ● Days Inn, ♿, I-40 and U.S. 21 North, 28677. Telephone: 704/873-5252. $22.88 for one; $27.88 for two.

Washington

   Accommodation: Econo-Travel Motor Hotel, 1220 West 15th St., 27889. Telephone: 919/946-7781. $16.95 for one; $20.95 for two in one bed; $23.95 for two in two beds.

Wilmington

   Help: Family Service/Travelers Aid, First Union National Bank Bldg., P.O. Box 944, 28402. Telephone: 919/763-5189.
   ● Open House/Crisis Line, 919/763-3695.
   Accommodations: Days Inn, ♿, U.S. 17 and U.S. 74, 5040 Market St., 28405. Telephone: 919/799-6300. $17.88 to $21.88 for one; $21.88 to $26.88 for two. Rates slightly higher from June 27 to July 12.
   ● Econo-Travel Motor Hotel, 4118 North Market St., 28403. Telephone: 919/762-4426. $15.95 to $17.95 for one; $18.95 to $20.95 for two in one bed; $21.95 to $23.95 for two in two beds.
   ● Motel 6, 2828 Market St., 28401. Telephone: 919/762-4496. See Charlotte listing for rates.

"I'd like to recommend Tuesday's, 4601 Oleander Dr., for anyone passing through Wilmington. It's a nice, well-done restaurant, reasonably priced, and particularly recommended for its all-you-can-eat salad plus bread and cheese. That was probably the best meal in my seven weeks of travel."

   Local residents also recommend Stock Market, also on Oleander Dr., and Valentino's for Italian food at two locations, 4410 Shipyard Blvd. and 5022 Market St.

Winston-Salem

Help: Family Service, Inc. (Travelers Aid), 610 Coliseum Dr., 27106. Telephone: 919/722-8173.

Accommodation: Motel 6, 3810 Patterson Ave., 27105. Telephone: 919/724-7240. See Charlotte listing for rates.

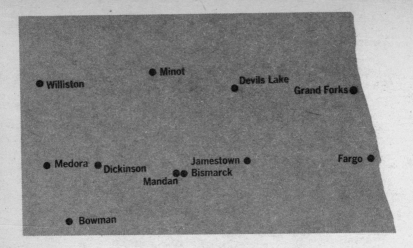

North Dakota

The sunsets, the thunderstorms, the cloud formations, and the northern lights of August are bound to dazzle anyone who has never before experienced "the plains" of North Dakota. The summers there are hot and dry, and the winters are cold and snowy. No matter what the time of year, the wide-open spaces are breathtaking.

North Dakota is primarily an agricultural state, with flatlands and wheat fields in the east and the rugged Badlands in the west. Most of the people who live there are of Scandinavian or German descent or they represent several tribes of native Americans including the Mandan and the Sioux.

Ten percent of the state's population lives in Fargo, the home of North Dakota State University. Not surprisingly, Fargo boasts a very active arts community—a symphony orchestra, opera company, community theater, and dance troupe. It's also the location of Bonanzaville, a restored western pioneer village, and Trollwood, a park devoted to the arts. During fair weather there are free outdoor concerts and arts and crafts exhibits, and during the winter there's cross-country skiing and ice skating. Fargo is near the border of Minnesota and its "sister city" of Moorhead, Minnesota. Moorhead State University and Concordia College, both liberal arts schools, are in Moorhead. The university has an excellent theater department with a good performing arts series and a summer theater workshop.

Other places to visit in North Dakota include the capital city of Bismarck, located on the Missouri River and the site of the Mandan Indian Mounds and Reservation; Fort Totten Indian Reservation; the International Peace Gardens, on the border between the U.S. and Canada; and most certainly, the Badlands at and around Medora, where you'll find the Theodore Roosevelt National Park. The park, definitely worth a visit, features restorations, museums, and, on summer nights, outdoor performances commemorating the history of the area through drama and music.

Some Special Events: Rodeos in Trenton and Binford (May); Turkey Barbecue in Lakota and Great River Race Weekend in Enderlin (June); Old-Fashioned Fourth of July in Langdon and Threshing Bee in Crosby (July); and Oktoberfest in Bismarck (in October, of course).

Hitching: A North Dakota law prohibits soliciting a ride from the roadway, which is defined as the main traveled portion of the highway. A friend from North Dakota State University says that although hitchhiking is not very well accepted, and hitchhikers are often considered to be nuisances by many people, hitching is probably safer in North Dakota than in many other states.

Tourist Information: North Dakota Tourism Promotion Division, State Capitol Grounds, Bismarck, ND 58505. Telephone: 701/224-2525.

Bismarck

Accommodations: Friendship Inn–Bismarck Motor Hotel, 2301 East Main St., 58501. Telephone: 701/223-2474. $21 for two in one bed; $25 for two in two beds.

● Econ-O-Inn of Bismarck, 1505 Interchange Ave., 58501. Telephone: 701/223-8060. $17.50 for one; $21.50 for two in one bed; $23.50 for two in two beds.

● Thrifty Scot Motel, 1300 Capitol Ave. East, 58501. Telephone: 701/223-9151. $17.90 to $22.90 for one; $21.90 to $23.90 for two in one bed; $26.90 to $28.90 for two in two beds.

● Motel 6, 2433 State St., 58501. Telephone: 701/255-1851. $12.95 for one; $16.95 for two; $19.95 for up to four.

Devils Lake

Accommodation: Motel 6, U.S. 2 and N.D. 19, 58301. To open in 1982. See Bismarck listing for rates.

Dickinson

Accommodations: Econ-O-Inn of Dickinson, I-94 and N.D. 22, 58601. Telephone: 701/227-1891. $15.50 to $18.50 for one; $20.50 for two in one bed; $23.50 for two in two beds.

● Friendship Inn–Nodak, East I-94 Business Loop, Hwy. 10 on East Villard St., 58601. Telephone: 701/225-5119. $17 to $21 for one; $20 to $24 for two in one bed; $24 to $27 for two in two beds.

● Friendship Inn–Queen City Motel, eight blocks west off N.D. 22 on I-94, Business Loop, 58601. Telephone: 701/225-5121. $17 to $21 for one; $19.50 to $23.50 for two in one bed; $24 to $36 for two in two beds.

Fargo

Help: Hotline, 701/235-SEEK.

On Campus: The Student Affairs Office at North Dakota State University is the best place to go for help in getting your bearings. At the Trader and Trapper in Moorhead and the Old Broadway in Fargo you'll run into lots of students.

Accommodations: YWCA, 411 Broadway, 58102. Telephone: 701/232-2547. Women only. $8.50 single. Weekly rate: $50. There's a reduction if you bring your own sleeping bag.

● Econ-O-Inn of Fargo, I-29 and 13th Ave. South, 58103. Telephone: 701/282-6300. $16.50 for one; $21.50 for two in one bed; $23.50 for two in two beds.

● Motel 6, 2202 South University Dr., 58102. Telephone: 701/235-4411. See Bismarck listing for rates.

● Thrifty Scot Motel, 901 38th St. SW, 58103. Telephone: 701/282-9100. $16.90 to $21.90 for one; $20.90 to $22.90 for two in one bed; $25.90 to $27.90 for two in two beds.

● Regal 8 Inn, 1202 36th St. South, 58103. Telephone: 701/232-9251. $17.88 for one; $20.88 for two in one bed; $23.88 for two to four in two beds.

Grand Forks

Accommodations: Regal 8 Inn, 1211 47th St. North, 58201. Telephone: 701/775-0511. See Fargo listing for rates.

● Econ-O-Inn, I-90 and U.S. 2, 58201. Telephone: 701/775-0555. $15.95 for one; $19.95 for two in one bed. $21.95 for two in two beds.

Jamestown

Accommodations: Motel 6, I-94 and U.S. 281, 58401. See Bismarck listing for rates.

● Friendship Inn–Tumbleweed Motor Hotel, 824 20th St. on I-94 and U.S. 281, 58401. Telephone: 701/252-5222. $16.50 to $18.50 for one; $18.50 to $20.50 for two in one bed; $22.50 to $26.50 for two in two beds.

Mandan

Accommodation: Best Value Lewis & Clark Hotel, 404 West Main, 58554. Telephone: 701/663-6465. $18 for one; $22 for two in one bed; $26 for two in two beds.

Medora

Camping: Theodore Roosevelt National Park, P.O. Box 7, 58645. Cottonwood and Squaw Creek campsites open year round at $2 per night; Halliday Wells campsite open May to September for free. Reservations accepted.

Minot

Accommodations: YMCA, 1st St. and First Ave. SE, 58701. Telephone: 701/852-0141. Men over 18 only. $9.77. Weekly rate: $27.28.

● YWCA, 205 Third Ave. SE, 58701. Telephone: 701/838-1812. Women only. $8 single; $11 double. "We have a large, recreation-type room and this is used by large groups of women and girls who bring their sleeping bags. The normal fee for use of this room is $2.50 per night per person." Reservations recommended.

● Econ-O-Inn of Minot, Hwy. 83 North at 22nd Ave. NW, 58701. Telephone: 701/852-3411. $16.50 for one; $20.50 for two in one bed; $22.50 for two in two beds.

Ohio

Ohio, the Iroquois word for "beautiful river," became a state in 1803. But its history dates back to the early Mound Builders, whose large earthworks can still be seen at places like Serpent Mound and Fort Ancient.

There is rich farmland in the northwestern part of the state, while the southeastern lands abound with recreational areas, including the caves of the Hocking Hills. There's a famous Pumpkin Festival each fall at Circleville, the gateway to the Hocking Hills.

Greenville is the site of the Greenville Treaty, which signified the unsuccessful effort of the great chief, Tecumseh, to unite tribes in order to withstand the usurping of their lands by the settlers. This story is depicted in the outdoor drama *Tecumseh!*, given each summer on Sugar Loaf Mountain, near Chillicothe.

Ohio played an important role in the story of the underground railroad. Many runaway slaves came up the Scioto and Olentangy Rivers after crossing the Ohio River through Columbus and Worthington. In the Worthington Historical Society's annual tours of old homes, you can see some of the slave hiding places.

The first organized settlement in the Northwest Territory was founded in 1788 at Marietta on the Ohio River. Marietta College, the Lafayette Hotel (named for its most famous guest), and an old riverboat and museum are among the attractions there.

In northern Ohio, Blossom Music Center, an outdoor amphitheater near Akron, is the summer home of the Cleveland Symphony.

Springfield, home of Wittenberg University, is located just off I-70 between Columbus and Dayton. The old National Road ended here at one time and the Pennsylvania House was the inn at the "end of the trail." A town of 80,000,

Springfield has a symphony, a theater group, an art center, and a long-established photographic society. The Summer Arts Festival offers performing arts throughout July, free to the public, in Cliff and Snyder Parks near the campus. And just nine miles south of Springfield is Yellow Springs, an interesting village of small shops and the home of Antioch Univeristy.

Ohio has 71 state parks, 59 of which have lakes. One of them, Hueston Woods, is located near Oxford, the home of Miami University and the place where McGuffey wrote his *Eclectic Readers*.

Ohio has produced eight presidents of the United States and a variety of other famous people from Thomas Edison (whose birthplace can be visited in Milan) to the Wright Brothers. The famous Air Force Museum near Dayton depicts the history of aviation and the Neil Armstrong Museum at Wapakoneta is named for the first man to walk on the moon.

For a good, understandably chauvinstic, source of general information on Ohio, get a copy of the state tourist office's booklet, *Your Passport to Ohio*.

Some Ohioans think of themselves as easterners, some as midwesterners. You'll have to decide for yourself whose side you're on. Ohio has many, many college towns where you'll be welcome.

Some Special Events: Winter Ski Carnival in Mansfield (February); Spring Art Fair in Columbus (March); Trout Festival in Jackson and Maple Festival in Chardon (April); Dulcimer Days in Coshocton (May); Ox Roast in Centerville (June); River Recreation Festival in Gallipolis (July); and Ohio Shaker Festival in Kettering (August).

Hitching: It's legal if you stay off the traveled portion of the road, except on freeways or Interstates. The State Highway Patrol says that, in general, hitching is discouraged in Ohio. From what we could figure out from information sent to us by several campuses, hitching is okay in the area around campus but not very good in more rural sections.

Tourist Information; Ohio Office of Travel and Tourism, P.O. Box 1001, Columbus, OH 43216. In Ohio call toll free 800-BUCKEYE.

Akron

Accommodations: YWCA, 146 South High St., 44308. Telephone: 216/253-6131. Women only. $9 plus 75¢ key deposit for room with no wash basin; $10 with basin; $11 with connecting bath. Weekly rate: $21 to $27.75. (10¢ per night membership fee for transients.) Reservations suggested.

● Red Roof Inn, 🔄, I-77 at Ohio 18. Telephone: 216/666-0566. $17.95 for one; $20.95 for two in one bed; $22.95 to $24.95 for two to four in two beds.

Alliance

Accommodation: YMCA, 205 South Union Ave., 44601. Telephone: 216/823-1930. Men only. $9.40 single. Weekly rate: $24.60. $15 key deposit.

Athens

Help: Careline, 614/593-3344, 596-5211, or 385-8484.

On Campus: Ohio University is in Athens, an "off-the-beaten-track college town," according to one Athenian. Another described it as "a nice place to live.

. . . Beautiful Appalachian countryside." For help and advice in finding your way around, check at the Information Center, Baker Center, 614/594-6811. There's a bulletin board in Baker Center on the ground floor where you'll find rides, apartments, etc. To meet students, go to CJ's, Bojangles, Crippled Creek Bar, or the Frontier Room in Baker Center. We've been told that there may be dorm rooms to rent for $9 per night; check at the International Student and Faculty Services Office (tel. 614/594-5773). You may also ask them for a mimeographed list of several inexpensive motels in the area.

Bowling Green

Help: The Link, 525 Pike St. Telephone: 419/352-1545.

Accommodation: Wintergarden Community Lodge Youth Hostel (AYH), Wintergarden Rd., 43402. Telephone: 419/352-9349. Open year round. $2 summer; $2.50 winter. AYH membership required (see page 21).

On Campus: Bowling Green State University is described by a student as "quite dull, really," but she does concede that you can call the Fact Line (tel. 419/372-2445) for information on the good variety of concerts and movies in Bowling Green. There are several bars where students congregate, including Uptown, Dixie Electric, Howard's Club H, and Mr. Bojangles, and there's Corner Kitchen, 183 South Main, for inexpensive full-course meals. The Union Hotel at the university has reasonably priced rooms. If all else fails, "there is a good, unobstructed view of tomato, wheat, and soybean fields".

Canton

Help: Crisis Center, 1341 Market North. Telephone: 216/452-6000.

Accommodations: YWCA, 🏠, 231 6th St. NE, 44702. Telephone: 216/453-7644. Near downtown. $8 per night; $40 weekly. Women only.

● Red Roof Inn, I-77 at Everhard Road, 44720. Telephone: 216/499-1970. $19.95 for one; $22.95 for two in one bed; $24.95 to $26.95 for two to four in two beds.

Chillicothe

Accommodation: Home Hostel (AYH). Telephone: 614/775-3632 or 773-3989. $2.50. AYH membership required (see page 21).

Cincinnati

"The downtown area of Cincinnati is thriving, unlike lots of other cities."

Help: Travelers Aid, 700 Walnut St., Room 307, 45202. Telephone: 513/721-7660.

Tourist Information Greater Cincinnati Convention and Visitors Bureau, Inc., 200 West 5th St., 45202. Telephone: 513/621-2142.

Accommodations: University of Cincinnati, Sander Hall, 🏠, Mail Location #45, 45221. Telephone: 513/475-6461 or 475-6580. $12 single; $8 per person double. Affiliation with the university is required. Space available in summer only. Reservations strongly suggested.

● Home Hostel (AYH). Telephone: 513/541-1972. $2. AYH membership required (see page 21).

● Red Roof Inn, 🔊, I-71 at Kennedy Rd., Norwood, 45213. Telephone: 513/531-6589. See Canton listing for rates.

● Red Roof Inn, I-75 at Sharon Rd. (Exit 15), Sharonville, 45246. Telephone 513/771-5141. See Canton listing for rates.

● Days Inn, I-75 and Ohio 63 (Exit 29), 150 Garver Rd., Monroe, 45050. Telephone: 513/539-9221. $20.88 to 23.88 for one; $25.88 to $28.88 for two. Rates higher June to August.

● Days Inn, 🔊, I-75 and Exit 189B, 1945 Dixie Hwy., Ft. Wright, KY 41011. Telephone: 606/341-8801. $22.88 for one; $27.88 for two.

● Days Inn, I-75 and Ohio 338, Exit 175, Walton, KY 41094. Telephone: 606/485-4151. $19.88 for one; $23.88 for two.

Cleveland

Help: Travelers Aid Center for Human Services, 1005 Huron Rd., 44115. Telephone: 216/241-6400 or 241-6402. Also at Greyhound Bus Terminal, 1465 Chester Ave. and Cleveland Hopkins International Airport.

Tourist Information: Cleveland Convention Bureau, 1301 East 6th St., 44114. Telephone: 216/621-4110, or toll free in Ohio, 800/362-1888; outside Ohio, 800/321-1999.

Accommodations: YWCA, 3201 Euclid Ave., 44115. Telephone: 216/881-6878, extension 158. Women only. $16.58 single. Weekly rate: $90.35.

● Red Roof Inn, I-71 at Bagley Rd. (Exit 235), Middleburg Hts., 44130. To open in 1982. See Canton listing for rates.

● Red Roof Inn, I-77 at Rockside Rd., Independence, 44131. Telephone: 216/447-0030. See Canton listing for rates.

● Red Roof Inn, I-71 at Ohio 82, Strongsville, 44136. Telephone: 216/238-0170. See Canton listing for rates.

● Red Roof Inn, 🔊, I-90 at Ohio 306 (Exit 193), Willoughby, 44094. Telephone: 216/946-9872. See Canton listing for rates.

● Best Value Travelers Inn, 32751 Lorain Rd., 44039. Telephone: 216/327-6311 or 777-7456. $14.95 to $17.95 for one; $19.95 to $25.95 for two in one bed; $22.95 to $29.95 for two in two beds.

● Best Value Yorktown Motorist Hotel, 11860 Clifton Blvd., 44107. Telephone: 216/228-5555. $16 to $22 for one; $20 to 25 for two in one bed; $21.50 to $26.50 for two in two beds.

Columbus

"A conservative city going through adolescence."

Tourist Information: Columbus Convention Bureau, 50 West Broad St., Suite 2540, 43215. Telephone: 614/221-6623.

Help: Community Information Referral, 614/221-2255.

On Campus: A piece of advice from a student at Ohio State University is "Don't jaywalk near OSU or in downtown Columbus." To meet students, go to Mr. Brown's, Stache and Little Brothers, High St. Brewing Co., or the Blue

Danube Restaurant. In spring there are quite a few on-campus festivals; just stop at the student union at 13th Ave. and North High St. for information.

Accommodations: YWCA, 65 South 4th St., 43215. Telephone: 614/224-9121. Women only. $12 per person.

● Central Branch, YMCA, (AYH-SA), ★, 40 West Long St., 43215. Telephone: 614/224-1131. Men only. $9.50. Weekly rate: $34.50. $4.50 for AYH members.

● Home Hostel (AYH). Telephone: 614/235-7669. Open all year. $2. Generally take foreign visitors or bicyclists only. AYH membership required (see page 21). Bring your own linen. Family provides meals.

● Red Roof Inn, I-70 at Brice Rd. 43068. Telephone: 614/864-3683. See Akron listing for rates.

● Days Inn, I-70 and Brice Rd., 5980 Scarsborough Rd., 43227. Telephone: 614/868-9290. $20.88 for one; $24.88 for two.

● Days Inn, I-270 and U.S. 62, 3131 Broadway, Grove City, 43123. Telephone: 614/871-0065. $20.88 for one; $24.88 for two.

● Red Roof Inn, I-71 at Morse Rd. (Exit 116), 43229. Telephone: 614/846-8520. See Akron listing for rates.

● Red Roof Inn, I-71 at Stringtown Rd., 43123. Telephone: 614/875-8543. See Akron listing for rates.

● Red Roof Inn, I-70 at Rome-Hilliard Rd., 43228. Telephone: 614/878-9245. See Akron listing for rates.

Dayton

Help: Travelers Aid, 184 Salem Ave., 45406. Telephone: 513/222-9481.

On Campus: For advice and general help during office hours you can call the Campus Information Center of the University of Dayton (tel. 513/229-3244). There's a bulletin board in the lower level of the Kennedy Union and you can meet University of Dayton students in the snackbar of the Union or in one of several bars in the Brown Street area adjacent to campus. At Ruffino's on Brown St. you'll find spaghetti, salad, and bread for $2.95.

Accommodations: Central YMCA, 117 West Monument Ave., 45402. Telephone: 513/223-5201. Men only. $10. Weekly rate: $33 single; $38 double. Cafeteria in building.

● YWCA, 141 West Third, 45402. Telephone: 513/461-5550. Women only. $5 to $12.60 single. Currently being renovated and will have cooking facilities.

● Red Roof Inn, I-75 at Ohio 725 West, Miamisburg, 45342. Telephone: 513/866-0705. See Akron listing for rates.

● Red Roof Inn, I-75 at Little York Rd. (Exit 60), 45414. Telephone: 513/898-1054. See Akron listing for rates.

● Days Inn, I-75 and Little York Rd. (Exit 60), 7470 Miller Lane, 45414. Telephone: 513/898-4946. $20.88 for one; $25.88 for two.

● Days Inn, I-75 and Springboro Rd. (Exit 50), 2455 Springboro Rd., Moraine, 45439. Telephone: 513/298-0380. $21.88 for one; $26.88 for two.

● Days Inn, ⬙, I-75 and Ohio 725 (Exit 44), 8101 Springboro Pike, 45342. Telephone: 513/434-8750. $22.88 for one; $26.88 for two.

● Travel Master Inn, 225 West 1st St., 45402. Telephone: 513/224-1121. $19 to $25 for one; $22 to $28 for two.

● Econo-Travel Motor Hotel, 316 Emma St., 45840. Telephone: 419/422-0154. $17.95 for one; $21.95 for two in one bed; $25.95 for two in two beds.

Fostoria

Accommodation: YMCA, 154 West Center St., 44830. Telephone: 419/435-6608. Men only. $8.95 plus $1 membership fee.

Gallipolis

Accommodation: Econo-Travel Motor Hotel, 389 Jackson Pike, 45631. Telephone: 614/446-7071. $22 for one; $25 for two in one bed; $28 for two in two beds.

Granville

On Campus: "The attraction of Granville is in its out-of-the-way, quiet atmosphere—you can enjoy the beauty of the natural surroundings." A student at Denison University here also mentioned that you can find home-style cooking at the Evergreens. Their specialty is red velvet cake. In Slayter Hall Union there is a bulletin board on the second floor with all kinds of listings.

Hebron

Accommodation: Motel 76, 10772 Lancaster Rd. SW, 43025. Telephone: 614/467-2311. $16.95 to $18.95 for one; $18.95 to $20.95 for two in one bed; $19.95 to $22.95 for two in two beds.

Hiram

Accommodation: Hiram College, 44234. Telephone: 216/569-3211. Men, women, and children. $10 single, $15 double in a converted college dorm.

Jeffersonville

Accommodation: Days Inn, I-71 and U.S. 35 (Exit 65), P.O. Box 127, 43128. Telephone: 614/948-2381. $20.88 to $21.88 for one; $24.88 to $25.88 for two. Rates slightly higher June to October.

Kent

Help: Town Hall II Help Line, 225 East College Ave., 44240. Telephone: 216/678-4357 (24 hours a day). The people here are willing to help: "We will do our best to help those who call or come to our door." They cannot, however, provide shelter except in emergencies.

On Campus: You can get from the Kent campus to other parts of the city cheaply on the KSU bus—it's available to nonstudents too. A good place to meet other students is at one of the cafeterias on the Kent State campus, Red Radish vegetarian restaurant, and Stone Jug restaurant and bar. You may be able to stay at Korb Guest Hall on campus; call 672-7000 for information.

Accommodation: Friendship Inn–Eastwood, Main St. between Kent and Ravenna, 44240. Telephone: 216/678-1111. $18.50 to $22 for one; $24 to $26 for two in one bed; $28 to $40 for two in two beds.

Lima

Accommodations: Home Hostel (AYH). Telephone: 419/222-7301 or 226-3169. 48-hour advance reservation advised. AYH membership required (see page 21).

● Susse Chalet Inn and Motor Lodge, I-75 (Exits 127, 127B) at junction of Rte. 81, 45801. Telephone: 419/225-9115. $19.70 to $22.70 for one; $23.70 to $26.70 for two; $29.70 to $32.70 for four.

Lucas

Accommodation: Malabar Farm State Park Youth Hostel (AYH), Rte. 1, 44842. Telephone: 419/526-9336. Open daily June to August; other times by reservation only. $1.50 summer; $2.50 winter. AYH membership required (see page 21).

Mansfield

Accommodation: YWCA, 455 Park Ave. West, 44906. Telephone: 419/522-1300. Women only. Weekly rates: $9 for members; $11 for nonmembers. Reservations requested one week in advance. $20 key deposit; $10 linen deposit.

Marietta

Accommodation: Home Hostel (AYH). Telephone: 614/374-5042 or 373-4667. Open all year. Reservations preferred. No smoking or drinking.

Marion

Accommodations: Susse Chalet Inn and Motor Lodge, on Ohio 423 (Delaware Ave.) by Harding Memorial, 43302. Telephone: 614/383-6771. See Lima listing for rates.

● Imperial 400 Motor Inn, 333 West Center St., 43302. Telephone: 614/383-6351. $16 to $20 for one; $21 to $24 for two in one bed; $23 to $26 for two in two beds.

Massillon

Accommodation: YMCA, 131 Tremont SE, 44646. Two blocks south of Rte. 30; five blocks east of Rte. 21. Telephone: 216/837-5116. Men only. $8.35. Weekly rate: $23.50.

Medina

Accommodation: Surburbanite Motel, 2909 Medina Rd., Box 611, 44258. Telephone: 216/725-4971. $17.95 for one; $20.95 for two in one bed; $22.95 for two in two beds.

Middletown

Accommodation: Regal 8 Inn, 2425 North Verity Pkwy., 45042. Telephone: 513/423-9403. $17.88 for one; $20.88 for two in one bed; $23.88 for two to four in two beds.

Montpelier

Accommodation: Friendship Exit 2 Motel, RR 3 (600 ft. from I-80), I-90 at Exit 2, 43543. Telephone: 419/485-3139. $18 to $20 for one; $21 to $23 for two in one bed; $26 to $29 for two in two beds.

New Philadelphia

Accommodation: Motel 6, 181 Bluebell Dr. SW, 44663. Telephone: 216/339-6530. $12.95 for one; $16.95 for two; $19.95 for up to four.

Orrville

Accommodation: Best Value Ridge Motel, 10355 East Lincolnway, 44667. Telephone: 216/682-4080. $15 for one; $20 for two in one bed; $22 for two in two beds.

Oxford

On Campus: Miami University is in Oxford, a small college town which is very receptive to young travelers. There are three inexpensive motels in the area, and you might be able to stay on campus if you speak with someone in the housing office. Miami U is known for its Apple Butter Festival and there are many other campus events year round.

You can meet students at Lottie Moon's, Mac & Joe's, the Circle, CJ's, the Balcony, Ozzies, and Dipaolo's.

"Oxford is definitely off any main path for travelers but provides a friendly student atmosphere and plenty of places to meet people, both on campus and in town."

Painesville

Accommodation: YMCA, 933 Mentor Ave., 44077. About 1½ miles north of Interstate 90 off 44. Telephone: 216/352-3303. Men only. $9.10. Weekly rate: $37. Call ahead to see if there's room.

Pomeroy

Accommodation: Best Value Meigs-Inn, 126½ East Main St., 45769. Telephone: 614/992-3629. $14 to $19 for one; $18 to $23 for two.

Portsmouth

Accommodation: Days Inn, ♿, Rte. 52 East (Wheelersburg Exit), 8402 Ohio River Rd., Wheelersburg, 45694. Telephone: 614/574-8431. $21.88 to $22.88 for one; $25.88 to $26.88 for two.

Sandusky

Accommodation: Days Inn, ♿, 4315 Milan Rd., 44870. Telephone: 419/627-8884. $16.88 for one; $20.88 for two. Rates higher May 15 to September 6.

Sidney

Accommodation: Days Inn, I-75 and Ohio 47 (Exit 92), Folkerth Ave., 45365. Telephone: 513/492-1104. $19.88 to $20.88 for one; $23.88 to $24.88 for two.

Springfield

On Campus: Wittenberg University is in Springfield, a city where "the people are very friendly" and which has "a small-town attitude about it." Snyder Park is a favorite attraction and another is the Springfield Art Center, which has a variety of exhibitions during the year. Cliff Park has free events during July.

You might find an available dorm room on campus for a night or two—check with the Admissions Office. The Press Box, 1024 North Plum St., is run by a Wittenberg graduate and serves good Mexican food. We received many other eating suggestions from a friend there, including Mike and Rosy's Deli, 330 West McCreight, which serves excellent sandwiches, homemade soups, carrot cake, etc., and O'Brien's Tavern on North Fountain, which serves a wide range of main dishes for $3 to $10. The campus is closed during August and September.

St. Clairsville

Accommodation: Friendship Inn–Twin Pines, National Rd. West, one-quarter mile east of I-70, Exit 213, on U.S. 40, 43950. $18 to $20 for one; $20 to $24 for two in one bed; $24 to $28 for two in two beds.

Strongsville

Accommodations: Friendship Inn–Pike View Motel, 10590 Pearl Rd., 44136. Telephone: 216/238-2888. $18 for one; $20 for two in one bed; $22 for two in two beds.

• La Siesta Motel, 🐾, 8300 Pearl Rd., Rte. 42, 44136. Telephone: 216/234-4488. $19 for one; $21 for two in one bed; $22 for two in two beds.

Toledo

Help: Travelers Aid, Information and Referral Center, 1 Stranahan Square, 43604. Telephone: 419/244-3728.

Accommodations: YWCA, 1018 Jefferson Ave., 43624. One block from bus terminal. Telephone: 419/241-3235. Women only. $11.

● Days Inn, I-75 and Ohio 20 at Exit 193 on I-75, Ohio Turnpike Exit 5, 43551. Telephone: 419/874-8771. $19.88 to $21.88 for one; $23.88 to $25.88 for two.

● Red Roof Inn, Ohio Turnpike at U.S. 20 (Exit 4), Maumee, 43537. Telephone: 419/893-0292. See Canton listing for rates.

● Red Roof Inn, I-475 at Airport Hwy. (Ohio 2), Holland, 43528. To open in 1982. See Canton listing for rates.

Warren

"This is the most overcast section of the country; we never see the sun. The fall is usually very short, winters are cold and damp. . . ."

Help: Contact Trumbull, Inc., 216/393-1565. In the Warren/Cortland areas, dial 393-1565; in the Niles/Girard/Hubbard areas, dial 545-4371; all other areas, dial "0" and ask the operator for Enterprise 1565. Open 24 hours.

Youngstown

Help: Hotline, 216/747-2696.

Accommodations: YWCA, 25 West Rayen Ave., 44503. Telephone: 216/746-6361. Women only. $8.44. Weekly rate: $42.20. Reservations suggested.

● Days Inn, &, I-80 and Ohio 46 (Niles Exit), 5425 Clarkins Dr., 44515. Telephone: 216/793-9806. $23 to $25 for one; $27 to $29 for two.

● Days Inn, &, I-80 and Ohio 193 (Belmont Exit), 1610 Motor Inn Dr., Girard, 44420. $22 to $25 for one; $26 to $29 for two.

● Motel 6, 1600 Motor Inn Dr., Girard, 44420. Telephone: 216/759-2183. See New Philadelphia listing for rates.

● Econo-Travel Motor Hotel, 1615 East Liberty St., Girard, 44420. Telephone: 216/759-9820. $22.95 for one; $26.95 for two in one bed; $30.95 for two in two beds.

Zanesfield

Accommodation: Marmon Valley Farm (AYH), Rte. 1, 43360. Telephone: 513/593-8051. Open year round except for December 15 to January 15, Thanksgiving, and Easter. Reservations required. $2 summer; $3 winter. AYH membership required (see page 21).

Oklahoma

More American Indians live in Oklahoma than in any other state in the U.S. Oklahomans, according to one we know, are generally open, friendly, and hospitable in the western style. Spring and fall are the best times to visit—the summer is very, very hot.

As you plan your stay in Oklahoma, consider visiting Anadarko, a town with an Indian museum and Indian City USA, an outdoor museum that depicts the life of the various tribes and is supervised by the anthropology department of the University of Oklahoma. Also try to include in your itinerary the Cowboy Hall of Fame and Western Heritage Center in Oklahoma City; the history of science collection at the University of Oklahoma in Norman; the Woolroc Museum in Bartlesville, the creation of the founder of Phillips Oil Company; the Thomas Gilcrease Institute of American History and Art in Tulsa, which has a fine collection of western paintings, Aztec manuscripts, and manuscripts of the early Spanish explorers; and the Cherokee Center in Tahlequah, which has both a museum and a pageant called the Trail of Tears that runs from early June through August.

Tent camping in Oklahoma is free in all 23 Oklahoma state parks and 23 recreation areas. The Tourism and Recreation Department tells you to "just pitch your tent by a beautiful lake, enjoy the Sooner State's clean air and pure water and have a ball." There are also many lakes with state-run lodges that are relatively inexpensive.

Some Special Events: Azalea Festival in Muskogee and Rattlesnake Hunt in Waureka (April); Strawberry Festival in Stilwell (May); Santa Fe Trail Daze in Boise City, Sequoyah Intertribal Pow Wow in Elk City, and Kiamichi Owa Chito Festival of the Forest in Broken Bow (June); Old Santa Fe Days in Shawnee (July); Watermelon Festival in Rush Springs and All-Night Gospel Sing in Seminole (August); State Fair in Oklahoma City (September); and Will Rogers Days in Claremore (November).

Hitching: Officially, hitchhiking is allowed except from roadways and turnpikes. The attitude in Oklahoma toward hitching doesn't seem to be enthusiastic. But a teacher friend at the University of Oklahoma in Norman polled his classes and about one-half said they'd pick up a hitchhiker. Nearly all said they did not recommend hitchhiking, though, and that "in this area nearly all interstate travel is on limited-access Interstate Highways."

Tourist Information: Marketing Services Division, Oklahoma Tourism and Recreation Department, 500 Will Rogers Memorial Bldg., Oklahoma City, OK 73105. Telephone: 405/521-2406. To order any brochures about the state, call 405/521-2409.

Alva

Accommodation: Friendship Inn Vista, 1400 Oklahoma Blvd., 73717. Telephone: 405/327-0431. Rates start at $16 for one, $18 for two in one bed, $20 for two in two beds.

Blackwell

Accommodation: Friendship Inn–Plainsman, Box 271, two miles west at junction of I-35 and Okla. 11, 74631. Telephone: 405/363-2911. $20 to $24 for one or two in one bed; $28 to $32 for two in two beds.

Chickasha

Accommodation: Friendship Inn–King's Inn, 702 South 4th St., 73018. Telephone: 405/224-3912. $17 to $19 for one; $20 to $24 for two in one bed; $22 to $26 for two in two beds.

Claremore

Accommodation: Friendship Inn–Long's Holiday Motel, 1000 West Will Rogers, 74017. Telephone: 908/341-4820. $20 for one; $21 for two in one bed; $23 for two in two beds.

Clinton

Accommodation: Friendship Inn Western, 801 South 8th, 73601. Telephone: 405/323-1790. $14 to $18 for one; $19 to $22 for two in one bed; $22 to $26 for two in two beds.

Duncan

Accommodation: Friendship Inn–Century Motel, 115 South 81 Bypass, 73533. Telephone: 405/255-8500. $16 for one; $18 for two in one bed; $20 for two in two beds.

Elk City

Accommodation: Friendship Inn–King's Inn, 1918 West 3rd St., 73644. Telephone: 405/225-1841. $13.95 to $16.95 for one; $15.95 to $18.95 for two in one bed; $19.95 and up for two in two beds.

El Reno

Accommodation: Friendship Inn–Western Sands Motel, Rte. 1, Box 108-B, 73036. Telephone: 405/262-6000. $22 for one; $25 for two in one bed; $27 for two in two beds.

Koiwa

Accommodation: Beacon Motel, √ 5%, P.O. Box 152, Hwy. 69, 74553. Telephone: 918/432-5321. $12.25 for one; $14.25 for two in one bed; $16.25 for two in two beds. Rates lower during winter.

Lawton

Accommodation: Friendship Inn–Coral Motel, 1709 Cache Rd. NW on Hwy. 62, 73501. Telephone: 405/353-2772. $16 to $20 for one or two in one bed; $22 to $35 for two in two beds.

McAlester

Accommodation: Friendship Inn–Mayfair, south on Business Rte. 69, 74501. $14 to $15 for one; $18 to $20 for two in one bed; $22 to $24 for two in two beds.

Miami

Accommodations: Friendship Inn–Thunderbird, 1307 Steve Owens Blvd., I-44 Will Rogers Turnpike, Miami Exit, 74354. Telephone: 918/542-4435. $19 to $21 for one; $22 to $24 for two in one bed; $25 to $27 for two in two beds.
● Townsman–Budget Host, √, 900 Steve Owens Blvd., 74354. Telephone: 918/542-6631. $19 to $21 for one; $21 to $23 for two in one bed; $25 to $27 for two in two beds.

Moore

Accommodation: Motel 6, 1417 North Moore Ave., 73160. Telephone: 405/799-9190. $12.95 for one; $16.95 for two; $19.95 for up to four.

Muskogee

Accommodation: Friendship Inn–Sooner Motel, 335 North 32nd St., 74401. Telephone: 918/687-4477. $11 to $16 for one; $13 to $18 for two in one bed; $17 to $23 for two in two beds.

Norman

Help: Number NYNE, Oklahoma University Crisis Hotline, 650 Parrington Oval, 73019. Telephone: 405/325-6963.
● Helpline, Inc., 405/364-3800. 8:30 a.m. to 5 p.m.

On Campus: For inexpensive lodging on campus, call 405/325-1011 and you might be able to stay in Walker Tower for $15 a night. To meet OU students, head for Mr. Bill's, Town Tavern, Service Station, Interurban, or Monte. You'll be able to have a beer as long as you're 18, mixed drinks only if you're 21.

Oklahoma City

Help: Travelers Aid, 601 NW 5th St., 73102. Telephone: 405/232-5507.

Accommodations: YMCA, 125 NW 5th St., 73102. Telephone: 405/232-6101. Men only. $10. Weekly rate: $40.

● Motel 6, 820 South Meridian Ave., 73108. Telephone: 405/946-6703. See Moore listing for rates.

● Regal 8 Inn, 5801 Tinker Diagonal, Midwest City, 73110. Telephone: 405/737-8851. $18.88 for one; $21.88 for two in one bed; $24.88 for two to four in two beds.

● Days Inn, ♿, I-40 and MacArthur, 720 South MacArthur, 73128. Five minutes from airport. Telephone: 405/947-0681. $23.88 to $24.88 for one; $27.88 to $28.88 for two.

● Days Inn, ♿, I-40 and Meridian, 4712 West I-40, 73128. Three miles from airport. Telephone: 405/947-8721. $23 to $24 for one; $27 to $28 for two.

● Friendship Inn–Carlyle Motel, 3600 NW 39th St., 73112. Telephone: 405/946-3355. $20 to $22 for one or two in one bed; $26 to $32 for two in two beds.

Okmulgee

Accommodation: Friendship–Carriage Inn, 1800 South Wood Dr. on Hwy. 75, 74447. Telephone: 918/756-6614. $16 for one; $19 for two in one bed; $22 for two in two beds.

Pauls Valley

Accommodation: Plaza Motel, √, U.S. 77 South, 73075. Telephone: 405/238-2712. $13 to $16 for one; $16 to $18 for two in one bed; $18 to $21 for two in two beds.

Sulphur

Camping: Chickasaw National Recreation Area, P.O. Box 201, 73086. Camping all year at Buckhorn and Rock Creek, and from April to October at Cold Springs, Guy Sandy, and the Point. $3 per campsite per night.

Tulsa

Help: Helpline, 918/583-HELP.

Tourist Information: Convention and Visitors Department, Metropolitan Tulsa Chamber of Commerce, 616 South Boston Ave., 74119. Telephone: 918/585-1201.

Accommodations: YMCA, 515 South Denver, 74103. Telephone: 918/583-6201. Men only. $9.88 ($10.98 with color TV). After four nights, $34.87 to $39.82 per week.

● Twin Towers Dormitory, University of Tulsa, 2821 East 8th St., 74104. Telephone: 918/592-6000, extension 2513 or 2375. **Mid-May to August 5.** $10 single; $14 double. Please bring your own linens.

● Days Inn, I-44 and 11th St., 11910 East 11th St., 74128. Telephone: 918/437-8980. $23.88 to $24.88 for one; $27.88 to $28.88 for two.

● Motel 6, 5828 South West Blvd., 74107. Telephone: 918/446-6661. See Moore listing for rates.

Vinita

Accommodation: Friendship Inn–Prairie Schooner Motel, RR 4, Hwy. 60/66/64, 74301. Telephone: 918/256-2832. $16 to $17 for one; $17 to $19 for two in one bed; $20 to $23 for two in two beds.

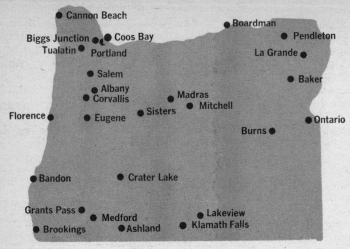

Oregon

Oregonians are so conscious and protective of the environment that they want to discourage visitors from falling in love with their state and staying, thereby changing the atmosphere of Oregon. Oregon "ungreeting cards" invite people to stay in Arizona for the summer.

The population in Oregon is a little over two million, so for those of you coming from a highly populated area, Oregon will give you a chance to breathe. Oregon has mountains, deserts, fields, and the ocean. From Eugene, for example, one can travel an hour west and be at the coast, or an hour east and be in the mountains.

Green is the color of Oregon. There's a lot of rain in winter (it's snow in the mountains); in color and scenery, late spring is the most beautiful season. In summer and fall, the weather is perfect for swimming in mountain lakes and hiking in the wilderness. Winter in Oregon is usually gray, but ski resorts like Mt. Bachelor near Bend, Mt. Hood (approximately 50 miles east of Portland), and Mt. Ashland near Ashland are worth a winter visit.

Most of Oregon's history is centered on Indian history, early settlers, explorers, and trappers. One of the small towns that has been restored to look as it did in the early days is Applegate, in southern Oregon near Ashland.

The major sightseeing attractions include Canon Beach, Newport, and Gold Beach along the coast. The "three sisters" area—Hood River Valley, Oregon Caves, and the mountains in southwestern Oregon (near Oregon Caves) —is probably the most spectacular in terms of mountain scenery. Eastern Oregon is very different geographically from the west. There is a lot of cattle raising in eastern Oregon, and the terrain is extremely dry. The area around Pendleton, the Steens mountains, and the Alvord desert are particularly attractive sections of the state.

Portland is an interesting city to visit. It's built into the trees so that it never seems as large as it is. It may not be spectacular as far as cities go (it could not really be compared to Seattle, San Francisco, Chicago, or New York, for example), but it is clean, quiet, and appealing. Eugene is somewhat more lively for a city of its size. The home of the University of Oregon, it has lots of ethnic restaurants, an extensive bike-path system, a public market, a Saturday market, some nice parks, and the cultural productions and sports activities that are part of the university. The Shakespeare Festival in Ashland in the summertime is quite well known and worth a stop.

"I guess the best thing I could say about Oregon is that it has lots more to offer than just large urban centers and that Oregon is there to explore. I think many people would find out a lot about Oregon if they were left on their own just to hike through the mountains or spend a day at the coast, drive through the back roads or swim in a mountain lake." [This quote is from a homesick Oregonian, in exile in Ohio.]

Some Special Events: Pear Blossom Festival in Medford (April); Pacific Northwest Championship All-Indian Rodeo in Tygh Valley (May); Strawberry Festival in Lebanon (June); World Championship Timber Carnival in Albany and Crooked River Round-Up in Prineville (July); Threshing Bee and Draft Horse Show in Dufur (August); Alpenfest in Wallowa Lake (September); Kraut and Sausage Feed and Bazaar in Verboot (November).

Hitching: Hitching is legal in Oregon, as long as you stand off the pavement. The official wording is: "It is illegal to solicit rides from drivers of private vehicles while standing in a road or on the paved or graveled shoulder designed for vehicle use." Friends from Oregon have been more enthusiastic than any others about hitchhiking in their state. Oregon is used to hitchhikers who are on their way from California to Canada on U.S. 101. Oregonians have tried to make things comfortable for travelers by setting up hostels along the route, and, in Eugene, a system of signs marking the best and safest places for hitchhikers to stand. The signs say "ride stop" and are blue with a yellow hand (thumb extended) on them. A New Yorker who hitched his way along the western coast of Oregon says that it is spectacular. He took 101 all the way from California to Washington: "Wild blueberries grow everywhere in August. Delicious, sweet and very distracting from hitching."

Tourist Information: Oregon Travel Information Section, Department of Transportation, 101 Transportation Bldg., Salem, OR 97310. Telephone: 503/378-6309.

Albany

Accommodation: Friendship Inn–Al-Ray Motel, 2727 East Pacific Blvd., 97321. Telephone: 503/926-4246. $23 for one; $27 for two in one bed; $32 for two in two beds.

Ashland

On Campus: According to someone from Southern Oregon State College, Ashland is a young, artistic, and cosmopolitan town with a relaxed atmosphere and a well-known summer Shakespeare festival. In summertime, he tells us that there is a hostel in the downtown area and that there may be rooms on campus for visitors. Call the International Travel and Study Office (tel. 503/482-7986, extension 6) for information.

Four restaurants recommended in Ashland are Brother's, a deli, at 95 North Main; Copper Skillet, for omelets, 1207 Siskiyou; Lithia Grocery, 47 North Main; and the Sandwich Shack, 397 Avery.

Accommodations: Residence Halls, Southern Oregon State College, ⬚, Indiana and Madrone Sts., 97520. Telephone: 503/482-6371. Five-night minimum for individuals; group of ten or more needn't stay as long. Must be student or educationally related. Open year round. $14.50 for one; $10 per person for two. Includes some meals.

● The Ashland Hostel (AYH), 150 North Main St., 97520. Telephone: 503/482-9217. Two blocks from bus station. Closed in December. Reservations suggested in July and August. $4 for AYH members; $6 for nonmembers.

Baker

Accommodation: Friendship Inn–Oregon Trail Motel, 211 Bridge St., P.O. Box 221, 97814. Telephone: 503/523-5844. $21 to $23 for one; $24 to $29 for two in one bed; $24 to $32 for two in two beds.

Bandon

Accommodation: Sea Star Traveler's Hostel (AYH), ⬚, 375 2nd St., 97411. Telephone: 503/347-9533. Open April 1 to October 31. $3.50 for AYH members.

"The hostel is owned and operated by a collective of five people. The building was a condemned structure which the collective brought back to life by completely renovating it with walls of natural cedar, big skylites, and many personal touches—one would never know the state it came from nor the work that went in. The town itself is a unique coastal town with a beautiful ocean beach. Many artists live in the town of 2500 which has two artist cooperatives and many shops."

Biggs Junction

Accommodation: Friendship Inn–Biggs' Nu-Vu Motel, Star Rte., Box 144, 97065. Telephone: 503/739-2525. $12 to $16 for one; $16 to $20 for two in one bed; $19 to $23 for two in two beds.

Boardman

Accommodation: Friendship Inn–Riverview Motel, Front and 1st South on I-80 North, 97818. Telephone: 503/481-2775. $18 to $22 for one; $22 to $26 for two in one bed; $25 to $30 for two in two beds.

Brookings

Accommodation: Friendship Inn–Brookings Thunderbird, 1144 Chetco Ave., P.O. Box AL, 97415. Telephone: 503/469-2141. $20 for one; $25.50 for two in one bed; $29 for two in two beds.

Burns

Accommodation: Motel 6, 997 Oregon Ave., 97720. Telephone: 503/573-6663. $12.95 for one; $16.95 for two; $19.95 for up to four.

Cannon Beach

Accommodation: Cannon Beach Hostel, Hemlock and Third, P.O. Box 398, 97110. Open June 1 through September 30. Beachcombing and good body surfing eight miles south of hostel. $3 per person; breakfast, $1; dinner, $1.50. There's a limit of a three-night stay in this dorm set up in a "nice old house."

Coos Bay

Help: Helpline, 503/267-5101.
Accommodation: The Seagull Youth Hostel (AYH-SA), First Presbyterian Church, Fourth and Elrod, P.O. Box 847, 97420. Telephone: 503/267-6114. Open May 31 through Labor Day. $4.50. Evening meals and breakfast provided.

"The rate at the Coos Bay Hostel includes two superb home-cooked meals provided by a group of local ladies—other towns would do well to copy!"

Corvallis

On Campus: Oregon State University is in this small city, and in Corvallis people love to bicycle. There are bike paths throughout the city and into the neighboring towns. For good, inexpensive food, friends suggest the Valley Restaurant on 3rd St. for sandwiches, soups, salads, and vegetarian main dishes; Olga's Ice Cream Parlour; Mazzi's, for Sicilian food; Woodstock's Pizza, Kings Blvd.; and Skipper's Seafood on 9th St. If you're looking for the students, check in at Allann Brothers Coffee House, the OSU Commons, Riverside Café, or a bar called Mother's Mattress Factory.

Crater Lake

Camping: Crater Lake National Park, P.O. Box 7, 97604. There's camping at Lost Creek and Mazama during the summer—the length of the season varies with snow.

Eugene

On Campus: The University of Oregon in Eugene is a popular stop for young people on their way from California to Canada. Erb Memorial Student Union Bldg., in the center of the campus at 13th and University Sts., is a good first stop. Pick up a copy of the *Daily Emerald,* the university's daily paper, which lists rides, jobs, housing, etc. For food, try Mama's Home Fried Truck Stop, 14th and Alder. Old Taylor's has a large variety of burgers and imaginative sandwiches on health breads; Rennies Landing has a similar menu. They are also popular nightspots along with DeFrisco's, Duffey's, and Max's.

We hear that the switchboard on KZEL 96 FM has a ride-assistance service. There are many excellent bicycle paths in Eugene, keep an eye out for plays on the mall during summer, and stop by at the wonderful public market at 5th St. on Saturday and Sunday.

Help: Eugene Switchboard, 503/686-8453. They'll help you find a place to stay in Eugene—stop at their office at 795 Willamette, Room 222. Check with them, too, for rides, odd jobs, and general information on the area.

Accommodations: Motel 6, 3690 Glenwood Dr., 97403. Telephone: 503/ 342-6177. See Burns listing for rates.

● Best Value Angus Inn, 2121 Franklin Blvd., 97403. Telephone: 503/342-1243. $20 to $22 for one; $22 to $24 for two in one bed; $26 to $28 for two in two beds.

● Continental Motel, ➦ 🖢, 390 East Broadway, 97401. Telephone: 503/ 343-3376. $15.75 for one; $18.90 for two. Pool and cable color TV.

● Check with Eugene Switchboard for crashing possibilities.

Florence

Accommodation: Friendship Inn–Silver Sands Motel, 1449 Hwy. 101 North, 97439. Telephone: 503/997-3459. $18 to $22 for one; $20 to $24 for two in one bed; $24 to $30 for two in two beds.

Grants Pass

Accommodations: Motel 6, 1800 North East Seventh, 97526. Telephone: 503/476-9096. See Burns listing for rates.

● Friendship Inn–Egyptian Motel, 728 NW Sixth Ave., 97526. Telephone: 503/476-6601. $14 to $20 for one; $18 to $28 for two in one bed; $24 to $32 for two in two beds.

Klamath Falls

Help: Hope-in-Crisis, Inc., Hotline 503/884-0636.

Accommodations: Motel 6, 5136 South 6th St., 97601. Telephone: 503/ 884-6273. See Burns listing for rates.

● Friendship Inn–North Entrance Motel, Hwy. 97, Box 1885, 97601. Telephone: 503/884-8104. $14 to $16 for one; $18 to $22 for two in one bed; $21 to $24 for two in two beds.

La Grande

Accommodations: Friendship Inn–Stardust Lodge, 402 Adams Ave., 97850. Telephone: 503/963-4166. $16 to $18 for one; $18 to $21 for two in one bed; $23 to $25 for two in two beds.

● Greenwell Motel, √, 305 Adams Ave., 97850. Telephone: 503/963-4134. $18 for one; $21 for two in one bed; $24 for two in two beds.

Lakeview

Accommodation: Friendship Inn–Lakeview Lodge, 301 G St. North, 97630. Telephone: 503/947-2181. $15 to $19 for one; $22 to $24 for two in one bed; $24 to $26 for two in two beds.

Madras

Accommodation: Friendship Inn–Juniper Motel, 415 North 5th St., 97741. Telephone: 503/475-6186. $16 to $18 for one; $22 to $24 for two in one bed; $24 to $26 for two in two beds.

Medford

Accommodation: Motel 6, 950 Alba Dr., 97501. Telephone: 503/779-6470. See Burns listing for rates.

Mitchell

Accommodation: Oregon Hotel (AYH-SA), P.O. Box 12, 97750. Telephone: 503/462-3534. Open all year. $3 per bunk.

Ontario

Accommodations: Friendship Inn–Fireside Motel, 1737 North Oregon, 97914. Telephone: 503/889-3101. $19 for two in one bed; $24 for two in two beds.
● Motel 6, 275 Butler St., 97914. Telephone: 503/889-6604. See Burns listing for rates.

Pendleton

Accommodation: Motel 6, 325 Southeast Nye Ave., 97801. Telephone: 503/276-6665. See Burns listing for rates.

Portland

Tourist Information: Portland Convention Bureau, 26 SW Salmon Ave., 97204. Telephone: 503/222-2223.
Help: Portland Metro Hotline, 503/248-5430.
On Campus: The University of Portland and Portland State University are here. One native Portlander says that she's in the minority since the city attracts many young people, especially from the East, who like its recreational opportunities, its reputation for being politically independent, and its friendly, liberal people.

There's no lack of places to eat in Portland, according to this same friend: Great American Sandwich Company, 7123 North Lombard, for submarines; Rhons, 3107 North Lombard, for especially large breakfasts; White Eagle Café, 836 North Russell, with good food and music at night, a favorite with railroaders; Euphoria Tavern, 320 Southeast Second; Hamburger Mary's, 840 Southwest Park; and Dave's Delicatessen, 445 Southwest Yamhill, a downtown kosher deli. The meeting place on campus is the Pilot House; off campus it's the Twilight Room, 5242 North Lombard, which has earned a solid reputation for its hamburgers.

Portland has an art museum and the Oregon Museum of Science and Industry. The downtown area is being restored and lots of interesting shops are opening all the time. The Saturday Market gives local artists and merchants a chance to show their wares under the Burnside Bridge.

Accommodations: YWCA, ♿, 1111 SW Tenth Ave., 97205. Telephone: 503/223-6281. Women only. $10.19 single without bath; $12.52 single with bath. Hostel rooms that sleep three or four: $4.36 per person; $3.49 if you bring your own sleeping bag. *"Exceptional value, very clean, with a friendly staff. A great supermarket next door."*

● The Ondine, c/o Portland Student Services, 1802 SW Tenth Ave., 97201. Telephone: 503/224-2727 or 228-2646. $15 single; $18 double. Modern high-rise building. Generally available during summer only; educationally related groups or individuals preferred. They might discount $5 if you provide your own linen and do without maid service.

● Best Value Paramount Heathman Hotel, 712 SW Salmon St., 97205. Telephone: 503/228-5262. $19 to $25 for one; $22 to $28 for two in one bed; $24 to $30 for two in two beds.

● Motel 6, 3104–06 SE Powell Blvd., 97202. Telephone: 503/233-8811. See Burns listing for rates.

● Motel 6, 17950 SW Lower Boones Ferry Rd., 97223. Telephone: 503/639-0631. See Burns listing for rates.

● Friendship Inn–Sands Motel, 3800 North Interstate Ave., 97227. Telephone: 503/287-2601. $18 to $20 for one; $21 to $23 for two in one bed; $24 to $27 for two in two beds.

● Friendship Inn–Town House, 4810 NE Sandy Blvd., 97213. Telephone: 503/282-7711. $20 to $24 for one; $24 to $28 for two in one bed; $27 to $31 for two in two beds.

Salem

Help: Cry of Love, 2303 Fairgrounds Rd. NE, 97303. Telephone: 503/581-5535.

"Boon's Treasury is a comfortable tavern here."

Accommodations: YMCA, 685 Court St. NE, 97301. Telephone: 503/581-9622. Men over 18 only. $6.50. "The Y is within walking distance of six or seven cafés and restaurants. Many of our residents walk to nearby Salem Memorial Hospital at Winter and Oak Sts., where the cafeteria has good meals and welcomes public patronage."

● YWCA, 768 State St., 97301. Behind State Capitol Building, next door to Willamette University, and near train and bus stations. Telephone: 503/581-9922. Women only. $8 single; $5 if you have a sleeping bag.

● Friendship Salem, 1855 Hawthorne NE, 97303. Telephone: 503/581-9410. $19 to $21 for one; $22 to $25 for two in one bed; $26 to $29 for two in two beds.

- Motel 6, 2250 Mission St. SE, 97302. Telephone: 503/588-0220. See Burns listing for rates.
- Western Saver Motel, 1401 Hawthorne Ave. NE, 97301. Telephone: 503/371-8024. $14.40 single; $21.90 double.

Sisters

Accommodation: Santiam Lodge Youth Hostel (AYH), Star Rte., 97759. Open May 1 to November 1. $3. A Presbyterian camp. AYH membership required (see page 21).

Tualatin

Accommodation: Western Saver Motel, 17959 SW McEwan, 97062. Telephone: 503/684-0760. $14.40 single; $21.90 double.

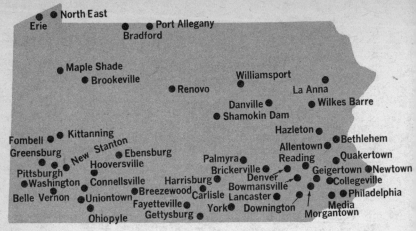

Pennsylvania

Pennsylvania is rich in history. Philadelphia was the patriots' capital through most of the Revolutionary War period. In this state one can visit the site of the country's greatest agonies as well as some of its greatest joys.

In Philadelphia you can visit Independence Hall, which still looks as it did 200 years ago when the Second Continental Congress gathered there to choose George Washington as the commander-in-chief of the Continental Army, where it heard the Declaration of Independence read, and where it convened throughout the war.

Valley Forge State Park, not far from Philadelphia, where Washington led over 10,000 ragged and starving men into an agonizing winter encampment in December 1777, has been called the most famous military camp in the world. More places to visit on the trail of the Revolutionary War are Washington Crossing State Park, the Betsy Ross House, and the Liberty Bell. And for those who are interested in the Civil War, Pennsylvania is the site of Gettysburg National Military Park, where 51,000 men fell in the bloodiest battle of the entire war.

Besides an abundance of historic sites, Pennsylvania has some very beautiful country, particularly in the Poconos and the often-visited Pennsylvania Dutch country. Urban types will gravitate toward Philadelphia and Pittsburgh; country types will want to explore Lancaster County and the Pocono Mountain area instead. Anyone planning to spend time in the Philadelphia area should look at a copy of *Philadelphia Resource Guide,* an access catalog put together by the Synapse Communications Collective and subtitled "Resources for Living Effectively in Philadelphia." For a copy of the third edition, write to Synapse, Inc., 3432 Sansom St., Philadelphia, PA 19104.

If the idea of a farm vacation strikes you, write to the Pennsylvania Department of Agriculture, Bureau of Rural Affairs, 2310 North Cameron St., Harrisburg, PA 17110, for their *Farm Vacation Directory,* which lists 28 Pennsylvania farms that offer accommodations and activities. Most are within our price range and are generally family oriented.

Some Special Events: Mummers Parade in Philadelphia (January); Cherry Blossom Festival in Wilkes-Barre (April); Northern Appalachian Festival in Bedford (May); Delco Scottish Games and Country Fair in Devon, and Annual Snake Hunt (prize for the longest snake, the snake with the most rattles) in Cross Fork (June); Freedom Week in Philadelphia (week before the Fourth of July); Woodsmen's Festival in Cherry Springs State Park (August); and Mountain Craft Days in Somerset (September).

Hitching: Hitchhiking is not legal in Pennsylvania, although many police departments do not enforce the law unless complaints are received about hitchhikers standing on the roadway. It seems to be an accepted means of travel but is not particularly encouraged. One friend from Pittsburgh said that "it is considered acceptable for males but is less acceptable for women. I myself use it for getting around and have as yet had no problems." The State Police think differently: "It is our contention that the hazards outweigh the advantages of this method of travel."

Tourist Information: Pennsylvania Department of Commerce, Bureau of Travel Development, 416 Forum Bldg., Harrisburg, PA 17120. Telephone: toll free 800/323-1717, or 717/787-5453 locally.

Allentown

Accommodation: Days Inn, I-78 and 15th St. Exit, Rte. 22 and 15th St., 18104. Telephone: 215/435-7880. $21.88 for one; $27.88 for two.

Belle Vernon

Accommodation: Motel 6, RD 4, Rte. 51 and I-70, 15012. Telephone: 412/929-4501. $12.95 for one; $16.95 for two; $19.95 for up to four.

Bethlehem

Accommodation: YMCA, ♿, 430 East Broad St., 18018. Telephone: 215/867-7588. Men only, 18 years and over. $7.67 per night. "Plenty of short-order places within two miles; fancier restaurants, too."

Bowmansville

Accommodation Bowmansville Youth Hostel (AYH), Rte. 625, P.O. Box 117, 17507. Telephone: 215/445-4831. Closed December 20 to January 5. Send stamped, self-addressed envelope with reservation request. $3.50. The houseparent at the hostel told us about a local Mennonite farmer who serves meals to travelers: Phares Hurst, RR 1, Narvon, PA 17555. Telephone: 215/445-6186. Reservations for meals should be made a few days in advance. AYH membership required (see page 21), or you may buy an introductory pass for $1.

Bradford

Help: Crisis Intervention Hotline, 814/362-4623. (People in area codes 814 and 412 can call toll free: 800/652-0562.)

Accommodation: YWCA, 24 West Corydon St., 16701. Telephone: 814/368-4235. Women only. $5. Weekly rate: $25. Cooking facilities available.

Breezewood

Accommodation: Superior Penn–Aire Motel, Box 156, 30 West at I-70, 15533. Telephone: 814/735-4351. $19 to $23 for two in one bed; $21 to $25 for two in two beds.

Brickerville

Accommodation: Cannon Hill Youth Hostel (AYH), Fox Rd., Rte. 1, P.O. Box 687, Newmanstown, 17073. Telephone: 717/626-6277. Open March 1 to December 1. Reservations advised. $3.50. AYH membership required (see page 21).

Brookville

Accommodation: Superior Hilton Motel, RD 3, Rtes. 322/28/36, 15825. Telephone: 814/849-7344. $20 for one; $24 for two in one bed; $32 to $37 for two in two beds.

Carlisle

Accommodation: Coast-To-Coast Motel, √ $2, 1252 Harrisburg Pike, 17013. Telephone: 717/243-8585. $19 to $22 for one; $21 to $26 for two in one bed; $24 to $29 for two in two beds.

Collegeville

Accommodation: Evansburg State Park Youth Hostel (AYH), 🦽 (completely on first floor), 837 Mayhall Rd., 19426. Telephone: 215/489-4326. $3.50. In 3400-acre state park.

Connellsville

Accommodation: Friendship Inn–Melody Motor Lodge, U.S. 119 South, Box 822, 15425. Telephone: 412/628-9600. $21 to $22 for one; $22 to $24 for two in one bed; $24 to $26 for two in two beds.

Danville

Accommodation: Red Roof Inn, I-80 at Pa. 54 (Exit 33). Telephone: 717/275-7600. $19.95 for one; $22.95 for two in one bed; $24.95 to $26.95 for two to four in two beds.

Denver

Accommodation: Denver Youth Hostel (AYH), Rte. 1, Stevens, 17578. Telephone: 215/267-5166. Open March 1 to December 1. Send stamped, self-addressed envelope with reservation request. $3.50. AYH membership required (see page 21).

Downingtown

Accommodation: Marah Creek State Park Youth Hostel (AYH), North Reeds Rd., Lyndell, 19354. Scheduled to open in late 1981. Located on the East Coast Bicycle Trail. Contact AYH National Office for details (see page 21).

Ebensburg

Accommodation: Friendship Cottage Restaurant and Inn, Rte. 22 West, 15931. Telephone: 814/472-8002. $20 to $24 for one; $22 to $26 for two in one bed; $24 to $28 for two in two beds.

Erie

Help: Hotline, 814/453-5656.
Accommodation: Red Roof Inn, ♿, I-90 at Pa. 97 (Exit 7). Telephone: 814/868-5246. $17.95 for one; $20.95 for two in one bed; $22.95 to $24.95 for two to four in two beds.

Fayetteville

Accommodation: Rite Spot Motel, 5651 Lincoln Way East, 17222. Telephone: 717/352-2144. $18 for one; $20 for two in one bed; $22 for two in two beds.

Fombell

Accommodation: Camp Silver Lake (AYH), Box 810, RD 1, 16123. Telephone: 412/452-6720. $2.50 summer; $3 winter; $1 tenting. No smoking. Reservations necessary. Ski lodge with fireplace as well as swimming pool, hiking, tobogganing, and cross-country skiing on hostel grounds.

Geigertown

Accommodation: Shirey's Hostel (AYH), P.O. Box 49, 19523. Telephone: 215/286-9537. Open March 1 to November 30. $5. Reservations necessary. 15 miles from bus or train; call hostel to be picked up. AYH membership required (see page 21).

Gettysburg

Accommodation: Superior Heritage Motor Lodge, 64 Steinwehr Ave., 17325. Telephone: 717/334-9281. $16 to $24 for one; $20 to $30 for two in one bed; $22 to $37 for two in two beds.

Greensburg

Accommodation: Friendship Inn of Greensburg, Rte. 30 East Bypass, 15601. Telephone: 412/836-1648. $23 to $25 for one; $27 to $30 for two.

Harrisburg

Accommodation: Days Inn, ♿, I-83 Exit 18 and Pennsylvania Turnpike Exit 18, 353 Lewisberry Rd., New Cumberland, 17070. Telephone: 717/774-4156. $21.88 to $23.88 for one; $27.88 to $29.88 for two.
● Red Roof Inn, I-81 at North Progress Ave. (Exit 24), 17110. Telephone: 717/657-1445. See Danville listing for rates.
● Red Roof Inn, I-283 at Pa. 441 (Exit 19), 17111. Telephone: 717/939-1331. See Danville listing for rates.

Hazleton

Accommodation: Superior Yale's Motel, Box 227A, 18222. Telephone: 717/788-4220. $19 for one; $25 for two.

Hooversville

Accommodation: Camp Harmony Youth Hostel (AYH), RD 1, 15936. Telephone: 814/798-8128. $2.50 summer; $3.75 winter. AYH membership required (see page 21).

Kittanning

Accommodation: Friendship Inn–Plaza Motel, RD 6, 422 East, 16201. Telephone: 412/543-1100. $22 for one; $25 for two in one bed: $29 for two in two beds.

La Anna

Accommodation: La Anna Youth Hostel (AYH), Rte. 2, P.O. Box 1026, Cresco, 18326. Telephone: 717/676-9076. Open year round. $3.50 April 16 to October 14; $4.50 October 15 to April 15. Water sports and skiing nearby. AYH membership required (see page 21).

Lancaster

Tourist Information: Pennsylvania Dutch Visitors Bureau, 1799 Hempstead Rd., 17601.

Help: Crisis Intervention, 717/394-2631.

Accommodation: YWCA, ♿ limited, 110 North Lime St., 17602. Telephone: 717/393-1735. Women only. $12. Reservations suggested.

Maple Shade

Accommodation: Superior Track and Turf Motel, Rte. 73, 08052. Telephone: 609/235-6500. $20 to $23 for one or two in one bed; $23 to $26 for two in two beds.

Media

Accommodation: Ridley Creek Park Youth Hostel (AYH), 841 Sycamore Mills Rd., 19063. Telephone: 215/LO 6-9846. Open year round. Located in a state park with hiking, biking, and bridle trails. $3.50. Call locally for directions. "A colonial stone farmhouse built in 1791 but fully modernized, with two bedrooms on second floor with several bunk beds in each and a large fireplace in the den." AYH membership required (see page 21).

Morgantown

Accommodation: Econo Lodge, Rte. 10 North, 19543. Telephone: 215/286-5521. $17.95 for one; $20.95 for two in one bed; $23.95 for two in two beds.

New Stanton

Accommodation: Superior New Stanton Motel, I-70, Exit 8, Pennsylvania Turnpike, 15672. Telephone: 412/925-7606. $20 to $22 for one; $22 to $24 for two in one bed; $28 to $32 for two in two beds.

Newtown

Accommodation: Tyler State Park Hostel (AYH), P.O. Box 94, 18940. Telephone: 215/968-0927. $3.50. Ten miles from Washington Crossing State Park. AYH membership required (see page 21).

Northeast

Accommodation: Best Value Lakeview Motel, 11021 Side Hill Rd., 16428. Telephone: 814/725-4567. $19 for one; $22 for two in one bed; $26 for two in two beds.

Ohiopyle

Accommodation: Ohiopyle Youth Hostel (AYH), P.O. Box 99, Ohiopyle State Park, 15470. Telephone: 412/329-4476. $4 summer; $4.50 winter. Whitewater rafting on Youghiogheny River. AYH membership required (see page 21).

Palmyra

Accommodation: Camp Seltzer Youth Hostel (AYH-SA), 17078. Telephone: 717/838-4957. Open year round. $5. Must bring sleeping bags.

Philadelphia

"Backpacking and hitchhiking types should try to get to the South Street area between 3rd and 6th—for all information and goings-on."

Help: Travelers Aid, 1218 Chestnut St., 19107. Telephone: 215/WA2-0950.
● People's Emergency Center, 3311 Chestnut St., 19104. Telephone: 215/382-7522 or 382-7521. If you find yourself in a destitute condition they will provide a free meal. They also suggest going to Cavanaugh's, 31 Market St.; Froggy's Saloon, 33 South 11th St.; or Smokey Joe's at 40 Walnut St. to meet young people.
● Help, 638 South St., 19147. Telephone: 215/925-4096 or 546-7766. "Drop-in and telephone counseling and referral for any type of problem."
● Philly Fun Phone, 215/864-1990. What's happening in Philadelphia.
● Council for International Visitors–Language Bank, 215/879-5248.
Tourist Information: Philadelphia Convention and Visitors Bureau, 1525 John F. Kennedy Blvd., 19102. Telephone: 215/864-1976. Open 9 a.m. to 5 p.m. every day except Christmas. The bureau offers personalized itineraries, information for the handicapped including braille maps and free guidebooks for wheelchair users, and tickets to various events including the New Year's Day Mummers Parade and the Mann Music Center.

"I would definitely recommend Philadelphia as a town to visit. I have been to many towns and have found Philadelphia to be the most exciting yet."

Accommodations: International House of Philadelphia, 3701 Chestnut St., 19104. Telephone: 215/EV7-5125. "For academically oriented Americans and foreign visitors." $22 single; $28 double (few). Reservations requested; room may be scarce. "Beautiful, modern, award-winning building." Someone at International House told us that the residence facilities at the University of Pennsylvania are available to their residents who stay a month or more.
● YMCA, 5722 Greene St., 19144. Telephone: 215/844-3281. Men only. $15 single. Weekly rate: $35 to $40.
● YWCA, ⬛, 2027 Chestnut St., 19103. Telephone: 215/564-3430. Women only. Weekly rates: for single with shared bath, $53; with private bath, $65.
● Chamounix Mansion–Philadelphia International Youth Hostel (AYH), West Fairmount Park, 19131. Three-quarters of a mile from #38 bus stop. In a house built in 1802. Telephone: 215/878-3676. Open year round except December 15 to January 15. Reservations recommended. $4 for AYH members; $5 for nonmembers. Former country estate overlooking Schuylkill River. They prefer that you bring your own linen or a sleeping bag.

Pittsburgh

Tourist Information: Pittsburgh Convention and Visitors Bureau, Inc., 200 Roosevelt Bldg., 15222. Telephone: 412/281-7711.
● Visitor's Information Phone: 412/391-6840. Offers 24-hour taped information on entertainment.
Help: Travelers Aid, Greyhound Bus Station, 11th St. and Liberty Ave., 15222. Telephone: 412/281-5474.
On Campus: Duquesne University, Carnegie-Mellon University, the University of Pittsburgh, and Point Park College are in this city. To meet students from Duquesne, go to Frank and Wally's on Forbes Ave., Van Braams Café on Van Braam off Forbes, or Sandroni's on Fifth Ave. near Magee. Since the University of Pittsburgh is a commuter campus, it's harder to find students in any one place. The Student Union might be a good place, though—worth a try.

Other places to meet people in a comfortable atmosphere are Wobblie Joe's bar, on the south side; CJ Barneys and the Wooden Keg, a bar in Oakland on the Pitt campus; Squirrel Hill Café, for cheap beer; or at the downtown YMCA's Tuesday night folk dancing.

For information on rides, apartments, odd jobs, etc., try the University of Pittsburgh Student Union's bulletin boards. Specifically for rides, mail the details of where you are going and where you can be reached to radio station WYEP/Rides America, 4 Cable Pl., 15213.

"Ethnic food abounds. Try Middle Eastern food restaurants in the Oakland area and for Italian food go to the Bloomfield section."

Accommodations: YMCA, 304 Wood St., 15222. Telephone: 412/227-6420. Men only. $19.02 single. Weekly rate: $54 first four weeks, $44 after that. Reservations requested three or four days in advance. Cafeteria in the building.
● YMCA, 600 West North Ave., 15212. Telephone: 412/321-8594. Men only. $14.91 single ($3 key deposit). Weekly rate: $45.94. "We are directly across the street from a park which is six blocks long and has everything you would want to do."
● Duquesne University Residence Hall, 1345 Vickroy, 15282. Near downtown. Telephone: 412/434-6655. Open May 15 to July 31. $8 to $10 single. Photo identification required. Reservations requested one week ahead. There is a charge for linen. Good recreational facilities on campus.
● Point Park College (AYH), ♿, 201 Wood St., 15222. Telephone: 412/391-4100. Open year round. $5. AYH membership required (see page 21).
● Red Roof Inn, Pa. 19 and I-76 (Pennsylvania Turnpike), Warrendale. See Danville listing for rates.
● Red Roof Inn, Old U.S. 22/33 at Pa. 60, 15205. Telephone: 412/787-7870. See Danville listing for rates.
● Motel 6, Rte. 19, RD 3, Box 107, Mars, 16046. Telephone: 412/776-9010. See Belle Vernon listing for rates.

Port Allegany

Accommodation: Best Value Canoe Place Inn, 101 Main St., 16743. Telephone: 814/642-2561. $14 to $20 for one; $17 to $23 for two in one bed; $19 to $25 for two in two beds.

Quakertown

Accommodation: Weisel Youth Hostel (AYH), RD 3, 18591. Telephone: 215/536-8749. AYH members: $2.50 summer; $3 winter. Introductory passes available for non-AYH members. Reservations strongly advised on weekends. Bring your own linen. "Rustic, a lovely manor house situated in a state park."

Reading

Accommodation: Econo-Travel Motor Hotel, 2310 Fraver Dr., 19605. Telephone: 215/378-1145. $22.95 for one; $26.95 for two in one bed; $30.95 for two in two beds.

Renovo

Accommodation: YMCA, 3rd and Huron Ave., 17764. Telephone: 717/923-0300. Men and women. $15 single; $20 double.

Shamokin Dam

Accommodation: Best Value Golden Arrow Motel/Restaurant, 128 South Susquehanna Trail, 17870. $17 to $18 for one; $21 for two in one bed.

Uniontown

Accommodation: YMCA, 6-8 North Gallatin Ave., 15401. Telephone: 412/438-2584. Men only. $12.91 single. Weekly rate: $43.81. Reservations are necessary.

Washington

Accommodation: Red Roof Inn, I-70 at U.S. 40 (Exit 4), 15301. Telephone: 412/228-5750. See Danville listing for rates.

West Reading

Accommodation: Friendship Inn–Penn-View, 250 Penn Ave., 19602. Telephone: 215/376-8011. $22 to $24 for one; $25 to $27 for two in one bed; $28 to $32 for two in two beds.

Wilkes-Barre

Accommodation: Best Value Imperial Motor Inn of Wilkes-Barre, 400 Kidder St. (Pa. 115 North), 18702. Telephone: 717/823-2171. $13 to $15 for one; $17 to $19 for two in one bed; $19 to $21 for two in two beds.

Williamsport

Accommodations: YMCA, 343 West 4th St., 17701. Telephone: 717/323-7134. Men and a limited number of women. $10.36 per night, tax and membership included. Vending machines and a microwave oven available. ($2.50 for AYH members, who must bring their own sleeping bags.)
● YWCA, 815 West 4th St., 17701. Telephone: 717/322-4637. Women only. $8.48. Weekly rate: $28.09. Kitchens available.

York

Help: Contact, 717/845-3656.
● Hotline, 717/843-0957..
Accommodations: YMCA, 90 North Newberry St., 17401. Telephone: 717/843-7884. Men only. $9 for a private room or $2 per person for a mat on the gym floor. A shower is provided—bring a towel, soap, and sleeping gear.
● YWCA, 320 East Market St., 17403. Telephone: 717/845-2631. Women only. $8 per night. Reservations suggested.

Rhode Island

Go directly to Newport on the coast and absorb the splendor of the Newport mansions. Once upon a time, before there was an income tax, the richest of the rich anchored their yachts at Newport and built themselves summer cottages along the shore. No one wants to rough it, after all, even in a resort home, so they included Tiffany windows, French ballrooms, Italian dining rooms, and animal topiary gardens in their plans. Extraordinary to see.

You'll notice that Rhode Island's listing is extremely short. We wrote to the Department of Economic Development for help, and someone there suggested that tourist homes are the best places to look for accommodations for under $25 in Rhode Island: "plain, old-fashioned room and board or room only arrangements." You can write to the Tourist Division, Rhode Island Department of Economic Development (address below) and ask for their *Rhode Island Tourist Guide.* They were kind enough to underline for us the places they thought would charge under $25—perhaps they'll do the same for you.

Some Special Events: May Day Breakfasts, which originated in 1867 and are now held throughout the state in church halls, grange halls, and private clubs (May 1); Strawberry Festival in Northgate (June); Newport County 4-H Fair in Portsmouth (July); Bristol County Fair in Warren (August); and Florentine Renaissance Fair in Providence (September).

Hitching: Hitchhiking is illegal in Rhode Island, says the law. It's done, but not to any great extent.

Tourist Information: Rhode Island Department of Economic Development, 7 Jackson Walkway, Providence, RI 02903. Telephone: 401/277-2601.

Charlestown

Accommodation: Friendship Willows Resort Motel and Restaurant, Box 236, Rte. 1, 02813. Telephone: 401/364-7727. $14 to $23 for one; $17 to $24 for two in one bed; $19 to $26 for two in two beds.

Kingston

Help: Sympatico, 401/783-0782.
Accommodations: University of Rhode Island Youth Hostel (AYH-SA), ★, Memorial Union, Rte. 138, 02881. Telephone: 401/789-3929. Men, women, and sometimes children. $4 for AYH members; $5 for others. Two-story farmhouse built around 1860; one mile west of the University of Rhode Island entrance. Closed December 20 to January 5.
● Aldrich Hall, Butterfield Rd., University of Rhode Island, 02881. Telephone: 401/792-2215. Ask for Summer Housing Office. Open June 1 to August 27. $18 single; $15 per person double. $3 linen charge. There's a bus station on campus; the train station is one mile away.
On Campus: A friend at the University of Rhode Island describes the attitude toward hitchhiking in Kingston as accepting for the most part. This contrasts with other reports so you'll have to feel it out for yourself. She suggests Mama Rosa's on Woodruff Ave. in Wakefield as a good place to get a meal, and the Sunnyside Bar in Narragansett as a good place to "hang out."

Newport

Tourist Information: Newport County Chamber of Commerce, P.O. Box 237 JB, 02840. Telephone: 401/847-1600.
● Newport Council for International Visitors, 40 Dearborn St., 02840. Telephone: 401/846-0222. A member of the council has provided us with some good tips about the area: Salve Regina College is here and you might be able to find ride and apartment information on their bulletin board. Also check the bulletin board at O'Hare Academic Center and Miley Hall. You can meet students at Newport Creamer, Harr's Bar and Grill, Spindrift Restaurant, and "many, many waterfront bars and grills." Basically, *"Newport is wall-to-wall people in the summer, accommodations are hard to find and everything is expensive."*
Accommodations: Armed Services YMCA (AYH), 50 Washington Square, 02840. Telephone: 401/846-3120. Open year round. $5 for AYH members. Reservations necessary.

Providence

Help: Travelers Aid, 46 Aborn St., 02903. Telephone: 401/521-2255. They can provide you with listings of rooming houses.
Tourist Information: Greater Providence Convention and Visitors Bureau, 10 Dorrance St., 02903. Telephone: 401/274-1636.
On Campus: Brown University dormitories are usually filled, but occasionally there will be an available room, so check with their housing office. The Rhode Island School of Design is also in Providence and it has a museum worthy of note. You can find an inexpensive meal ($3 to $6) at Camille's Coffee Shop, 178 Mathewson St.; Alexander's Restaurant, 110 Mathewson St. (where

the specialty is a variety of hamburgers); and Andrea's on Thayer St., primarily Greek food.

Accommodations: YMCA, 160 Broad St., 02903. Telephone: 401/456-0100. Men and women. $14 single. Weekly rate: $50.

● Susse Chalet Inn, U.S. 6 and 114A off I-195, Seekonk, MA 02771. Telephone: 617/336-7900. $22.70 for one; $26.70 for two; $32.70 for four.

Woonsocket

Help: Road Counseling Services, 401/769-3100.

Accommodation: Best Value Woonsocket Motor Inn, 333 Clinton St., 02895. Telephone: 401/762-1224. $23 for one; $26 for two in one bed; $29 for two in two beds.

South Carolina

Most of South Carolina has been left the way it was in the beginning—and that's good. You'll find beaches, subtropical islands, mountains, streams, and lakes. The city of Charleston is as aristocratic a city as the U.S. can claim. If your time in South Carolina is limited, you'll probably want to spend most of it in Charleston and the area around it.

Historic Charleston, founded in 1670, is a lovely place to explore on foot. Start your stroll at Battery Park and then walk slowly by the beautiful 18th-century homes. Save time for a visit to the Heyward-Washington House; the second-oldest synagogue in the U.S.; the Charleston Museum; the Dock Street Theater (dating from 1736); and Cabbage Row, the inspiration for *Porgy and Bess.* And only ten miles from this wonderful city, you'll enjoy the 25-acre Magnolia Gardens, where the camellias, oaks, and cypresses draped with moss and wisteria are breathtaking. You may walk the trails, ride a bicycle through, rent a canoe, or take a guided boat tour of the area.

Two areas that are enormously popular with young people, because of the beaches and the nightlife, are the Grand Strand and one of the beaches on it, Myrtle Beach. The Grand Strand is 55 miles of uninterrupted beach that stretches from Little River at the state line south to Pawley's Island.

Some Special Events: Spoleto Festival, one of the world's most comprehensive arts festivals in Charleston (May and June); Hampton County Watermelon Festival in Hampton (June); Water Festival in Beaufort and Tobacco Festival in Lake City (July); Governor's Frog Jump and Egg Striking Contest in Springfield (April); South Carolina State Fair in Columbia (October); and Chitlin' Strut (a day of country music, dancing, a Pig Calling Contest, parade, chicken and chitlin' barbecue) in Salley (November).

Hitching: A friend at the University of South Carolina says that hitchhiking around the university area—Columbia—is a common practice. Since the school is not on a major road, not many people hitch through. If they do, though, they'll find university people "nice and helpful." Although the tourist office doesn't recommend hitchhiking anywhere, the Department of Highways and Public Transportation says it's legal except on the "roadway," the traveled portion of a street or highway.

Tourist Information: Division of Tourism, South Carolina Department of Parks, Recreation and Tourism, P.O. Box 71, Columbia, SC 29202. Although it is possible to rent cabins in South Carolina's state parks, it gets a bit complicated for the months of June to September when assignments for cabin rentals are made in a public drawing. However, from September to June cabins are rented on a first-come, first-served basis. Write to the tourist office (address above) for information and the brochure *South Carolina State Parks.*

Allendale

Accommodation: Carolina Motor Lodge, √, Hwy. 301 North, 29810. Telephone: 803/584-2195. $14.92 for one; $17.76 for two in one bed; $19.80 for two in two beds.

Bamberg

Accommodation: Ziggy's Superior Motel, U.S. 310 and 601, 29003. Telephone: 803/245-2429. $13 to $16 for one; $14 to $18 for two in one bed; $16 to $20 for two in two beds.

Beaufort

Accommodation: Budget Host Motel, ✦ ★ 5%, 👤 (limited), U.S. 21, Box 4236, 29902. Telephone: 803/524-3322. $17 to $18 for one; $19 to $20 for two in one bed; $24 to $25 for two in two beds.

Charleston

Tourist Information: Charleston County Park, Recreation and Tourist Commission, P.O. Box 834, 29402.

Accommodations: Econo-Travel Motor Hotel, 4500 Arco Lane, 29405. Telephone: 803/747-3672. $19.95 for one; $23.95 for two in one bed; $27.95 for two in two beds.

• Econo-Travel Motor Hotel, 5169 Rivers Ave., 29405. Telephone: 803/747-0404. $18 for one; $23 for two in one bed; $26 for two in two beds.

• Econo-Travel Motor Hotel, 2237 Savannah Hwy., 29407. Telephone: 803/571-1880. $19.95 for one; $23.95 for two in one bed; $27.95 for two in two beds.

• Days Inn, 👤, I-26 and West Montague Ave., 3016 West Montague Ave., 29405. Telephone: 803/747-4101. $21.88 for one; $25.88 for two.

• Days Inn, 👤, 260 Hwy. 17 Bypass, Mt. Pleasant, 29464. Telephone: 803/881-1800. See above listing for rates.

• Motel 6, 2058 Savannah Hwy., 29407 (intersection of Hwys. 17 and 7). Telephone: 803/571-0560. $12.95 for one; $16.95 for two; $19.95 for up to four.

Clemson

Help: Clemson University/Campus Hotline, 803/654-1040. "They will try to help most anyone." Hours 8 p.m. to 7 a.m. daily.

On Campus: Although the housing situation is tough around the campus area, stop at the University Union Travel Center (tel. 803/654-2461) for help in finding a place to stay. According to our friend at the Travel Center, Clemson isn't a bad place at all, "just a little behind the times." Another friend says it's not behind at all, only marching to the beat of a different drummer. There is one place you are sure to meet people in Clemson: Edgar's Night Club in the University Union complex. There are also lots of nightclubs downtown, within walking distance from the campus. Go to Sourdough's for a meal under $5.

Accommodation: Days Inn, I-85 and S.C. 187, Exit 14, P.O. Box 1914, 29621. Telephone: 803/287-3550. $21.88 for one; $25.88 for two.

Clinton

On Campus: Presbyterian College is here in this small town which is filled with "beautiful old houses and lovely gardens." You can meet college students in the canteen at the student center or at the local disco. Keep an eye out for the free movies shown on campus most weekends. You can probably stay in the college dorm for $1. Unlike most, they are not coed. There is a good smörgåsbord for $4.50 at Duff's Restaurant, or you can eat a full meal at the school cafeteria for $2.50.

Columbia

Help: Family Service Center (Travelers Aid), 1800 Main St., 29201. Telephone: 803/779-3250.

Accommodations: Days Inn, 🖢, I-20 and U.S. 1 (Two Notch Rd.), 7128 Parkland Rd., 29204. Telephone: 803/736-0000. $22.88 for one; $26.88 for two.
• Days Inn, 🖢, I-26 and S.C. 215 (Airport Exit), 29169. Telephone: 803/796-9900. $20.88 to $21.88 for one; $24.88 to $25.88 for two.
• Econo-Travel Motor Hotel, 127 Morninghill Dr., 29210. Telephone: 803/772-5833. $19.95 for one; $23.95 for two in one bed; $27.95 for two in two beds.
• Econo-Travel Motor Hotel, 1617 Charleston Hwy., West Columbia, 29169. Telephone: 803/796-3714. $19.95 for one; $23.95 for two in one bed; $27.95 for two in two beds.

Dillon

Accommodation: Days Inn, I-95 and S.C. 9 (Exit 193), Rte. 1, 29536. Telephone: 803/774-6041. $17.88 to $19.88 for one; $21.88 to $23.88 for two.

Florence

Accommodations: Econo Lodge, I-95 at U.S. 52, 29501. Telephone: 803/ 665-8558. $17.95 for one; $19.95 for two in one bed; $21.95 for two in two beds.
● Days Inn, I-95 and U.S. 76 (Exit 157), P.O. Box 3806, 29501. Telephone: 803/665-8550. $18.88 for one; $22.88 for two.

Greenville

Help: Family Counseling Service/Travelers Aid for Greenville County, "300" Building, Suite 108, University Ridge, P.O. Box 10306, Federal Station, 29603. Telephone: 803/232-2434.
Tourist Information: Discover Upcountry Carolina Association, P.O. Box 3132, 29602.
Accommodations: Days Inn, I-85 and U.S. 276, P.O. Box 6552, 29606. Telephone: 803/288-6600. $20.88 for one; $24.88 for two.
● Econo-Travel Motor Hotel, 536 Wade Hampton Blvd., 29609. Telephone: 803/232-6416. $17.95 for one; $21.95 for two in one bed; $25.95 for two in two beds.

Hardeeville

Accommodations: Days Inn, I-95 and U.S. 17, Exit 5, P.O. Box 613, 29927. Telephone: 803/784-2221. $19.88 to $21.88 for one; $23.88 to $25.88 for two.
● Econo-Travel Motor Hotel, I-95 at Exit 5 (Rte. 17), P.O. Box 581, 29927. Telephone: 803/784-2201. $16 for one; $20 for two in one bed; $23 for two in two beds.

Manning

Accommodation: Days Inn, I-95 and U.S. 301 (Exit 115), Rte. 4, 29102. Telephone: 803/473-2596. $16.88 to $19.88 for one; $20.88 to $23.88 for two.

Myrtle Beach

Accommodations: Best Value Plantation Motel, South Kings Hwy. at 11th Ave., 29577. Telephone: 803/448-5617 or 448-6150. $12 to $24 for one or two in one bed; $12 to $32 for two in two beds.
● Econo Lodge, 3301 Hwy 17 South, 29582. Telephone: 803/272-6196. $12.95 to $16.95 for one; $16.95 to $20.95 for two in one bed; $19.95 to $24.95 for two in two beds. Rates slightly higher May 22 to September 7.

Orangeburg

Accommodation: Superior Slumberland Motel, 1440 Five Chop Rd., Rte. 2, Box 582, 29115. Telephone: 803/534-5081. $19 for one; $21 for two in one bed: $24 for two in two beds.

Santee

Accommodation: Days Inn, I-95 and S.C. 6 (Exit 98), P.O. Box 9, 29142. Telephone: 803/854-2175. $19.88 to $20.88 for one; $23.88 to $24.88 for two.

Spartanburg

Accommodation: Best Value University Inn, 1019 Frontage Rd., 29303. Telephone: 803/578-9450. $13.88 for one; $18.88 for two in one bed; $20.88 for two in two beds.

Walterboro

Accommodation: Econo-Travel Motor Hotel, Rte. 4, Box 218-D, 29488. Telephone: 803/538-3830. $15.95 for one; $19.95 for two in one bed; $23.95 for two in two beds.

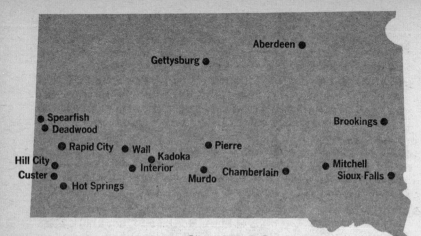

South Dakota

As you plan your days in South Dakota, you'll concentrate on the natural wonders of the state because they are quite spectacular. The most interesting geological formations are the Black Hills and the Badlands. The Black Hills are the highest mountains east of the Rockies. The Badlands, caused by centuries of erosion, are beautifully colored cliffs, ridges, and spires.

Once a prehistoric swamp, the Badlands National Monument is one of the richest fossil beds in the world. Along the Fossil Walk you can examine pieces of the past, like a dog-size camel, a three-toed horse, and a sabre-toothed cat. For children, there's a special "Feelie Room" at the Park Visitor Center.

And no one would want to leave the state before getting a look at sculptor Gutzon Borglum's Mount Rushmore National Memorial. This granite monument to Washington, Jefferson, Lincoln, and Theodore Roosevelt is bound to astound you. Every night during the summer there's a lighting ceremony at the monument.

And for those who like the romance of the Old West, there should certainly be a visit to Deadwood, a town that once had wide-open gambling and bawdy houses and the Number 10 Saloon, where Wild Bill Hickok never did hear Jack McCall's six-gun go off.

Some Special Events: Old Time South Dakota Fiddlers Jamboree in Lake Norden (April); Jackrabbit Stampede (includes a rodeo) in Brookings (May); Czech Days in Tabor and High Plains Art Fair in Spearfish (June); Sitting Bull Stampede Rodeo in Mobridge and Black Hills Roundup in Belle Fourche (July); Frontier Days in White River and Sioux Empire Fair in Sioux Falls (August); State Fair in Huron and Annual Appreciation Hoedown in Wall (September).

Hitching: Hitching, at least in the area of South Dakota State University, is good, and rides are not difficult to get. Forget about hitchhiking in winter, though. South Dakotans are accepting of people on the road as long as they are open and friendly in return. The South Dakota Highway Patrol sent us a list of the best roads for hitchhikers: I-90, I-29, U.S. 12, U.S. 212, U.S. 14, U.S.

18, U.S. 81, U.S. 281, U.S. 83, U.S. 385, and S.D. 79, but they don't recommend hitchhiking. It is prohibited on the roadway; hitchhike on ramps only.

Tourist Information: Division of Tourism, Pierre, SD 57501. Telephone: 605/773-3301. Statewide, toll-free information and referral service: 800/843-1930. Open 8 a.m. to 5 p.m. Monday through Friday.

Aberdeen

Accommodations: Sands Motel, 1111 6th Ave. SE, 57401. Telephone: 605/225-6000. $16.89 for one; $18.89 for two in one bed; $21.89 for two in two beds.

● Best Value Avalon Motel, 1923 6th Ave. SE, 57401. Telephone: 605/225-1325. $13.50 to $16 for one; $16.50 to $18 for two in one bed; $18.50 to $20 for two in two beds.

● Best Value Riverview Motel, 1409 6th Ave. SE, 57401. Telephone: 605/225-5300. $11.85 to $16.85 for one; $15.85 to $20.85 for two in one bed; $17.85 to $22.85 for two in two beds.

Brookings

Help: Help Phone, South Dakota State University. Telephone: 605/688-5146. Open 7:30 p.m. to 2:30 a.m.

On Campus: Go to the University Center of South Dakota State University to meet students and to find out whether you can stay in a dorm on campus. You can also try United Ministries, and if that doesn't work, Brookings has two parks suitable for camping in good weather. There is a good bulletin board in Off Campus Housing, University Student Union (tel. 605/688-5818). For a bite to eat, try the Ram Pub or Pheasant Lounge, both on the Main Ave. of town.

Accommodations: New Life Educational Foundation, 317 Third Ave., 57006 (near South Dakota State University). Telephone: 605/692-9753. Men, women, and children. $5 per night, but "if people have no money at all we will allow them to stay provided they help with the work that needs to be done around the center. We are a Christian organization that lives and works together in a converted hotel." Meals are served for $1.50 extra per meal.

● Friendship Inn–Malinda, 144 Main Ave. South, 57006. Telephone: 605/692-6338. $11 for one; $14 for two in one bed; $16.50 for two in two beds.

● Motel 6, U.S. 14 and I-29, 57006. To open in 1982. $12.95 for one; $16.95 for two; $19.95 for up to four.

Chamberlain

Accommodation: Friendship Inn–Bel Aire, 312 East King, 57325. Telephone: 605/734-5595. $18 to $25 for two in one bed; $20 to $29 for two in two beds.

368 WHERE TO STAY USA

Custer

Accommodation: Best Value Chief Motel and Café, 120 Mt. Rushmore Rd., 57730. Telephone: 605/673-2318. $15 to $24 for one; $18 to $28 for two in one bed; $22 to $32 for two in two beds.

Deadwood

Accommodation: Friendship Inn–76 Motel, 68 Main St., Box 442, 57732. Telephone: 605/578-3476. $18 to $23 for one; $21 to $29 for two in one bed; $23 to $35 for two in two beds.

Gettysburg

Accommodation: Superior Trail Motel, 211 East Garfield, 57442. Telephone: 605/765-2482. $13 to $16 for one; $16 to $18 for two in one bed; $18 to $20 for two in two beds.

Hill City

Accommodation: Pines Edge Motel, √10%, junction of Rtes. 16 East and 385, P.O. Box 454, 57745. Telephone: 605/574-2236. $16.64 for one; $20 for two in one bed; $25 for two in two beds.

Hot Springs

Camping: Wind Cave National Park, 57747. Camping at Elk Mountain (one mile north of headquarters) from May 15 to September 15. $4 per campsite per night.

Interior

Camping: Badlands National Park, P.O. Box 6, 57750. Camping at Cedar Pass, $4 per campsite per night. Camping at Sage Pass, with primitive facilities, no fee.

Kadoka

Accommodations: Best Value West Motel, P.O. Box 1, 57543. Telephone: 605/837-2427. $12 for one; $14 to $18 for two in one bed; $16 to $26 for two in two beds.
● Cuckleburr Motel, Exit 150, I-90, P.O. Box 293, 57543. Telephone: 605/837-2151. $18 to $22 for one; $22 to $24 for two in one bed; $24 to $28 for two in two beds.

Mitchell

Accommodations: Friendship Inn–Anthony, 1518 West Havens, 57301. Telephone: 605/996-7518. $14 to $20 for one; $16 to $25 for two in one bed;

$18 to $27 for two in two beds.

● Motel 6, 1309 South Ohlman St., 57301. Telephone: 605/996-9696. See Brookings listing for rates.

Murdo

Accommodation: Friendship Inn–Zoart, I-90 Business Loop, 57559. Telephone: 605/669-2322. $16 to $22 for two in one bed; $20 to $27 for two in two beds.

Pierre

Accommodations: Motel 6, 815 Wells Ave., 57501. Telephone: 605/224-6666. See Brookings listing for rates.

● Thrifty Scot Motel, 520 West Sioux Ave., 57501. Telephone: 605/224-0411. $17.90 to $19.90 for one; $21.90 to $23.90 for two in one bed; $26.90 to $30.90 for two in two beds.

Rapid City

Accommodations: Marion's Guest House, 830 Quincy, 57701. About 4½ blocks from bus station. Telephone: 605/342-1790. $12 single; $18 double; $21 triple. Recommended by a reader from Belgium who said it was "an excellent place to spend the night."

● YMCA (AYH-SA), 815 Kansas City St., 57701. Telephone: 605/342-8538. Men and women. Open June 1 to August 30. $3 includes dormitory cot, toilet, shower, pool, and tourist information. Must bring your own bedding. They prefer foreign students, hostelers, and readers of *Where to Stay.*

● Home on the Range, 2422 Canyon Lake Dr., 57701. Telephone: 605/343-1368. $8 single. Weekly rate: $40. Many recreational facilities nearby. "There are 16 eating places less than 10 blocks away."

● Colonial Motel, ♥ ★ 5%, 511 East North St., 57701. Telephone: 605/342-1417. $15 to $22 for one; $17 to $27 for two. Heated pool at motel.

● Best Value Budget Inn Motel, 610 East North St., 57701. Telephone: 605/342-8594. $15 to $20 for one; $20 to $25 for two in one bed; $22 to $27 for two in two beds.

● Best Value Four Seasons Motel, 930 East North St., 57701. Telephone: 605/343-7822. $14 to $23 for one; $16 to $26 for two in one bed; $18 to $30 for two in two beds.

● Motel 6, 620 East Latrobe St., 57701. Telephone: 605/343-1220. See Brookings listing for rates.

● Friendship Inn–Fantasy Inn, 3737 Sturgis Rd., 57701. Telephone: 605/342-2892. $18.50 to $22.50 for one; $20.50 to $24.50 for two in one bed; $22.50 to $28.50 for two in two beds.

● Superior Price Motel, √10%, 401 East North St., 57701. Telephone: 605/343-1806. $16 to $22 for one; $20 to $26 for two in one bed; $22 to $30 for two in two beds.

Sioux Falls

Help: Volunteer and Information Center, 605/334-6645. The center is open 24 hours and also has a crisis line. They recommend several inexpensive eateries in the area: Kirk's, 2605 West 12th; Country Kitchen, 2708 East 10th; Crack'd Pot, 1420 North Minnesota and 2700 South Minnesota; and Walt and Mary's, 3201 East 10th. Generally you can get a meal at these places for $3 to $5, some including salad bar. They also mentioned Zac's, a local disco, and Firehouse Coffeehouse for the evening hours.

Accommodations: YWCA, 300 West 11th St., 57102. Telephone: 605/336-3660. Women only. $8.50 single; $15 double. Weekly rate: $45. Reservations requested.

"This is a warm, neat and friendly place; however, most of the residents are between the ages of 17 and 21 and are rather noisy."

● Motel 6, 3009 West Russell St., 57104. Telephone: 605/336-0071. See Brookings listing for rates.

● Econ-O-Inn of Sioux Falls, I-29 and 41st St. West, 57106. Telephone: 605/334-5600. $15.50 for one; $19.50 for two in one bed; $21.50 for two in two beds.

● Thrifty Scot Motel, 5001 North Cliff Ave., 57104. Telephone: 605/331-5959. $16.90 to $18.90 for one; $20.90 to $22.90 for two in one bed; $25.90 to $29.90 for two in two beds.

● Thrifty Scot Motel, 3401 Gateway Blvd., 57106. Telephone: 605/339-9240. $16.90 to $18.90 for one; $20.90 to $22.90 for two in one bed; $25.90 to $29.90 for two in two beds.

● Exel Inn, ♿, 1300 West Russell St., 57104. Telephone: 605/331-5800. $11.50 for one; $16.50 for two in one bed; $18.50 for two in two beds.

● Friendship Inn–Arena Motel, 2401 West Russell St., 57104. Telephone: 605/336-1470. $12 to $18 for one; $15 to $22 for two in one bed; $17 to $28 for two in two beds.

● Friendship Inn–Pine Crest, S.D. 42, U.S. 16 (old), and I-29, Exit 79, 57106. Telephone: 605/336-3530. See above listing for rates.

Spearfish

Accommodation: Friendship Inn–Royal Rest, 444 Main, 57783. Telephone: 605/642-3842. $16 to $22 for one; $18 to $26 for two in one bed; $20 to $30 for two in two beds.

Wall

Accommodation: Friendship Inn–Elk Motel, P.O. Box 287, corner of Hwys. 14, 16, and 16A, 57790. $12.50 to $24.50 for one; $16.50 to $30.50 for two in one bed; $22.50 to $34.50 for two in two beds.

Tennessee

We'll let someone who lives in Tennessee tell you about it: "The main things I like around here are the mountains and tiny towns where people live set apart from a lot of the world—like the tiny area near Knoxville where the Melungeons live. Stories vary about who the Melungeons are—some say they're descendants of Spaniards who got lost in the New World and some think that they're a mixture of the Spaniards and some escaped slaves. Whatever the truth is, they remain aloof and apart and have kept alive some old crafts like making buckets of wood with no nails. There are dulcimer makers here too, and I suppose I should mention Gatlinburg—the tourist center of Tennessee. Lots of people like it, but it's too touristy for me—too many Ye Olde Shoppes, etc. But on the way to Gatlinburg there's a grist mill dating back to 1850 where corn and wheat are still ground by water power. It's a pretty place."

Some Special Events: Dogwood Arts Festival in Knoxville (17-day salute to spring and the beauty of the dogwood trees), Mule Day in Columbia, and the World's Largest Fish Fry in Paris (all in April); Appalachian Music Days in Bristol and Spring Music and Crafts Festival in Rugby (May); Dulcimer Convention in Cosby, Country Music Days in Elizabethton, and Rhododendron Festival in Roan Mountain (all in June); Old-Time Fiddler's Jamboree in Smithville and Gatlinburg Craftsmen's Fair in Gatlinburg (July); Memphis Music Festival: A Tribute to Elvis in Memphis (August); and the Tennessee State Fair in Nashville (September).

Note: No event can compare to the next World's Fair, which will be held in Knoxville from May to October 1982.

Hitching: It can be tricky to hitchhike in Tennessee. Legally you must stay off the "roadway." Police tend to be hard on hitchhikers. Some discouraging words from a student at the University of Tennessee: "Very few hitchhikers are able to get a lift, even around the university area. People are leary of hitchers lately." Perhaps it would be best to do what many students do instead of hitchhiking—they hike or ride their bikes.

Tourist Information: Department of Tourist Development, P.O. Box 23170, Nashville, TN 37202. Telephone: 615/741-2158.

Caryville

Accommodation: Tennessee Motel, 101 Tennessee Dr., Box 75, 37714. Telephone: 615/562-9595. $18 to $20 for one or two in one bed; $20 to $22 for two in two beds.

Chattanooga

Help: Family and Children's Services of Chattanooga (Travelers Aid), 323 High St., 37403. Telephone: 605/267-0021.

Tourist Information: Chattanooga Area Convention and Visitors Bureau, 1001 Market St., 37402. Telephone: 615/756-2121.

Accommodations: YWCA, 🐟 ★, 300 East 8th St., 37403. Telephone: 615/267-5493. Women only. $10 single. Weekly rate: $50 first two weeks; $23 following weeks.

● Days Inn, I-75 and U.S. 41 (East Ridge Exit 1-B), 1401 Mack Smith Rd., 37401. Telephone: 615/894-7480. $18.88 to $19.88 for one; $22.88 to $23.88 for two.

● Days Inn, I-75 and Ga. 146 (Ft. Oglethorpe-Rossville Exit), Ringgold, GA 30736. Telephone: 404/891-9910. $19.88 for one; $24.88 for two.

● Econo Lodge, 6650 Ringgold Rd., 37412. Telephone: 615/894-1860. $18.75 to $20.75 for one; $21.75 to $25.75 for two in one bed; $24.75 to $27.75 for two in two beds.

● Scottish Inn, I-75 and Hwy. 41, Exit 1, East Ridge, 37412. Telephone: 615/894-0911. $16.95 for one; $19.95 for two in one bed; $22.95 for two in two beds.

Clarksville

Accommodation: Motel 6, 881 Kraft St., 37040. Telephone: 615/552-3315. $12.95 for one; $16.95 for two; $19.95 for up to four.

Cleveland

Accommodation: Friendship Diplomat Motor Lodge and Restaurant, 720 South Lee Hwy., 37311. Telephone: 615/476-6586. $14 to $16 for one; $18 to $20 for two in one bed; $22 to $28 for two in two beds.

Cookeville

Accommodation: Days Inn, I-40 and Tenn. 111 (Exit 288), Rte. 8, 38501. Telephone: 616/528-5411. $18.88 to $21.88 for one; $22.88 to $25.88 for two.

Gatlinburg

Tourist Information: Gatlinburg Chamber of Commerce, 37738. Telephone: 615/436-4178, or toll free 800/251-9868 outside of Tennessee.

Camping: Great Smoky Mountains National Park, 37738. There are several campgrounds in this immensely popular park. Some are open all year, some during the summer season only. There are also trail shelters along the Appalachian Trail—one day's journey apart. Permits required for backcountry use. Reservations can be made through Ticketron, April through October.

Accommodations: Bell's Wa-Floy Retreat Hostel (AYH), 🐟 ♿, P.O. Box 212, Rte. 3, 37738. Telephone: 615/436-5575 or 436-7700. $5 to $6 for AYH members; $10 to $12 for nonmembers. "We have 22 buildings total. A two-

TENNESSEE **373**

story lodge, a motel, and cottages and apartments of various sizes." Restaurants on premises.

● Econo Lodge, 167 Pkwy., Hwy. 441, 37830. Telephone: 615/436-5652. $18.95 for one or two in one bed; $22.95 for two in two beds.

Greenville

Accommodation: Star Motel, √, 1633 Tusculum Blvd., 37743. $14.95 to $16.95 for one; $16.95 to $18.95 for two in one bed; $18.95 to $20.95 for two in two beds.

Jackson

Accommodations: Friendship Inn–Thunderbird, U.S. 45, 38301. Telephone: 901/422-5536. $24.98 for one or two in one bed; $29.42 for two in two beds.

● Days Inn, I-40 and U.S. 45, 2295 North Highland St., 38301. Telephone: 901/668-1145. $19.88 for one; $25.88 for two.

Jellico

Accommodation: Days Inn, I-75 and U.S. 25 West, Exit 160, P.O. Box 299, 37762. Telephone: 615/784-7281. $17.88 to $18.88 for one; $21.88 to $22.88 for two.

Kingsport

Accommodation: Econo-Travel Motor Lodge, 1704 East Stone Dr., 37660. Telephone: 615/245-0286. $18.95 for one; $21.95 for two in one bed; $23.95 for two in two beds.

Knoxville

Tourist Information: Knoxville Area Council for Conventions and Visitors—KNOXVISIT, 901 East Vine Ave., P.O. Box 15012, 37901. Telephone: 615/523-7263.

Help: University Center Information Desk, 615/974-3453.

● Knoxville Travelers Aid Society, Inc. 203 East Fifth Ave., 37917. Telephone: 615/522-8718.

On Campus: According to someone at the University of Tennessee, Knoxville is "a great place to live, a fair place to visit, and a great place to travel through." If you are passing through, you can count on meeting students in the Student Center or at any of the bars and restaurants that appear and disappear on Cumberland Ave. between the 1500 and 2000 blocks.

To find out what's going on on campus, get a copy of the *Daily Beacon,* the university paper. Everyone reads it, so if you want to put a notice somewhere about a ride, apartment, etc., put it in the *Beacon.* The various bulletin boards in the Student Center are also a good source of information.

For food, try the Torch, 1701 Cumberland Ave., where you can eat well for $2; the L and N Tavern, 723 Western Ave., where you can get Chinese food served at homemade heavy tables; and Ramsey's Restaurant on 16th St., for a meat or fish and vegetable dinner. Anyone can take advantage, too, of the University Food Service meals or Smokey's, in the dorms in the Student Center, where a full meal is $2.75.

For help finding a place to stay, both foreign and U.S. students can stop in at the International Student Affairs Office, Room 201, Alumni Hall. Telephone: 615/974-3177.

Accommodations: YMCA, 605 West Clinch Ave., 37902, P.O. Box 2776, 37901. Telephone: 615/522-9622. Men over 18 only. $9.50. Weekly rate: $23.50 to $25.50.

● Days Inn, I-75/I-40 and Lovell Rd. (Exit 374), Concord, 37720. Telephone: 615/966-5801. $19.88 to $23.88 for one; $23.88 to $27.88 for two.

● Ranch House Motel, 3207 East Magnolia Ave., 37914. Telephone: 615/523-7155. $15.95 for one; $19.95 for two in one bed; $21.95 for two in two beds.

● Econo Lodge, 104 Bridgewater Rd., 37919. Telephone: 615/693-5331. $19.95 for one; $21.95 for two in one bed; $24.95 for two in two beds.

Lebanon

Accommodations: Dix's Best Value Plaza Motor Lodge, 319 West Main St., 37087. Telephone: 615/444-3163 or 444-3164. $15 to $18 for one; $18 to $20 for two in one bed; $24 to $30 for two in two beds.

● Days Inn, I-40 and U.S. 231 South, 37087. Telephone: 615/449-2900. $20.88 for one; $23.88 for two. Rates higher June to September.

Manchester

Accommodation: Days Inn, I-24 and U.S. 41 (Exit 114), P.O. Box 886, 37355. Telephone: 615/728-9530. $18.88 to $22.88 for one; $22.88 to $26.88 for two.

Memphis

Help: Travelers Aid, 1025 Dermon Bldg., 38103. Telephone: 901/525-5466.

Tourist Information: Convention and Visitors Bureau of Memphis, 12 South Main St., Suite 107, 38103. Telephone: 901/526-1919.

Accommodations: Regal 8 Inn, 1360 Springbrook Rd., 38116. Telephone: 901/396-3620. $19.88 for one; $22.88 for two in one bed; $25.88 for two to four in two beds.

● Red Roof Inn, 🖾, I-40 at Sycamore and Bartlett Rds. (Exit 12), 38134. Telephone: 901/388-6111. $17.95 for one; $20.95 for two in one bed; $22.95 to $24.95 for two to four in two beds.

● Tennessee Hotel, 88 South 3rd St., 38103. Telephone: 901/525-6621. Across the street from the bus station. $12 single; $17 double. Moderately priced restaurant in hotel.

● Days Inn, I-240/I-40 and 5301 Summer Ave., 38122. Telephone: 901/761-1600. $21.88 for one; $26.88 for two. Rates higher May 16 to September 6.

● Days Inn, 🖾, I-55 and Brooks Rd., 38116. Telephone: 901/345-2470. Five minutes from airport. $20.88 to $22.88 for one; $24.88 to $26.88 for two.

● Days Inn, I-55 and East Shelby Dr. Exit, 1970 East Shelby Dr., 38116. Telephone: 901/332-0222. $21.88 to $22.88 for one; $26.88 to $27.88 for two.

Murfreesboro

Accommodations: Days Inn, I-24 and U.S. 231 (Exit 81), 2036 South Church St., 37130. Telephone: 615/893-1090.

● Motel 6, 114 Chaffin Place, 37130. Telephone: 615/890-1910. See Clarksville listing for rates.

Nashville

Help: Travelers Aid, 122 Seventh Ave. North. Telephone: 615/256-3168 or 256-3169.

Tourist Information: Convention and Visitors Division, Nashville Area Chamber of Commerce, 161 Fourth Ave. North, 37219. Telephone: 615/259-3900.

Accommodations: Scottish Inn, I-65 and James Robertson Pkwy. Exit 85, 37206. Telephone: 615/255-8361. $14.95 to $23.95 for one; $17.95 to $32.95 for two.

● Motel 6, 95 Wallace Rd., 37211. Telephone: 615/834-1231. See Clarksville listing for rates.

● Superior Travelers Rest Inn Inc., Franklin Rd. and Old Hickory Blvd., Brentwood, 37027. Telephone: 615/373-3033. $19 to $25 for one; $24 to $27 for two in one bed; $29 to $33 for two in two beds.

● Days Inn, I-65 and Trinity Lane, Exit 87B, 37207. Telephone: 615/226-4500. $21.88 to $23.88 for one; $25.88 to $27.88 for two.

● Days Inn, I-40 and Old Hickory Blvd., Hermitage, 37076. Telephone: 615/889-8940. $21.88 for one; $25.88 for two. Rates higher June to September.

● Days Inn, I-24 and Murfreesboro Rd. (Exit 52), 321 Plus Park Blvd., 37217. Telephone: 615/367-9180. $22.88 to $23.88 for one; $26.88 to $27.88 for two. Rates higher May 16 to September 11.

● Days Inn, I-24 at Bell Rd. (Exit 59), 1101 Bell Rd., Antioch, 37013. Telephone: 615/834-8440. $20.88 to $22.88 for one; $25.88 to $27.88 for two. Rates higher May 16 to September 11.

Newport

Accommodation: Best Value Bryant Town Motel, 1510 Cosby Rd., 37821. Telephone: 615/623-6006. $18 to $21 for one; $21 to $24 for two in one bed; $27 for two in two beds.

South Pittsburg

Accommodation: Scottish Inn, I-24 junction at Kimball and South Pittsburg Exit, Jasper, 37347. Telephone: 615/837-7933. $18 for one; $20 for two in one bed; $23 for two in two beds.

Sweetwater

Accommodation: Best Value Mar-Vel Motel East, South Main St., 37874. Telephone: 615/337-3585. $14.98 for one; $19.26 for two in one bed; $26.95 for two in two beds.

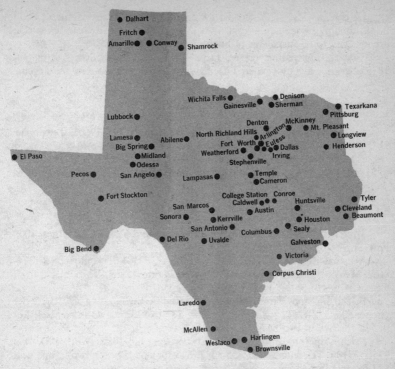

Texas

Texas is big—maybe not as big as Alaska but still very, very big (7½% of the total U.S. land area). Texans love the bigness and don't seem to mind being teased about it. Texas cities are some of the fastest growing and most prosperous urban areas in the U.S. at a time when most cities are on the decline. It's eastern Texas that's the most developed; western Texas is still a land of vast deserts, mountains, and prairies, with all the huge ranches that you've seen in John Wayne movies. There are tropical areas in the south, along the Mexican border and Gulf of Mexico.

Because of the general prosperity in much of Texas, there are part-time unskilled jobs to be had in most of the cities—Houston and Dallas especially.

Some Special Events: Tip of Texas Orchid Show in Los Fresnos and Frontier Days in Lajitas (April); Pioneer Heritage Week in Del Rio and Rodeo in Mesquite every Friday and Saturday (May); Ethnic Folk Festival in Austin and Pow Wow at the Indian Reservation in Livingston (June); Fishing Fiesta in Freeport and Watermelon Festival in McDade (July); Pioneers and Old Settlers Reunion in Alvarado and International Barbecue Cookoff in Taylor (August); and the World Championship Barbecue Goat Cookoff and Arts and Crafts Fair in Brady (September).

Hitching: Most of the people we heard from on Texas campuses don't think hitchhiking is such a great idea in their state and seem to agree that drivers tend to be suspicious of hitchhikers.

Tourist Information: Texas, Dept. OHT, P.O. Box 5064, Austin, TX 78763. Ask for a copy of their 170-plus-page booklet *Texas! Live the Legend.*

Abilene

Accommodations: Motel 6, 4951 West Stamford St., 79603. Telephone: 915/673-2561. $12.95 for one; $16.95 for two; $19.95 for up to four.

● Sunset Lodge, 3801 South 1st St., 79605. Telephone: 915/677-8546. $13 to $18 for one; $16 to $22 for two in one bed; $20 to $26 for two in two beds.

Amarillo

Tourist Information: Board of Conventions and Visitors Activities, 1000 Polk St., 79101. Telephone: 806/374-9812.

Accommodations: YMCA, 816 Van Buren, 79101. Telephone: 806/374-4651. Men only; age 18 and over. $6.75. Weekly rate: $28.50. Three blocks from bus.

● Friendship Inn–Farrell Manor, 100 East Amarillo Blvd., 79107. Telephone: 806/372-1261. $18 to $20 for one; $21 to $23 for two in one bed; $24 to $30 for two in two beds.

● Friendship Inn–Broncho Lodge, 6005 Amarillo Blvd. West, P.O. Box 3356, 79106. Telephone: 806/355-3321. $15 for one; $19 for two in one bed; $22 for two in two beds.

● Motel 6, 2032 Paramount Blvd., 79109. Telephone: 806/355-9861. See Abilene listing for rates.

● Regal 8 Inn, 6030 I-40 West, 79106. Telephone: 806/359-7651. $18.88 for one; $21.88 for two in one bed; $24.88 for two to four in two beds.

● Scottish Inn, Mirror St. at Hwys. 60 and 66, 79107. Telephone: 806/373-8316. $16 to $18 for one; $18 to $20 for two in one bed; $20 to $22 for two in two beds.

Arlington

On Campus: One friend at the University of Texas in Arlington says "You should feel at home at UTA—one out of every 12 students is an 'international.'"

Accommodations: Bauder Fashion College, 508 South Center St., 76010. Telephone: 817/277-6666 or 261-2812. Men, women, and children. Open June 10 to August 10. $13 single; $8.50 per person double. Reservations requested two weeks in advance. Must provide own linens and towels. Meals available in cafeteria. Swimming pool available.

● Friendship Oasis Motel, 818 West Division, 76012. Telephone: 818/274-1616. $14 to $16 for one; $16 to $20 for two in one bed; $20 to $24 for two in two beds.

● Motel 6, 2626 Randol Mill Rd. East, 76011. Telephone: 817/649-1101. See Abilene listing for rates.

Austin

Tourist Information: Tourist and Convention Information, Austin Chamber of Commerce, P.O. Box 1967, 78767. Telephone: 512/478-9383.

Help: Room Locator Service, 512/474-8885.

● Information and Crisis Center Hotline, 512/472-2411.

On Campus: The largest campus of the University of Texas is in Austin. Students can be found all over Austin with an especially high concentration in the Student Union. International students traveling in the area may contact the International Office at 512/471-1211 for general help and advice.

When you're hungry, go where the Austin Texans go—to Mad Dog & Beans for hamburgers and trimmings, 512 West 24th St.; Mr. Gatti's Pizza, 503 West Martin Luther King Jr. Blvd.; Matt's El Rancho at 303 East 1st or Fonda San Miguel at 2330 West North Loop, both for Mexican food.

Taos Dormitory, 2612 Guadalupe, has single rooms for $15 and double rooms for $20.

Accommodations: The Castilian, 🎓 ★ 10%, ♿ (limited), 2323 San Antonio St., 78705. One block west of university campus. Telephone: 512/478-9811. Men, women, and children. May 25 to August 15. $19 single; $23 double.

● Austin Youth Hostel (AYH), 1312 Newning Ave., 78704. Telephone: 512/442-1584. Open year round. $4. AYH membership required (see page 21). Closed first Sunday of every month.

● Motel 6, 2707 Interregional Hwy. South, 78741. Telephone: 512/444-4842. See Abilene listing for rates.

● Motel 6, 9420 North I-35, 78753. Telephone: 512/836-0714. See Abilene listing for rates.

● Western 6 Motel, 8010 North I-35, 78753. Telephone: 512/837-9890. $14.40 single; $21.90 double.

Beaumont

Accommodations: YWCA, 660 Calder St., 77701. Telephone: 713/832-7765. Women 17 and over only. $10 single. Two blocks from bus; three miles from train. Bring your own linen.

● Days Inn, ♿, I-10 and Rusk St., 77702. Telephone: 713/838-0581. $22.88 for one; $28.88 for two.

● Motel 6, 2640 I-10 East, 77703. Telephone: 713/898-2770. See Abilene listing for rates.

Big Bend

Camping: Big Bend National Park, 79834. There's camping year round at Cottonwood, Chisos, Rio Grande, and Panther Junction. $1 to $2 per campsite per night.

Big Spring

Accommodations: Friendship American Motor Inn, Hwy. 87 and I-20, 79720. Telephone: 915/263-7357. $15 to $17 for one; $18 to $20 for two in one bed; $22 to $24 for two in two beds.

● Motel 6, 600 West I-20, 79720. Telephone: 915/263-6243. See Abilene listing for rates.

Brazosport

Accommodation: Motel 6, Texas 332 and Lazy Lane, Clute, 77531. Telephone: 713/265-6766. See Abilene listing for rates.

Brownsville

Accommodation: Motel 6, 2255 North Expressway, 78521. Telephone: 512/546-6699. See Abilene listing for rates.

Caldwell

Accommodation: Friendship Inn–Varsity Inn Motel, P.O. Box 716, 77836. Telephone: 713/567-4661. $22 to $25 for one; $25 to $28 for two in one bed; $29 to $33 for two in two beds.

Cameron

Accommodation: Friendship Inn–Varsity Motel, Hwy. 190-77 and 36 South, 76520. Telephone: 817/697-6446. $20 to $23 for one; $23 to $26 for two in one bed; $28 to $31 for two in two beds.

Cleveland

Accommodation: Best Value Pine Forest Motel and Restaurant, Hwy. 59 North, Rte. 6, Box 732, 77327. Telephone: 713/592-8707. $18.49 for one; $19.52 for two in one bed; $21.58 for two in two beds.

College Station

Accommodation: Motel 6, 2327 Texas Ave., 77840. Telephone: 713/696-1631. See Abilene listing for rates.

Columbus

Accommodation: Friendship Inn–Baker Motel, 1136 Walnut St., 78934. Telephone: 713/732-2315. $21 to $23 for one; $23 to $29 for two in one bed; $25 and up for two in two beds.

Conroe

Accommodation: Motel 6, west side of I-45 at Gladstell St., 77301. See Abilene listing for rates.

Conway

Accommodation: Friendship Inn–L.A. Motel and Restaurant of Conway, I-40 and Hwy. 207, 79020. Telephone: 806/537-5127 or 537-9927. $17 for one; $19 for two in one bed; $22 for two in two beds.

Corpus Christi

Camping: Padre Island National Seashore, 9405 South Padre Island Dr., 78418. There are campgrounds at Malaquite Beach for $2, and primitive camping on other beaches.

Accommodation: Motel 6, 845 Lantana St., 78408, Telephone: 512/882-5231. See Abilene listing for rates.

Dalhart

Accommodation: Friendship Inn–Xit Ranch Motel, 209 Liberal St., 79022. Telephone: 806/249-4589. $17 for one; $18 for two in one bed; $21 for two in two beds.

Dallas

Tourist Information: Dallas Convention and Visitors Bureau, Dallas Chamber of Commerce, 400 South Houston (in person) or 1507 Pacific (mailing address), 75201. Telephone: 214/651-1020.

Accommodations: Western 6 Motel, 4220 Independence Dr., 75237. Telephone: 214/296-3331. $14.40 single; $21.90 double.

• Days Inn, I-35 East and Camp Wisdom Rd., 220 West Camp Wisdom Rd., 75232. Telephone: 214/224-8261. $21.88 to $23.88 for one; $25.88 to $27.88 for two.

• Motel 6, 3629 Hwy. 80, 75150. Telephone: 214/279-7249. See Abilene listing for rates.

• Motel 6, 4610 South R. L. Thornton Freeway, 75224. Telephone: 214/372-1456. See Abilene listing for rates.

• Motel 6, 9626 C. F. Hawn Freeway, 75217. Telephone: 214/286-5206. See Abilene listing for rates.

• Days Inn, I-35 East and 2275 Valley View Lane, 75234. Telephone: 214/243-6868. $21.88 to $23.88 for one; $25.88 to $27.88 for two.

• Days Inn, I-635 and 2753 Forest Lane, 75234. Telephone: 214/620-2828. See above listing for rates.

• Days Inn, 9386 LBJ Freeway, 75231. Telephone: 214/690-1220. See above listing for rates.

• Days Inn, I-30 and 6222 Beltline Rd., 75041. Telephone: 214/226-7621. $23.88 for one; $27.88 for two.

• Days Inn, Airport Freeway and O'Conner Rd., 110 West Airport Freeway, 75062. Telephone: 214/438-8500. $21.88 to $23.88 for one; $25.88 to $27.88 for two.

• Days Inn, U.S. 80 at Town East Blvd., 3817 Hwy. 80 East, 75150. Telephone: 214/270-7551. $23.88 for one; $27.88 for two.

● Days Inn, Texas 360 and Ave. J, 1195 North Watson Rd., 76011. Telephone: 817/649-8881. $23.88 to $24.88 for one; $27.88 to $28.88 for two.

"Two blocks from the bus station was the Lawrence Hotel, which I would highly recommend. It is on the corner of Houston and Jackson Sts. and it has a beaut disco around the corner, 'City Lights.' Back to the hotel, the rooms are large with double bed and private bathroom, and they don't charge extra for the bugs in the bath."

Del Rio

Accommodations: Friendship Inn–Desert Hills, Hwys. 90, 277, and 377, 1912 Ave. F, 78840. Telephone: 512/775-3548. $12 to $14 for one; $14 to $15 for two in one bed; $15 to $17 for two in two beds.

● Motel 6, 2115 Ave. F, 78840. Telephone: 512/775-6635. See Abilene listing for rates.

Camping: Amistad National Recreation Area, Star Rte. 2, Box 5A, 78840. Camping all year at primitive campsites.

Denison

Accommodation: Friendship Inn–La Villa Motel, Hwys. 69 and 75. Telephone: 214/465-8811. $23.50 to $25 for one; $26 to $27.50 for two in one bed; $30 to $39 for two in two beds.

Denton

Accommodation: Motel 6, 4125 I-35 East, 76201. Telephone: 817/387-0571. See Abilene listing for rates.

El Paso

Help: El Paso Crisis Services, 915/779-1800.

Accommodations: YMCA, 701 Montana, 79902. Telephone: 915/533-3941. Men, women, and one child. $11 single with bath, $10 without bath; $17 double with bath.

● Armed Services YMCA, 315 East Franklin St., 79901. Telephone: 915/532-4957. $11 single; $16 double. *"After visiting the Armed Services YMCA on two occasions, I thought I must write to tell you of their excellence. The rooms are large, spotlessly clean, and all the staff very helpful."*

● Gardner Hotel, 311 East Franklin Ave., 79901. Telephone: 915/532-3661. Five blocks from bus; eight blocks from train. $11.50 single with private bath, $8.50 to $10 single with shared bath; $12.50 double with private bath, $11.50 to $13 double with shared bath. "A 60-year-old hotel which is safe, clean, and friendly."

● Friendship Inn–La Posta Motor Lodge, 4111 North Mesa St., 79902. Telephone: 915/533-3986. $18 to $22 for one; $19 to $24 for two in one bed; $22 to $29 for two in two beds.

● Friendship Inn–Beverly Crest Motor Inn, 8709 Dyer St., 79904. Tele-

phone: 915/755-7631. $16 to $18 for one; $18 to $20 for two in one bed; $21 to $24 for two in two beds.
- Motel 6, 11049 Gateway Blvd. West, 79935. Telephone: 915/591-6600. See Abilene listing for rates.
- Motel 6, 7840 North Mesa St., 79932. Telephone: 915/584-3485. See Abilene listing for rates.

Euless

Accommodation: Western 6 Motel, 110 West Airport Freeway, 76039. Telephone: 817/267-8454. $14.40 single; $21.90 double.

Fort Stockton

Accommodations: Friendship Inn–Silver Saddle Lodge, 803 East Dickinson Blvd., 79735. Telephone: 915/336-3311. $16 to $18 for one; $22 to $24 for two in one bed; $24 to $26 for two in two beds.
- El Rancho Motel, 901 East Dickinson Blvd., Box 1612, 79735. Telephone: 915/336-2251. $15 for one; $17 for two in one bed; $19 for two in two beds.
- Motel 6, 3001 West Dickinson Blvd., 79735. Telephone: 915/336-6631. See Abilene listing for rates.

Fort Worth

Help: Crisis Intervention, 817/336-3355.
- First Call For Help, 817/336-8757.
Tourist Information: Convention and Visitors Bureau, 700 Throckmorton St., 76102. Telephone: 817/336-2491.
- Visitor Information Center, 817/625-5082.
Accommodations: YWCA, ♿, 512 West 4th St., 76102. Telephone: 817/332-6191. Women only. $10 per night plus $5 key and linen deposit. Less for Y members. Ten blocks from bus; 13 blocks from train. A 24-hour restaurant nearby. Reservations not accepted. If you are in need of access facilities, call to make sure they have been completed. "Historic old building with beautiful original furnishings."
- YMCA, 512 Lamar St., 76102. Telephone: 817/332-3281. Men only. Weekly rate: $35. $5 key deposit. You must stay at least one week.
- Motel 6, 6401 Airport Freeway, Haltom City, 76117. Telephone: 817/834-3851. See Abilene listing for rates.
- Motel 6, 5701 South Freeway, 76134. Telephone: 817/293-6112. See Abilene listing for rates.
- Motel 6, I-35 and Highland Terrace, 76134. See Abilene listing for rates.
- Motel 6, 8701 I-20 West, 76116. Telephone: 817/244-6060. See Abilene listing for rates.
- Motel 6, 3271 I-35 West, 76106. Telephone: 817/624-8476. See Abilene listing for rates.
- Days Inn, I-20 and Las Vegas Trail, 76108. Telephone: 817/246-4961. $21.88 to $23.88 for one; $25.88 to $27.88 for two.
- Days Inn, I-35 West and Felix St., 812 East Felix St., 76115. Telephone: 817/926-9211. See above listing for rates.

● Western 6 Motel, 1236 Oakland Blvd., 76103. Telephone: 817/834-7361. $14.40 single; $21.90 double.

● Caravan Motor Hotel, 2601 Jacksboro Hwy., 76114. Telephone: 817/626-1951. $22 for one; $26 for two in one bed; $30 for two in two beds.

Fritch

Camping: Lake Meredith National Recreation Area, P.O. Box 1438, 79036. Camping at six sites along the shoreline all year.

Gainesville

Accommodation: Caravan Motor Hotel, P.O. Box 856, 76240. Telephone: 817/665-5555. $22 for one; $26 for two in one bed; $30 for two in two beds.

Galveston

Accommodation: Motel 6, 7404 Ave. J, 77551. Telephone: 713/744-6666. See Abilene listing for rates.

Harlingen

Accommodation: Motel 6, 224 South U.S. Expressway 77, 78550. Telephone: 512/425-3731. See Abilene listing for rates.

Henderson

Accommodation: Friendship Inn–Woodlawn Hills Motel, 1204 North Hwy. 79, 75652. Telephone: 214/657-2511. $17 to $19 for one; $19 to $21 for two in one bed; $22 to $24 for two in two beds.

Houston

Houston is the fastest-growing city in the U.S. and seems to have escaped the economic problems that other U.S. cities face. Twenty-four of the 25 largest U.S. oil companies are active in Houston, along with 400 other not-so-large companies. Houston is, indeed, a modern-day boom town that seems to be bursting at the seams. An excellent guide to this big, rich, and aggressively modern city is *Texas Monthly's Guide to Houston,* by Felicia Coates and Harriet Howle ($3.95). *Texas Monthly* itself is a good guide to places to eat and things to do; look, too, at *Houston City Magazine* for the same kind of information. For free maps and information about tours and sightseeing, stop at the Greater Houston Convention and Visitors Council, 1522 Main St., 77002. Telephone: 713/658-4200. They also have two toll-free numbers: 800/392-7722, inside Texas; and 800/231-7799, outside Texas. And be warned: Houston can be incredibly hot and steamy. Hot enough, in fact, to have made it necessary to build air-conditioned tunnels connecting the downtown buildings.

Getting There: There's an airport limousine bus service from Intercontinental Airport to the Downtown Air Terminal in the Hyatt Regency Hotel. The 25-mile ride costs $5.50; the same trip by taxi would be $25.

• The Greyhound station is at 1410 Texas Ave. (tel. 222-1161), Trailways is at 2121 Main St. (tel. 759-6560), and Amtrak's terminal is at 902 Washington St. (tel. 224-1577).

Getting Around: *"This is a very difficult city to get around in if you don't have a car."*

• For 10¢ you can ride any bus within the boundaries of a Shoppers Special Route: Buffalo Bayou on the north, Pierce St. on the south, the Eastex Freeway on the east, and I-45 on the west. On weekdays, minibuses serve the downtown area for 10¢ a ride. For information on public transportation you can visit the Metro Information Center in the lobby at 403 Louisiana or call 651-1212. But the best way, by far, to see Houston is by car. If you don't have your own, you can get a good rental deal at Scher Rent-A-Car, 6400 Southwest Freeway (tel. 782-9911), at $12.50 per day.

Accommodations: YMCA, 1600 Louisiana St., 77002. Telephone: 713/ 659-8501. Men only. $13 per night the first week; $7 per night thereafter. Weekly rate is $93 for the first week; $45 to $50 thereafter. Air-conditioned; color television in each room. "We have a complete referral service here. . . . any traveler coming here will find that he will get assistance when needed."

• YMCA, 7903 South Loop East, 77012. Telephone: 713/643-4396. Men only. $10.30 single with air conditioning; $9.10 without.

• The Grant Motel, &, 8200 South Main St., 77025. Telephone: 713/668-8000. Near Rice University–Texas Medical Center area. Quiet, clean rooms with extra-long beds. $25 single; $28 double.

• Auditorium Hotel, 701 Texas Ave., 77002. Telephone: 713/227-3351. Convenient downtown location. Clean rooms. $20.80 single; $25.61 double.

• Texas State Hotel, 720 Fannin at Rusk, 77002. Telephone: 713/227-2271. A very "basic" hotel in the heart of downtown. $21.94 single; $26.22 double.

If you have a car, try these motels:

• Regal 8 Inn, 4045 North Freeway, 77022. Telephone: 713/691-6671. See Amarillo listing for rates.

• Scottish Inn, 310 South Heights Blvd., 77007. Telephone: 713/869-4541. $18 for one; $21 for two in one bed; $24 for two in two beds.

• Days Inn, I-10 and F-M Rd., P.O. Box 848, 77423. Telephone: 713/934-8511. $23.88 for one; $27.88 for two.

• Days Inn, I-45 and Cavalcade, 100 West Cavalcade, 77009. Telephone: 713/868-7121. $23.88 for one; $27.88 for two. Rates slightly higher December 15 to May 31.

• Days Inn, I-45 at South Wayside, 2200 South Wayside, 77023. Telephone: 713/928-2800. See above listing for rates.

• Best Value Alamo Plaza Motel, 4343 Old Spanish Trail, 77021. Telephone: 713/747-6900. $17 to $18 for one or two in one bed; $20 to $21 for two in two beds.

Where to Eat: The Original Ninfa's (there are three others), 2704 Navigation Rd. In the Port of Houston area near the bayou. Call 228-1175 for hours. "Just about the best Mexican food in Houston." The atmosphere is pure fiesta. Tacos al carbon, the specialty of the house, costs about $6 at dinnertime.

• Goode Company, 5107 Kirby Dr., in the Rice University area. Telephone: 522-2530. Texas-style barbecue that you've got to try at least once while you're in Houston.

• The Old Spaghetti Warehouse, 901 Commerce St. at Travis (downtown).

Telephone: 229-9715. Antiques, plants, and of course, spaghetti. A special spaghetti dinner with soup, salad, and a beverage costs about $4.

● James Coney Island, 1142 Travis. Telephone: 652-3819. Chili, sandwiches, salads, and hot dogs. Conveniently located and usually open from 7 a.m. to 10 p.m. every day of the week. Two Coney Islands (hot dogs), fries, and a beer are $3.

● Green Leaf Café, 2602 Navigation. Telephone: 226-9917. Closed Monday. South of Downtown, along the Ship Channel. Authentic Mexican food and atmosphere. $2.75 for a plate of beans, rice, tacos, and an enchilada.

● Leo's Coffee Shop, 1203 Fannin (downtown). Telephone: 652-5955. Open 24 hours. American food, with nothing over $6. "The atmosphere is interesting —especially in the wee hours."

What to See and Do: From May to September, the arts go outdoors to Miller Theater in Hermann Park near the Medical Center. Ballet, symphony, opera, plays—almost every night there's something to see and it's all free. Call 224-4240 for information.

● The Alley Theater, 615 Texas Ave., is reputed to be one of the best regional theaters in the U.S. Call 228-8421 for ticket information. There are student discounts of up to 25%—ask about them.

● NASA's Lyndon B. Johnson Space Center, 20 miles south of Houston. Here you can see Mission Control, where space flights from Gemini to the Space Shuttle *Columbia* have been monitored. Free walking tours are available Monday through Friday. Call 713/483-4321 for reservations.

● The Astrodome Sports Stadium claims to be the largest single attraction in the state of Texas. There are tours every day. Call 749-9500 for details.

● Rothko Chapel, 1411 Sul Ross. Fourteen of Mark Rothko's paintings hang in this ecumenical chapel in an interesting neighborhood southwest of downtown. For information, call 524-9839.

● Museums: The Museum of Fine Arts, 1001 Bissonnet (tel. 526-1361), is open Tuesday through Sunday, and the Contemporary Arts Museum (tel. 526-3129) at 5216 Montrose Blvd. follows the same schedule. Admission is free to both.

● If you're lucky enough to be in Houston at the end of March you'll be able to enjoy the Houston Festival, a celebration of the city that goes on all around the town.

At Night: Paradise Island Club, 4705 Main St. Open until 2 a.m. Tuesday through Sunday. This is a smoky and usually loud spot where you can hear progressive jazz and rock 'n' roll, but probably not each other.

● Comedy Workshop, San Felipe at South Shepherd. Every night, for a $3 cover, you can see a comedy revue. Next door, at the Comic's Club Annex, you can hear stand-up comics. Call 524-7333.

● Todd's, 5050 Richmond. Nice dance bar with free buffet from 6 p.m. to 9:30 p.m.

● Gilley's Club, 4500 Spencer Hwy. "A real honky-tonk immortalized by the film *Urban Cowboy.*"

● Corky's, 623 Hawthorne. A converted old wood-frame house where you can hear jazz from 6 p.m. to 2 a.m.

Shopping: Anything you could possibly desire should be somewhere in the Galleria Shopping Center, 5015 Westheimer Rd., which is becoming a tourist attraction in itself. The complex is covered, so you'll never know what the weather is like outside, and inside you can eat a Big Mac, go to a movie, or look at Gucci's latest.

Help: Travelers Aid, 5501 Austin St., P.O. Box 88061, 77004. Telephone: 713/522-3846.

• Crisis Hotline, 713/228-1505.

Huntsville

Accommodations: Motel 6, 1607 I-45, 77340. Telephone: 713/295-6666. See Abilene listing for rates.

• Regal 8 Inn, I-45 and Texas 30, 77340. Telephone: 713/295-6401. $17.88 for one; $20.88 for two in one bed; $23.88 for two to four in two beds.

Irving

Accommodation: Western 6 Motel, 510 South Loop 12, 75060. Telephone: 214/445-1151. $14.40 single; $21.90 double.

Kerrville

Accommodation: Friendship Inn–Del Norte, Hwy. 27 West, 78028. Telephone: 512/257-6112. $19 to $25 for one; $23 to $26 for two in one bed; $25 to $29 for two in two beds.

Lamesa

Accommodation: Friendship Inn–Westerner, 915 North Dallas, 79331. Telephone: 806/872-2115. $16 to $19 for one; $19 to $21 for two in one bed; $23 to $25 for two in two beds.

Lampasas

Accommodation: Friendship Inn–Saratoga Motel, 1408 South Key Ave., 76550. Telephone: 512/556-6244. $15 for one; $18.50 for two in one bed; $21.50 for two in two beds.

Laredo

Accommodation: Motel 6, 5310 San Bernardo Ave., 78041. Telephone: 512/722-4666. See Abilene listing for rates.

Longview

Accommodations: YMCA, 1230 South High St., 75602. Telephone: 214/758-7323. Men only. $8 single, Weekly rate: $45. There are several restaurants nearby offering inexpensive meals. "This is a modern, $2½-million, air-conditioned building." One mile from bus and train stations.

• Motel 6, 110 West Access Rd., 75603. Telephone: 214/753-1631. See Abilene listing for rates.

● Imperial 400 Motor Inn, 1019 East Marshall St., 75601. Telephone: 214/753-0276. $19 to $21 for one; $22 to $24 for two in one bed; $24 to $25 for two in two beds.

Lubbock

On Campus: People from Texas Tech University congregate at Fat Dawg's, 2408 4th St., or J. Patrick O'Malley's, 1211 University. When they're hungry they go to Gardski's Loft, 2009 Broadway, for great hamburgers, or Mesquite's, 2409 Broadway.

Accommodations: Friendship Inn–Sands Motel, 310 Ave. Q, Jet Hwys: 82 and 84, 79415. Telephone: 806/763-2861. $16 to $20 for one; $17 to $21 for two in one bed; $21 to $25 for two in two beds.

● Motel 6, 909 66th St., 79413. Telephone: 806/745-6666. See Abilene listing for rates.

McAllen

Accommodation: Motel 6, 700 U.S. 83 Expressway, 78501. Telephone: 512/682-1071. See Abilene listing for rates.

McKinney

Accommodation: Friendship Inn–Woods Motel, one mile east of U.S. 75 on Hwys. 121 and U.S. 380, 75002. $17 to $20 for one; $20 to $23 for two in one bed; $23 to $26 for two in two beds.

Midland

Accommodation: Motel 6, 1000 South Midkiff, 79701. Telephone: 915/694-1655. See Abilene listing for rates.

Mt. Pleasant

Accommodation: Friendship Inn–Sands Motel and Café, 227 Ferguson Rd., 75455. Telephone: 214/572-6681. $18 to $20 for one; $20 to $22 for two in one bed; $23 to $25 for two in two beds.

North Richland Hills

Accommodation: Western 6 Motel, 7804 Bedford Euless Rd., 76118. Telephone: 817/485-3000. $14.40 single; $21.90 double.

Odessa

Accommodations: Motel 6, 2925 East Hwy. 80, 79762. Telephone: 915/333-6666. See Abilene listing for rates.

● Friendship Inn–Travelers Lodge, 2325 East 2nd St., 79761. Telephone:

915/332-9131. $16 for one; $18 for two in one bed; $20 to $22 for two in two beds.

● Friendship Inn–Imperial Motel, 221 West 2nd St., 79760. Telephone: 915/332-0791. $16.05 for one; $18.19 for two in one bed; $23.54 for two in two beds.

Pecos

Accommodations: Motel 6, 3002 South Cedar, 79772. Telephone: 915/445-3666. See Abilene listing for rates.

● American Motor Inn, 2116 West Hwy. 80, 79772. Telephone: 915/445-5431. Ten blocks from bus station. $18 single; $24 double.

Pittsburg

Accommodation: Scottish Inn, 611 Greer Blvd., 75686. Telephone: 214/856-3666. $18.50 to $22.50 for one or two in one bed; $19.50 to $24.50 for two in two beds.

San Angelo

Accommodation: Motel 6, 311 North Bryant, 76901. Telephone: 915/655-6666. See Abilene listing for rates.

San Antonio

"This is a beautiful and charming city."

Help: Help Line, 512/227-4357.

Tourist Information: San Antonio Convention and Visitors Bureau, P.O. Box 2277, 210 South Alamo St., 78298. Telephone: 512/223-9133. Outside Texas: toll free, 800/531-5700.

● Visitor Information Center, 512/226-2345.

Accommodations: Friendship Inn–Siesta, 4441 Fredericksburg Rd., 78201. Telephone: 512/733-7154. $20 to $24 for one; $26 to $28 for two in one bed; $27 to $29 for two in two beds.

● Motel 6, 9503 I-35 North, 78233. Telephone: 512/653-7320. See Abilene listing for rates.

● Motel 6, 138 North W. W. White Rd., 78219. Telephone: 512/333-2330. See Abilene listing for rates.

● Regal 8 Inn, 4621 East Rittiman Rd., 78218. $19.88 for one; $22.88 for two in one bed; $25.88 for two to four in two beds.

● Alden Hotel, 223 3rd St., 78205. Telephone: 512/223-7480. Close to bus station. $10 and up for a single; $13 and up for a double. Downtown location. Shangra Lah restaurant connects with lobby.

San Marcos

Accommodation: Motel 6, 1321 I-35 North, 78666. Telephone: 512/392-0093. See Abilene listing for rates.

Sealy

Accommodation: Ranch Motel, 443 U.S. 90 East, 77474. Telephone: 713/885-7401. $16 for one; $19 for two in one bed; $22 for two in two beds.

Shamrock

Accommodation: Friendship Inn–Western, 104 East 12th, 79079. Telephone: 806/256-3244. $13 to $15 for one; $17 to $19 for two in one bed; $20 to $23 for two in two beds.

Sherman

On Campus: Austin College is in Sherman. Sherman is a "dry" town but Denison nearby is "wet." You can meet students at the "Pouch Club"—it requires membership, although two guests are allowed and you could be one of them. "The Chefette" on West Houston has good, home-style cooking to satisfy your hunger pangs.
Accommodation: Trade Winds Motel, 🍴 ★, 1530 Hwy. 75 North, P.O. Box 610, 75090. Telephone: 214/892-2171. $21 for one; $23 for two in one bed; $26 for two in two beds. Restaurant on premises.

Sonora

Accommodation: Friendship Inn–Twin Oaks, west on Hwy. 290 (junction of Hwys. 277 and 290), P.O. Box 371, 76950. Telephone: 915/387-2551. $20 for one; $23 for two in one bed; $30 for two in two beds.

Stephenville

Accommodation: Caravan Interstate Inn, 811 East Rd., 76401. Telephone: 817/965-5043. $15 to $17 for one; $17 to $20 for two in one bed; $20 to $23 for two in two beds.

Temple

Accommodations: Friendship Inn–Temple Motor Inn, 1001 North General Bruce Dr., 76501. Telephone: 817/778-4900. $20 to $22 for one; $24 for two in one bed; $26 for two in two beds.
● Motel 6, 1100 North General Bruce Dr., 76501. Telephone: 817/773-1766. See Abilene listing for rates.

Texarkana

Accommodation: Motel 6, 1924 Hampton Rd., 75503. Telephone: 214/792-7666. See Abilene listing for rates.

Tyler

Accommodation: Motel 6, 3236 Brady Gentry Pkwy., 75702. Telephone: 214/595-2222. See Abilene listing for rates.

Uvalde

Accommodation: Amber Sky Motel, 2005 East Main, 78801. Telephone: 512/278-5603. $16 for one; $21 for two.

Victoria

Accommodation: Motel 6, 3716 Houston Hwy., 77901. Telephone: 512/578-6351. See Abilene listing for rates.

Weatherford

Accommodation: Best Value Wayside Motel, DSR Box 18, Old Dennis Rd. and I-20, 76086. Telephone: 817/594-3816. $20.14 for one; $23.32 for two in one bed; $27.56 for two in two beds.

Weslaco

Accommodation: Friendship Inn–Vali-Ho, 2100 East Business Hwy. 83, 78596. Telephone: 512/968-2173. $18 to $21 for one; $19 to $21 for two in one bed; $22 to $25 for two in two beds.

Wichita Falls

Help: CONCERN, 817/723-0821.

Accommodations: YMCA, 1010 9th St., 76301. Telephone: 817/322-7816. Men only; age 18 and over. $5 single. Weekly rate: $22. Four blocks from bus.

● YWCA, 803 Burnett, 76301. Telephone: 817/723-0991. Women only. $5 for semiprivate rooms; $10 for private rooms. Weekly rates: $35 and $70. Cafeteria nearby.

● Motel 6, 1812 Maurine St., 76305. Telephone: 817/723-6666. See Abilene listing for rates.

Utah

Brigham Young and his Mormon followers are the ones to thank for Utah. Brigham Young took one look, said "This is the place," and founded Salt Lake City in 1847. The Mormons have been behind just about everything that goes on in Salt Lake City, and therefore the rest of Utah, ever since.

What to see in Utah? In Salt Lake City: Mormon Temple Square, Beehive House (where Brigham Young lived with several of his wives), Trolley Square, Kennecott Copper Mines, This Is the Place Monument, and the Hogle Zoo. Not to be missed, too, are the natural wonders of the state: Arches National Park, Bryce Canyon National Park ("a helluva place to lose a cow" is what one of the first settlers is reputed to have said of these beautiful badlands), Canyonlands National Park, Capitol Reef National Park, Dinosaur National Monument, and Zion National Park. The Great Salt Lake, 75 miles long and 30 miles wide, is what is left of a lake that was once ten times that size. If you take a dip, you'll bob like a cork.

The Utah Travel Council told us that "Utahans take pride in the appearance of their state and their personal appearance as well. To produce the most desirable effect on the population, a tidy appearance is suggested."

Some Special Events: Dairy Days in Logan (May); Strawberry Days in Pleasant Grove (June); Handcart Days in Bountiful (July); Swiss Days in Midway and Tomato Days in Hooper (August); Miner's Day in Tooele, Utah State Fair in Salt Lake City, and Threshing Bee in Hyrum (September); and the Annual Lighting of Temple Square in Salt Lake (December).

Hitching: When we asked someone at Brigham Young about the general attitude toward people on the road in his area, he said they thought of it as a "very good learning experience if with good supervision." It seems that their idea of "on the road" is a bit different from ours. Legally, hitching is prohibited from the roadway or the shoulder of the highway. A trooper in the Utah Highway Patrol said simply, "Please do not hitchhike."

Tourist Information: Utah Travel Council, Council Hall, Capitol Hill, Salt Lake City, UT 84114.

Bryce Canyon

Camping: Bryce Canyon National Park, 84717. Two campgrounds. North open May 1 to November 1; Sunset open June 1 to Labor Day. The exact season depends on the weather. Horseback riding. $2 per campsite per night.

Cedar City

Camping: Cedar Breaks National Monument, P.O. Box 749, 84720. Campground at Point Supreme (two miles north of southern entrance). Open June 15 to September 15. $2 per campsite per night.
Accommodation: Friendship Inn–Village Inn Motel, 840 South Main (Hwy. 130), 84720. Telephone: 801/586-9926. $22 to $24 for one; $28 to $32 for two.

Fillmore

Accommodation: Friendship Inn–Fillmore Motel, 61 North Main St., 84631. Telephone: 801/743-5454. $15 to $17 for one; $17 to $19 for two in one bed; $23 to $25 for two in two beds.

Green River

Accommodations: Friendship Inn–Green River Motel, West City Limits on U.S. 6, 50, and I-70, 84525. Telephone: 801/564-3234. $20 to $24 for one or two in one bed; $22 to $30 for two in two beds.
• Motel 6, I-70 and Green River, 84525. Telephone: 801/564-3266. $12.95 for one; $16.95 for two; $19.95 for up to four.

Hatch

Accommodation: Friendship Inn–Galaxy Motel, Hwy. 89 North, 84735. Telephone: 801/735-4211. $20 to $22 for one; $24 to $26 for two in one bed; $26 to $28 for two in two beds.

Heber

Accommodations: Friendship Inn–Hy-Lander Motel and Restaurant, 425 South Main St., 84032. Telephone: 801/654-2150. $15 to $19 for one; $19 to $24 for two in one bed; $23 to $26 for two in two beds.
• Green Acres Lodge, √, 989 South Main St., 84032. Telephone: 801/654-2202. $18 to $24 for one; $20 to $26 for two in one bed; $22 to $28 for two in two beds.

Kanab

Accommodation: K Motel, ♥ ★ 10%, 330 South 100 East, P.O. Box 1301, 84741. Telephone: 801/644-2611. $16 to $18 for one; $18 to $20 for two in one bed; $20 to $22 for two in two beds.

Mexican Hat

Accommodation: Friendship Inn–San Juan Motel Café and Lounge, Hwy. 163, Utah 47, P.O. Box 156, 84531. Telephone: 801/683-2220. $19 for one; $23 for two in one bed; $25 for two in two beds.

Moab

Camping: Canyonlands National Park, 84532. Campground at Squaw Flat and Willow Flat. Open all year. No water at Willow Flat.
● Arches National Monument, c/o Canyonlands National Park, 84532. Campground at Devil's Garden (18 miles north of Visitor Center). Open March to October. $4 per campsite per night. Free during the rest of the year, but there is no water.
● Natural Bridges National Monument, c/o Canyonlands National Park, 84532. Campground with 14 sites (four miles off Utah 95).

Monticello

Accommodation: Friendship Inn–Canyonlands Lodge, 389 North Main St., 84535. Telephone: 801/587-2266. $22 to $24 for one; $24 to $28 for two in one bed; $28 to $32 for two in two beds.

Nephi

Accommodation: Friendship Inn–Safari, 413 South Main St., 84638. Telephone: 801/623-1071. $18 to $24 for one; $22 to $26 for two in one bed; $23 to $28 for two in two beds.

Ogden

Accommodations: Friendship Inn–Millstream, 1450 Washington Blvd., 84404. Telephone: 801/394-9425. $20 for one; $22 for two in one bed; $24 to $26 for two in two beds.
● Motel 6, 1455 Washington Blvd., 84404. Telephone: 801/399-9261. See Green River listing for rates.

"By far, my most enjoyable stay was in Ogden at the Hotel Ben Lomond, the tallest building in the city, one block west of the bus terminal. Ogden is a very pleasant town nestled in the shadows of the Wasatch Mountains. All of Ogden can be seen from the windows of a city bus—a round trip to and from the edge of town was 40¢ and the mountains are only a 15-minute walk from the hotel. The people, predominantly Mormon, were almost all friendly and went out of their way to make me feel at ease."

Panguitch

Accommodations: Friendship Inn–Bryce Way, 429 North Main St., 84759. Telephone: 801/676-8881. $19 to $22 for one; $21 to $24 for two in one bed; $25 to $29 for two in two beds.

● Friendship Inn–Sand's Motel, 390 North Main St., 84759. Telephone: 801/676-8874. $14 to $20 for one; $18 to $24 for two in one bed; $20 to $28 for two in two beds.

Provo

Accommodations: Motel 6, 1600 South University Dr., 84601. Telephone: 801/377-4666. See Green River listing for rates.
● Friendship Inn Uptown, 469 West Center St., 84601. Telephone: 801/373-8248. $17 to $22 for one; $20 to $25 for two in one bed; $24 to $29 for two in two beds.
● Friendship Inn–City Center, 150 West 300 South St., 84601. Telephone: 801/373-8489. $14.90 to $17.90 for one; $16.90 to $19.90 for two in one bed; $19.90 to $23.90 for two in two beds.
● Imperial 400 Motor Inn, 40 West 300 South St., 84601. Telephone: 801/373-0660. $20 to $22 for one; $22 to $26 for two in one bed; $22 to $28 for two in two beds.

Richfield

Accommodation: Friendship Inn–Topsfield Lodge, 1200 South Main, P.O. Box 556, 84701. Telephone: 801/896-5437. $12.50 to $16.50 for one; $15.50 to $19.50 for two in one bed; $17.50 to $21.50 for two in two beds.

St. George

Accommodations: Motel 6, 205 North 1000 East St., 84770. Telephone: 801/673-6666. See Green River listing for rates.
● Friendship Inn–Sands, 581 East St. George Blvd., 84770. Telephone: 801/673-3501. $14 to $16 for one; $17 to $20 for two in one bed; $19 to $22 for two in two beds.

Salina

Accommodation: Friendship Inn–Safari, 1425 South State St., 84654. Telephone: 801/529-7447. $18 to $24 for one; $24 to $30 for two in one bed; $26 to $32 for two in two beds.

Salt Lake City

Help: University of Utah Helpline, 801/581-8228.
● Travelers Aid, 160 West South Temple, 84084. Telephone: 801/328-8996.
● Information and Referral, 801/487-4716.
● Listening Post, 801/278-4716.
Tourist Information: Salt Lake Valley Convention and Visitors Bureau, The Salt Palace, Suite 200, 84101. Telephone: 801/521-2822. According to someone at the tourist office, "Salt Lake is a very friendly city. Please come to visit us."

Accommodations: YWCA, 🔄, 322 East 3rd South St., 84111. Telephone: 801/355-2804. Women only. $10 to $12 single; $8 and $11 per person double; $7 per person triple. *"This place is neat and clean."*

● Carlton Hotel, 140 East South Temple, 84111. Telephone: 801/355-3418. $25 single; $30 twin room. Lower rates November to March. Just 2½ blocks from bus station.

● Friendship Inn Townhouse, 245 West North Temple St., 84103. Telephone: 801/532-7200. $18 to $24 for one; $22 to $28 for two in one bed; $24 to $30 for two in two beds.

● Motel 6, 176 West 6th South St., 84101. Telephone: 801/521-3280. See Green River listing for rates.

● Motel 6, 1990 West North Temple St., 84116. Telephone: 801/322-3061. See Green River listing for rates.

On Campus: From July 1 to September 15, you might be able to stay at 1002 Austin Hall for $7 a night on the University of Utah campus. Contact Residential Living at the same address. While you're there you can have a reasonable meal at the Union Cafeteria in the student union, where there is also a ride board. Ballif Hall has apartment listings on its bulletin board.

Springdale

Camping: Zion National Park, 84767. Three campgrounds: South open April 15 to September 15; Watchman open year round; Lava Point open June to October 15. $2 per campsite per night at South and Watchman. Lava Point has no water.

Torrey

Camping: Capitol Reef National Park, 84775. Camping at Capitol Reef and Cedar Mesa. Open all year. No water at Cedar Mesa. $2 per campsite per night at Capitol Reef.

Accommodation: Friendship Inn–Rim Rock Motel, RR Box 1, Hwy. 24, 84775. Telephone: 801/425-3843. $20 to $23 for one; $25 to $26 for two in one bed; $26 to $28 for two in two beds.

Wendover

Accommodation: Motel 6, U.S. 40 and E St., 84083. Telephone: 801/665-2848. See Green River listing for rates.

Colchester
Stowe
Burlington
Waterbury Center
South Burlington
Plainfield
Warren
Montpelier
Fairlee
Rochester
West Hartford
White River
Junction
South Wallingford
Ludlow
Bennington
Brattleboro
Woodford

Vermont

Known as the "Green Mountain State," Vermont has tried zealously and successfully to protect its natural beauty. Some would say it's the most attractive state east of the Mississippi.

Vermont is a state of small, picturesque villages. Its largest city, Burlington, has fewer than 50,000 inhabitants. Its geography is characterized by a pleasant mix of mountain and valley, unmarked by intrusive billboards and commercial advertising. Its Long Trail is a mountain footpath extending the length of the state with free shelters every 10 to 20 kilometers.

As the state in which the United States' first ski tow was installed (in 1932), it has long been a leader in the field of winter sports. It has more than 20 major downhill ski areas and more than 50 cross-country ski touring centers. Ski-country accommodations range from austere dormitories to luxurious condominiums.

In summer, many of the ski areas are available for hiking, swimming, and mountain climbing, and there are numerous opportunities for water sports on the many lakes that dot the state. Besides physical beauty, the state offers a great deal in the way of cultural attractions: summer theaters, music festivals (the one at Marlboro is the best known), outstanding language schools at Middlebury College and the School for International Training, and a host of arts and crafts fairs.

The most popular time of the year for tourists to visit Vermont is in late September and early October, when fall weather turns the green of the mountains into an unbelievably colorful splash of red, orange, and yellow. But if you were to consult with the residents, you'd be told that late spring is equally colorful, when the apple blossoms turn the hillsides pink.

Because of its rather rugged winter climate, Vermont's people tend to be independent individualists. It is one of the few states that was once a republic; the founding fathers refused to join the original 13 colonies until it was proven that the experiment in federal government wasn't designed to concentrate too much power in one person. Life in Vermont today is an echo of those early days—the state is warmly hospitable to new ideas, to experimentalists, to people seeking freedom from urban pressures.

Some Special Events: Winter Carnival in Stowe (January); Winter Carnival at Middlebury College (February); Maple Sugar Square and Round Dance Festival in Burlington (March); Maple Festival in St. Albans (April); Fiddlers Concert in Calais (June); Strawberry Festival in Clarendon and Old-Time Fiddler's Contest in Craftsbury (July); Horse Show in South Woodstock and Bread Loaf Writers' Conference in Middlebury (August); "A Day With Robert Frost in Frost Country" in Ripton and Vermont State Fair in Rutland (September).

Hitching: The law prohibits hitchhiking from the "roadway" and on the Interstate system, and the Department of Public Safety suggests you "confine hitchhiking to the daylight hours. Many sections of Vermont's roads are remote and uninhabited; therefore, they may be dangerous from the standpoint of traffic safety and personal security." Young people hitchhike quite often; many who are at colleges in Vermont have no other choice since extensive public transportation isn't available, and unless they have their own wheels they have to hitch rides with others.

Tourist Information: Vermont Travel Division, 61 Elm St., Montpelier, VT 05602.

Bennington

Accommodation: Colonial Guest House, Orchard Rd. and Rte. 7 North, 05201. Telephone: 802/442-2263. $12 to $20 per room. An old, restored colonial farmhouse with six bedrooms.

Brattleboro

Help: Hotline for Help, 17 Elliot St. Telephone: 802/257-7989. General counseling and referrals. They suggested the Latchis Hotel on South Main St., which is rundown but inexpensive, or the Holly Motel. Call them and they'll be happy to provide you with any information they can. Some places to go to meet local people are Common Ground Restaurant, Spring Tree Café, Mole's Eye, Via Conditti, and the Chelsea House, a folklore center on Rte. 9, West Brattleboro.

Accommodation: Susse Chalet Motor Lodge, I-91 (Exit 3) on Route 5 North, 05301. Telephone: 802/254-6007. $19.70 for one; $23.70 for two; $29.70 for four.

Burlington

On Campus: During the school year you'll find a high concentration of students at the Billings Student Center at the University of Vermont. While you're there you can pick up a copy of the student newspaper, the *Vermont Cynic,* to find out what's going on on campus and around town. Some of the favorite student haunts downtown include B.T. McGuire's on Church St. and Finbar's on Main St. For a reasonably priced meal (mainly vegetarian) try the Fresh Ground Coffee House, 175 Church St.; Carbur's for a sandwich (they have a 25-page sandwich menu so be sure to have plenty of time for reading), 119 St. Paul St.; or the Bakery Lane Soup Bowl, 209 Battery St. For great ice cream, it's Ben and Jerry's Homemade at 107 St. Paul St. If you'd rather be outdoors, take a ferry ride across Lake Champlain at sunset or hike on the Long Trail of the Green Mountains.

Inquire at Trinity College about the possibility of spending a night or two on campus.

Accommodation: YWCA, 278 Main St., 05401. Telephone: 802/862-7520. Women only. Bedrooms that sleep 12 plus floor space for sleeping bags. $7 per night; $23 per week. You must be a YWCA member at a fee of $5.50.

Colchester

Accommodation: Mrs. Farrell's Youth Hostel (AYH), Williams Rd., RD 4, 05446. Telephone: 802/878-8222. $3.50 with your own linen, $4.50 without. Reservations required. AYH membership preferred.

Fairlee

Accommodation: Hulbert Outdoor Center, 05045. Telephone: 802/333-9766. Open September to May. $4. Generally a group facility which will accommodate individuals if space permits. Be sure to call ahead.

Ludlow

Accommodation: Ludlow Youth Hostel (AYH-SA), 44 Pleasant St., 05149. Telephone: 802/228-8646, or 228-5127. Open May 15 to October 1. $3. Reservations necessary.

Montpelier

Accommodation: Lackey's Tourist Home, 153 State St., 05602. Telephone: 802/223-7292. Family-run Victorian with nine rooms for guests. $12.60 single; $18.90 double.

Plainfield

On Campus: According to a friend at Goddard College, Plainfield is "a unique community of musicians, artists and students; a very addictive lifestyle exists here." If you want to visit this beautiful area you can spend a night at Goddard for $7 to $10 (check with the housing office), or you might be able to stay for free by getting to know a student. You can meet students at the campus cafeteria or in Montpelier at the Horn of the Moon Café or M.J. Friday's Bar and Restaurant. It seems that hitchhiking is quite common and accepted here.

Rochester

Accommodation: School House Youth Hostel (AYH), 146 Main St., 05767. Telephone: 802/767-9384. Open May 15 to October 15, and November

15 to April 15. $2.50 summer; $5 winter. The hostel was built in 1827 as a church, was converted to a gym and school in 1940, and became a hostel in 1963. Near Killington and Sugarbush ski areas. AYH membership required (see page 21).

South Burlington

Accommodation: Econo Lodge, 🔲, 1076 Williston Rd., 05401. Telephone: 802/863-1125. $17.95 to $24.10 for one; $22.95 to $29.95 for two; $24.95 to $32.15 for two to four in two beds.

South Wallingford

Accommodation: Green Mountain Tea Room and Guest House, Rte. 7, 05773. Telephone: 802/446-2611. $8 to $9 single. Vermont Transit and Greyhound buses stop in front of Tea Room. Meals served at reasonable prices, "and afternoon tea is most definitely served. We have 15 varieties."

Stowe

Accommodation: Timberholm Inn, Cottage Club Rd., 05672. Telephone: 802/253-7603. European-style country inn which serves breakfast as part of the fee. $12 to $16 single; $18 to $26 double.

Warren

Accommodation: Old Homestead Youth Hostel (AYH), East Warren Rd., 05674. Telephone: 802/496-3744. Open year round. $3.50 summer. From November 15 to May operates as a ski lodge only. $10 single. "A homelike atmosphere."

Waterbury Center

Accommodation: Ski Hostel Lodge Youth Hostel (AYH), 05677. Telephone: 802/244-8859. Open April 1 to November 15. Skiing at Mt. Mansfield six miles away. $4.50 for AYH members. Summer rates are $12 for a single for nonmembers. From November 15 to April, operates as a ski lodge only. $20 includes overnight and two meals in a dorm; $25 for a private room. Weekends are $40 to $55 in the dorm, with two breakfasts and Saturday dinner included. Bring your own sleeping bag.

West Hartford

Accommodation: Clifford's Guest House, Pomfret Rd., 05084. Telephone: 802/295-3554. $9 per person, including breakfast.

White River Junction

Accommodations: Motel 6, I-90 and I-89, 05001. To open in 1982. $12.95 for one; $16.95 for two; $19.95 for up to four.

● Susse Chalet Motor Lodge, junction I-91, I-89 on Rte. 5. Telephone: 802/295-3051 or toll free 800/258-1980. $22 single; $26 double.

Woodford

Accommodation: Greenwood Lodge (AYH), Rte. 9 (mailing address in season: P.O. Box 246, Bennington, 05201; off-season: Ed and Ann Shea, 197 Lyons Rd., Scarsdale, NY 10583). Telephone: 802/442-2547. Open July, August, and October for fall foliage weekends. $5.80; tenting $3.15. Ten miles from Bennington; three miles from Appalachian and Long Trail hiking. Reservations required.

Virginia

Northern Virginia is physically and philosophically the gateway to the South. The state is rich with the echoes of history: Jamestown was the site of the first English settlement in North America, in 1607; a Virginian, Richard Henry Lee, introduced the motion to separate the 13 colonies from England in 1776; Thomas Jefferson was the guiding hand behind the Declaration of Independence; and no one has to be reminded that George Washington was from this state as well. Much of the agony of the Civil War took place in Virginia: it was at Appomattox that Robert E. Lee surrendered in 1865. To get a sense of Virginia's history—and the history of the entire U.S., in fact—you should plan a visit to Williamsburg, the beautifully reconstructed capital of 18th-century Virginia, George Washington's residence at Mount Vernon, Jefferson's Monticello in Charlottesville, and Yorktown, where the American Revolution ended with the British soldiers marching out to the tune of "The World Turned Upside Down." Somewhat less well known but still worth a visit are the Art Museum in Richmond, with its fine collection of Fabergé jewelry made for Russia's last czar, and the Mariners' Museum in Newport News.

For the people who like the out-of-doors, Virginia has lots of excellent camping. Shenandoah National Park and the Blue Ridge Parkway (see listing under Asheville, North Carolina) stretch from western Virginia through to North Carolina and present campers with some exquisite spots to spend a night or two. The Skyline Drive, which winds through Shenandoah National Park, is a spectacular 105 miles of overlooks and trails that are a treat for city-worn tourists.

Virginia Beach, 28 miles of shoreline from Cape Henry to Virginia's Outer Banks, is a popular fair-weather retreat. And for the curious, there's Tangier Island in Chesapeake Bay, an unspoiled spot where some of the natives still speak "old English" and work as fishermen; there's a boat that connects the mainland with the island from Reedville, Virginia, at certain times of the year and from Crisfield, Maryland, all year.

Some Special Events: Colonial Weekends in Williamsburg (January and February); Dogwood Festival in Charlottesville (April); Salt Water Fishing Tournament at Virginia Beach (May); Potomac River Festival at Colonial Beach (June); Wild Pony Round-up in Chincoteague (July); Old Fiddler's Contest in Galax and East Coast Surfing Championships at Virginia Beach (August); State Fair in Richmond (September); and Oyster Festival in Chincoteague (October).

Hitching: Virginia is one of those states that does have laws prohibiting hitchhiking except on the Interstate System or controlled-access highways. Our campus friends from all over Virginia don't recommend hitchhiking, though.

Tourist Information: Virginia State Travel Service, 9th St. Office Bldg., Richmond, VA 23219.

Alexandria

Help: Alexandria Hotline, 703/548-3810.

Accommodation: YMCA, 420 East Monroe Ave., 22301. Telephone: 703/549-0850. $11 single; $15 double.

Ashland

Accommodations: Econo-Travel Motor Hotel, P.O. Box 308, 23005. Telephone: 804/798-9221. $22.95 for one; $26.95 for two in one bed; $30.95 for two to four in two beds.

● Days Inn, I-95 and Va. 54 West (Exit Rte. 54 West), P.O. Box 2117, 23005. Telephone: 804/798-4262. $19.88 to $20.88 for one; $23.88 to $24.88 for two.

Blacksburg

Accommodation: Econo-Travel Motor Hotel, 3333 South Main St., 24060. Telephone: 703/951-4242. $16.95 for one; $20.95 for two in one bed; $23.95 for two in two beds.

Bristol

Accommodation: Econo-Travel Motor Hotel, 912 Commonwealth Ave., 24201. Telephone: 703/466-2112. $17.95 for one; $21.95 for two in one bed; $25.95 for two in two beds.

Carmel Church

Accommodation: Days Inn, I-95 and Va. 207, Carmel Church Rd., P.O. Box 35, Ruther Glen, 22546. Telephone: 804/448-2011. $20.88 to $21.88 for one; $24.88 to $25.88 for two.

Charlottesville

There's an organization in Charlottesville called Guesthouses, Bed & Breakfast, Inc. (P.O. Box 5737, 22901), which matches travelers with people who have room in their homes to take in overnight guests. Prices can be as low as $18 single and $28 double, including breakfast. Most homes are near the University of Virginia. Write for details. Certain homes have access facilities.

Accommodations: Econo-Travel Motor Hotel, 2014 Holiday Dr., 22901. Telephone: 804/295-3185. $22.95 for one; $26.95 for two in one bed; $29.95 for two in two beds.

● Econo Lodge, 400 Emmet St., 22903. Telephone: 804/296-2104. $22.50 to $24.50 for one; $26.45 to $28.45 for two in one bed; $29.95 to $31.95 for two in two beds.

Chesapeake

Accommodations: Econo-Travel Motor Hotel, 1439 George Washington Hwy. North, 23323. Telephone: 804/487-8861. $18.95 for one; $21.95 for two in one bed; $24.95 for two in two beds.

● Econo-Travel Motor Hotel, 3244 Western Branch Blvd. (Rte. 17), 23321. Telephone: 804/484-6143. $17.95 for one; $22.95 for two in one bed; $27.95 for two in two beds.

● Econo-Travel Motor Hotel, 4725 West Military Hwy., 23321. Telephone: 804/488-4963, $18.95 for one; $22.95 for two in one bed; $24.95 for two in two beds.

Chester

Accommodation: Days Inn, I-95 and Va. 10 (Exit 6 West), P.O. Box AN, 23831. Telephone: 804/748-5871. $18.88 to $19.88 for one; $22.88 to $23.88 for two.

Christiansburg

Accommodations: Econo-Travel Motor Hotel, 2430 Roanoke St. SE, 24073. Telephone: 703/382-6161. $17.95 for one; $21.95 for two in one bed; $25.95 for two in two beds.

● Days Inn, ♿, I-81 and U.S. 11 (Exit 37), P.O. Box 768, 24073. Telephone: 703/382-0261. $20.88 for one; $23.88 for two.

Collinsville/Martinsville

Accommodation: Econo-Travel Motor Hotel, 800 South Virginia Ave., 24078. Telephone: 703/647-3941. $18.95 for one; $22.95 for two in one bed; $24.95 for two in two beds.

Culpeper

Accommodation: Econo-Travel Motor Hotel, U.S. 15 and U.S. 29 Bypass, P.O. Box 407. Telephone: 703/825-5097. $19.95 for one; $23.95 for two in one bed; $27.95 for two in two beds.

Danville

Accommodation: Econo-Travel Motor Hotel, 1390 Piney Forest Rd., 24541. Telephone: 804/797-4322. $18.95 for one; $22.95 for two in one bed; $26.95 for two in two beds.

Dumfries/Quantico

Accommodation: Econo-Travel Motor Hotel, ♿, 17005 Dumfries Rd., 22026. Telephone: 703/221-4176. $21.95 to $23.95 for one; $25.95 to $27.95 for two in one bed; $28.95 to $30.95 for two in two beds.

Emporia

Accommodation: Days Inn, I-95 and U.S. 58 (Exit 58 West), P.O. Box 1036, 23847. Telephone: 804/634-9481. $19.88 to $20.88 for one; $23.88 to $24.88 for two.

Ferrum

Accommodation: Ferrum College Summer Programs, 24088. Telephone: 703/365-2121. Men, women, and children. Primarily summer. "There is a special 'Leisure Learning Family Vacation' program during the summer featuring seminars, swimming, horseback riding, hiking, fishing, tennis, white-water tubing, evening programs, field trips, and special activities for children." $18 per day per person or $30 per couple, including meals. Special rates for children, too. Reservations necessary.

Fredericksburg

Accommodations: Countryside Inn, ➤ ★, I-95 and U.S. 1, 22401. Telephone: 703/898-1000. $15.95 for one; $19.95 for two.
● Econo-Travel Motor Hotel, junction of I-95 and Rte. 3, P.O. Box 36, 22401. Telephone: 703/786-8374. $17.95 to $19.95 for one; $20.95 to $23.95 for two in one bed; $23.95 to $26.95 for two to four in two beds.
● Econo Lodge, 5321 Jefferson Davis Hwy., 22401. Telephone: 703/898-5440. $19.95 to $24.95 for one or two in one bed; $24.95 to $29.95 for two in two beds.
● Days Inn, ♿, Falmouth and Warrenton Exit, I-95 and U.S. 17 North, Rte. 12, Box 36, 22401. Telephone: 703/373-5340. $17.88 to $22.88 for one; $21.88 to $26.88 for two.

Front Royal

Accommodations: Cool Harbor Motel, 15th and Shenandoah Ave., 22630. Telephone: 703/635-2191. $18 to $20 for one; $20 to $24 for two in one bed; $22 to $26 for two in two beds.
● Friendship Inn–Skyline Motel Hotel, P.O. Box 942, Rte. 340, 22630. Telephone: 703/636-6739. $12 to $20 for one; $20 to $22 for two in one bed; $20 to $24 for two in two beds.

Hampton

Help: Peninsula Family Service and Travelers Aid, Inc., 1520 Aberdeen Rd., P.O. Box 7315, 23666. Telephone: 804/838-1960.

Accommodations: Days Inn, ☺, I-64 and Mercury Blvd., 1918 Coliseum Blvd., 23669. Telephone: 804/826-4810. $22.88 for one; $26.88 for two. Rates higher June to August.

● Econo-Travel Motor Hotel, 1781 North King St., 23669. Telephone: 804/723-0741. $19.50 to $21.50 for one; $22.50 to $24.50 for two in one bed; $25.50 to $27.50 for two to four in two beds.

● Econo-Travel Motor Hotel, 2708 West Mercury Blvd., 23666. Telephone: 804/826-8970. $19.95 for one; $23.95 for two in one bed; $26.95 for two in two beds.

Harrisonburg

Accommodation: Econo-Travel Motor Hotel, Rte. 33 and I-81, 22801. Telephone: 703/433-2576. $19.95 for one; $24.95 for two in one bed; $27.95 for two in two beds.

Leesburg

Accommodation: Youth Hostel (AYH), Caldwell, 88 Shenandoah St., 22075. Telephone: 703/777-1234. Open all year. $4.50. Call before coming.

Lexington

"This is a rural area, most of the people are farming or working in factories. There is a strong work ethic—Scottish-Irish Presbyterian roots; people don't relate too well to folks who don't settle down to work, raise crops and kids."

Accommodations: Econo-Travel Motor Hotel, I-64 and U.S. 11, P.O. Box 1088, 24450. Telephone: 703/463-7371. $20.95 for one; $24.95 for two in one bed; $28.95 for two in two beds.

● Days Inn, ☺, I-81 and U.S. 11 (Exit 53), Rte. 5, P.O. Box 1329, 24450. Telephone: 703/463-9131. $20.88 for one; $23.88 for two.

Luray

Camping: Shenandoah National Park, 22835. There are four major campgrounds with a total of over 600 sites, plus backcountry campsites and trail shelters. $3 per campsite per night. Big Meadows open all year; others open from April or May to October. You can make reservations through Ticketron. Luray Caverns are nearby.

Lynchburg

Accommodations: YWCA, 626 Church St., 24504. Telephone: 804/847-7751. Women only. $6.50 single; $6 per person double. Weekly rate: $22 to $24. Make reservations.

● Econo-Travel Motor Hotel, 2400 Stadium Rd., P.O. Box 2028, 24501. Telephone: 804/847-1045. $19.95 for one; $24.95 for two in one bed; $27.95 for two in two beds.

Marion

Accommodation: Village Superior Motel, Exit 18 on I-81, 24368. Telephone: 703/783-4936. $18 for one; $20 for two in one bed; $22 for two in two beds.

Mt. Sidney

Accommodation: Augusta Motel, Rte. 1, Box 23, 24467. Telephone: 703/248-8040. $15.60 for one; $20.80 for two.

Newport News

Help: Contact Peninsula, 211 32nd St. Telephone: 804/245-0041.
Accommodation: Econo-Travel Motor Hotel, ⬡, 11845 Jefferson Ave., 23606. Telephone: 804/599-3237. $15.95 to $17.95 for one; $18.95 to $21.95 for two in one bed; $22.95 to $23.95 for two to four in two beds.

Norfolk

Help: Family Service/Travelers Aid, Inc., 222 19th St. West, 23517. Telephone: 804/622-7017.
Tourist Information: Norfolk Convention and Visitors Bureau, 208 East Plume St., 23510. Telephone: 804/441-5266.
Accommodations: YMCA, 312 West Bute St., 23510. Telephone: 804/622-6328. $12.75. Reservations required one week in advance during summer.
● Econo-Travel Motor Hotel, 865 North Military Hwy., 23502. Telephone: 804/461-4865. $24.95 for one; $28.95 for two in one bed; $32.95 for two in two beds.
● Econo-Travel Motor Hotel, 3343 North Military Hwy., 23518. Minutes from airport. Telephone: 804/855-3116. $21.95 for one; $25.95 for two in one bed; $29.95 for two in two beds.
● Econo-Travel Motor Hotel, 1050 Tidewater Dr., 23504. Telephone: 804/623-6353. $23.95 for one; $27.95 for two in one bed; $31.95 for two in two beds.
● Econo Lodge, 1850 East Little Creek Rd., 23518. Telephone: 804/583-1561. $22.95 for one; $26.95 for two in one bed; $30.95 for two in two beds.
● Econo-Travel Motor Hotel, ⬡, 5819 Northampton Blvd., Virginia Beach, 23455. Telephone: 804/464-9306. $21.95 for one; $25.95 for two in one bed; $28.95 for two to four in two beds. Rates slightly over our maximum June 11 to September 15.

Petersburg

Accommodations: Countryside Inn, ➤ ⬡, I-95 and Rte. 460 East, 900 Winfield Rd., 23803. Telephone: 804/861-8480. $22.68 for one; $28.08 for two double beds.

- Econo-Travel Motor Hotel, 25 South Crator Rd., 23803. Telephone: 804/861-4680. $19.95 for one; $23.95 for two in one bed; $26.95 for two in two beds.
- Days Inn, I-95 and Walthall Exit 5, 2310 Indian Hill Rd., Colonial Heights, 23834. Telephone: 804/520-1010. $18.88 to $19.88 for one; $22.88 to $23.88 for two.

Portsmouth

Accommodation: Imperial 400 Motor Inn, 333 Effingham St., 23704. Telephone: 804/397-5806. $23 to $25 for one; $25 to $27 for two in one bed; $26 to $28 for two in two beds.

Richmond

"A beautiful city representing four centuries of legend, history, and tradition."

Help: Hot Line, 804/643-0888.
- Travelers Aid, 515 East Main St., 23219. Telephone: 804/643-0279 or 648-1767.
Accommodations: Massad's House Hotel, ☛ $1, 11 North 4th St., 23219. Telephone: 804/648-2893. $20.50 for one; $27 for two. Just 2½ blocks from bus station.
- Days Inn, I-64 and Broad St., Dickens Rd., 23230. To open in December 1981. Call toll-free number for rates.
- Days Inn, Sandston-Byrd Airport Exit 47-A and I-64, 5500 Williamsburg Rd., Sandston, 23231. Telephone: 804/222-2041. $22.88 to $23.88 for one; $26.88 to $27.88 for two.
- Econo-Travel Motor Hotel, 5408 Williamsburg Rd., 23150. Telephone: 804/222-1020. $21.95 for one; $25.95 for two in one bed; $28.95 for two in two beds.
- Econo-Travel Motor Hotel, 🔣 6523 Midlothian Turnpike, 23225. Telephone: 804/276-8241. See above listing for rates.
- Econo-Travel Motor Hotel, 2125 Willis Rd., 23234. Telephone: 804/271-6031. $19.95 for one; $23.95 for two in one bed; $27.95 for two in two beds.
- Scottish Inn, I-64 and U.S. 60 at Bottoms Bridge Exit, Quinton, 23141. Telephone: 804/932-4479. $18 for one; $20 for two in one bed; $22 for two in two beds.

Roanoke

Help: TRUST, 703/563-0311. They provide accommodations, too. See below.
- Family Service–Travelers Aid, Suite 518, Carlton Terrace Bldg., 920 South Jefferson St., 24016. Telephone: 703/344-3253.
- Free Clinic, 703/344-5156.
Accommodations: TRUST, 3515 Williamson Rd., 24012. About 1½ miles from I-81. Telephone: 703/563-0311. Provides emergency overnight housing and facilities for 24 hours. Men and women. No charge for services. Cooking facilities available. The people at TRUST invite you to stop by for information on Roanoke.

- Days Inn, 🛇, I-581 and U.S. 460, P.O. Box 12325, 24024. Telephone: 703/342-4551. $21.88 for one; $24.88 for two.
- Econo-Travel Motor Hotel, 6621 Thirlane Rd. NW, 24019. Telephone: 703/563-0853. $19.95 for one; $23.95 for two in one bed; $25.95 for two in two beds.
- Econo-Travel Motor Hotel, 🛇, 3816 Franklin Rd., 24014. Telephone: 703/774-1621. $19.95 for one; $23.95 for two in one bed; $25.95 for two in two beds.
- Econo-Travel Motor Hotel, 308 Orange Ave. NW, 24012. Telephone: 703/343-2413. $17.95 for one; $21.95 for two in one bed; $23.95 for two in two beds.
- Best Value Thrifty Inn, 6520 Thirlane Rd. NW, 24019. Telephone: 703/563-2871. $15.95 for one; $18.95 for two in one bed; $21.95 for two in two beds.

Salem

Accommodation: Econo-Travel Motor Hotel, 1535 East Main St., 24153. Telephone: 703/366-2426. $19.95 for one; $23.95 for two in one bed; $25.95 for two in two beds.

South Hill

Accommodation: Econo-Travel Motor Hotel, 623 East Atlantic St., 23970. Telephone: 804/447-7116. $16.50 for one; $20 for two in one bed; $23 for two in two beds.

Staunton

Accommodations: Econo-Travel Motor Hotel, Rte. 4, Box 105A, 24401. Telephone: 703/885-5158. $18.95 for one; $20.95 for two in one bed; $23.95 for two in two beds.
- Days Inn, 🛇, I-81 and Va. 654 (Exit 55A), P.O. Box 2307, Mint Springs, 24401. Telephone: 703/337-3031. $20.88 for one; $23.88 for two.

Suffolk

Accommodation: Econo-Travel Motor Hotel, 1017 North Main St., 23434. Telephone: 804/539-3451. $14.95 to $16.95 for one; $17.95 to $19.95 for two in one bed; $20.95 to $22.95 for two to four in two beds.

Triangle

Camping: Prince William Forest Park, P.O. Box 208, 22172. Oak Ridge campground (six miles west of the entrance) is open all year. $2 per campsite per night.

Urbana

Accommodation: Sangraal-by-the-Sea (AYH), ✦ ★ 25%, 🛇, P.O. Box 187, 23175. Telephone: 804/776-6500 evenings and weekends or 887-2500 weekdays. Call the hostel for a pickup from bus or train station in Williamsburg or Saluda (call ahead). Open year round. Sangraal is a Swiss-style château lodge on the waterfront with canoeing, sailing, and hiking trails. $5.75 for AYH members; $7 for nonmembers. Discount applies to lodging, meals, and rental of sailboats, canoes, and bicycles.

Verona

Accommodation: Econo Lodge, intersection of I-81 and Va. 612, P.O. Box 586, 24482. Telephone: 703/248-8981. $17 for one; $20 for two in one bed; $23 for two in two beds.

Virginia Beach

Accommodation: The Sinclair Inn, 2607 Atlantic Ave., 23451. Telephone: 804/428-4733. European-style inn on the oceanfront. Open May 15 to September 15. $12 for a single or double with shared bath, May 15 to June 18; $16 for private bath. Rates in season (June 18 to September 1) are a little above our maximum at $28 for a single or double with shared bath, $38 with private bath, but since rates tend to be very high in this area these are fairly reasonable.

Williamsburg

Accommodation: Motel 6, 3030 Richmond Rd., 23185. Telephone: 804/565-2710. $12.95 for one; $16.95 for two; $19.95 for up to four.

On Campus: According to our correspondent at the College of William and Mary, the college itself does not have many activities that would be of interest to travelers, but Williamsburg is "a re-creation of an 18th-century colonial city—beautiful, fascinating, and definitely worth some time and effort." Busch Gardens, a beer and amusement park, also merits a stop.

Word has it that the Greenleaf Café on Scotland St. serves excellent, cheap meals; another good place to eat is George's Campus Restaurant on Prince George St. Also recommended are Milton's Pizza, Sal's Italian Restaurant, and Hsing Ling Chinese Restaurant—all at Williamsburg Shopping Center. If you're up for a ferry ride, take the Jamestown ferry to (guess where?) Jamestown, and four or five miles down the only road is the Surrey House, which serves excellent southern cooking for $3 to $10.

Late fall and very early spring are good times to visit, when there is a minimum of tourists.

Winchester

Accommodations: Econo-Travel Motor Hotel, 1020 Millwood Pike, 22601. Telephone: 703/667-5000. $19.95 for one; $22.95 for two in one bed; $25.95 for two in two beds.
● Econo Lodge, Sunnyside Station, Rte. 522, 22601. Telephone: 703/667-1033. $17.95 for one; $21.95 for two in one bed; $24.95 for two to four in two beds.

Woodbridge

Accommodations: Econo-Travel Motor Hotel, 13317 Gordon Blvd., 22191. Telephone: 703/491-5196. $22.95 for one; $26.95 for two in one bed; $29.95 for two in two beds.
● Econo Lodge, 13964 Jefferson Davis Hwy., 22191. Telephone: 703/494-4144. See above listing for rates.

Wytheville

Accommodation: Econo-Travel Motor Hotel, 1190 East Main St., 24383. Telephone: 703/228-5517. $18.95 for one; $22.95 for two in one bed; $25.95 for two in two beds.

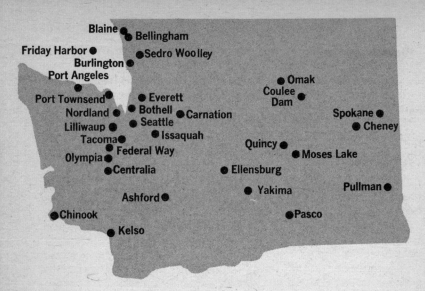

Washington

Let's start with the Olympic Peninsula, with its 8000-foot mountains, permanent glaciers, and hot springs. Much of the peninsula is un- or underinhabited and occupied by the Olympic National Park; its principal sight is the world's only nontropical rain forest, in the Hoh River Valley. This is great country for *experienced* hikers and backpackers, but mountain treks should be done in groups with someone who knows the terrain and how to survive when lost.

The ocean beach at Kalaloch is part of the national park and has highway access; there is a lodge on the beach, but it is always booked, summer and winter, far in advance and there is nowhere else to stay for miles. To get around the peninsula by road on Hwy. 101 takes a full day at top speeds without stopping. To see anything and to enjoy the country at all requires a minimum of three days. For those going on to Canada there is ferry service several times daily from Port Angeles to Victoria, B.C. The peninsula is exceptionally rainy and the water off all beaches is much too cold for swimming. There's a summer arts and music festival at Port Townsend.

Southwest Washington is bordered by the Cascade Range on the east, the Pacific on the west, the Columbia River on the south, and the Olympic Peninsula on the north. Most of the area is densely forested and heavily logged. There's very little population here except in pulp mill towns, the deep-sea fishing port of Ocean Shores, the dunes and beach area near Long Beach, the industrial town of Aberdeen, and the dull strip along Interstate 5 running from the state capital at Olympia to the Portland suburb of Vancouver, Washington.

The Puget Sound area extends from the Canadian border south to the state capital at Olympia along an inland sea over 100 miles in length and dotted with wooded islands and peninsulas, many of which are reachable via an extensive state ferry system. The sound is noted for its delicious (and ever-dwindling) salmon, oysters, clams, mussels, octopus, and other marine life. Although this area contains the bulk of the population of the state of Washington, one is never far from mountain and coastal scenery.

Not all of the cities and towns of Puget Sound are notable, but the following rate a mention: Bellingham, with its Western Washington University, superb local museum in the 19th-century former city hall, interesting restored urban area with good restaurants, and rose gardens; Everett, a horror of air pollution and uncontrolled urban sprawl, but with redeeming features nearby including the harbor, lighthouse, and seafood restaurants at the ferry port of Mukilteo and the views of the Cascades as one travels up toward Stevens Pass. And then there's Puyallup (anyone able to pronounce the name of this place correctly is recognized as a Northwest native) with its fine views of Mount Rainier, daffodil festival in the spring, and state fair in September.

Tacoma is an interesting city that tries hard to live up to its reputation as the area's organized crime capital. On the surface, Tacoma doesn't have much going for it. One Seattle wit says Tacoma is the place where you find Velveeta in the gourmet cheese shop. And yet the north end of the city has some of the prettiest shoreline in the area, the bridge over the Narrows is an attractive replacement for the famous Galloping Gertie of the 1940s, and the city center is an attractive mix of new urbanism, pedestrian malls, and a few sensationally grotesque Victorian public buildings. Many of the inhabitants are descendants of Yugoslav fishermen who came to the Northwest in the early part of the century.

Olympia features tours of the Olympia Brewery in Tumwater with a nice little waterfall tumbling into the south end of Puget Sound and a beautiful view of the Capitol building overlooking the sound. Once you leave the public buildings on Capitol Hill, you descend to the midst of what looks like an unkempt Norwegian fishing village—no beauty, but great character.

For something about Seattle, see page 418.

Some Special Events: International Plowing Match in Lynden (April); Apple Blossom Festival in Wenatchee and Washington State Garden Show in Tacoma (May); Folk Life Festival in Seattle (June); Pioneer Rodeo in Roy, Festival of People in Montesano, and Indian Celebration in Nespelem (all in July); Threshing Bee in Lynden and Grant County Fair and Rodeo in Moses Lake (August); Harbor Days Festival and Tug Boat Races in Olympia (September); and Scandinavian Festival in Tacoma (October).

Hitching: Until recently, hitchhiking was illegal everywhere in Washington. Now that has been changed, and it's legal on all roads except limited-access facilities or freeways. Hitching, according to a friend, is good to excellent except in Olympia, which he says you should most definitely avoid if you're hitching. A friend at Central Washington State College in Ellensburg says that hitching from there to the coast is excellent, but getting rides to the eastern part of the state is not as easy. A friend in Bellingham says: "Both inside and outside of town, there is lots of thumb riding. In fact, it's the major means of transportation for a big piece of the population."

Tourist Information: Travel Development Division, Department of Commerce and Economic Development, General Administration Bldg., Olympia, WA 98504.

Ashford

Accommodation: The Lodge Youth Hostel (AYH), P.O. Box 86, 98304. Hwy. 706, one-quarter mile outside Nisqually entrance to Mount Rainier National Park. Telephone: 206/569-2312. Open year round. $3 summer; $4.50 winter. AYH membership required (see page 21).

Camping: Mount Rainier National Park, 98304. Six campgrounds. Sunshine Point and Longmire open year round; others open during summer season only. $1 to $3 per campsite.

Bellingham

Tourist Information: Bellingham Chamber of Commerce, P.O. Box 958, 98227. Telephone: 206/734-1330.

Help: Whatcom County Crisis Service, 124 East Holly, Mason Bldg., Room 201. Telephone: 206/734-7271 or 384-1485. "Emergency counseling for individuals and families with temporary crises; information and referrals on just about anything in Whatcom County. Phones are open 24 hours."

"Bellingham is a fine town and has a lot of alternative lifestyle people living in it. The south side of town is a traveler's dream, with restored buildings, easy-living people, and lots of local color. People here are always helping each other and keeping up on the most recent information concerning politics, energy use, pollution, etc. There are a few places that house people for free, but the problem is that these houses are privately owned and do not advertise as places of refuge. Most people just stumble across them. If you come to Bellingham, walk our coastline. Although we haven't escaped pollution, there are some very fine places along the shore. Just follow the railroad tracks south of town."

Accommodations: YWCA, 1026 North Forest St., 98225. Telephone: 206/734-4820. Women; limited space for men. $9 single; $12 double. Weekly rate: $45. Reservations necessary (one month in advance preferred). "An elegant historical building."

● Motel 6, 3701 Byron St., 98225. Telephone: 206/734-6940. $12.95 for one; $16.95 for two; $19.95 for up to four.

Blaine

Accommodation: Imperial 400 Motor Inn, 288 D St., 98230. Telephone: 206/332-5603. $19 to $23 for one; $23 to $27 for two in one bed; $26 to $30 for two in two beds.

Bothell

Accommodation: Northshore YMCA International Youth Hostel (AYH), 20208 Bothell Way NE (Wash. 527), 98011. Telephone: 206/483-6208. Open year round. Reservations required October 1 to March 31. $4.50 summer, $5.50 winter for AYH members; $6.50 summer, $7.50 winter for nonmembers. Space for camping is available.

Burlington

Accommodation: Friendship Inn–Cocusa, 200 West Rio Vista, 98233. Telephone: 206/757-6044. $20 to $24 for one; $27 to $29 for two in one bed; $29 to $31 for two in two beds.

Carnation

Accommodation: Carnation Hostel (AYH), 6602 Tolt River Rd. NE, 98014. Telephone: 206/333-6275 or 333-4981. Call the houseparents from the bus station (three miles) and they will pick you up. $3 for adults; $1.50 for children. The hostel is located on a 20-acre farm. "There are gardens, bees, and sheep." They prefer that you bring your own sleeping bag. There is also room for camping.

Centralia

Accommodation: Motel 6, 1310 Belmont, 98531. To open in 1982. See Bellingham listing for rates.

Cheney

Help: Rap-In, Eastern Washington University, 509/359-7979 or 800/838-5273 (toll free from Spokane). Closed during university vacations.

Accommodation: Eastern Washington State College Dormitories, &, Louise Anderson Hall, 99004. Telephone: 509/359-7022. Open year round but space is limited during fall, winter, and spring. $12.50 single; $10 per person double. Reservations are not necessary during summer.

Chinook

Accommodation: Fort Columbia Youth Hostel (AYH), P.O. Box 224, 98614. Telephone: 206/777-8755 (after 5 p.m.). Open June 1 to September 31. $3. AYH membership required (see page 21).

Coulee Dam

Camping: Coulee Dam National Recreation Area, P.O. Box 37, 99116. Twenty-one campgrounds. Most open year round. Six are accessible by boat only. Some are $3; most are free.

Ellensburg

On Campus: Central Washington University is here in this friendly, rural farming/college community. You might be able to find a place to stay on campus by calling the Central Washington University Conference Center at 509/963-1141.

To meet students, try Webster's, 319 North Pearl; Adeline's, 315 North Main; the Tave, 117 West 4th; or Pizza Place, 716 East 8th.

Accommodation: Ponderosa Motel and Trailer Court, 🐦 $1, ⬛ (limited), 700 South Main, 98926. Telephone: 509/925-9388. $16 for one; $18 for two in one bed; $21 for two in two beds. Rates lower in winter. Two of the rooms have cooking facilities.

Everett

Accommodations: Western 6 Motel, 24 128th St. SW, 98204. Telephone: 206/353-8120. $14.40 single; $21.90 double.
● Motel 6, 10006 Hwy. 99 South, 98204. Telephone: 206/355-1811. See Bellingham listing for rates.

Federal Way

Accomodation: Home Hostel (AYH-SA). Telephone: 206/927-1558. Ten miles from Tacoma; 20 miles from Seattle. Reservations necessary. $3 hostel members; $4 nonmembers.

Friday Harbor

Help: San Juan Community Services, 206/378-2669.
Accommodation: Elite Hotel, 🐦, 55 1st St., 98250. Telephone: 206/378-5555. Friday Harbor is on San Juan Island, and the Elite is 1½ blocks from the ferry landing. $17 for a single or double. There is also dorm space, which costs $7 for six to eight people or $6 for ten people. Bring a sleeping bag. The hotel has a café, sauna, and hot tubs. Three weeks' advance reservation necessary in summer.

Issaquah

Accommodation: Motel 6, 1885 15th Pl. NW, 98027. Telephone: 206/392-9666. See Bellingham listing for rates.

Kelso

Accommodation: Motel 6, 1505 Allen St., 98626. Telephone: 206/636-3660. See Bellingham listing for rates.

Lilliwaup

Accommodation: Mike's Beach Hostel and Resort (AYH-SA), 🐦 ★ ⬛, Rte. 1, Box 95 N, 98555. Telephone: 206/877-5324. Open April 15 to October 15. $5 summer. AYH membership required (see page 21).

Moses Lake

Accommodations: Motel 6, 2822 Wapato Dr., 98837. Telephone: 509/765-6676. See Bellingham listing for rates.
● Imperial 400 Motor Inn, 905 West Broadway, 98837. Telephone: 509/765-

8626. $19 to $24 for one; $23 to $28 for two in one bed; $26 to $31 for two in two beds.

Nordland

Help: Office of Human Affairs, 206/385-4040.

Accommodation: Fort Flagler State Park Hostel (AYH), 98358. Telephone: 206/385-1288. Open May 1 to September 30. Rest of year by reservation only. Men, women, and children. $3.50 for AYH members; $4.50 for nonmembers (includes purchase of temporary pass).

Olympia

Accommodations: Friendship Inn–Golden Gavel Motor Hotel, 909 Capitol Way, 98501. Telephone: 206/352-8533. $21 to $25 for one; $24 to $29 for two in one bed; $26 to $30 for two in two beds.

● Motel 6, 400 West Lee St., Tumwater, 98501. Telephone: 206/943-5000. See Bellingham listing for rates.

Omak

Accommodation: Best Value Stampede Motel, P.O. Box 955, 215 West 4th, 98841. $18 for one; $20 for two in one bed.

Pasco

Accommodation: Motel 6, 1520 North Oregon St., 99301. Telephone: 509/547-6666. See Bellingham listing for rates.

Port Angeles

Camping: Olympic National Park, 600 East Park Ave., 98362. Seventeen campgrounds. Three are open year round; others just for the summer season. $3 per campsite for some; others are free.

Port Townsend

Help: Human Affairs, City Hall, 607 Water. Telephone: 206/385-2322.

Accommodation: Fort Worden Youth Hostel (AYH), 98368. Telephone: 206/385-0655. Open year round, except December 15 to January 3 and Thanksgiving Day. $3.50 for AYH members; $4.50 for others. *"Hostels like the one at Port Townsend were fantastic—that place is a home away from home."*

Pullman

On Campus: There is a hotel in the student union at Washington State University where you can get a single for about $20. The union building is also the place to eat and to meet students, although services are very limited during the summer.

Quincy

Accommodation: Friendship Villager Inn Motel, 711 Second Ave. SW, 98848. Telephone: 509/787-3515. $18 for one; $24 for two in one bed; $26 for two in two beds.

Seattle

Built on seven hills (remind you of another famous city?), settled in between the Olympic and Cascade Mountain ranges, and right alongside the shores of Puget Sound and several freshwater lakes, Seattle is an appealing town. From the Observation Deck of the Space Needle, in Seattle Center (the park that was the site of the 1962 World's Fair), you can get a good look at it all: downtown, the Pike Place Market, the Waterfront, Pioneer Square, Fisherman's Terminal, Woodland Park and Zoo, Capitol Hill (Seattle's equivalent of Greenwich Village), Seattle University, the University of Washington, and 14,000-foot-high Mount Rainier. Anyone who's going to spend more than just a day or two in the Queen City should probably take a look at some of these guidebooks:

1978-79 Seattle #1 Guide—Weekly's Guide to Washington, Madrona Publishers, Inc., Seattle ($4.95).

Seattle Then and Now, by Roland Morgan, Bodima, 13 Estates Dr., Orinda, California ($6.95).

The Poor Man's Guide to Seattle Area Restaurants, by Mary and Marvin Braunstein, West Seattle Associates, Inc. ($2.95).

Washington State National Parks, Historic Sites, Recreation Areas and Natural Landmarks, by Ruth Kirk, University of Washington Press, Seattle ($1.95).

Footsore: Walks and Hikes Around Puget Sound, by Harvey Manning, Mountaineers Press, Seattle (four volumes, $5.95 each).

Seattle, Past to Present, by Roger Sale, University of Washington Press, Seattle ($6.95).

To find out what's happening and when, check any of the following newspapers: *Weekly, Sun, Tempo, Daily, Argus, Seattle Times,* and *Post Intelligencer.* For maps and answers to tourist questions of any kind, stop at the Convention and Visitors Bureau at 1815 Seventh Ave. or at Sea-Tac International Airport. Both are open seven days a week. Anyone who speaks a foreign language and needs help can call the Foreign Language Bank (tel. 622-4250). At the University of Washington, there's an information center at 4014 University Way NE (tel. 543-9198).

Getting There: The airport, Sea-Tac International (the Tac is for neighboring Tacoma), is about 15 miles from downtown Seattle. You can get from the airport to town by bus for 75¢. It's a two-zone ride. The return bus to the airport can be boarded at 2nd and Union Sts. downtown, but you'll have to ask for a transfer as you get on. There's also something called a "Hustle Bus" that connects the airport with the downtown airline terminal at 415 Seneca St. for a $4 fare. True to its name, the bus takes 20 minutes.

● The bus station is at 7th and Stewart Sts., and the train station is at 3rd and South Jackson; both are served by Metro bus. There are Metro information booths at each station, where you can pick up maps and bus schedules and directions to where you're heading.

Getting Around: To get into a taxi costs $1 and it's $1 for every mile you ride. You can flag a taxi but that's tricky; it's best to call ahead one of the following: Farwest (tel. 622-1717); Yellow Cab (tel. 622-6500); or Grey Top (tel. 622-4949).

● The monorail links downtown Seattle and Seattle Center; a ride costs 35¢. The buses run often and cost 50¢ for a one-zone ride and 70¢ for one that covers two zones. Zone 1 covers the entire city, Zone 2 the periphery and surrounding King County. For bus information, dial 447-4800. If you have a bike and you want to take it on the bus with you, call the Bicycle Hot Line (tel. 522-BIKE) and find out how. Another rather unique feature of Seattle Metro Transit, called Magic Carpet, lets you ride for free in the downtown core area. The driver will explain how far you can travel without paying a fare. This certainly simplifies visits to the Pioneer Square and Pike Place Market areas, theaters, movies, shopping, and sports events at the Kingdome.

Accommodations: Occasionally there's space in the University of Washington dormitories; telephone Campus Housing at 206/543-6222 to check.

● Seahaven Youth Hostel (AYH), 1431 Minor Ave., 98101. Four blocks from the center of downtown. Telephone: 206/382-4170. Open all year. For AYH members the rates are $5.50 for a dorm room and $12 for a private room. For the same accommodations, nonmembers pay $6.50 and $14, respectively; they must also purchase a temporary Hostel Pass and leave a refundable deposit. This hostel has been set up in a grand old hotel, an echo of Seattle's past with its brass doors, terrazzo floors, and inch-thick marble everywhere. Right in the hostel is a social center which serves pastry and coffee all day long.

● YMCA, 🐝 ★ $1, Downtown Branch, 909 Fourth Ave., 98104. Telephone: 206/447-4511. One mile from bus station, a free bus ride from the train station. Men, women, and small children. $16 to $18 single; $21 to $23 double without bath; $28 to $30 with bath. Lots of athletic facilities, laundry, and restaurant.

● YWCA, 1118 Fifth Ave., 98101. Telephone: 206/447-4888. Women only. $12.75 to $15.50 single; $10.50 per person double without bath. Exercise equipment and a pool in the building; a deli and coffeeshop for post-exercise hunger.

● University Motor Inn, 4140 Roosevelt Way NE, 98105. Telephone: 206/632-5055. In the university district. $24 single; $29 double.

● College Inn Guest House, 4000 University Way NE, 98105. Telephone: 206/633-4441. A reconverted old inn with rooms without bath, as they were in the 1890s, but with period furnishings. Young and friendly management. College Inn Café and Pub downstairs are both student hangouts with moderately priced food and drink. Room rates range from $18 to $39, depending on the size and number of persons per room. The price of the room includes a continental breakfast.

● Friendship Inn–Three Bears Motel, 2717 South 216th St., 98188. Telephone: 206/824-2331. $21 to $23 for one; $23 to $26 for two in one bed; $26 to $28 for two in two beds.

● Western 6 Motel, 16500 Pacific Hwy. South, 98188. Telephone: 206/246-4101. $14.40 single; $21.90 double.

● Motel 6, 18900 47th Ave. South, 98188. Telephone: 206/246-5520. See Bellingham listing for rates.

Where to Eat: Pike Place Market has a number of eateries, ranging from what many people consider Seattle's best restaurant—Labuznik, 1924 First Ave. (tel. 682-1624), with Central European food that's expensive—to ethnic places serving moderately priced French food (Le Bistro, 93A Pike St.; tel. 682-3049); inexpensive Greek food (Athenian Inn, Pike Pl.; tel. 624-7166); and not-very-expensive Bolivian food (Copacabana, Pike Pl.; tel. 622-6359). We've been told that the saltenas, deep-fried meat pastries, are especially good in this small but cozy restaurant.

● Pier 59 Seafood Bar and Deli, Pier 59, Alaskan Way. Telephone: 624-0312. On the waterfront right by the Seattle Aquarium.

● Ivar's Salmon House, 401 NE Northlake Way, in the university district. Telephone: 632-0767. You can get a classic meal of alder-smoked salmon, Indian style, with cole slaw and cornbread for $5.25 at lunch; expect to pay approximately $8 to $9 for dinner. There is also a takeout stand on Northlake Way near the restaurant entrance, and you can take your salmon ($4.25) or fish and chips ($2.09) down to the floating pier in front of the restaurant.

● Russian Samovar, 806 East Roy. Telephone: 323-1465. Located on Capitol Hill, near the Seattle Art Museum. Enjoy a Russian meal in an atmosphere made special by stained glass, Russian fairytale murals, and examples of Russian craftwork.

● Sergio's, 321 East Pine. Telephone: 623-0258. Near Seahaven Hostel. The specialty here is international cuisine with a Filipino flavor, and the prices are very reasonable. It's a good place to read the morning paper with croissants and café au lait or espresso for about $2. Sergio's is open throughout the day and evening.

● Lox, Stock and Bagel, 4552 University Way NE. Telephone: 634-3144. Near the University of Washington campus. A typical university-type place— burgers, omelets, and deli sandwiches if you don't want lox.

● Last Exit on Brooklyn, 3930 Brooklyn Ave. NE. Telephone: 545-9873. Good coffee, sandwiches, chess, and conversation.

● Woerne's European Café, 4108 University Way NE. Telephone: 632-7893. German food and pastries.

● El Tapito, 4116 University Way NE. Telephone: 633-2038. Good, inexpensive Mexican food in the university area.

What to See and Do: You'll have to visit the Seattle Center, the site of the World's Fair almost 20 years ago, which has been transformed into a park that offers performing arts, museums, the Pacific Science Center, shops, an amusement park, and the Space Needle.

● The Waterfront along Alaskan Way is another must-see. Here you'll find shops, restaurants, harbor tours, an aquarium, and a fine park.

● Pioneer Square, Seattle's birthplace, has been restored to the splendor of 1889, the year that the Seattle fire struck. Leaded windows, wrought iron, restored brick and stone storefronts, and two cobblestone plazas are all wonderful reminders of Seattle's Klondike Gold Rush Days. After the fire of 1889, the streets of Pioneer Square were raised. The original sidewalk level remained beneath, leaving shopfronts in large caverns that were forgotten over the years. Now it's possible to take an underground tour of the area. Telephone 682-4646 for information.

At Night: If you like theater, Seattle is a goldmine of small and large companies that often perform original material which has never, or not yet, been to Broadway. Try particularly the Seattle Rep, A.C.T., the Intiman Theater, the Empty Space, and the many small theaters around Pioneer Square. Many of these theaters offer student discounts or reduced-price last-minute tickets.

- The Seattle Symphony performs at the Opera House in Seattle Center. There are also many chamber music, vocal recitals, and University of Washington musical events all through the year. Check the newspapers.
- Parnell's, 313 Occidental South. Telephone: 624-2387. A low-key lounge atmosphere where you can hear excellent jazz. Can be expensive though, with a hefty cover charge.
- People who like their music country and western style congregate at the Central Tavern and Café, 207 1st South St. near Pioneer Square. Telephone: 622-0209. The crowd stands around the bar or sits, but either way they obviously enjoy themselves.
- Call the Seattle Folklore Society, 311 First Ave. South. Telephone 292-9419 for the schedule of folk music events in town.
- There is lots of dance in Seattle, both from touring companies and resident troupes. The Pacific Northwest Ballet (tel. 447-4655) is functioning as of this writing, but some of the smaller, innovative companies may very well fall victim to "Reaganomics." Check newspapers for current dance events.
- Be sure to check the University of Washington *Daily* for university events: rap sessions, concerts, plays, film series, lectures, visiting celebrities, etc.
- Pier 70 Restaurant and Chowder House, Alaskan Way and Broad. There's a big terrace dance floor right on the waterfront, which attracts a large singles crowd because of its live music and the chance to dance. Expect a cover charge.

Shopping: Pike Place Market, 1st and Pike, downtown. A series of roofed-over and open-air stalls where truck farmers and hawkers sell their wares—produce, flowers, antiques, crafts, art, etc. Open Monday to Saturday, 9 a.m. to 6 p.m.

- People in the Northwest love the out-of-doors. They hike, they ski, and they climb mountains with a vengeance. If you'd like to do the same, you might want to stop at Recreational Equipment, Inc., 1525 11th Ave., to take a look at the tents, packs, boots, etc. If you don't want to buy, you can rent here instead.
- University Book Store, 4326 University Way NE. Over 60,000 books to choose from.
- The Elliott Bay Book Company, 1st South and South Main (Pioneer Square). Lots more books.
- A Different Drummer, 420 Broadway East (Capitol Hill). New and used books, a wide selection.
- Shorey's, 110 Union and 119 South Jackson. Books in Pioneer Square.
- Peaches, 811 NE 45th St. All kinds of records in the university district.
- Wide World of Music, 215 Pike. Records downtown.
- Filippi's, 1351 East Olive. A great stock of used records and books.

Tourist Information: Seattle-King County Convention and Visitors Bureau, 1815 Seventh Ave., 98101. Telephone: 206/447-7273.

Help: Travelers Aid, 909 Fourth Ave., 98104. Telephone: 206/447-3888.
- Crisis Clinic (for emotional crises), 1530 Eastlake Ave. East. Telephone: 447-3222.

Sedro Woolley

Camping: North Cascades National Park, 98284. Seven campgrounds open from May to October or November.
- Ross Lake National Recreation Area, c/o North Cascades National Park,

98284. Five campgrounds accessible by car; three of them are open April to October; two are open all year. Fifteen campgrounds are accessible by boat only or by boat and trail, and are open from June to November.

● Lake Chelan National Recreation Area, c/o North Cascades National Park, 98284. Five campgrounds all accessible by boat and trail. Boat launching at Chelan. Open April to November. No fee.

Spokane

Tourist Information: Spokane Area Convention and Visitors Bureau, West 609 Spokane Falls Blvd., 99201. Telephone: 509/624-1341.

On Campus: On the Gonzaga University campus, near Crosby Library, you'll find a bulletin board with rides and apartments listed. For food, try the Chef Restaurant, North 1329 Hamilton, where they offer meat, potatoes, salad, vegetable, and bread for $3.25. Two places to go to meet students are Bulldog, 1300 block on Hamilton, and the Forum, 1400 block on Hamilton.

Accommodations: Friendship Tiki Lodge Inn, West 1420 Second Ave., 99204. Telephone: 509/838-2026. $18 to $20 for one; $20 to $26 for two in one bed; $22 to $28 for two in two beds.

● Friendship West Wynn Motel and Restaurant, West 2701 Sunset Blvd., 99204. Telephone: 509/747-3037. $20 to $24.50 for one; $22.50 to $30.50 for two in one bed; $24.50 to $32.50 for two in two beds.

● Motel 6, 1508 South Rustle St., 99204. Telephone: 509/838-6401. See Bellingham listing for rates.

Tacoma

Accommodations: Friendship Inn–Calico Cat Motel, 8821 Pacific Ave., 98444. Telephone: 206/535-2440. $18 to $22 for one; $20 to $25 for two in one bed; $25 to $35 for two in two beds.

● Motel 6, 5201 20th St. East, Fife, 98424. Telephone: 206/922-6612. See Bellingham listing for rates.

Yakima

Accommodation: Motel 6, 1104 North 1st St., 98901. Telephone: 509/452-0407. See Bellingham listing for rates.

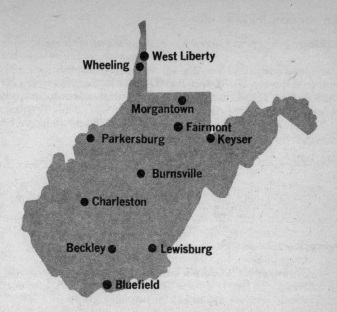

West Virginia

West Virginia offers a great deal of natural beauty. The eastern part of the state has the highest mountains, several caverns and glades. The western part, although more urbanized, has its share of rural scenery. West Virginia has 36 state parks and forests, many with camping facilities.

One of the most popular of the state's tourist attractions is Harpers Ferry National Historic Park, where the Shenandoah and Potomac Rivers meet. In the mid-19th century, this thriving town fell victim to the Civil War. Remains of the arsenal, some restored buildings, and special exhibits are on view in summer.

Some Special Events: Black Cultural Festival in Charleston (March); Heritage Days in Parkersburg (April); Blue Ridge Quilt Show in Harpers Ferry (May); Monroe County Arts and Crafts Fair in Peterstown and West Virginia Folk Festival in Glenville (June); Mountaineer Days in Thomas and Hot Air Balloon Races in Huntington (July); Hancock County Fair in Newell (August); and Tucker County Fair and Firemen's Homecoming in Parsons (September).

Hitching: Hitchhiking is prohibited on Interstate routes and limited-access highways. Otherwise it is legal and, according to the Department of Public Safety, best on U.S. routes and state routes; however, they don't really approve of hitching in general.

Tourist Information: Travel Development Division, Governor's Office of Economic and Community Development, State Capitol Complex, 1900 Washington St., Charleston, WV 25305.

Beckley

Accommodations: Days Inn, &, Rte. 3 (Harper Rd.) and I-77 (West Virginia Turnpike), 102 Harper Park Dr., 25801. Telephone: 304/255-5291. $24.88 for one; $28.88 for two. Rates slightly higher June to October.
• Best Value Laurel Lodge, √, 1909 Harper Rd., 25801. Telephone: 304/255-2161. $23 for one; $26 for two in one bed; $28 for two in two beds.

Bluefield

Accommodation: Econo-Travel Motor Hotel, 3400 Cumberland Rd., 24701. Telephone: 304/327-8171. $23.95 for one; $27.95 for two in one bed; $30.95 for two in two beds.

Burnsville

Accommodation: Friendship Inn Motel 79, on I-79 at junction of W.Va. 5 and Main St., 26335. Telephone: 304/853-2554. $16 to $21 for one; $20 to $25 for two in one bed; $22 to $25 for two in two beds.

Charleston

Accommodations: Red Roof Inn, I-64 at W.Va. 34, Winfield Exit, Hurricane, 25526. Telephone: 304/757-6392. $19.95 for one; $22.95 for two in one bed; $24.95 to $26.95 for two to four in two beds.
• Red Roof Inn, West Virginia Turnpike at MacCorkle Ave. To open in 1982. See above listing for rates.

Fairmont

Accommodations: Friendship Inn–Avenue Motel, 816 Fairmont Ave., 26554. Telephone: 304/366-4960. $17 for one; $20 for two in one bed; $23 for two in two beds.
• Red Roof Inn, I-79 at W.Va. 250, 26554. To open in 1982. See Charleston listing for rates.

Keyser

Accommodation: Best Value Potomac Motel, P.O. Box 421, 26726. Telephone: 304/788-1671. $22.38 for one; $24.40 for two in one bed; $30 for two in two beds.

Lewisburg

Accommodation: Friendship Inn–Sunset Terrace Motel, Box 627, U.S. 60 West, 24901. Telephone: 304/645-2363. $16 to $22 for one; $23 for two in one bed; $23 to $30 for two in two beds.

Morgantown

On Campus: You're bound to meet students of West Virginia University at the Mountainlair Blue Tic Tavern on campus, or nearby at the Chestnut Pub on Chestnut St. where people gather to play backgammon. Morgantown is known for its glass factories; if you're interested, you can arrange a tour of one.

Accommodation: Chestnut Ridge Camp Youth Hostel (AYH), P.O. Box 590, 26505. Telephone: 304/292-4773. Open year round. $1.25. Hostel is 15 miles east of Morgantown. There is no public transportation from town to the hostel. In the surrounding area are 13,000 acres of state forest with numerous hiking trails, and swimming, fishing, and skiing.

Parkersburg

Accommodations: Red Roof Inn, ⬤, I-77 at U.S. 50 West (Exit 176), 26101. Telephone: 304/485-1741. See Charleston listing for rates.

● Days Inn, ⬤, I-77 and W.Va. 31, P.O. Box 39, 26187. Telephone: 304/485-9596 or 375-3730. $22.88 to $24.88 for one; $26.88 to $28.88 for two.

West Liberty

Accommodation: Krise Hall, West Liberty State College, Attention Dean of Students Office, Room 1, 26074. West Liberty is ten miles from Wheeling. Telephone: 304/336-8016 on weekdays, 8:30 a.m. to 4:30 p.m. Men and women. Open May 20 to August 15. $12 per person per day. There's a large park nearby "with all imaginable recreational facilities." Reservations requested 24 hours in advance.

Wheeling

Help: Crisis Line, 304/234-8161.

Accommodations: YWCA, ⬤, 1100 Chapline St., 26003. Telephone: 304/232-0511. Women only. $7.21. Weekly rate: $43.26.

● Wheeling College Dormitories, ⬤ ⬤, 316 Washington Ave., 26003. Telephone: 304/243-2295 or 243-2000. Open June 1 to August 1. $10 single. Oglebay Park, one of the 25 best in the country in terms of recreational facilities, and Wheeling Park, also well equipped, are right nearby.

● Econo Lodge, Rte. 1, Box 184A, Triadelphia, 26059. Telephone: 304/547-1380. $19.95 for one; $24.95 for two.

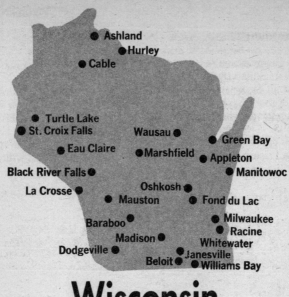

Wisconsin

The northern two-thirds of the state is heavily forested and thickly populated with literally thousands of lakes. The Wisconsin Division of Tourism, in fact, says that "Wisconsin is water." The state has over 14,000 lakes in all. As you'd expect, water sports abound. Wisconsin's weather is moderate in summer, but watch out for the severe cold in winter. There's a long, pleasant fall, but don't expect any spring.

The rich prairieland in the southern part of the state attracted settlers in droves in the mid-1800s and eventually large numbers of immigrants—Germans, Poles, and Scandinavians—came to join them.

Some of the things to see in Wisconsin include Apostle Islands National Lakeshore, where Longfellow's Hiawatha lived by the "Shining Big Sea Water" of Lake Superior; Wisconsin Dells, a stretch of the Wisconsin River that has many man-made attractions including a water show and an amusement park.

Since much of Wisconsin's economy depends on pulp and paper products, it would be interesting to pay a visit to the U.S. Forest Products Laboratory in Madison. Operated by the U.S. Forest Service and the University of Wisconsin, the laboratory is always experimenting with ways to use wood and wood products and to conserve the state's resources. Madison is also the home of the University of Wisconsin system, which has campuses in several other cities.

Two other products closely associated with Wisconsin are cheese and beer, so if you have enough time, consider a tour of a cheese plant or a brewery.

Some Special Events: Maifest in Jacksonport (May); International Picnic in Green Bay and Sawdust City Days in Eau Claire (June); King Richards Renaissance Faire in Kenosha (July); State Fair in Milwaukee's suburb of West Allis (August); U.S. Watermelon Seed-Spitting Championship (September); Fall Festival in Sister Bay and Harvest Festival and Grape Stomping Contest in Prairie du Sac (October).

Hitching: Officially, there's no hitchhiking on the roadway. To quote the State Protective Service: "It has been done on the curb or grassy part of the highway right-of-way."

"I have hitchhiked 12,000 miles in many states and countries and have found Wisconsin the best state. I would recommend it, but hitching on the Interstates will get you a ticket. Stay on the ramps."

Tourist Information: Wisconsin Division of Tourism, P.O. Box 7606, Madison, WI 53707. Telephone: 608/266-2161; toll free 800/362-9566 in Wisconsin and 800/356-9508 from neighboring states.

Appleton

Accommodations: Q.A. Inn, ♿, 2000 Holly Rd., P.O. Box 206, 54912. Telephone: 414/734-9872. $18 to $22 for one; $23 to $28 for two. Good recreational facilities nearby.
● Exel Inn, ♿, 210 North Kools St., 54911. Telephone: 414/733-5551. $17.95 for one; $22.95 for two in one bed; $24.95 for two in two beds.

Ashland

Accommodation: Friendship Inn–Ashland Motel, 2300 West Lake Shore Dr., 54806. Telephone: 715/682-5503. $20 to $25 for one; $25 to $28 for two in one bed; $28 to $36 for two in two beds.

Baraboo

Accommodation: Friendship Inn–Campus Motel, Rte. 4, Box 70, 53913. Telephone: 608/356-8366. $16 to $20 for one; $22 to $26 for two in one bed; $24 to $28 for two in two beds.

Beloit

On Campus: You'll meet students and find out about rides and apartments in the Student Union of Beloit College. If you're hungry while you're in the neighborhood of the campus, try Domenico's for pizza, on the main downtown street (534 East Grand Ave.); the Olde Banque, 417 State, for sandwiches and full dinners; and for Mexican food, el Jacalito on Rte. 2. At night you'll find good company by going to Goody's Bar, Sue Dahl House, or Coughy House. You might be able to find a student willing to put you up for a night or two if you're friendly and lucky.

Black River Falls

Accommodation: Best Value Pines Lodge Motor Inn, RR 4, Box 297, 54615. Telephone: 715/284-5311. $16 for one; $20 for two in one bed; $24 for two in two beds.

Cable

Accommodation: Ches Perry Youth Hostel (AYH), P.O. Box 164, 54821. Telephone: 715/798-3367. Ski season, from Thanksgiving to the end of April, $3.50. By reservation only during other months, $2.50. Reservations must be sent to Mark Leonard, 3712 North Clark St., Chicago, IL 60613.

Dodgeville

Accommodations: Spring Valley Trails (AYH-SA), Rte. 2, P.O. Box 170, 53533. Telephone: 608/935-5725. Open year round. $4.
● Folklore Village Farm (AYH), Rte. 3, 53533. Telephone: 608/924-3725. Reservations required. Open all year; Saturday overnights only. $2.50 summer; $3 winter. Hostelers welcome to pot-luck supper and community folk dance every Saturday at 7 p.m.

Eau Claire

On Campus: If you need anything while you're in Eau Claire, put a notice up in one of the local bars or at the university union, Davies Center. To meet students, go to any of the places on Water St. like the Old Home Tavern, the Joynt, Papa Bear's, and Shenannigan's. To find a place to stay, stop at the Lobby Shoppe information desk, one of the dorms, the housing office, or a bar near campus—"some of the local customers usually have a line on places where people can be accommodated temporarily."

Two possibilities for on-campus stays are Katherine Thomas Hall (tel. 715/836-5821) or Oak Ridge Hall (tel. 715/836-5611). To eat inexpensively— all you can eat for $2.50—just get on line at the campus cafeteria.

For a tour of the campus, go to the Admissions Office at 11 a.m. or 2 p.m. Chippewa Valley Museum is outstanding for a regional museum, Water St. is an interesting old business section, and Putnam Park is a good place for a hike.
Accommodation: Exel Inn, ♿, 2305 Craig Rd., 54701. Telephone: 715/834-3193. $16.95 for one; $21.95 for two in one bed; $23.95 for two in two beds.

Fond du Lac

Accommodations: Motel 6, 738 West Johnson St., 54935. Telephone: 414/923-1990. $12.95 for one; $16.95 for two; $19.95 for up to four.
● Thrifty Scot Motel, 107 North Pioneer Rd., 54935. Telephone: 414/923-6790. $16.90 to $21.90 for one; $20.90 to $22.90 for two in one bed; $25.90 to $27.90 for two in two beds.

Green Bay

"Green Bay is a provincial town, big on bowling and football."

Help: Green Bay Area Free Clinic, 414/437-9773.
● Crisis Line, 414/432-8832.

Accommodations: YMCA, ♿, 235 North Jefferson St., P.O. Box 490, 54301. Telephone: 414/435-5361. Men only. $8 single. Weekly rate: $34. Six blocks from bus station.
- Motel 6, 1614 Shawano Ave., 54303. Telephone: 414/499-1407. See Fond du Lac listing for rates.
- Exel Inn, ♿, 2870 Ramada Way, 54304. Telephone: 414/499-3599. See Appleton listing for rates.

Hurley

Accommodation: Crystal Springs Dairy Youth Hostel (AYH), 223 Silver St., 54534. Telephone: 906/932-2222. $3.25 summer; $4.25 winter. Reservations required December 15 to December 31. AYH membership required (see page 21).

Janesville

Accommodation: Motel 6, 2422 Fulton St., 53545. Telephone: 608/756-4541. See Fond du Lac listing for rates.

La Crosse

On Campus: Here is the home of the University of Wisconsin at La Crosse. The town is big on water sports and beer. You can entertain yourself by taking a brewery tour or going to the Octoberfest during the first week of October. You can't miss it since the entire town is involved. "With 127 bars in a city of 50,000, this is definitely a party town."

Accommodations: Exel Inn, ♿, 2150 Rose St., 54601. Telephone: 608/781-0400. See Appleton listing for rates.
- Best Value Bluff View Motel, 3715 Mormon Coulee Rd., 54601. Telephone: 608/788-0600. $20 to $25 for one or two in one bed; $25 to $30 for two in two beds.
- Friendship Inn Guest House, 810 South 4th St., 54601. Telephone: 608/784-8840. $23 to $26 for two in one bed; $26 to $29 for two in two beds.

Madison

Help: Dane County Mental Health/Crisis Intervention, 608/251-2341 or 251-2345.
- Near East Side Community Health Center, 1133 Williamson St., 53703. Telephone: 608/255-0704. Provides low-cost health care.

On Campus: A friend at the University of Wisconsin in Madison gave us five telephone numbers for travelers to use if they need advice or help: Wisconsin Union Main Desk, 608/262-1331; Campus Assistance Center, 608/263-2400; Counseling Center, 608/262-1744; Visitors Information Booth, 608/262-3318; and the Union Travel Center, second floor, Memorial Building, 608/262-6200. To meet students, have an inexpensive meal, and check the ride boards, stop at the Wisconsin Union, 800 Langdon St., or Union South, corner of Randall Ave. and Johnson St. According to one Madisonian, his city is "a great place to visit or go to school. It welcomes young people and student travelers."

What to do in Madison? Visit the State Capitol, visit the university, bike or hike through the arboretum, walk down State St. and see the State St. Mall. In spring, summer, and fall, visit the Saturday Farmer's Market on Capitol Square.

For up-to-date information on many entertainment events, pick up an *Isthmus* newspaper at any State St. store. It comes out every Thursday.

Accommodations: YWCA, 🔌, 101 East Mifflin, 53703. Telephone: 608/257-1436. Women, couples, or small families (no men alone). $11.25 to $12.25 single; $19 double.

● University YMCA (AYH), 306 North Brooks St., 53715. Telephone: 608/257-2534. Men and women. $15 single; $20 double. Weekly rate: $45 single; $58 double. AYH members pay $4; however, space is available for AYH May 15 to August 15 only. Restaurant called "The Main Course" on the first floor, one block from University of Wisconsin.

● Friendship Inn–Aloha Inn Motel, 3177 East Washington Ave., 53704. Telephone: 608/249-7667. $20 for one; $24 for two in one bed; $27 for two in two beds.

● Red Roof Inn, 🔌, I-90 at U.S. 151 (Exit 151). Telephone: 608/241-1787. $17.95 for one; $20.95 for two in one bed; $22.95 to $24.95 for two to four in two beds.

● Exel Inn, 🔌, 4202 East Towne Blvd., 53704. Telephone: 608/241-3861. $18.50 for one; $23.50 for two in one bed; $25.50 for two in two beds.

● Motel 6, 6402 East Broadway, 53704. Telephone: 608/221-2291. See Fond du Lac listing for rates.

Manitowoc

Accommodation: Thrifty Scot Motel, 4004 Calumet Ave., 54220. Telephone: 414/684-7841. $18.90 to $22.90 for one; $22.90 to $26.90 for two in one bed; $27.90 to $29.90 for two in two beds.

Marshfield

Accommodations: Best Value Murray Inn, ✓ 🔌, 2121 Arnold (Hwy. 13 North), 54449. Telephone: 715/387-2511. $21 for one; $26 for two in one bed.

● Friendship Inn–Downtown Motel, 750 South Central Ave., 54449. Telephone: 715/387-1111. $14 to $17 for one; $18 to $22 for two in one bed; $21 to $25 for two in two beds.

Mauston

Accommodation: Friendship Inn–Willows Motel, Hwys. 12 and 16, 53948. Telephone: 608/847-6800. $19.50 for two in one bed; $24 to $26 for two in two beds.

Milwaukee

Help: Travelers Aid Department, 1730 North 7th St., P.O. Box 08517, 53208. Telephone: 414/265-5544.

Tourist Information: Greater Milwaukee Convention and Visitors Bureau, Inc., 756 North Milwaukee St., 53202. Telephone: 414/273-3950.

On Campus: The University of Wisconsin has a campus in Milwaukee. For a good and inexpensive meal in the area, you could try Riegelman's Pharmacy, on Downer Ave. (for sandwiches, malts, and sundaes); Kalt's, on Oakland Ave. (restaurant and bar); or William Ho's, on North Oakland Ave. (for Chinese food).

Still another campus in Milwaukee is that of Marquette University. According to a friend at Marquette, some favorite eating and drinking places in the area are Wales on Wells, 1508 West Wells, for good fast food; Angelo's, 1601 West Wells, for pizza; and Cousins, 1634 West Wisconsin, for subs. For drinks, there's the Circle Inn, 735 North 16th St. (which also has good hamburgers), and on the same street, the Ardmore Bar, J. V. Grunts, and the Gym.

Accommodations: Milwaukee School of Engineering Residence Hall, 1121 North Milwaukee St., 53201. Telephone: 414/277-7400. Men and women; students only. Open June 1 to August 20. $10 per night. $15 double (there is a waiting list) for two days or longer.

● Red Barn Youth Hostel (AYH), 🚻, 6750 West Loomis Rd., Greendale, 53129. Telephone: 414/529-3299. Open May 1 to October 31. $3. AYH membership required (see page 21). Reservations preferred.

● YMCA, 🚻 (partial), 915 West Wisconsin Ave., 53233. Telephone: 414/276-5077. Men, women, and children. $14 to $18 single. Restaurant on premises.

● Motel 6, 5037 South Howell Ave., 53207. Telephone: 414/481-7800. See Fond du Lac listing for rates.

● Exel Inn, 🚻, 115 North Mayfair Rd., Wauwatosa, 53226. Telephone: 414/257-0140. $23.50 for one; $28.50 for two in one bed; $30.50 for two in two beds.

● Red Roof Inn, 🚻, I-94 at College Ave. East (Exit 319), 53154. Telephone: 414/764-3500. $19.95 for one; $22.95 for two in one bed; $24.95 to $26.95 for two to four in two beds.

Oshkosh

Accommodation: Motel 6, 1015 South Washburn St., 54901. Telephone: 404/235-6720. See Fond du Lac listing for rates.

Racine

Help: Hotline, 826 Park Ave. Telephone: 414/637-9557.

Accommodation: YMCA, 725 Lake Ave., 53403. Telephone: 414/634-1994. Men and women. $17 to $19 single. Reservations recommended. Overlooks Lake Michigan.

St. Croix Falls

Camping: St. Croix National Scenic Riverway, P.O. Box 708, 54024. Two campgrounds open April 1 to October 31.

Turtle Lake

Accommodation: Timberlake Lodge (AYH), 🦌 ★ 10%, Rte. 2, 54889. Telephone: 715/986-2484. Open all year. $4 for AYH members; $5 for nonmembers. Also has campground, backpack sites, and canoe-to sites. "An excellent place for peace and quiet."

Wausau

Accommodation: Exel Inn, ♿, 116 South 17th Ave., 54401. Telephone: 715/842-0641. See Appleton listing for rates.

Whitewater

Accommodation: The Dock (AYH-SA), 🦌 ★ (AYH price), Rte. 2, 53190. Telephone: 608/883-2856. Open June 1 to September 1, sometimes longer. $5 summer; $6 winter. Reservations recommended by mail or phone.

Williams Bay

Accommodation: Conference Center, George Williams College, Lake Geneva Campus, 53191. Telephone: 414/245-5531. Open year round. $24.50 for a single or double except during the summer. Summer rates, including meals, are $23 to $35 per person.

Wyoming

Wyoming is blessed with a great number of tourist attractions and just about all of them are natural. Yellowstone National Park, our biggest national park with over two million acres, was set aside in 1872 and preserved to this day in all its beauty. The geyser Old Faithful still spouts. And now 300 miles of paved roads connect the park's various features and its campsites. And then there's Grand Teton National Park—another beautiful place to fish, hike, or camp. Wyoming can also claim two national monuments—Devil's Tower (the oldest, designated by Teddy Roosevelt) and Fossil Butte. There are nine national forests in Wyoming, including Shoshone—the nation's first. Two regions are designated national recreation areas—Big Horn Canyon and Flaming Gorge. And there are historic spots to visit all along the Oregon Trail, the first road west, which crosses Wyoming from Fort Laramie to Fort Bridger. It seems to be no exaggeration for Wyoming to claim the title of the "First State in Outdoor America." Rodeo is king in Wyoming during the summer and nearly every community has one of its own.

The Wyoming Travel Commission (address below) offers a variety of travel publications including *Self-Guided Tours,* a series of four brochures giving drive-yourself itineraries; *Accommodations; The Oregon Trail;* and *Wyoming's Heritage and Recreation Areas.* All are free.

Some Special Events: Wyoming State Winter Fair in Lander (January); Winter Festival in Pinedale (February); Old Time Fiddle Contest in Shoshoni (May); Woodchoppers Jamboree in Encampment and Indian Tribal Pow Wows and Sun Dances in Fort Washakie (June); Jubilee Days Rodeo in Laramie and Frontier Days in Cheyenne, the world's largest outdoor rodeo that lasts for nine days (July); Gift of the Waters Pageant (commemorating the deeding of the hot springs from the Shoshone Indians to the people of Wyoming) in Thermopolis (August).

434 WHERE TO STAY USA

Hitching: Wyoming has traditionally been hard on hitchhikers, and there's no reason to suspect that will change in the near future. It's one of the states (see page 15) that uses the word "highway" in its law.

Tourist Information: Wyoming Travel Commission, Cheyenne, WY 82002. Telephone: 307/777-7777.

Afton

Accommodation: Friendship Inn–Lazy B Motel, P.O. Box 675, 83110. Telephone: 307/886-3187. $18 to $22 for one; $20 to $24 for two in one bed; $22 to $26 for two in two beds.

Buffalo

Accommodations: Friendship Z-Bar Motel, 626 Fort St., 82834. Telephone: 307/684-5535. $18 to $20 for one; $18 to $22 for two in one bed; $22 to $26 for two in two beds.
• Best Value Canyon Motel, 997 Fort St., P.O. Box 56, 82834. Telephone: 307/684-2957. $16 to $20 for one or two in one bed; $19 to $24 for two in two beds.

Casper

Accommodation: Motel 6, I-25 and Big Horn Rd., 82601. To open in 1982. $12.95 for one; $16.95 for two; $19.95 for up to four.

Cheyenne

Accommodations: YWCA, 222 East 17th St., 82001. Telephone: 307/632-9506 or 635-5212. Women only. $10.40. Weekly rate: $46.50. Three blocks from bus and train. Three restaurants within one block of YWCA.
• Motel 6, 1735 Westland Rd., 82001. Telephone: 307/635-1676. See Casper listing for rates.

Cody

Accommodation: Best Value 7K's Motel, Northford Star Rte., 82414. Telephone: 307/587-2532 or 587-5890. $14 to $20 for one; $20 to $24 for two in one bed; $24 to $26 for two in two beds.

Devils Tower

Camping: Devils Tower National Monument, 82714. Campground at Belle Fourche River open May to September. $2 per campsite.

Douglas

Accommodations: Friendship Inn–Chieftain, 815 East Richards on Hwys. 20, 26, and Business I-25, 82633. Telephone: 307/358-2673. $22.50 for one; $24.50 for two in one bed; $28.50 to $29.50 for two in two beds.

● Friendship Inn–Vagabond, 5th and Richards, 82633. Telephone: 307/358-4311. $22.50 for one; $24.50 for two in one bed; $28.50 for two in two beds.

Dubois

Accommodations: Friendship Inn–Stagecoach Motor Inn, P.O. Box 216, 82513. Telephone: 307/455-2303. $18 to $24 for one; $20 to $26 for two in one bed; $22 to $28 for two in two beds.

● Best Value Branding Iron Motel, U.S. 26 and 287, 82513. Telephone: 307/455-2893. $16 to $18 for one; $18 to $20 for two in one bed; $20 to $22 for two in two beds.

● Sage Motel, 505 West Ramshorn, P.O. Box 595, 82513. Telephone: 307/455-2344 or 455-2626. $18 to $22 for one; $18 to $24 for two in one bed; $20 to $26 for two in two beds.

Greybull

Accommodation: Best Value Antler Motel, 1116 North 6th, 82426. Telephone: 307/765-4404. $16 to $18 for one or two in one bed; $18 to $20 for two in two beds.

Jackson

Accommodation: Motel 6, 600 South Hwy. 89, 83001. Telephone: 307/733-9666. See Casper listing for rates.

Jackson Hole

Accommodation: The Hostel (AYH-SA), P.O. Box 546, Teton Village, 83025. Telephone: 307/733-3415. Open all year. Reservations necessary during winter. $25 single or double. 10% discount for AYH members.

Kemmerer

Accommodation: Friendship Inn–Lazy U Motel, 521 Coral, 83110. Telephone: 307/877-4428. $19 to $20 for one; $22 to $24 for two in one bed; $26 to $28 for two in two beds.

Lander

Accommodation: Best Value Silver Spur Motel, 340 North 10th, 82520. Telephone: 307/332-5189. $18 to $20 for one or two in one bed; $22 to $30 for two in two beds.

Laramie

Accommodation: Motel 6, 621 Plaza Lane, 82070. Telephone: 307/742-0542. See Casper listing for rates.

Lovell

Accommodation: Friendship Inn–Horseshoe Bend, 375 East Main, 82431. Telephone: 307/548-2221. $17 to $19 for one; $20 to $22 for two in one bed; $23 to $25 for two in two beds.

Moose

Camping: Grand Teton National Park, P.O. Drawer 170, 83012. Six campgrounds. Open May to September or October. $4 per campsite per night.
● John D. Rockefeller, Jr., Memorial Parkway, c/o Grand Teton National Park, P.O. Drawer 170, 83012. Telephone: 307/733-2880. Trailer village at Flagg Ranch, tent/trailer campground at Huckleberry Hot Springs, small tent/trailer campground at Snake River. $3 to $7 and up per campsite. Camping June 15 to early September, depending on weather.

Newcastle

Accommodation: Friendship Inn–Buckaroo Motel, 1309 South Summit, 82701. Telephone: 307/746-4435. $20.50 to $22.50 for one; $22.50 to $26.50 for two in one bed; $26.50 to $30.50 for two in two beds.

Pine Bluffs

Accommodation: Friendship Inn–Travelyn, at Pine Bluffs Exit Ramp I-80 at 7th St., 82082. Telephone: 307/245-3226. $18 to $24 for one; $22 to $30 for two in one bed; $24 to $32 for two in two beds.

Powell

Accommodation: Northwest Community College, ♿, 231 West Sixth, 82435. Telephone: 307/754-6510. Ask for Mrs. K. Christiansen, Supervision Housing Arrangements. Foreign students only. June 1 to July 31. $7 per person based on double occupancy. Reservations requested eight weeks in advance. "We are in the heart of the Rockies." The bus will deliver guests to the college campus on request.

Rawlins

Accommodation: Sunset Motel, 1302 West Spruce, 82301. Telephone: 307/324-3448. $18 to $24 for one; $18 to $26 for two in one bed; $24 to $30 for two in two beds.

Riverton

Accommodation: Friendship Inn–El Rancho, 221 South Federal, 82501. Telephone: 307/856-2268. $20 to $24 for one or two in one bed; $25 to $35 for two in two beds.

Rock Springs

Accommodation: Motel 6, I-80 and Dewar Dr. 82901. See Casper listing for rates.

Sundance

Accommodation: Arrowhead Motel, ♿, P.O. Box 191, 82729. Telephone: 307/283-3307. $16 to $22 for one; $18 to $26 for two in one bed; $22 to $28 for two in two beds.

Teton Village

Accommodation: The Hostel (AYH-SA), 🎒 ★ 10% May 15 to October 1, P.O. Box 546, 83025. Twelve miles northwest of Jackson. Ten miles from Grand Teton National Park. Telephone: 307/733-3415. Men, women, and children. Room for one or two, $25. 10% discount to AYH members May 15 to October 1. Reservations necessary.

Torrington

Accommodations: Best Value/Oregon Trail Lodge, El Hwy., P.O. Box 186, 82240. Telephone: 307/532-2101. $16 to $18 for one; $20 to $22 for two in two beds.

Wheatland

Accommodation: Friendship Inn–Wyoming Motel, 1101 9th St., 82201. Telephone: 307/322-2574. $18 to $20 for one; $20 to $22 for two in one bed; $26.50 to $30.50 for two in two beds.

Yellowstone

Accommodations: The Yellowstone Park Division, TWA Services, Inc., 82190. There are cabins operated by the Yellowstone Park Division throughout the park that are reasonably priced:

● At Lake Yellowstone, open June 10 to September 5. Family cabins: one or two, $21; $4.50 for each additional person.

● At Old Faithful Lodge and Cabins, open May 30 to September 26. Budget cabins (bring your own towels): one or two, $16. Budget shelters (bring your own linens, bedding, and towels): one to four, $10.50.

● At Old Faithful Snow Lodge and Cabins, open May 30 to November 2. Budget cabins (bring your own towels): one or two, $16; $4.50 for each additional person.

● At Mammoth Hot Springs Hotel and Cabins, open May 23 to September 21. Budget cabins (bring your own towels): one or two, $16; $4.50 for each additional person.

Note: Reservations at all of the above are highly recommended. Write to Yellowstone Park Division for a detailed brochure and instructions on how to go about reserving space, or telephone 307/344-7311.

● Best Value City Center Motel, P.O. Box 211, 214 Madison, MT 59758. Telephone: 406/646-7337. $20 for one; $22 for two in one bed; $24 for two in two beds. Three blocks from West Yellowstone Park entrance.

Camping: Yellowstone National Park, 82190. Thirteen campgrounds open June to August, September, or October. Mammoth Campgrounds open all year. Bridge Bay, three miles southwest of Lake Junction, is the largest with 438 sites. $3 or $4 per campsite per night.